POLITICAL CHANGE IN THE METROPOLIS

EIGHTH EDITION

RONALD K. VOGEL
University of Louisville

JOHN J. HARRIGAN
Hamline University

D1416970

PEARSON
Longman

New York • San Francisco • Boston
London • Toronto • Sydney • Tokyo • Singapore • Madrid
Mexico City • Munich • Paris • Cape Town • Hong Kong • Montreal

Editor-in-Chief: Eric Stano
Senior Marketing Manager: Elizabeth Fogarty
Supplements Editor: Kristi Olson
Production Manager: Eric Jorgensen
Project Coordination and Text Design: Pre-Press Company, Inc.
Electronic Page Makeup: Laserwords Private Limited.
Cover Design Manager: Nancy Danahy
Cover Image: (*top image*) © The Image Bank/Getty, Inc. and (*bottom image*) © CORBIS, Inc.
Photo Researcher: Rona Tuccillo
Senior Manufacturing Buyer: Dennis J. Para
Printer and Binder: RR Donnelley & Sons Company
Cover Printer: Phoenix Color Corp.

For permission to use copyrighted material, grateful acknowledgment is made to the copyright holders, which are hereby made part of this copyright page.

Cataloging-in-Publication Data on file at the Library of Congress

Credits: Page 5: Photo by Andrea Booher/FEMA News Photo, "New York City, October 4, 2001"; Page 9: Photo by AFP/Getty Images; Page 10: Photo by Michael Reiger/FEMA, "New Orleans, La., September 8, 2005"; Pages 12-16: Transcript of Radio Interview with New Orleans' Nagin, "Mayor to feds: 'Get off your asses,'" CNN Image Source. Used with permission; Page 19: Table 1.1: Robert Fishman, "The American Metropolis at Century's End: Past and Future Influences," Housing Facts & Findings, Volume 1, Issue 4 (Winter 1999), p. 9. ©1999 Fannie Mae Foundation, Washington, D.C. Used with permission. Source. Used with permission; Page 59: Table 2.5: "Downtown Population Change." ©Fannie Mae Foundation and The Brookings Institution 2001. Used with permission; Page 98: Table 4.3: "Frequency of Local Government Forms" adapted and reprinted with permission of the International City/County Management Association, 777 North Capitol Street NE, Suite 500, Washington, D.C. 20002. All Rights Reserved; Page 122: Figure 5.1: "Diversity Experienced in Each Group's Typical Neighborhood—National Metropolitan Average," Lewis Mumford Center; Page 166-68: Table 6.1, "If U.S. City/County Metro Economies Were Nations: World Rankings on Gross Domestic and Metropolitan Product, 2000," DRI-WEFA; Page 175: Table 6.3, "Underclass Census Tracks in 20 Largest Metropolitan Areas, 1990 and 2000," Paul A. Jargowsky and Rebecca Yang/Brookings Institution; Pages 178-79: Table 6.4, "City-Suburban Disparities—Median Household Income," John Logan, Lewis Mumford Center; Page 236: Table 8.1: "Household Spending on Transportation in 28 Metropolitan Areas," Surface Transportation Policy Project/Center for Neighborhood Technology; Pages 241–43: Congress for the New Urbanism, "Charter of the New Urbanism."

Please visit us at www.ablongman.com

ISBN 0-321-20228-7

1 2 3 4 5 6 7 8 9 10—DOC—09 08 07 06

To my wife Jeanie and my son Alex

R.K.V.

To Sandy, with respect and appreciation

J.J.H.

generation in urban America. In this edition of *Political Change in the Metropolis,* the authors continue to update the text and strive to balance the historical treatment of cities and the metropolis with more contemporary trends. Throughout the book, the authors update tables and figures to provide the latest available data on trends in metropolitan areas including numbers and types of governments; population; social, economic, and fiscal conditions; crime rates; and poverty. The most significant changes from the last edition include a new discussion of the concept of resilient cities; an update on the status of redevelopment of lower Manhattan; a new section on the New Orleans flooding following Hurricane Katrina; a review of the new census terminology for metropolitan areas; updated trends on concentrated poverty; and greater treatment of George W. Bush's urban policies. We hope that the text retains its familiarity to past users while also appealing to those who seek more contemporary coverage of urban affairs.

The authors want to express their appreciation to the editorial team at Longman, especially to Eric Stano, editor-in-chief, and Donna Garnier, editorial assistant. They greatly facilitated the revisions and ensured the manuscript was completed in a timely fashion. Rona Tuccillo, Visual Researcher at Longman, was a great help in finding photos of the New Orleans flooding. We also want to thank Abi Smith, graduate research assistant in the Ph.D. program in Urban and Public Affairs program at the University of Louisville. Abi provided invaluable assistance by gathering data and articles for the updates of tables in the text, responding to editorial queries, and ensuring that the production process stayed on schedule. Melissa Morrison, a graduate assistant in the Master's in Urban Planning program at the University of Louisville, did an excellent job of putting together the index.

The production team at Pre-Press Company, Inc., especially Patrick Franzen, was extremely efficient and professional in editing the manuscript and ensuring that the final product is readable and understandable. Finally, we would like to thank those anonymous reviewers of the previous edition whose helpful feedback proved to be invaluable guidance in shaping this revision: Craig W. Allin, Cornell College; Christopher A. Cooper, Western Carolina University; and Jennifer L. Pfeifer, University of Minnesota.

—*Ronald K. Vogel and John J. Harrigan*

PART ONE

METROPOLITAN CITIES IN THE TWENTY-FIRST CENTURY

Hurricane Katrina hit New Orleans on August 29, 2005, all but destroying the city. The storm riveted the attention of the American people, reminding us of the destructive forces of nature and the fragility of urban infrastructure and the modern systems we depend upon for public services and daily living. Terrorists hijacked two planes and crashed them into the World Trade Center in New York City on September 11, 2001, causing the collapse of the Twin Towers, spreading fear and panic throughout lower Manhattan and indeed the nation at large. The attack led to the grounding of all commercial flights, disrupted all transportation in and out of the city, and left a gaping hole in the skyline of New York. Studies of contemporary urban politics cannot ignore these events. Yet the response—federal, state, and local—must be considered in light of "enduring tensions" in urban politics in the United States. Indeed, the New Orleans flood reminds us of the persistence of widespread poverty and racial inequalities that are the underlying conditions associated with the urban crisis in American cities. Moreover, for the near future, the aging infrastructure in American cities and threats posed by sprawl and overdevelopment to the environment may pose a greater long-term danger to cities and urban life. The goal of this book is to balance understanding contemporary phenomena affecting cities, such as globalization, terrorism, or natural disasters, against a longer-term perspective on urban politics in the United States.

By way of introduction, Chapter 1 highlights the major challenges cities face today and puts them in historical context. These challenges include natural disasters, domestic and international terrorism, concentrated poverty, racial and ethnic tension, and continuing population sprawl beyond the boundaries of cities. Current urban problems are considered against the historical backdrop of the development and politics of the cities.

Chapter 1 traces the organization of urban politics through three historical periods, each with its own biases. The first era, *machine- and ethnic-based politics,* is associated with European immigrants who governed the larger cities of the Northeast and Midwest from the 1840s through the 1920s. The second era, *functional fiefdoms,* began in the 1930s and continued to gain momentum in the post–World War II period. Expansion of governmental services and activities led to the organization of political influence on a functional basis rather than on the ethnic and geographic bases that had predominated in the earlier era. A number of special districts, public authorities, and independent agencies were created under the reform banner to prevent politics from interfering with the judgments of experts, such as local boards of health run by medical professionals.

The third era is that of the *dependent city*. It emerged in the late 1960s and is characterized by a concern about the viability of the city in the face of dramatic contemporary political, economic, and social change. The city is buffeted about by external forces such as reduced federal aid, the rise of a world economy, and continued suburbanization beyond the city limits. Local leaders must respond to these external forces as much as or more than to internal urban politics. The threat of terrorism, both foreign and domestic, may indicate the emergence of a fourth era of urban politics in cities—that of the *vulnerable city*. Adding to the vulnerable city is the growing propensity for natural disasters to affect more people, possibly because more people now live nearer threats, as well as the rise of more complex and fragile urban systems that can easily be disrupted accidentally or deliberately.

Some of the implications of these changes are discussed in Chapter 1. Chapter 2 defines some basic concepts of urbanization, explains why and how America became urbanized, and examines the political biases that have accompanied urbanization and metropolitanization in the United States.

CHAPTER 1

TWENTY-FIRST CENTURY CITIES AND THE CHALLENGE OF URBAN GOVERNANCE

CHAPTER SYNOPSIS

Resilient Cities: *New York City and the World Trade Center Attack; New Orleans and Hurricane Katrina* • Urban Politics and the Bias of Political Organization • Three Historical Periods of Urban Politics: *Ethnic- and Geographic-Based Politics and the Era of the Political Machines; Functional Fiefdoms and the Era of Reform; The Dependent City* • A Fragmented System of Local Government • Defining Politics and Power in the City

Resilient Cities

In the 1980s, cities were viewed as dangerous places associated with urban decline, violent crime, and volatile race relations. This image of the city was somewhat exaggerated but not entirely inaccurate. Crime rates were high, central cities were losing population, and there were growing economic and social disparities between residents of the central cities and of the suburbs.

In contrast, the period from about 1993 to 2001 was one of economic growth and prosperity for American cities. Many declining cities saw their populations stabilize or even increase modestly. Income, economic opportunity, and revenues grew greatly in the urban centers, even if they were sometimes outpaced by the suburbs. Massive investment in central business districts occurred with many cities boasting new stadiums, arenas, performing arts centers, waterfront parks, and the like. Even if inner-city neighborhoods were plagued by severe poverty and (along with first-ring suburbs) showed signs of decline, the cities had shiny new downtowns and enhanced infrastructure and services. Even if the public schools were failing, the cities themselves seemed to be thriving. This was most evident in flush city budgets and in the decline in violent crime (see Chapter 11).

Just as we became more optimistic about the fate of American cities, the terrorist attacks of September 11, 2001, raised new fears about the health and future of cities.[1] Cities are not just threatened by international terrorists. The bombings at the Atlanta Olympics in 1996 and the Oklahoma City federal building in 1995 were the work of domestic terrorists. In addition, as the Cincinnati riots in 2001 reminded us, circumstances that might spawn a race riot are present in many cities; that is, the

3

presence of a significant group at the bottom of the social ladder whose members believe they have little chance of advancing. The immediate catalysts for riots are usually charges of police brutality, a shooting of a minority youth, or the acquittal of a police officer charged with excessive force.

Although cities have long been vulnerable to natural and human disasters, almost all of these cities are rebuilt and few cities actually perish.[2] Lawrence J. Vale and Thomas J. Campanella, in a book called *The Resilient City,* distinguish natural disasters from human disasters, which are further classified as accidental or deliberate. Examples of natural disasters that nearly destroyed American cities are the Chicago Fire (1871), the San Francisco Earthquake (1906), and the Yellow Fever Epidemic in Memphis (1878). Human disasters may be accidents such as the chemical release in Bhopal, India (1984) and the nuclear reactor meltdown in Chernobyl, Ukraine (1986). Human disasters also include civil war, for example, the killings and destruction due to bombing and gunfire in Beirut (1980s) and the burning of Atlanta (1864). World War I and World War II destroyed parts or all of places such as London, Berlin, and Tokyo as nations bombed each other's major cities. The U.S. used nuclear bombs to destroy the Japanese cities of Hiroshima (1945) and Nagasaki (1945). International terrorism by Al Qaeda hijacking planes and using them as missiles to destroy the World Trade Center and severely damage the Pentagon (2001) are the most recent human disasters. Cities also face domestic terrorism by right-wing extremists often linked to white supremacist movements as in the case of the bombings at the Atlanta Olympics (1996) by Eric Rudolph and the Oklahoma federal building (1995) by Timothy McVeigh.

The rebuilding of cities reveals the underlying urban politics as well as the way the natural or human disaster may have altered urban politics. As Lawrence J. Vale and Thomas J. Campanella state:

> The process of post-disaster recovery is a window into the power structure of the society that has been stricken. Understanding the meaning of urban disasters therefore entails more than examining the various institutions every society sets up to manage recovery. These institutions—such as civil defense organizations, law enforcement agencies, charities, insurance brokers, and victims compensation funds—are certainly vital aspects of urban resilience. Yet the broad cultural question of recovery is more than a problem of "disaster management," however daunting and important that may be. What we call "recovery" is also driven by value-laden questions about equity. Who sets the priorities for the recovering communities? How are the needs of low-income residents valued in relation to the pressing claims of disrupted businesses? Who decides what will be rebuilt where, and which voices carry forth the dominant narratives that interpret what transpires? Who gets displaced when new facilities are constructed in the name of recovery? What roles do nonlocal agencies, national disaster-assistance policies, and international relief organizations have in setting guidelines for reconstruction? How can urban leaders overcome the lingering stigma inflicted by their city's victimization? What place is there for visionary architecture and long-range planning?[3]

In other words, rebuilding the city is a function of and reflects the urban politics of that city. This becomes clear as we review the cases of New York City and New Orleans.

New York City and the World Trade Center Attack

At 8:45 a.m. on September 11, 2001, a passenger jet struck the north tower of the World Trade Center (WTC), and 18 minutes later a second airliner hit the south tower.

New York City, October 4, 2001—An aerial view of the recovery operation under way in lower Manhattan at the site of the collapsed World Trade Center.
Source: Photo by Andrea Booher/FEMA News Photo. http://www.fema.gov/.

At 9:43 a.m., a third plane crashed into the Pentagon, and a fourth flight went down at 10:10 a.m. in Pennsylvania. At 10:28 a.m., the WTC collapsed, watched on television by millions of Americans. Later, it was learned that the four planes had been hijacked by terrorists connected to Osama bin Laden, who was also connected to the bombing of two U.S. embassies in Africa in 1998, to that of the *Cole* battleship in 2000, and to the earlier (1993) bombing of the WTC. All flights in the United States were grounded for several days. New York City was virtually shut down, as bridges and tunnels connecting Manhattan to the mainland were closed. In the following days and weeks, the city searched in vain for survivors and began to clear the rubble.[4] Mayor Rudolph Giuliani emerged as a national hero, universally praised for his courage and resolve in the immediate aftermath of the attack.

The total cost of the terrorist attack on New York City was astounding. At the World Trade Center 2,726 people lost their lives. Among the dead were 23 New York City police officers and 343 firefighters killed when the towers unexpectedly collapsed shortly after the planes crashed into them.[5] The New York City Partnership and Chamber of Commerce estimated the total economic impact on New York City's economy will exceed $83 billion. Even after federal and state assistance and insurance reimbursements, the city faced $16 billion in "net damage to the economy." The chamber study reported 125,000 jobs were lost in the immediate aftermath of the attack—100,000 in lower Manhattan—the heart of the city's financial services industry. In addition, about 25 million square feet of office space, about 30 percent of the office space in lower Manhattan, was lost or damaged. A subway, a power station, and a telephone switching station also need to be rebuilt.[6]

Our Darkest Day; Our Finest Hour

On September 11, New York City suffered the darkest day in our long history. The destruction of the World Trade Center, and the resulting loss of thousands of lives, has broken our City's heart. But our heart still beats and our City remains strong. We will emerge from this stronger than we have ever been before.

This vicious, unprovoked attack on our City, and our Nation, demonstrates the depths of human cowardice and cruelty. Yet the reaction of New Yorkers to this tragedy has shown us the heights of human generosity and courage. Within moments after the first plane struck, ordinary men and women showed extraordinary bravery in assisting one another to safety, even at the cost of their own lives. Our Fire Fighters and Police Officers have personified courage, and though the losses to their ranks have been terrible, they have set the example for the rest of us by continuing to work with renewed vigor.

The Fire Department, in particular, has suffered greatly. More than 300 members of the Department are dead or missing as of this writing, and we have already held funerals for three of the most beloved and valued members of New York's Bravest: Chief Peter Ganci; First Deputy Commissioner William Feehan; and Father Mychal Judge. These legendary leaders and their many courageous fallen colleagues will never be forgotten.

This tragedy, along with the nearly simultaneous bombing of the Pentagon in Washington and the crash of a hijacked commercial plane near Pittsburgh, has touched the lives of millions of people throughout our City, across the Nation, and around the world. Family members, friends, and co-workers have been suddenly taken from us. This enormous loss provokes our sadness, and it also stirs a sense of outrage and anger. President Bush is right to call this an act of war. He is also right to declare that the terrorist enemies of the United States will face retaliation. Basic justice—and the national interest—demand no less.

Yet even as we mourn our dead and prepare for what could be a long and bitter war against an elusive enemy, let us always remember that our greatest national strengths are our openness, our diversity, our inclusiveness, and our freedom. These are the assets that our terrorist foes seek to destroy, but these are also the values that will guarantee our eventual and total victory. The people of the City of New York will demonstrate that we are stronger than these barbarians. We are not going to participate in group blame or group hatred, because those are the sicknesses that caused this tragedy. Our City is going to continue to honor its immigrant heritage. Through the strength of our example, we are going to send the message that life in our City goes on, undeterred. We will continue to embody the highest ideals of America.

I have always had full confidence in the people of this City, and that confidence has risen even higher as I have watched the behavior of New Yorkers in the wake of this tragedy. They evacuated the scene of destruction in good order; they almost immediately formed long lines to donate blood; they have made generous corporate and individual donations of money and supplies; they have offered welcome encouragement and solace to the relatives of the missing and to our exhausted rescue workers. We are a united City, and I have never been so proud to be a New Yorker.

Source: Mayor Rudolph Giuliani's weekly column, New York City, September 24, 2001, from http://www.nyc.gov/html/om/html/2001b/weekly/wkly0924.html.

New York City's main concern is that the site where the World Trade Center stood be redeveloped and that businesses return to the area to ensure that the key corporate and finance sectors remain vital and that New York's status as a global city not be threatened. The federal government, even in the midst of the crisis, was concerned about limiting federal assistance. President George W. Bush initially offered $17 billion, which was subsequently raised to $20 billion, to help rebuild New York City (Governor George Pataki had requested $54 billion).[7] Much of this money is for cleanup from the disaster.[8] New York City's business and civic elite pressured the federal government to do more. In addition to the $20 billion, they sought another $5 billion in tax breaks to returning businesses. An initial concern was whether the promised money would actually appear. Many recall that federal aid promised to Los Angeles after the 1992 riots never materialized. Former President Bill Clinton advised the New York Partnership to "Get the money now."[9] Insurance companies ($19 billion), government ($16 billion), and private charities ($3 billion) paid an additional $38 billion of relief to victims, businesses, and other government agencies.[10]

Initial unity in New York City in the aftermath of 9/11 did not last long. Even during the cleanup, firefighters clashed with city police when the city ordered the police to limit the number of firefighters at "ground zero," because in their concern with recovering victims' remains, they were obstructing efforts to clear the site. Another conflict occurred over a planned memorial depicting three firefighters raising the American flag amid the ruins. It happened that the actual firefighters were white, but the scene in the memorial was made "politically correct" to include an African American and a Hispanic.

Nowhere is the reemergence of urban politics clearer than in the debate over how to rebuild lower Manhattan. John Mollenkopf has identified the politics and interests of those who will decide how to rebuild on the WTC site.[11] They include:

- The Port Authority of New York and New Jersey, which owns the land where the World Trade Center stood. It is a public authority with members appointed by the governors of New York and New Jersey.
- Mr. Larry Silverstein, who holds a 99-year lease on the World Trade Center. He claims the legal right to redevelop the site and is preparing to build Freedom Tower.
- The Lower Manhattan Redevelopment Corporation, a 16-member authority created by New York Governor Pataki and charged with overseeing redevelopment.
- The City of New York and Mayor Michael Bloomberg, who has little formal role in the rebuilding. However, the city and the mayor have the resources to obstruct or facilitate all plans for rebuilding lower Manhattan.

Many other groups are also taking an interest. They include victims groups representing families, police officers, and firefighters seeking to memorialize the victims; organizations seeking to encourage the return of small businesses; major corporate interests seeking to ensure that New York City retains a strong base in the corporate service sector and finance; and citizens and neighborhood groups hoping for more balanced development, especially residential. Mollenkopf indicates that a major question will be whether redevelopment will be a top-down or a bottom-up process. At present, it is top-down. He suggests that this does not bode well for future redevelopment, because the fact that the city is only weakly integrated into the formal decision process and that citizens and neighborhood interests have no direct role will undermine the long-term support necessary for successful redevelopment.

The rebuilding indeed stalled while the developer Larry A. Silverstein and the Port Authority argued over who would develop the project. Silverstein may receive as much as $2.2 billion in insurance claims from the collapse of the Twin Towers. He will use the settlement to develop Freedom Tower, which is destined to be the tallest building in the world when finished in 2009. He is already building a 52-story office building to replace one of the destroyed buildings in the 9/11 attack. He also has plans for four other buildings.[12] However, Mayor Bloomberg believes developer Silverstein should focus on building Freedom Tower and allow the Port Authority, owner of the land leased to Silverstein, to proceed with the rest of the site's development. The mayor says the developer does not have sufficient financial resources to proceed with the development of the entire site. Freedom Tower has been delayed by about a year when design changes were required to improve the building's security, which will likely be a continuing target of terrorists. The Port Authority wants to reclaim land from the lease with Silverstein and take responsibility for the rest of the development, including a building to house its own offices. There is also doubt that businesses will want to rent space in Freedom Tower due to the risk of terrorism. The city and state have agreed to rent 40 percent of the space in Freedom Tower to ensure the project's success. The mayor's criticism of Silverstein is also an attack on the governor in that he controls the Lower Manhattan Redevelopment Corporation, which is in favor of Silverstein's development efforts rather than the Port Authority's proposal.[13]

Mayor Bloomberg and U.S. Senator Charles Schumer have also disagreed over "competing visions for rebuilding ground zero." The mayor has called for building apartments and a hotel rather than just commercial office space. Schumer calls this a "lack of confidence in downtown." He also criticized the plan for the Port Authority to construct a building for its own offices on site rather than move into Freedom Tower. Schumer called for the mayor to provide $1.75 billion of tax-exempt bonds, Liberty Bonds, which were part of the federal aid package to support New York City's economic revitalization. The mayor said he would not use the Liberty Bonds to support a project that he does not think is financially feasible, returning to his doubts about Silverstein's ability to finance his plans. The mayor also expressed doubt that the World Trade Center memorial and museum will be able to raise the $1 billion required to realize their plans and that the city may not be able to help. Governor Pataki is considering running for president so problems with redevelopment would greatly undermine his candidacy.[14] The National Trust for Historic Preservation has also objected that the memorial will cause "substantial destruction" to the historic preservation of the Twin Towers foundation and slabs that the building sat on.[15] Moreover, some family members disagree vehemently with the memorial being placed underground or indeed with any structures being built on the site.

New Orleans and Hurricane Katrina

On August 29, 2005, Hurricane Katrina came ashore with devastating effects on the Gulf Coast region including Florida, Mississippi, Louisiana, and Alabama. The course of the hurricane seemed to spare New Orleans from the worst of the storm. However, initial relief turned to horror as officials realized that the dam levees failed, resulting in the flooding of 80 percent of the city.[16] Although most citizens evacuated, some 100,000 people were left behind, mostly poor and black. The city was ill-prepared to evacuate so many people and insufficient shelters or provisions were in place. About 25,000 people were trapped in the Superdome without enough water or food and with poor sanitary conditions. Another 20,000 people went to the Convention Center, which was never intended as a shelter.[17] People watched images on their televisions of survivors having to fend for themselves with no sign of local, state, or federal officials coming to the rescue. Many tried to leave on foot, crossing the Crescent City Convention Bridge only to be turned back at gunpoint by Gretana, Louisiana, sheriffs[18] apparently fearing invasion by mobs of black looters. Viewers had trouble believing this was a disaster in a modern America city rather than a Third World country. The hurricane was a natural disaster but it appears that the flooding was the result of human disaster, a poorly maintained levee system.[19] The effects of the flooding are chronicled by Louise Comfort, who reports on the impact of the disaster in New Orleans and Louisiana.

> The costs are indeed staggering: more than 1,300 dead; 1.5 million people displaced from their homes; 60,000 homes totally destroyed; an estimated $200 billion in disaster assistance and rebuilding costs in addition to the $52 billion already appropriated by Congress, and a possible long-term negative impact on the U.S. economy, given the damage to the oil refineries and production operations of the Port of New Orleans.[20]

New Orleans, La., September 1, 2005—Soldiers watch people boarding buses near the Superdome.
Source: AFP/Getty Images.

New Orleans, La., September 8, 2005—FEMA's US&R teams, in route by helicopter to conduct a search in St. Bernard Parish, view the flooding in New Orleans.
Photo: Michael Rieger/FEMA http://www.photolibrary.fema.gov/photodata/original/19250.jpg.

Following 9/11, the framework for emergency planning was changed. The Office of Homeland Security was created and the Federal Emergency Management Agency (FEMA) and other agencies were brought under the new cabinet department's auspices. The emphasis of homeland security was planning and responding to terrorism. Although FEMA has a role to play in this, as evidenced in the response to the destruction of the Twin Towers, FEMA lost its direct access to the president and Congress as it was no longer an independent agency. As initial assessments are made regarding the disaster in New Orleans, the national reorganization certainly appears to have significance.[21] The testimony of Michael Brown, former FEMA head, before a congressional committee pointed out that FEMA was down one-fourth of its workforce and that Secretary Michael Chernoff of Homeland Security would not support FEMA budget requests for more equipment and personnel. The testimony also highlighted the Republican view of the president and Congress that the federal government take a secondary role in emergency planning and response. Of course, this explanation does not match the expectations of citizens and emergency planning laws that the federal government responds when the scale of the disaster overwhelms state and local capacity or resources.

In the case of New Orleans, the flood destroyed the local communication and transportation infrastructure. First responders either abandoned their posts or had no resources or ability to assess the situation and intervene. No doubt, local officials and the mayor are responsible for inadequate planning. The scale of the disaster also overwhelmed the state of Louisiana. There is also concern that the state had insufficient National Guard or equipment available due to the Iraq War. In addition, there are questions about lack of communication and coordination between state officials and the city on the one hand, and the federal government on the other. Nevertheless, FEMA and the federal government took five days to show up.

Hurricane Katrina and the flooding of New Orleans in August 2005 revealed significant weaknesses in the intergovernmental system to deal with emergency planning. First, the current federal budget process that supports emergency response emphasizes the response and recovery side over mitigation and preparedness (Donaue and Joyce, 2001, p. 728). The failure of the levee system and the difficulty of evacuating New Orleans and the Gulf of Mexico region were anticipated in a simulation exercise in 2004. Moreover, the levee system was built to protect New Orleans from a Category 3 hurricane, not a Category 5. Little effort was made to plan or mitigate flooding in New Orleans. Observers have warned of the consequences of the decline in the coastal wetlands as a brake on a hurricane as well as the migration to coastal regions where half the nation's population now resides.[22]

Some amount of blame for the disaster has to rest with local officials. Researchers Peter Burns and Matthew Thomas trace the failure to evacuate the city and deal with the immediate crisis facing the citizens as result of a poorly developed local governing coalition or regime (see Chapter 7). The mayor had few networks or established patterns of relations to draw upon to help evacuate the city, relate to state and federal officials, or draw upon the aid and resources of private and nongovernmental agencies that could assist him. The lack of trust and bonds was an obstacle. In the aftermath of the storm, Governor Blanco created the Louisiana Recovery Authority to lead the effort to restore the economy, rebuild housing, and assist in the recovery of New Orleans and Louisiana. Mayor Ray Nagin has created the Bring New Orleans Back Commission to develop a master plan to direct federal and state aid to ensure New Orleans recovery. Burns and Thomas are hopeful that these may lead to a stronger regime that may more effectively govern New Orleans. However, they acknowledge that there is still a lack of consensus about the rebuilding agenda.[23] There is still serious concern about whom the city will serve and whether the African American majority will return. The mayor was widely criticized for his speech calling for the return of a *chocolate* city. However, many blacks fear that there is an agenda to prevent New Orleans from returning as a black city by depriving the poorer black residents the location or means to return. Nagin was reelected mayor in a runoff primary against Louisiana Lieutenant Governor Mitch Landrieu, who is white, in May 2006.

Others, such as urbanist Peter Dreier, point a finger more directly at the federal government and the ideology of conservatives such as President Bush who favor market solutions over government action and have eroded the capacity of governments at all levels to act positively and provide effective services and address urban problems. He says:

> Katrina was a human-made disaster more than a natural disaster. The conditions that led to the disaster, and the response by government officials, were the result of policy choices. Government incompetence was an outgrowth of a more serious indifference to the plight of cities and the poor. As a result, the opportunity to reconstruct New Orleans as part of a bold regional renewal plan was lost. Whatever positive things happen in Katrina's aftermath will be

due, in large measure, to the long-term work of grassroots community and union-organizing groups who mobilized quickly to provide a voice for the have-nots and who found allies among professionals to help formulate alternative plans to those developed by business and political elites.[24]

Dreier denounces the Bush administration for its "crony capitalism" and reliance on "disaster profiteers" to rebuild the Gulf area.[25] He cites the fact that many no-bid contracts worth billions of dollars went to companies such as Kellogg Brown & Root, which is a subsidiary of Haliburton. Little effort was made to steer rebuilding jobs and resources to New Orleanors. He also highlights that the president suspended the Davis-Bacon law to allow companies to avoid paying prevailing wages (union level), thus lowering wages.

For Dreier, the real tragedy is that the rebuilding effort in New Orleans could have set the stage for really dealing with urban problems in America. With more than $100 billion in federal money going toward the rebuilding of housing, schools, transportation, parks, and commercial redevelopment, there was an opportunity to cooperatively and democratically set a vision for rebuilding the city and region. Moreover, the disaster could have led to a more ambitious urban agenda that would provide a model for cities throughout the nation with the return of a federal partner for cities.

Undoubtedly, local, state, and national officials were unprepared to deal with the disaster. While the specific failures of various officials, agencies, and systems is likely to be studied in detail over the next several years, there is no doubt that the intergovernmental system and lack of coordination are a major part of the story.

Mayor to feds: 'Get off your asses'

Transcript of Radio Interview with New Orleans' Nagin

(CNN)—New Orleans Mayor Ray Nagin blasted the slow pace of federal and state relief efforts in an expletive-laced interview with local radio station WWL-AM.

The following is a transcript of WWL correspondent Garland Robinette's interview with Nagin on Thursday night. Robinette asked the mayor about his conversation with President Bush:

NAGIN: I told him we had an incredible crisis here and that his flying over in Air Force One does not do it justice. And that I have been all around this city, and I am very frustrated because we are not able to marshal resources and we're outmanned in just about every respect.

You know the reason why the looters got out of control? Because we had most of our resources saving people, thousands of people that were stuck in attics, man, old ladies. . . . You pull off the doggone ventilator vent and you look down there and they're standing in there in water up to their freaking necks.

And they don't have a clue what's going on down here. They flew down here one time two days after the doggone event was over with TV cameras, AP reporters, all kind of goddamn—excuse my French everybody in America, but I am pissed.

WWL: Did you say to the president of the United States, "I need the military in here"?

NAGIN: I said, "I need everything."

Now, I will tell you this—and I give the president some credit on this—he sent one John Wayne dude down here that can get some stuff done, and his name is [Lt.] Gen. [Russel] Honore.

And he came off the doggone chopper, and he started cussing and people started moving. And he's getting some stuff done.

They ought to give that guy—if they don't want to give it to me, give him full authority to get the job done, and we can save some people.

WWL: What do you need right now to get control of this situation?

NAGIN: I need reinforcements, I need troops, man. I need 500 buses, man. We ain't talking about—you know, one of the briefings we had, they were talking about getting public school bus drivers to come down here and bus people out here.

I'm like, "You got to be kidding me. This is a national disaster. Get every doggone Greyhound bus line in the country and get their asses moving to New Orleans."

That's—they're thinking small, man. And this is a major, major, major deal. And I can't emphasize it enough, man. This is crazy.

I've got 15,000 to 20,000 people over at the convention center. It's bursting at the seams. The poor people in Plaquemines Parish. . . . We don't have anything, and we're sharing with our brothers in Plaquemines Parish.

It's awful down here, man.

WWL: Do you believe that the president is seeing this, holding a news conference on it but can't do anything until [Louisiana Gov.] Kathleen Blanco requested him to do it? And do you know whether or not she has made that request?

NAGIN: I have no idea what they're doing. But I will tell you this: You know, God is looking down on all this, and if they are not doing everything in their power to save people, they are going to pay the price. Because every day that we delay, people are dying and they're dying by the hundreds, I'm willing to bet you.

We're getting reports and calls that are breaking my heart, from people saying, "I've been in my attic. I can't take it anymore. The water is up to my neck. I don't think I can hold out." And that's happening as we speak.

You know what really upsets me, Garland? We told everybody the importance of the 17th Street Canal issue. We said, "Please, please take care of this. We don't care what you do. Figure it out."

WWL: Who'd you say that to?

NAGIN: Everybody: the governor, Homeland Security, FEMA. You name it, we said it.

(continued)

Mayor to feds: *(continued)*

And they allowed that pumping station next to Pumping Station 6 to go under water. Our sewage and water board people . . . stayed there and endangered their lives.

And what happened when that pumping station went down, the water started flowing again in the city, and it starting getting to levels that probably killed more people.

In addition to that, we had water flowing through the pipes in the city. That's a power station over there.

So there's no water flowing anywhere on the east bank of Orleans Parish. So our critical water supply was destroyed because of lack of action.

WWL: Why couldn't they drop the 3,000-pound sandbags or the containers that they were talking about earlier? Was it an engineering feat that just couldn't be done?

NAGIN: They said it was some pulleys that they had to manufacture. But, you know, in a state of emergency, man, you are creative, you figure out ways to get stuff done.

Then they told me that they went overnight, and they built 17 concrete structures and they had the pulleys on them and they were going to drop them.

I flew over that thing yesterday, and it's in the same shape that it was after the storm hit. There is nothing happening. And they're feeding the public a line of bull and they're spinning, and people are dying down here.

WWL: If some of the public called and they're right, that there's a law that the president, that the federal government can't do anything without local or state requests, would you request martial law?

NAGIN: I've already called for martial law in the city of New Orleans. We did that a few days ago.

WWL: Did the governor do that, too?

NAGIN: I don't know. I don't think so.

But we called for martial law when we realized that the looting was getting out of control. And we redirected all of our police officers back to patrolling the streets. They were dead-tired from saving people, but they worked all night because we thought this thing was going to blow wide open last night. And so we redirected all of our resources, and we hold it under check.

I'm not sure if we can do that another night with the current resources.

And I am telling you right now: They're showing all these reports of people looting and doing all that weird stuff, and they are doing that, but people are desperate and they're trying to find food and water, the majority of them.

Now you got some knuckleheads out there, and they are taking advantage of this lawless—this situation where, you know, we can't really control it, and they're doing some awful, awful things. But that's a small majority of the people. Most people are looking to try and survive.

And one of the things people—nobody's talked about this. Drugs flowed in and out of New Orleans and the surrounding metropolitan area so freely it was scary to me, and that's why we were having the escalation in murders. People don't want to talk about this, but I'm going to talk about it.

You have drug addicts that are now walking around this city looking for a fix, and that's the reason why they were breaking in hospitals and drugstores. They're looking for something to take the edge off of their jones, if you will.

And right now, they don't have anything to take the edge off. And they've probably found guns. So what you're seeing is drug-starving crazy addicts, drug addicts, that are wrecking havoc. And we don't have the manpower to adequately deal with it. We can only target certain sections of the city and form a perimeter around them and hope to God that we're not overrun.

WWL: Well, you and I must be in the minority. Because apparently there's a section of our citizenry out there that thinks because of a law that says the federal government can't come in unless requested by the proper people, that everything that's going on to this point has been done as good as it can possibly be.

NAGIN: Really?

WWL: I know you don't feel that way.

NAGIN: Well, did the tsunami victims request? Did it go through a formal process to request?

You know, did the Iraqi people request that we go in there? Did they ask us to go in there? What is more important?

And I'll tell you, man, I'm probably going get in a whole bunch of trouble. I'm probably going to get in so much trouble it ain't even funny. You probably won't even want to deal with me after this interview is over.

WWL: You and I will be in the funny place together.

NAGIN: But we authorized $8 billion to go to Iraq lickety-quick. After 9/11, we gave the president unprecedented powers lickety-quick to take care of New York and other places.

Now, you mean to tell me that a place where most of your oil is coming through, a place that is so unique when you mention New Orleans anywhere around the world, everybody's eyes light up—you mean to tell me that a place where you probably have thousands of people that have died and thousands more that are dying every day,

(continued)

Mayor to feds: (continued)

that we can't figure out a way to authorize the resources that we need? Come on, man.

You know, I'm not one of those drug addicts. I am thinking very clearly.

And I don't know whose problem it is. I don't know whether it's the governor's problem. I don't know whether it's the president's problem, but somebody needs to get their ass on a plane and sit down, the two of them, and figure this out right now.

WWL: What can we do here?

NAGIN: Keep talking about it.

WWL: We'll do that. What else can we do?

NAGIN: Organize people to write letters and make calls to their congressmen, to the president, to the governor. Flood their doggone offices with requests to do something. This is ridiculous.

I don't want to see anybody do anymore goddamn press conferences. Put a moratorium on press conferences. Don't do another press conference until the resources are in this city. And then come down to this city and stand with us when there are military trucks and troops that we can't even count.

Don't tell me 40,000 people are coming here. They're not here. It's too doggone late. Now get off your asses and do something, and let's fix the biggest goddamn crisis in the history of this country.

WWL: I'll say it right now, you're the only politician that's called and called for arms like this. And if—whatever it takes, the governor, president— whatever law precedent it takes, whatever it takes, I bet that the people listening to you are on your side.

NAGIN: Well, I hope so, Garland. I am just—I'm at the point now where it don't matter. People are dying. They don't have homes. They don't have jobs. The city of New Orleans will never be the same in this time.

WWL: We're both pretty speechless here.

NAGIN: Yeah, I don't know what to say. I got to go.

WWL: OK. Keep in touch. Keep in touch.

Source: http://www.cnn.com/2005/US/09/02/nagin.transcript.

Return to Normalcy: Urban Politics and the Bias of Political Organization

As the preceding discussion illustrates, conflicting values and institutional structures shape the way community decisions are made. Immediately after the World Trade Center collapse, the city and country rallied around New York and Mayor Giuliani. However, even as the city began the recovery effort, the mayor was attempting to extend his term in office by state legislative fiat, and the federal government was trying to reduce its obligations to the city. The disaster creates a large bloc of land available for redevelopment—but as what? Should the towers be rebuilt? Should the site be devoted to a large memorial to the victims? Should a park and commercial space share the site? What about residential housing? And who should decide? The mayor, the residents, or the Port Authority that owned the land and the World Trade Center? How will the redevelopment be financed? And what role should various groups play in the decision making?

Governmental structures are not politically neutral. They are biased in terms of the interests and policy directions they would favor or disfavor. One objective of this book is to identify the biases inherent in the organization of political and governmental power in metropolitan America. *Political bias,* as that term is used here, does not necessarily imply that the political actors are purposely and consciously biased for or against given groups of people. It does imply, as political scientist Harold Lasswell has argued, that the political process in itself in some measure determines *who* gets *what* political or economic benefits, *when* they get them, and *how* they get them.[26] Political bias in the metropolis, then, involves two questions: Who benefits from the ongoing political structure and process in the metropolis? And who pays the cost of those benefits? These political biases can occur either in the input into the political decision-making process or in the resulting policy outcomes.[27]

One must distinguish between the bias of specific actions and the *patterns of bias* that underlie a series of actions. Patterns of bias are indicated when some groups are systematically excluded from the governmental decision-making process and their interests are systematically neglected in governmental policy outcomes. Are some groups or categories of people systematically disadvantaged or ignored or hurt by the nature of the urban political process? And conversely, do some other people systematically benefit from the same process?

The Nature of Change in Metropolitan Politics

Closely related to the bias of political structures and processes are the changes that occur in the ways in which power is organized in the metropolis. Political change in the United States has been especially marked by its evolutionary nature.[28] Some political analysts believe that changes in the American political system historically have been evolutionary, incremental, and marginal. That is, there has never been a revolutionary overthrow of the class structure of the society or a widespread disavowal of the sanctity of private ownership of the major economic institutions. One political scientist, Kenneth M. Dolbeare, argues that even the Civil War and Reconstruction, which destroyed slavery and set the stage for the far-reaching Fourteenth Amendment to the Constitution, did not provoke fundamental political change in the United States.[29] In Dolbeare's view, all political change in this country has been marginal and has left the basic socioeconomic structure of the nation intact.

Most political changes have also been *interdependent* with socioeconomic changes.[30] As the nation's population has become increasingly metropolitan, for example, and as the nation's economy has become dominated by nationally based corporations rather than locally based proprietorships, there have been political reactions to these changes. To cope with the increasingly metropolitan population, the amount of governance in metropolitan areas increased markedly. And to cope with the transition from a regionally based to a nationally based economy, the regulatory capacity of government—particularly that of the federal government—increased substantially. Much of this change, however, in the view of political scientist Murray Edelman, has been *symbolic* rather than *substantive*. For example, the increase in regulatory capacity has been primarily a symbolic change that appeases the public and diverts attention from the fact that there have been few substantive changes in the distribution of power and wealth.[31] Political changes, in this view, normally focus on the symbols of power and seldom touch the substance.

These perceptive insights regarding change are relevant to metropolitan politics. However, we should be careful not to confuse change with instability. Some political systems can undergo rapid changes in the admission of new elites—such as happens following an election—and yet remain quite stable in terms of the class structure, the tenure of governments, and the widespread acceptance of the shared, underlying political and cultural values of the society.[32] This seems to have been the pattern in the United States. Some other political systems become quite unstable precisely because they are not able to tolerate political changes that would admit new elites into the political decision-making process. Thus it may well be that continuous, incremental, evolutionary change leads to political stability and forestalls the need for drastic revolutionary change. Change that allows emerging sectors in the society to share symbolically and vicariously in the exercise of power may also enable the elites of these emerging sectors to be co-opted into the decision-making structure or to bring about major redistributions of wealth.

In the American metropolises, political change has also occurred in an incremental, not a revolutionary, fashion. But this is change nonetheless. For example, the Tammany Hall political machine was not destroyed overnight. However, the tight control of this machine over New York City government, as it existed under Boss Tweed and some of his successors, was eventually destroyed. And the destruction of that control helped make a significant difference in how New York City is governed and in who benefits from its governance.[33] Thus the mayor of New York now struggles to retain a role in the most important development project the city may undertake in the next 100 years, eclipsed by independent public authorities, private actors and interests, and state-led redevelopment agencies. Table 1.1 reports the most important influences on the American metropolis according to a survey of urban scholars.

Three Historical Periods

The evolutionary nature of metropolitan political change can be seen in the historical development of political power in American cities. Three distinct evolutionary changes can be noted. First, roughly coterminous with the age of political machines and extensive European immigration was an era in which political power was ethnically and geographically based. (How this came about is described in considerable detail in Chapter 3.) Prior to 1830, political power in many American cities was controlled by very small circles of economic elites labeled variously as patrician, Brahmin, Yankee, Bourbon, or (much later)

TABLE 1.1   Past and Future Influences on the American Metropolis

The Top Ten Influences on the American Metropolis of the Past 50 Years	The Ten Most Likely Influences on the American Metropolis for the Next 50 Years
1. The 1956 Interstate Highway Act and the dominance of the automobile	1. Growing disparities of wealth
2. Federal Housing Administration mortgage financing and subdivision regulation	2. Suburban political majority
3. Deindustrialization of central cities	3. Aging of the baby boomers
4. Urban renewal: downtown redevelopment and public-housing projects (1949 Housing Act)	4. Perpetual "underclass" in central cities and inner-ring suburbs
5. Levittown (the mass-produced suburban tract house)	5. "Smart growth": environmental and planning initiatives to limit sprawl
6. Racial segregation and job discrimination in cities and suburbs	6. Internet
7. Enclosed shopping malls	7. Deterioration of the "first-ring" post-1945 suburbs
8. Sunbelt-style sprawl	8. Shrinking household size
9. Air conditioning	9. Expanded superhighway system of "outer beltways" to serve new edge cities
10. Urban riots of the 1960s	10. Racial integration as part of the increasing diversity in cities and suburbs

Reprinted from Robert Fishman, "The American Metropolis at Century's End: Past and Future Influences," *Housing Facts & Findings,* Volume 1, Issue 4 (Winter 1999), p. 9. ©1999 Fannie Mae Foundation, Washington, D.C. Used with permission. http://www.fanniemaefoundation.org/programs/hff/v1i4-metropolis.shtml.

WASP (white Anglo-Saxon Protestant). The members of these elites typically belonged to the higher-status Protestant churches in their localities. They viewed with considerable distrust both the egalitarian principles of Jacksonian democracy and the Catholic European immigrants who stood to benefit from those principles. From the 1830s until at least the end of the century, there was a steady evolution in the political influence of these European ethnic groups. Much of their political influence was founded on indigenous institutional power bases developed within the ethnic communities. The institutions that formed the base for their indigenous power remained the dominant urban political institutions until the 1930s. The major institutions thus created were the political machines, the urban organization of the Catholic Church dioceses, organized crime, certain labor unions, and some sectors of business. In many instances, these institutions are still influential in today's metropolitan politics, although they are seldom dominant.

The second evolutionary change began with the progressive reform movement at the turn of the century and reached its zenith between the 1940s and the 1970s. The evolutionary change during this period was the emergence of political organization on a *functional basis,* as distinguished from the ethnic and geographic bases of the earlier period. Within given functional areas, public bureaucracies and private interests developed. In public education, for example, the top administrators in the school systems, the teachers' unions, the superintendents' offices, and the state departments of education came to dominate public education and to reduce the power of the boards of education—the elected public officials.[34] A similar phenomenon occurred in public safety. The police bureaucracies, the police officers' associations, and conservative citizens' groups concerned with law and order insulated the police from effective control by locally elected city councils and mayors.* But the most dramatic example of the emergence of functionally organized power occurred in the arena of public housing and urban renewal. The formulation of urban renewal policy soon got beyond the control of elected officials in most cities. Semiautonomous local public authorities were created in response to federal legislation, and they were financed largely by federal funds. In a sense, functional fiefdoms emerged in which the decision makers acted with considerable independence from control by elected public officials. The mayor of New York may find it difficult to shape the redevelopment of lower Manhattan because independent public bodies retain a great deal of authority over the decisions involved.

The functional organization of power enabled technicians and specialists to supersede elected politicians in making the most fundamental decisions about rebuilding the cities. Equally important, major decisions on metropolitan growth came to be made by specialized agencies called *special districts* rather than by general-purpose governments. Within each functional area the public bureaucracies, the special districts, and the related private interests acted in a fashion somewhat reminiscent of feudal fiefdoms in the Middle Ages, when each fiefdom was virtually autonomous and its nobility was answerable only to itself. In the 1950s and the 1960s, an analogous situation occurred in American metropolitan areas. Within many functional areas of public activity, the appropriate influential people of the community were answerable virtually to themselves alone. Highways, redevelopment, low-income public housing, public health, and public education were all fiefdoms acting independently of one another. Little thought was given to coordinating their activities.

The third evolutionary change began in the mid-1960s; we call it the period of the *dependent city*. In this stage of development, local autonomy has been sharply challenged by outside economic forces over which the local government has little control. Local autonomy has also been reduced by policy mandates from the federal and state governments, which influence not only what policies city governments can pursue but also the procedures for implementing those policies.[35] Some of the chief characteristics of this period of the dependent city are an effort to coordinate the various functional

---

*The extent of police department insulation is difficult to measure at best, and elected officials certainly affect the overall environment within which the police departments function. Nevertheless, evidence suggests that police law-enforcement practices are the product more of a bureaucratic imperative than of legislative policy made by the city council in response to broad community demands. Jeffrey Pressman found that the mayor and city council in Oakland were unable to alter the police department's policies regulating handgun use by police officers; see p. 515 of Pressman's "The Preconditions for Mayoral Leadership," *American Political Science Review* 66, no. 2 (June 1972): 511–524. John A. Gardiner studied the enforcement of traffic laws in 697 communities throughout the United States and concluded that there was "almost no evidence to suggest that the police are carrying out publicly established enforcement policies"; see p. 171 of Gardiner's "Police Enforcement of Traffic Laws: A Comparative Analysis," in *City Politics and Public Policy*, ed. James Q. Wilson (New York: Wiley, 1968), pp. 151–172. Input from council members and influential citizens almost always occurred on an ad hoc basis with little implication for overall policies (p. 167). And a study by James Q. Wilson of different approaches toward juvenile delinquency by a professionalized police department and a more traditional, fraternally oriented police department found that the more bureaucratized and professionalized police force was much less sensitive to subtle community mores, was much less flexible in dealing with first offenders, and acted more in accord with the model of "an army of occupation" (p. 190 of James Q. Wilson, "The Police and the Delinquent in Two Cities," in Wilson, *City Politics and Public Policy*, pp. 173–195).

fiefdoms, an attempt to subordinate them to policy-making bodies at the metropolitan level, an overriding concern for public-private partnerships in the quest for economic development, and halfhearted attempts to cope with the massive social problems of poverty, crime, poor education, family breakdown, and racial separation that are increasingly the burden of the central cities.

The central city cannot by itself cope well with all its problems. As the redevelopment of the WTC site illustrates, it depends on state government for legal authority, on the state government and the federal government for whatever financial help it can get, on the business community for participation in economic development projects, and on surrounding suburbs for cooperation in addressing the multitude of problems (such as pollution, transportation, and education) that cross city boundaries. Making all these interdependent relationships work for the benefit of metropolitan residents has required acknowledging the need in recent decades for effective political leaders, especially for effective central-city mayors.

In summary, then, three broad evolutionary changes have been observed in the structure of political power in the metropolis:

- The first change was the emergence of power organized on an ethnic basis and a ward, or geographic, basis.
- Second was the emergence of power organized on a functional basis.
- Third has been the emergence of the dependent city, in which effective political power has become highly fragmented among dozens of local governments, and the central city has lost its dominance over the metropolis.

Urban politics in this contemporary period has become metropolitan in scope. From desegregation of schools to economic development, rarely is there a major public issue that can be dealt with effectively wholly within the boundaries of the central city alone. And often the federal government becomes involved through political mandates or financial incentives.

These evolutionary changes are of more than simple historical interest. Each of these three ways of organizing power *continues* to exist. The first way of organizing power did not destroy the older, closed circles of urban elites of the early nineteenth century. But it did open up new channels of political access for groups in the metropolis that did not have access under the older order. The second political change did not destroy the ethnic organization of power,[36] but it did create new channels of political access beyond the control of the ethnic-dominated political machines. Nor has the third political change destroyed the functional fiefdoms. But it has made the domestic policy and philosophy of whoever controls the White House of great importance to cities and metropolitan areas.

Political change in the metropolis, then, does not mean that one form of political organization replaces a previous form. On the contrary, it means that several forms of political organization have evolved side by side. The net result has been the emergence of a patchwork—an incredibly complex structure that is continually evolving in an incremental fashion. For those who know how to navigate them, there are numerous channels of political access to decision makers. Each channel has its own set of biases. And any one channel offers an opportunity to influence decisions only within a very limited scope of activities.

Even the largest, most extensive general-purpose government in the metropolis as it now exists—the central-city government—has only a very limited scope of action available to it. And in most instances, the evolution of a decision-making capacity at the metropolitan level is not very far advanced. What exists in most metropolises is an open political situation. Anyone with sufficient resources can do something of limited scope (for example, construct an apartment building or delay the extension of a free-way through a residential neighborhood). But no one has the capacity to do something comprehensive that covers several functional sectors or the metropolis at large (for example, to integrate highway construction with planning public transit with sewer construc-tion with residential construction with prior metropolitan land-use planning with equalizing social access to housing, education, and employment opportunities).

A Fragmented System of Local Government

Kenneth Newton points to "fragmentation as a structural attribute of U.S. urban govern-ment" with serious consequences for urban politics and policy.[37] The U.S. Constitution provides for a federal system: the central government and the state governments. The states then set up their own systems of local government, and these 50 systems result in 87,453 local governments in the United States (see Table 1.2 and Figure 1.1). Not only that, but these governments overlap with each other in boundaries and functions.

Although social scientists have noted this fragmentation, their theories, according to Newton, have stressed individualistic explanations. This has led some of them to conclude wrongly that fragmentation is good rather than bad. For example, public-choice theorists focus on how fragmented local government provides individuals with

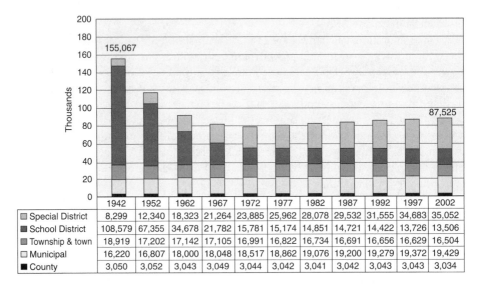

	1942	1952	1962	1967	1972	1977	1982	1987	1992	1997	2002
Special District	8,299	12,340	18,323	21,264	23,885	25,962	28,078	29,532	31,555	34,683	35,052
School District	108,579	67,355	34,678	21,782	15,781	15,174	14,851	14,721	14,422	13,726	13,506
Township & town	18,919	17,202	17,142	17,105	16,991	16,822	16,734	16,691	16,656	16,629	16,504
Municipal	16,220	16,807	18,000	18,048	18,517	18,862	19,076	19,200	19,279	19,372	19,429
County	3,050	3,052	3,043	3,049	3,044	3,042	3,041	3,042	3,043	3,043	3,034

FIGURE 1.1   Number of Local Governments in the United States

Source: Statistical Abstract of the United States, 2006, Table 415.

TABLE 1.2 Description of Local Government

	Description	Services Provided	Comment
Counties	General-purpose governments that are subdivisions of a state and are set up to carry out traditional state functions at the local level. In some states, counties are referred to as boroughs (Alaska) or parishes (Louisiana). All but two states have this unit of government.	Tax assessment and collection; official record keeping of property transfers; registering births, deaths, marriages, and divorces; elections; road maintenance; law enforcement and jails.	Traditionally, counties were the only government in a rural area. In more modern times, counties have added services, reflecting the urban populations they now serve. These services include health care, mass transit, pollution control, social services, and economic development.
Cities	General-purpose governments set up to provide urban services to more densely populated areas. Cities, or incorporated places (municipal corporations), are set up under state law. This usually involves citizens petitioning the state legislature to establish a municipality formally. The legislature then grants the city a charter that specifies the boundaries, organization, and powers of the municipality.	Police, fire, sewers, garbage collection, zoning, urban renewal, parks and recreation, roads.	Cities typically were created because urban residents demanded a higher level of public services than that provided by rural county governments. Population growth on the fringe of the city was often brought within the boundaries of the city by a process known as *annexation*, wherein the territory would be appended to the city, usually after a referendum (a vote of the affected citizens). In most instances today, a dual-majority-vote requirement (annexation must be favored by a majority in both the area to be annexed and the city as a whole) results in defeat of the

(continued)

TABLE 1.2 Description of Local Government (continued)

	Description	Services Provided	Comment
			annexation proposal because suburbanites nearly always vote against it. Cities are often created in the suburbs to prevent an older central city from annexing territory. This enables the more affluent residents to isolate themselves from the central city and its taxes and problems.
Towns and Townships	General-purpose governments that are set up as subdivisions of counties and carry out county services in a subset of the county. These may be rural or urban services.	Roads, law enforcement.	This type of government is found in 20 states in the Northeast and Midwest. In some states towns are more significant than in others.
Special Districts	Special-purpose governments designed to perform selected functions or services in specified geographic areas. These may be created for any purpose one can imagine, limited only by state law or the state constitution. In some instances, the state may grant city or county government the right to create special districts.	Fire, water supply and management, library, sewers, urban renewal, mosquito control (Florida).	In most cases, these government are insulated from direct control of the voters, and appointed board members make decisions. The rationale for this is that these governments deal with technical issues wherein it is thought that professional expertise should guide action. This type of government has been increasing greatly in the last several decades.

(continued)

TABLE 1.2 Description of Local Government *(continued)*

	Description	Services Provided	Comment
School Districts	A particular type of special district with an elected board that oversees the public school system.	Setting educational standards and building, maintaining, and operating the public elementary, middle, and high schools.	In some cases, city governments may provide this service. In addition, there may be more than one school district in a county. In the 1970s, many middle-class whites withdrew their children from public schools or moved to the suburbs to avoid busing and school integration. Many school consolidations occurred because of the high expense of providing public education.

the ability to choose what community to live in on the basis of the level of services and taxes that best meets their needs. They are hypothesized to behave as consumers in the marketplace. Competition among localities for business firms and residents is said to be beneficial because it results in more efficient urban services and lower tax rates.[38]

Pluralist theory focuses on how fragmentation allows greater democracy by providing many access points for groups and individuals to influence decisions that affect them. Pluralism's focus on the question "Who governs?"[39] points to "the power of individuals rather than the power of groups, rules, [and] institutions, or to a consideration of the ways in which certain sorts of structures shape the very nature and distribution of power."[40] Newton believes that the reliance on individualist explanations of urban politics (choices of individual consumers or elites) ignores the more important social and political consequences for urban areas of a fragmented system of local government.

For Newton, the real cause of the fragmentation is the desire of the affluent to separate themselves by creating autonomous suburban communities and leaving the poor and minorities behind in declining central cities. Governments in the metropolitan area strive to use all their powers (such as zoning and taxes) to protect their tax base and limit their responsibility for metropolitan problems outside their own boundaries. One economic consequence of this is that central cities are placed in an untenable position. If they spend money to address the problems of poverty and inner-city decay, they will drive out the affluent individuals and businesses that are the major source of revenue through property and other taxes.[41] Thus the individualist, pluralist, and public-choice theories obscure the larger structural imperatives that drive urban policy. Here, individual behavior and the choices of consumers, businesses, and political and economic leaders operate in the context of the political structure of the metropolis. There exist a myriad of local governments in which certain parts of the community can escape and isolate themselves.

According to Newton:

> The very drawing of political boundary lines may represent the victory of one social group over another, and it may be that different forms of city government and the structure of government within political units are much less important as basic determinants of the patterns of urban politics in the United States than is the drawing of political boundaries around and between different communities. Simply giving a middle-class suburb its autonomy as a unit of local government affects the total system of the metropolis, since money, the life blood of public services, is redirected along different arteries to different bodies politic.[42]

In addition, political fragmentation makes it difficult to assemble sufficient political resources to address problems. It may be impossible to arrive at consensus among so many different jurisdictions, and this may lead to "immobilism and non-decision-making."[43] The structure of political institutions in the metropolis, and the biases associated with them, become permanent. This is usually less of a problem for more affluent residents who can utilize their own resources to meet their needs (e.g., private schools, private security, private health care, private recreation). According to Newton, "fragmentation is a solution to problems—the middle-class solution which tries to ensure that other people's problems do not encroach on their suburbs."[44]

Newton explains that the fragmented system of local government leads to weak "public political authorities" and "strong private interests" whose actions have greater weight in community decisions—and hence a greater effect on outcomes—than do urban politics confined to city councils and the like. The net result of all this fragmentation in metropolitan areas is that we have "too many governments and not enough government": very weak governments that lack the capacity actually to address problems.[45] Another effect is that the private sector is virtually unregulated, because the local public sector lacks the means to make or enforce regulations. Further, citizens and politicians lower their expectations of what local government can accomplish.

Newton's ideas have not gone unnoticed. Scholars and practitioners alike have periodically called for a restructuring of local government in the United States. David Rusk, former mayor of Albuquerque, has proposed massive consolidation of central cities and county government.[46] He believes that this would help reconnect central cities to the suburbs and ensure that they have an adequate resource base. Rusk also believes this would allow for fair-share housing throughout the region; at present, suburban cities can, through their zoning powers, prevent low-income housing from being built within their boundaries. However, Rusk's proposals would leave most suburban cities intact and would not greatly reduce the fragmentation of local government. Moreover, city-county consolidation would undo the political gains of minorities who have taken over the central cities, because white, middle-class suburbanites would retake control of the city governments. In addition, there is evidence that some central cities today are no longer the ineffectual entities that they were when the boundary changes were originally proposed.[47] Here the calculation of whether the poor and minorities would be better off under the consolidation that Rusk advocates may vary from city to city. We shall revisit these issues in Chapters 9 and 10.

Bias, Change, and Political Power

To summarize the argument to this point: Urban political structures change slowly in an incremental, evolutionary fashion. As these changes occur, they have the potential to alter the existing patterns of bias concerning the ways in which political power is organized in the metropolis.

In presenting this argument, we have used the terms *politics* and *political power* in a very broad sense. Politics has referred to the struggle over public decisions that determine public policies and allocate values, goods, and services; hence *politics,* as used in this book, refers not only to the election of government officials but also to the making of public decisions and the results of public policy established by those decisions.[48]* It also refers to the broader social and economic processes that establish the constraints, needs, and capabilities that limit governmental action. In the next section, we take a more detailed look at *political power.*

---

*Political power also involves what are referred to as *nondecisions*. Nondecisions are the potential issues that never get placed on the agenda for public decision making because they are beyond the pale of what is politically acceptable. The importance of nondecisions to the exercise of power is argued by Peter Bachrach and Morton S. Baratz in "The Two Faces of Power," *American Political Science Review* 56, no. 4 (December 1962): 947–952. The significance of decisions and nondecisions in urban politics is discussed in Chapter 7.

Political Power

Public policies quite often result from pressure exerted on government by groups and individuals whose interests will be affected by those policies. To the extent that a given group or individual has influence on what a government does or does not do, that group or individual is said to possess political power.[49] To the extent that a given group or individual lacks influence on what a government does or does not do, that group or individual is said to lack political power. Some political scientists have suggested that the concept of power is so vague and so susceptible to multiple interpretations that it ought to be avoided whenever possible.[50] However, because some individuals, groups, and public officials do have the capability to influence government actions, it seems useful to have a term to represent that idea; thus we will use the term *political power* for this purpose. Mayors, city councils, and a host of other governmental officials and agencies are politically powerful because they have the capacity to take official action directly. Interest groups are politically powerful to the extent that they can influence what the governmental actors do.

Three aspects of political power are important to understanding how metropolises function.

Context of Power   First, metropolitan political power is generally contextual; that is, a given group usually has power only in a given context. It has power in those areas of public interest in which it chooses to, or is able to, assert itself. Thus, for example, real estate developers usually exert considerable influence on zoning and land use, but they are seldom influential in questions of air pollution control.

Structure of Power   A second important aspect of metropolitan political power is that it is structured: There are patterns to the distribution of power in the metropolis, and some categories of people are more powerful than others. The participating electorate possesses power to the extent that it chooses many of the political leaders and some-times acts as a restraint on what policy makers can accomplish. Further down the power scale from this real, if somewhat limited, power of the participating electorate is the extremely limited political power of unorganized people and of those who do not participate. In particular, the unorganized and the poor typically exert very little influence on the making of public decisions.[51] In contrast to the limited power of the participating electorate and the extremely limited power of the unorganized and the poor, some highly organized groups consistently exert great influence on public decisions that affect them. Certain businesspeople (especially those from the utilities, the major financial institutions, and the major local retailers) generally have a considerable voice in projects that promote their metropolitan area's economic expansion.[52] The political influence of other groups—groups such as labor unions, political parties, church organizations, and organized crime—varies from one metropolis to another. In Detroit, for example, labor unions are a very strong political force,[53] whereas unions tend to be much weaker in cities of the South and Southwest. But the important point here is that there is always a structure to the organization of political influence in metropolises. This does not necessarily mean that a small elite controls events. It does mean that political decisions do not occur randomly.

Public Power and Private Power   Political power is not only contextual and structured; it is also inseparable from private power. The broad sense of the term *political power,* as it is currently used by political scientists, makes drawing fine distinctions between the private and public aspects of power increasingly difficult. To take just one example, for the purely private financial reasons of trying to maximize profit and minimize losses, mortgage banks historically have been reluctant to make mortgage loans in declining areas of American cities. This practice is known as *redlining,* because the bankers supposedly draw a red line around the areas not eligible for loans.[54] Some other neighborhoods are allegedly *greenlined.* The target neighborhoods for urban redevelopment and gentrification, for example, encounter no shortage of mortgage bankers and real estate entrepreneurs who want to redevelop historic buildings or put up new projects.

Although mortgage lenders' decisions to redline neighborhoods are motivated by private reasons and private profits, these decisions have far-reaching public ramifications. The urban neighborhoods that are denied mortgage loans begin to deteriorate. Governments become obliged to spend public funds on stepped-up police and fire protection, public welfare assistance, renewal, and other services to deal with the consequences of that deterioration. The greenlined neighborhoods, by contrast, thrive and see their property values go up. For these reasons, the mortgage lenders' exercise of private power is equally an exercise of public power. Furthermore, if the cities' public authorities do not or cannot use their influence to induce lenders to make loans in redlined areas, then for all practical purposes, the public authorities have publicly acquiesced in and legitimized* these privately made decisions that determine which neighborhoods of the metropolis will deteriorate and which prosper. It is very difficult to call decisions of such magnitude private rather than public decisions, even though they might be made privately, by private businesspeople, for private motives. In this sense, the distinction between private and public has become vague. Private decisions can be public decisions in certain circumstances.

Privatism and Power

This reliance on private decision makers to decide on developments of extreme public importance we will call *privatism.* According to historian Sam Bass Warner, Jr., privatism has been characteristic of American urban history.[55] But this too is changing. One of the most marked political differences between 1900 and 2000 is the increased ability of governments today to influence private decisions that have public ramifications. In the case of redlining, for example, government has applied pressure on banks to cease the practice.

---

*Legitimacy has been defined as the "quality of being justified or willingly accepted by subordinates that converts the exercise of political power into 'rightful' authority"; see Jack C. Plano and Robert E. Riggs, *Dictionary of Political Analysis* (Hinsdale, Ill.: Dryden Press, 1973), p. 45. In this example, the acquiescence of the public authorities in the actions of the mortgage bankers enhances the likelihood of popular acceptance of the notion that bankers have a "rightful authority" to take actions that have such far-reaching consequences. According to Dolbeare, fundamental political change is first of all a process of "delegitimizing" existing institutions and then "legitimizing" new political institutions; see Kenneth M. Dolbeare, *Political Change in the United States* (New York: McGraw-Hill, 1974), p. 8. Thus, in this example, fundamental change would first of all involve delegitimizing the existing right of mortgage bankers to decide which areas of a metropolis qualify for mortgage loans. The second step would be to give this right to a new institution.

By contrast, one of the most important goals of the Reagan administration was to put an end to the public sector's encroachment into areas of economic life that had traditionally been private; hence the Reagan administration's support for privatization—that is, the contracting out of many public services to providers in the private sector.

Finally, privatism has its own patterns of bias. It helps make the urban system of politics more responsive to existing powerful and affluent institutions (especially banks and real estate developers) than to low-income individuals. In making the urban system of politics less responsive to low-income people, privatism inhibits the development of lower-class-based political institutions that might give the poor more influence over their city governments. How does privatism do this? By fostering a set of attitudes that encourage in people a self-centered individualism in which their personal ambitions for family, career advancement, and consumption of consumer goods take precedence over concerns for the community as a whole or concerns that all members of the community enjoy a decent living standard.[56] The essence of privatism, according to Warner, is that

> the individual should seek happiness in personal independence and in the search for wealth; socially, privatism meant that the individual should see his first loyalty as his immediate family, and that a community should be a union of such money-making, accumulating families; politically, privatism meant that the community should keep the peace among individual money-makers, and, if possible, help to create an open and thriving setting where each citizen would have some substantial opportunity to prosper.[57]

In such a privatistic value system, there is little room for the notion that the state is responsible for helping those people who fail to prosper. The privatistic person is not receptive to a welfare system and supports the political system only to the extent that the system assists his or her personal advancement. Gone is the ancient Greek belief that the purely private person is useless.

Privatism has different effects on different social classes. It induces the upper middle class to support city governments that would subsidize downtown redevelopment projects and not to support city governments that would dramatically increase welfare or social services in poor neighborhoods.[58] The effect of privatism on the poor classes is the inhibition of voter turnout and of involvement in political activities (such as protest demonstrations and collective bargaining) that would increase their collective influence on city government.

That, at least, is the theory of privatism. To date there is not much empirical research devoted to issues of privatism. But one survey did indeed find that people who scored high on a privatism index were less inclined than others to engage in political or protest activity, cared less about politics, were more materialistic, and were less liberal.[59] Unless the findings of this survey are reinforced by others, we would not be justified in concluding that privatism is as pervasively biased as the argument here suggests. But these findings are suggestive enough for us to take the privatism argument seriously. If the privatism argument is correct, the biases of privatism are quite apparent. Privatism helps the wealthy and the upper middle classes retain their privileged status in our society. And by discouraging a class-based politics, privatism hinders the ability of the urban poor to pursue their own collective self-interest.[60]

SUMMARY

1. Cities are challenged by a host of natural and human disasters ranging from terrorist attacks on the World Trade Towers in New York City to Hurricane Katrina damaging the levees leading to flooding in New Orleans. Cities are *resilient* and most of the time return, although not necessarily to pre-disaster levels. Modern complex administrative systems require coordination among and between numerous public and private actors at the local, regional, state, and national levels. The New Orleans flooding especially revealed defects in the intergovernmental system and reminded us of the underlying persistence of poverty and racial inequality in American cities. These serious urban problems are largely unaddressed by the American political system at any level.

2. In examining the process of urban politics, this book will look for *patterns of bias* to see whether certain groups of people systematically benefit from the process and whether other groups of people are systematically excluded from the process or are put at a disadvantage by it.

3. Urban political change has been predominantly incremental change rather than revolutionary change.

4. Three distinct periods of urban political change can be noted in America:
   A. 1830s–1930s: the period of ethnic and machine politics
   B. 1930s–1970s: the period of functional fiefdoms
   C. 1960s–present: the period of the dependent city

5. Local government is fragmented in the United States. This fragmentation leads to biases in urban politics and policy. Notably, the middle and upper classes are able to isolate themselves from the problems of the central city and to exclude the poor from their suburban communities.

6. We use the term *politics* in a broad sense to refer to the struggle over public decisions that determine public policies and allocate values, goods, and services.

7. *Political power* is the ability to influence these public decisions. Urban political power is characterized by three features. First, it is contextual. That is, a given group usually has power only in a given context. Second, it is structured. The most powerful groups are those that are permanent and that maintain an ongoing relationship with government. Third, public power is inseparable from private power. Private institutions (such as mortgage banks) make private decisions (such as discouraging mortgage loans in redlined neighborhoods) that have consequences (such as neighborhood deterioration) to which governments must respond.

8. Finally, it can be argued that the tradition of privatism in urban America is itself biased in favor of the upper middle classes and against the interests of the urban poor.

NOTES

1. H. V. Savitch and Grigoriy Ardashev, "Does Terror Have an Urban Future?" *Urban Studies* 38 (December 2001): 2515–2533.
2. Lawrence J. Vale and Thomas J. Campanella, *The Resilient City: How Modern Cities Recover from Disaster* (Oxford: Oxford University Press, 2005).

3. Ibid., 12–13.

4. http://www.com/2001/US/09/11/chronology.attack/index.html.

5. Centers for Disease Control, "Deaths in World Trade Center Terrorist Attacks—New York City, 2001," *Morbidity and Mortality Weekly Report*, September 11, 2002: 51: 16–18; http://www.nyc.gov/html/nypd/pdf/viewlist.pdf; http://www.nyc.gov/html/fdny/html/general/commstat.html.

6. New York City Partnership and Chamber of Commerce, "Working Together to Accelerate New York's Recovery: Economic Impact Analysis of the September 11th Attack on New York City (New York: Author, November 2001), 5–6. http://www.nycp.org; "The $105 Billion Question," *Newsweek*, October 22, 2001, 62.

7. Jennifer Steinhauer, "City Proposes Priority Uses of Federal Aid," *New York Times*, October 24, 2001, 1.

8. Steven Stehr, "The Political Economy of Assistance," *Urban Affairs Review* 41 (March 2006): 495.

9. Robert Kolker, "The Power of Partnership," *New York*, November 26, 2001.

10. Steven Stehr, "The Political Economy of Assistance," *Urban Affairs Review* 41 (March 2006): 495.

11. John Mollenkopf, "Who Decides and How? Government Decision-Making After 9/11." Unpublished manuscript, January 29, 2002.

12. "Verdict Favors World Trade Center Leaseholder," http://www.cnn.com/2004/LAW/12/06/wtc.trial/ (downloaded March 8, 2006).

13. Charles V. Bagli, "Deadline for Ground Zero Plan Nears," *New York Times*, February. 6, 2006 (downloaded from nytimes.com on March 8, 2006).

14. Charles V. Bagli and Sewell Chan, "Schumer and Bloomberg Clash on Ground Zero Plan," *New York Times*, February 28, 2006, 3.

15. David W. Dunlap, "Critics Say Memorial Plan Imperils Towers' Remnants," *New York Times*, March 2, 2006 (downloaded from nytimes.com March 8, 2006).

16. *The Federal Response to Hurricane Katrina: Lessons Learned*, http://www.whitehouse.gov/reports/katrina-lessons-learned/.

17. Louise Comfort, "Cities at Risk: Hurricane Katrina and the Drowning of New Orleans," *Urban Affairs Review* 41 (March 2006): 501, 506.

18. Ibid., 506.

19. Ibid., 503.

20. Ibid., 507.

21. Steven Stehr, "The Political Economy of Assistance," *Urban Affairs Review* 41 (March 2006): 496.

22. Ibid., 493.

23. Peter Burns and Matthew Thomas, "The Failure of the Nonregime: How Katrina Exposed New Orleans as a Regimeless City," *Urban Affairs Review* 41 (March 2006): 517–527.

24. Peter Dreier, "Katrina and Power in America," *Urban Affairs Review* 41 (March 2006): 528.

25. Ibid., 533.

26. Harold Lasswell, *Politics: Who Gets What, When, How* (New York: McGraw-Hill, 1936).

27. Students not familiar with the input-output model of political analysis might find it useful to examine one of the many "systems analysis" models of politics. Much of the systems analysis terminology stems from the writings of David Easton and Gabriel Almond. See David Easton, *A Systems Analysis of Political Life* (New York: Wiley, 1965) and Gabriel Almond and G. Bingham Powell, *Comparative Politics: A Developmental Approach* (Boston: Little, Brown, 1966). Some interesting attempts to concentrate on the output side of this model in order to analyze the costs and benefits of policy outputs are Thomas R. Dye, *Politics, Economics, and the Public: Policy Outcomes in the American States* (Chicago: Rand McNally, 1966) and Brett W. Hawkins, *Politics and Urban Policies* (Indianapolis: Bobbs-Merrill, 1971).

28. *Political change* has proved to be an elusive term for political scientists to define precisely. The literature on political change has focused primarily on non-Western countries that are perceived as undergoing a modernizing or developmental process. Another focus has been the revolutionary aspects of some change. Prominent examples of these focal points can be found in John H. Kautsky, *Political Change in Underdeveloped Countries: Nationalism and Communism* (New York: Wiley, 1962); David E. Apter, *The Politics of Modernization* (Chicago: University of Chicago Press, 1965); Leonard Binder, *Iran: Political Development in a Changing Society* (Berkeley and Los Angeles: University of California Press, 1962); Peter H. Merkl, *Political Continuity and Change* (New York: Harper & Row, 1967); and Chalmers A. Johnson, *Revolutionary Change* (Boston: Little, Brown, 1966).

29. Kenneth M. Dolbeare, *Political Change in the United States: A Framework for Analysis* (New York: McGraw-Hill, 1974), p. 7.

30. This point is made particularly by Anthony Downs, *Urban Problems and Prospects* (Chicago: Markham, 1970), p. 1; and by Daniel N. Gordon, "The Bases of Urban Political Change: A Brief History of Developments and Trends," in *Social Change and Urban Politics: Readings,* ed. Daniel N. Gordon (Englewood Cliffs, N.J.: Prentice-Hall, 1973), pp. 2–21. Dolbeare, however, argues that political change is an independent process because the political system has often failed to change with changes in the economic system. See his *Political Change in the United States,* p. 3.

31. Murray Edelman, *The Symbolic Uses of Politics* (Urbana: University of Illinois Press, 1964).

32. This point is made by Yasumasa Kuroda in a study of a Japanese community. See his *Reed Town, Japan: A Study in Community Power Structure and Political Change* (Honolulu: University of Hawaii Press, 1974), pp. 7–8.

33. See Theodore Lowi, *At the Pleasure of the Mayor* (New York: Free Press, 1964). See also Edward C. Banfield and James Q. Wilson, *City Politics* (Cambridge, Mass.: Harvard University Press, 1963), pp. 107–110.

34. Political scientist Marilyn Gittell has described the difficulty of exercising electoral control over the New York City public school system. See her "Professionalization and Public Participation in Educational Policy Making: New York City, a Case Study," *Public Administration Review* 27, no. 3 (September 1967): 237–251. A similar point is developed by Norman I. Fainstein and Susan S. Fainstein in "The Political Evaluation of Educational Policies," in *Neighborhood Control in the 1970's,* ed. George Frederickson (New York: Chandler, 1973), pp. 195–216. See Harmon L. Zeigler et al., *Governing American Education* (Belmont, Calif.: Duxbury Press, 1974). See also Chapter 7.

35. See Chapter 11 for a fuller discussion of the attempts made during the 1970s to articulate a national urban policy.

36. See Michael Patrenti, "Ethnic Politics and the Persistence of Ethnic Identification," *American Political Science Review* 61 (September 1967): 717–726; and Raymond E. Wolfinger, "The Development and Persistence of Ethnic Voting," *American Political Science Review* 59 (December 1965): 896–908.

37. Kenneth Newton, "American Urban Politics: Social Class, Political Structure and Public Goods," *Urban Affairs Quarterly* 11 (December 1975): 241–264.

38. See Robert Bish and Vincent Ostrom, *Understanding Urban Government: Metropolitan Reform Reconsidered* (Washington, D.C.: American Enterprise Institute for Policy Research, 1979); Ronald Oakerson and Roger Parks, "Metropolitan Organization: St. Louis and Allegheny County," *Intergovernmental Perspectives* 17 (Summer 1991): 27–34; Roger Parks and Ronald Oakerson, "Metropolitan Organization and Governance—A Local Political Economy Approach," *Urban Affairs Quarterly* 25 (1989): 5–17.

39. See Robert Dahl, *Who Governs?* (New Haven, Conn.: Yale University Press, 1961).

40. Kenneth Newton, "American Urban Politics: Social Class, Political Structure and Public Goods," *Urban Affairs Quarterly* 11 (December 1975): 245.

41. See Paul Peterson, *City Limits* (Chicago: University of Chicago Press, 1981).

42. Kenneth Newton, "American Urban Politics: Social Class, Political Structure and Public Goods," *Urban Affairs Quarterly* 11 (December 1975): 255.

43. Ibid., 257.

44. Ibid., 258.

45. Ibid.

46. See David Rusk, *Cities Without Suburbs,* 2d ed. (Washington, D.C.: Woodrow Wilson Center Press, 1995).

47. H. V. Savitch and Ronald K. Vogel, "Metropolitan Consolidation versus Metropolitan Governance in Louisville," *State and Local Government Review,* 32, no. 3 (Fall 2000): 198–212.

48. The definition of politics as the allocation of values, goods, and services is adapted from David Easton, *The Political System* (New York: Knopf, 1953). The definition of politics in terms of decision making is adapted from Robert A. Dahl, *Who Governs? Democracy and Power in an American City* (New Haven, Conn.: Yale University Press, 1961) and Nelson Polsby, *Community Power and Political Theory* (New Haven, Conn.: Yale University Press, 1963).

49. This approach to defining power is analyzed extensively by Robert A. Dahl in *Modern Political Analysis,* 2d ed. (Englewood Cliffs, N.J.: Prentice-Hall, 1970), pp. 19–25 and 32–34. Dahl asserts that power is merely an extreme form of influence in which coercion is involved. "Severe losses for non-compliance can be invoked by the power holder" (p. 32).

50. Raymond E. Wolfinger, *The Politics of Progress* (Englewood Cliffs, N.J.: Prentice-Hall, 1974), pp. 7–9.

51. This viewpoint is discussed in Chapter 7. On the political efficacy of the poor and the unorganized, see Michael Parenti, "Power and Pluralism: A View from the Bottom," *Journal of Politics* 32, no. 3 (August 1970): 501–532.

52. On central-city business interests, see especially Edward C. Banfield and James Q. Wilson, *City Politics* (Cambridge, Mass.: Harvard University Press, 1963), pp. 261–276. On suburban business interests, see especially Charles Gilbert, *Governing the Suburbs* (Bloomington: University of Indiana Press, 1967), 145.

53. On Detroit, see Edward C. Banfield, *Big City Politics* (New York: Random House, 1965). On Chicago, see Banfield and Wilson, *City Politics*, pp. 277–278.

54. For background on this practice, see the *Wall Street Journal*, April 5, 1974, p. 1.

55. Historian Sam Bass Warner, Jr., has asserted the importance of privatism in American urban history. See his *The Private City: Philadelphia in Three Periods of Its Growth* (Philadelphia: University of Pennsylvania Press, 1968); Warner asserts, "The tradition of privatism is . . . the most important element of our culture for understanding the development of cities" (pp. 38–39).

56. See Juergen Habermas, *Legitimation Crisis* (Boston: Beacon Press, 1973), pp. 37, 75, and Robert D. Holloway and J. Harry Wray, *American Politics and Everyday Life* (New York: Wiley, 1982), p. 60.

57. Warner, *The Private City*, pp. 3–4.

58. Although he did not use the term *privatism*, the argument against city governments financing substantial welfare or social services is made quite persuasively by Paul E. Peterson in his *City Limits* (Chicago: University of Chicago Press, 1981).

59. Steven A. Peterson, "Privatism and Politics: A Research Note," *Western Political Quarterly* 37, no. 3 (September 1984): 483–489.

60. Another downside to increased privatism is discussed by Evan McKenzie in *Privatopia: Homeowner Associations and the Rise of Residential Private Government* (New Haven, Conn.: Yale University Press, 1996). He argues that private homeowner associations are taking on local governmental functions and that this usurpation of power threatens the constitutional rights of individuals.

CHAPTER 2

THE EMERGENCE
OF METROPOLITAN AMERICA

CHAPTER SYNOPSIS

Urban Characteristics of the American Population: *Definition of Urban;*
Census Terminology • Basic Determinants of Metropolitan Growth: *Agricultural Surplus;*
Innovations in Transportation Technology; Reduction in Death Rates in Cities • Urbanization
in the U.S.: *Historical; Contemporary Metropolitan America; Postindustrial Metropolitan*
Development • Implications and Biases of Metropolitan Development Patterns:
Role of Government and Politics in Shaping Development; Privatism and Segregation

For most of its history, America was shaped by rural people and small-town residents. Today, by contrast, 93 percent of all Americans live in metropolitan areas. This dramatic transformation has deeply affected the political culture and economy of the United States. Chapter 2 explores several broad questions about the process through which contemporary metropolises emerged in the United States.

- What is meant by the terms *urban* and *metropolitan?* What are the essential urban characteristics of the American population?
- Why do metropolises grow? How has the character of American urbanization changed as the cities grew into metropolises? In what ways does urbanization today differ from earlier patterns of urban growth?
- What are the political implications of these changes? Do these changes involve any political bias? That is, have they diminished some people's access to the political decision makers and to the social amenities of the metropolis, such as good schools and employment opportunities? If so, who are the people whose political and social access has been diminished?

Urban Characteristics of the American Population

The classic definition of *urban* has three elements: volume, density, and heterogeneity of population. The first two elements are basically demographic, and the third is sociological.[1] The key criteria for distinguishing urban from nonurban places thus become: How large must a population be to be called urban? How dense must it be? And how heterogeneous must it be?

Urbanists usually rely on data from the United States Census Bureau to study urban trends and statistics. The Office of Management and Budget (OMB), which is responsible for defining metropolitan boundaries and classifications used by the U.S. Census Bureau, recently led an interagency Metropolitan Standards Review Committee that recommended a new set of concepts and definitions to better capture urban settlement patterns. These criteria took effect in 2003 and completely revise the units of analysis employed to describe and analyze urban trends. The metropolis is now defined as the *core-based statistical area* (CBSA). The CBSA "is a geographic entity associated with at least one core . . . plus adjacent territory that has a high degree of social and economic integration with the core as measured by commuting ties." A CBSA with an urban cluster of 10,000 to 50,000 is designated a *micropolitan statistical area.* A CBSA with an urbanized area of 50,000 or more is classified as a *metropolitan statistical area* (see Figure 2.1 and Table 2.1). Counties remain the "building blocks" (or minor civil divisions in New England) for designating the CBSA.

One important change is that the threshold for commuting has been raised. Outlying counties will now be included in the CBSA only "if (a) 25 percent of the employed residents of the county work in the CBSA's central county or counties, or (b) at least 25 percent of the jobs in the potential outlying county are accounted for by workers who reside in the CBSA's central county or counties."[2] Population density will no longer be a factor in whether to include an outlying county in the metropolitan area. This definition should more accurately reflect the city-region's boundary on the basis of its economy operationalized through commuting patterns. However, this is still a fairly restrictive definition of commuting, focusing as it does on work. In today's multicentered metropolis, many commute daily for education, and their trips will not be factored into this equation.

Although the 2000 census reports data according to the older classification system, the new definitions are coming into use and researchers are shifting to the new terminology. William Frey, Jill Wilson, Alan Berube, and Audrey Singer outline some of the significant changes associated with the new definitions in a Bookings Institution report.[3] They report the following changes:

- Under the new system, 81 of the nation's 102 largest metropolitan areas have undergone changes in territory and population. The most common changes involved the addition of new counties to an existing metropolitan area, and the combination of two or more metro areas to form a new, larger metropolis.
- Both metropolitan and micropolitan areas contain *principal* cities, which replace central cities in the new names given to these areas. Roughly 40 percent of the combined metropolitan population lived in principal cities in 2000, compared to 35 percent in central cities.
- The new definitions alter the social and economic attributes of many metropolitan areas as well as their national rankings on these attributes. For instance, New York has replaced Los Angeles as the nation's most populous metropolitan area. San Francisco drops from fourth to fourteenth in metropolitan rankings of college degree attainment.[4]

TABLE 2.1   Largest Metropolitan Areas

Rank	Metropolitan Area (2000)	Population in 1990	Population in 2000	Population in 2003	Percent Change, 1990–2000	Percent Change, 2000–2003
1	New York-Northern N.J.-Long Island, N.Y.-N.J.-Pa.	16,846,000	18,323,000	18,641,000	8.8%	1.7%
2	Los Angeles-Long Beach-Santa Ana, Calif.	11,274,000	12,366,000	12,829,000	9.7	3.7
3	Chicago-Naperville-Joliet, IL-IN-WI	8,182,000	9,099,000	9,334,000	11.2	2.6
4	Philadelphia-Camden-Wilmington, PA-NJ-DE-MD	5,435,000	5,687,000	5,773,000	4.6	1.5
5	Dallas-Fort Worth-Arlington, TX	3,989,000	5,162,000	5,590,000	29.4	8.3
6	Miami-Fort Lauderdale-Miami Beach, FL	4,056,000	5,008,000	5,289,000	23.5	5.6
7	Washington-Arlington-Alexandria DC-VA-MD-WV	4,123,000	4,796,000	5,090,000	16.3	6.1
8	Houston-Baytown-Sugar Land, TX	3,767,000	4,715,000	5,076,000	25.2	7.6
9	Atlanta-Sandy Springs-Marietta, GA	3,069,000	4,248,000	4,610,000	38.4	8.5
10	Detroit-Warren-Livonia, MI	4,249,000	4,453,000	4,484,000	4.8	0.7
11	Boston-Cambridge-Quincy, MA-NH	4,134,000	4,392,000	4,440,000	6.3	1.1
12	San Francisco-Oakland-Fremont, CA	3,687,000	4,124,000	4,157,000	11.9	0.8
13	Riverside-San Bernardino-Ontario, CA	2,589,000	3,255,000	3,642,000	25.7	11.9
14	Phoenix-Mesa-Scottsdale, AZ	2,238,000	3,252,000	3,593,000	45.3	10.5
15	Seattle-Tacoma-Bellevue, WA	2,559,000	3,044,000	3,142,000	18.9	3.2
16	Minneapolis-St. Paul-Bloomington, MN-WI	2,539,000	2,969,000	3,084,000	16.9	3.9
17	San Diego-Carlsbad-San Marcos, CA	2,498,000	2,814,000	2,931,000	12.6	4.2
18	St. Louis, MO-IL	2,581,000	2,699,000	2,736,000	4.6	1.4
19	Baltimore-Towson, MD	2,382,000	2,553,000	2,616,000	7.2	2.5
20	Tampa-St. Petersburg-Clearwater, FL	2,068,000	2,396,000	2,532,000	15.9	5.7

Source: U.S. Census Bureau, Current Population Reports, Population Change in Metropolitan and Micropolitan Statistical Areas: 1990–2003, Table 6.

FIGURE 2.1   Metropolitan Areas of the United States and Puerto Rico: 2004

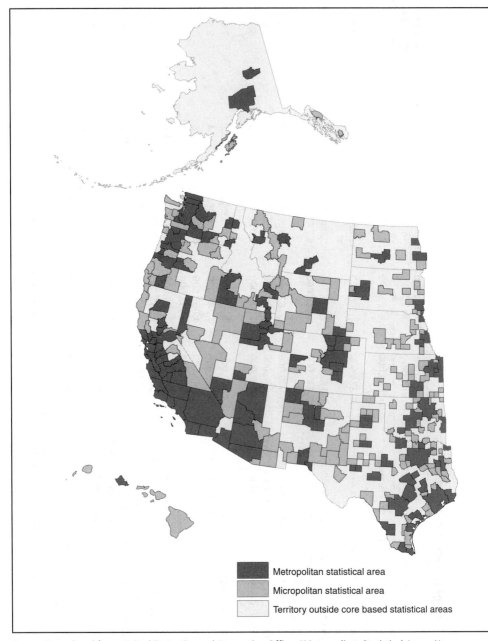

Metropolitan statistical area

Micropolitan statistical area

Territory outside core based statistical areas

Source: Reproduced from: United States General Accounting Office, "Metropolitan Statistical Areas: New Standards and Their Impact on Selected Federal Programs (June 2004), GAO-04-758, p. 15.

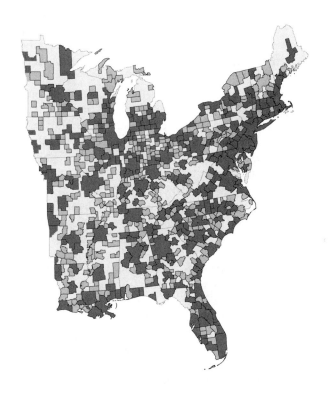

The search for an appropriate definition of the *metropolitan area* (MA) is not new. One approach has been to define as metropolitan any area with a population of at least 100,000 people that contains a central city or cities and has at least 65 percent of its economically active population engaged in nonagricultural activities.[5] This fairly restrictive definition would exclude many areas now considered metropolitan.

A different approach to defining a metropolitan area has been to avoid putting precise political boundaries on what is considered metropolitan. This is done by defining an area not in terms of counties (as the MA is defined) but in terms of commuting distance. One advocate of this approach is geographer John Friedmann, who rejects the term *metropolitan area* and introduces *urban field*. He defines an urban field as a core area of 300,000 people plus all areas within a radius equivalent to a two-hour automobile drive.[6] Friedmann prefers such a definition—which would probably classify about 90 percent of the American population as urbanized—because, he asserts, most of the American people exhibit urban social traits regardless of where they live or what their occupations. Whatever the relative advantages of these other approaches to defining metropolitan areas, the MA definition is the most widely accepted method of identifying American metropolises, and it is the definition according to which all federal statistical data are compiled.

In addition to urban places and MAs, another level of urbanization, called *megalopolis* by French geographer Jean Gottmann,[7] is found along the North Atlantic seacoast where the metropolitan areas are growing into one another. The Northeast megalopolis centered around New York City includes a chain of metropolises stretching from southern New Hampshire to northern Virginia and containing about 45 million people. The Northeast megalopolis contains distinguishing features other than a continuous metropolitan strip. Covering some 50,000 square miles, with an average density of 700 people per square mile, it is one of the largest dense areas in the world. It is one of the world's wealthiest concentrations of people. It also embraces one of the world's greatest concentrations of political and economic power and artistic and literary leadership.

Metropolitan areas in three other regions are increasingly growing together to the megalopolis point. One of these regions, with 25 million people, is along the southern shore of the Great Lakes, particularly along Lake Michigan. Numerous MAs branch out contiguously from key lake ports at Milwaukee-Chicago, Detroit-Toledo, Cleveland, and Buffalo-Rochester. A third megalopolis, with 30 million people, is emerging on the southern Pacific coast from San Francisco to the Mexican border. A fourth megalopolis with about 10 million people is developing along the Florida peninsula from Jacksonville to Miami on the Atlantic Coast and spreading out to include Orlando in Central Florida across to Tampa on the Gulf Coast. Together, these four megalopolises comprise a very small percentage of the land area of the United States, but they contain more than 38 percent of the U.S. population.

The Basic Determinants of Metropolitan Growth

The emergence of giant megalopolises did not happen by accident. Metropolitan growth is shaped by basic economic, technological, and political forces. Only within the last hundred years have these forces converged to create great metropolises of several million people. The great cities of antiquity and the Middle Ages were relatively small. Babylon covered an area of no more than 3.2 square miles. Athens, at the height of its glory in the fifth century B.C., contained fewer than 200,000 people. Florence in the fourteenth century was a city of no more than 90,000 people, and Venice in the fifteenth century contained about 190,000. Of all the leading premodern cities, only Rome approached a population of a million.[8]

There are three reasons why giant metropolises and megalopolises began to emerge only in the late nineteenth and early twentieth centuries. First, it was not until that time that a large enough *agricultural surplus* was produced to enable a majority of the population to live off the agricultural production of a dwindling minority of the population. The level of urbanization is inversely proportional to the number of farmers it takes to support one nonfarmer who lives in the city.

This fact led some urbanists to argue that urbanization is dependent on increased agricultural production.[9] Although this may imply that city dwellers are parasites living off the agricultural surplus, in fact, farmers and city dwellers are mutually dependent. Farmers would be forced to live at a subsistence level if cities and towns did not exist to perform valuable services for farmers. Urbanites transport farmers' goods, finance their investment in crops, import or manufacture consumer goods that farmers can purchase with the earnings from their crops, and administer the safety and well-being of the countryside. Without these services, modern agriculture would be impossible.[10]

In the contemporary era, this ecological balance has been altered by the second factor in the rise of the large metropolis: the *innovations in transportation technology.*[11] The contemporary metropolis requires a sophisticated transportation network in order to "import" food and raw materials and to move the area's production out to its markets. The availability of steamships, railroads, motor transport, and air transport makes it possible to supply increasingly larger populations over increasingly longer distances. These forms of transport are also much more energy-intensive than the forms of transport that supplied any previous forms of urbanization. Unless new forms of transport or new sources of energy are discovered before existing supplies of petroleum are exhausted, contemporary metropolises and megalopolises will not remain viable.

In addition to the transportation network and the agricultural surplus made possible by modern technology, a third factor contributing to the growth of giant metropolises has been increasing *control over death rates.* Until the nineteenth century, life in towns and cities was much more hazardous than life in the rural areas. Sanitary conditions were so poor and death rates so high that the growth of towns and cities was often very sporadic. Even as late as 1878, a two-month epidemic of yellow fever in the city of Memphis, Tennessee, killed 5,000 people, struck another 12,000, and caused 25,000 people to flee the city. In just two months, the city's population was reduced from about 50,000 people to fewer than 20,000.[12] Cities like Memphis could not grow into metropolises until people learned how to keep their excretion from polluting their drinking water; until they learned some elementary principles of hygiene; and until the improving practice of medicine began to eliminate the scourge of contagious diseases such as typhoid, typhus, cholera, and yellow fever. When these things occurred, the human population began to grow at an exponential rate, and, in an economic sense, an excess population was created.

Because of the ecological balance between the rural areas and the small rural towns, this excess population could not sustain itself in rural areas and had to migrate elsewhere.

The problem became particularly acute during the nineteenth century in western Europe and England, where there was no more open land to be colonized and cultivated. Much of the excess population therefore migrated to the first great cities of the Industrial Revolution—Liverpool, Birmingham, Sheffield, and London. And much of it migrated to the Western Hemisphere, where it stimulated the urbanization of the United States.

How the United States Urbanized: Small Town to Megalopolis

The Urbanization of America, 1840–1920

The same three factors that permitted the development of large cities in general influenced the growth of cities in the United States. From 1730 to the end of the eighteenth century, the percentage of the population living in cities actually declined.[13] Large cities did not become commonplace until well into the nineteenth century. At the time of the War of Independence, the largest city, Philadelphia, contained only about 40,000 people. The first city of 100,000 population did not emerge until almost 1820, and even as late as 1840, there were only three such cities. By 1850 that number had doubled.[14] The decade of the 1840s thus marks the beginning of intensive urbanization in the United States. The city-building phase of urbanization reached its peak by 1920, when for the first time a majority of the population lived in urban places. These 80 years of urbanization resulted from three historical forces:

- Immigration and migration
- Improved transportation
- The emergence of a national corporate economy

Urban Migrations   The first of these forces was extensive immigration. Thirty-seven million people migrated to the United States between 1841 and 1930. Politically, they were a very important force, for they created the basic institutions of urban politics that are influential in many of the central cities even today.

As can be seen in Table 2.2, urban migrants arrived in different stages. The first stage was dominated by Irish and German immigration, with the Irish settling primarily in urban places in the Northeast and the Germans settling in both urban and rural places in both the Northeast and the Midwest.

During the second stage, from the 1890s until the 1920s, immigrants came primarily from southern and eastern Europe and settled both in the Northeast and in the cities of the Midwest. These two waves of European immigration had a profound impact on the composition of the American population. In a 1972 survey, the Census Bureau estimated that over 30 percent of the population of the United States traced its heritage to just six of these ethnic nationalities: German, Irish, Russian, Polish, Italian, and French.[15] Because the Irish, Russian, Polish, and Italian immigrants settled mainly in the metropolitan cities, they represent an even larger percentage of the metropolitan population than of the overall American population. The urban political institutions created by these immigrants have had a disproportionate influence on the development of metropolitan America.

TABLE 2.2   Four Waves of Immigration/Migration to Cities

Group	Era	Number
First Wave: Mainstream Immigrants		
English	1845–1895	4,114,023
Germans	1845–1885	5,747,710
Second Wave: European Ethnic Minorities		
Irish	1845–1885	4,437,610
Italians	1900–1914	4,648,503
Catholic Poles	1900–1914	
Jews[a]	1882–1924	2,300,000
Third Wave: Rural South to North		
American blacks	1940–1970	
	1910–1920	300,000
	1920–1930	1,300,000
	1930–1940	500,000
	1940–1950	2,500,000
Fourth Wave: Contemporary Urban Migrants[b]		
Hispanics	1961–1998	8,949,000
Asians	1961–1998	6,984,000

[a]Jewish immigrants prior to 1880 were mostly Germans. After 1880 they were mostly Russians and Poles.

[b]Hispanic and Asian immigration is probably greatly understated because of the large number of illegal immigrants.

Sources: U.S. Bureau of the Census, *Historical Statistics of the United States from Colonial Times to 1957* (Washington, D.C.: U.S. Government Printing Office, 1957), pp. 56–59. U.S. Bureau of the Census, *Statistical Abstract of the United States: 1971* (Washington, D.C.: U.S. Government Printing Office, 1971), p. 92. Jewish immigration is taken from Arthur A. Goren, "Jews," *Harvard Encyclopedia of American Ethnic Groups,* ed. Stephen Thernstein (Cambridge, Mass.: The Belknap Press of Harvard University Press, 1980) p. 571. Data are taken from U.S. Bureau of the Census, *Statistical Abstract of the United States: 1990* (Washington, D.C.: U.S. Government Printing Office, 1991), p. 10; U.S. Bureau of the Census, *Statistical Abstract of the United States: 2000* (Washington, D.C.: electronic version), p. 10; and Lerone Bennett, Jr., "10 Most Dramatic Events in African American History," *Ebony* 56 (February 2001), p. 122.

A third migration wave that profoundly altered the composition of American cities was that of American blacks coming out of the rural South into the cities. Because the black migrants were American citizens rather than foreign immigrants, their migration into cities has been called *in-migration* rather than immigration. This migration wave was at its peak from about 1940 to the early 1970s. Today, there is evidence of a modest *reverse migration* of African Americans returning to the South. The 2000 census reveals that the black population in the South grew by more than 3.5 million people between 1990 and 2000 (a net increase of more than 500,000), while the Northeast, Midwest, and West had a net loss in black population. Interestingly, those returning are settling in the suburbs rather than in central cities.[16]

Finally, as African American urban in-migration began to taper off in the 1970s, a fourth wave of Hispanic and Asian immigrants began moving into American cities. These immigrants are dramatically altering the demographic composition and politics of cities.[17]

Transportation Technology   The combination of innovation in the technology of transport and the frontier movement to the West also contributed to the establishment of U.S. cities.[18] The discovery of gold in California, the existence of fertile farmland from the Appalachian Mountains almost to the Pacific Coast, and the generous subsidization of the railroads to expand westward spurred a continual westward migration of the population. Along these railroad lines there began to emerge "gateway" cities, which functioned as transfer points for the exchange of goods between the railroads and the surrounding agricultural communities.[19]

In many instances the railroads created the cities. When southern Illinois towns refused to grant concessions that the Illinois Central Railroad desired in order to run its tracks through those towns, the Illinois Central ran its tracks through other locations and established its own gateway towns in competition with existing cities. A typical practice was for the railroad to acquire title to empty land, survey it, parcel it out for city lots, and then sell the lots for a profit. At Kankakee, Illinois, for example, the railroad bought land for $18,000, sold some of the subdivided lots for $50,000, and held the remainder, valued at $100,000, for future sales. When the Illinois Central was chartered in 1851, there were only ten towns along its route. Twenty years later there were 81, and the total population of all these places, excluding Chicago, increased 14-fold, from 12,000 to 172,000.[20] The creation of these western railroad towns opened up western farmlands and turned the United States into the world's greatest agricultural producer. The agricultural surplus that began to emerge in the nineteenth century in turn became a further stimulus to growth of American cities.

Growth within the cities was also conditioned by the technology of transportation. Sam Bass Warner, Jr., has shown how transit innovations affected the growth of Boston.[21] Until the 1850s, Boston was a pedestrian city with no transit system, and the outer boundaries of the residential areas were naturally limited to a radius of about 2 miles. The introduction of horse-drawn railways extended the city's boundaries to perhaps 2.5 miles by 1873 and to 4 miles by 1887. In the 1890s, electric streetcars were introduced, and the city's boundaries were extended to a radius of 6 miles.

The streetcar had other important effects on city development. It facilitated a form of retail strip shopping areas along the streetcar routes where retailers found it lucrative to establish their shops. Later, in the age of the automobile, these strip shopping areas would decline in most cities, and the more successful retailers would move to the suburban shopping centers and malls. The streetcars also made possible the first extensive urbanization by connecting the central business district with newly urbanized places beyond the city proper. The streetcar outlined the physical growth of the eastern central cities as we know them today.

The other major technological innovations in transportation were the elevated and subway railways. New York introduced the first steam elevated trains in the 1870s, but because of their dirtiness and their tendency occasionally to spew hot ashes on pedestrians walking beneath the elevated structures, they were replaced with electric elevated trains in the 1890s and with subways in the early 1900s.

It is difficult to overestimate the importance of these technological changes to the prosperity of individual cities.[22] Table 2.3 indicates how dependent most cities are on prevailing modes of transportation technology and how vulnerable they are to sudden innovations. Although budding nineteenth-century river cities such as Galena, Illinois; Wheeling, West Virginia; and Louisville, Kentucky, seemed destined to grow into another Chicago, they found their growth stunted when transportation technology changed. They were bypassed because of newer, more efficient means of transporting goods and

TABLE 2.3 Transportation Technology and the Growth of Cities

| Mode of Transport | Time Period of Most Importance | Source of Locomotion | Intensiveness | | | Representative City |
			Capital	Labor	Energy	
Turnpike Most important cargo: people, supplies for personal needs	1800–1840	Animal and foot	Low	Very high	Very low	Cumberland, Md.
Canal Most important cargo: grain from West to East	1820–1850	Barge: first animal, then steam	Medium	High	Very low	Rome, N.Y.
River Most important cargo: grain, agricultural products generally, people	1840–1875	Steam, then diesel	Low	High	Very low	Galena, Ill.
Railroad Most important cargo: agricultural products, coal, manufacturing goods, people	1850–1920	Steam, then diesel	High	High	Medium	Vandalia, Ill.
Auto/truck/air Most important cargo: people, manufactured products	1920–?	Gasoline, diesel, and jet engines	Very high	Medium	Very high	Las Vegas, Nev.
Electronic Communications Most important cargo: information	1965–?	Telecommunications, computers, facsimile, Internet	Very high	Low	High	Suburb or satellite city of a metropolis

people. The newer forms of transport are highly energy-intensive, and contemporary cities that are dependent solely on them are vulnerable to fluctuations in the availability of energy. If the petroleum problems of the 1970s were to recur and to signal a permanent petroleum shortage, sharp declines would probably be suffered by cities such as Las Vegas, which is exclusively dependent on air and motor transport. The same could occur in many suburbs and satellite cities in the megalopolises. On the other hand, if sources of electrical energy are sufficient to sustain the increasingly widespread applications of electronic telecommunications technology, then settlement patterns within the megalopolises seem likely to continue dispersing and decentralizing.

Emergence of a National Corporate Economy   The third factor that led to the growth of the metropolis in the United States was the transformation of the economy from a small-enterprise base into a national corporate economy. Until late in the nineteenth century, most business enterprises in American cities were small-scale, family-owned companies that maintained few permanent employees.[23] After the Civil War, more and more business corporations set up national or regional headquarters in large cities such as New York, Chicago, and Boston.

Not only did this concentration of business headquarters provide economic activity to make those regional cities grow, but the modern business offices of those corporate headquarters also created millions of new and peculiarly urban jobs in fields such as advertising, marketing, financing, accounting, typing, office management, and general office work. The creation of these occupations in turn contributed to the demand for a growing urban labor force and population. Hence the corporate business office arose and provided another stimulus to the growth of large cities.[24]

Contemporary Metropolitan America

More recent urbanization differs from past patterns in three significant respects. First, population in the last century shifted south and west. Second, suburbanization has occurred at a remarkable pace, especially since World War II. Third, central cities, especially in the Northeast and Midwest, have experienced dramatic losses in population in the last three decades.

The Westward Drift   A marked slowdown occurred in the growth of many places that had been urbanizing prior to 1920—specifically, the central cities in the Northeast and the small towns that served rural areas, particularly those east of the Mississippi River.[25] Whereas in 1930 the Southwest and Northwest accounted for only a quarter of all cities over 100,000 in population, today they account for more than half of those cities and 8 of the nation's 12 largest cities are now located in the Sunbelt.

Politically, the westward drift is important for several reasons. With few exceptions, such as San Francisco, the cities in these regions did not receive the millions of European immigrants that the cities of the Northeast had received, so the style and ethnic base of their politics are different. Asians and Hispanics have a much larger presence in politics in the West than in most cities of the Northeast. The cities of the Southwest are also much more dependent on motor and air transport than on water and rail transport, and this makes them more vulnerable to potential energy shortages in the future.

These cities also tend to benefit more from the new sources of wealth—Texas oil, federal defense and aerospace expenditures, and the tourist and recreation boom—than do the cities of the Northeast and the Midwest. For all of these reasons, the style and character of urban politics in these new cities differ markedly from those of the older cities of the Northeast and Midwest.

Suburbanization   The second significant change in the urbanization process since 1920 has been the shifting of urban growth away from the central cities and into the suburbs. The 1920 census was distinctive for being the first to show that more people lived in urban than in rural places; the 1970 census was the first to show that the suburban population outnumbered the central-city population.

As Figure 2.2 shows, suburban growth has been increasing greatly in all regions. The one exception is Pittsburgh, which had a small negative (−0.04%) loss in suburban population between 1990 and 2000. This is related to the overall contraction of population in Pittsburgh, where even the metropolitan area declined by 1.5 percent over the last decade. Suburban growth was most pronounced in the South and West.

FIGURE 2.2   Suburbanization in Largest 25 Metropolitan Areas, 1990–2000

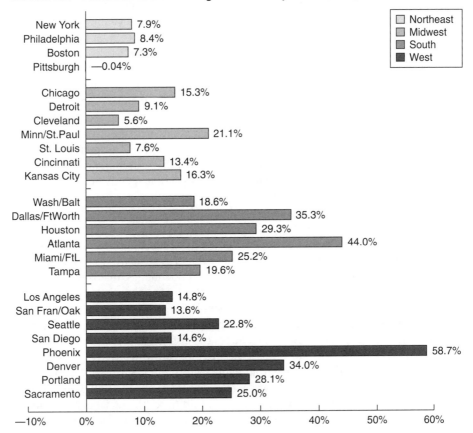

Atlanta, for example, saw a 44 percent growth in its suburban population, and Phoenix a 59 percent increase. Even Portland, Oregon, noted for its efforts to rein in sprawl through strong growth management policies and an urban growth boundary, experienced a 28 percent increase in suburban population over the last decade.

Four factors have been responsible for the suburbanization of the United States: the automobile, the new technology in road and residential construction, the cultural dislike of big cities, and the invention of long-term, low-down-payment home mortgages.

The role of the automobile and of road construction in stimulating suburbanization derived partly from the ease with which they extended the acceptable commuting distance for large numbers of people. The advent of the automobile and of improved roads also liberated real estate developers and retail businesspeople from having to build their residences and shops along the streetcar lines.

The spread of the automobile was greatly facilitated by federal and state government highway and freeway construction. Particularly since the passage of the Federal Aid Highway Act of 1956, which earmarked the revenue from a gasoline tax for a highway trust fund to build and maintain the interstate highway system, freeway construction has stimulated the dispersion of the population throughout the suburbs. Where the roads were constructed, the population moved, and shopping facilities soon followed. The shopping centers in turn attracted more people to move into nearby areas.

The introduction of the automobile and of the freeway systems made suburbanization possible but not inevitable. To make suburbanization inevitable, several other things had to occur. For one, the mass of the population had to *want* to move to the suburbs. In the United States, historical-cultural developments worked in that direction. As far back as the writings of Thomas Jefferson, one common theme of American intellectual literature has been disparagement of city life.[26] The popular media have generally idealized the small town as the epitome of American civilization.

For the metropolis to become suburbanized, people not only had to *want* to live in suburbia, they also had to *be able to afford* to live there. One device that helped make this possible was the long-term, low-down-payment mortgage loan pioneered by the Federal Housing Administration (FHA) and Veterans Administration (VA) after World War II. These agencies' mortgage guarantees made it possible for any qualifying person to purchase a home with a small down payment or no down payment at all, with monthly payments spread over a 30-year period, and with an interest rate slightly below the prevailing conventional-mortgage interest rates. Once the government-guaranteed mortgages proved that long-term, low-down-payment mortgages were financially viable, mortgage banks began to use them in conventional mortgage loans. Because the cheapest large plots of land existed beyond the central-city boundaries, that is where most of this new mortgage money was lent. For the first time in American history, home ownership was open to the majority of the urban population.

The government-backed mortgages were not without their critics. They greatly increased home ownership in the United States but also led to the development of the segregated metropolis. For many years the FHA agreed to restrictive covenants in deeds that prohibited the property from being sold to non-Caucasians.[27] Even after restrictive covenants were struck down by the Supreme Court in 1948,[28] the FHA instructed its officers not to approve loans that would upset the racial composition of neighborhoods.[29] It was not until 1962 that President Kennedy issued an executive order prohibiting discrimination in FHA loans. Government-backed mortgages also were accused of being biased against the lower-middle-income and lower-income strata of the society, because most of the mortgages went to upper-middle-class families. And to observers concerned about the development of communities (as distinguished from the proliferation of housing projects), the government-backed mortgages were accused of existing primarily as a government prop to the construction industry and real estate developers.[30]

Thus the suburbanization of America after 1920—and especially after 1945—was virtually predetermined by a number of converging factors:

The intellectual disrepute of the city
The cultural value placed on living in single-family homes in open spaces
The availability of cheap land beyond the city's boundaries
The unprecedented access to that land via new roadways and extensive use of the
   automobile
The availability of long-term, low-down-payment mortgages

It must be noted that this analysis of the causes of suburbanization places very little weight on the cause most often cited: the flight of the white population away from the racial minorities that were moving into the central cities. Although there can be no doubt that much of the white population did move to the suburbs to avoid living with African Americans, this fails as a sufficient explanation of suburbanization. The fact is that suburbanization occurred equally in metropolises with very small African American populations (such as Seattle, Portland, and Minneapolis) and in metropolises with very large African American populations (such as Washington, D.C., Philadelphia, and New York).

Finally, it must also be noted that the rapid expansion of the urban population into suburbia does not necessarily represent an exercise of individual free choice. As indicated earlier, people migrated to suburbs because those were the places where acceptable housing was most likely to be found. That the acceptable housing occurred in the form of single-family homes in suburbs was not a consequence of individual choices. Rather it was a consequence of the transit, housing, employment, and finance policies of the federal and state governments and the major mortgage banking institutions. How many single-family homes are built each year and who gets the credit to buy them are much less a consequence of individual choice than a consequence of government credit policies and of the policies of real estate developers and financial institutions.

Central-City Decline   In addition to population shifts to the South and West and continued suburbanization, the population exodus from the central cities of the Northeast and Midwest was becoming alarming. The magnitude of these population changes is staggering. For example, census figures reveal that between 1980 and 1990, Chicago lost about 221,000 people, Philadelphia lost over 100,000, and Detroit lost about 175,000 persons.

These three trends—Sunbelt growth, suburbanization, and central-city decline in the Northeast and Midwest—are highlighted in Figures 2.3 and 2.4. Central cities in 18 of the largest 25 metropolises, including every large city in the Northeast and Midwest,

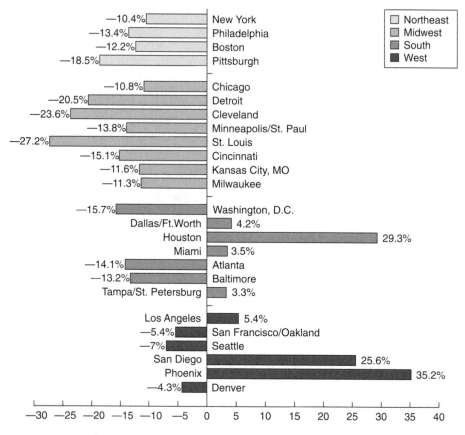

FIGURE 2.3   Central-City Growth/Decline in Largest 25 Metropolitan Areas, 1970–1980

Note: Data report in the figure is for all central cities in the metropolitan area.
Source: U.S. Bureau of the Census.

lost population between 1970 and 1980. Even a number of cities in the South and West, including Washington, Atlanta, Baltimore, Seattle, San Francisco–Oakland, and Denver, were experiencing dramatic population losses. Central cities in only 3 large metropolitan areas grew substantially in this time frame—Houston, San Diego, and Phoenix, all with growth rates of 25 to 35 percent.

The 1980s were only slightly better; during this period, central cities in 14 of the largest 25 metropolises lost population. All the largest cities in the Midwest, as well as most in the Northeast, continued to lose population. The exceptions were New York and Boston, which actually experienced modest growth between 1980 and 1990. Again, some cities even in the South and West continued to have problems, including Washington, Atlanta, Baltimore, and Denver. But most central cities in the largest metropolises of the South and West gained population and there was rapid growth in Los Angeles, San Diego, Dallas–Fort Worth, Houston, and Phoenix.

The 2000 census reveals that central cities in 7 of the largest 25 metropolitan areas are still losing population: Philadelphia, Pittsburgh, Detroit, Cleveland, St. Louis, Cincinnati,

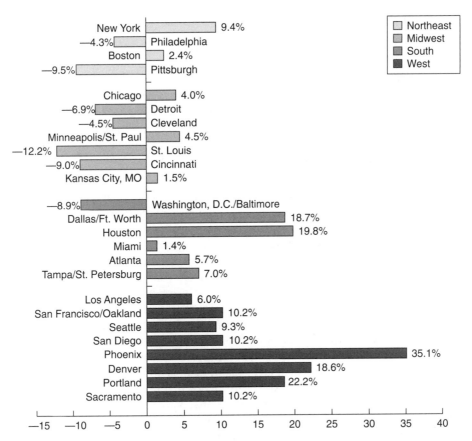

FIGURE 2.4 Central-City Growth/Decline in Largest 25 Metropolitan Areas, 1990–2000

Note: Data reported in the figure is for all central cities in the metropolitan area.

Source: U.S. Bureau of the Census.

and Washington–Baltimore. Only one of these is in the South, and none are in the West. Thus a number of central cities in the Northeast and Midwest continue to experience population loss. Several southern and western central cities, including those in the Dallas–Ft. Worth, Houston, San Francisco–Oakland, San Diego, Phoenix, Denver, Portland, and Sacramento metropolises, are growing rapidly. The latter two metropolises joined the top 25 metropolitan areas for the first time in the 2000 census. Thus, although we may speak generally of central-city decline, it is probably more accurate to speak of some cities declining and others, notably in the South and West, growing.

What was behind the central-city population losses? The changing economy and the middle-class exodus from the city were major factors. Other factors cited in a government report on metropolitan trends were the decline in household size and population displacement. Household size has declined by 16.5 percent over a 20-year period in the largest 40 metro areas. More people are remaining single, refraining from having children, or residing in single-parent households. Population displacement also occurs when commercial space in the central business district (CBD) encroaches on neighboring residential areas.[31]

The Dual Migration

Although suburbanization cannot be traced directly to racial discord and prejudice or to individual free choices, the fact of suburbanization has had profound consequences for race relations and the kinds of choices that are available in such social amenities as housing, jobs, and schools. Suburbanization was an integral part of the most far-reaching demographic trend of the post–World War II era: the *dual migration*. The first part of the dual migration was an in-migration of relatively poor, rural, and racial-minority peoples into the large central cities. The second part of the dual migration was the out-migration of more affluent, middle-class whites to the suburbs.

Who Were the In-Migrants?   The third and fourth waves of urban migration shown in Table 2.2 were dominated by people who did not share the European backgrounds of the majority of the American population.

From about 1940 to 1970, there was a steady migration north and west of African American sharecroppers who were driven off southern farms and plantations by policies of agricultural subsidies and by the mechanization of farm labor. Coming at the tail end of the period when the great industrial city was dominant, this migration led to huge concentrations of African Americans in large industrial cities such as New York, Chicago, Detroit, St. Louis, and Los Angeles, and in other big commercial centers such as Washington, where the best jobs were found in those years. Disastrously for many African American in-migrants, however, industrial manufacturing did not turn out to be the great employer of unskilled labor that it had been in the past. The result was the development of huge African American ghettos that in many ways resembled an underdeveloped country more than a modern city. As we will see in Chapter 5, these underdeveloped ghettos had large concentrations of unskilled people, a decreasing supply of jobs, poor access to credit or investment capital, and an economy that was dominated by outsiders.[32] Even today, almost three decades after the African American urban in-migration peaked, urban blacks still live in a greater state of segregation than other urban minorities.[33]

Contemporary urban migration has been dominated by Hispanics and Asians. There are 35.3 million people of Spanish-speaking origin in the continental United States (excluding 3.8 million Hispanics in Puerto Rico), making it the third-largest Spanish-speaking country in the world.[34] More than half (20.6 million, or 58.5%) are Mexicans ("Chicanos"), about 10 percent (3.4 million) are Puerto Ricans, and about 3.5 percent (1.2 million) are Cubans. Two states, California and Texas, account for half of all Latinos in the United States. Mexican Americans have concentrated in the West (55 percent), Puerto Ricans in the Northeast (61 percent), and Cubans in the South (74 percent).

The large number of Hispanics and their geographic concentration significantly affect urban politics. However, the Hispanic population is not undifferentiated. Cuban Americans, heavily concentrated in Miami, differ from Puerto Ricans and Mexican Americans in two respects. First, they came to the United States mainly for political rather than economic reasons, many of them being middle-class people who escaped from Castro's Cuba in the 1960s. Second, they tend to be much more conservative in their politics than either Puerto Ricans or Mexican Americans. This is most apparent in matters of U.S. foreign policy; the Miami Cuban community consistently supported the Reagan administration's attempt to overthrow the Sandinista government of Nicaragua and has opposed Castro's Cuba whenever possible.[35]

The Elian Gonzales case further cemented Cuban solidarity in Miami. Elian was a six-year-old boy whose mother perished trying to reach the Florida shores on a small boat. After being plucked from the sea by a Cuban refugee, Elian was temporarily placed with a refugee uncle in Miami. The boy's father, back in Cuba, sought the return of Elian. Ordinarily, this would have been a simple case because the law recognizes the right of parents to have custodial care and to determine what is in the child's best interests. However, young Elian became a *cause célèbre* within the Cuban exile community, and many Americans questioned whether the youngster should have to return to Communist-ruled Cuba. A protracted legal case ensued. After the Miami family defied a federal court order to return Elian, U.S. Attorney General Janet Reno ordered a raid to "rescue" the boy and return him to his father in Cuba. The fallout from the case continues as an issue in Florida and national politics. Vice President Gore sought to distance himself from the Clinton administration's decision to return Elian, and the case may have been a factor in his close election loss in Florida. The refugee family's attorney, Manny Diaz, was subsequently elected mayor of Miami in November 2001. Janet Reno continued to face the exile community's wrath, contributing to her loss in the Florida governor race in 2002.

Constituting still another category of Latin Americans is the growing number of immigrants, about 1.7 million, who come from Central America to settle in the southwestern states and in southern Florida. Conditions of warfare and strife in Central America have prompted the gradual but steady entry of these refugees into U.S. cities.

The influx of Asians stems from the change in immigration statutes in 1965, which removed the previous ceiling of 100 persons per Asian country per year. Especially after the Vietnam War, there was also a significant inflow of refugees from Indochina. These groups have an important political impact in cities such as San Francisco. But the nature of their impact is difficult to predict, because the Asian immigrants are even more diverse ethnically, linguistically, and economically than are the Hispanics. Between 1981 and 1998, the greatest number of Asian immigrants came from the Philippines (8,438,000), followed by Vietnam (7,192,000), China (6,575,000), India (4,984,000), and Korea (4,529,000).[36]

Finally, there also has been a migration of Native Americans into the cities, although in much smaller numbers. In 1952 the Bureau of Indian Affairs began a relocation program to move families and individuals from the reservations to big cities including Cleveland, Chicago, Denver, Dallas, Los Angeles, San Francisco, Oakland, and San Jose. Others migrated to the cities on their own. In 1960 about 166,000 Native Americans lived in big cities. Of the 33,000 voluntarily relocated by the government, about one-third moved back to their former residences. Native Americans have become more organized through intertribal conferences since 1961 and through growth of the Pow Wow circuit since the 1970s. Pow Wows are gatherings and celebrations that help maintain cultural ties; more than 2,000 are now held annually.[37] In the substantial Native American communities found in Minneapolis and Los Angeles, these in-migrants exist in a state of poverty and disorganization that is perhaps greater than that of any other ethnic or racial group in those cities.

The Dual Migration's Effects on the Cities   These migrations of relatively nonaffluent people into the central cities constitute the first part of the dual migration. The second part consists of the migration of more affluent people out of the central cities. The large metropolitan areas have been compared to huge doughnuts with a hole in the middle. Because the suburbs become separate tax entities, the central cities do not share the increased tax revenue from more expensive homes, the increasing number of shopping centers, and the growing number of business establishments in the suburbs. Furthermore, the suburbs normally do not belong to the same school districts as the central cities, so there is less and less mingling between poor and upper-middle-class children in the schools. Although it is not completely true that the suburbs became affluent while the central cities became impoverished, it is true that the largest number of poor people settled in the central cities. And because suburbanization brought changes in the metropolitan political structure, the central cities found it more and more difficult to come up with the resources required to handle the social problems of the poor.

The Dual Migration and Ethnic Succession   The dual migration of the poorer people and the racial minorities into the central cities and of more affluent, upper-middle-class people out to the suburbs has deep historical roots. As the early Irish immigrants became affluent enough to move into the better neighborhoods, their slums were inherited by Italians, Jews, and Poles. As these ethnic minorities moved out of the slums, they in turn were followed by the post–World War II urban minorities. By 1970 the African American urban in-migration slowed to a trickle in most areas, while the out-migration of affluent whites continued. The slowdown of the in-migration of the poor has not been a great boon for cities, however. As African American in-migration from the South began to taper off, that reduced the pressure on housing in lower- and working-class black neighborhoods. At the same time, open housing policies and a general rise in the incomes of middle-class, young African American families enabled unprecedented numbers of African Americans to migrate out of the slums into more attractive neighborhoods. The net result was a rapid deterioration in lower- and working-class African American neighborhoods, which were abandoned to what one group of commentators called "a destructive residual underclass."[38] This process of decline occurred in many large cities.

Neighborhoods such as Woodlawn in Chicago and New York's South Bronx gained notoriety for their abandoned or burned-out blocks. Woodlawn is a neighborhood just south of the University of Chicago campus. The neighborhood changed in the 1950s from a predominantly white neighborhood to a predominantly African American one. During the 1960s, Woodlawn also became the locale for the most highly organized and powerful of Chicago's teenage gangs, the Blackstone Rangers. Violence precipitated by the Rangers, together with the availability of nonsegregated housing elsewhere in the city, drove out of the neighborhood most of the working-class and middle-class families who could afford to leave. At the same time, pressure on absentee landlords to bring their properties up to the standards of the city's building codes meant that for many owners, increased rents would not offset increased maintenance and repair costs. Many landlords responded by abandoning their buildings. The abandoned buildings then fell prey to vandals, looters, and arsonists. Woodlawn went from 81,279 people in 1960 to just 27,473 by 1990, leaving 70 percent of the neighborhood vacant land.

By the 1990s, the abandonment process in places like Woodlawn and the South Bronx slowed down. There is now evidence that a reversal is under way. In 1988, a neighborhood development corporation bought an old and decaying Woodlawn complex from HUD and renovated it into 400 apartments for low-income residents and 31,000 square feet of commercial development. A sign of success was the arrival of a new grocery store and a bank in the neighborhood. Then a new project was undertaken to renovate a 117-unit complex into apartments for the working poor. In 1994, this was followed by an initiative to build new homes that sell for about $149,000. The housing was close to the University of Chicago and the 28 new homes were sold. Another 41-home development was undertaken in 1995. The hope is that these projects will cumulatively turn the tide. This is occurring in communities such as Cleveland, Baltimore, St. Louis, Boston, and Louisville. The New York City Housing Partnership has built thousands of homes in the South Bronx, Brooklyn, and Harlem.

If this reversal continues in places like Woodlawn and the South Bronx, it will fit into a life cycle theory of neighborhoods that was articulated many years ago by urban scholars Edgard M. Hoover and Raymond Vernon. They argued that there are five stages in the life cycle of a neighborhood. The cycle starts with the creation of subdivisions of single-family homes, which is followed by the development of apartment buildings. As the original residents die or move out to other neighborhoods, they are replaced, in the third stage, by less affluent residents, who downgrade the neighborhood by dividing the single-family homes into duplexes and apartments. This is followed by a fourth stage of population decline and abandonment. Finally, new developers see potential in the neighborhood and a fifth stage, renewal, completes the cycle.[39]

This neighborhood cycle is not limited to the inner city. Many older suburbs in the first ring around cities are now experiencing great difficulty. One estimate by the U.S. Department of Housing and Urban Development concluded that as much as 30 percent of the suburbs could be in decline. Some suburbs actually are smaller industrial cities that have been overtaken by metropolitan expansion and are now considered suburbs to the central city. Other suburbs have been overtaken by in-migration of the poor or were working-class suburbs that declined when industry closed down and people could no longer afford to keep up their homes or support businesses.[40]

Changes in Growth Patterns in the Next Century: Postindustrial Metropolitan Development

As we move into the twenty-first century, we see both continuities with and changes from the historical urbanization patterns we've just described. Among the continuities, the most significant is the population drift toward the southern and western Sunbelt regions. A second continuity with the past is in the continuous growth of the suburbs in metropolitan areas. There is no evidence that either of these trends will slacken in the new millennium.

But existing patterns of urbanization are not simply a continuation of the past. We are in a new phase of urbanization, *postindustrial metropolitan development*. The Office of Technology Assessment (OTA), a now disbanded congressional agency, describes this stage of urbanization in a report prepared for policy makers and entitled *The Technological Reshaping of Metropolitan America*:

> The current and emerging phase of urban development, beginning in the 1970s, is best understood as post-industrial metropolitan development, where business spreads throughout

the metropolis; residential growth spreads to the outer suburbs and to exurban areas; some parts of the central cities, especially central business districts (CBDs) revive (at least in the 1980s); and many parts of older central cities and inner suburbs, particularly those formerly dependent on mass production manufacturing, stagnate or decline. . . . Goods-related employment declines as a share of metro jobs, and services, particularly information-based services (e.g., banking, insurance), increase.[41]

As we discussed earlier, changes in urbanization are stimulated in part by changes in technology. According to OTA, advance technologies "are changing the locational patterns of individuals and industries." Historically, cities in the United States grew up around commerce and industry. Businesses needed to locate in the core areas to gain access to labor markets, transportation infrastructure (such as ports and railroads), and other businesses (warehouse, distribution, legal, and administrative support services). New technology has allowed individuals and businesses to be "physically farther apart, yet functionally still . . . close." In the industrial era, this led to physical expansion of metropolitan areas (suburbanization of people and business) and later to a regional redistribution of population and employment (growth in the South and West).[42]

Now, new technologies are likely to lead to even greater decentralization and deconcentration. As OTA explains,

Many of the early applications of information technology improved internal operations (e.g., mainframe and desk top computing) and often created "islands of automation" with little interconnection between components. It is only recently that technologies that facilitate real-time and wide-spread linkages and communication among operations have begun to be widely adopted. These technologies are getting cheaper and more powerful, and will become pervasive. This report puts these technologies into three groups: (1) technologies to transform information into electronic form (e.g., fax, videophones, computers, optical scanners, and bar code readers); (2) switching and routing technologies (internet communications and e-mail, call forwarding systems, local and wide area networks, and wireless communications and computing); and (3) transmission (e.g., fiberoptics, digital switching systems, and satellites).

   Digitized and electronic processes have the potential to replace many paper transactions, some face-to-face functions, and some physical transport of goods. Because a rapidly growing share of the economy consists of information transactions—be they stock trades, insurance forms, or point-of-sale data—the potential of information technologies to shape spatial patterns of employment is greater than ever before. . . . For example, industries that in the past had to be close to customers and other firms because they constantly transmitted information are now more free of the need for proximity because of electronic digital transactions. Within goods industries, information technology is transforming the logistics chain, making it possible for goods distribution and transportation to consolidate operations and locate farther from the customer. Similarly, industries requiring frequent face-to-face contact . . . will be able to adequately meet many communication needs electronically through e-mail, video telephones, and easy-to-use data transfer protocols. In sum, technology is connecting economic activities, enabling them to be physically farther apart, reducing the competitive advantage of high-cost, congested urban locations, and allowing people and businesses more (but not total) freedom to choose where they will live and work.[43]

These trends are reflected in the decentralization of the population to new urban centers in the countryside. Corporations that open new executive offices or new plants show an increasing tendency to favor the smaller Sunbelt urban centers. When General Motors, for example, decided to build a new automobile called the Saturn, it also decided to locate the plant in Spring Hill, Tennessee, rather than in Detroit or in some other traditional automobile-manufacturing city of the Midwest.

However, "OTA concludes that the new wave of information technologies will not prove to be the salvation of a rural U.S. economy that has undergone decades of population and job loss as its natural resource-based economy has shrunk." OTA suggests that economic and population growth will occur in the middle and large metropolitan areas, which are more "conducive to innovation and learning." In addition, there has been a tendency for companies to consolidate service operations in fewer cities to achieve economies of scale and to close down distribution centers in smaller towns and metropolitan areas. This is possible because of advances in information technology, such as *just-in-time inventory supply systems* for manufacturing and increased reliance on overnight delivery systems offered by firms such as UPS and Federal Express.[44]

Although isolated rural areas are unlikely to benefit from the new postindustrial economy, rural areas close to existing metropolitan areas, especially those linked to a metropolis by interstate highways, are likely to be overtaken by metropolitan expansion as businesses and people continue to suburbanize seeking cheaper land, lower taxes, and open spaces. In the 1970s, we mistook urban expansion as a *back-to-the-farm movement*. We now see more clearly that people were not moving to embrace rural lifestyles. Instead, rural areas were becoming suburbs and industrial parks to nearby metropolitan areas.

The 2000 census reveals that several large cities are still losing population (see Figure 2.4 and Table 2.4). However, there are hopeful signs of *reurbanization* as we enter the twenty-first century. Two factors have helped cities stem the outflow of population: immigration and gentrification. Professor Dowell Meyers points out that the era of urban decline coincided with sharp reductions in immigration and that urban revitalization in the last several decades is associated with a liberalization of immigration policy. The main gateway cities for new international migrants are New York, Los Angeles, Chicago, San Francisco, Miami, and Houston. Immigration has been an important factor in reversing population losses in New York and Chicago in the last decade.

A number of cities have experienced a so-called urban renaissance that began in the late 1970s, when a number of factors combined to attract young and middle-aged professional people into certain areas of central cities. At that time, federal housing policies introduced incentives for urban neighborhood redevelopment, and energetic individuals and couples seized the opportunity to buy up deteriorated urban homes and restore them. Because this process brings upper-middle-income people back into these neighborhoods, it is sometimes called *urban gentrification*.

In view of these forces, corporations found it advantageous to increase rather than decrease employment opportunities in the cities. After virtually deserting the central cities during the 1950s and 1960s to establish their plants in more economical settings, they seemed to discover in the late 1970s that the central-city downtown areas were lucrative places to relocate their headquarters and other office facilities. Many city governments encouraged these developments by granting generous tax abatements, below-market interest rates, and other subsidies. As white-collar job opportunities expanded in downtown areas, mortgage lending institutions found themselves pressured to modify their blatant redlining practices and agree to finance homes, townhouses, apartments, and condominiums for the influx of upper-middle-income service workers who wanted to live within quick commuting distance of their new jobs.

TABLE 2.4 Population Change in the 25 Largest Cities, 1960–2004

	1960	1990	2000	2004	Percent Change 1990–2000	Percent Change 1960–2000	Percent Change 2000–2004
1. New York	7,781,984	7,322,564	8,008,278	8,104,079	9.4%	2.8%	1.2%
2. Los Angeles	2,479,015	3,485,398	3,694,820	3,845,541	6	32.9	4.1
3. Chicago	3,550,404	2,783,726	2,896,016	2,862,244	4	−22.6	−1.7
4. Houston	938,219	1,630,553	1,953,631	2,012,626	19.8	52	3.0
5. Philadelphia	2,002,512	1,585,577	1,517,550	1,470,151	−4.3	−32	−3.1
6. Phoenix	439,170	983,403	1,321,045	1,418,041	34.3	200.8	7.3
7. San Diego	573,224	1,110,549	1,223,400	1,263,756	10.2	53.1	8.3
8. San Antonio	587,718	935,933	1,144,646	1,236,249	22.3	48.7	8.0
9. Dallas	679,684	1,006,877	1,188,580	1,210,393	18	42.8	1.8
10. San Jose	204,196	782,248	894,943	904,522	14.4	77.2	1.1
11. Detroit	1,670,144	1,027,974	951,270	900,198	−7.5	−75.6	−5.4
12. Indianapolis[a]	476,258	741,952	791,926	784,242	6.7	40	−1.0
13. Jacksonville[a]	201,030	635,230	735,617	777,704	15.8	72.7	5.7
14. San Francisco	740,316	723,959	776,733	744,230	7.3	4.7	−4.2
15. Columbus	471,316	632,910	711,470	730,008	12.4	33.8	2.6
16. Austin	186,545	465,622	656,562	681,804	41	71.6	3.8
17. Memphis	497,524	610,337	650,100	671,929	6.5	23.5	3.4
18. Baltimore	939,024	736,014	651,154	636,251	−11.5	−44.2	−2.3
19. Fort Worth	356,268	448,181	534,694	603,337	19.3	50.1	12.8
20. Charlotte	201,564	426,984	540,828	594,359	26.7	168.3	9.9
21. El Paso	276,687	515,342	563,662	592,099	9.4	50.9	5.0
22. Milwaukee	741,324	628,088	596,974	583,624	−5	−24.2	−2.2
23. Seattle	557,087	516,259	563,374	571,480	9.1	1.1	1.4
24. Boston	697,197	574,283	589,141	569,165	2.6	−18.3	−3.4
25. Denver	493,887	467,610	554,636	556,835	18.6	11	0.4

[a]Consolidated city-counties.

Sources: U.S. Bureau of the Census, Annual Estimates of the Population for Incorporated Places Over 100,000, Ranked by July 1, 2004 Population: April 1, 2000 to July 1, 2004.

Link: http://www.census.gov/popest/cities/SUB-EST2004.html (December 2005).

There is some evidence that all this investment in downtowns has paid off. A Fannie Mae/Brookings report found that 18 of 24 cities examined had *downtown* population growth between 1990 and 2000 (see Table 2.5). However, we must be cautious in interpreting this. In a place such as Los Angeles, there are many suburban downtowns, some of which may be more vital than that of the core City of Los Angeles. Although increased investment in downtowns may make cities attractive for tourists and affluent residents, this investment may come at the expense of surrounding inner-city neighborhoods. Finally, few of these downtowns really contain the full range of amenities needed for urban living. Downtown residents in many cities must go to the suburbs to do their grocery shopping.[45]

Overall, the number of urban neighborhoods undergoing revitalization is still very small. Gentrification by itself is clearly not strong enough to reverse the long-term decline of older central cities.[46] Nevertheless, gentrification is an important phenomenon. The

TABLE 2.5   Downtown Population Change

		Percent Change	
Category	Area	Downtown	City
Downtown Up,	Houston	69.0%	19.8%
City Up	Seattle	67.4	9.1
	Chicago	51.4	4.0
	Denver	51.4	18.6
	Portland, Ore.	35.4	21.0
	Atlanta	25.1	5.7
	Memphis	18.2	6.5
	San Diego	16.1	10.2
	Colorado Springs	7.2	28.4
	Los Angeles	5.7	6.0
	Boston	4.5	2.6
	Des Moines	0.3	2.8
Downtown Up,	Cleveland	32.2	−5.4
City Down	Norfolk, Va.	20.5	−10.3
	Baltimore	5.1	−11.5
	Philadelphia	4.9	−4.3
	Detroit	2.9	−7.5
	Milwaukee	2.5	−5.0
Downtown Down,	Charlotte	−0.7	36.6
City Up	San Antonio	−5.9	22.3
	Lexington, Ky.	−6.1	15.6
	Phoenix	−9.1	34.3
Downtown Down,	Cincinnati	−16.9	−9.0
City Down	St. Louis	−17.5	−12.2

Source: University of Pennsylvania Department of City and Regional Planning; U.S. Bureau of the Census 1990 and 2000. Reproduced from: Rebecca R. Sohmer and Robert E. Lang, "Downtown Rebound," Table 3 (p. 5), Fannie Mae Foundation and Brookings Institution Center on Urban and Metropolitan Policy Census Note 03 (May 2001), http://www.fanniemaefoundation.org/census_notes.shtml.

restoration of old, previously run-down neighborhoods has an important symbolic impact on how people think about cities. For young, single people and those who are recently divorced, for middle-aged professionals, and for the elderly, the city can be a very desirable place to live. Partially because of this, it has become commonplace to speak of a "new vitality" in the cities.[47] Although this urban vitality is most prominent in the newer cities of the South and West, old northern cities such as Chicago, Philadelphia, Baltimore, Boston, New York, and Washington, D.C., are also experiencing gentrification.

Gentrification is not always viewed positively. Existing neighborhood residents, including the poor, are often pushed out as landlords undertake renovations and increase rents to appeal to the young, urban professionals (*yuppies*). Many of the original urban pioneers, often artists and owner-renovators who began the gentrification process, found that they could no longer afford to live there because of increased rental prices or higher property taxes. As the neighborhoods became more attractive, property values increased and stores catered to tourists and more affluent shoppers, stocking higher-end goods that cost more. Commercial development changed the character of these neighborhoods and displaced poorer populations.

All this led to a backlash against gentrification that exerted pressure on city officials to restrict commercial conversion of residences, to limit the size of redevelopment projects, and to pursue affordable-housing policies.[48] One study of gentrification in Baltimore between 1980 and 1990 suggests a more complicated picture. Although gentrification did lead to increased property values and lower densities, it also raised the minority population and the number of subsidized housing units. Thus the relationship between gentrification and population displacement is not entirely clear and requires further investigation.[49]

Today, revitalization of poorer, minority, inner-city neighborhoods is probably of greater importance than gentrification. The Clinton administration introduced policies to try to bring about this revitalization. Shortly after taking office in 1993, President Clinton was able to gain congressional support for his Empowerment Zone program. Under this program, Atlanta, Baltimore, Chicago, Detroit, New York, and Philadelphia/Camden received $100 million to tackle the problems of inner-city neighborhoods afflicted by poverty. Cleveland and Los Angeles received supplemental grants. Another 60 cities were designated Enterprise Communities with grants of $3 million.

To obtain the grants, the cities had to work with grass-roots groups in designated poor neighborhoods to develop a strategic plan on how to turn the neighborhoods around and overcome severe poverty and economic, social, and physical deterioration. Most zones focused on a combination of business incentives, job training, social services, and physical redevelopment. Cities were also encouraged to include community development banks in their strategies to counter the effects of redlining and create a new source of capital in minority communities. (A community development bank must limit its investments to particular geographic boundaries.)

These programs have been in place for about a decade now. The actual amount of money allocated to address the problems is small. Further, the geographic scope of intervention is limited; communities were required to target poor, minority neighborhoods with no more than 20,000 people permitted to live in the designated boundaries. It is difficult to see how this program can significantly alter the cities' fate. However, it was the first new urban policy initiative in a long time and has caused cities to refocus their attention on poor neighborhoods. The Clinton administration expanded the

Empowerment Zone program in a second round, hoping that these local strategies would serve as catalysts to broader neighborhood and community redevelopment. If successful, these neighborhoods should gain population and businesses.[50] However, most assessments of the Empowerment Zone program found gains were quite limited.

Urban Economic Transformation

Even if urban gentrification returned the middle class to the cities and even if empowerment and enterprise zones stemmed further urban decline, most cities, especially older cities, would still have trouble prospering in the face of an economic transformation that is robbing them of their historical economic base. Earlier we cited industrialization as a motivating force behind nineteenth- and early-twentieth-century urbanization. Buffalo, Pittsburgh, Cleveland, Gary, Milwaukee, and dozens of smaller Great Lakes cities grew up and prospered as blue-collar factory towns. But since World War II, blue-collar jobs have been declining in the central cities and expanding in the suburbs. Today there are many more industrial-manufacturing jobs in suburbs than there are in central cities.

If the city has been losing its vocation as a factory town, what economic activities have evolved to replace the factories? The answer, according to John H. Mollenkopf, is government jobs, third-sector institutions (for example, hospitals, universities, and foundation headquarters), and advanced corporate services (such as legal, accounting, computing, advertising, and investment banking).[51] The explosion of advanced corporate services has been especially important, because cities with many such services become very attractive sites for corporation headquarters.

These economic changes have affected different cities in different ways, contributing to the vitality of some but retarding the growth of others. Mollenkopf argues that three types of cities are emerging. First are the old industrial cities such as Gary, Indiana, and Youngstown, Ohio. Despite dramatic changes in the national economy that have caused the industrial-manufacturing sector to decline relative to the service sector, these old cities have clung to their industrial economic bases. Gary and Youngstown are especially good examples, because their basic industry (steel manufacturing) is heavily dependent on the fortunes of the automobile industry. As that industry suffered major setbacks in the last several decades, Gary, Youngstown, and many other old industrial cities were economically shattered.

In an entirely different situation are the newer service and administrative centers of the Southwest—cities such as San Diego, for example. They attracted administrative and service corporations and high-technology industries that weathered the economic storms of the 1970s better than the old basic industries of the Midwest.

Finally, contends Mollenkopf, a third type of city has transformed its economy from old industry to banking, service sectors, and advanced corporate services. Typical of this category are New York, Chicago, Philadelphia, Boston, and San Francisco. Though all have suffered significant population declines, they have maintained themselves as significant locales for corporation headquarters and service-sector activities. The 2000 census seems to bear this out.

These economic changes pose a difficult dilemma for city leaders who want to avoid future dependence on dying industries and thus feel they must compete successfully for high-technology industries or dynamic service-sector enterprises. In this competitive quest for revitalization, can cities afford *not* to give tax concessions, community development funds, and other incentives to corporations, even though the resulting downtown revitalization may cause severe hardship for many of the urban poor and may divert investment money from residential neighborhoods?

Central-city mayors, newspaper editors, business corporations, and construction union officials tend to view this urban renaissance as a necessary process for stabilizing city populations,[52] making the city physically attractive, and creating job opportunities. On the other hand, many minority-group spokespersons and some scholars look at the same phenomenon and ask for whom the cities are being saved.[53] They charge that displacement and other changes central to the urban renaissance mainly benefit corporations, mortgage institutions, and real estate speculators. Few benefits, in their view, trickle down to the poor or even to the mass of the city's working- and middle-class residents.

In city after city, there has been an absolute decline in the number of unskilled jobs available to the large mass of unskilled and undereducated people who concentrate in the cities. At the same time, the fields where central-city jobs are growing usually have fairly stiff educational or post-high-school training requirements for them. Adding to this *job-skills mismatch* is that new jobs for lower-paid and less skilled workers are locating in the suburbs. For example, in the early 1990s, 87 percent of all such entry-level unskilled jobs were created in the suburbs.[54]

Some Political Implications of Metropolitan Growth Patterns

An underlying assumption of this chapter has been that demographic and technological forces have significant political implications. Three implications in particular stand out:

- The nature of urban growth is shaped by political decisions.
- Urban growth inevitably leads to greater governmental activity and expenditures.
- Urban growth obliges governments to assume the role of arbiter between conflicting groups in the urban arena.

The effect of political decisions on urban growth can be seen by reviewing some of the items previously covered in this chapter. For example, political decisions shaped the technological innovations that caused urban growth. At every stage of new technological implementation listed in Table 2.3, governments made significant public investments. In an early stage, government lands were given to the railroads, and the railroads in turn sold these lands to construct their railroad cities. Later, in the automobile/motor-transport stage, the federal government utilized the highway trust fund to provide a continual source of funding for the highways and the interstate road system.

Not only have governmental decisions contributed directly to the application of new transportation technologies, but also many governmental decisions have had a profound impact on where urbanization would occur. The rapid post–World War II urbanization of southern California was due in large measure to federal expenditures in the aerospace and defense industries. The decision in Nevada to legalize gambling contributed to the urbanization of Reno and Las Vegas. Finally, as indicated earlier, state and federal decisions on highway construction, home-mortgage-loan terms, and the subsidization of farmers to reduce acreage have contributed immensely to decentralization of the metropolis and to the dual migration that has characterized the metropolitan United States since the 1920s.

A second political implication of metropolitan growth is that increasing levels of urbanization inevitably lead to increasing levels of governmental activity and governmental expenditure. The yellow fever epidemic in Memphis that we cited earlier indicates how important it is for urban governments to take the initiative in such matters as sewage disposal, water supply, and public health. At the metropolitan level, suburban growth has meant greater expenditures for streets, utilities, fire and police protection, and public education. This inevitable increase in governmental activity as urbanization proceeds conflicts sharply with the political value, widely held in the United States, that governments should engage in as little activity as possible.

A third political implication of metropolitan growth is that governments are increasingly obliged to satisfy demands put forward by emerging groups in the growing metropolis. Often these groups ask the government to redress grievances they have against other actors in the metropolis. At other times they ask the government to help them satisfy certain needs they cannot satisfy themselves because they lack the economic resources to compete on an equal footing in the economic system. This has been true particularly in relation to the struggle of racial minority leaders and others to gain equal access to the social amenities of the metropolis—housing, jobs, and education. When they do not succeed in bargaining directly with institutions that control that access, they seek redress from the government, and government officials are called upon to assist in the conflict.

Compared to the countryside, the urban ghetto is more conducive to militant political activity such as protesting, demonstrating, and rioting; the city brings potential leaders into direct contact with many more potential followers, and it is also more receptive to traditional forms of redressing grievances. In the city, lawsuits are brought before the courts. Lobbying is conducted before the legislatures and city councils. Candidates run for public office. All this indicates that the more urbanized an area becomes, the more involved will its governments become in social conflicts.

These three political implications have special significance for the South and the Southwest, where urban growth rates are currently most intensive. Historically, the South and Southwest have been the most conservative regions of the nation, resisting both extensive public welfare programs and political movements such as organized labor that often represent the interests of dissatisfied groups. Southwestern metropolises such as Houston and Dallas have received large numbers of in-migrating Hispanics and northern laborers driven from their native regions by economic recession and lured to the Southwest by the hope of jobs. Alfred A. Watkins argues that these migrants will create considerable political tensions as they seek to improve their economic status and political influence.[55]

Political Bias in the Changes in Urban Growth

It may seem absurd to suggest that demographic movements might be biased politically, for demographic movements are neutral phenomena. Nevertheless, urban growth in contemporary America has patterns and consequences that favor certain groups of people above others. Three of these phenomena stand out:

The tradition of privatism
Segregation of classes
Limited mobility of the poor

First, a persistent motive force behind urban growth throughout U.S. history has been what Sam Bass Warner, Jr., called privatism (see p. 29). Warner wrote, "The tradition of privatism is . . . the most important element of our culture for understanding the development of cities."[56] City growth was not promoted because of a sense of community so much as it was promoted by private speculators and entrepreneurs who needed the growth to maximize their profits. Land, in particular, was seldom viewed as a public asset. On the contrary, it was a private asset on which the shrewd person not only could speculate wisely but also could build a city. The nineteenth-century masters in real estate speculation were the railroaders. The twentieth-century masters were the central-city and suburban real estate developers. The provision of cultural facilities such as libraries and museums was left to philanthropists or to private subscription.[57] There was no concept of the *public good* for which the government could make such provisions. Although it is not uncommon today for cities to build such facilities, John Logan and Harvey Moltoch argue that what is really happening is that local growth and development interests are using public resources to enhance their own greed and profit, while hiding behind the veil of serving the public interest (see Chapter 7).[58]

As cities grow larger, the tradition of privatism conflicts sharply with the government's role as a provider of services and a redresser of grievances. The extent to which governments at the metropolitan, state, and federal levels should try to guide urban growth is a hotly debated question. There are probably very few people who would argue any longer for leaving metropolitan growth entirely to private initiative. But there is no general agreement on how much guidance government should provide or even on which governments should provide it.[59]

A second bias of the contemporary metropolis is that it is probably more class-segregated than in the past. When the cities were so small and densely populated that all classes were concentrated within a few miles of the central business district, the residential areas of the poor, the working class, the middle class, and the wealthy were necessarily very close to one another. The contemporary metropolises are so much larger and so much less densely populated that this is no longer true. A study of census tracts in Milwaukee and Buffalo found a very high level of class segregation in both the cities and the suburbs.[60] Although some gains have been made in African American suburbanization and in reducing racial residential segregation within big cities,[61] most urban poor people and most racial minorities still live in inner-city neighborhoods.[62] According to a 1995 HUD report,

> For the average large metropolis of the Northeast and the Midwest, two-thirds of the population would have to be moved to achieve perfect racial integration, 73.4 percent and 69 percent, respectively. For the South 64.4 percent and for the West 50.3 percent of the population would have to move to achieve racial integration. More importantly, for the Northeast and the Midwest, the percentages for 1990 exceeded their 1970 counterparts, confirming an increase in racial polarization.[63]

A third bias is that the changes over the past 50 or 60 years have made the contemporary metropolis less amenable to promoting the social mobility of the poor. The European immigrants lived within easy commuting distance of the urban growth areas where the greatest job and entrepreneurial opportunities existed. Today these opportunities have shifted to the suburban fringe. But the poor, urban in-migrant typically moves into an old residential neighborhood far removed from suburban job locations. In most metropolises, public transportation systems are not very efficient. The poor in-migrants' geographic distance from the growth area makes it much more difficult for them to partake in the metropolitan growth either as employees or as speculative entrepreneurs than it was for the European immigrants who migrated into a city still rapidly growing. Furthermore, the economic transformations in the past several decades have greatly reduced the number of unskilled and semiskilled jobs and have in large measure replaced small, owner-run retail stores with large retailing outlets and franchises.

In summary, urban America in the days of European immigration was biased toward the entrepreneurial type who had the imagination and the capacity to profit from growth opportunities. Urban America at the close of the twentieth century was much less conducive to the upward social mobility of the poor classes, particularly the poor classes within the racial minority communities. The apparent exceptions to this have been the Vietnamese, Korean, and other Asian entrepreneurs who have achieved remarkable success in developing stores, restaurants, and retail shops.

Finally, the redistricting of Congress and the state legislatures after the 1990 and 2000 census is reducing the political representation of the cities. Containing the largest concentrations of poor people, the cities will be in a much worse position to get federal and state assistance in the new millennium than they were before.

SUMMARY

1. In the twentieth century, the American population became overwhelmingly urban. A *metropolitan area* consists of an urbanized area of 50,000 or more people plus those areas that are economically and socially integrated with the core area. A *micropolitan statistical area* consists of an urbanized area of 10,000–50,000 people and adjacent areas that are economically or socially integrated.

2. Three basic determinants of metropolitan growth have been identified: an agricultural surplus, transportation innovations, and declining death rates.

3. The urbanization of America (1840–1920) was stimulated by the immigration of millions of Europeans, the opening of the western frontier, and the creation of a national corporate economy.

4. The metropolitanization of America (1920–1975) was characterized by a shifting of the population westward and by the growth of suburbs. The 1950s and 1960s were marked by dual migration. As affluent whites moved out of the cities, their place was taken by rural African Americans and by Hispanics, Asians, and poor whites.

5. The last decade of the twentieth century witnessed the completion of the transformation to a postindustrial city. Older, central cities, especially in the Northeast and Midwest, lost millions of people and jobs. Central-city revitalization, including gentrification and a downtown development boom, has occurred

over the last decade, although it is not clear how much the poor and minorities have benefited from these processes and whether these trends can reverse central-city decline.

6. These urbanization patterns have definite political implications and biases. American urbanization historically has been marked by privatism. The metropolitan areas have become more class- and race-segregated as time has progressed, and the great cities now provide less of a stimulus to the upward social mobility of the poor.

NOTES

1. The definition of *urban* in terms of volume, density, and heterogeneity was formulated by sociologist Louis Wirth in his article "Urbanism as a Way of Life," *American Journal of Sociology* 44 (July 1938): 1–24. The distinction between the sociological and demographic concepts of urbanization has been made by several other scholars as well. See especially John Friedmann, "Two Concepts of Urbanization: A Comment," *Urban Affairs Quarterly* 1, no. 4 (June 1966): 78–79.

2. Office of Management and Budget, "Standards for Defining Metropolitan and Micropolitan Statistical Areas," *Federal Register,* vol. 65, no. 249, December 27, 2000/Notices.

3. William Frey, Jill H. Wilson, Alan Berube, and Audrey Singer, *Tracking Metropolitan America in the 21st Century: A Field Guide to the New Metropolitan and Micropolitan Definitions* (Washington, D.C.: The Brookings Institution, 2004).

4. Ibid., p. 1.

5. Peter Hall, *The World Cities* (New York: World University Library, 1971), p. 19.

6. John Friedmann and John Miller, "The Urban Field," *Journal of the American Institute of Planners* 21 (November 1965): 314.

7. Jean Gottmann, *Megalopolis: The Urbanized Seaboard of the United States* (New York: Twentieth Century Fund, 1961). For an updating of Gottmann's ideas, see *Since Megalopolis,* ed. Jean Gottmann and Robert A. Harper (Baltimore, Md.: Johns Hopkins University Press, 1989).

8. Kingsley Davis, "The Origin and Growth of Urbanization in the World," *American Journal of Sociology* 60 (March 1955): 530–532.

9. On the primacy of agriculture thesis, see ibid.

10. On the primacy of urbanization thesis, see Jane Jacobs, *The Economy of Cities* (New York: Vintage, 1970), chap. 1.

11. The importance of transportation technology is cited by many urbanists. See especially Friedmann and Miller, "The Urban Field," and Gino Germani, "Urbanization, Social Change, and the Great Transformation," in *Modernization, Urbanization, and the Urban Crisis,* ed. Gino Germani (Boston: Little, Brown, 1973), pp. 29–30.

12. Gerald M. Capers, Jr., "Yellow Fever in Memphis in the 1870's," *Mississippi Valley Historical Review* 24, no. 4 (March 1938): 483–502.

13. U.S. Bureau of the Census, *A Century of Population Growth: 1790–1900* (Washington, D.C.: U.S. Government Printing Office, 1909), p. 15.

14. U.S. Bureau of the Census, *Historical Statistics of the United States: Colonial Times to 1957* (Washington, D.C.: U.S. Government Printing Office, 1957), p. 14. Philadelphia's 1790 population was found in U.S. Department of Commerce and Labor, Bureau of the Census, *A Century of Population Growth: 1790–1900,* p. 11.

15. U.S. Bureau of the Census, *Current Population Reports,* ser. P-20, no. 249, "Characteristics of the Population by Ethnic Origin: March 1972 and 1971" (Washington, D.C.: U.S. Government Printing Office, 1973).

16. William H. Frey and Milken Institute, "Census 2000 Shows Large Black Return to the South, Reinforcing the Region's 'White-Black' Demographic Profile," Population Studies Center, University of Michigan, May 2001.

17. For an excellent interpretation of some of the political consequences of the third and fourth urban migration waves, see Steven P. Erie's "Rainbow's End: From the Old to the New Urban Ethnic Politics," in

Urban Ethnicity in the United States: New Immigrants and Old Minorities, vol. 29, *Urban Affairs Annual Reviews,* ed. Lionel Maldonado and Joan Moore (Beverly Hills, Calif.: Sage, 1985), pp. 249–275.

18. The classic interpretation of the importance of the western frontier to American history was made by Frederick Jackson Turner in his famous essay *The Frontier in American History* (New York: Henry Holt, 1920). His argument was rejected by historian Arthur M. Schlesinger, Sr., in "City in American History," *Mississippi Valley Historical Review* 27 (June 1940): 43–66, who argued that urbanization was the motive force behind the frontier movement and most of the important historical-political movements. For a reformulation of the importance of the frontier in the urbanization process, see Daniel J. Elazar, *Cities of the Prairie: The Metropolitan Frontier and American Politics* (New York: Basic Books, 1970).

19. Roderick D. McKenzie, *The Metropolitan Community* (New York: McGraw-Hill, 1933), pp. 4–5.

20. See Charles N. Glaab and A. Theodore Brown, *A History of Urban America* (New York: Macmillan, 1967), pp. 113–144. For a fascinating, in-depth account of the creation of one city by the Northern Pacific Railroad, see Waldo O. Kliewer, "A Railroad City: The Foundations of Billings, Montana," *Pacific Northwest Quarterly,* July 1940.

21. Sam Bass Warner, Jr., *Streetcar Suburbs: The Process of Growth in Boston, 1870–1890* (Cambridge, Mass.: Harvard University Press, 1962).

22. For a study of the impact of a subway on big-city growth, see James Leslie David, *The Elevated System and the Growth of Northern Chicago* (Evanston, Ill.: Northwestern University, Department of Geography, 1965).

23. Sam Bass Warner, Jr., documents the small-scale nature of business in Philadelphia in the late eighteenth century in *The Private City: Philadelphia in Three Periods of Its Growth* (Philadelphia: University of Pennsylvania Press, 1968), chap. 1. Oscar Handlin documents the late-nineteenth-century transition of Boston's economy from small-scale to large-scale enterprise in *Boston's Immigrants* (Cambridge, Mass.: The Belknap Press of Harvard University Press, 1941), chap. 3.

24. Chapter 1, "The Metropolitan Explosion," in Hall, *The World Cities,* contains a more thorough explanation of this idea.

25. Schlesinger, "City in American History."

26. For a summary of this antiurban tradition, see Morton White and Lucia White, *The Intellectual Versus the City: From Thomas Jefferson to Frank Lloyd Wright* (Cambridge, Mass.: Harvard University Press, 1962).

27. Mark L. Gelfand, *A Nation of Cities: The Federal Government and Urban America 1933–1965* (New York: Oxford University Press, 1975), p. 220.

28. *Shelley v. Kraemer,* 334 U.S. 1 (1948).

29. Gelfand, *A Nation of Cities,* p. 220.

30. On the charge of economic discrimination, see Eugene Lewis, *The Urban Political System* (Hinsdale, Ill.: Dryden Press, 1973), pp. 221–223.

31. U.S. Congress, Office of Technology Assessment, *The Technological Reshaping of Metropolitan America,* OTA-ETI-643 (Washington, D.C.: U.S. Government Printing Office, 1995), p. 78.

32. William K. Tabb, *The Political Economy of the Black Ghetto* (New York: Norton, 1970), pp. 22–23. See also William Julius Wilson, *When Work Disappears: The World of the New Urban Poor* (New York: Vintage Books, 1996).

33. Douglas S. Massey and Nancy A. Denton, "Hypersegregation in U.S. Metropolitan Areas: Blacks and Hispanics Segregated Along Five Dimensions," *Demography* 26, no. 3 (August 1989): 373–391.

34. Data on Hispanics are taken from U.S. Bureau of the Census, *The Hispanic Population: Census 2000 Brief* (May 2001), http://www.census.gov/prod/2001pubs/c2kbr01-3.pdf.

35. See Joan Didion, "Miami: 'La Lucha,'" *New York Review of Books* 34, no. 10 (June 11, 1987): 15–18.

36. Calculated from *Statistical Abstract of the United States: 2001* (Washington, D.C.: U.S. Government Printing Office, 1991), Table 7, p. 11.

37. Helen Hornbeck Tanner, ed., *The Settling of North America: The Atlas of Great Migrations into North America from the Ice Age to the Present* (New York: Macmillan, 1995), pp. 168–169, 192–193.

38. Winston Moore, Charles P. Livermore, and George F. Galland, Jr., "Woodlawn: The Zone of Destruction," *Public Interest* (Winter 1973): 42; Cal McAllister, "Building for the Future," *Chicago Tribune,* April 15, 1995, CN 3; Charles J. Orlebeke, *New Life at Ground Zero: New York, Home Ownership, and the Future of American Cities* (Albany, N.Y.: The Rockefeller Institute Press, 1997), pp. 195–196. On this phenomenon, see also Ben Wattenberg, *The Real America* (Garden City, N.Y.: Doubleday, 1974), pp. 142–143.

39. Edgard M. Hoover and Raymond Vernon, *Anatomy of a Metropolis* (Garden City, N.Y.: Anchor Books, 1959), p. 198.

40. U.S. Congress, Office of Technology Assessment, *The Technological Reshaping of Metropolitan America,* OTA-ETI-643 (Washington, D.C.: U.S. Government Printing Office, September 1995), p. 78; Myron Orfield, *Metropolitics: A Regional Agenda for Community and Stability* (Washington, D.C.: The Brookings Institution, 1997), pp. 15–16.

41. U.S. Congress, Office of Technology Assessment, *The Technological Reshaping of Metropolitan America,* OTA-ETI-643 (Washington, D.C.: U.S. Government Printing Office, September 1995), p. 3.

42. Ibid., p. 5.

43. Ibid., pp. 5–6.

44. Ibid., pp. 6–7.

45. See "Downtown Housing as an Urban Redevelopment Tool: Hype or Hope?" in *Housing Policy Debate,* vol., 10, no. 2, 1999: 477–505.

46. On this point, see especially Brian J. L. Berry, "Islands of Renewal in Seas of Decay," in *The New Urban Reality,* ed. Paul E. Peterson (Washington, D.C.: The Brookings Institution, 1985), pp. 72–74.

47. See, for example, George Sternlieb and James W. Hughes, eds., *Revitalizing the Northeast* (New Brunswick, N.J.: Center for Urban Policy Research, 1978). See also Donald B. Rosenthal, ed., *Urban Revitalization,* vol. 18, *Urban Affairs Annual Reviews* (Beverly Hills, Calif.: Sage, 1980).

48. See, for example, Tony Robinson, "Gentrification and Grassroots Resistance in San Francisco's Tenderloin," *Urban Affairs Review* 30 (March 1995): 483–513; Richard DeLeon, *Left Coast City: Progressive Politics in San Francisco, 1975–1991* (Lawrence: University Press of Kansas, 1992).

49. George Wagner, "Gentrification, Reinvestment, and Displacement in Baltimore," *Journal of Urban Affairs* 17 (1995): 81–96.

50. U.S. Department of Housing and Urban Development, *Empowerment: A New Covenant with America's Communities—President Clinton's National Urban Policy Report* (Washington, D.C.: Department of Housing and Urban Development, Office of Policy Development and Research, 1995); Robin Hambleton, "The Clinton Policy for Cities: A Transatlantic Assessment," *Planning Practice and Research* 10, nos. 3–4 (1995): 359–377.

51. John H. Mollenkopf, *The Contested City* (Princeton, N.J.: Princeton University Press, 1983), pp. 31–36.

52. See Marc Levine, "'A Third-World City in the First World': Social Exclusion, Racial Inequality, and Sustainable Development in Baltimore, Maryland," in Mario Polèse and Richard Stren, *The Social Sustainability of Cities* (Toronto: University of Toronto Press, 2000), p. 156.

53. For example, see Paul Levy and Dennis McGrath, "Saving Cities for Whom?" *Social Policy* 10, no. 3 (November–December 1979): 20–28.

54. See U.S. Department of Housing and Urban Development, "The State of the Cities" (Washington, D.C.: U.S. Government Printing Office, 1997).

55. Alfred A. Watkins, "Intermetropolitan Migrations and the Rise of the Sunbelt," *Social Science Quarterly* 59, no. 3 (December 1978): 553–561.

56. Warner, *The Private City,* pp. 38–39.

57. Bayrd Still, "Patterns of Mid-nineteenth Century Urbanization," *Mississippi Valley Historical Review* 28 (September 1941): 187–206.

58. *Urban Fortunes* (Berkeley: University of California Press, 1987). See also J. Allen Whitt, "Mozart in the Metropolis: The Arts Coalition and the Urban Growth Machine," *Urban Affairs Quarterly* 23 (1987): 15–36.

59. See David C. Ranney, *Planning and Politics in the Metropolis* (Columbus, Ohio: Merrill, 1969), especially chap. 7, "Conflict and the Planning Process: The Politics of Planning," pp. 109–138.

60. See Richard Hamilton, *Class and Politics in the United States* (New York: Wiley, 1972), pp. 155–180.

61. Karl Taeuber, "Racial Residential Segregation, 28 Cities, 1970–1980," Center for Demography and Ecology, University of Wisconsin, Madison, Working Paper 83-12; Joint Center for Political Studies, *Blacks on the Move: A Decade of Demographic Change* (Washington, D.C.: Joint Center for Political Studies, 1982).

62. See Katharine L. Bradbury, Anthony Downs, and Kenneth A. Small, *Urban Decline and the Future of American Cities* (Washington, D.C.: The Brookings Institution, 1982), pp. 187, 214–215.

63. U.S. Department of Housing and Urban Development, Office of Policy Development and Research, "Measuring the Performance of Our Cities," *U.S. Housing Market Conditions,* 4th Quarter 1995 (March 1996): 8.

PART TWO

THE ETHNIC AND RACIAL BASE OF POLITICS

The tone of contemporary urban politics in the United States has been greatly influenced by late-nineteenth-century machine politics and the events that caused their decline. So true has this been that contemporary urban politics is incomprehensible without some understanding of these historical forces. Machine politics emerged as the great industrial cities were born along the North Atlantic seacoast and the Great Lakes states. As governing devices, the machines were often deeply rooted in the social structure of the ethnic groups that inhabited these cities. The basic unit of political organization was a geographic unit—the *ward* or *precinct*.

Because the political machines were rooted in the social organization of certain ethnic communities, machine politics were biased toward and benefited those communities and certain businesspeople. In contrast, other groups, such as the racial minorities, benefited very little, for machine politics was effectively biased *against* them. However, there were very few cities with sizable racial minority populations until the twentieth century.

Reformers promoted several devices to remove city government from the control of the political machines. They were aided in their antimachine efforts by the patterns of metropolitan growth and by some actions taken by the federal government.

CHAPTER 3

ETHNIC-BASED POLITICS
IN THE CITY

CHAPTER SYNOPSIS

Immigrants in Late Nineteenth and Early Twentieth Centuries: *Size and Distribution of Ethnic Settlements; Politics of Developing Indigenous Power Bases* • Ethnic Networks as Ethnic Traps: *Success for the Irish—Yes, and No; Limits of a Political Strategy as a Means of Group Advancement for Contemporary Racial and Ethnic Groups in the City*

Chapter 2 indicated that the first major change in patterns of urbanization in the United States took place between 1840 and 1930, when hundreds of medium-size and large cities were created in the Northeast and Midwest by the settlement there of most of the 37 million immigrants who arrived during that period. Politically, this process gave birth to the organization of urban political power on *geographic and ethnic bases*. Many powerful contemporary institutions in urban politics developed out of the indigenous community structures of four European ethnic minorities: the Irish, Italians, Jews, and Poles.

Irish, Italian, Jewish, and Polish people settled almost exclusively in urban centers and, as much as any other ethnic group, shaped the institutions that dominated urban politics prior to World War II. Today, the descendants of these four ethnic groups number some 63 million. Most are settled in urban areas, and their ethnicity continues to be important in modern urban politics. This is especially so as they come into conflict with the newer urban ethnic minorities: African Americans, Hispanics, and Asians (see Chapter 5).

The Size and Distribution of Ethnic Settlements

Table 3.1 divides the major ethnic groups represented in the U.S. metropolitan population of the year 2000 into three general categories:

1. The mainstream nationalities that were assimilated the most thoroughly into the native white American population (especially English and Germans)

TABLE 3.1   Estimated Ethnic and Racial Composition of the Metropolitan Population (2000)

Nationality or Racial Group	Approximate Number in the United States
Mainstream Nationalities	
English	28,264,856
Germans	46,488,992
European Ethnics	
Irish	33,067,131
Italians	15,942,683
Polish	9,053,660
Jews[a]	6,041,000
Contemporary Urban Minorities	
Blacks[b]	36,419,434
Hispanics	35,305,818
Asians[b]	11,898,828

[a]Taken from U.S. Bureau of the Census, *Statistical Abstract of the United States, 2000,* No. 74. Religious Bodies-Selected Data (Data 1998).

[b]Race alone or in combination.

Source: U.S. Bureau of the Census, *Census 2000 Supplementary Summary Tables Geographic Area;* U.S.

Bureau of the Census, *Census 2000 Redistricting* (Public Law 94-171) Summary File, Tables PL1 and PL2.

2. The European ethnic minorities that immigrated principally before World War I and still exhibit political characteristics of ethnic cohesion (especially the Irish, Italians, Polish, and Jews)
3. The newer racial and ethnic minorities that migrated into the cities primarily since World War II either from the American South or from abroad (especially African Americans, Hispanics, and Asians)

At the end of the nineteenth century, when some of the most important urban political institutions were being formed, the European ethnics constituted a majority of the population in most cities of 100,000 or more.[1] The European ethnic minorities are important not only because they still constitute a huge percentage of the urban population, but also because they shaped the dominant models of ethnic advancement that still influence urban politics today. For this reason, the political institutions developed by these European ethnic minorities are important to the study of contemporary urban politics.

The Politics of Developing Indigenous Power Bases

Table 3.2 summarizes the bases of ethnic group politics in cities during the era of the political machines (1870s–1930s). Contrasting different ethnic and racial groups' *upward mobility* path allows us to consider whether an economic strategy or a political

TABLE 3.2 Immigrant Ethnic Groups in Machine Era

Ethnic Solidarity	Institutional Base of Ethnic Group Power	Economic Base	Benefits to Ethnic Group of Strong Identity	Costs to Ethnic Group of Strong Identity/ Problems Maintaining Identity
		The Irish		
Potato famine, Catholicism, hostility of mainstream population (Irish were a huge voting bloc with a high degree of ethnic cohesiveness).	Catholic Church— organized around parish boundaries. Church becomes an agency for collecting and distributing resources for the good of the community and is central to social life. Democratic Party (political machine)— organized around ward boundaries. The machine becomes a way to make city government serve interests of the group—specifically, to attain city jobs and use city budgets to enhance neighborhood assets and life (e.g., parks).	Construction, real estate, and development. Building large numbers of new churches and schools, providing employment, and developing an entrepreneurial class. Politics: securing city jobs and contracts through machines and patronage; enhancing construction and real estate development by getting government and private contracts to build the physical city (office buildings, infrastructure).	Community-based economy: money from small contractors, tradespeople, grocers, saloon owners, retailers, and doctors and lawyers stays in community and is reinvested through contributions to social and religious institutions (e.g., Knights of Columbus, Catholic hospitals). Politics as an avenue of upward mobility for group. Irish were the primary beneficiaries of machine politics.	Political strategy held group back. Ethnic network of social mobility reduced development of a broader entrepreneurial class and thus undermined group progress.

(continued)

TABLE 3.2 Immigrant Ethnic Groups in Machine Era *(continued)*

Ethnic Solidarity	Institutional Base of Ethnic Group Power	Economic Base	Benefits to Ethnic Group of Strong Identity	Costs to Ethnic Group of Strong Identity/ Problems Maintaining Identity
		The Italians		
Strong family loyalty, link to others from hometown in Italy, and lack of trust of outsiders (non-family members).	Social organization built upon kinship relations and personal loyalties.	Business leaders mobilized capital that was reinvested to produce jobs and more business.	Rise of strong middle class.	Lack of trust made it difficult to pursue cooperative ventures (e.g., build a school or hospital).
This lack of trust was reinforced by exploitation of new immigrants, as well as by hostility from established groups.	Small business and professional class arose to serve the needs of a tight community. Tended to support and employ other Italians.	High savings rate among Italians resulted in captial available to invest in community enterprises such as small businesses (e.g., restaurants, taverns, construction, trucking, produce and fruit marketing, roofing) as well as professional services (e.g., doctors, lawyers).	Community-based economy. Business leaders used economic power to support Italian candidates. Business leaders formed Italian community and civic organizations that fostered greater ethnic solidarity (e.g., Italian-American Labor council).	Organized crime undermined group progress and cast shadow on all Italians.

(continued)

TABLE 3.2 Immigrant Ethnic Groups in Machine Era (continued)

Ethnic Solidarity	Institutional Base of Ethnic Group Power	Economic Base	Benefits to Ethnic Group of Strong Identity	Costs to Ethnic Group of Strong Identity/ Problems Maintaining Identity
		The Jews		
Emigrated to escape political or religious persecution	Social organization based on family life and private and religious organizations.	Skilled labor and small businesses.	Independent of political machine and often participated in reform efforts.	Success bred resentment in other groups.
United in opposing anti-Semitism. Highly concentrated in a few major cities.		High value placed on education leading to large professional class of doctors, lawyers, dentists, teachers, etc.		Difficult to assimilate into American "Christian" culture while maintaining Jewish identity.
		The Poles		
Low national consciousness; Polish identity developed after arrival through the activities of two large, national organizations (see next cell).	Polish Roman Catholic Union (PRCU) organized lodges in each Polish Roman Catholic parish. Set up by the Polish clergy to underwrite a network of Polish parishes and schools.	Unskilled laborers arrived in large cities at time of Industrial Revolution and got jobs in auto, steel, and other factories.	Gained symbolic rewards and "lower tier" patronage jobs and welfare services" in return for machine support.	Difficult to maintain community social structure because of assimilation and suburbanization of younger generations.
	Polish National Alliance (PNA) not restricted to Catholics and organized by community rather than parish. Goal was to liberate Poland from German, Austro-Hungarian, and Russian conquerors. After liberation in 1919, goal became promotion of Polish heritage.	High value placed on education of children led to large professional class.		

strategy is more beneficial to the group in the long run. This has particular relevance to the efforts of later arrivals to the city—blacks, Hispanics, and Asians—to attain their share of the American dream.

The Irish

The Irish were the first European ethnic group to migrate in massive numbers directly into the American city. The Irish faced persistent political repression by the British in Ireland, as well as periodic famines. Irish immigration to the United States began to swell in the 1840s.[2] Half a million Irish reportedly starved to death during the potato famine of that decade, and out of a total population of no more than 8 million, over 1 million people migrated to the United States in the seven years between 1847 and 1854.

As their numbers increased, a *nativist movement* arose to protect the integrity of American society from the supposed debilitating consequences of allowing the immigrants access to that society.[3] Like most later immigrants, the Irish found themselves in an alien and hostile environment, and their churches and convents were periodically burned and sacked by angry mobs.

Religion as Community Development   Largely because of this distrust, Catholicism made several important contributions to the development of the social structure of the Irish community. First, Catholicism gave the Irish their own set of distinguishing characteristics that bound them together. Irish Catholics were clearly distinguished from Protestants and from virtually everybody else by several practices and beliefs: confession, Sunday Mass, meatless Friday, Lenten observance, the belief that Catholicism is the only means of salvation, ashes on the forehead when Lent began and Easter palms for decoration when it ended, religious relics carefully placed on the walls of Irish homes, and the lack of a fundamentalist puritanism about liquor and gambling.

These ritualistic observances gave the Irish the symbols of identity that were to become very useful to aspiring civic leaders in the American cities. Once a group of people begins to think of itself as different and unique, this sense of uniqueness can be exploited for purposes of political mobilization. Ethnic solidarity thus gave the professional politicians an effective way of building electoral coalitions that could cut across class lines.[4]

A second contribution of the Catholic Church to Irish development was the creation of parish churches and parish schools.[5] By developing parishes, the Irish were bound together in *geographic* units. Catholic churchgoers not only attended church in their neighborhood; they also lived there, educated their children there, and often worked there. This would prove to be an enormous advantage in electoral politics, which was organized on the basis of the geographic units of wards and precincts.

Parish development stimulated considerable construction activity that channeled business opportunities to Irish contractors and job opportunities to Irish laborers.[6] Quite naturally, the Irish Catholic bishops and pastors awarded these construction contracts to Irish businessmen. The success of these early entrepreneurs was highly dependent on the very limited base of the Irish community, and their hopes for continued success made it imperative for them to reinvest a portion of their profits in religious and social institutions of the Irish community.[7] Irish communities soon blossomed with insurance organizations, fraternal and service organizations, Catholic hospitals, high schools, Knights of Columbus centers, colleges, and even universities. An institutional framework was established to advance young men in society, to provide help for the less fortunate, and at the same time to bind the community together.

Through the parochial school and the Sunday collection plate, the parish and the diocese efficiently mobilized both human and financial resources to build the business, educational, and religious institutions through which individual Irish could live what they considered to be productive and dignified lives. The church not only provided jobs and business opportunities; for a long time it also constituted the focal point of institutionalized Irish social life. Indeed, during the early years of immigration, the only locale that seriously competed with the parish as an Irish gathering place was the saloon, which served as an informal communications network in the Irish social structure.[8]

Politics as a Business Venture The social institutions built through the church dovetailed neatly with urban political developments in the late nineteenth century. Already bound together symbolically, geographically, and economically by the church, the Irish developed into a cohesive voting bloc that eventually gained great influence over the Democratic party in city after city.

In the days of the long ballot, the spoils system, patronage, and other innovations of Jacksonian democracy, control over the Democratic party and the elected city officials soon developed into the well-known phenomenon of *machine politics*. (Machine politics as such will be discussed in the next chapter. For now, we will focus on the implications of the machines for the Irish community.) For the Irish, the period of dominance in machine politics enabled them to secure two advantages. First, they were able to get patronage jobs in the bureaucracy. For example, the Irish were disproportionately employed as public servants.[9]

Second, by controlling the city government, Irish political leaders could make sure that a disproportionate share of the jobs and business contracts went to their fellow Irish political supporters. Until the Great Depression of the 1930s, the relationships between city growth and business contracts provided enormously productive channels for social mobility in the Irish community. In a sense, control over the Democratic party enabled politicians to reverse the truism of American politics that political power results from great wealth. In the case of some of the Irish, wealth was acquired as a result of political power.

The Irish did not invent the political machine, political patronage, political corruption, or the awarding of government contracts for political purposes. These existed long before the arrival of the Irish.[10] What the Irish *did* do was eventually to take control of preexisting Democratic party organizations in some key cities such as New York and Chicago. They then used that control to remain in office by giving out such favors as government contracts, patronage, or whatever scarce resource they possessed to lower-status Irish constituents in exchange for their votes. By keeping themselves in power, they helped create another channel of upward mobility for their fellow Irish.

The Italians

Italian ethnic networks of political influence and social mobility were similar to those of the Irish in some general respects, but they were very different in terms of the politically important institutions that the Italians created.

Like the Irish, most Italian immigrants were unskilled laborers, and very few of them had experience as merchants or skilled tradespeople.[11] The majority of Italian immigrants after 1880 came from impoverished southern Italy. They settled mostly in northeastern and midwestern cities, where their initial economic niche was to compete with the Irish for jobs in the general unskilled labor force.[12] Italians who migrated to California were mostly northern Italians, who were a little less destitute than the southern Italians and did not get along well with them.[13] The northern Italians also had immigrated much earlier and were much less alienated from the surrounding society.

The southern Italian immigrants tended to settle in eastern and midwestern big-city neighborhoods called "Little Italies." Normally there were several Little Italies in a big city; Chicago had 17.[14] Usually people from other ethnic backgrounds also lived in the Italian neighborhoods. People from the same district in Italy would settle in a particular building or block. Thus the buildings and sometimes the blocks were homogeneous, whereas the neighborhoods themselves were usually heterogeneous.[15]

Competition with the Irish   Although the Italians started with an occupational base and a settlement pattern similar to those of the Irish, they created an entirely different network of social mobility. No doubt much of the difference was due to the fact that the Italians arrived later, when the channels of social advancement that earlier had been open to the Irish—that is, the Catholic Church and the Democratic party—were closed.[16]

Many Italians were estranged both from the Irish clergy and from the institutional church, which was much more puritanical than the churches they had known in Italy.[17] Consequently, they demanded parishes with Italian priests and Italian-language services. The Italians were also skeptical of the parish school and preferred to send their children to the public schools.[18] This estrangement of the Italians from the Irish-dominated church institutions was termed the *Italian problem* by some of the clergy.[19] The church has not performed economic and organizational services for the Italians to the same extent that it performed them for the Irish.

Italians found the Democratic party less closed to their ambitions than the church, but it took many years for them to capitalize on the opportunities it offered. One reason why the Italians took until the 1930s to gain political prominence involves the skill with which the deeply entrenched Irish politicians played elements of the Italian communities against one another and minimized the potential voting strength of Italians. In both New York and Chicago, the Irish political leaders gerrymandered council and legislative district lines through the Little Italies and thus divided the Italian vote among several districts.[20] Italians took many years to develop an indigenous power base capable of effectively challenging the Irish. When this indigenous power base finally did develop, three elements were of prime importance: the nature of the social structure of the Italian communities, Italian business, and organized crime.

Political Relevance of Italian Social Structure   One theme that pervades most of the commentary on Italian social structure is the tremendous importance of kinship and personal relations. Italians preferred to interact with relatives and other Italians rather than with nonrelatives and non-Italians. As late as the 1960s, researchers found that Italians were much more inclined than other European ethnic groups to live in ethnic neighborhoods, to visit their relatives regularly, and to visit often with others of the same ethnicity. They also were much less likely than any other European ethnics except Jews to marry outside of their ethnic group.[21]

The Italian-American ethnic community was bound together by a strong web of kinship and personal relationships. There was a high level of mistrust and suspicion about people who fell outside the web (especially non-Italians), and there was a tendency toward authoritarian relationships in which roles were relatively stable, well defined, and well understood. Insiders were to be trusted insofar as they conformed to the well-defined role patterns for family members and friends. Outsiders were to be trusted only after they had established a stable personal relationship.[22] This emphasis on mistrust and this ethnocentricity were much stronger among immigrants from southern Italy than among newcomers from northern Italy. In researching a village in southern Italy, Edward L. Banfield found the lack of trust between families to be so pervasive that the community was virtually immobilized and incapable of any cooperative action for community projects such as getting a hospital or improving schools.[23]

This dual importance of the family in politics and of close personal relationships is probably an outgrowth of the conditions under which Italians immigrated to and settled in the American cities. These conditions did little to make the Italians trust outsiders, and they virtually demanded that the immigrants learn cooperation in order to avoid perpetual exploitation.

The first exploiter that the isolated immigrant was likely to encounter was the *padrone*. Immigrants were required to have the means to support themselves before they could enter the country. If there were no family members to meet an immigrant at the port of entry and vouch for him, labor contractors called padrones would meet him, find him lodging, and offer him employment. For these services the padrone received a share of the immigrant's wages, and he dominated an exploitive relationship with his workers that not only included their work but often extended to other aspects of their life. The padrone system lasted from the 1880s until about 1920.[24]

At about the same time, a violent form of extortion known as the *Black Hand* appeared. Black Handers sent notes demanding payment of money under the threat of murder or bodily harm if the money was not paid. Until strong Italian community organizations were created, there was no one to whom the isolated Italians could turn for help when threatened. The police were ineffective against Black Handers. Black Hand activities flourished until about World War I.[25]

Not only did the immigrants face exploitation from within the Italian community; they faced open hostility from without. In the 1890s, eleven Italian prisoners in New Orleans were lynched after a jury had found them *not* guilty of murdering the city's police chief. Italian residents of an Illinois town were driven out of their homes and beaten, and their houses burned, in a fit of mob hysteria. And in one of the most famous trials of the 1920s, two Boston Italians (Nicola Sacco and Bartolomeo Vanzetti) were condemned to death in a trial that included a judge who apparently was prejudiced against Italians and a jury that included no Italians and that based its decision on evidence that appeared circumstantial.[26] Apart from such egregious incidents, Italian immigrants commonly were cheated by non-Italian merchants or lost their savings when bankers went bankrupt.

Political Ramifications of an Ethnic Business Class   Facing these circumstances, Italians perhaps naturally turned to relatives, friends, and fellow Italians when they sought to establish business enterprises. The earliest businesses were small newspapers and retail operations that catered to the particular needs and tastes of Italian communities. Soon every city with a sizable Italian population had its Italian newspaper and was dotted with numerous small, autonomous family restaurants. Fruit peddlers, peanut sellers, and pushcart vendors soon plied their trade on the major commercial streets. Non-Italians increasingly dined at Italian restaurants and purchased goods from Italian merchants. These Italian businesspeople began to perform for the Italian community a *capital mobilization function* similar to that which the parish performed for the Irish.

Italian entrepreneurs and workers had an enormous capacity to save, sometimes salting away half or more of their monthly wages in the late 1800s and early 1900s. Among Italian immigrant families in New York, 35 percent took in roomers, even though the typical tenement apartment contained only three or four rooms.[27] Many of the tenants were young men who had traveled ahead without their families. And much of the saving, of course, was by these same men, who wished to finance an eventual return to Italy or passage for their families to the New World. Whatever the reason for this high level of saving, the net result was that the Italians amassed capital to invest in their own community enterprises.[28]

In a community organized around strong family loyalties and personal relationships, it was perhaps inevitable that accumulated savings were deposited with Italian bankers rather than in non-Italian financial institutions. The Italian banker became an intermediary between the immigrant and the institutions of the outside world. The most successful of the Italian bankers was A. P. Giannini, who founded the Bank of America. He started his banking operations by making credit available to immigrant fishermen, fruit peddlers, small ranchers, and working people who lacked the collateral or the credit standing to get loans from the already established banks. As his banking operations stabilized and he built up trust among the immigrants, Giannini also attracted their savings deposits. Many of these people would not put their money in a non-Italian bank. Of course, the employees he hired were also Italian.[29]

As the Italian business, professional, and middle classes developed, they maintained their preference for conducting their affairs with Italians. They developed strong ethnic networks: "The Italian doctor sees an Italian lawyer when he wants legal advice, both of them have their expensive suburban house built by an Italian contractor, and all of them vote for an Italian political leader to represent the interests of their community at city hall or the state house."[30]

Politically, the business and professional people used their new wealth to advance Italian candidates and Italian causes. The Italian business leaders not only were helpful to politicians; they also helped form many Italian community organizations. Some of the organizations, such as the Sons of Italy, promoted general ethnic solidarity. Others, such as the Italian-American Labor Council and the Italian-American Chamber of Commerce, had a narrower functional base.

Italian businesspeople thus performed at least three functions in the development of the Italian community. They mobilized capital that was reinvested to produce jobs and more businesses. They contributed financially to certain Italian politicians and Italian political causes. And they helped form civic organizations that in turn promoted solidarity and cohesion among Italians.

Organized Crime and Italian Community Development   Few aspects of Italian-American life are more controversial than its supposed relation to organized crime. Rather than being a Sicilian import, Italian-American organized crime was probably created in the United States. This would be entirely consistent with the experiences of other ethnic groups—both Irish and Jewish slums were plagued by organized criminal gangs.[31] It must be stressed that in *many* cities, organized crime has had no political impact on Italian community development.[32] But in *some* cities, it has.

Where organized crime played a role in Italian community development, three features stand out. First, many of the criminal leaders were bound together by the "web of kinship."[33] Second, Italian organized crime helped finance some Italian businesses and some community organizations. Because much, if not most, of the revenue generated by the organized gangs came from non-Italians who used the services of gang-controlled numbers games, alcohol, narcotics, and prostitutes, great sums of capital flowed into Italian hands. By the mid-twentieth century, much of this money was being invested in legitimate enterprises, especially hotels, nightclubs, vending machines, real estate, and even stock markets.[34] How extensive this legitimate investment is, and how important it was for the development of Italian business, are impossible to determine. But it cannot be ignored. Nor can it be assumed that such investments were always made for nefarious purposes.[35] Whatever their purposes, to the extent that investments were made within the Italian community, they helped provide jobs for Italian workers and helped businesspeople get established.

A third way in which the Italian experience with organized crime affected Italian community development was through its use of political influence. When New York's reform mayor Fiorello La Guardia sought to deny the Democratic organization of Tammany Hall as much patronage as he could, the organization became desperate. With its traditional sources of funds (kickbacks from the patronage job holders) drying up because of La Guardia's opposition, the Tammany organization needed a new source of money. And one source was organized crime, which gradually used its newly found wealth to get Italians appointed to judgeships and elected to other offices in New York City.[36]

In Boston, a process of "reciprocal obligations" was established, wherein a loosely knit, interlocking organization worked through both political parties by paying off the appropriate political bureaucratic leaders. The racketeers were virtually given a free hand in their business enterprises, and they were able to obtain favors for their constituents. In Chicago, a direct relationship was formed between Italian acquisition of political influence and the emergence of strong crime leaders.[37]

There is a pattern of ethnic succession in organized crime.[38] Just as Italian dominance of organized crime succeeded Irish and Jewish dominance of organized crime, the Italians themselves began ceding dominance to different Hispanic and Asian groups in the 1980s. By the mid-1980s, Colombians and Cubans had come to rival Italian crime groups as the dominant intermediaries in the importation of illegal narcotics, especially cocaine.[39]

This loss of Mafia hegemony over organized crime in the 1980s was a consequence of three setbacks the Mafia suffered in those years. First, as increasing numbers of the younger generations of Italians went to college, they found that they had opportunities for upward social mobility in the professions and the corporate world that had been denied their parents and grandparents. Thus the recruitment base for future leadership was narrowing, causing the leadership ranks to become quite aged by the 1980s and leading to generational conflicts.[40]

The second setback can be attributed to ethnic succession in housing. A stroll through lower Manhattan makes it obvious that Little Italy is being invaded by Chinatown. As one ethnic group vacates the slums and is replaced there by another, the first group loses its recruitment base and becomes estranged from the new customers in the slums. If there is a market for numbers, narcotics, and other illegal services in the slums today, the Italians are probably not so readily able to service that market as are elements of the African Americans, Hispanics, and Asians who have been moving into the slum areas. The third setback to the Mafia came at the hands of federal prosecutors who succeeded in winning several key convictions in the 1980s and 1990s.[41]

Italian Power Base: Summary   What, then, is one to conclude about the emergence of ethnic-based political power among the Italians? Four conclusions seem apparent. First, by themselves the political parties and the Catholic parishes that had worked well for the Irish were of extremely limited utility to the Italians who sought political power. Second, Italian ethnic-based political power did not materialize until a distinctive social organization, built in great measure on the basis of kinship and personal loyalties, began to emerge in Italian communities. Third, Italian ethnic-based political power was dependent on large numbers of immigrants who vitally needed this kind of personalized social structure in order to survive in the very impersonal and remote big city.

Finally, the rise of Italian politicians was related directly to the rise of an Italian middle class that had developed the skills and the financial resources needed to sustain political campaigning. This middle class had a diverse economic base in business, in the professions, and sometimes in organized crime.[42] When all three of these developments (the kinship-based social structure, the large number of immigrants, and the middle class to provide leadership) matured, as they did in many cities in the 1930s and 1940s, an indigenous base of political power was created.

The Jews

The political influence of the Irish and the Italians in the United States developed through what can be called traditional channels of urban politics. The urban experience of Jews in this country has been very different and probably much more successful. The differences emerge in four major respects.

The Primacy of Ideology   Whereas Irish and Italian involvement in urban politics has been marked by pragmatism rather than ideology, the Jewish involvement has had a strong ideological component. Jews were much more willing to support liberal, socialist, and antimachine reform policies.[43] There have been a few Jewish bosses, but not very many. In opinion surveys, Jews consistently outscore other whites on indexes of liberalism and racial tolerance.[44]

A Varied Partisan Background   Whereas the Irish and Italians have been strong Democrats, the Jews have had a much more varied partisan background. Until the 1920s, Jews were mostly Republican. This stemmed in part from what Lawrence Fuchs called "enormous gratitude toward the Republic which granted them refuge," in part from dislike of the Irish-controlled Democratic machines,[45] and in part from the Republican party's abolitionist and Reconstruction origins. Jewish influence was also strongly felt in the organization of socialist movements in the early twentieth century. Much of this support was dissipated by the administration of Franklin Roosevelt, and Jews have been predominantly Democratic ever since.

On the local level, since 1932, Jewish political influence has been the greatest in the Northeast, where Jews are the most heavily concentrated. Particularly in New York, Jews have fluctuated between reformism within the Democratic party and support for reform candidates put forward by the Republican and Liberal parties. Reform mayors Fiorello La Guardia and John Lindsay garnered some of their strongest support in Jewish precincts.[46]

Experience as Skilled Laborers and Merchants   The economic base of the Jewish middle class differed significantly from that of the Irish and Italian communities. In comparison to the Irish and Italian male immigrants, who were mostly unskilled laborers, only 14 percent of Jewish immigrants from 1899 to 1910 were unskilled laborers; two-thirds of these immigrants were skilled laborers, many of them tailors. In addition, Jewish immigrants included a higher proportion of people who had experience as merchants.[47] A common enterprise among the early-twentieth-century Jewish immigrants was to open "sweatshops." These were often begun in the entrepreneur's own apartment, where he could set up sewing machines, employ many Jewish tailors to operate them, and bid for contracted work from the large garment manufacturers in New York or Boston. If successful, he could eventually move the establishment from his apartment to an actual shop; and if he were very successful, he might even become a garment manufacturer.[48]

In addition to the garment trade, Jewish merchants established small retail businesses such as delicatessens, restaurants, and bakeries. Much of the capital accumulated through these Jewish enterprises was reinvested in the professional and graduate training of the immigrants' children. More than any other ethnic group, the Jews have placed a high value on formal education and have produced a disproportionate percentage of the nation's doctors, dentists, scholars, intellectuals, and creative artists.[49]

This economic base of the Jewish community has had politically important consequences. Fewer Jews than Irish or Italians became economically dependent on political patronage jobs or on benefits to be derived from allegiance with the political machines. Even where large numbers of Jews did work for local bureaucracies, they were usually in professions such as teaching or social work that were not under the direct control of political machines. The conditions of their employment were structured by professional standards rather than political connections. Because of this, fewer Jewish leaders than Irish or Italian leaders had to support the machine for reasons of economic dependence.

Community Structure   The fourth difference between the Jews and the Irish and Italians lies in the social structure of their communities. The Irish and Italians had left their countries largely for economic reasons, so a substantial number of these immigrants returned to their homeland once they had saved enough money. The Jews, in contrast, emigrated largely to escape political or religious persecution, and for this reason, Jewish emigration was a one-way trip. Even if they became economically successful, Jews had nothing to return to in Europe except more persecution. Accordingly, Jews were often said to be more eager to integrate into the mainstream of American life.[50]

One of the pervading themes of American Jewish community development has been that of reacting to anti-Semitism.[51] This was probably the most unifying element in what otherwise was a very heterogeneous people. Although all Jews nominally shared the same religion, there were strongly felt differences between those of reform, orthodox, and conservative persuasions, as well as between the earlier German immigrants and the later Russian and Polish immigrants. Even within the same economic arena—the garment industry, for example—there were sharp differences between the Jewish union leaders and the Jewish owners. In spite of these differences, they became united because, as Jews, they were all endangered by outbreaks of anti-Semitism. Jews, wealthy or not, faced discrimination and exclusion from the most prestigious clubs, schools, and residential areas. Even in the working-class neighborhoods of big cities, anti-Semitism erupted. Where Jewish and Irish neighborhoods abutted in northern Manhattan, Jews were sometimes beaten up by young Irish gangs.[52] Anti-Semitism led to the formation of a bond between many Jews—a connection that crossed class lines. The bonds were strengthened by the rise of the Nazi regime in Germany, the horrors of World War II, and the establishment of the state of Israel. Perhaps the most obvious indicator of these bonds was the low rate of intermarriage between Jews and gentiles, although more recently this pattern has been breaking down.[53]

The political consequences of these developments in the Jewish communities have been very important. As noted, the economic base of most Jews made them independent of the urban political machines. The social conditions of Jewish life and the oppression of anti-Semitism led them to support liberal causes such as civil rights and social welfare legislation that the political machines quite often opposed. Given these differences between Jews and the machines, it was probably inevitable that much of the anti–Tammany Hall reform leadership in New York's Democratic party came from the Jewish community.

The Poles

The fourth-largest urban European ethnic community in the United States is that of the Poles.[54] Large-scale Polish immigration began in the 1870s and continued until World War I; the motivating force behind it was primarily economic. About three-fourths of the Polish immigrants were Catholic, and the overwhelming majority entered the economy as unskilled laborers in great manufacturing cities such as Buffalo, Detroit, Cleveland, Pittsburgh, Milwaukee, New York, and Chicago. Many of them found their economic base in the automobile industries, steel mills, foundries, and other heavy industries.

Much of Polish community development resulted from the activities of two large, national organizations that established local lodges in each Polish community. The first was the Polish Roman Catholic Union (PRCU), established in 1873. The PRCU was organized with a local in each Polish Roman Catholic parish. It was dominated by the Polish clergy, who sought to use the PRCU to establish a network of Polish parishes and Polish parochial schools. The Polish clergy resented the dominance of the Catholic Church by the Irish, and they thought that if they could establish a strong parish and school network, the Irish-dominated church hierarchy would have to become open to the Poles as well as to the Irish.

The larger organization is the Polish National Alliance (PNA). The PNA was not restricted to Roman Catholics, and it was organized by community rather than by parish. Founded in 1880, its major goal was to achieve the liberation of Poland from its German, Austro-Hungarian, and Russian conquerors. So divided was Poland by its conquerors that many Poles acquired a consciousness of their national character only after they arrived in America and such organizations as the PNA made them aware of it.[55] So successful was the PNA in attracting members through its goal of Polish liberation that the PRCU was also forced to adopt liberation as a major objective. Once that objective was accomplished in 1919, both organizations turned their attention toward maintaining the Polish heritage among the immigrants and their children. The PRCU discouraged participation in non-Polish institutions. Both organizations ran a variety of activities and enterprises, which ranged from selling insurance to conducting English classes for the immigrants.

As a result of these and similar mutual-benefit organizations, a vibrant institutional life was created in Polish communities. By 1960 an estimated 830 Polish parishes and more than 500 Polish elementary schools existed in the United States. Polish convents were established, a Polish college was established in Pennsylvania, and the PRCU subsidized a seminary that trained Polish priests. Polish-language newspapers abounded. Polish businesspeople's organizations flourished. Like the Jews, the Poles made special efforts to provide higher education for their young. Both major organizations and several others maintained scholarship programs. In short, a strong ethnic community developed.

The Ethnic Network as an Ethnic Trap

The Irish benefited the most from the machine era. For contemporary urban minorities—African Americans, Hispanics, and Asians—intrigued with the Irish avenue of advancement, it is important to note that there were limits to the amount of upward mobility that could be promoted through the church and the political machine. The person who relies on that network as a channel of mobility often becomes trapped in it and has difficulty gaining recognition outside of it.[56] Some contend that the financial sacrifices the Irish made in contributing to the extensive construction of parish schools and churches hindered the formation of an Irish upper class in the United States.[57]

What was true of the church as an avenue of advancement was also true of the political machine. Steven P. Erie studied the political channel of advancement and concluded that an Irish upper middle class developed more rapidly in cities without an Irish machine than it did where the machines existed. There were several reasons for this. First, political patronage work could employ only a limited number of Irish laborers. The machine most successful at employing Irish was probably that of Tammany Hall in New York, but even at the peak of that machine's influence in 1930, the public sector employed less than a fourth of the Irish workforce in the city. That meant the overwhelming majority of Irish workers had to find nonpatronage jobs. Expansion of public-sector jobs for Irish laborers was often limited by machine politicians who were pressured by their big-business campaign contributors to follow conservative fiscal policies that would hold down government expenses and public payrolls. Most important, in Erie's analysis, was that the political jobs were predominantly unskilled, low-paying, dead-end jobs. The greater the number of Irish who became elevator operators, maintenance workers, firefighters, or low-level clerks in City Hall, the less the number of Irish who had an incentive to develop professional skills and become lawyers, doctors, accountants, or entrepreneurs. For all of these reasons, Erie argues, the political machines did more to inhibit upward social mobility among the Irish than they did to promote that mobility.[58]

Although it is important to recognize that the ethnic network can become a trap, it is also important to remember that the vast majority of early Irish immigrants were so impoverished, so lacking in entrepreneurial skills, so deficient in the skilled trades, often so poorly educated, and held in such low esteem by the rest of society that they had no other realistic choice than to band together and seek advancement as a group. For these people, passing up a low-level government job in hopes of becoming an accountant in the private sector was not an option. For some Irish families, in fact, the government connection became a source of steady income that helped them provide their children with training in marketable skills.

Furthermore, the machine itself was only one of several channels for gaining political influence and social mobility. The channels created by the Irish were based on the hierarchically organized church, the Democratic Party, control over the city's elective offices, and the use of that control to provide jobs and business opportunities. All of these elements were mutually reinforcing, and most important, they provided an indigenous base of Irish political power. The Irish were symbolically bound together by a strong sense of ethnic and religious identification that gave rise, in city after city, to the founding of fraternal and social groups such as the Sons of Erin and the Ancient Order of Hibernians.

In the next chapter, we will examine the political machines more carefully and consider whether reforms have permanently limited the ability of more recent ethnic and racial groups in the city to use City Hall in their efforts to advance.

SUMMARY

1. In the pre–World War II city, urban political power was ultimately based on the social organization of ethnic communities. The largest of the ethnic communities were the Irish, Italians, Jews, and Poles. Each had its own particular social base for fostering political influence and upward social mobility.

2. For these urban ethnic groups, political power rested in great measure on a substantial number of middle-class people serving as clergy, lawyers, politicians, racketeers, businesspeople, or professionals who could contribute money and talent to political causes that furthered the group's cohesion.

3. Institutions such as parish churches, local businesses, and (in some instances) crime organizations were created to mobilize money and a workforce that would constitute a new investment in the community.

4. The political power derived from these ethnic groups was indigenous; it was not dependent on outside benevolence.

NOTES

1. U.S. Bureau of the Census, Twelfth Census of the United States: 1900, vol. 1, Population, p. cxxii.

2. Two political novels that capture the flavor of the political and economic conditions spurring Irish emigration are Thomas Flanagan's The Tenants of Time (New York: Warner, 1988) and Leon Uris's Trinity (Garden City, N.Y.: Doubleday, 1976).

3. For a history of nativist movements and their effects on the immigrants, see John H. Higham, Strangers in the Land (New Brunswick, N.J.: Rutgers University Press, 1955).

4. Robert Dahl, Who Governs? Democracy and Power in an American City (New Haven, Conn.: Yale University Press, 1966), p. 38.

5. John Tracy Ellis, American Catholicism (Chicago: University of Chicago Press, 1963), p. 102.

6. John Tracy Ellis, Perspectives in American Catholicism (Baltimore, Md: Helicon, 1963), p. 61. See Edwin Scott Gaustad, Historical Atlas of Religions in America (New York: Harper & Row, 1962), p. 169; John F. Maguire, The Irish in America (London: Longmans, Green, 1968); George Potter, To the Golden Door: The Story of the Irish in Ireland and America (Boston: Little, Brown, 1960), p. 359.

7. Shannon, The American Irish, pp. 36–37.

8. Ibid., p. 116. See also Edward M. Levine, *The Irish and Irish Politicians: A Study of Cultural and Social Alienation* (Notre Dame, Ind.: University of Notre Dame Press, 1966), p. 119.

9. Ibid., p. 120; Dahl, *Who Governs?* pp. 41–52; Herbert Gans, *The Urban Villagers: Group and Class in the Life of Italian-Americans* (New York: Free Press, 1962), p. 167.

10. This is a main thesis of Amy Bridges in *A City in the Republic: Antebellum New York and the Origins of Machine Politics* (Ithaca, N.Y.: Cornell University Press, 1987).

11. One source estimates that 75 percent of the Italian immigrants were general laborers, 15 percent were skilled tradespeople, 6 percent were farmers, and about 5 percent were merchants and dealers. See Rudolf Glanz, *Jews and Italians: Historic Group Relations and the New Immigration, 1881–1924* (New York: Shulsinger Brothers, 1970), pp. 31–33.

12. David Ward, "The Emergence of Central Immigrant Ghettoes in American Cities, 1840–1920," *Annals of the American Association of Geographers* 58 (June 1968): 343–351.

13. Glanz, *Jews and Italians*, p. 10.

14. Rudolph J. Vecoli, "Contadini in Chicago: A Critique of the Uprooted," *Journal of American History* 64 (1964): 404–417.

15. John S. MacDonald and D. Leatrice, "Urbanization, Ethnic Groups and Social Segmentation," *Social Research* 29 (Winter 1962): 435.

16. Carl Wittke, *The Irish in America* (Baton Rouge: Louisiana State University Press, 1956), p. 92.

17. One scholar of Italian Americans writes that "they did not feel that they could speak intimately with priests in America as they had in the old country," and consequently they tried at first to sustain their religious contacts with the village priests in Italy [Lawrence Frank Pisani, *The Italian in America: A Social Study and History* (New York: Exposition Press, 1957), p. 165]. Another scholar argues that even in Italy the peasantry was alienated from the clergy [Joseph Lopreato, *Italian Americans* (New York: Random House, 1970), pp. 88–89]. In either interpretation, early Italian immigrants had difficulty relating to the American Catholic Church.

18. Humbert S. Nelli, *Italians in Chicago, 1880–1930: A Study of Ethnic Mobility* (New York: Oxford University Press, 1970), pp. 67, 189. This changed as the Italians grew more affluent in the post–World War II era, and Italians became strong supporters of the parochial schools (Lopreato, *Italian Americans*, pp. 89–90).

19. Pisani, *The Italians in America,* p. 166.

20. On New York, see Lowi, *At the Pleasure of the Mayor,* p. 40. On Chicago, see p. 68 in Humbert S. Nelli, "John Powers and the Italians: Politics in a Chicago Ward, 1896–1921," *Journal of American History* 57 (June 1970): 67–84.

21. Andrew M. Greeley, *Why Can't They Be Like Us? America's White Ethnic Groups* (New York: Dutton, 1971), pp. 87, 92; Nelli, *Italians in Chicago,* p. 196.

22. Andrew M. Greeley, *That Most Distressful Nation: The Taming of the American Irish* (Chicago: Quadrangle Books, 1972), pp. 147, 152.

23. Edward C. Banfield, *The Moral Basis of a Backward Society* (New York: Free Press, 1958).

24. Glanz, *Jews and Italians*, pp. 27–28.

25. Francis A. J. Ianni, "The Mafia and the Web of Kinship," *Public Interest* 22 (Winter 1971): 88.

26. On the New Orleans incident, see Richard Gambino, *Vendetta: A True Story of the Worst Lynching in America* (Garden City, N.Y.: Doubleday, 1977). On the Boston execution of Sacco and Vanzetti, see Leonard Dinnerstein and Frederic Cople Jaher, *The Aliens: A History of Ethnic Minorities in America* (New York: Appleton-Century-Crofts, 1970), p. 216; *New York Times,* August 23, 1977, p. 47, and February 1, 1978, p. 10. For a fictional account of contemporary Italian reactions to the Sacco and Vanzetti trial, see Rick Boyer, *The Penny Ferry* (New York: Warner, 1984).

27. Pisani, *The Italians in America,* p. 62.

28. Andrew F. Rolle, *The Immigrant Upraised* (Norman: University of Oklahoma Press, 1968), p. 305; Pisani, *The Italians in America,* p. 65.

29. Rolle, *The Immigrant Upraised,* p. 379.

30. Greeley, *American Catholics—Making It or Losing It?* p. 32.

31. See Herbert Asbury, *The Gangs of New York: An Informal History of the Underworld* (New York: Capricorn Books, 1970; originally published 1927).

32. See, for example, Wolfinger's comments on the lack of influence of organized crime in New Haven politics (*The Politics of Progress,* p. 75n.).

33. Ianni, "The Mafia and the Web of Kinship," pp. 96–98.

34. Whyte, *Street Corner Society,* pp. 140–146; Daniel Bell, *The End of Ideology: On the Exhaustion of Political Ideas in the Fifties* (Glencoe, Ill.: Free Press, 1960), p. 130.

35. Former attorney general Ramsey Clark argues that many legitimate investments by crime figures are not made for the purpose of control [Ramsey Clark, *Crimes in America* (New York: Simon & Schuster, 1970), p. 73]. Others also note significant legitimate investment by organized crime figures but look on it much more suspiciously than Clark. See, for example, Richard D. Knudten, *Crime in a Complex Society* (Homewood, Ill.: Dorsey Press, 1970), p. 193.

36. Ibid., pp. 128–136.

37. Humbert S. Nelli, "Italians and Crime in Chicago: The Formative Years, 1890–1920," *American Journal of Sociology* 74 (January 1969): 389.

38. Ianni, "The Mafia and the Web of Kinship," p. 97; Bell, *The End of Ideology,* pp. 128–136.

39. This is noted by several writers. See Gage, *The Mafia Is Not an Equal Opportunity Employer,* p. 135; Ianni, "The Mafia and the Web of Kinship," p. 97; and Salerno and Tompkins, *The Civic Confederation,* p. 376. Also see Joan Didion, "Miami: 'La Lucha,'" *New York Review of Books* 34, no. 10 (11 June 1987): 15–18.

40. *Minneapolis Star and Tribune,* January 14, 1987, p. 3A.

41. See *The New York Times,* November 7, 1983, p. 1; October 25, 1984, p. 1; September 19, 1986, p. 1; November 15, 1986, p. 9; and March 11, 1987, p. 1.

42. Raymond E. Wolfinger, "The Development and Persistence of Ethnic Voting," *American Political Science Review* 59 (December 1965): 896–908.

43. Lawrence Fuchs comments that the early-twentieth-century socialists won more votes with their denunciations of local corruption than with their socialist programs. See *The Political Behavior of American Jews* (Glencoe, Ill.: Free Press, 1956), p. 124.

44. Several surveys of the National Opinion Research Center (NORC) conducted at various times in the 1960s demonstrate this. Relevant examples can be found in Greeley, *Why Can't They Be Like Us?* pp. 74, 75, 204, 207, and 208.

45. Fuchs, *The Political Behavior of American Jews,* p. 51.

46. On La Guardia, see Fuchs, *The Political Behavior of American Jews,* p. 158.

47. Glanz, *Jews and Italians,* pp. 31–32.

48. Ibid., p. 28.

49. Charles S. Liebmann, *The Ambivalent American Jew: Politics, Religion and Family* (Philadelphia: Jewish Publication Society of America, 1973), p. 136.

50. Glanz, *Jews and Italians,* p. 21.

51. For an interpretation of Jewish unity as motivated primarily as a reaction to anti-Semitism, see George Friedmann, *The End of the Jewish People?* trans. Eric Mosbacher (Garden City, N.Y.: Doubleday, 1967).

52. Katznelson, *City Trenches,* pp. 84, 101–102.

53. Fred Massarik and Alvin Chenkin, "United States National Jewish Population Study: A First Report," *American Jewish Yearbook: 1973–74* (American Jewish Committee, New York, and Jewish Publication Society of America, Philadelphia, 1973), p. 295.

54. Despite the large size of America's Polish population, there is still a shortage of serious scholarship published on Polish politics. Except where otherwise noted, most of the interpretations in this book are taken from Joseph A. Wytrwal, *America's Polish Heritage: A Social History of the Poles in America* (Detroit: Endurance Press, 1961). Two more recent studies are Neil C. Sandberg, *Ethnic Identity and Assimilation: The Polish-American Community—Case Study of Metropolitan Los Angeles* (New York: Praeger, 1974); and Edward R. Kantowicz, *Polish-American Politics in Chicago* (Chicago: University of Chicago Press, 1975). The classic scholarly treatment of Poles in English is W. I. Thomas and Florian Znaniecki, *The Polish Peasant in Europe and America* (Boston: Richard C. Badger, 1918).

55. Oscar Handlin, *The American People in the Twentieth Century* (Cambridge, Mass.: Harvard University Press, 1954), p. 68.

56. Greeley, *Why Can't They Be Like Us?* pp. 50–51.

57. Nathan Glazer and Daniel Patrick Moynihan, *Beyond the Melting Pot: The Negroes, Puerto Ricans, Jews, Italians, and Irish of New York* (Cambridge, Mass.: M.I.T. Press, 1963), p. 230. Moynihan was the Irish contributor to this team.

58. Steven P. Erie, *Rainbow's End: Irish-Americans and the Dilemmas of Urban Machine Politics, 1840–1985* (Berkeley: University of California Press, 1988), pp. 60–61.

CHAPTER 4

MACHINE POLITICS AND REFORM

CHAPTER SYNOPSIS

Rise of Political Machines: *Definition of Political Machine; Machine Politics and the Growth of Cities; Tammany Hall* • The Reform Movement: *Clash of Cultural Perspectives; Social and Structural Reformers* • Structural Reforms to Weaken Machine Rule: *Electoral Reform (e.g., nonpartisan elections, at-large elections); Civil Service; Other* • Restructuring City Government: *Weak and Strong-Mayor Systems; Council-Manager Model; Commission Form* • Did Reform Kill the Machines?: *Role of Reform; Federal Role; Demographic Change* • Have Machines Really Disappeared? • The Reform Legacy

The Political Machines: Outgrowth of Ethnic-Based Politics

The last chapter traced the upward-mobility path of newly arrived immigrants in the late 1800s and early 1900s. Ethnic-based politics naturally led to machine-based politics. Fred I. Greenstein presents the classic definition of a political machine. He suggests that machine politics entails four main elements:

1. There is a disciplined party hierarchy led by a single executive or a unified board of directors.
2. The party exercises effective control over nomination to public office, and through this, it controls the public officials of the municipality.
3. The party leadership—which quite often is of lower-class social origins—usually does not hold public office and sometimes does not even hold formal party office. At any rate, official position is not the primary source of the leadership's strength.
4. A cadre of loyal party officials and workers, as well as a core of voters, is maintained by a mixture of material rewards, including patronage and *nonideological* psychic rewards—such as personal and ethnic recognition, camaraderie, and the like.[1]

The machine is a political party organization (Democratic or Republican) centralized under the control of a "boss" who oversees the selection of party nominees for local elected offices. The machine relies on patronage—awarding of government contracts and other material incentives—to secure campaign workers and campaign contributions. Machines appealed to immigrant voters on the basis of ethnic identity and rewarded loyal supporters with jobs. The machines were nonideological. They did not attack the capitalist system or seek to adopt a radical program of reform. Rather, the machines would intercede on behalf of individuals who had machine connections and offer modest assistance to those in need—for example, after the outbreak of a fire. Of course, the recipients of the machine's help would undoubtedly be grateful and would reward the machine with continued support. The primary purpose of the machines was to get and keep political power.

The city was geographically divided into wards or voting districts for city council. The immigrants were concentrated geographically in the city, so the wards closely paralleled the boundaries of ethnic neighborhoods. It was in these neighborhoods that the Irish, Italians, and Poles developed institutions that served as avenues of upward mobility. Because these wards served as the boundaries for election to city council, it was here that the political machine took root and became an additional avenue for upward mobility by the immigrants.

Wards were divided into precincts. Each precinct would have one or more precinct captains, depending on the population size. The precinct captains were responsible for turning out a good vote for the machine on election day and were also the link between the immigrant and the machine. Those with problems could readily approach a precinct captain and seek assistance in dealing with the city bureaucracy. Those who rendered continuous and loyal service to the machine could also seek a job. Patronage was allocated by the boss to the ward leaders. Wards that continuously provided greater support to the machine's victories could expect to receive an increasing share of the patronage positions and other benefits.

The wards also served as the boundaries for city council (sometimes called assembly or board of aldermen) seats. The party, under the boss's direction, would select nominees for mayor, council members, and other elected positions, including judges, prosecutors, legislators, and county commissioners. A disloyal councilor or mayor could be disciplined by giving the party nomination to someone else in the next election. There was no open primary or other avenue to contest the nomination. In some instances, ward leaders also served as councilor members or the boss might run for mayor. However, the actual power was rooted in the political machine, not in the official position in city government.

Party officials needed a way to earn a living while working for the machine. They usually held an official position in city government and drew a salary, although their real duties were to serve the party organization. Of course, they were expected to contribute financially to the party to help sustain the party's organization. Winning and keeping office required much money. Businesses that wanted city contracts were also expected to make financial contributions to the machine in the form of kickbacks. Some of the money undoubtedly went into the hands of machine politicians, but much of it was used to sustain the machine organization.

Virtually every large city in the late 1800s and early 1900s was governed by a political machine. As we have seen, the fuel for the political machines was the immigrant population in the cities, who were the majority of the population. Alan DiGaetano points out that there is a "link between the expansion of the municipal work force between 1870 and 1900 and the rise of party machines" (see Table 4.1).[2] It was during this time that big cities rapidly expanded their urban services—including police, fire, and public works. The expansion of municipal services provided the patronage jobs needed to reward loyal workers.

TABLE 4.1 Expansion of the Municipal Workforce and the Rise of Urban Party Machines

	1870		1880		1900		Rise of Party Machine
	Total City Employees	Per 1,000 Population	Total City Employees	Per 1,000 Population	Total City Employees	Per 1,000 Population	
Baltimore	1,074	4.29	1,470	4.42	2,549	5.05	1880s
Boston	1,258	5.02	2,218	6.11	3,725	6.64	1880s
Chicago	1,386	4.64	1,977	3.93	9,946	5.86	1910s
Cincinnati	715	3.31	1,285	5.04	1,862	5.71	1880s
Cleveland	315	3.50	695	4.34	1,798	4.71	1880s
Detroit	306	3.85	468	4.02	1,801	6.30	1880s
Jersey City	360	4.36	462	3.83	1,183	5.73	1870s
Kansas City	—	—	177	3.17	946	5.78	1890s
Milwaukee	215	3.01	393	3.40	1,264	4.43	1880s
New Orleans	1,547	8.08	1,271	5.88	1,682	5.86	1870s
New York	4,222	2.86	6,305	3.30	20,516	5.97	1870s
Philadelphia	2,372	3.52	3,928	4.64	7,446	5.76	1870s
Pittsburgh	360	2.59	532	2.26	1,662	3.68	1880s
St. Louis	878	2.82	1,597	4.56	3,946	6.86	1880s
San Francisco	716	4.79	1,568	6.70	2,356	6.87	1870s

Source: U.S Bureau of the Census (1872, 1, Table 32; 1882, 1, Table 36; 1904, Tables 41 and 43).

Reproduced from: Alan DiGaetano, "The Origins of Urban Political Machines in the United States: A Comparative Perspective," *Urban Affairs Quarterly* 26 (March 1991): 345.

The political machines tapped into the ethnic institutions and networks in the immigrant communities and became an added path of upward mobility for some. Those people who did not get tangible payoffs from machine politics could still receive symbolic payoffs. Nominating an Italian or a Pole to high office granted recognition to that ethnic group. And either because this recognition gave them vicarious pleasure or because they hoped that their own children might rise in a similar fashion, the members of the group remained loyal to the nominating party.

The oldest and most famous combination of ethnic and machine politics occurred in the Tammany Hall machine in Manhattan.[3] The Tammany Society was founded in 1789 primarily as a social fraternal organization. It slowly became politicized and, particularly under the Irish, served as the mechanism for controlling the activities of the neighborhood district clubs. The district clubs were the heart of the organization. They dispensed patronage and controlled nominations within their jurisdictions. But for citywide nominations and patronage or for settling disputes between clubs, a citywide organization was needed, and this was the role reserved for Tammany Hall. Tammany reached its greatest strength in the era that extended from the Civil War until the early 1900s under the leadership of William Marcy "Boss" Tweed, Charles F. Murphy, and Richard Croker.

Boss Tweed was surely the most colorful of the bosses. He rose from foreman in the fire department through the positions of alderman and congressman to the position of boss of Tammany Hall. As boss he controlled the dispensing of government contracts to the point where he was able to steal millions of dollars from the New York City treasury. Tweed was finally arrested and served a jail sentence for his crimes, but few other Tammany bosses ended their careers in prison.

Despite their inefficiencies and high levels of graft, the machines, including Tammany Hall, did serve to integrate the competing demands of various ethnic groups for patronage jobs and representation in government. They also served as a link between the government and the impoverished immigrants (particularly the Irish) and provided a channel through which the larger ethnic groups (particularly the Italians and Poles) were able to demand concessions from city governments and to get a share of the representation and patronage. The fact that ethnic groups could be represented as such through the machines meant that machine politics offered a way of diffusing class divisiveness in the cities: Aspiring ethnic politicians, in order to rise, had to mold a core of followers from all classes within the ethnic group.

The Reform Movement

Who were the Reformers?

To understand the *reform movement*, it is necessary to understand that its conflict with the political machines was in great measure a conflict between cultures. The machine leaders usually rose from the working and lower classes in the immigrant communities. In contrast, the reformers were primarily upper-class and upper-middle-class businesspeople, lawyers, professionals, and university people. They were Protestant rather than Catholic.

The reformers could never reconcile themselves to the fact that city government was dominated by the kind of people on whom the machines relied for their leadership. Historian Richard Hofstadter has described the conflict between the reformers and the machine leaders in terms of two incompatible perceptions of the very *raison d'être* of politics. The immigrant politician viewed politics in personal terms. "Political relations were not governed by abstract principles; they were profoundly personal."[4] The payoffs from political involvement also were highly specific—a job for a relative, a government contract, perhaps, or advance information on a proposed government land purchase that could enable one to make a quick profit by buying it beforehand and reselling it later to the government. Even those who were not close enough to the bosses to make money from their political involvement often received special payoffs—the proverbial bucket of coal or Christmas turkey, the intercession of the ward leader with the police in certain circumstances, or even just the friendship of the precinct captains and the ward leaders.[5]

In contrast to the immigrants' highly personal view of politics, the upper-middle-class reformers looked upon politics as "the arena for the realization of moral principles of broad applications—and even, as in the case of temperance and vice crusades—for the correction of private habits."[6] The reformers were convinced that the immigrants and machine politics were detrimental to their concepts of a democracy in which the business of the town was to be conducted directly, and in a businesslike fashion, by the best-qualified citizens.[7]

Social and Structural Reformers   Many reformers had complete faith in the ultimate rightness and efficacy of the system. They, after all, had benefited from it. These reformers tended to concentrate on reforms in governmental structure that would make city government more efficient and less costly to the corporate and business taxpayers. For this reason they can be called *structural reformers.*

Many other reformers were critical of the capitalist system. They were appalled by the degrading living conditions of the urban lower classes, the social irresponsibility of many industrial corporations, and the obvious graft that seemed to characterize the relations between the business leaders and the big-city political machines. They tended to concentrate more on social than on structural reforms.[8] They can be called *social reformers.*

The ideological differences between these two kinds of reformers were reflected in their practical activities. One avenue of social reform was the *muckraking* and *reform journalism* exemplified by the work of observers such as Joseph Lincoln Steffens.[9] A second channel of social reform activity was *social work,* particularly the settlement house movement. A prominent social worker was Jane Addams, who founded the Hull House settlement house in Chicago to facilitate assimilation of the immigrants and to influence governmental activities in progressive directions.[10] The third tactic of social reform activity was to *take over the government* and use it to implement progressive policies. A good example is the activity of Detroit's mayor Hazen Pingree, described in the accompanying box.

Historian Samuel P. Hays carefully examined several reform movements and concluded that the major initiators of the structural reforms came primarily from the cities' top business leadership and upper-class elite. According to Hays, the movement to reform governmental structures "constituted an attempt by upper class, advanced professional, and

Social and Structural Reformers in Power

Many social reformers sought election to public office, and a few became mayors in major cities. Some of the more prominent were Tom Johnson of Cleveland (1901–1909), Samuel "Golden Rule" Jones (1897–1903) and Brand Whitlock (1906–1913) of Toledo, and Hazen Pingree of Detroit (1890–1897). Hazen Pingree was elected mayor of Detroit just before the depression of 1893. Through his efforts at regulating the public utilities, he succeeded in getting the public lower rates on electricity, gas, and telephone service. When a stubborn privately owned transit company refused to lower streetcar fares, he put the city in the transit business and promoted a competing streetcar line. In addition to these kinds of objectives, the social-reform mayors also sought free swimming pools, park expansion, school construction, and public relief for the unemployed.

In contrast to the social-reform mayors who were willing to spend public money to improve social conditions for the lower classes, most of the reform mayors were structural reformers who were most interested in honesty, efficiency, and cost cutting. Prominent examples were John Purroy Mitchell in New York, Grover Cleveland in Buffalo, and James Phelan in San Francisco. Rather than increasing expenditures on services to the poor, these mayors cut payrolls, reneged on contracts to pave streets, and cut back on school expenditures. There is little argument that the structural reformers made a more honest accounting of their tax revenues than did the political bosses, but it is also true that the costs of their honest accounting were paid largely by the poor and by the residents of poor neighborhoods.

Source: Melvin G. Holli, *Reform in Detroit: Hazen S. Pingree and Urban Politics* (New York: Oxford University Press, 1969), pp. 393–403.

---

large business groups to take formal political power from the previously dominant lower- and middle-class elements so that they might advance their own conception of desirable public policy."[11] Among the many reform movements that Hays examined, he found none in which small-business people, white-collar workers, or artisans were represented.

The Goal of Reform   The reformers focused their attack on breaking the links between the bosses and (1) an untutored immigrant electorate and (2) businesspeople who were willing to partake in the "honest graft" that the machines offered them. If these links could be broken, then higher-quality people, not dominated by the machine, could be elected to city office. City government could then be administered according to accepted practices of efficiency and administrative honesty—and probably at considerably less expense. These beliefs in the inherent goodness of efficiency and honesty underlay the programs of the structural reformers.

The Programs of Structural Reform

The devices for accomplishing these strategic aims were quite simple, although it took several years for them to evolve. The heart of the problem was the party bosses. Because the bosses were very difficult to eliminate, the key to the solution lay in making them

TABLE 4.2   Structural Reforms to Weaken Machine Rule

Facilitated Machine Rule	Reform
Party Boss Control of Electoral Process	
Party nominating conventions	Direct primary or open primaries
Single-member districts (ward elections)	At-large elections
Long ballot	Short ballot
Partisan elections	Nonpartisan elections
Balloting abuses (such as buying votes)	Election laws and enforcement (such as voter registration and campaign practices)
Party Boss Control of City Government	
Patronage	Civil service
Favoritism in awarding contracts	Open-bidding requirements, ethics laws
Weak-mayor form of government	Restructure city government (shift to strong-mayor, then commission, and finally council-manager form of government)
Little accountability of city government to voters	Referendum, recall, initiative

ineffective. This was largely accomplished through two broad movements: (1) breaking the control of the party bosses over the electoral process and (2) administering the city government according to designs that would make it efficient and honest. This demanded a restructuring of city government (see Table 4.2).

Breaking the Bosses' Control Over the Electoral Machinery   Under the existing rules of the game of urban politics, reformers could not compete with the bosses. If the reformers were to be effective in the long run, they would have to change the rules of the game. The devices for doing this were relatively simple. If the party bosses controlled the nomination process through control of the party nominating conventions, then conventions had to be replaced with *direct primaries* in which the people would nominate their own candidates without the interference of corrupt political middlemen.

If another source of the bosses' strength lay in the geographic or ward organizations through which they could channel limited welfare benefits to the needy in exchange for their votes, the logical solution was to eliminate wards and hold *at-large elections*, with every candidate for a particular city office running against every other candidate. Reformers argued that the single-member district (ward) elections promoted parochial neighborhood interests, whereas at-large elections promoted citywide interests (that is, public interests).

If the long ballot meant that 50 or 100 offices had to be voted on at local elections—numbers so large that voters relied heavily on machine endorsements to distinguish friendly from unfriendly candidates—then the logical solution was a *short ballot* so that people would have to learn about the candidates for only a limited number of offices.

If the machine's strength depended on its ability to control party nominations, the machine might be permanently crippled by holding *nonpartisan elections* in which partisan nominations were banned. And if the machines controlled the margin of votes in close elections by dishonest election practices—such as repeating, voting in the names of people who had died or moved away, buying votes, substituting premarked ballots for unmarked ballots, or simply having the election officials add up the tallies incorrectly—then the final *coup de grâce* might be given to the machine simply by making such practices illegal and clamping down on violations of election law.

The standard mechanisms for breaking the control of the party bosses, then, were the direct primary, at-large elections, the short ballot, nonpartisan elections, and fair-campaign laws, along with the separation of local elections from national elections. Referendum, recall, and initiative devices also were instituted in some cities. By *initiative,* a group of citizens could draft a bill by petition and submit it directly to the voters for approval. Through the *referendum,* legislation passed by councils or legislatures could be overturned by the voters at the ballot box. Through the *recall,* voters could directly remove from office any officials who displeased them. To complete the assault on boss-controlled politics, many states permitted *open primaries,* in which voters did not have to prove their party affiliation in order to vote in a party's primary election.

It was easier to get the reforms instituted in places like California, where progressive movements had been able to gain temporary control over the state government. Thus states with strong progressive movements—Minnesota, Oregon, Wisconsin, and California—became the leaders in the reform movements to put the political machines out of business. Where reforms were put into effect, political machines often found themselves severely contained. Studies of the effect of cross-filing and open primary elections in California concluded that these devices did indeed weaken the control of the party bosses.[12]

Restructuring City Government   At the same time that reformers sought to break the bosses' control over the election process, they also sought to have the city itself administered competently in a politically neutral manner. Specifically, they wanted to eliminate patronage as a basis for employing city government workers, and they wanted to eliminate partisan favoritism from the delivery of public services.

Strong- and Weak-Mayor Forms of Government   The mayor-council form of government is predicated on a separation of powers between the legislative and executive branches via checks and balances. There are two variants of this model, the *weak-mayor* and the *strong-mayor* form. Most machine-dominated cities had the weak-mayor form. Reformers viewed the weak-mayor model as susceptible to machine dominance and proposed the strong-mayor system as a reform.

The weak-mayor form of government derived from the traditional American distrust of executive authority. Powers over the bureaucracy and budget were typically divided into several offices, many of which were elective and most of which had considerable patronage to dispense. This division of budget-making and policy-making powers into many hands made it extremely difficult for citizens to know which officers were responsible for what policies. It also inhibited any coordinated policy control over city government services.

The weak-mayor form of government thus came under attack from several points of view. It hindered public accountability. It fostered the dominance of city government by machines. And it proved incapable of coordinating all public policies in the city.

One proposed solution to these defects was to create a strong mayor who would not be subordinated to a political boss and who would be able to coordinate all the policies of city government departments.

The differences between the weak- and strong-mayor forms of government are illustrated in Figure 4.1. Under the strong-mayor form, the mayor actually assumes authority over administration of the city government, leaving to the council the responsibility for legislative functions. Because department heads are appointed by the mayor, they become more accountable to him or her. Through the mayor they are (theoretically, at least) accountable to the voters. The strong-mayor form does not eliminate politics from city administration, but it does in theory limit the government fragmentation that was felt to be conducive to machine dominance.

The Council-Manager Plan of Government   The council-manager plan, sometimes referred to as the *city-manager plan,* of government was an attempt to obtain unified control over the city administration and at the same time to isolate city administration even further from political influence. All policy was to be established by the city council. Day-to-day operations were turned over to the city manager, who took care of the administrative details and stayed out of political questions.

FIGURE 4.1   Weak- and Strong-Mayor Forms of Government

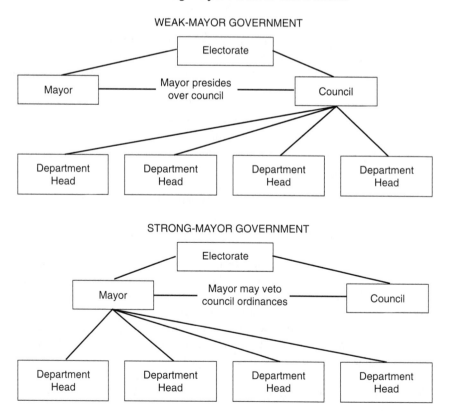

TABLE 4.3   Frequency of Local Government Forms

Population Size	All Cities	Form of Government (number and percentage)			
		Mayor-Council	Council-Manager	Commission	Town Meeting[a]
Over 1,000,000	9	6 (67%)	3 (33%)	—	—
500,000–1,000,000	23	15 (65%)	7 (30%)	1 (4%)	—
250,000–499,999	45	24 (53%)	20 (44%)	1 (2%)	—
25,000–249,999	1365	443 (32%)	871 (64%)	23 (2%)	28 (2%)
10,000–24,999	1892	722 (38%)	996 (53%)	48 (3%)	126 (7%)
2,500–9,999	5229	2374 (45%)	2509 (48%)	72 (1%)	274 (5%)
Total, all cities over 2,500	7144	3096 (43%)	3505 (49%)	143 (2%)	400 (6%)

[a]Includes representative town meeting.

Source: Adapted and reprinted with permission of the International City/County Management Association, "Inside the Year Book," Table 2, in *The Municipal Year Book 2006* (Washington, D.C.: International City/County Management Association, 2006), p. xii.

The city-manager plan of government quickly became popular in the United States. As noted in Table 4.3, it was adopted by a majority of all cities in the 10,000 to 250,000 population range. The incidence of city-manager government drops off in cities of fewer than 10,000, because the cost of hiring a manager becomes prohibitive for very small communities. It also begins dropping off in cities above 250,000, because the sheer size of such cities increases the number of conflicting interest groups concerned about city administration. City managers function best in cities where there is a broad consensus on local politics. As cities become larger, a broad consensus is difficult to achieve, because the number of interest groups tends to be considerable. Large cities also tend to have more heterogeneous populations, which put conflicting demands on city government, especially if the council is elected from districts rather than at-large.[13] The largest cities with council-manager systems are Dallas and San Diego; as their populations have grown, both cities have seen the city-manager system subjected to pressure. Some civic leaders in Dallas have suggested a move to a strong-mayor system. In San Diego, the mayor's office was substantially strengthened in the 1970s.

James Svara has challenged the conventional wisdom that the council-manager form of government embodies a dichotomy between politics and administration—that is, a strict separation or line between policy making and politics on the one hand, and administration on the other. According to Svara, early reform scholars recognized that some responsibilities would be *shared* between policy makers (elected council members) and administrators (city managers). He believes that the dichotomy has been overstated in efforts to more easily explain the reform model. In addition, the myth of the dichotomy "shields administrators from scrutiny and serves the interests of elected officials who can pass responsibility for unpopular decisions to administrators."[14]

Svara acknowledges that there was a period of time when public administration as a field did embrace the dichotomy. However, he argues that this was never the perspective of the original formulators of the council-manager model. Critics of the reform model usually point to this false dichotomy between politics and administration as the fatal flaw in the council-manager system. After all, council members rarely accept the boundaries between policy making and administration and seek to intervene in administrative decisions. Similarly, in cities where managers await policy direction from the council or fail to engage in politics, little gets done. Svara agrees that the dichotomy is false but argues that it was never part of the model and that it completely distorts the way the system was intended to work. He believes the dichotomy perspective evolved from the 1950s onward and became the dominant understanding of the model.[15]

Svara seeks a more sophisticated understanding of the reform model stripped of the simplistic trappings of the politics-administration dichotomy. According to Svara,

> The *complementarity of politics and administration* holds that the relationship between elected officials and administrators is characterized by interdependency, extensive interaction, distinct but overlapping roles, and political supremacy and administrative subordination coexisting with reciprocity of influence in both policy making and administration. Complementarity means that politics and administration come together to form a whole in democratic governance.[16]

In this view, politicians "respect" administrative expertise and therefore limit their intervention in administrative matters. Similarly, administrators seek political guidance and direction from politicians because they are committed to democratic accountability. However, complementarity is a pattern of city governance that prevails only when mutual respect is present. In some cities, where elected officials have a high degree of control, "political dominance" will be the pattern. In cities where managers have greater independence and elected officials a low degree of control, "bureaucratic autonomy" will be the pattern of city governance.

The structure of city government and accompanying reforms (such as civil service) can strengthen or reduce administrator independence. Svara points out that in the machine era, administrators had little independence and this allowed for political dominance. Svara's notion of complementarity is not limited to reform government. This pattern can also occur in the mayor-council model. However, there is probably a tendency for the mayor-council model to tilt in the direction of the political dominance pattern. In medium-size suburban cities, the council-manager model will probably approximate the complementarity pattern outlined by Svara.

The Commission Form of Government Another reform-style city government is the *commission form*. It was first developed in 1901 in Galveston, Texas, after a tidal wave inundated the city and killed 6,000 people. Because the disaster was too great to permit the politics-as-usual conduct of government, a commission of three leading businessmen was established to run the city during the crisis. Their administration proved so popular that after the crisis was over, Galveston adopted the commission form of government permanently.

The number of cities adopting commission government spread rapidly in the early twentieth century, to about 500.[17] But commission government has not endured. As Table 4.3 shows, fewer than 150 cities use commission government today, and this figure includes only two cities with populations over 250,000 (Tulsa, Oklahoma, and Portland, Oregon).

A commission form of government uses the council members as administrators as well as legislators. As shown in Figure 4.2, each council member (commissioner) is

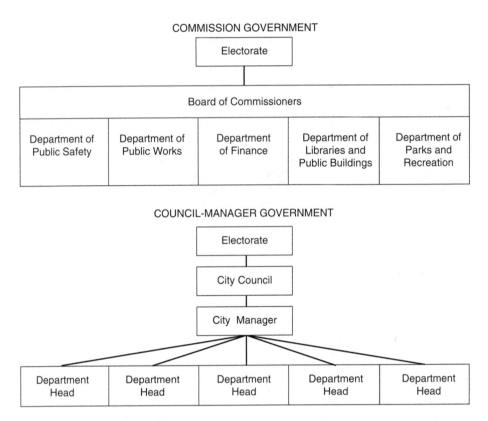

Figure 4.2   Commission and Council-Manager Forms of Government

elected directly by the voters, usually in an at-large election. In addition to being a legislator, the commissioner is also the head of a particular department of government. The commission format has not proved effective in either running the government or managing political conflict. Because the council members are also department heads, budget meetings frequently turn into logrolling sessions in which no overall capacity exists to budget for the city government as a whole. Coalitions form, as is normal on city councils, but council members who are left out of the coalitions find their departments left with smaller appropriations.

It should be noted that the three forms of city government we have discussed represent ideal patterns. In any real-world city, the form of government is likely to deviate from these models. This is because each state sets the parameters for what form of government cities may adopt, and cities vary in the extent to which they adopt the form of government. In some strong-mayor cities, for example, the mayor may have the right to appoint department heads but not the right to remove them without cause or approval of the city council. Cities that adopt council-manager forms of government usually also reform their electoral systems (to nonpartisan, at-large elections, for example) and adopt civil service. However, this is not always the case. And some unreformed cities have electoral reforms and civil service requirements. Some council-manager cities now even give the mayor a veto.

Over time, then, there has been a certain blurring of the distinctions among these models. H. George Frederickson, Gary A. Johnson, and Curtis H. Wood refer to the "adapted city." In the "political city" using the traditional strong-mayor system, administrative reforms are frequently adopted including merit systems, appointment of a chief executive officer, and use of bidding to award contracts. In the "administrative" or reform city, the authors find electoral reforms such as partisan and district elections replacing nonpartisan and at-large elections.

Did Reform Kill the Machines?

The developments we have been examining did not themselves necessarily destroy the old political machines. Ironically, restructuring of city government from the weak-mayor form to the strong-mayor, commission, or even council-manager form of government may have strengthened the political machines in some cities. In Kansas City, for example, the Pendergast machine did not fully develop until after a council-manager form of government was adopted. According to Alan DiGaetano,

> The rise of the administrative local state, where executive authority was enhanced and the power of the city council curtailed, afforded local party bosses the means to organize centralized political machines. A local party leader in control of a strong executive could impose order on lower-level party officials by threatening to cut off their supply of patronage. The consolidation of administrative authority enabled city-wide party bosses to orchestrate the distribution of patronage from above and thus united previously autonomous ward bosses into a single, centralized machine.[18]

DiGaetano considers whether urban reform actually led to the demise of the political machines. He examines the relationship between organizational reforms (adoption of a strong-mayor, commission, or council-manager system), electoral reforms (adoption of nonpartisan and at-large elections), and administrative reforms (adoption of civil service and centralized purchasing and bidding policies) and the political machines in the 33 cities with a population of 100,000 or more people in 1930 (see Table 4.4).

In the case of unreformed cities, 4 out of 5 continued to be dominated by political machines until the 1970s and 1980s. In another 14 cities, reforms were implemented but did not lead to the decline of machines. In yet another 14 cities, structural reforms were associated with the demise of the political machines, either leading to their defeat or preventing them from returning to power. DiGaetano believes that reform "may have been a necessary step in eliminating political machines, but it was not a sufficient one."[19] He looks to demographic changes and economic restructuring of the local economy to account for the machines' decline. Significant community change weakens the machines' organization and support and makes it easier for reformers to attack and organize an alternative reform governance coalition or regime.

The Federal Government and the Decline of Machines

The Great Depression was such a disaster that federal action to curb its effects was widely demanded. By the winter of 1932–1933, 25 percent of the national workforce was unemployed. Traditional forms of assistance proved inadequate to cope with the

TABLE 4.4   Reform and the Decline of Machines

Cities Where Reform Succeeds in Destroying the Machine or Preventing Its Return	Cities Where Reform Fails to Destroy the Machine	Cities That Did Not Adopt Reforms
Major Reforms Adopted	*Major Reforms Adopted*	Albany (1980s)
Cincinnati (1925)[a]	Boston (1951)	Louisville (1970)
Dayton (1914)	Denver (1947)	Jersey City (1938)
Dallas (1931)	Kansas City (1939)	New Haven (1980s)
Detroit (1912)	Memphis (1955)	Providence (1976)
Grand Rapids (1916)	New Orleans (1946)	
Los Angeles (1909)	Philadelphia (1978)	
Portland (1912)	San Antonio (1951)	
Rochester (1932)		
Modest Reforms Adopted	*Modest Reforms Adopted*	
Baltimore (1928)	Chicago (1983)	
Bridgeport (1935)	Cleveland (1941)	
Milwaukee (1910)	Gary (1967)	
Minneapolis (1913)	New York (1933)	
San Francisco (1911)	Omaha (1933)	
Seattle (1918)	Pittsburgh (1970)	
	St. Louis (1941)	

[a]The year the machine declined is enclosed in parentheses.

Source: Adapted from Alan DiGaetano, "Urban Political Reform: Did It Kill the Machine?" *Journal of Urban History* 18 (November 1991): Tables 1, 2, and 3.

immediate needs of the families of these workers. Charitable organizations were overloaded with requests for help, and state governments saw their revenues drop precipitously as the Depression curtailed economic activity. When the federal government finally began to act in an extensive way to cope with the Depression, two aspects of its actions had a detrimental effect on the political machines.

First, the New Deal administration of President Franklin D. Roosevelt instituted a form of individual public assistance that bypassed the political machines. For workers who were dismissed from their jobs, unemployment compensation was initiated. For workers who were injured on the job, worker's compensation was begun. For mothers who were widowed or who had been deserted by their husbands, Aid for Dependent Children (ADC) programs were established. As a supplement to pension plans, the Social Security Act was passed. Other welfare programs were established for the blind, the aged, and the disabled.

Two key features of all these programs made the recipients independent of the political machines. First, the recipients had a *legal right* to assistance under these programs. They did not, in effect, have to buy the assistance by voting for the machine's candidates or by doing precinct work during the campaigns. Second, the assistance came *directly* to the recipients, usually through the mail in the form of a check. There was nothing that the ward leaders could do to increase the value of the checks being sent to supporters of the party or to decrease the value of the checks being sent to supporters of the opposition.

Machine leaders could still give advice to welfare recipients on their welfare rights and benefits, and they could try to intercede on behalf of recipients with the welfare agencies,[20] but machine leaders no longer had a significant welfare-dispensing function to perform. This deprived the party bosses of some of the material incentives they had implemented in order to maintain voter support.

A second general effect of the New Deal came from the rapidly expanding role of the federal government in urban areas. To support bankrupt cities, the federal government began making grants and loans to help them finance public improvements such as water supply systems, sewage systems, hospitals, and other public works. Increasingly, however, federal programs were carried out not by city governments but by agencies especially created to handle particular services. The Federal Housing Act of 1937, for example, enabled federal housing projects to be administered not through city governments but through quasi-public corporations called *housing authorities*. Federal aid for airport construction was usually dispensed to a separate airport commission, not a city government. Federal highway aid was channeled through state highway departments, not the mayor's office. The general pattern was to isolate these federally funded agencies as much as possible from the influence of city hall and the political machines.[21]

A third way the federal government affected machines was through federal court decisions. The most important of these were rulings that sharply restricted the ability of the party in power to fire workers for patronage reasons.[22]

Demographic Change and the Decline of Machines

The decline of the political machines was also hastened by the basic demographic and technological forces described in Chapter 2. The dual migration, the westward drift of the population, the decline in dominance of the Northeast, the encirclement of the central city by suburbs, and the shift of urban growth from the central city to the suburbs all made it impossible for the political machines to expand their influence.

The dual migration was detrimental to machine politics because the political machines never had as much success in absorbing the new urban minorities as they had with the European immigrants. The westward drift of the population and the rise of urban centers in the West are also relevant to the decline of machine politics. In the Southwest, the machines' reinforcing social institutions were much weaker. Labor unions were not traditionally strong in the Southwest. Although ethnic communities developed in the West, they seldom evolved a strong machine style of politics.[23] Even within the Northeast, suburbanization and the rising middle class reduced the machine's reach.

Has Machine Politics Really Disappeared?

The years immediately before and immediately after World War II stand as a symbolic period in urban political history. One after another, several famed central-city machines suffered significant losses. James Curley, the boss-mayor of Boston, was sent to prison, as was Thomas Pendergast, head of the political machine in Kansas City. The Crump machine in

Memphis was defeated in 1949. In an attempt to defuse complaints about the corrupt practices of the incumbent Kelly-Nash machine in Chicago, the Chicago Democrats dumped boss-mayor Ed Kelly in 1947 in favor of a reform candidate, businessman Martin Kennelly. They hoped that Kennelly would draw the support of the good-government reformers. Through their astuteness, the Chicago bosses were able to maintain their power for at least another generation. But a general feeling persisted that the day of the boss was past, that urban political machines were on their way out. Novelist Edwin O'Connor portrayed the decline of the urban political boss in his novel *The Last Hurrah,* a story well worth reading because its romanticization of machine politics contrasts sharply with the negative view of machines that prevailed among most observers.[24]

So widespread has been the view that political machines have disappeared that it has become part of the conventional wisdom about American urban politics.[25] Yet the persistence of machine-style politics in Chicago and the perseverance of the Tammany organization in New York City suggest that machine politics is not entirely dead.[26] In the middle and late 1980s, indeed, New York's political organization was racked by scandals over patronage, graft, organized crime, and laundering of money of a magnitude that the city had not seen for 50 years. In Boston, Mayor Kevin White (1967–1983) kept himself in power in no small measure by using several traditional tactics of machine politics (such as patronage, dispensing of favors on a political basis, and pressuring city employees to make campaign contributions).[27]

Even though there are remnants of machine politics in cities, there are four fundamental differences from the earlier machine era.

Hierarchical party organization and discipline have been destroyed by factionalism and racial and ethnic divisions. First, in reference to Greenstein's criterion that machine politics demand a party hierarchy, very few such hierarchies remain. The Democratic party in Chicago outlasted most other machine hierarchies, but it too is on the ropes as we begin the twenty-first century. Following the death in 1976 of the city's legendary boss, Mayor Richard J. Daley, the machine was rent by persistent infighting and racial conflict. With the election of African American Harold Washington to the mayor's office in 1983, and his reelection in 1987, the machine was widely viewed as having been dealt a death blow. Washington had campaigned for mayor on a platform of reform, pledging that he would dance on the grave of patronage and open up the political process to those who had previously been left out. In practice, reform under Washington meant using affirmative-action hiring procedures to increase the number of African American and Hispanic employees in city government.[28]

In this respect, Washington did not abolish the machine so much as he sought to take command of it and use it to advance the minority populations of the city. He seemed well on the road to achieving that goal when he died of a heart attack late in 1987. His death opened once again a bitter struggle between the various political factions in the city to achieve dominance over the machine. In 1989 the African American electorate split between two candidates, African American voting turnout declined, Hispanic voters dropped out of the coalition that Washington had forged six years earlier, and the mayor's office was recaptured by the traditional machine's heir apparent, Richard J. Daley, Jr., son of the city's former boss. Today, however, the Chicago machine is a pale imitation of what it was 20 years earlier. Bitter divisions between the city's political factions, along with technological and social pressures on political parties, are certain to erode the Chicago machine's base of support as they have that of other machines around the country.

Patronage has declined in importance. A second development that has under-mined the old-style machines in Chicago and elsewhere has been increasing impediments to the use of patronage jobs to staff the machine. For many reasons, patronage is much less attractive to politicians than it used to be.[29] Patronage is difficult to administer without losing more supporters than are gained;[30] because there are always more applicants than patronage positions available, most applicants end up disappointed. In addition, civil service reforms have reduced the number of patronage jobs at the same time that increasing general affluence has made low-paying government jobs unappealing to many people.[31] Although traditional patronage is still important in parts of the East and Midwest,[32] patronage has also come under attack by the courts. Recent Supreme Court decisions have outlawed the dismissal of government workers for partisan reasons.[33] Traditional patronage will become increasingly difficult to maintain.

In contrast to the decline of traditional patronage, recent years have seen a growth in the use of other forms of governmental incentives to reward supporters. Consider the increased use of outside consultants to conduct studies or to carry out government projects.[34] These forms of incentives differ from traditional patronage in two major respects. First, many of these public-related jobs today go to middle-class people rather than to working-class or lower-class people. Second, in most instances, the awarding of these newly created material incentives is not controlled by political party machines. In this sense, non-civil-service material incentives actually may have increased during the past 20 years. But except where strong party hierarchies exist,[35] the political parties do not usually control how the incentives are passed out. However, there are exceptions. According to one of New York City's most experienced observers, Jack Newfield,

> The machine is an infrastructure of permanent institutions. It contains law firms, landlords who make contributions, judges who channel judicial patronage to clubhouse lawyers, printing companies that get all the petitions and literature business, community newspapers that receive judicial advertising, and friendly unions. In the Bronx, it controls the community school boards and picks principals on the basis of politics, not education.[36]

New immigrants are less dependent on the political machines for upward social mobility. A third change in the workings of machine politics has occurred in its role of providing a channel of social mobility for the urban-dependent populations. Historically, the machines received electoral support from the immigrant-dependent populations.[37] In turn, the machines provided certain welfare services on a sporadic basis to the poor. Furthermore, they existed as a channel for social mobility for some immigrants who were aggressive and ambitious. As these few were nominated for high office, their ethnic supporters received symbolic recognition.

As immigration was curtailed in the late 1920s, the immigrant-dependent population was replaced by a new mass of urban immigrants that consisted mainly of racial minorities, Hispanic minorities, and poor whites. These new urban minorities have voted overwhelmingly Democratic. But the machines have not provided them with the same resources they provided the European immigrants. Theodore J. Lowi's study of the class origins of high public officials in New York City over a 60-year period found that the Democratic party in that city was "no longer the clear channel of social mobility."[38] In this sense, the party is less able than before to provide benefits for the racial minorities, the Hispanic minorities, and the poor whites, who together constitute the dependent populations of today. This does not suggest that parties are useless to the new minorities; to the extent that parties control nomination for electoral office, they can be very useful.[39] But the parties do not fit into networks of social mobility for the new urban minorities as they once did for the Irish, Italians, and Poles.

New institutions have taken over functions previously provided by central-city political machines. A fourth change in machine politics is that new organizations have been created to meet many of the needs that the political machines once met. Machines originally evolved in part because they filled certain needs of urban society in the late nineteenth century. In addition to meeting some of the welfare needs of the immigrant-dependent populations, they filled at least two other needs.

First, because of the rapid growth of cities in the late nineteenth century, city governments were faced with overwhelming demands to provide services such as streets, sewers, water, lights, transportation, public safety, and health inspections. But city governments were organized to perform very few of these functions. Even elementary functions such as police and fire protection were provided on a voluntary basis well into the nineteenth century. The machine offered a mechanism for getting the services provided.

Second, the machines filled a need of the cities' business sector. The business sector needed appropriate responses from the city governments in the form of licenses and franchises to operate streetcar lines, install natural gas, or provide electric power. By allowing themselves to be bought, machine politicians provided the appropriate responses to the business sector.[40]

Central-city machines can no longer fulfill these needs. Welfare is highly institutionalized. And the most dynamic growth in public services has been occurring in the suburbs, which are usually controlled by county governments or suburban municipalities that are beyond the reach of central-city machines.

The Reform Legacy

If individual political reforms did not necessarily destroy the old machines or the ethnic basis of politics, then what difference did they make? Did the reform movement make any difference at all in urban politics? There has been considerable empirical research on various aspects of these questions.

Reform-Style Governments: Their Success in Certain Kinds of Cities

Non-reform-style city government is most likely to be found in central cities, in the East, in cities with high percentages of ethnic concentrations, in slowly growing cities, and in older, industrial cities. Conversely, reform-style city government is most likely to be found in suburban cities, in the West, in cities with low percentages of ethnic concentrations, in rapidly growing cities, and in newer, non-industry-based cities.[41]

The Class Bias of Political Reforms

In the 1960s and 1970s, social scientists carried out many studies identifying the effects of urban reform. These studies produced considerable empirical evidence that nonpartisan and at-large elections are biased in that they reduce council representation of lower-income people and racial minorities and depress voter turnout.[42]

Are *policy outcomes* of reformed governments equally biased against the lower classes? There is some evidence that reformed cities spend less and tax less than do nonreformed cities. The reformed cities are also less responsive to sharp racial, ethnic, and socioeconomic divisions in the electorate. These findings confirm some of the expectations of both the early reformers and the political bosses. Recall that many political reforms had been supported by businesspeople who hoped that the reformed governments would hold down both expenditures and taxes. In contrast, the bosses had opposed the reforms because they would diminish the political voice of the lower classes (through diminishing patronage).[43]

Two more recent studies suggest that structure may not really affect taxing or spending policies. David R. Morgan and John P. Pelissero traced taxing and spending patterns in 23 cities over an 11-year period. They found that 12 cities changed governmental structure within this period, whereas 11 cities kept the same structure throughout. The authors concluded that the changes in governmental structure had "almost no impact on changes in taxing and spending levels."[44] David R. Morgan and Kenneth Kickham recently examined the effects of changing the form of county government on revenue and expenditure patterns. They compared 10 counties that had reorganized from a commission to an elected or appointed executive to 10 that had not. They found that "changes in form of government have virtually no effect on rates of change in county fiscal behavior."[45]

Another way of looking at the output side of government is to consider the orientation of city council members. Some have a policy orientation, focusing their efforts on overall city policies. Others have a service orientation, focusing on helping to improve the delivery of city services to residents. Bledsoe and Welch's survey of 975 city council members from all cities of 50,000 or more in 1982 found that council members from district cities were much more inclined to have a service orientation than were those from at-large cities.[46] Council members from district cities are also much more likely than those from at-large cities to play the ombudsman role of handling constituent complaints about city government and city services.[47]

Fragmentation Increased by Reform

Reform-style government tends to increase the fragmentation of urban political power. From the 1930s to the 1970s, urban services expanded unrelentingly. Welfare services were greatly expanded. Increasing numbers of public hospitals were built. More and more urban areas began purchasing private transit systems and operating them publicly. Public employment offices were established. Airports had to be built to handle the rapid growth of airlines—and then rebuilt to accommodate the jetliners. After passage of the United States Housing Act in 1949, cities were able to tear down dilapidated buildings in blighted neighborhoods and could try to replace them with housing and redevelopment projects.

Few of these new services were turned over to the traditional city governments. Expanded welfare and hospital services became the province of the county governments. When privately-owned transit systems were sold to the public, the general pattern was to create a metropolitan district to operate them. Usually airports were also operated by metropolitan districts. Public employment offices were generally run by the states or the federal government. Housing authorities that administered the urban renewal programs often were appointed by the city councils, but they operated under rigid federal guidelines and rarely served as an arm of the city government. Redevelopment plans for central business districts were usually initiated by businesspeople who had a stake in the survival of the downtown business district. Funds for redevelopment usually came from federal urban renewal programs or from private investors, and the participation of city councils was often limited to making the appropriate zoning changes and setting up bond referenda when they were needed.

Public Accountability Decreased by Reform

Another consequence of the political reform movements was to reduce the public officials' accountability to the electorate. As in the fragmentation of local government authority, this was a result that the reformers had not counted on: The reformers had not intended to reduce government accountability, but a decrease in accountability did result from the reform measures.

Charles R. Adrian has asserted that nonpartisan elections prevent the groups that control the government from being held collectively accountable to the voters.[48] And Robert Wood has argued that nonpartisanship is based on some very faulty assumptions about the ability of individuals to determine who in government is responsible for what policies: "Inescapably, there is a belief that the individual can and should arrive at his political convictions untutored and unled; an expectation that in the formal process of election and decision making a consensus will emerge through the process of right reason and by higher call to the common good."[49]

Furthermore, as authority shifted increasingly from the hands of the elected officials into the hands of the large public bureaucracies, it became exceedingly difficult for the elected officials to control the bureaucrats. The doctrine embraced by public administration that policy making should be separated from policy implementation further served to insulate the bureaucracies from accountability to elected officials. When bureaucrats did not want to suffer the interference of elected officials on some controversial action, they could insist that the action dealt with policy implementation rather than policy making and consequently was not subject to scrutiny by the elected officials. As the public bureaucracies became more and more insulated, they began to develop into *functional fiefdoms*.

These changes in city politics significantly affected the fortunes of African Americans, Hispanics, Asians, and other minorities who were growing to sizable numbers in many American cities. This effect will be examined in the next chapter.

SUMMARY

1. Large cities in the late 1800s and early 1900s were populated by recent immigrants. These cities were governed by political machines made up of members of the immigrant population.
2. A prime motive of the early-twentieth-century progressive reformers was to drive the political bosses and the political machines out of business. The reform movements were started by upper-class and professional people who reacted

negatively to the dominance of city politics by the lower-class immigrants and their political machines.

3. The programs of the political reformers to end the dominance of the machines were many, most notably direct primaries, nonpartisan elections, at-large elections, and separation of local elections from national elections. In addition to reforming the electoral structure, the reformers also sought to alter the forms of city government itself. They particularly opposed the weak-mayor system of government and particularly favored the council-manager form and the commission form.

4. Not only the progressive reform movement but also the federal government contributed to the decline of the political machines. The expansion of federal welfare and assistance programs made poor people less dependent on the political machines for governmental assistance. Federal programs also led to an expansion of governmental services in urban areas, but the new services were often turned over to special districts and specialized agencies that were not under the direct control of the old-style machines.

5. Metropolitan growth has also contributed to the decline of machines. Machine politics has not fared well in the suburbs or in the South and West, where the most dramatic urban growth has occurred since the 1940s.

6. Although political machines have declined in recent years, we still see remnants of machine politics in some large cities. However, these machines pale in comparison to those of the late nineteenth and early twentieth centuries.

7. Several biases can be attributed to the progressive reform movements. First, the political reforms were most likely to take place in suburban cities, in the West, in cities with low percentages of ethnic populations, in rapidly growing cities, and in newer, non-industry-based cities. The political reforms generally worked to the disadvantage of the lower-income groups and the racial minorities while increasing the access of the upper- and middle-income groups. The reforms tended to weaken the political machines, to fragment government, and to decrease the accountability of urban governments to the residents of urban areas.

NOTES

1. Fred I. Greenstein, "The Changing Pattern of Urban Party Politics," *Annals of the American Academy of Political and Social Science* 353 (May 1964): 3.
2. Alan DiGaetano, "The Origins of Urban Political Machines in the United States: A Comparative Perspective" *Urban Affairs Quarterly* 26 (March 1991): 345.
3. Tammany Hall has been the subject of many fascinating studies. Among them see Seymour Mandelbaum, *Boss Tweed's New York* (New York: Wiley, 1955); Harold Zink, *City Bosses in the United States* (Durham, N.C.: Duke University Press, 1930); and Gustavus Meyers, *The History of Tammany Hall* (New York: Boni and Liveright, 1917).
4. Richard Hofstadter, *The Age of Reform: From Bryan to F.D.R.* (New York: Knopf, 1935), p. 181.
5. Edward C. Banfield and James Q. Wilson [*City Politics* (New York: Vintage, 1963), p. 117] argue that friendship was perhaps the most important thing that the political leaders gave to the masses.
6. Hofstadter, *The Age of Reform*, p. 181.
7. Ibid.
8. Melvin G. Holli, *Reform in Detroit: Hazen S. Pingree and Urban Politics* (New York: Oxford University Press, 1969), pp. 393–403.

9. Joseph Lincoln Steffens, *Shame of the Cities* (New York: McClute, Phillips, 1940).

10. Jane Addams, *Twenty Years at Hull House* (New York: Macmillan, 1911).

11. Samuel P. Hays, "The Politics of Reform in Municipal Government in the Progressive Era," *Pacific Northwest Quarterly* 55 (October 1964): 157–166.

12. Herbert Kaufman, "Emerging Conflicts in the Doctrines of Public Administration," *American Political Science Review* 50 (1956): 1057–1060.

13. A study of district versus at-large elections in five cities found that changing to the district system did not produce more conflict in council meetings, but it did tend to produce more factions among the newly represented groups. See Peggy Heilig and Robert J. Mundt, *Your Voice at City Hall* (Albany: State University of New York Press, 1984). A survey of city council members also revealed that district elections tend to produce factions on the council more often than at-large elections do. See Susan Welch and Timothy Bledsoe, *Urban Reform and Its Consequences: A Study in Representation* (Chicago: University of Chicago Press, 1988), p. 99.

14. James H. Svara, "The Myth of the Dichotomy: Complementarity of Politics and Administration in the Past and Future of Public Administration." *Public Administration Review* 61, no. 2 (March–April 2001): 177.

15. James H. Svara, "The Politics-Administration Dichotomy Model as Aberration," *Public Administration Review* 58, no. 1 (January–February 1998): 51–59.

16. James H. Svara, "Complementarity of Politics and Administration as a Legitimate Alternative to the Dichotomy Model," *Administration and Society* 30, no. 6 (January 1999): 678.

17. George S. Blair, *American Local Government* (New York: Harper & Row, 1964), p. 213.

18. Alan DiGaetano, "The Rise and Development of Urban Political Machines: An Alternative to Merton's Functional Analysis," *Urban Affairs Quarterly* 24 (December 1988): 264.

19. Ibid., p. 42.

20. In his study of Boston, William F. Whyte found this to occur. See his *Street Corner Society* (Chicago: University of Chicago Press, 1970), pp. 196–197. Steven Erie asserts that it also occurred in Chicago. See his *Rainbow's End: Irish-Americans and the Dilemmas of Machine Politics, 1840–1985* (Berkeley: University of California Press, 1988).

21. See William G. Colman, "The Role of the Federal Government in the Design and Administration of Intergovernmental Programs," *Annals of the American Academy of Political and Social Science* 359 (1965): 28–29. See also Roscoe Martin, *The Cities and the Federal System* (New York: Atherton Press, 1965), pp. 176–181.

22. *Rutan v. Republican Party of Illinois*, 110 S. Ct. 2729 (1990). For an assessment of earlier Supreme Court rulings on patronage, see Neil D. McFeeley, "The Supreme Court and Patronage: Implications for Local Government," *National Civic Review* 71, no. 5 (May 1982): 257–258.

23. Erie, *Rainbow's End.*

24. Edwin O'Connor, *The Last Hurrah* (Boston: Little, Brown, 1956). Examples of favorable treatments of machine politics are Frank R. Kent, *The Great Game of Politics* (Garden City, N.Y.: Doubleday, 1923; rev. ed., 1930); Sonya Forthal, *Cogwheels of Democracy: A Study of the Precinct Captain* (New York: William Frederick Press, 1946); and Harold F. Gosnell, *Machine Politics: Chicago Model* (Chicago: University of Chicago Press, 1937; 2d ed., 1967).

25. Raymond E. Wolfinger applied the term *conventional wisdom* to the notion that political machines have disappeared. See his "Why Political Machines Have Not Withered Away and Other Revisionist Thoughts," *Journal of Politics* 34 (May 1972): 365–398.

26. On Chicago, Philadelphia, New Haven, and Tammany, see Wolfinger, "Why Political Machines Have Not Withered Away." On upstate New York, see James A. Riedel, "Boss and Faction," *Annals of the American Academy of Political and Social Science* 353 (May 1964): 14–26.

27. These scandals occupied much newspaper space during 1986 and 1987. For a succinct interpretation of their relationship to machine politics, see Jack Newfield, "Mayor Daley Is Alive and Well in N.Y.C.," *Nation* (April 4, 1987): 429–434. See also Michael Tager, "Municipal Corruption in New York City," *Urban Politics and Urban Policy Section Newsletter* 1, no. 2 (Spring 1987): 14. On Boston, see Fox Butterfield, "Troubles of Boston's Mayor Are Tied to Political Machine," *New York Times,* December 20, 1987.

28. See Paul M. Green, "Making the City Work: Machine Politics and Mayoral Reform," paper presented at the annual meeting of the American Political Science Association, Chicago, September 3–6, 1987.

29. Bernard Hennessey refers to the decline of patronage as a "received wisdom." See his "On the Study of Party Organization," in *Approaches to the Study of Party Organization,* ed. William J. Crotty, Jr. (Boston: Allyn and Bacon, 1968), p. 32.

30. Frank J. Sorauf, "Patronage and Party," *Midwest Journal of Political Science* 3 (May 1959): 115–126. Although much of the belief in the decline in patronage is apparently traced to Sorauf's article, this article itself dealt with only one rural county in Pennsylvania. The belief also appeared in many government texts that antedated Sorauf's article.

31. Greenstein, "The Changing Pattern of Urban Party Politics," pp. 7–8.

32. On state-level patronage, see Daniel P. Moynihan and James Q. Wilson, "Patronage in New York State, 1955–1959," *American Political Science Review* 58 (June 1964): 286–301. On patronage at the state level in Illinois, Indiana, and Ohio, see John H. Fenton, *Midwest Politics* (New York: Holt, 1966). On patronage in New England, see Duane Lockard, *New England State Politics* (Princeton, N.J.: Princeton University Press, 1959). On county-level patronage, see W. Robert Gump, "The Functions of Patronage in American Party Politics: An Empirical Reappraisal," *Midwest Journal of Political Science* 15, no. 1 (February 1971): 87–107. On urban-level patronage, see Martin Tolchin and Susan Tolchin, *To the Victor: Political Patronage from the Clubhouse to the White House* (New York: Vintage, 1972), chaps. 2 and 4.

33. *Rutan v. Republican Party of Illinois,* 110 S. Ct. 2729 (1990).

34. See Wolfinger, "Why Political Machines Have Not Withered Away."

35. A study of the strong machine in New Haven, for example, found that CETA jobs were tightly controlled by party boss Arthur T. Barbieri, but the jobs were apparently dispensed much more for reasons of ethnic favoritism than to maximize votes for the party. See Michael Johnston, "Patrons and Clients, Jobs and Machines: A Case Study of the Uses of Patronage," *American Political Science Review* 73, no. 2 (June 1979): 385–398.

36. See Newfield, "Mayor Daley Is Alive and Well in N.Y.C."

37. Elmer E. Cornwell, Jr., "Bosses, Machines, and Ethnic Groups," *Annals of the American Academy of Political and Social Science* 353 (May 1964): 27–39. For a counterargument that there was no necessary relationship between immigrant populations and the existence of machines, see Wolfinger, *The Politics of Progress* (Englewood Cliffs, N.J.: Prentice-Hall, 1974), pp. 122–130.

38. Theodore J. Lowi, *At the Pleasure of the Mayor* (New York: Free Press, 1964), p. 112.

39. Joyce Gelb, "Blacks, Blocs and Ballots: The Relevance of Party Politics to the Negro," *Polity* 3, no. 1 (Fall 1970): 44–69.

40. Greenstein, "The Changing Pattern of Urban Party Politics." See also Alan DiGaetano, "The Rise and Development of Urban Political Machines: An Alternative to Merton's Functional Analysis," *Urban Affairs Quarterly* 24 (December 1988): 243–267.

41. John H. Kessel, "Governmental Structure and Political Environment," *American Political Science Review* 56 (1962): 615–620. Raymond Wolfinger and John Osgood Field, "Political Ethos and the Structure of City Government," *American Political Science Review* 60 (June 1966): 306–326. On the impact of education and Catholicism, see Terry N. Clark, "Community Structure, Decision-Making, Budget Expenditures, and Urban Renewal in 51 American Communities," *American Sociological Review* 33, no. 4 (August 1968): 576–593. For an analysis of the impact of these variables on government forms, see Thomas R. Dye and Susan A. MacManus, "Predicting City Government Structure," *American Journal of Political Science* 20, no. 2 (May 1976): 257–271.

42. Robert Lane, *Political Life* (Glencoe, Ill.: Free Press, 1959), pp. 269–271; Albert K. Karnig, "Private-Regarding Policy, Civil Rights Groups, and the Mediating Impact of Municipal Reforms," *American Journal of Political Science* 19, no. 1 (February 1975): 91–106; Robert H. Salisbury and Gordon Black, "Class and Party in Partisan and Nonpartisan Elections," *American Political Science Review* 67, no. 3 (September 1963): 590; Albert K. Karnig and B. Oliver Walters, "Decline in Municipal Turnout: A Function of Changing Structure," *American Politics Quarterly* 11, no. 4 (October 1983): 491–505; Charles E. Gilbert and Christopher Clague, "Electoral Competition and Electoral Systems in Large Cities," *Journal of Politics* 24 (1962): 338–347. In 88 San Francisco-area cities, Willis Hawley found that nonpartisanship favored Republicans twice as often as it favored Democrats. See his *Non-Partisan Elections and the Case for Party Politics* (New York: Wiley, 1973), pp. 31–33. See also Oliver P. Williams and Charles R. Adrian, "The Insulation of Local Politics Under the Nonpartisan Ballot," *American Political Science Review* 53 (1959): 1052–1063; Heinz Eulau, Betty H. Zisk, and Kenneth Prewitt, "Latent Partisanship in Nonpartisan Elections: Effects of Political Milieu and Mobilization," in *The Electoral Process,* ed. M. Kent Jennings and L. Harmon Ziegler (Englewood Cliffs, N.J.: Prentice-Hall, 1966), p. 215; Karnig and Walter, "Decline in Municipal Turnout," pp. 491–505 Howard Hamilton, "The Municipal Voter: Voting and Nonvoting in City Elections," *American Political Science Review* 65, no. 4 (December 1971): 1135–1140; Welch and

Bledsoe, *Urban Reform and Its Consequences;* Carol A. Cassell, "Social Background Characteristics of Nonpartisan City Council Members," *Western Political Quarterly* 38, no. 3 (September 1985): 495–501.

43. Robert L. Lineberry and Edmund P. Fowler, "Reformism and Public Policies in American Cities," *American Political Science Review* 61, no. 3 (September 1967): 701–716. Clark, "Community Structure, Decision-Making, Budget Expenditures, and Urban Renewal," pp. 587–591. Clark found high correlations between reform-style government and centralized decision-making structures. Decentralization was measured by the number of actors involved in making key decisions and by the extent of overlap among the makers of decisions in the issue areas of urban renewal, the election of the mayor, air pollution, and the antipoverty program. For the controversiality of decisions and their vulnerability to disruption by community pressures, Clark used the term *fragile.* He wrote, "For less fragile decisions, the more centralized the decision-making structure, the lower the level of outputs" (p. 588).

44. David R. Morgan and John P. Pelissero, "Urban Policy: Does Political Structure Matter?" *American Political Science Review* 74, no. 4 (December 1980): 1005.

45. David R. Morgan and Kenneth Kickham, "Changing the Form of County Government: Effects on Revenue and Expenditure Policy," *Public Administration Review* 59, no. 4 (July/August 1999): 315.

46. Timothy Bledsoe and Susan Welch, "Some Predictors of Service Representation in Urban Politics," paper presented at the annual meeting of the American Political Science Association, Chicago, September 14, 1983.

47. Heilig and Mundt, *Your Voice at City Hall,* p. 96.

48. Charles R. Adrian, "Some General Characteristics of Non-Partisan Elections," *American Political Science Review* 46 (1952): 775.

49. Robert Wood, *Suburbia, Its People and Their Politics* (Boston: Houghton Mifflin, 1958), p. 157.

PART THREE

POLITICS IN THE CONTEMPORARY CITY

Although the contemporary city has inherited much of its political structure and style from the older American city discussed in Part Two, today's city also differs in many important respects from the historical American city. In contrast to the European immigrants who predominated in the older city, today's most visible urban minorities are African Americans, Hispanics, and Asians. The most important question facing the American city today is whether the city is still a place of opportunity for the upward mobility of its poorest residents and its most recent in-migrants. Chapter 5 examines this question by focusing on the changing impact that the racial and Hispanic minorities are having on city politics. Chapter 6 analyzes the economic environment that affects how much upward mobility central cities can offer.

Chapter 7 focuses on the various groups and interests that compete for control of city government and for the ability to shape local development and policy. In many cities, there is evidence of the formation of urban regimes—coalitions of public officials and private business leaders who work together to govern the local community. The chapter also considers the consequences of regime politics for local democracy.

CHAPTER 5

THE CITY AS A PLACE OF OPPORTUNITY: THE POLITICS OF RACIAL AND SOCIAL CHANGE

CHAPTER SYNOPSIS

African Americans and Urban Politics: *Increased Diversity in the City*; *Urban Segregation and the Ghetto*; *The Civil Rights Movement*; *Black Power and Racial Violence*; *The Politics of Advancement* • African American Political Incorporation: *Black Mayors*; *Dual Strategy*; *Limits of Incorporation* • Fourth-Wave Immigrants: *Hispanics*; *Asians*; *Issues of Concern to Immigrants* • Search for a Rainbow: *Race, Class, and Ethnicity—Obstacles to Cooperation*; *Minority Opportunities and Biases in the Contemporary City*

In earlier times American cities played a pivotal role as a place of economic opportunity for poor migrants. From the mid-nineteenth century to the mid-twentieth century, European immigrants and their offspring used the city as a source of jobs, business opportunities, education, political influence, and upward social mobility. Many European ethnics, of course, did not rise up the social ladder. Many returned to Europe. Many died in squalor at an early age. Some turned to anarchism in rebellion against a system they saw as hopeless. And in most cases, it took three or four generations for the families of immigrants to achieve middle-class status. Nevertheless, most of today's grandchildren and great-grandchildren of yesterday's Irish, Polish, Russian, Italian, and other European immigrants enjoy a better position on the socioeconomic ladder than their ancestors did.

Few of today's urban minorities are from Europe. Rather, they are predominantly African Americans who have migrated from the rural South since World War II; Hispanics from Mexico, Central America, and the Caribbean; or Asians whose families immigrated from strife-ridden places such as Vietnam, Cambodia, and Laos or are former inhabitants of Hong Kong and China seeking economic security or political and religious freedom.

At the dawn of the twenty-first century, is the American city still a place of opportunity for its poorest residents and its most recent in-migrants? This chapter addresses that question by focusing on the largest of these urban groups—the African Americans, Hispanics, and Asians. How have their current political positions evolved out of historical circumstances? What institutions have they developed for exercising leadership in their urban communities? What themes underlie their politics today? Are their political

TABLE 5.1   Economic and Social Status of Racial/Ethnic Groups in the United States

	Hispanic					Non-Hispanic		
	Mexican American	Puerto Rican	Cuban	Central and South American	Other Hispanic Total	Asians	White	Black
Percentage completing 4 years of high school (25 years of age and over)	51.9[a]	71.8[a]	72.1[a]	66.5[a]	73.8[a]	83.3[b]	85.1[c]	79.9[c]
Percentage who completed 4 years of college (25 years of age and over)	7.9[a]	14.0[a]	24.0[a]	21.8[a]	19.7[a]	43.1[b]	27.6[c]	17.3[c]
Median family income	$34,206[d]	$36,350[d]	$45,233[d]	$41,897[d]	$38,630[d]	$60,984[b]	$54,633[c]	$33,525[c]
Median age (in years)[c]	25.4[d]	27.4[d]	41.5[d]	30.4[d]	28.6[d]	33.7[e]	37.3[e]	30.6[e]

Sources:

[a]U.S. Census Bureau, Current Population Survey, Annual Social and Economic Supplement, 2004, Ethnicity and Ancestry Statistics Branch, Population Division.

[b]U.S. Census Bureau, *Statistical Abstract of the U.S., 2004–2005*, Table 38.

[c]U.S. Census Bureau, *Statistical Abstract of the U.S., 2004–2005*, Table 38.

[d]U.S. Census Bureau, *Statistical Abstract of the U.S. 2004–2005*, Table 33.

[e]U.S. Census Bureau, Current Population Survey, 2004, Annual Social and Economic Supplement: Link:

http://www.census.gov/population/socdemo/hispanic/ASEC2004/median_tab_04.xls.

[f]U.S. Census Bureau, *Statistical Abstract of the U.S. 2004–2005*, Table 14.

situations today analogous to those of the European ethnics discussed in Chapter 3? And what prospects for upward mobility are offered them through the political arena in the 1990s? Table 5.1 provides a quick comparison of the current status of contemporary minorities in the city. African Americans lag significantly behind non-Hispanic whites in income and education levels. Cubans and Asians have surpassed blacks in educational attainment and income levels. Let us explore more fully the experiences of minority groups in the city.

African Americans and Urban Politics

The most dramatic social change in American cities in the last 50 years has been the increased racial and ethnic diversity due to great in-migration of African Americans and Hispanics to the cities. Focusing on the largest 100 cities, about 24 percent of all central-city residents are now African American. Another 22.5 percent of the population of cities is Hispanic. Asians make up about 7 percent of city residents. Non-Hispanic whites now are a minority of city residents (44 percent), and this number is expected to shrink further in the next decade.[1]

Suburbs are also more diversified. In metropolises of over 500,000 persons (the largest 102 metropolises), 27 percent of the suburban population is now minority. This is up from 19 percent in 1990. Moreover, 47 percent of all minorities in these largest metropolises lived in the suburbs in 2000, an increase from 40 percent in 1990.[2]

Urban Segregation

Table 5.2 lists all cities over 100,000 people with large African American populations. Interestingly, all are *majority-minority* cities (non-Hispanic whites make up less than 50 percent of the population). African Americans are much more likely to live in segregated environments than are other large urban minorities such as Asians and Hispanics. So much more concentrated is the African American urban population that we now speak of "hypersegregation."[3]

Segregation between two racial/ethnic groups is measured by an "index of dissimilarity" on a scale of 0 to 100. An index score of 50 on white-black segregation would mean that 50 percent of blacks in the city or metropolis would have to move in order for each neighborhood (census tract) to reflect the distribution of blacks in the community (city or metropolis). As Table 5.3 indicates, none of the 50 largest metropolises has a low rate of segregation (below an index of 30), and more than half are hypersegregated (above an index of 60). Although American metropolises remain highly segregated, there was a 5.5 percent decrease in African American residential segregation between 1990 and 2000, the third decade of decline. More disheartening is that white-black school segregation rates are actually increasing, even while metropolitan index rates are declining. On average, school segregation rates increased 2 points while residential segregation rates decreased 3–4 points. This is related to changes in school desegregation policies, not to changes in residential patterns.[4]

Growing areas are more likely to be less segregated as a result of more African Americans moving into areas that were formerly all white. Thus growing metropolitan

TABLE 5.2   Cities with Large Black Populations

Rank	City	City Population (2000)	City Population Black (2000)	Share of Population That Is Black (2000)	Black Mayors
1	New York, NY	8,008,278	1,962,154	24.50%	David N. Dinkins (1989–1993)
2	Chicago, IL	2,896,016	1,053,739	36.40%	Eugene Sawyer (1987–1989) Harold Washington (1983–1987)
3	Detroit, MI	951,270	771,966	81.20%	Kwame Kilpatrick (2002–) Dennis Archer (1994–2002) Coleman Young (1974–1993)
4	Philadelphia, PA	1,517,550	646,123	42.60%	John F. Street (1999–) W. Wilson Goode (1983–1991)
5	Houston, TX	1,953,631	487,851	25.00%	Lee P. Brown (1997–2004)
6	Baltimore, MD	651,154	417,009	64.00%	Kurt Schmoke (1987–1999)
7	Los Angeles, CA	3,694,820	401,986	10.90%	Thomas Bradley (1973–1993)
8	Memphis, TN	650,100	397,732	61.20%	W. W. Herrenton (1992–)
9	Washington, DC	572,059	340,088	59.40%	Anthony Williams (1998–) Marion Barry (1994–1998) Sharon Pratt Dixon (1990–1993) Marion Barry (1979–1990)
10	New Orleans, LA	484,674	323,392	66.70%	C. Ray Nagin (2002–) Marc Morial (1994–2002) Sydney Barthelemy (1986–1993) Ernest Morial (1978–1986)

(continued)

TABLE 5.2   Cities with Large Black Population *(continued)*

Rank	City	City Population (2000)	City Population Black (2000)	Share of Population That Is Black (2000)	Black Mayors
11	Dallas, TX	1,188,580	304,824	25.60%	Ron Kirk (1995–2001)
12	Atlanta, GA	416,474	254,062	61.00%	Shirley Clarke Franklin (2001–) Bill Campbell (1994–2001) Maynard Jackson (1990–1994) Andrew Young (1982–1990) Maynard Jackson (1973–1982)
13	Cleveland, OH	478,403	241,512	50.50%	Frank Jackson (2006–) Michael R. White (1991–2001) Carl Stokes (1967–1971)
14	Milwaukee, WI	596,974	220,432	36.90%	
15	Jacksonville, FL	735,617	211,252	28.70%	
16	Indianapolis, IN	781,870	198,252	25.40%	
17	Birmingham, AL	242,820	177,709	73.20%	
18	St. Louis, MO	348,189	177,446	51.00%	Bernard Kincaid (1999–) Richard Arrington (1997–1999)
19	Charlotte, NC	540,828	175,661	32.50%	
20	Columbus, OH	711,470	172,750	24.30%	Michael B. Coleman (2000–)
21	Nashville-Davidson, TN	545,524	145,483	26.70%	
22	Newark, NJ	273,546	142,083	51.90%	Sharpe James (1986–)
23	Cincinnati, OH	331,285	141,534	42.70%	Mark Mallory (2005–)
24	Boston, MA	589,141	140,305	23.80%	
25	Oakland, CA	399,484	140,139	35.10%	

Source: Center on Urban and Metropolitan Policy, The Brookings Institution, Living Cities Databook Series, National Conference of Black Mayors, http://www.ncbm.org/index.html; U.S Conference of Mayors, http://www.usmayors.org, and various city and news websites.

TABLE 5.3   White-Black Index of Dissimilarity[a] (Segregation), 50 Largest Metropolitan Areas, 1980, 1990, 2000*

Metropolitan Area	1980	1990	2000
1. Detroit, MI PMSA	87.46	87.48	84.72
2. Milwaukee-Waukesha, WI PMSA	83.95	82.78	82.16
3. New York, NY PMSA	81.61	82.23	81.82
4. Chicago, IL PMSA	88.39	84.44	80.85
5. Newark, NJ PMSA	82.85	82.71	80.42
6. Cleveland-Lorain-Elyria, OH PMSA	85.47	82.71	77.32
7. Cincinnati, OH-KY-IN PMSA	79.02	76.78	74.84
8. Nassau-Suffolk, NY PMSA	77.64	77.24	74.38
9. St. Louis, MO-IL MSA	82.80	78.27	74.35
10. Miami, FL PMSA	80.48	73.21	73.57
11. Bergen-Passaic, NJ PMSA	80.42	76.73	73.24
12. Philadelphia, PA-NJ PMSA	78.28	77.05	72.33
13. Indianapolis, IN MSA	79.66	75.17	70.66
14. New Orleans, LA MSA	71.70	68.68	69.25
15. Kansas City, MO-KS MSA	77.84	72.64	69.12
16. Baltimore, MD PMSA	74.54	71.63	67.93
17. Los Angeles-Long Beach, CA PMSA	81.22	73.19	67.55
18. Houston, TX PMSA	76.08	67.28	67.49
19. Pittsburgh, PA MSA	73.45	70.86	67.27
20. Boston, MA-NH PMSA	76.46	69.55	65.68
21. Atlanta, GA MSA	77.04	68.63	65.61
22. Tampa-St. Petersburg-Clearwater, FL MSA	78.92	70.86	64.47
23. Washington, DC-MD-VA-WV PMSA	69.60	65.65	63.12
24. Columbus, OH MSA	73.26	68.38	63.10
25. Oakland, CA PMSA	74.18	68.13	62.81
26. Fort Lauderdale, FL PMSA	83.95	70.86	62.25
27. Denver, CO PMSA	69.12	64.49	61.76
28. San Francisco, CA PMSA	67.82	64.12	60.87
29. Fort Worth-Arlington, TX PMSA	78.30	62.59	60.33
30. Dallas, TX PMSA	78.37	63.30	59.36
31. Greensboro-Winston-Salem-High Point, NC MSA	66.56	61.61	59.01
32. Providence-Fall River-Warwick, RI-MA MSA	72.12	64.60	58.69
33. Minneapolis-St. Paul, MN-WI MSA	67.72	62.31	57.83

HYPERSEGREGATION

(continued)

TABLE 5.3 White-Black Index of Dissimilarity[a] (Segregation), 50 Largest Metropolitan Areas, 1980, 1990, 2000 (continued)

Metropolitan Area	1980	1990	2000	
34. Nashville, TN MSA	65.95	60.78	57.05	HIGH SEGREGATION
35. Orlando, FL MSA	74.13	60.93	57.04	
36. Sacramento, CA PMSA	58.58	56.26	55.97	
37. Charlotte-Gastonia-Rock Hill, NC-SC MSA	61.92	55.78	55.16	
38. San Diego, CA MSA	64.01	58.41	54.15	
39. Austin-San Marcos, TX MSA	65.47	55.01	52.28	
40. San Antonio, TX MSA	61.86	55.08	50.40	
41. Seattle-Bellevue-Everett, WA PMSA	67.95	56.56	49.62	MODERATE SEGREGATION
42. Portland-Vancouver, OR-WA PMSA	68.89	63.69	48.07	
43. Riverside-San Bernardino, CA PMSA	54.80	45.21	46.28	
44. Norfolk-Virginia Beach-Newport News, VA-NC MSA	59.57	48.92	46.20	
45. Raleigh-Durham-Chapel Hill, NC MSA	52.33	48.71	46.17	
46. Phoenix-Mesa, AZ MSA	61.63	50.44	43.72	
47. Las Vegas, NV-AZ MSA	63.38	51.98	43.32	
48. San Jose, CA PMSA	48.94	43.70	40.51	
49. Salt Lake City-Ogden, UT MSA	56.37	48.21	36.91	
50. Orange County, CA PMSA	46.25	38.71	36.80	

*Metropolitan classifications are those used in the 2000 census. PMSA stands for primary metropolitan statistical area and MSA stands for metropolitan statistical area. An MSA is a freestanding metropolitan area. A PMSA is a metropolitan area that is part of a larger consolidated metropolitan area. For example, Nassau-Suffolk (Long Island) and New York PMSAs together make up part of a consolidated metropolitan area of New York.

[a]The dissimilarity index measures whether one particular group is distributed across census tracts (neighborhoods) in the metropolitan area in the same way as another group. A high value indicates that the two groups tend to live in different tracts. The index ranges from 0 to 100. A value of 60 (or above) is considered very high. It means that 60 percent (or more) of the members of one group would need to move to a different tract in order for the two groups to be equally distributed. Values of 40 or 50 are usually considered a moderate level of segregation, and values of 30 or below are considered fairly low.

Source: Table produced from data downloaded from Lewis Mumford Center for Comparative Urban and Regional Research, Metropolitan Racial and Ethnic Change, http://mumford1.dyndns.org/cen2000/WholePop/WPdownload.html.

areas in the South and West have lower segregation rates than those in the Northeast or Midwest.[5] At the present slow rate of decline in the segregation index, it will take at least 40 years for black-white segregation to reach the level of Hispanic-white segregation.[6]

There has been a large increase in African American suburbanization in recent decades. In the year 2000, again looking at the largest 102 metropolises, 39 percent of all African Americans lived in the suburbs, up from 34 percent in 1990.[7] Blacks made up about 9 percent of the suburban population overall. And in places such as Atlanta, Richmond, New Orleans, Fort Lauderdale, Miami, and Washington, D.C., blacks make up more than 20 percent of the suburban population.

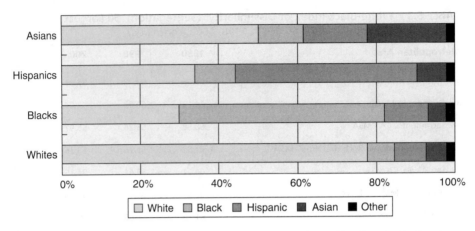

FIGURE 5.1   Diversity Experienced in Each Group's Typical Neighborhood—National
Metropolitan Average

Source: Reproduced from Lewis Mumford Center, "Ethnic Diversity Grows, Neighborhood Integration Lags
Behind," April 3, 2001, revised December 18, 2001, p. 3.

However, reduced metropolitan segregation and increased black suburbanization
do not mean that blacks and whites live in integrated neighborhoods in the suburbs.
Although there has been a great increase in suburbanization of blacks, this has not been
accompanied by a reduction in suburban segregation. African Americans moving to the
suburbs tend to move into black enclaves.[8] As Figure 5.1 reveals, a typical white person lives in a neighborhood that is 80 percent white. Minorities, on the other hand, live
in much more diversified neighborhoods. The average African American lives in a
neighborhood that is 51 percent black.

Consequences of Urban Segregation

Social Consequences   Breaking down the social segregation of African Americans is
one of the most important challenges facing America today. The continuing segregation
of most African Americans has many negative consequences. And the consequences are
most severe on those poor African Americans who live in inner-city ghettos and lack
the money needed to move out to the suburbs or to better central-city neighborhoods.
Concentrating hundreds of thousands of poor people into small sections of the city ag-
gravates the severe social problems posed by trying to hold families together and provide an environment conducive to the educational development of children. It also
keeps African Americans physically removed from the much larger job markets in the
suburbs. This physical and economic segregation reinforces social segregation. To the
extent that young ghetto African Americans become isolated from the mainstream of
society, they lose touch with the standard English, the social mores, and the behavior
skills that get rewarded in the job market. As these disadvantages accumulate, they
contribute to despair, resentment, anger, and dysfunctional violence among many
youths who feel trapped in the urban ghettos.[9]

To some observers, the ghetto seems more like a Third World country than like a modern American city. It suffers from low per capita income and high birthrates, an abundance of unskilled laborers during an economic era that has decreasing demand for such laborers, and a very limited ability to raise investment capital through either savings or credit. Most goods and services are imported from outside, most of the institutions in the ghetto are owned or controlled by outsiders, and feelings of relative deprivation and resentment are common.[10]

Political Consequences   Politically, the segregation of urban African Americans into central-city neighborhoods eventually came to be a source of strength. Segregation facilitated political activities that had been more difficult when African Americans were spread throughout the rural South. The effect of the spontaneous outburst of hundreds of civil disturbances and the demand for black power in the 1960s was to mobilize African American political forces in ways that had not been possible earlier.[11] Especially critical were the Civil Rights Act of 1964 and the Voting Rights Act of 1965. To understand urban African American politics, it is necessary to understand these laws and the events that led up to their enactment.

The Civil Rights Movement

The major impetus for African American political organization during the first half of the twentieth century was civil rights. Although the Civil War and the Thirteenth Amendment ended slavery, most African Americans were trapped for the next hundred years in a degrading and violent segregation system. In southern states, segregation statutes prohibited African Americans from marrying whites; eating in the same restaurants as whites; sitting in the same sections on buses, trains, or in theaters; using the same restrooms; drinking from the same fountains; going to the same schools; and even being buried in the same cemeteries. Voting was restricted to a handful of African Americans, and during the early part of the twentieth century, African American officeholders virtually disappeared. For African Americans who rebelled or tried to assert their civil rights, there was always the threat of economic sanction such as being fired from a job. And there was often the threat of lynching and mob violence.

Accompanying this political, psychological, and social oppression was extensive discrimination in the workplace. This job discrimination eased during the two world wars, when labor was in short supply and African Americans were deliberately enticed from the rural South to take factory jobs in cities. Also, during the labor strife of the 1930s, some employers hired African Americans as strikebreakers—even though the African Americans seldom realized that these job offers were extended simply to break the unions and would be withdrawn as soon as the strikes were over.

In the face of this oppression and manipulation, early African American leadership split into two styles that still exist in today's African American politics. First, Booker T. Washington's accommodationist style of leadership stressed African American economic improvement and downplayed political activity and civil rights agitation.[12] Washington's philosophy was best articulated in a speech at the Atlanta Exposition in 1895 when he called on African Americans to improve themselves individually and integrate individually into the larger society rather than attempting group advancement through political agitation. Committed to his belief in individualism, Washington was a key figure in establishing the nation's first African American college, the Tuskegee Institute, where young African Americans could get training to enter the middle-class mainstream of American society.

In opposition to Washington's individualistic approach, other African Americans insisted that few, if any, African Americans would be able to enter the middle-class mainstream of American society until African Americans advanced as a group and broke down the barriers of racial segregation and discrimination. A key leader was W. E. B. Du Bois, who with others started the Niagara movement in 1905 to press for political and civil rights. Although the Niagara movement quickly died, its ideals were embraced in 1909 by a new organization, the National Association for the Advancement of Colored People (NAACP). The NAACP eventually became the largest and one of the most successful of the African American civil rights organizations. Particularly effective was the NAACP/Legal Defense Fund, which financed and fought court battles to get segregation statutes overturned.[13] Its most significant victory was the Supreme Court's ruling in *Brown v. Board of Education* (1953),[14] which struck down the segregation of public schools.

Through these early victories, the NAACP was critical to the black movement, but its commitment to judicial strategies was very time-consuming, and many African Americans sought to speed up the move toward civil rights. A turning point in this process can be traced to an afternoon in 1955 when an African American woman, Rosa Parks, refused to give up a seat in the "white section" of a bus in Montgomery, Alabama, and was jailed as a result. The Montgomery African American community, led by Baptist minister Martin Luther King, Jr., staged a very effective bus boycott and at the same time sued in the federal courts to get the bus segregation policy overturned. By winning that suit, the Montgomery leaders showed dramatically that legal tactics could be successfully combined with *direct action tactics* such as boycotts. The next few years saw the creation of two new organizations devoted to direct action tactics: the Southern Christian Leadership Conference (SCLC) under King's direction and the Student Non-Violent Coordinating Committee (SNCC). These organizations systematically organized civil disobedience tactics. Typically they would get a group of people to violate segregation statutes (for example, blacks and whites would sit down together to eat at a segregated lunch counter) and get themselves arrested. They appealed their convictions in the federal courts, but the appeals route was a slow, tortuous process, which often required going as high as the United States Supreme Court. And there was never any certainty that one's conviction would be overturned.

Just as important as the legal battle was the media coverage of these direct confrontations and protests. National television exposed the brutality of segregation and helped build public support for civil rights. These efforts came to fruition in the Civil Rights Act of 1964, which outlawed discrimination in public accommodations such as motels, restaurants, and theaters. The key provisions of this act are outlined in the accompanying box.

Key Provisions of the 1964 Civil Rights Act

Public Accommodations

Prohibited discrimination in public accommodations.

Desegregation of Government Facilities

Authorized the Justice Department to initiate suits to desegregate facilities owned or managed by state or local governments.

School Desegregation

Authorized the Justice Department to initiate suits to desegregate public schools and colleges.

Authorized the Office of Education to give technical and financial aid to school districts in the process of desegregation.

Civil Rights Commission

Strengthened the commission's role in investigating civil rights complaints.

Federally Funded Programs

Prohibited racial discrimination in programs that receive federal funds.

Equal Employment Opportunity

Prohibited private-sector employers from discriminating in employment on the basis of race, religion, sex, or national origin.

Voting Rights

Strengthened the role of the federal courts and the attorney general in dealing with violations of voting rights.

Black Power and Racial Violence

Despite the historic achievements of the civil rights movement, by the mid-1960s African American leadership was facing a crisis. The most prominent civil rights leader, Martin Luther King, Jr., was assassinated in 1968. Furthermore, although the passage of civil rights laws gave middle-class African Americans access to public accommodations such as restaurants and motels, it provided no immediate improvement in the depressed economic conditions of the overwhelming majority of African Americans. New leaders began to question whether African Americans could ever hope to enter the mainstream of American society. Some argued that the African American community was an internal colony within American society. The dominant institutions operating within the urban ghettos (banks, schools, stores, and apartment buildings) were run by white outsiders who took the money generated by these institutions out of the ghetto. A study of Chicago found that black-owned and black-run institutions were dependent on and inferior to the dominant white institutions.[15]

Those who saw the African American ghetto as a colony within American society rejected the belief that African Americans could ever hope to integrate individually into the mainstream of American society. In this view, the only route was to rebel against the colonizing society and declare black independence. This train of thought led some African American leaders during the 1960s to turn to *black nationalism* as a solution to African American problems. The ensuing intellectual debate was reminiscent of W. E. B. Du Bois's arguments 60 years earlier against the individual-integration philosophy of Booker T. Washington.

Perhaps the most dynamic new leader—until his assassination in 1965—was Malcolm X, a successful recruiter and spokesman for the Nation of Islam (Black Muslims). Where the civil rights leaders had worked primarily with a middle-class African American clientele, Malcolm X appealed directly to poor blacks. His rejection of American patriotism in favor of black nationalism brought him into direct conflict with mainstream American liberalism, which had long supported civil rights movements.

Other developments in the 1960s also led toward a politics of *confrontation*. Stokely Carmichael made a speech in 1966 calling for "black power."[16] The Black Panther party was organized in Oakland, California, in 1966 and began preparing itself for violent confrontation with the police. In Chicago, a police squad assaulted the city's Black Panther headquarters and killed several Black Panther leaders.

The most startling change in African American politics during the late 1960s, however, resulted from the urban riots. In city after city during those years, each spring and summer saw African American people looting stores in their neighborhoods, burning buildings, and engaging in confrontations with the police. Between 1964 and 1968 at least 220 people were killed, over 8,300 were injured, and more than 52,000 were arrested.[17] In the single month following the assassination of Martin Luther King, Jr., in 1968, riots broke out in 172 cities and 27,000 people were arrested.[18]

After the very destructive Watts riot in Los Angeles in 1965, the governor of California appointed the McCone Commission to investigate it, and the McCone Commission assigned blame for the Watts riot to a few troublemakers in the African American community.[19] As riots broke out in other cities, however, and literally hundreds of thousands of African American people participated in them, it became apparent that much more was involved than simply the instigation of a few troublemakers. One alternative explanation was that the rioting was an African American reaction to the oppression of racism in American society.[20] Another viewpoint was that the riots constituted an act of political rebellion, an attempt to break out of the colonial bonds that held African Americans in subjugation to the white community.[21]

Joe R. Feagin and Harlan Hahn surveyed the research on urban rioting during the 1960s and pointed to two recurring background factors. First, cities with large African American populations were more likely to have riots than cities with small African American populations, and their riots tended to be more serious. Second, Feagin and Hahn traced a growing acceptance, by African Americans during the 1960s, of collective violence as a legitimate means to achieve their goals in a political system whose conventional political channels were unresponsive.[22]

In addition to underlying background factors, a precipitating set of events is needed to trigger a riot. The most common triggering event during the ghetto riots of the 1960s was some action on the part of the police—shooting an African American teenager, treating someone roughly, or engaging in some other perceived brutalities. The National Advisory

Commission on Civil Disorders studied several riot cities in 1967 and found that more than 60 percent of the major and serious riots were precipitated by police actions.[23] Rumors about the incident would spread rapidly, a crowd would gather to discuss it, and violence would begin. Further police action would fail to contain the violence, and National Guard reinforcements would be called in to maintain the peace. These circumstances created an adversarial situation. The police and the National Guard acted much like an occupying army. Community leaders would try unsuccessfully to gain control of the scene. Moderate leaders often came out on the streets urging people to go back to their homes. Militant leaders often mingled on the streets but made no effort to discourage people from looting stores or engaging in other riot activities.

It is not clear whether the riots benefited the African American community. One study found that the Watts riot brought an immediate influx of federal poverty funds into Los Angeles.[24] However, businesses left. (It was not until 1985, 20 years after the riot, that Watts got another full-service supermarket.[25]) City governments reacted politically by pouring money into police services that could maintain order rather than into social services to address the grievances of African American residents. This was attributed by one scholar to a negative white backlash against the African American community.[26]

Since the 1960s there had been very few riots on the scale of those in the 1960s until the outbreak of a major riot in Miami, Florida, in May 1980. The circumstances surrounding the Miami riot were strikingly similar to those surrounding the riots of the 1960s. Such background factors as high African American unemployment and smoldering resentments prevailed. Miami African Americans apparently resented that while these grievances went unattended, special help was being given to over 100,000 Cuban refugees pouring into the city in the spring of 1980. Many African Americans looked upon these refugees as competitors for scarce jobs. The spark that ignited the riot involved the local police. Six months earlier, an African American insurance salesman had been brutally beaten to death while in the custody of a team of white police officers. Despite trial testimony of eyewitnesses about the beating, an all-white jury acquitted the four white officers charged with the killing. The riot erupted the day that the jury's decision was announced. When the riot ended three days later, 18 people were dead and another 400 were injured. In December 1982, another Miami African American neighborhood rioted following the fatal police shooting of an African American youth in a videogame arcade.[27]

Ten years later, in 1992, the most devastating riot in history took place in Los Angeles. Again, the precipitating event was the acquittal of police officers who had badly beaten an African American man, Rodney King. The event had been recorded on videotape. Mark Baldassare identifies what he calls the defining characteristics of the Los Angeles riots:

> First, the conditions of poor, urban blacks or the "underclass" have not improved and remain a critical source for urban uprisings. Next, black-white tensions remain high, as race relations are in a troubled state due to personal and institutional racism, and can easily explode into violent episodes. Third, the combined effects of foreign immigration and economic restructuring, present in many U.S. cities in the 1990s, are leading to interethnic hostilities.[28]

Baldassare suggests that given the prevalence of these conditions in many American cities, riots in the cities may not be such unusual events in the twenty-first century.

Indeed, a serious riot occurred in Cincinnati following the shooting by police of an unarmed African American in April 2001. Looting and fires damaged some 120 businesses, and police made over 800 arrests. Only a four-day citywide curfew restored order to the community. The main rioting occurred in a black neighborhood, but one being transformed into an upscale shopping and entertainment district. Here, gentrification and redevelopment were accompanied by a significant and aggressive style of policing to ensure the safety—both physical and psychological—of the white and middle-class visitors.[29]

In the aftermath of the rioting, a "de-policing" occurred, and police stopped addressing "suspicious behavior" and responded only to 911 calls. This practice is becoming more common when police departments feel maligned or not backed up by public officials and citizens. The police made 50 percent fewer arrests following the riots than in the previous year.[30] The riots initially led to a broader airing of black grievances, and a commission was appointed to study the situation and recommend ways to improve overall race relations in the city. Calls are being made for more black economic opportunity, for more diversity in the police department, and for acknowledgment of the racial profiling that occurs in policing.[31] The city was criticized for moving too slowly, and black leaders initiated a boycott of the city. The city struck back with an ad campaign highlighting the city's progress in race relations, including its having hired a black female city manager.[32] Conservative urban critics suggest that Cincinnati fell victim to "riot ideology," wherein the city essentially pays off rioters and racial activists to avoid conflict and civil disturbances.[33] It is hoped that the election of a black mayor—Mark Mallory, a state senator—in December 2005 will help reduce interracial tension and lead to an end to the economic boycott of Cincinnati.

Black Power and the Politics of Advancement

It is clear that the riots of the 1960s were a major dividing line in African American urban history. If African American politics before the decade of urban rioting was characterized by a unified struggle for civil rights and for an end to segregation, African American politics since 1970 has broadened the focus to many other concerns. Among the great civil rights organizations, the NAACP and the NAACP/Legal Defense Fund were beset by internal strife,[34] while CORE (Congress on Racial Equality) and the SCLC lost their earlier dynamism. African American leadership became somewhat fragmented after 1970, but steady progress was made as African Americans gained representation in most sectors of the mainstream of American life and the American economy. In terms of urban politics, in contrast with the fundamental struggles of the civil rights movement, urban African American political leaders now focus on the more commonplace tasks of getting representation on city councils, getting African American mayors elected, increasing job and economic opportunities, trying to reverse the deterioration of the city, and trying to target the city's resources more directly at the social problems of its minority populations.

The events of the 1960s had set the stage for significant electoral success in the 1970s. Removal of the legal restrictions on African American voting (such as poll taxes, white primaries, literacy tests, and other forms of discrimination), and especially the federal government's enforcement of the 1965 Voting Rights Act (see the accompanying

---

Key Provisions of the 1965 Voting Rights Act

Voting Examiners

Authorized the Justice Department to appoint voting examiners who could register people to vote in counties or municipalities that (1) had used a literacy test in determining voter registration for the 1964 presidential election or (2) had a voter turnout of less than 50 percent of the voting-age population in the 1964 presidential election.

Literacy Test

Authorized the Justice Department to suspend literacy tests if it was found that they had the effect of discriminating.

Prior-Approval Requirement

In political subdivisions in which federal voting examiners had been appointed, no change in voting laws, voter qualification laws, or municipal boundaries could be approved without prior approval of either the Justice Department or a three-judge federal court in Washington, D.C.

Enforcement Machinery

Gave the attorney general and the Civil Service Commission authority to enforce the act. Provided fines and imprisonment for convictions of violating the act.

---

box), led to a massive increase in the African American electorate, which in turn led to a dramatic increase in the number of elected African American officials. Whereas only 1,469 elected African American officials could be identified in 1970, the number had increased to 8,896 by 1999. Today there are almost 500 African American mayors, compared to only a handful 25 years ago.[35]

Implementing the Voting Rights Act   All of the provisions of the Voting Rights Act were controversial, but the most enduring controversy surrounded the Section 5 *prior-approval* (or preclearance) requirement, which prohibited 9 states and portions of 13 other states from making any changes in election laws or municipal boundaries without prior federal approval. This provision was due to expire after five years, but it was renewed several times after repeated attempts to water it down. In 1982 it was renewed for a 25-year period to expire in 2007. It now covers language minorities as well as racial minorities.

What makes the Section 5 prior-approval requirement so important, from the African American perspective, is that it prevents the deliberate alteration of election laws, boundaries, and systems of representation to negate the impact of African American voters. For example, in the 1950s the city of Tuskegee, Alabama, had changed the shape of its boundaries from a square to a 28-sided polygon for the specific purpose of keeping enough African Americans outside the city boundaries to ensure white control of the city council. Although the Supreme Court struck down that act as blatantly unconstitutional,[36] many African Americans feared that less blatant manipulations would be effected without the prior-approval requirement.

Do At-Large Elections Discriminate?   The techniques most likely to dilute African American voting influence were probably annexation and at-large elections. *Annexation* is felt to reduce African American influence when a city annexes suburban white residents and thereby decreases the proportion of the city's electorate that is African American. At-large elections, it is charged, enable the white majority to minimize if not prevent African American representation on the city council. As an example, one midwestern city had a ward system of elections in which the African American ward repeatedly elected a very militant council member who was disliked by the rest of the council. To get around this member, the city changed to an election system in which each ward nominated two members for its city council seat, and these nominees competed against each other in a citywide at-large election. Under this system the African American ward nominated the militant African American council member as its first choice and a more moderate African American as its second choice. But in the citywide at-large runoff, the moderate was elected and the first-choice, more militant African American was unseated.[37]

Whether this was an atypical result of electoral changes or whether at-large elections do in fact systematically discriminate against racial minorities has been subjected to considerable research. One study of 16 New Jersey cities found that African American representation was not seriously hampered by nonpartisan elections, at-large elections, or reform-style government.[38] This conclusion was supported by some broader studies that attempted to assess the impact of at-large elections throughout broader regions.[39] Particularly in cities with minority populations that are too small or too scattered to dominate a single ward, the at-large system might well be more conducive to getting minorities elected. And one study found that the switch from at-large to ward elections did not significantly improve African American representation.[40]

Most systematic studies, however, have come to the opposite conclusion. Albert Karnig's study of African American representation and reformism on a national scale, for example, found that the district system of representation definitely made it easier for African Americans to get a fair number of council members elected than did at-large representation.[41] A number of other studies that focused on cities of different sizes have tended to support Karnig's conclusions. For example, a study of Texas cities that switched from at-large to ward systems found that minorities increased their representation after the switch.[42] A statistical examination (called multiple regression) of the impact of several variables—such as form of representation, socioeconomic development, and percentage of the population minority—discovered that these other variables affected African American representation much less than did the factor of at-large versus ward representation. The ward system consistently gave the African Americans more representation than the at-large system.[43]

Court Rulings on At-Large Elections   With the preponderance of research in the 1970s showing that annexation and at-large elections dilute African American voting strength, it is not surprising that numerous prior-approval-requirement cases were brought to the federal courts. On annexation cases, the Supreme Court has not consistently struck down annexation as violating the Voting Rights Act. The Court allowed

Richmond, Virginia, to annex a large suburban area, thereby reducing African Americans from a majority to 42 percent of the city's electorate. The mitigating factors here were that the annexation could be justified on economic grounds of increasing the city's tax base and the fact that the expanded city adopted a nine-ward city council that assured African Americans a majority in four wards.[44] (African Americans in 1977 won control of the fifth ward as well, giving them a majority in the council.) Although the Supreme Court approved Richmond's suburban annexation, the Department of Justice in 1979 disallowed an annexation in Houston, Texas, that would have diluted the African American and Hispanic percentage of the city population by only a few percentage points.[45] In this case, however, it is not clear what constituted the best interests of those minorities. On the one hand, annexation would have slightly diluted their share of the city population; on the other hand, the motive of the proposed annexation was not racial deprivation but increasing the city's tax base, and that clearly would have benefited the minorities.

In dealing with at-large versus ward elections, the Supreme Court has shown a tendency to follow three patterns. First, it has tended to reject attempts to move from ward to at-large elections. Second, however, it has tended not to strike down existing at-large systems, even if they do have a discriminatory effect, unless there has been a past history of deliberately using the system to deprive minorities of their right to vote. That was the precedent established in a case involving Mobile, Alabama, which has had a three-member, at-large commission since 1911. By the 1970s, African Americans accounted for 40 percent of Mobile's voters, but they had never elected a city council member. They charged that the at-large system denied them representation and asked the Court to force Mobile to adopt a ward election system. The Supreme Court refused to do so, however,[46] on the grounds that the system had not been established with the intent of diluting African American votes.

The third tendency has emerged in instances when at-large cities have sought to make some other change that brought them under federal court jurisdiction; the federal courts have tended to force such cities to modify their at-large elections to guarantee representation for minorities. Thus when Port Arthur, Texas, sought to annex a suburban white community, the Supreme Court forced it to adopt a plurality-vote rule that would give African Americans (35 percent of the population) a fair chance to win two city council seats.[47] The largest cities forced to modify their at-large systems were Houston and Dallas. In these instances, the Department of Justice pressured the two cities into setting up, in their at-large systems, some wards that would guarantee representation for African Americans and Hispanics.[48] And the nation's three largest cities (New York, Los Angeles, and Chicago) were forced to redraw their ward boundaries in order to give better representation to Hispanics.

Revisionist Thought on At-large Elections   By the mid-1980s, extensive court action and repeated research findings had made it an article of faith in urban politics that at-large systems discriminated against African Americans. But a revisionist viewpoint began to emerge, suggesting that the at-large system had been excessively maligned. Court action in the 1970s and 1980s had reversed the most flagrant abuses of the at-large system, and it was conceivable that in a nondiscriminatory setting, African Americans might be better off with an at-large system. Charles S. Bullock, for example, argued that there are instances when ward elections promote little more than token representation.

In such systems, council members from exclusively white districts have no electoral reason to respond to African American concerns, but at-large council members may have such reasons because they want African Americans as part of their voter base.

Further, African American council members from exclusively African American wards may hesitate to cooperate with white council members for fear of being branded Uncle Toms. In such instances, the African American council members would be less influential in bargaining with the rest of the council than would an African American at-large member or perhaps even a white member with African American sympathies.

In short, Bullock argues that ward elections may reinforce racial barriers and at-large elections may break them down.[49] In this view, some ward elections give African Americans symbolic representation at the cost of substantive representation. There has also been some research indicating that white voters will sometimes cross over and vote for African American or Hispanic candidates, particularly those with higher education levels, those who are homeowners, and those in integrated neighborhoods.[50]

In light of this revisionist view of at-large elections, Susan Welch in the late 1980s surveyed all cities of 50,000 or more people to see whether at-large elections still discriminated against African Americans as they had in the 1970s. Although the discriminatory impact of at-large elections had diminished greatly in the intervening years, she found that African Americans still achieved greater numerical representation in ward elections than in at-large elections.[51]

The Voting Rights Act and Redistricting

Following the 1990 census, all states began redrawing the boundaries for their congressional and state legislative districts. But the 1982 amendments to the Voting Rights Act put a new wrinkle in the normal redistricting process. States were now required to create specific congressional districts and state legislative districts for racial and language minorities whenever possible. Failure to do so might put the state in violation of the Voting Rights Act's 1982 provision that minorities no longer had to prove that governments intended to discriminate in drawing election boundaries. It was sufficient to prove that the boundaries had a discriminatory effect, regardless of the government's intent.

This new situation created some strange alliances and conflicts. The National Republican Committee, not normally sympathetic to African American causes but eager to unseat some powerful white urban representatives in Congress, aligned itself with African American civil rights activists in the attempt to create more African American districts in cities such as Chicago and Houston. In Chicago, this move pitted African Americans against Hispanics as they jockeyed with each other in the attempt to win congressional seats.[52]

In determining how much minority population a minority district must have, the courts have often relied on the 65 percent rule of thumb: that it takes an African American or Hispanic population concentration of 65 percent to ensure that a district will elect a minority representative.[53] It is assumed that if 65 percent of the population is African American, 50 percent of the voters will be African American. Whether African American or Hispanics are any better represented by being packed into safe seats of this sort is still subject to question.[54] In places where African American or Hispanic voter turnout is equal to that of whites, it would obviously be a waste of minority votes to follow the 65 percent rule. Following that rule would pack too many minorities into one district and would necessarily reduce their electoral influence on representatives from neighboring districts.

The push to increase the number of minority districts has been hampered by new Supreme Court decisions ruling that the federal Voting Rights Act does not permit what the court deems racial *gerrymandering*—that is, drawing district lines solely on the basis of racial criteria. It is unclear just how far a state can go to remedy past discrimination. The Court is concerned that districts have become too "bizarre" in shape in an effort to obtain a large enough minority population to ensure African American and Hispanic victories.[55] States and localities are caught between the U.S. Department of Justice's enforcement of the Voting Rights Act and the Supreme Court's rulings against what it considers overreaching. This has also created confusion among localities that had been voluntarily adopting ward or mixed-election systems in negotiated settlements with minority groups in several communities. Now, localities are subject to lawsuits on both sides whether they switch or not.

African American Political Incorporation

To assess the influence of the Voting Rights Act on African American advancement, we need to examine the *political incorporation* of African Americans. This term is increasingly used by political scientists for the accession to governmental and civic power by African Americans and other minorities. Four levels of political incorporation have been identified by Rufus Browning, Dale Marshall, and David Tabb, who coined the term.

  Weak mobilization and exclusion. Minorities vote, but they lack the population size and other resources to elect minorities to government office.

  Protest and exclusion. The prime example was Oakland before 1977. Not only did a large minority population exist, but they also voted. However, there was substantial white opposition to African American incorporation, and lack of unity of minority leaders made it impossible for African Americans to overcome a hostile white governing coalition. African Americans remained excluded from government.

  Weak mobilization and incorporation. The prime example was San Francisco during the 1960s and early 1970s. White liberal major Joseph Alioto was able to win election by mobilizing the vote of minorities. He appointed minority leaders to minor positions in his administration and channeled government contracts to minority organizations. This gave the African American community partial incorporation, but some saw it as co-opting the African American leadership and as limiting, rather than maximizing, the advancement of San Francisco African Americans.

  Biracial electoral alliance and strong incorporation. The prime example was Berkeley, California, from the late 1950s to the 1980s. African American leaders and liberal whites formed an electoral alliance in the 1950s. African Americans got onto the city council in the 1960s, and the biracial coalition gained a majority on the council. By 1980 there were an African American mayor and an African American city manager, and African Americans held a significant number of top administrative positions. One consequence of the early incorporation of African Americans in Berkeley was that during the 1960s, "protest by blacks in Berkeley did not come so close to the edge of violence as it did in other cities."

In a reexamination of their study in 1995, Browning, Marshall, and Tabb found that "exclusion is far less common, and in six of the ten cities, including all the largest cities, these groups [African Americans, Latinos, and Asians] are, overall, well established, politically important, and strongly incorporated." In addition, protest is no longer a significant characteristic of these cities' politics.[56]

How much improvement African American incorporation has made in the living conditions of urban African Americans has been subject to different interpretations. But three generalizations can be made. Incorporation, especially in cities with African American mayors, has brought material benefits to African Americans. Nevertheless, there are limits on how much an African American mayor can achieve. And African American incorporation itself probably is not sufficient to bridge the sharp class differences between the growing African American middle class and the still-substantial African American working and lower classes.

African American Mayors and the Benefits of Incorporation　In their investigation of ten California cities, the inventors of the term *incorporation* found that cities with the highest levels of African American incorporation were indeed more responsive to African American concerns than were cities with lower levels of incorporation.[57] A study of four cities in Florida yielded similar findings. The more elected and appointed positions African Americans held in local government, the more responsive that government was to African American complaints about discrimination in hiring, police brutality, the paving of streets, and the quality of recreational services.[58]

Peter K. Eisinger examined six large cities with African American mayors and concluded that those mayors enjoyed considerable success at expanding public-sector opportunities for African Americans during the 1970s.[59] Perhaps the most successful tactic for expanding public-sector opportunities was the aggressive pursuit of affirmative action policies. In five of the six cities, an African American was named to head the city personnel office, and this resulted in substantial increases in African American employees on the city payroll. In Atlanta and Detroit, this increase in African American employees occurred despite the fact that overall city employment was declining. Affirmative action was also used to award city contracts to minority businesses. Atlanta mayor Maynard Jackson encouraged joint ventures that would enable small African American firms to bid jointly with larger companies. Detroit mayor Coleman Young instituted a policy of preferential bidding in which city firms were preferred over firms from outside the city that were less likely to hire African Americans. Newark mayor Kenneth Gibson set aside 25 percent of all federal public-works funds for minority contractors.

The net impact of these strategies, according to Eisinger's research, was substantial improvement in African American city employment and African American firms doing business with the city. In Detroit, for example, the African American share of city administrators nearly doubled, from about 12.1 percent to 23.5 percent, between 1973 and 1977, and the African American share of professional employment increased from

22.8 to 41.1 percent. The percentage of African Americans on Detroit's police force increased sixfold, from 5 percent to 30 percent, between 1967 and 1978.

Eisinger's findings on the policy impact of African American mayors were buttressed by Albert Karnig and Susan Welch's statistical analysis of policy impacts of African American mayors in all cities of 50,000 or more in population. Welch and Karnig found that cities with African American mayors had significantly higher expenditures for welfare services and significantly lower expenditures for parks, libraries, and fire protection. Additionally, cities with African American mayors raised more money generally than did cities without an African American mayor, and they gained these additional revenues in part by importing a greater share of federal aid.[60] These data should not be interpreted to mean that the mere presence of an African American mayor will substantially reduce black poverty. In fact, a recent study found that election of minority mayors did not result in fiscal policies significantly different from those cities without minority mayors.[61] However, there is a substantive difference in the kinds of policies that minority mayors pursue, which tend to reflect more concern for social welfare.

A Dual Strategy for African American Mayors   African American mayors achieve these advantages for their African American constituents by following what Peter Eisinger called a *dual strategy*.[62] The first part of the dual strategy is to stimulate economic development that will increase job opportunities for African Americans in the private sector. The second part of the dual strategy is to expand African American opportunities in the public sector.

The private-sector strategy of promoting economic growth in the city, so that jobs will be created for African American workers, means getting big corporations to invest in substantial redevelopment—usually downtown. This approach has been followed with substantial results in Detroit, Los Angeles, Newark, Baltimore, and Atlanta, as well as in many cities not run by African American mayors. However necessary this strategy might be to producing jobs in the private sector, it has many political consequences for the African American mayors who follow it. It forecloses alliances of the mayor with lower-income whites, working-class whites, and middle-class whites.[63] If the mayor aligns lower-income African American constituents with poor whites, that can produce a class-based politics that may alienate business interests and discourage them from investing in the city. Indeed, V. O. Key argued many years ago that the imposition of the segregation system in the South in the 1880s was partly a reaction to Populist attempts to unite African American and white lower-class voters against the dominating upper-class elites.[64] The strategy of downtown development also minimizes alliance with working- and middle-class whites, who will be competing directly with the African Americans for the jobs to be created. And it does not seem to leave any meaningful role for middle-class whites to play in city politics. The strategy of downtown development also brings African American mayors constantly under fire in the African American community for "selling out" to the white power structure. Thus, Eisinger maintains, the African American entrepreneurial mayors spend considerable time reassuring their African American constituents that they have not sold out.[65]

If they want to expand private-sector economic opportunities, however, the African American mayors may have little choice but to ally themselves with the downtown business community. Downtown redevelopment generates many construction jobs during the development phase and also attracts many white-collar service jobs as the new facilities go into operation. Whether this economic development strategy will actually do much to promote African American economic advancement is open to question. We will examine this issue in Chapter 6.

The second strategy for African American mayors is to expand opportunities for African Americans in the public sector by aggressively implementing affirmative action policies, by channeling city government contracts to African American businesses and businesses that hire African American workers, and by installing a substantial number of African American political appointees who can bring more African Americans into city government employment. As Peter Eisinger's research suggests, these tactics can have considerable success in expanding employment opportunities for African American residents of cities.

To make a broader test of whether African American mayors could significantly improve public employment of their African American constituents, Eisinger later examined the factors governing African American municipal employment in 43 cities whose populations were 10 percent or more African American.[66] He found that African American employment was only slightly affected by social and demographic variables such as the city's size, whether the city was growing or declining, whether the African American population was well educated, and whether public employment was expanding. The key variables were the size of the African American population and whether the city had an African American mayor. The larger an African American population is, the more it constitutes a potential voting bloc able to compete successfully for city jobs. African American mayors have a greater impact on appointments of African Americans to professional and administrative positions than on the general city government workforce. Because these appointed administrators become "gatekeepers" with the power to hire in their departments, they are able to use their positions to ease the entry of African Americans into the city bureaucracy. Strong mayors like Detroit's, of course, are able to use the strategy more successfully than weak mayors, because they have more administrative appointments to make. This strategy also is more likely to bear fruit in economically healthy cities whose governments are not under fiscal pressure to cut back on public services.[67]

The Limits on African American Mayors   Just as Steven Erie showed that there were limits on what could be achieved by Irish power and machine politics (see Chapter 3), so are there limits on what African American mayors can achieve following the dual strategy. Two examples illustrate this. Carl Stokes experience as Cleveland's first black mayor in the late 1960s showed the limits of a mayor operating in a situation of only limited incorporation. Atlanta showed the limits on the mayor in a city with a great deal of incorporation.

The tenure of Cleveland's first African American mayor, Carl Stokes (1967–1971), illustrates the mayor's dependence on two conditions: (1) the mayor's ability to respond to African American constituents without alienating white political and civic leaders and (2) the willingness of white political leaders to cooperate with the African American mayor. In the case of Carl Stokes, neither condition seems to have been present. Stokes was elected mayor of Cleveland in 1967 and reelected in 1969, the first African American elected to head any major American city. Although he sought to be mayor of all the people of Cleveland, Edmond J. Keller states that "his primary commitment was to the black community."[68] In his first term, he added 5,200 public-housing units, which more than doubled the existing number. This put him at odds with the white-dominated city council, and when he envisioned a series of low-income housing projects spread throughout the city, he was strongly opposed not only by the city council but also by a majority of whites and by many middle-class African Americans as well.

In his second term, Stokes sought to improve the city's tax base by raising the city income tax and ending the city's sharing taxes with suburbs. This would have enabled property taxes to be lowered while still raising an additional $26 million for the city. The council opposed this plan and submitted its own tax proposal to the voters. Faced with these two competing proposals, the voters polarized, with African American precincts favoring Stokes's plan and white precincts opposing both plans. When both plans were rejected by the voters, the city was forced to lay off some city workers and reduce some public services. Edmond Keller writes that this episode left Stokes's image severely tarnished. He was branded as incompetent and would have had a difficult time restoring the white community's confidence in him even if he had tried.[69] To Stokes's credit, he created a strong political organization in Cleveland's African American community that dominated several diverse local elections and gave the African American community an influential voice in the city's government. But after Stokes declined to run for reelection in 1971, the African American organization splintered.[70]

In contrast to Cleveland, Atlanta had a substantial African American middle class that had begun achieving political incorporation as early as the 1940s. In that decade, a white mayor perceived that he could mold a political coalition of the city's business community and its African American middle class. Policies of racial moderation (in contrast to existing segregation policies in the rest of the state) would attract enough African American votes to maintain his coalition in office, and policies of downtown development would draw support from the business community. This led to an accommodationist style of African American politics. By making substantial contributions to African American organizations, depositing sums in African American banks, and working with African American churches on housing and other projects, Atlanta's business community may in some respects have co-opted local African American leaders from pursuing more militant tactics. This accommodationist period lasted until the period of protest and racial violence that occurred in the 1960s.

In 1973 Atlanta elected its first African American mayor, Maynard Jackson. African Americans eventually took majority control of the city government, and Jackson and his successors in the mayor's office followed the dual strategy discussed earlier: affirmative action combined with promotion of economic development. As in most cities, economic development in essence meant rebuilding the downtown central business district.

However, according to political scientist Clarence N. Stone, political incorporation of Atlanta's middle-class African Americans has not necessarily brought great benefits to the mass of the African American population. He charges that working-class African Americans, lower-class African Americans, and neighborhood groups have been virtually excluded from the governing regime that predominates in Atlanta.[71]

The Limits of Political Incorporation   What is suggested by the limits on African American mayors in promoting black advancement is that there may be limits on what can be accomplished by African American incorporation within the central city itself.

As we shall see in the next chapter, the central city exists within a broader economic setting. Large cities such as New York, Chicago, and Los Angeles have become the settling places for a large African American underclass. Even if every city government position were filled by an African American and even if the maximum number of development dollars were spent on rebuilding the downtown, the central-city government left on its own still would not have the resources to end the poverty of the large underclass. And politically no mayor, no matter what race, could devote all of the city's resources to solving the problems of a single ethnic group to the exclusion of all other groups. One implication is that a much broader assault is needed on the educational problems, the social deterioration, the economic deprivation, and the racial discrimination facing the African American underclass than can be waged by the central-city government on its own. For this reason, many call for a new infusion of federal aid for cities.

J. Phillip Thompson in a new book on black mayors distinguishes two waves of black mayors. First were the "'civil rights' mayors elected in highly racially polarized elections taking place in cities that had become majority black or were approaching a black majority." But by the 1980s, black voters became disenchanted with limited successes, due in part to declines in federal aid and changing city economies.

> Black mayors were increasingly criticized for assuming a role of race leader rather than as city manager, and accused of antagonizing white businesses and failing to entice them to their cities (Ross and Levine 2001, 120). New, younger black mayoral candidates replaced the mayors of the civil rights era, promising to deemphasize race, promote efficient government, and offer strategies to lure investors to strengthen downtown businesses and create jobs.

Examples of such mayors are Mike White in Cleveland elected in 1989 who Thompson points out "was elected with only a third of the black vote and 80 percent of the white vote." Other examples are Dennis Archer in Detroit (1993), William Campbell in Atlanta (1993), Wilson Goode in Philadelphia (1984–1992), and Ray Nagin in New Orleans (2002).[72] At the end of the day, however, Thompson finds the new black mayors have been no more effective than the old.

> In short, the nation's technocratic black mayors have suffered fates not unlike their predecessors. They came to office promising change and significant improvements, and they were often blamed when they could not stem the tide of urban decline; their primary success seemed to be providing grander facilities for professional sports. Neither the "civil rights" black mayors nor the technocratic managers addressed two characteristics of government structure that consistently undermined efforts to improve cities: the first, the fiscal and political isolation of cities within larger regional and state governments; and the second, the lack of empowerment of black civic organizations.[73]

David Imbroscio believes black leaders could challenge the structural and resource constraints operating in the city. At present, black elected officials accept these constraints, and this leads them into alliances with the business community and encourages them to pursue corporate-centered growth strategies or else look to the federal and state governments for greater aid. Imbroscio suggests that these leaders have more room to maneuver and that they could actually restructure the situation so that they could better serve those who elected them. He proposes that black leaders pursue an alternative development strategy that loosens the regime's reliance on business support and allows it greater latitude to respond to the preferences of the population.

According to Imbroscio, economic constraints can be reduced by encouraging greater local business capacity rather than relying on a strategy of attracting businesses from without. Institutional constraints can be lowered by adopting a partial strategy of municipal enterprise and retaining public control over projects. Linkage policies, wherein the city extracts payment for the right to development could replace incentive policies to entice development. Imbroscio acknowledges that it is an open question whether these alternative development strategies would have made more headway in addressing inner-city problems. However, he believes this alternative strategy could not be worse than the present corporate-centered strategy that has failed to improve the plight of the lower-class minorities.[74]

Fourth-Wave Immigrants and Urban Politics

As we saw in Chapter 2, Hispanics and Asians constitute a fourth historical wave of migrants into American cities. Today there are more than 35 million Hispanics and over 10 million Asians in the United States, and these are the fastest-growing groups in the country. Are they likely to follow the paths of ethnic succession and upward social mobility traced by the European ethnics? Or are they following a pattern different from the European ethnics or the African Americans?

Hispanics and Urban Politics

The 35 million Hispanics in the United States account for about 12.5 percent of the total American population. As Table 5.4 shows, the three largest Hispanic groups in America are Puerto Ricans, Cubans, and Mexican Americans. Although Hispanics are found throughout the United States, they are concentrated most heavily in the Southwest, New York, Florida, and Illinois. The Southwest has relatively few Cubans or Puerto Ricans. It is heavily Mexican American, although it has sizable concentrations of people from Central and South America as well. Florida's Hispanic population is dominated by Cubans and to a lesser extent by people from Central and South America. Illinois is unique in that it has large numbers of both Mexican Americans and Puerto Ricans (mostly in Chicago).

TABLE 5.4   Hispanic Peoples in the United States

Country of Origin	Number	Percent
Mexico	26,630,000	65.9
Puerto Rico	3,840,000	9.5
Cuba	1,614,000	4
Other Hispanic origin[a]	8,341,000	20.6
Total	40,425,000	100

[a]Central America, South America, Spain, and all other Hispanic or Latino.

Source: U.S. Census Bureau, Current Population Survey, Annual Social and Economic Supplement, 2004, Ethnicity and Ancestry Statistics Branch, Population Division.

Because these diverse peoples all share the same mother tongue, there is a tendency to think of Hispanics as one group of people. In most key respects, however, the groups are distinct. Racially, for instance, Mexican Americans tend to be of Spanish-Indian backgrounds, whereas most Cubans and Puerto Ricans are of Caucasian or black African descent or some mixture of both. In Puerto Rico's Spanish history, color differences were much less important than in the United States, which has provoked powerful emotional reactions in some Puerto Ricans who were required to make this adjustment.[75] Reasons for entering the mainland United States also differ for each group. Most Mexican American immigrants seek economic opportunity, whereas Cubans are political refugees from the Castro regime. Puerto Ricans are United States citizens, free to travel back and forth between Puerto Rico and the mainland. For this reason, the Puerto Rican community is free of the illegal-alien problems that plague other Hispanic communities. Finally, there are important political differences among these groups. Cubans, as we shall see, tend as a group to be much more politically conservative than Puerto Ricans or Mexican Americans.

Because the space limitations of this text make it impossible to do justice to all the nuances and divisions of Hispanic America, we will focus here on the largest Hispanic-American group, the Mexican Americans, and take a short look at the Cubans, because their experience is so distinctive.

The Political Legacy of Mexican American History

As a result of the Mexican-American War of 1846, about 75,000 Mexicans living in the newly annexed territories that are now California, Arizona, and New Mexico suddenly became Americans.[76] Although the Mexicans numerically dominated this territory before 1846, they were soon outnumbered by "Anglos" attracted to the West by the California gold rush, the completion of the transcontinental railroad, the Army's pacification of the West, and the hope of economic prosperity. In Texas, Americans had begun settling while that area was still under Mexican domination. When they achieved sufficient numbers, they proclaimed the independence of Texas from Mexico and in 1845 were annexed to the United States. The history of Mexican Americans has left a threefold political legacy for the twenty-first century: economic deprivation, oppression, and cultural nationalism.

Economic Deprivation   That the Mexican Americans as well as most Spanish-speaking Americans are economically deprived is well documented. As shown in Table 5.1, non-Cuban Hispanics lag far behind the non-Hispanic population in both educational attainment and income, and Mexican Americans are among the poorest groups. The low average income of Mexican Americans results in part from their high concentrations in poorly paying, dead-end jobs in the garment industry, agricultural harvesting, fast-food restaurants, and other service occupations. As we observed in Chapter 3, one of the key resources in any ethnic group's rise to power is the existence of a substantial middle class that can provide leadership and begin moving into positions of political and economic importance. The long history of economic deprivation slowed the entrance of Mexican Americans into the mainstream of middle-class American politics.

Oppression   The lag in resources caused by economic deprivation is compounded by a history of oppression. Current Mexican American writers describe a long history of maltreatment by various government agencies. Particularly resented have been the Border Patrol and the immigration authorities, whose job has been to stem illegal immigration through projects such as "Operation Wetback" in the 1950s. Under Operation Wetback,

> United States–born children were known to have been expelled with their parents. Many American-born adults were stopped and asked for proof of citizenship in cities far removed from the border—and some, reacting with anger as well as amazed incredulity, came into conflict with the officers. Because of its large scale and allegations of rough treatment, Operation Wetback became one of the most traumatic recent experiences of the Mexican-Americans in their contacts with government authority. No Mexican-American community in the Southwest remained untouched.[77]

During the Great Depression of the 1930s, welfare officials in Los Angeles and Detroit attempted to reduce welfare costs by repatriating Mexican Americans to Mexico, even though many of those repatriated were United States citizens who objected to being deported.[78] One of the most bitterly detested governmental units was the Texas Rangers. Formed in 1835 to protect the frontier, the Texas Rangers, according to one historian, subsequently engaged in a "reign of terror against the Mexicans."[79] Nor have Mexican American grievances against government agencies all been far in the past. In the 1960s, Mexican American sheep grazers came into violent conflict with the National Forest Service, which attempted to drive them off the forest for conservation purposes.[80] And in 1978, Mexican American groups in Houston, Texas, charged that city's police officers with police brutality in their relations with the Mexican American community.[81]

Cultural Nationalism   Given this history of conflict, it is not surprising that cultural nationalism came to be a significant part of the Mexican American drive to political empowerment in the 1970s and 1980s. In some respects this was symbolized by the term *Chicano,* which came to prominence in the 1970s. Although the origins of the term are not clear, it is clear that Chicano implies a sense of pride in the unique Mexican American culture. The term also is "associated with all Mexican-American militant and separatist groups."[82] The political effect of this growing sense of cultural nationalism was a heightened militancy that F. Chris Garcia and Rudolph O. de la Garza called *Chicanismo,* a call for greater attentiveness to Mexican American needs in several problem areas that are partially urban in nature: bilingual and bicultural education, community control of schools, fairer treatment by law enforcement agencies, better employment opportunities, an end to housing discrimination, and better health care. Only a small percentage of Mexican Americans identified with the term Chicano,[83] however, and militant cultural nationalism among Mexican Americans peaked with the rise and fall of the La Raza Unida (LRU) party in the 1970s.[84]

In sum, the political legacy of Mexican American history is the heightened awareness among Mexican Americans of past and present discrimination against them and a sense of cultural nationalism. Although historically, Mexican Americans were marginally involved in electoral politics, today they are a major political force, especially in the Southwest.

Mexican American organizations can be divided into three categories. First are the early accommodationist organizations that stressed patriotism to the United States.[85] Some of these, such as the *Orden Hijos de Americas* (Order of the Sons of America), were similar to the fraternal and mutual-benefit societies of other immigrant groups. Most important was the League of United Latin American Citizens (LULAC). Viewing themselves primarily as an educational and civic group, LULAC leaders did not engage in any political activities or even attempt to increase Mexican American voter turnout.

A second category of groups began emerging after World War II. They were much more politically oriented than the earlier accommodationist groups. The most politically oriented of these were the Mexican American Political Association (MAPA) in California and the Political Association of Spanish-Speaking Organizations (PASSO) in Texas. Both groups tried to improve Mexican American voter turnout, endorsed and campaigned for candidates, and engaged in a variety of community organization tactics. One of the most visible of the Mexican American groups was Cesar Chavez's United Farm Workers (UFW).[86] Affiliated with the AFL-CIO, the UFW successfully organized grape pickers and field workers in California, battled with the Teamsters, gained for Mexican Americans the support of prominent Anglo liberals such as Senator Robert Kennedy, and organized a moderately successful nationwide boycott of grapes (and the resulting wines) and lettuce that had not been picked by members of the United Farm Workers. Despite these early successes, the UFW did not adapt well to the more conservative environment that prevailed after 1980, and it lost membership and suffered financial difficulty.[87]

A third category of Mexican American groups consists of the more radical organizations that emerged in the 1970s, when *cultural nationalism* was at its peak. The net result of cultural nationalism was the proliferation of newer, more militant groups such as the Brown Berets, the Federal Alliance of Free City-States, the Crusade for Justice, and various student organizations. Some of these accepted the use of violence if they thought it necessary to attain Mexican American goals. Like the leadership of the earlier groups, that of the radical groups was middle-class, but these leaders differed from those of the earlier groups in that they sought to appeal to lower- and working-class Mexican Americans.[88]

The best-known radical group was La Raza Unida (LRU), which rejected collaboration with traditional Democrats. Running its own candidates for office, LRU took electoral control of Zavalas County in Texas and used that position as a springboard to set up LRU chapters throughout the Southwest. However, LRU leaders were too suspicious of other Mexican American leaders (even such militant ones as Cesar Chavez of the UFW)[89] to establish broad-based political coalitions. In the late 1970s the LRU suffered a major setback when its candidate for governor of Texas drew only a handful of votes, and by the middle 1980s the party had disappeared. It would be a mistake to dismiss the party as a failure, however. It filled a leadership vacuum among Mexican Americans in the early 1970s, and it may well have opened the way for Mexican American entrance into the political mainstream of the United States.[90]

Mexican American Mayors   As the Mexican American population has grown and participation rates have gone up, its political influence in urban politics has increased accordingly. What form this influence will take is not fully determined yet. It seems unlikely that very many cities will see a Mexican American political dominance on the model of the African American dominance of cities such as Detroit and Atlanta. Mexican Americans dominate very few large cities numerically to the extent that African Americans do (see Table 5.5). Furthermore, a higher percentage of Hispanics than of African Americans live in the suburbs, and in few areas of the country do Hispanics suffer the extreme hypersegregation experienced by African Americans.[91] Although this greater dispersion of Hispanics reduces their social isolation in comparison to African Americans, it also disperses their voting potential, makes it more difficult for them to elect city council members, and requires successful mayoral candidates to construct voting coalitions that include Anglo as well as Mexican American voters. The three most prominent examples of Mexican American mayors constructing such coalitions probably occurred in San Antonio, Denver, and most recently Los Angeles.

San Antonio   With a Mexican American majority in its population, San Antonio may have seemed tailor-made for Mexican American political incorporation. However, San Antonio, like most cities in the Southwest, had historically expanded by annexing surrounding suburban settlements. As central cities annexed white suburbs, the voting power of Mexican Americans was diluted.

Furthermore, from the mid-1950s to the mid-1970s, San Antonio had been dominated by an organization called the Good Government League, which was composed of major business interests. Ninety-five percent of all city council members during this period were also members of the Good Government League.[92] But Good Government League dominance splintered in 1975 when the so-called Independent Team, a coalition of newer businesses, pledged to concentrate city development on the growing north side of the city. The city's Hispanic population was poorly represented in both of those governing coalitions. In 1974, the Mexican Americans lost on a proposal to create several district seats for the city council and end the at-large system of elections.

They got a second shot at this goal after 1975, when the Voting Rights Act was amended to cover voting discrimination against language minorities. The following year the Department of Justice objected to San Antonio's plan to annex 65 square miles with a population that was 75 percent Anglo on the grounds that such an annexation would dilute the Mexican American voting strength from 52 percent to a minority. San Antonio ultimately was allowed to make the annexation, but only on condition that ten city council districts be created to ensure representation from the city's African American and Hispanic neighborhoods.[93] The eleventh vote on the council was given to a weak mayor who was elected at-large.

Under this plan, the Mexican Americans took control of the San Antonio city council in 1977 and in 1981 elected Henry Cisneros as mayor. Under Mexican American control, the city government restricted suburban construction activities over an aquifer supplying the city's water and pursued affirmative action policies that brought more minorities into city government. Cisneros maintained his support in the Mexican American neighborhoods while working with business leaders to promote economic growth.[94] He put together an effective governing coalition between the business community and neighborhood groups.[95] During Cisneros's eight-year reign as mayor, economic development in San Antonio virtually exploded,[96] with thousands of jobs created for Hispanics as well as other workers. Cisneros brought the city extensive favorable

TABLE 5.5   Cities with Large Hispanic Populations

	City	City Population (2000)	City Hispanic or Latino Population (2000)	Share of Population That Is Hispanic or Latino, 2000	Hispanic Mayor
1	New York, NY	8,008,278	2,160,554	27.00%	
2	Los Angeles, CA	3,694,820	1,719,073	46.50%	Antonio Villaraigosa (2005–)
3	Chicago, IL	2,896,016	753,644	26.00%	
4	Houston, TX	1,953,631	730,865	37.40%	
5	San Antonio, TX	1,144,646	671,394	58.70%	Ed Garza (2001–2005)
					Henry Cisneros (1981–1989)
6	Phoenix, AZ	1,321,045	449,972	34.10%	
7	El Paso, TX	563,662	431,875	76.60%	Raymond C. Caballero (2001–)
					Carlos Ramirez (1997–2001)
8	Dallas, TX	1,188,580	422,587	35.60%	
9	San Diego, CA	1,223,400	310,752	25.40%	
10	San Jose, CA	894,943	269,989	30.20%	Ron Gonzales (1998–)
11	Santa Ana, CA	337,977	257,097	76.10%	Miguel Pulido (1994–)
12	Miami, FL	362,470	238,351	65.80%	Manny Diaz (2001–)
					Joe Carollo (1996–2002)
					Xavier Suarez (1985–1994)
					Maurice Ferre (1973–1984)
13	Hialeah, FL	226,419	204,543	90.30%	Raul L. Martinez (1993–2005)
					Julio J. Martinez (1991–1993)
					Raul L. Martinez (1981–1990)
14	Austin, TX	656,562	200,579	30.50%	
15	Albuquerque, NM	448,607	179,075	39.90%	
16	Denver, CO	554,636	175,704	31.70%	
17	Tucson, AZ	486,699	173,868	35.70%	
18	Fresno, CA	427,652	170,520	39.90%	
19	Long Beach, CA	461,522	165,092	35.80%	
20	Fort Worth, TX	534,694	159,368	29.80%	
21	Anaheim, CA	328,014	153,374	46.80%	
22	Corpus Christi, TX	277,454	150,737	54.30%	
23	Philadelphia, PA	1,517,550	128,928	8.50%	
24	Las Vegas, NV	478,434	112,962	23.60%	
25	San Francisco, CA	776,733	109,504	14.10%	

Source: Center on Urban and Metropolitan Policy, The Brookings Institution, Living Cities Databook Series Population data: on mayors: *Who's Who in American Politics 1997–1999,* Marquis Who's Who, New Providence, New Jersey, 1997. *Who's Who Among Hispanic Americans 1992–1993,* Gale Research, Detroit and London, 1992. *The Municipal Yearbook* (1982–1998), Washington, D.C., International City/County Management. U.S. Conference of Mayors; http://www.mayors.org, and individual city and news websites.

national publicity, and in 1988 he was being pushed to run for governor of Texas. Instead, he retired from the mayor's office to start a financial services business and devote more time to an ailing son who had been born with severe birth defects. Shortly thereafter, he accepted President Clinton's appointment as Secretary of the Department of Housing and Urban Development (1993–1997). Since then, his record has been somewhat tarnished by allegations that he had an affair, paid hush money, and then lied to federal agents about this so as not to threaten Senate confirmation of his appointment.

Denver   More typical than San Antonio, with its Mexican American majority, is Denver, where Hispanics account for only about 20 percent of the population. Denver elected Federico Peña mayor in 1983. Denver Hispanics were able to win the mayor's office because they possessed several of the key resources that have been identified by Rufus P. Browning, Dale R. Marshall, and David H. Tabb as critical for political incorporation.[97] Among these resources was a population large enough to influence elections, the existence of middle-class Hispanics with the socioeconomic status and resources to support political campaigns, the absence of a hostile Anglo-dominated governing coalition, and the absence of reformed political structures (such as city manager government and an at-large city council) that could be used to impede minority-group influence. Peña won the election by putting together a voting coalition of minorities and white liberals. As mayor, he worked hard to bring other Mexican Americans into government. By the late 1980s, Mexican Americans had achieved electoral positions roughly proportionate to their size in the population, and the number of Hispanics in appointive positions had increased dramatically. Peña did not do nearly so well at shoring up his support with the business community or with white voters, however. Denver's economy was badly hurt by sliding energy prices in the mid-1980s. The mayor's plans to stimulate economic growth by building a new airport and convention center did not materialize. He barely won reelection in 1987[98] and then lost the office in 1989. President Clinton later tapped him to be Secretary of Transportation (1992–2000).

Los Angeles   In 1973, Tom Bradley was elected the first and only black mayor of Los Angeles. Bradley won with the support of a biracial coalition including liberal white Democrats, Jews, Latinos, and blacks. Bradley governed for 20 years promoting affirmative action, police reform to reduce concerns about police brutality, and seeking greater federal aid for urban problems.[99] When Bradley retired, it was expected that Mike Woo, a liberal Chinese-American council member, would succeed him.[100] However, millionaire Republican businessman Richard Riordin defeated Woo, running on a conservative platform. The election of Richard Riordin, just one year after the Los Angeles riot, signaled an abrupt end to the rainbow coalition that had sustained Bradley for many years. The Riordin agenda included fighting crime, fiscal conservatism, and greater attention to economic development. Riordin was succeeded by Jim Hahn in 2001. Hahn, a liberal Democrat, won with black votes in the inner city and white affluent votes in suburban San Fernando Valley, seeming to restore at least part of the biracial coalition of Bradley.

However, Hahn confronted a secession movement in the San Fernando Valley that threatened the unity and integrity of Los Angeles. Although the referendum to withdraw from Los Angeles failed, the pressures to decentralize continued. Sometimes referred to as "Mayor Pothole," Hahn lacked the broader vision and strategy of Riordin to make L.A. a global city. The black community was angered by Hahn's failing to reappoint Bernard Parks, the black police chief who went on to win a seat in the city Assembly. Hahn's chief challenger for the mayoralty, Antonio Villaraigosa, former speaker of the California Assembly, who had strong support in the Latino community also went on to win a seat in the Assembly.[101] Although credited with much success in defeating the secession effort, during his reelection campaign Hahn faced charges that the $5 million campaign finance effort against succession involved improprieties, including strong-arm fundraising tactics among city contractors or vendors. There also were investigations of the way contracts were let in a number of city departments and several senior city employees resigned amidst investigations. Hahn opposed the expansion of Los Angeles International Airport, saying it was time for others in the region to absorb the costs and congestion of continued airport expansion.

Hahn was challenged by both former police chief Bernard Parks and Antonio Villaraigosa in elections in June 2005.[102] The shooting death of a black youth by police in February 2005 further undermined Hahn's support in the black community, which voted 71 percent in his favor in 2001 although making up only 14 percent of the vote in Los Angeles.[103] Hahn also lost his strong base of support in suburban San Fernando Valley. With about 33 percent of the voters turning out, Villaraigosa was elected in a landslide (59 percent to 41 percent) becoming the first Latino elected to mayor in Los Angeles in more than a century. A major campaign theme was Hahn's inadequacies as mayor of a global city. In an effort to bolster support, Hahn's campaign themes revolved around charges that Villaraigosa was weak on crime.[104] The fact that Los Angeles is now almost half Latino substantially improved Villaraigosa's chances. When Hahn angered the black community and the white suburban vote in San Fernando Valley, Villaraigosa's victory was assured.

Cuban Urban Politics

Cuban political influence is most markedly felt in Miami, a city in which Hispanics are a majority and Cubans are the dominant Hispanic group. But there are at least two Cuban communities in Miami. Most Miami Cubans are middle-class Caucasians who came into the country as refugees when Fidel Castro took over the island in 1959. These Cubans, many of them business and professional people, did not take long to enter the middle-class mainstream of American life, assisted as they were with about $1 billion in federal assistance between 1961 and 1974. As Table 5.1 shows, they enjoy a much better economic position than Mexican Americans or Puerto Ricans. In contrast to this middle-class, older Cuban community, Miami also houses the "Marielitos," about 100,000 Cubans who escaped from Castro or were let go by him in 1980. Mostly black and poor, these more recent arrivals are not viewed positively by the older Cuban immigrants.[105]

Politically, Cubans, who are motivated by a fierce anticommunism, are much more Republican and conservative than the other Hispanic groups. Most Cubans felt a deep disappointment with the Democrats when President Kennedy failed to overthrow the Castro regime. They provided many of the Spanish-speaking operatives for numerous

CIA missions against communism in the Western Hemisphere, and when President Reagan began supporting the Contra war against the Sandinista regime in Nicaragua, large numbers of Cubans gave him and the Republicans their allegiance,[106] using their economic power and political savvy, to marshal community support for the Contra effort. A few have become intimately involved in illegal drug trafficking.[107]

The Cubans have dramatically transformed Miami politics. The city is divided tri-ethnically among Cubans, who are a slight majority of the city's population; African Americans, who account for another 27 percent; and a small non-Hispanic white population of about 11 percent. Politically, the gaps among these three ethnic groups are huge. Cuban mayor Xavier Suarez won election in 1985 by maximizing his Hispanic vote, while his opponent sought to put together a coalition of Hispanics, African Americans, and non-Hispanic whites. By 1987 Suarez solidified his political support and won majorities in all three of those ethnic groupings while winning a reelection runoff.[108] Manny Diaz succeeded him in 2001 and was reelected in 2005.

Black-Cuban relations in Miami, never warm, were exacerbated by the influx of the Marielitos in 1980 and by an influx of impoverished immigrants from other Latin American nations. These newer immigrants have greatly displaced black Americans from low-income service jobs in hotels, hospitals, and restaurants and by doing so have created a great deal of resentment in the African American community. The Marielitos enjoy little of the middle-class achievements of the early white Cuban immigrants. Their plight received national attention in 1987 when Cubans in two federal prisons rioted because they thought they were going to be deported to Cuba. The depth of black-Cuban animosity was seen in 1991 when South African leader Nelson Mandela visited Miami after praising Castro for having supported South African blacks. This praise for Castro so enraged Cubans in the city that Mayor Suarez denounced Mandela's remarks and refused to hold an official welcome for him. This in turn enraged African American leaders, who interpreted the snubbing of Mandela as a snubbing of themselves.

Miami has been beset by financial scandals, corruption, and fierce interethnic and racial infighting. A federal investigation in 1996 uncovered bribery and fraud involving the Hispanic city manager, Cesar Odio, and the only African American commissioner, Miller Dawkins, both of whom pled guilty and went to jail. That year the city was also found to have a $68 million deficit, a discovery that prompted the governor to appoint a fiscal-oversight board. The Cuban community itself was fractured. The 1997 mayoral elections resulted in a runoff between two Cuban candidates, incumbent Mayor Joe Carollo and the challenger, former Mayor Xavier Suarez. The race was rife with accusations of voter fraud. Suarez won the runoff, but the court later ruled the election void because of rampant voter fraud. Carrollo was found to have won the original general election and was officially named mayor after fraudulent absentee ballots were thrown out. Non-Hispanic white residents of affluent Coconut Grove and other neighborhoods unsuccessfully sought to disincorporate the City of Miami in a referendum in the same 1997 election. Also in that election, the voters did approve a charter change setting up a strong-mayor system with single-member district elections.[109]

The Elian Gonzales case mentioned in Chapter 2 further inflamed politics in Miami. Following the federal raid to take Elian from his Miami relatives, Mayor Carollo fired the city manager. Shortly thereafter, the police chief resigned. He had been criticized for cooperating with federal officials in their efforts to regain custody of Elian to return him to his father in Cuba. In the November 2001 elections, Manny Diaz—the attorney who had handled the Miami relatives' efforts on behalf of Elian—was elected mayor. And the case overshadowed the 2002 race for governor as President Bush's brother sought to retain his seat against the challenge of former Attorney General Janet Reno, who had ordered the raid.[110]

Asians and Urban Politics

The second-largest group of fourth-wave urban immigrants are from Asia and the western Pacific area. But being from this region is about all they have in common, because they represent different nationalities, different languages, different religions, and different socioeconomic levels. The largest of these migrant groups are from the Philippines, Korea, China, Vietnam, Japan, and India. For the most part, however (the main exceptions being Southeast Asian Vietnamese, Cambodians, and Hmongs), Asian immigrants have much better educational levels and enjoy more prestigious occupations than do African Americans or Mexican Americans. Although they are not yet earning incomes comparable to those of whites with similar education, they seem, according to one study, to face "very few barriers to socioeconomic achievement . . . [and their] . . . story seems to be quite rosy."[111] In addition to enjoying better socioeconomic positions than most of the fourth-wave urban immigrants, Asian Americans are also much less segregated than African Americans and Hispanics.[112]

Despite this more favorable picture for Asians, they do face some distinct discrimination problems in America. The United States Civil Rights Commission in 1987 warned of a high level of racially motivated violence against Asians. Quite frequent were fire bombings and attacks on Korean retail stores.[113] This was certainly evident in the Los Angeles riot in 1992 (discussed earlier in the chapter). Asians have also complained that elite universities have imposed quotas on the admission of Asian students, not because the Asians do poorly in college but because they outperform most other students.

Issues of Concern to Fourth-Wave Immigrants

The three main issues of concern to fourth-wave immigrants are probably immigration, bilingualism, and jobs.

Immigration   Immigration is an issue because of the millions of people who seek better economic opportunities in the United States. The Immigration and Naturalization Service (INS) estimates that there are about 5 million illegal immigrants in the United States. Of these, 2.7 million are estimated to be from Mexico, and about 2.1 million of the 5 million illegal immigrants have overstayed their visas.[114] The U.S. *war against terrorism* is expected to reduce this number dramatically.

Immigration today is shaped principally by the Immigration Act of 1965 and the Immigration Reform and Control Act of 1986 (usually called the Simpson-Rodino Act). The first of these laws repealed previous restrictions on the immigration of Asians, effectively reduced the proportion of European immigrants, and turned Asia and Latin America into the two main sources of immigrants.[115]

The second, the Simpson-Rodino Act, sought to cope with the problem of illegal immigrants, the bulk of whom are impoverished rural laborers from Mexico. The 1986 Simpson-Rodino Act sought to come to grips with illegal immigration by

1. Requiring employers to verify the U.S. citizenship or legal status of all employees and imposing stiff penalties on employers who violate the law.
2. Granting amnesty to all aliens who had resided permanently in the United States since January 1, 1982, and giving them an amnesty period of one year (until May 1987) to apply for citizenship.
3. Granting temporary status to alien agricultural workers who had worked at least 90 days in the United States between May 1985 and May 1986 and also giving them an amnesty period of one year to apply for citizenship.

During the amnesty period, nearly 2 million aliens applied for citizenship,[116] but since then the number of illegal immigrants appears to have increased rather than decreased.[117] Substantial numbers of businesses that suffer from shortages of cheap labor do not really want to curb immigration,[118] and they often successfully exploit legal loopholes—using contract workers instead of payroll employees, accepting false documentation of alien status, and employing aliens for such short periods (three days or less) that they do not fall under the law.

Whether illegal Mexican aliens take jobs away from Americans, whether they should enjoy free public services such as education and welfare, and whether they pay more in taxes than they receive in free public services are hotly debated questions in both Hispanic and non-Hispanic communities. And there is no more unanimity among Mexican Americans on these issues than among non-Hispanics.[119]

Bilingualism   A second issue of concern to fourth-wave immigrants is bilingualism. Should immigrants be obliged to learn English in order to get jobs and go to school? Or should schools be obliged to offer instruction in the native tongues of recent immigrants as a means of helping them keep up with their studies until their command of English is sufficient for them to enter regular classes? And should employers be obliged to hire workers who cannot understand written or spoken instructions in English?

The usual argument for bilingualism is that it should be used, especially in schools to prevent immigrant children from dropping out and to improve their academic performance. Although there is some evidence that bilingual instruction does indeed accomplish these goals, opponents point out the absurdity of a city such as Los Angeles having to provide instruction in the native tongues of Mexican, Japanese, Indian, Philippine, Korean, Vietnamese, Cambodian, and other immigrant children who inhabit that city.[120] Opponents also fear that providing schooling in the languages of non-English speakers could lead to Spanish being recognized as a second official language and to a cultural separatism problem such as that of Québec, Canada. By 1990, 11 states had passed laws mandating English as the official state language, but the constitutionality of such legislation is unclear.[121]

Jobs   The third issue of crucial importance to fourth-wave urban immigrants is whether they can find jobs to maintain themselves and whether in doing so they take jobs away from native-born low-income Americans,[122] or whether the jobs they take are so menial and arduous that native-born Americans are unwilling to do them.[123] Social science research on these questions has not yet provided definitive answers, but four generalizations seem apparent.[124]

First, there is some evidence that immigration has added jobs to the overall American economy, especially in California, by providing a pool of low-wage laborers that may make some American manufacturers more competitive with low-wage foreign manufacturers. Second, this process does indeed drive down wages for existing workers, especially in manufacturing and agricultural areas. Third, some researchers fear that reliance on low-wage immigrant laborers may inhibit American manufacturers from modernizing their production processes with high technology and may in the long run undermine the competitiveness of American industry. Finally, some researchers fear that demographic trends will eventually cause a labor shortage in the United States and that large-scale immigration will have to be stimulated to compensate for this shortage.

The Search for a Rainbow Coalition

If low-income Mexican Americans, Puerto Ricans, American Indians, non-Hispanic whites, and Asians could form an electoral coalition capable of swinging election results, that act alone would vastly increase their political influence. The most prominent spokesperson for this movement is, of course, Jesse Jackson, who in his 1984 and 1988 presidential campaigns coined the term *rainbow coalition*. Just as the rainbow's natural beauty lies in the spectrum of colors it presents, the political rainbow coalition would embrace a spectrum of people of different colors: whites, browns, reds, yellows, and blacks.

Scholars have devoted considerable energy to the question of why a cross-nationality electoral coalition did not emerge among lower-class European immigrants in the late nineteenth and early twentieth centuries. Ethnic divisions, religious divisions, the tradition of privatism, the hope of upward social mobility, workplace-oriented unions (as distinct from class-oriented unions), nonideological machine politics, and repression of ideological movements by the law, the police, and various national guards all conspired in the past to prevent the emergence of institutions that would enable the lower classes to advance their political and economic self-interests. Have any changes occurred that might permit the emergence of something akin to Jesse Jackson's electoral coalition in the twenty-first century?

Let us analyze this question first from the viewpoint of the central-city African American leader seeking to put together a multiethnic electoral coalition capable of winning office. The most logical allies would seem to be lower-class whites, who face many of the same economic problems faced by lower-class African Americans (poor housing, poor schools, need for social services, and need for more jobs). The capacity of lower-class African Americans and lower-class whites to form a united constituency has not been analyzed thoroughly, but one study of voting patterns in the South between 1960 and 1977 suggests that such alliances are very difficult to forge. In partisan elections, lower-income whites had a fairly strong tendency to support the same candidates as those supported by African Americans—so long as the candidates were white.

But this support dissipated when the candidate was African American or when elections were nonpartisan.[125]

A more successful voting alliance for African Americans has been with white liberals. In Berkeley, California, for example, a sizable African American middle class coalesced with liberal academic whites to get African American representation on the city council.[126] The most successful citywide African American candidates have retained the loyalty of a small minority of whites while getting an extraordinary turnout of African Americans. In the 1977 election of Ernest N. Morial as the first African American mayor of New Orleans, for example, Morial received only 19 percent of the white vote but 95 percent of the African American vote; three-quarters of the city's eligible African American voters turned out.[127] In Richard Arrington's election as the first African American mayor of Birmingham, Alabama, in 1979, Arrington also won only 10 to 15 percent of the white vote but was aided by a large African American voter turnout.[128] The same pattern held for more recent African American mayors elected for the first time. Philadelphia's W. Wilson Goode won about 20 percent of that city's white vote but an estimated 97 percent of the African American vote in 1983.[129] Chicago's Harold Washington won few white votes but an estimated 97 percent of the African American vote in 1983.[130] Both men were aided by extraordinary turnouts of African American voters—over 95 percent in Philadelphia and 82 percent in Chicago. Of all the big-city African American mayors, only Los Angeles's Thomas Bradley won a majority of white votes in his initial election to the office in 1973.

A third possible voting alliance for African Americans is with Hispanics. An important example of an African American–Hispanic coalition emerged in Chicago, where Mayor Harold Washington won an estimated 57 percent of the Hispanic vote in 1987[131] and relied on Hispanic support to gain control of the city council.[132] We also saw that Hispanic mayors Henry Cisneros in San Antonio and Federico Peña in Denver were able to draw African Americans as well as Hispanics into their alliances with white liberals. But in most cities, African Americans and Hispanics do not coalesce easily into a unified voting bloc. Houston mayor Kathy Whitmire was supported by a majority of African Americans in her 1983 election but was opposed by a majority of Mexican Americans. Former New York mayor Edward Koch enjoyed warm support from Puerto Rican leaders but encountered coolness from African American leaders. A number of California cities have both African American and Hispanic populations, and in a few of these cities, such as Sacramento, African American–Hispanic coalitions did emerge. But the preeminent analysis of minority-group politics in northern California describes African American–Hispanic alliances as difficult to achieve.[133] Across the continent, in Miami, black-Cuban relations are openly hostile.

If African American leaders face innumerable problems in building a rainbow coalition, can the same be said of Hispanic leaders? On the face of it, urban Hispanics could logically ally themselves with several other disadvantaged groups in the city—principally American Indians, African Americans, and lower-class whites. Garcia and de la Garza think that racial and cultural differences preclude a successful coalition with lower-class whites.[134] They do point out, however, that some successful alliances have been made between American Indians and African Americans. As we discussed earlier, however, several pitfalls hinder African American–Hispanic alliances, despite the fact that both groups suffer from similar economic and discriminatory handicaps.

Ironically, Hispanics' most successful political alliances have been with upper- and upper-middle-class whites, who provided considerable financing and support for the UFW's struggle with the Teamsters and various agricultural landowners in California.

Los Angeles illustrates the difficulties of forging a durable rainbow coalition. African Americans lost the mayoralty after Tom Bradley (1973–1993) stepped down. No one has been able to rebuild his coalition. Certainly the 1992 riot played a role in driving a wedge between members of Bradley's coalition. However, blacks are becoming a smaller group in the wake of suburbanization and the growth of the Hispanic population. Even Watts, the notorious black ghetto, is now majority Latino. In addition, Asians have been greatly increasing in population. As more Latinos gain citizenship, they seek to replace blacks in elected office. Rather than form coalitions, black leaders have been resisting Latino efforts to gain more benefits from control of local government.[135]

Bias in Contemporary City Politics

In the arena of city politics, the newer urban minorities (especially African Americans and Hispanics) possess strengths in the new century that they lacked in earlier decades. Their greatest assets are their large share of the urban population and the growing number of middle-class minorities who have the economic resources and social know-how to influence local politics. These assets, combined with the politically important development of a sense of cultural uniqueness (African American and Hispanic pride), facilitate a race- and ethnic-based voting pattern that has elevated increasing numbers of African Americans and Hispanics to positions of political influence in urban America. Furthermore, a number of outside political forces benefited African American and Hispanic causes. The federal government's espousal of affirmative action, for example, worked hand in hand with minority demands for better job opportunities.

Despite these strengths, the non-middle-class portions of minority communities still face definite biases in the urban political system. Three kinds of biases have been identified in this chapter. First, several internal aspects of the minority communities work to the disadvantage of the lower-class and working-class portions of those communities. These groups largely lack the extensive personal resources (such as money, self-esteem, confidence, and leisure time) that are so important in politics.[136] Further, they have high transiency levels that hinder long-term political allegiances. Welfare families are often relocated around the city, breaking up political communication networks. Competent and upwardly mobile minorities get co-opted into managerial positions with established institutions, which drains off the lower class's ability to maintain internal leadership.

If the first bias stems from the internal social structure of the minority communities, a second bias stems from the political and governmental reforms discussed in Chapter 4—especially at-large elections, nonpartisan elections, civil service hiring procedures, and racially motivated boundary changes. Although none of these procedures has eliminated minority influence in local politics, the general conclusion of the empirical research on this question is that such reform dilutes minority influence.

A third bias of contemporary urban politics stems from the inability of low-income minorities and low-income whites to establish political coalitions. This is the missing element of the rainbow coalition. In South Boston, for example, low-income whites and

African Americans found themselves in disastrous competition for public housing, neighborhood development funds, government jobs, and public school resources. Although those lower-income whites have predominantly been portrayed as implacably racist, one sympathetic article argues that they, more than any other group of whites in Boston, have borne the major costs of desegregation.[137] As long as low-income whites stay out of a city's attempted rainbow coalition, the dominant alliance will usually be one between middle-class minorities, liberal middle-class whites, and upper-income business interests. If someday a political genius figures out how to bridge the huge cultural gap between lower-income whites and lower-income minorities, there will be a major upheaval in the tone of city politics.

The structure of city government does not facilitate upward mobility for African Americans and Hispanics nearly as much as it did a century ago for European immigrants. Newer minority groups have been less able to use the city government for social and economic advancement, and, as we have seen, they have not had the same success in creating institutions that bind them together internally or in coalitions. The political machine is no longer available or open to the new minorities, and they have failed to create alternative institutions. As William Nelson points out,

> In contrast to the European ethnic incorporation pattern, the election of black politicians to high public office has not led to effective black penetration of other sectors of the economic and political system. Blacks have not used their control over mayorships to substantially infiltrate existing party structures, or to build permanent independent organizations of their own.[138]

This would apply to Hispanics as well.

Finally, even if a true rainbow coalition of lower-status city dwellers does emerge, they may still face enormous obstacles in using politics to improve their economic well-being. These obstacles stem from the economic and fiscal conditions of the cities in the twenty-first century. Does the city still offer the same economic opportunities to unskilled laborers that it did a century ago? Career-ladder positions now inevitably require some schooling or training. There are fewer unskilled-labor jobs in industrial factories than there were a generation ago. The most dynamic growth areas of the metropolitan economies are on the suburban fringes. The inner-city minorities no longer live where job opportunities are rapidly expanding. This was not true a century ago, when inner-city job opportunities were expanding rapidly and were within easy commuting distance of the poorest neighborhoods. Finally, does the fiscal condition of many cities enable them to expand their workforces and function as employers for lower-income populations, as the political machines did a century ago? These questions about the economic and fiscal abilities of the city to perform its historical role as an arena of social mobility are so important that we will devote all of the next chapter to them.

SUMMARY

1. As a result of African American and Hispanic migration into the cities, the white population is becoming a minority in most big cities. The new urban minorities initially brought to urban politics a tone infused with militant rhetoric. It has

not fit very well into the mold of machine politics, and the old political machines have not met the needs of these new minorities.

2. African American urban politics has shifted away from emphasis on the struggle for civil rights that characterized African American politics before and during the 1960s. In the new century, African American urban politics is focusing on gaining or holding representation in city government, increasing job and economic opportunities, trying to reverse the deterioration of the city, and trying to target the city's resources more directly at the social problems of minority populations. African American mayors have had some limited success with a dual strategy of encouraging business investment to increase jobs in the private sector and using affirmative action strategies to increase job opportunities for African Americans in the public sector.

3. Hispanic politics strives to frame electoral strategies and mold political coalitions to maximize Hispanic influence. San Antonio serves as an example of Mexican Americans seeking political control through conventional means and using that control to promote economic development. Key issues for Mexican Americans involve bilingualism, immigration, and jobs. Cubans dominate Miami, are much more economically successful than other Hispanics, and are much more conservative.

4. Asians constitute the largest block of legal immigrants today. They are more successful economically and are less segregated than African Americans or Hispanics.

5. Despite the appeal of a rainbow coalition among lower-income racial minorities, several obstacles stand in the way of such a coalition materializing.

6. Four patterns of bias affect today's urban politics. First, several internal aspects of African American and Hispanic politics reduce their potential political influence. Second, the reform-style politics discussed in Chapter 4 inhibit the political influence of African Americans and Hispanics. Third, lower-income whites are usually absent from rainbow coalitions, leaving the coalitions dominated by upper-middle-class and business-community leaders. Fourth, there are limits to the socioeconomic advancement that can be achieved through political power.

NOTES

1. The Brookings Institution Center on Urban and Metropolitan Policy, "Racial Change in the Nation's Largest Cities," http://www.brook.edu.
2. William H. Frey, "Melting Pot Suburbs: A Census 2000 Study of Suburban Diversity." Washington, D.C.: The Brookings Institution (June 2001), pp. 1–2, 5.
3. Douglas S. Massey and Nancy A. Denton, "Hyper-Segregation in U.S. Metropolitan Areas: Black and Hispanic Segregation Along Four Dimensions," Demography 26, no. 3 (August 1989): 373–391; Edward L. Glaeser and Jacob L. Vigdor, "Racial Segregation in the 2000 Census: Promising News," The Brookings Institution, Survey Series (April 2001), p. 3.
4. John R. Logan, "Choosing Segregation: Racial Imbalance in American Public Schools, 1990–2000, Lewis Mumford Center for Comparative Urban and Regional Research, January 18, 2002.
5. Edward L. Glaeser and Jacob L. Vigdor, "Racial Segregation in the 2000 Census: Promising News," The Brookings Institution, Survey Series (April 2001), http://www.brook.edu/urban/mediaalerts/glaeserrelease.htm.
6. Report by the Lewis Mumford Center, "Ethnic Diversity Grows, Neighborhood Integration Lags Behind," (April 3, 2001, revised December 18, 2001), p. 1.
7. Ibid.

8. Ibid., "The New Ethnic Enclaves in America's Suburbs."

9. William Julius Wilson, *The Truly Disadvantaged* (Chicago: University of Chicago Press, 1987); Elijah Anderson, *Streetwise* (Chicago: University of Chicago Press, 1990). See Spencer Rich's interview with Douglas S. Massey in "Our Very Segregated Cities," *Washington Post National Weekly*, August 28–September 30, 1989, p. 37.

10. William K. Tabb, *The Political Economy of the Black Ghetto* (New York: Norton, 1970), pp. 22–23.

11. Robert C. Smith, "The Changing Shape of Urban Black Politics: 1960–1970," *Annals of the American Academy of Political and Social Science* 439 (September 1978): 24.

12. Howard Brotz, ed., *Negro Social and Political Thought, 1850–1950* (New York: Basic Books, 1966), p. 359.

13. Milton D. Morris, *The Politics of Black America* (New York: Harper & Row, 1975), pp. 215–220.

14. *Brown v. Board of Education of Topeka, Kansas,* 347 U.S. 483 (1954).

15. For a summary and critique of the internal colonialism argument, see Robert Blauner, "Internal Colonialism and Ghetto Revolt," *Social Problems* 16, no. 4 (Spring 1969): 393–408.

16. Carmichael's ideas are discussed in Stokely Carmichael and Charles V. Hamilton, *Black Power* (New York: Random House, 1967).

17. Bryan T. Downes, "A Critical Reexamination of the Social and Political Characteristics of Riot Cities," *Social Science Quarterly* 51, no. 2 (September 1970): 349–360.

18. Joe R. Feagin and Harlan Hahn, *Ghetto Revolts: The Politics of Violence in American Cities* (New York: Macmillan, 1965), p. 105.

19. See Milton D. Morris, *The Politics of Black America* (New York: Harper & Row, 1975), p. 229.

20. This was in essence the conclusion of the National Advisory Commission on Civil Disorders, *Report of the National Advisory Commission on Civil Disorders* (Washington, D.C.: U.S. Government Printing Office, 1968).

21. Blauner, "Internal Colonialism and Ghetto Revolt."

22. Feagin and Hahn, *Ghetto Revolts,* pp. 122, 127, 132.

23. Ibid., p. 146.

24. James David Greenstone and Paul E. Peterson, "Reformers, Machines, and the War on Poverty," in *City Politics and Public Policy,* ed. James Q. Wilson (New York: Wiley, 1968), pp. 286–289.

25. *New York Times,* August 12, 1985, p. 1.

26. Susan Welch, "The Impact of Urban Riots on Urban Expenditures," *American Journal of Political Science* 19, no. 4 (November 1975): 741–760.

27. See *New York Times,* February 18, 1983, p. 8; and *Newsweek,* January 10, 1983, p. 23; Bruce Porter and Marvin Dunn, *The Miami Riot of 1980* (Lexington, Mass.: Lexington Books, 1984); Ronald K. Vogel and Genie N. L. Stowers, "Miami: Minority Empowerment and Regime Change" in H. V. Savitch and John Clayton Thomas, *Big City Politics in Transition* (Thousand Oaks, Calif.: Sage, 1991).

28. Mark Baldassare, "Introduction" in *The Los Angeles Riots: Lessons for the Future,* ed. Mark Baldassare, (Boulder, Colo.: Westview Press, 1994), p. 3.

29. Michelle Cottle, "Boomerang: Did Integration Cause the Cincinnati Riots? *New Republic,* May 7, 2001, *Economist,* April 21, 2001, p. 25.

30. John Leo, "Cincinnati Cops Out" *U.S. News & World Report,* July 7, 2001, p. 10.

31. National Report, "What Can Cities Do to Ease Racial Tension?" *Jet.*

32. Kevin Osborne, "City to Fight Boycott with Ads?" February 12, 2002.

33. Ibid.

34. See Kenneth Clark, "The NAACP: Verging on Irrelevance," *New York Times,* July 14, 1983, p. 23

35. U.S. Bureau of the Census, *Statistical Abstract of the United States, 2001,* Table 399 [http://www.census.gov]; National Conference of Black Mayors, http://www.blackmayors.org/members/members.html.

36. *Gomillion v. Lightfoot,* 81 S.Ct. 125 (1960).

37. Lee Sloan, "Good Government and the Politics of Race," *Social Problems* 17 (Fall 1969): 161–175.

38. Leonard A. Cole, "Electing Blacks to Municipal Office: Structural and Social Determinants," *Urban Affairs Quarterly* 10, no. 1 (September 1974): 17–39.

39. See especially Susan MacManus, "City Council Procedures and Minority Representation: Are They Related?" *Social Science Quarterly* 59, no. 1 (June 1978): 153–161.

40. Ibid.

41. Albert Karnig, "Black Representation on City Councils: The Impact of District Elections and Socioeconomic Factors," *Urban Affairs Quarterly* 12, no. 2 (December 1976): 223–242.

42. Chandler Davidson and George Korbel, "At-Large Elections and Minority Group Representation: A Re-examination of Historical and Contemporary Evidence," *Journal of Politics* 43, no. 4 (November 1981): 982–1005. Also in support of the thesis that at-large elections diluted the African American vote were Clinton B. Jones, "The Impact of Local Election Systems on Black Political Representation," *Urban Affairs Quarterly* 11, no. 2 (March 1976): 345–356; Margaret K. Latimer, "Black Political Representation in Southern Cities: Election Systems and Their Causal Variables," *Urban Affairs Quarterly* 15, no. 1 (September 1979): 65–86; Theodore P. Robinson and Thomas R. Dye, "Reformism and Black Representation on City Councils," *Social Science Quarterly* 59, no. 1 (June 1978): 133–141; and Delbert Taebel, "Minority Representation on City Councils: The Impact of Structure on Blacks and Hispanics," *Social Science Quarterly* 59, no. 1 (June 1978): 142–152.

43. Richard L. Engstrom and Michael D. McDonald, "The Election of Blacks to City Councils: Clarifying the Impact of Electoral Arrangements on the Seats/Population Relationship," *American Political Science Review* 75, no. 2 (June 1981): 344–354.

44. *City of Richmond v. U.S.,* 442 U.S. 358 (1975). See Thomas P. Murphy, "Race-Based Accounting: Assigning the Costs and Benefits of a Racially Motivated Annexation," *Urban Affairs Quarterly* 14, no. 2 (December 1978): 169–194.

45. *New York Times,* March 28, 1979, p. 1.

46. *City of Mobile v. Bolden,* 446 U.S. 55 (1980). Although Mobile has not yet been forced to abandon its at-large system, the Supreme Court in 1982 did establish a precedent that may lead to Mobile's undoing. An at-large county commission in Burke County, Georgia, was forced to establish wards when the Supreme Court ruled that its at-large system was being *maintained* for the purpose of preventing representation of the county's African Americans (about half the county population). Because this situation is so similar to Mobile's, it suggests that Mobile's at-large council may eventually be struck down. *Rogers v. Lodge,* 102 S.Ct. 3272 (1982). See *New York Times,* July 2, 1982, p. 9.

47. *City of Port Arthur v. United States,* 103 S.Ct. 530 (1982).

48. *New York Times,* January 9, 1980, p. A-14; January 21, 1980, p. A-12.

49. Charles S. Bullock III, "Symbolics or Substance: A Critique of the At-Large Election Controversy," *State and Local Government Review* 21, no. 3 (Fall 1989): 91–99.

50. Lana Stein, "Equal Opportunity in the City" in *Handbook of Research on Urban Politics and Policy,* ed. Ronald K. Vogel (Westport, Conn.: Greenwood Press, 1997), pp. 372–373.

51. Susan Welch, "The Impact of At-Large Elections on the Representation of Blacks and Hispanics," *Journal of Politics* 52, no. 4 (November 1990): 1050–1076.

52. Congressional Quarterly Weekly Report, May 4, 1991, pp. 1104–1105.

53. Kimball Brace, Bernard N. Grofman, Lisa R. Handley, and Richard G. Niemi, "Minority Voting Equality: The 65 Percent Rule in Theory and Practice," *Law & Policy* 10, no. 1 (January 1988): 43–63.

54. Ibid.

55. *Shaw v. Reno,* 113 S.Ct. (1993); *Miller v. Johnson,* 63 LW (1995). See Michael Pagano and Ann Bowman, "The State of American Federalism, 1994–1995" *Publius* (Summer 1994): 15–16; Mark Rush, "From *Shaw v. Reno* to *Miller v. Johnson:* Minority Representation and State Compliance with the Voting Rights Act" *Publius* 25, no. 3 (Summer 1995): 155–172.

56. Rufus P. Browning, Dale R. Marshall, and David H. Tabb, *Protest Is Not Enough* (Berkeley: University of California Press, 1984); Rufus P. Browning, Dale Rogers Marshall, and David H. Tabb, "Mobilization, Incorporation, and Policy: Ten California Cities Revisited," paper presented at the American Political Science Association, 1995. In this paper, the authors slightly changed the labels, dropping the term *co-optation* because they believed it was misinterpreted as "wholly manipulative and destructive of minority mobilization and power, which was not what we mean at all" (pp. 3–4).

57. Ibid.

58. James W. Button, *Blacks and Social Change: Impact of the Civil Rights Movement in Southern Communities* (Princeton, N.J.: Princeton University Press, 1989).

59. Peter K. Eisinger, "Black Mayors and the Politics of Racial Economic Advancement," in *Culture, Ethnicity, and Identity,* ed. William C. McReady (New York: Academic, 1983), pp. 95–109.

60. Albert K. Karnig and Susan Welch, *Black Representation and Urban Policy* (Chicago: University of Chicago Press, 1980), pp. 122–128, 141.

61. John Pelissero, David Holian, and Laura Tomaka, "Does Political Incorporation Matter?" *Urban Affairs Review* 36 (September 2000): 84–93.

62. Eisinger, "Black Mayors and the Politics of Racial Economic Advancement," p. 106.

63. Ibid., pp. 105–198.

64. V. O. Key, *Southern Politics* (New York: Vintage, 1949).

65. Eisinger, "Black Mayors and the Politics of Racial Economic Advancement," p. 106.

66. Peter K. Eisinger, "Black Employment in Municipal Jobs: The Impact of Black Political Power," *American Political Science Review* 76, no. 2 (June 1982): 380–392.

67. Peter K. Eisinger, "The Economic Conditions of Black Employment in Municipal Bureaucracies," *American Journal of Political Science* 26, no. 4 (November 1982): 754–771.

68. Edmond J. Keller, "The Impact of Black Mayors on Urban Policy," *Annals of the American Academy of Political and Social Science* 439 (November 1978): p. 51.

69. Ibid.

70. William E. Nelson, Jr., "Cleveland: The Rise and Fall of the New Black Politics," in *The New Black Politics: The Search for Political Power,* ed. Michael B. Preston, Lenneal J. Henderson, Jr., and Paul Puryear (New York: Longman, 1982), pp. 187–208.

71. Clarence N. Stone has developed this theme in his carefully researched studies of Atlanta. For a synopsis of his thesis, see his "Race and Regime in Atlanta," *Racial Politics in American Cities,* ed. Rufus P. Browning, Dale Rogers Marshall, and David H. Tabb (New York: Longman, 1990), pp. 125–139. See also William E. Nelson, Jr., "Black Mayoral Leadership: A Twenty-Year Perspective" *National Political Science Review* 2 (1990): 188–195.

72. J. Phillip Thompson III, *Double Trouble: Black Mayors and Social Change* (New York: Oxford University Press, 2006), p. 6.

73. Ibid., p. 10.

74. David Imbroscio, "Structure, Agency, and Democratic Theory," *Polity* 32, no. 1 (Fall 1999): 45–66.

75. Joseph P. Fitzpatrick and Lourdes Travieso Parker, "Hispanic Americans in the Eastern United States," *Annals of the American Academy of Political and Social Science* 454 (March 1981): 99. For a graphic discussion of the question of color for Puerto Ricans, see Piri Thomas, *Down These Mean Streets* (New York: Knopf, 1967).

76. Harry P. Pachan and Joan W. Moore, "Mexican Americans," *Annals of the American Academy of Political and Social Science* 454 (March 1981): 114.

77. Leo Grebler, Joan W. Moore, and Ralph C. Guzman, *The Mexican-American People: The Nation's Second Largest Minority* (New York: Free Press, 1970), pp. 521–522.

78. Ibid., pp. 524–525.

79. Walter Prescott Webb, *The Texas Rangers: A Century of Frontier Defense* (Boston: Houghton Mifflin, 1935), pp. 479, 486.

80. Grebler et al., *The Mexican-American People*, p. 528.

81. *New York Times,* July 17, 1978, p. A-8.

82. F. Chris Garcia and Rudolph O. de la Garza, *The Chicano Political Experience: Three Perspectives* (North Scituate, Mass.: Duxbury Press, 1977), p. 15.

83. A 1976 survey of Mexican Americans found that 50 percent preferred the term *Mexican American* to refer to themselves, 20 percent preferred the term *Mexican,* and only 4 percent preferred the term *Chicano.* John A. Garcia, "Yo Soy Mexicano . . . : Self-Identity and Sociodemographic Correlates," *Social Science Quarterly* 62, no. 1 (March 1981): 90.

84. Ignacio M. Garcia, *United We Win: The Rise and Fall of La Raza Unida Party* (Tucson: University of Arizona, Mexican-American Studies and Research Center, 1989), p. 232.

85. Garcia and de la Garza, *The Chicano Political Experience,* p. 38.

86. Juan Gomez-Quinones, *Chicano Politics: Reality and Promise, 1940–1990* (Albuquerque: University of New Mexico Press, 1990), pp. 105–107, 137–139.

87. *New York Times,* September 15, 1985, p. 43.

88. Garcia and de la Garza, *The Chicano Political Experience,* p. 82.

89. Gomez-Quinones, *Chicano Politics,* pp. 137–139.

90. Garcia, *United We Win,* p. 232.

91. Massey and Denton, "Hyper-Segregation in U.S. Metropolitan Areas," pp. 373–391.

92. Tucker Gibson, "Mayoralty Politics in San Antonio, 1955–1979," in *The Politics of San Antonio: Community Progress and Power,* ed. David R. Johnson, John A. Booth, and Richard J. Harris (Lincoln, Nebr.: University of Nebraska Press, 1983), p. 116.

93. Charles L. Cotrell and R. Michael Stevens, "The 1975 Voting Rights Act and San Antonio, Texas: Toward Federal Guarantee of a Republican Form of Government," *Publius* 8, no. 1 (Winter 1978): 79–100.

94. Neal R. Peirce and Jerry Hagstrom, "San Antonio's Mexican-American Mayor Seeks New Agenda for Minorities, Poor," *National Journal* 14, no. 42 (October 16, 1982): 1758–1759.

95. John A. Booth, "Political Change in San Antonio, 1970–82: Toward Decay or Democracy," in *The Politics of San Antonio*, pp. 209–211.

96. Henry Flores, "Structural Barriers to Chicano Empowerment," in *Latino Empowerment: Progress, Problems, and Prospects,* ed. Roberto E. Villarreal, Norma G. Hernandez, and Howard D. Neighbor (New York: Greenwood Press, 1988), p. 34.

97. Browning, Marshall, and Tabb, *Protest Is Not Enough.*

98. Rodney E. Hero, "Hispanics in Urban Government and Politics: Some Findings, Comparisons, and Implications," *Western Political Quarterly* 43, no. 2 (June 1990): 403–414; "The Election of Hispanics in City Government: An Examination of the Election of Federico Pena as Mayor of Denver," *Western Political Quarterly* 40, no. 1 (March 1987): 93–106.

99. Raphael J. Sonenshein and Susan H. Pinkus, "The Dynamics of Latino Political Incorporation: The 2001 Los Angels Mayoral Election as Seen in Los Angeles Times Exit Polls," *PS* (March 2002), 67–74.

100. Karen M. Kaufmann, *The Urban Voter* (Ann Arbor: University of Michigan Press, 2004), pp. 94–102.

101. S. B. Jeffe, "Southern Exposure," *California Journal,* 33, no. 3 (March 1, 2002); L. Mecoy, "Mayor James Hahn's L.A. Story," *California Journal*, 32, no. 7 (July 1, 2002): 32.

102. "Los Angeles Mayoral Race," *Economist* 371, no. 8371 (April 17, 2004): 30.

103. M. Finnegan, "Driven by Events, Hahn Turns to a Familiar Bloc," *Los Angeles Times,* February. 22, 2005.

104. Ibid.

105. See Stuart Taylor, Jr., "Rising Voice of Cuban-Americans," *New York Times,* March 7, 1984, p. 20; Bernard Weinraub, "Wooing Cuban-Americans in G.O.P.," *New York Times,* May 22, 1987, p. 8; Joan Didion, "Miami: La Lucha," *New York Review of Books* 34, no. 10 (June 11, 1987): 15; and David Rieff, "The Second Havana," *New Yorker* 63 (May 1987): 65–83.

106. See "Miami: America's Casablanca," *Newsweek,* January 25, 1988, 22–29.

107. Browning, Marshall, and Tabb, *Protest Is Not Enough.*

108. Ronald K. Vogel and Genie N. L. Stowers, "Miami: Minority Empowerment and Regime Change" in H. V. Savitch and John Clayton Thomas, *Big Cities in Transition* (Thousand Oaks, Calif.: Sage), p. 119.

109. Robyne S. Turner, "Tropical Heat: Lessons in Miami Politics," *Urban News* 12, no. 1 (Spring 1998): 1–2, 4–11.

110. Oscar Corral, "Learning to Be Mayor," *Miami Herald,* November 25, 2001; *Economist,* "Joe Carollo, Still Crazy," May 13, 2000, p. 32; Janet Ward, "City's Local Leaders Are Not Exactly *Miami* Nice," *American City & County* 114 (11) (September 1999): 6.

111. *Wall Street Journal,* October 15, 1985, p. 64; *New York Times,* November 7, 1985, p. 1. On the 1987 runoff, see *New York Times,* November 12, 1987, p. 11.

112. Morrison G. Wong, "Post-1965 Immigrants: Demographic and Socioeconomic Profile," in *Urban Ethnicity in the United States: New Immigrants and Old Minorities,* vol. 29, *Urban Affairs Annual Reviews,* ed. Lionel Maldonado and Joan Moore (Beverly Hills, Calif.: Sage, 1985), p. 69.

113. Philip Garcia, "Immigration Issues in Urban Ecology: The Case of Los Angeles," in *Urban Ethnicity in the United States: New Immigrants and Old Minorities,* vol. 29, pp. 84–86.

114. U.S. Department of Justice, Immigration and Naturalization Services, Office of Policy and Planning, Annual Report, *Legal Immigration, Fiscal Year 2000,* pp. 56, 59.

115. *Minneapolis Star and Tribune,* February 8, 1987; Ronald K. Vogel and Genie N. L. Stowers, "Miami: Minority Empowerment and Regime Change."

116. *Christian Science Monitor,* January 8, 1982, p. 1.

117. *New York Times,* December 1, 1988, p. 9; Alvar Carlson, "America's New Immigration: Characteristics, Destinations, and Impact, 1970–1989," *Social Science Journal* 31 (1994): 213–236.

118. This argument is stated by former Colorado governor Richard D. Lamm, who wrote, "I do not believe that massive immigration is the only cause of unemployment or poverty, but I know it is a significant cause of them. I do not think we can cure the ills of unemployment by eliminating illegal immigration, but I know that allowing it to continue certainly makes unemployment worse." See Richard D. Lamm and Gary Imhoff, *The Immigration Time Bomb* (New York: Dutton, 1985), p. 155.

119. A 1980 survey of 200 Hispanic registered voters in Houston, for example, found that 56 percent approved of tuition-free schooling for undocumented aliens and 44 percent disapproved. Leon F. Bouvier and Robert W. Gardner, "Immigration to the U.S.: The Unfinished Story," *Population Bulletin* 41, no. 4 (November 1986): 13–18; Susan A. MacManus and Carol A. Cassel, "Mexican-Americans in City Politics: Participation, Representation and Policy Preferences," *Urban Interest* 4, no. 1 (Spring 1982): 66.

120. See Julian L. Simon, *The Economic Consequences of Immigration* (New York: Blackwell, 1989). Also see his op-ed article in the *Wall Street Journal,* January 26, 1990, p. 12.

121. See Ricardo R. Fernandez and William Velez, "Race, Color, and Language in the Changing Public Schools," in *Urban Ethnicity in the United States: New Immigrants and Old Minorities,* vol. 29, p. 132.

122. *New York Times,* February 8, 1990, p. A-1.

123. This charge is exemplified by a *Wall Street Journal* editorial of June 12, 1987, which claimed that restrictions on immigration begun in 1987 would cause one-third of Oregon's strawberry crop to rot because there would not be enough pickers.

124. These generalizations are taken from Bouvier and Gardner, "Immigration to the U.S.," pp. 28–32.

125. Richard Murray and Arnold Vedlitz, "Racial Voting Patterns in the South: An Analysis of Major Elections from 1960 to 1977 in Five Cities," *Annals of the American Academy of Political and Social Science* 439 (September 1978): 29–39.

126. Browning, Marshall, and Tabb, *Protest Is Not Enough*, pp. 46–53.

127. Alvin J. Schexnider, "Political Mobilization in the South: The Election of a Black Mayor in New Orleans," *New Black Politics*, pp. 221–237.

128. *Focus* 7, no. 11 (November 1979).

129. *New York Times*, January 5, 1984, p. 9; November 10, 1983, p. 17.

130. Michael B. Preston, "The Election of Harold Washington: Black Voting Patterns in the 1983 Chicago Mayoral Race," *PS* 16, no. 3 (Summer 1983): 486–488.

131. *New York Times*, April 9, 1987, p. 11.

132. Paul Green, "The Message from the 26th Ward," *Comparative State Politics Newsletter* VII, no. 4 (August 1986): 16.

133. Browning, Marshall, and Tabb, *Protest Is Not Enough*, pp. 121–124.

134. Garcia and de la Garza, *The Chicano Political Experience*, p. 130.

135. Daniel Wood, "New Diversity Meets First Big Political Test," *Christian Science Monitor,* April 9, 2001. "The Fading of Black Power," *Economist*, May 16, 1998, p. 27.

136. Harold V. Savitch, "Powerlessness in an Urban Ghetto: The Case of Political Biases and Differential Access in New York City," *Polity* 5, no. 1 (Fall 1972): 19–56.

137. David R. Novack, "Forced Busing in South Boston: Class, Race, and Power," *Journal of Urban Affairs* 9, no. 3 (1987): 277–292.

138. William E. Nelson, Jr., "Black Mayoral Leadership: Twenty-Year Perspective" *Enduring Tensions in Urban Politics,* ed. Dennis Judd and Paul Kantor (New York: Macmillan, 1992), p. 455.

CHAPTER 6

THE CITY AS A PLACE OF OPPORTUNITY: THE CHANGING URBAN POLITICAL ECONOMY

CHAPTER SYNOPSIS

Economic Restructuring and Cities: *Shift from Industrial to Service-Based Economy; Globalization and Cities; Rising Inequality; Declining Poverty* • Inner-City Poverty: *Increasing Ghetto Poverty; The Bipolar City; Central-City and Suburban Disparities* • An Urban Renaissance? *Revived Downtowns? Urban Neighborhoods—Some Renewed Vitality?* • Urban Economic Development Strategies: *Redeveloping the Physical City; Business Climate; Incentives for Economic Development; Assessing Urban Development Strategies*

As earlier chapters have documented, nineteenth- and early-twentieth-century European immigrants found the American city a useful place for gaining political influence and economic advancement. In today's American cities those ethnic groups have been succeeded to a great extent by African Americans, Hispanics, and Asians. Chapter 5 described how African Americans and Hispanics have begun to use their growing numbers to gain city council seats, mayoral office, and other positions of political influence. On the face of it, this suggests that the process of ethnic succession is working for today's urban minorities just as it worked for the European ethnics a century ago. At least the process of ethnic succession seems to be working in the urban political sphere.

Whether the process of ethnic succession is also working in the economic sphere raises a very important question. As we enter the twenty-first century, is the American city still a place of opportunity for its poorest residents, its minorities, and its most recent in-migrants?

This chapter addresses that question by focusing on four major changes that took place in the political economy of American cities in the latter part of the twentieth century:

- The shift from an industrial economy to a postindustrial economy.
- A large underclass in central cities and high disparities between the central cities and the suburbs.
- An urban renaissance that has seen the rebuilding of many downtowns.
- Increasing reliance on economic and urban development strategies to improve the economic and fiscal position of the city.

The Changing Economic Climate of Urban America

To appreciate how the prospects for African American and Hispanic upward mobility differ from those of the European ethnics a century ago, we must first examine three broad trends taking place in the American economy:

The transformation from an industrial to a postindustrial economy.

The rise of globalization and the global city stemming from the increased flow of goods, services, and ideas across and between cities, nations, and corporations.

The changing class structure of American society.

From Industrial to Postindustrial Economy

American cities grew up in an industrial era, roughly from the late 1800s to the end of World War II. During this time, cities were built to meet the needs of industrial production. Industrial production was centered in the cities because that is where the labor force and infrastructure (transportation, communication, and support services) to produce and transport material goods were located. In the United States, the most important cities were the industrial cities of the Northeast and Midwest. Cities were associated with the particular goods or segment of the economy they served. For example, Pittsburgh produced steel, and Detroit was the center of auto production.

National and international commerce required efficient transportation routes. Prior to the proliferation of the automobile and the building of the interstate highway system in the 1950s, goods were shipped along rail lines and waterways. Factories had to be near ports and railways to receive raw materials and transport finished goods to their final destinations. This meant that cities were also important as commercial and trade centers, because they housed most of the nation's population and were connected by rail and air transport for efficient shipment and distribution of goods.

The economy has shifted in recent decades from an industrial-based economy to a service-based economy. That is, the main economic function is now the "processing of information and knowledge" instead of the manufacture of raw materials into finished goods. Cities are now in a postindustrial era.[1] White-collar employment (managerial functions, technical services, and professions) are more important than blue-collar work (manual labor) in this new postindustrial economy. The shift to a postindustrial economy, with the accompanying loss of manufacturing jobs, had a devastating impact on many central cities, especially those in the Northeast and Midwest. This deindustrialization process has reached the point where manufacturing constitutes only a small part of total city employment.

Even in a postindustrial economy, manufacturing is still important. Indeed, in some cities, the number of jobs in manufacturing is increasing (see Figure 6.1). The most dynamically growing parts of the manufacturing sector have been manufacturing of high-technology products such as computers, lasers, and sophisticated medical equipment. Growth in manufacturing jobs in San Jose is clearly indicative of these types of industries. These are among what economist Lester C. Thurow calls the "sunrise industries,"[2]

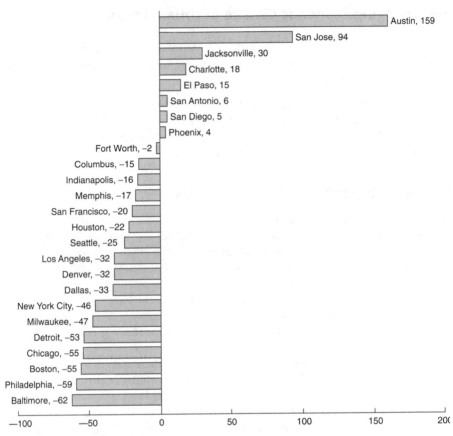

FIGURE 6.1   Percent Change in Manufacturing Jobs, 1980–2000
Source: State of the Cities Data Systems (SOCDS).
Link: http://socds.huduser.org/Census/Census_Home.html.

those whose day in the sun is just beginning. In contrast are radio and television manufacturing and the old, heavy-industry manufacturing of steel and automobiles. These "sunset industries" have been badly damaged by foreign competition and have lost a considerable portion of their share of the market.

In a dynamic economy, jobs are always disappearing and new jobs are being created to replace them, so on the face of it, that sunrise industries are replacing the sunset industries should not cause much alarm. But two important questions about the current process of job loss and job creation are relevant to urban America.

First, are the new jobs in the sunrise industries and the service sector as plentiful and as lucrative as the disappearing jobs in the sunset industries (with corresponding requirements in terms of education and skill levels)? There were about 2 million fewer jobs in manufacturing production in the United States in 2000 than in 1990. In the same time frame, the number of non-retail service jobs exploded, with an increase of close to 21 million new jobs, and the number of retail sales jobs jumped by just over

6 million.[3] About 5.3 million workers "lost or left a job between January 2001 and December 2003 because of plant closings or moves, slack work, or the abolishment of their positions."[4]

Many of the newly created service jobs pay less and provide fewer hours of work than the manufacturing jobs that are disappearing. The Bureau of Labor Statistics estimated that in 2004 the average manufacturing worker earned $659 per week, whereas the retail trade worker earned only $371 per week. On the other hand, the professional and technical service worker earned $828 per week.[5] However, these jobs require high levels of education and training that most factory workers would not be qualified for. In short, on the average, the jobs that are disappearing pay much better than the jobs that are being created.

The second question about the dynamics of the relationship between jobs lost and jobs created is whether the new jobs are being created in the places where the old jobs are being lost. And the answer is no, not for the most part. With a few significant exceptions, most industrial job losses are occurring in the belt of northern industrial cities stretching from the Hudson River on the east to the Mississippi on the west (see Figure 6.1).[6] Overall, most new jobs are being created in suburbs (see Figure 6.2) rather than in central cities and disproportionately in the southern and southwestern regions. Certainly the long-term economic growth trends have worked to the disadvantage of the central-city poor, especially those in the Northeast and the Midwest, where the industrial belt has been eroding.

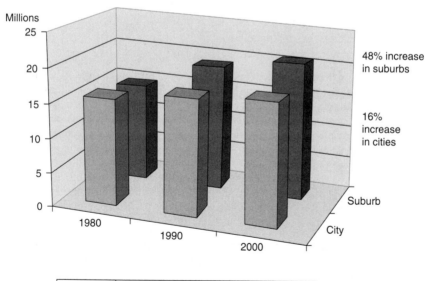

	1980	1990	2000
▢ City	15437977	17300163	17871295
▪ Suburb	14285578	18597666	21164246

FIGURE 6.2 Total Employment, Largest Cities and Their Suburbs, 1980–2000
Source: State of the Cities Data Systems (SOCDS)
http://socds.huduser.org/Census/Census_Home.html

Globalization and the Rise of the Global City

Although the United States has never been totally independent of the world economy, our economic interdependence with the rest of the world today dwarfs any interdependence of the past. According to Paul Knox,

> What is distinctive about the globalization of the past 25 years or so is that there has been a decisive shift in the proportion of the world's economy that is transnational in scope. . . . After World War II, an increasing number of large corporations began to invest in overseas production and manufacturing operations as a means of establishing a foothold in foreign consumer markets. . . . By 1970, almost 75 percent of U.S. imports were transactions between the domestic and foreign subsidiaries of transnational conglomerates. By the end of 1970, overseas profits accounted for a third or more of the overall profits of the 100 largest transnational corporations. By the early 1980s, 40 percent of all world trade was in the form of intra-firm trade (that is, between different branches and companies of the same transnational conglomerate).
>
> Between 1990 and 1995, U.S. overseas investment in manufacturing grew at twice the rate of exports of U.S.-manufactured goods. By the mid-1990s, there were nearly 40,000 transnational corporations in the world, 90 percent of which were headquartered in the United States, Japan, or the European Union. Between them, these corporations control about 180,000 foreign subsidiaries and account for over $6 trillion in worldwide sales.[7]

Globalization of industry was accompanied by a globalization of finance and by the rise of global or world cities. Knox tells us that "today, with the globalization of the economy, the key roles of world cities are concerned less with the deployment of imperial power and the orchestration of trade [as in past ages] and more with transnational corporate organization, international banking and finance, supranational government, and the work of international agencies."[8] He explains,

> The complicated interdependence of these transnational relationships was seen in the global financial crises of 1997–1999. Large banks, mutual funds, and pension funds lost confidence in the currencies of developing nations and pulled out hundreds of billions of dollars of investment capital from Asia, Latin America, and Eastern Europe. As a result the capital markets in these places plunged. To stem the capital outflows and prop up the currencies, the International Monetary Fund arranged bail financing for several countries. These bailouts, however, imposed stringent budgetary restraints that helped worsen the local economies, drive up unemployment in Brazil, provoke food riots and inter-ethnic fighting in Indonesia, and bring Korea's export industry to a halt. Nor was the United States immune to this global crisis. The stock market swooned and the U.S. balance of trade deficit soared due to rising imports and a sharp drop in exports.[9]

As for American cities, Knox argues that they are intricately linked to these "vast webs of interdependence."[10] Some cities, such as New York and Los Angeles, play key strategic roles, whereas other American cities occupy a much more dependent position in the global economy. Researchers have identified several tiers in the new international hierarchy of cities. As the reader will note (see the accompanying box), many American cities are not considered central to the global economy.

Global cities share certain attributes, according to Saskia Sassen. First, employment is substantially based in services rather than in manufacturing. Multinational corporations housed in the global cities require an extensive array of specialized support services, including financial, advertising, accounting, and legal services. Second,

---

The New International Hierarchy of Cities in the Global Economy

First tier: the key command and control centers for the global economy: London, *New York*, Tokyo

Second tier: "cities with influence over large regions of the world economy": Brussels, *Chicago*, Frankfurt, *Los Angeles*, Paris, Singapore, *Washington, D.C.*, Zurich

Third tier: "more limited or more specialized international functions": Amsterdam, *Houston*, Madrid, Mexico City, *Miami, San Francisco, Seoul*, Sydney, Toronto, Vancouver

Fourth tier: "cities of national importance and with some transnational functions": *Boston*, Barcelona, *Dallas*, Manchester, Montreal, Munich, Melbourne, *Philadelphia*

Fifth tier: "places where an imaginative and aggressive local leadership has sought to carve out distinctive niches in the global marketplace": *Atlanta, Rochester, Columbus, Charlotte*

Source: Paul Knox, "Globalization and Urban Economic Change," *Annals of the American Academy of Political and Social Science* 551 (May 1997): 23.

---

the spatial organization of global cities is altered by the increasing concentration of corporate headquarters and support services in the central business districts crowding out other functions, especially residential. The middle class finds it exceedingly difficult to afford to live in the global city. At the same time, an increased lower class, usually immigrant, is drawn to the city to provide the low-paying personal services needed by the corporate elite.[11] Some criticism has been leveled at the global-cities thesis for overemphasizing the role of cities at the top of the hierarchy, such as New York, London, and Tokyo, in driving international trade and commerce. Questions have also been raised about whether the major characteristics of global cities have been overstated. For example, Tokyo still has a large share of its economy based in manufacturing and has a relatively small foreign population compared to New York and London.[12]

The more important point is that virtually all American cities are linked in one fashion or another to the global economy. International trade has become a mainstay of metropolitan economies in the United States. In 1999, exports from 253 metropolitan areas totaled $536 billion. Export sales in 93 of these metros totaled more than $1 billion, and overall exports rose by 46 percent between 1993 and 1999.[13] Moreover, as the United States Conference of Mayors reminds us in Table 6.1, American city-region economies exceed those of many nation-states (see Table 6.1).

The rise of the global economy has profoundly affected American cities and their fortunes.[14] On the positive side, this interdependence enriches the quality of American life by making a greater variety of imported goods and services available. Moreover, aggressive expansion of American exports opens up larger world markets to American companies, thus creating more jobs and income. In theory, the increased need to compete in both the import and the export markets leads to better products at

TABLE 6.1   If U.S. City/County Metro Economies Were Nations: World Rankings on Gross Domestic and Metropolitan Product, 2000 (U.S. Billions, Current)

Rank	Nation or Metro Area	GP 2000	Rank	Nation or Metro Area	GP 2000
1	United States	9,963.00	43	Minneapolis-St. Paul, MN-WI	121.30
2	Japan	4,614.00			
3	Germany	1,873.00	44	Finland	118.00
4	United Kingdom	1,410.00	45	Seattle-Bellevue-Everett, WA	115.00
5	France	1,286.00			
6	China	1,104.00	46	Phoenix-Mesa, AZ	114.20
7	Italy	1,074.00	47	Greece	110.90
8	Canada	699.00	48	Israel	108.00
9	Brazil	665.00	49	San Francisco, CA	107.30
10	Mexico	578.00	50	Nassau-Suffolk, NY	106.80
11	Spain	557.00	51	San Diego, CA	104.60
12	India	510.00	52	Venezuela	102.90
13	Korea, South	480.00	53	Portugal	100.50
14	New York, NY	437.80	54	Newark, NJ	96.30
15	Australia	428.00	55	Baltimore, MD	96.20
16	Los Angeles-Long Beach, CA	363.70	56	Ireland	95.10
			57	Singapore	93.70
17	Netherlands	360.00	58	Oakland, CA	92.10
18	Chicago, IL	332.80	59	Egypt	91.50
19	Taiwan	323.00	60	Denver, CO	91.10
20	Argentina	284.00	61	Colombia	90.00
21	Russia	247.00	62	St. Louis, MO-IL	89.60
22	Switzerland	241.30	63	Malaysia	88.80
23	Boston, MA	238.80	64	San Jose, CA	85.40
24	Belgium	227.00	65	Riverside-San Bernardino, CA	84.10
25	Sweden	224.10			
26	Turkey	217.60	66	Tampa-StPetersb-Clrwater, FL	82.20
27	Washington, DC-MD-VA-WV	217.00			
			67	Cleveland-Lorain-Elyria, OH	80.80
28	Austria	184.90			
29	Philadelphia, PA-NJ	182.40	68	Pittsburgh, PA	80.70
30	Houston, TX	177.50	69	Philippines	78.00
31	Hong Kong	164.60	70	New Haven-BrPt-Stamford-Danbury-Waterbury, CT	76.80
32	Atlanta, GA	164.20			
33	Norway	164.00			
34	Poland	163.00	71	Chile	73.00
35	Dallas, TX	160.00	72	Miami, FL	71.60
36	Denmark	158.00	73	Portland-Vancouver, OR-WA	71.50
37	Detroit, MI	156.30			
38	Indonesia	147.60	74	Iran	67.10
39	Saudi Arabia	145.30	75	Puerto Rico	65.30
40	South Africa	132.30	76	Kansas City, MO-KS	64.80
41	Orange County, CA	130.00	77	Hartford, CT	64.30
42	Thailand	128.20			

(continued)

**TABLE 6.1   If U.S. City/County Metro Economies Were Nations: World Rankings
on Gross Domestic and Metropolitan Product, 2000
(U.S. Billions, Current)** *(continued)*

Rank	Nation or Metro Area	GP 2000	Rank	Nation or Metro Area	GP 2000
78	Middlesex-Somerset-Hunterdon, NJ	63.60	111	Memphis, TN-AR-MS	38.90
			112	Louisville, KY-IN	38.70
79	Sacramento, CA	63.10	113	Bangladesh	38.50
80	Fort Worth-Arlington, TX	63.00	114	Kuwait	38.05
81	Pakistan	62.70	115	Albany-Schenectady-Troy, NY	37.80
82	Peru	62.70	116	Syria	35.53
83	Charlotte-Gastonia-Rock Hill, NC-SC	61.30	117	Morocco	34.80
			118	West Plam Beach-Boca Raton, FL	33.20
84	Columbus, OH	60.70	119	Honolulu, HI	33.00
85	United Arab Emirates	60.70	120	Monmouth-Ocean, NJ	33.00
86	Orlando, FL	59.50	121	Romania	33.00
87	Cincinnati, OH-KY-IN	59.40	122	Providence-Warwick, RI	32.50
88	Bergen-Passaic, NJ	59.30	123	Oklahoma City, OK	32.30
89	Indianapolis, IN	57.70	124	Birmingham, AL	32.00
90	Nigeria	54.90	125	Ukraine	31.70
91	Milwaukee-Waukesha, WI	54.80	126	Wilmington-Newark, DE	31.40
92	Las Vegas, NV-AZ	54.60	127	Dayton-Springfield, OH	31.20
93	San Antonio, TX	53.70	128	Vietnam	30.60
94	Algeria	52.80	129	Manchester-Nashua, NH	30.20
95	New Zealand	52.10	130	Syracuse, NY	30.10
96	Norfolk-Virginia Beach-Newport News, VA-NC	51.70	131	Greenville-Spartanburg-Anderson, SC	29.90
97	Czech	50.80	132	Jersey City, NJ	28.10
98	Austin-San Marcos, TX	48.20	133	Harrisburg-Lebanon-Carlisle, PA	27.10
99	Buffalo-Niagra Falls, NY	47.80	134	Fresno, CA	26.30
100	Hungary	47.40	135	Omaha, NE-IA	26.20
101	Fort Lauderdale, FL	46.70	136	Tulsa, OK	25.70
102	New Orleans, LA	46.50	137	Albuquerque, NM	25.60
103	Salt Lake City-Ogden, UT	46.40	138	Iraq	25.50
104	Greensboro-Winston-Salem-HighPoint, NC	46.30	139	Ventura, CA	24.50
105	Rochester, NY	45.70	140	Tucson, AZ	22.90
106	Richmond-Petersburg, VA	45.70	141	Akron, OH	21.90
107	Nashville, TN	45.20	142	Knoxville, TN	21.50
108	Raleigh-Durham-Chapel HIll, NC	44.30	143	Toledo, OH	21.20
109	Jacksonville, FL	43.00	144	Springfield, MA	20.90
110	GrRapids-Muskegon-Holland, MI	42.30	145	Allentown-Bethlehem-Easton, PA	20.60

(continued)

Table 6.1   If U.S. City/County Metro Economies Were Nations: World Rankings on Gross Domestic and Metropolitan Product, 2000 (U.S. Billions, Current) *(continued)*

Rank	Nation or Metro Area	GP 2000	Rank	Nation or Metro Area	GP 2000
146	Scranton-Wilkes-Barre-Hazelton, PA	20.60	160	Oman	18.82
			161	Fort Wayne, IN	18.60
147	Santa Rosa, CA	20.50	162	El Paso, TX	18.60
148	Uruguay	20.49	163	Trenton, NJ	18.50
149	Baton Rouge, LA	20.40	164	Slovenia	18.47
150	Slovakia	20.20	165	Little Rock-North	18.40
151	Tunisia	19.96		Little Rock, AR	
152	Dominican Republic	19.67	166	Madison, WI	18.40
153	Des Moines, IA	19.10	167	Lafayette, LA	18.20
154	Ann Arbor, MI	19.10	168	Kazakhstan	18.20
155	Columbia, SC	19.10	169	Luxembourg	18.10
156	Guatemala	19.05	170	Lexington, KY	17.80
157	Tacoma, WA	19.00	171	Colorado Springs, CO	17.60
158	Croatia (Hrvatska)	19.00			
159	Bakersfield, CA	18.90	172	Wichita, KS	17.50

Source: Reproduced from U.S. Conference of Mayors, "U.S. Metro Economies: The Engines of Growth" (July 2001) (http://www.usmayors.org/citiesdrivetheeconomy/index3.html).

the most reasonable prices. Cities that house these corporations or subsidiary plants and operations may grow with the companies.

On the negative side, many corporations and communities are poorly prepared to compete in international markets. Costs for labor, environmental protection, and occupational safety are significantly less in developing countries such as Brazil, Mexico, and Korea. For much of the past 30 years, many of these developing countries have been run by authoritarian governments that curbed free labor unions, held down wage costs, and did not force their factories to adhere to the kinds of environmental and safety standards that prevail in the United States. Because of these lower costs, many American corporations closed down domestic factories and built offshore manufacturing plants in developing countries. Additionally, the host governments often subsidize the export of their products to the United States (what American-based manufacturers call dumping). Despite huge transportation costs, these and other factors combined to give many imported products a distinct price advantage over comparable American products.

Paradoxes: Rising Inequality But Less Poverty

As the American economy adapts to these technological and global challenges, that adaptation has profound consequences for the social and political structures of metropolitan America. Economist Lester Thurow flatly charged that the American middle class has shrunk.[15] A 2000 census report provides some support for this thesis. The report found that between 1947 and 1968, income inequality among families declined by 7.5 percent. After 1968 through 1998, inequality of family income increased substantially.[16]

The census report attributes the increased inequality to changes in the economy and in household composition. As the authors of the report explain,

> More highly skilled, trained, and educated workers at the top are experiencing real wage gains, while those at the bottom are experiencing real wage losses making the wage distribution considerably more unequal. Changes in the labor market in the 1980s included a shift from goods-producing industries (that had disproportionately provided high-wage opportunities for low-skilled workers) to technical service industries (that disproportionately employ college graduates) and low-wage industries, such as retail trade.
>
> But within-industry shifts in labor demand away from less-educated workers are, perhaps, a more important explanation of eroding wages than the shift out of manufacturing. Other factors related to the downward trend in wages of less-educated workers include intensifying global competition and immigration, the decline of the proportion of workers belonging to unions, the decline in the real value of the minimum wage, the increasing need for computer skills, and the increasing use of temporary workers.
>
> At the same time, changes in living arrangements have occurred that tend to exacerbate differences in household incomes. For example, increases in divorces and separations, increases in births out of wedlock, and the increasing age at first marriage may have all led to a shift away from traditionally higher-income married-couple households and toward typically lower-income single-parent and nonfamily households. Also, the increasing tendency for men with higher-than-average earnings to marry women with higher-than-average earnings may have contributed to widening the gap between high-income and low-income households.[17]

Although historically, there appears to be some erosions in the size of the middle class, the last decade has been relatively stable. Figure 6.3 reports household income for the 100 largest cities from 1990 to 2000. The change has been slight. It is difficult to draw any major conclusions regarding Thurow's thesis from this data. An examination of poverty trends might provide more of a basis to evaluate whether standard of living is increasing or declining.

Between 1959 and 1969, great progress was made in reducing poverty from over 22 percent to only 12.1 percent of the total population. As Figure 6.4 shows, poverty dropped in 1973 to its lowest level of 11.1 percent, or about 23 million people. This was 42 percent fewer people in poverty than in 1959. Poverty rates in terms of the actual numbers of people in poverty rose overall by 50 percent between 1970 and 1993. The economic boom of the 1990s appears to have significantly reduced poverty. In 2000, 11.3 percent, or 31.1 million people, in the United States were below the poverty level.[18] However, from 2000 to 2004, the poverty level has increased dramatically with an additional 6 million people and rising to 12.7 percent.[19]

African Americans and Hispanics are disproportionately living in poverty. In 2004, 25 percent of all African Americans and 22 percent of all Hispanics were living in poverty, compared with 9 percent of all non-Hispanic whites and 10 percent of Asians (see Figure 6.5). Although minorities have higher rates of poverty, black poverty rates have declined substantially. In 1993 about one-third of blacks were in poverty compared to less than one-fourth in 2000.[20] However, the recession in 2001 caused the black poverty rate to jump from 22 percent in 2000 to 25 percent in 2004.

The poverty rate is based on a definition developed by the Social Security Administration in 1964. Originally, poverty was defined by identifying a nutritionally adequate food plan. On the basis of a survey, it was assumed that families spent about one-third of their income on food, so this budget was multiplied by three. It was then adjusted on the

Household Income Distribution in 100 Largest Cities, 1990

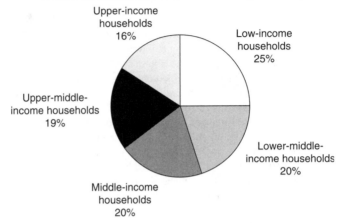

Household Income Distribution in 100 Largest Cities, 2000

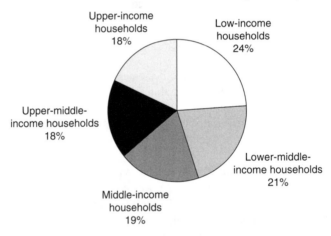

FIGURE 6.3   Size of Middle Class, 1990 and 2000

Source: Data for pie charts taken from Living Cities Databook Series, The Brookings Institution, http://www.brookings.edu/es/urban/livingcities/databooks.htm.

basis of the size of the family, rural or urban residence, and other factors. Every year, the food plan was adjusted to reflect price changes, and then new poverty thresholds were determined. In 1969 and 1981, some minor changes were made in the definition of poverty, including eliminating the separate thresholds for farm and nonfarm families and eliminating the gender of the head of household (male/female). In addition, rather than being pegged to recalculation of the thrifty-food-plan costs, the poverty level is adjusted on the basis of changes in the consumer price index (CPI).[21] Table 6.2 reports the poverty thresholds for 2004.

It is important to remember that although an individual may fall within the poverty guidelines, this does not mean he or she qualifies for or receives welfare. There has

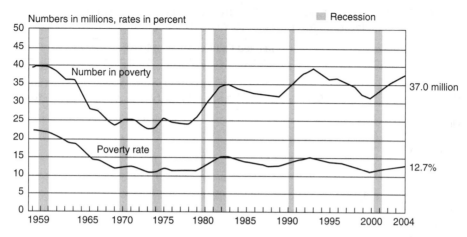

FIGURE 6.4   Number of Poor and Poverty Rate, 1959–2004

Note: The data points are placed at the midpoints of the respective years.

Source: U.S. Census Bureau, Figure 3, *Income, Poverty and Health Insurance Coverage in the United States: 2004*, p.9 Link: http://www.census.gov/prod/2005pubs/p60-229.pdf

always been concern that the welfare programs encouraged welfare dependence and a *culture of poverty*—reflecting a view that the poor are poor because they have individual failings in their values and their abilities. The poor are said to have a present-time orientation—that is, to be more interested in immediate self-gratification than in planning and sacrificing to create a better future for themselves and their families. In this view, the poor are undeserving because they are lazy and engage in undesirable social behaviors. Welfare is seen as part of the problem because the poor will be supported in their undesirable behaviors, which will then be transmitted to the next generation. Recent welfare reform legislation will be considered in Chapter 12.

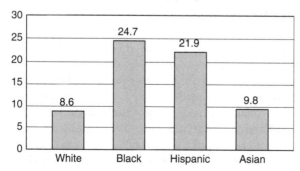

FIGURE 6.5   Poverty Rates by Race and Hispanic Origin, 2004

Source: U.S. Census Bureau, *Income, Poverty, and Health Insurance Coverage in the United States, 2004*, Table B-1: pp. 48–51.

Link: http://www.census.gov/prod/2005pubs/p60-229.pdf.

TABLE 6.2 Poverty Thresholds for 2004, by Size of Family and Number of Related Children Under 18 Years (Dollars)

Size of Family Unit	Related Children Under 18 Years								
	None	One	Two	Three	Four	Five	Six	Seven	Eight or More
One person (unrelated individual)									
Under 65 years	9,827								
65 years and over	9,060								
Two persons									
Householder under 65 years	12,649	13,020							
Householder 65 years and over	11,418	12,971							
Three persons	14,776	15,205	15,219						
Four persons	19,484	19,803	19,157	19,223					
Five persons	23,497	23,838	23,108	22,543	22,199				
Six persons	27,025	27,133	26,573	26,037	25,241	24,768			
Seven persons	31,096	31,290	30,621	30,154	29,285	28,271	27,159		
Eight persons	34,778	35,086	34,454	33,901	33,115	32,119	31,082	30,818	
Nine persons or more	41,836	42,039	41,480	41,010	40,240	39,179	38,220	37,983	36,520

Source: Reproduced from U.S. Bureau of the Census (http://www.census.gov/hhes/poverty/threshld/thresh04.html).

The Changing National Economy and the City as a Place of Opportunity—New Urban Poverty and the Ghetto Underclass

How have these trends affected the ability of cities to perform their historical roles as places of opportunity for the poor? Disastrously, argues sociologist William Julius Wilson in his seminal book *The Truly Disadvantaged* and in *When Work Disappears*.[22] The economic changes of the late twentieth century provoked a migration of jobs and population from inner-city neighborhoods to the suburbs. Especially in the large metropolises of the Northeast and Midwest, huge inner-city ghettos have become holding pens for a desperate urban underclass that is substantially African American and is living in dangerous social isolation from the mainstream American middle class.

The New Underclass

Wilson explains that poverty in the inner cities today differs from that of the past. For the first time, most adults in inner-city ghettos do not work. This disappearance of work has led to high rates of joblessness in poor and minority inner-city neighborhoods. High levels of joblessness have contributed to crime, to the breakup of family structure, and to dependence on welfare, and have undermined the social organization of the ghetto. The disappearance of work is traceable to the changes in urban economies and to the exodus of the middle class, including African Americans, from central-city neighborhoods. There are still working people in the ghetto, but their presence is overshadowed by those who do not work. These neighborhoods are socially and economically isolated from the rest of society.

This is a structural explanation for the rise of underclass neighborhoods. According to Wilson, the problem is not a *culture of poverty* but a *disappearance of work*. This disappearance of work is due to changes in the economy that eliminated work opportunities for low-skilled, poorly educated workers in the central cities. The loss of manufacturing jobs and the movement of lower-skilled jobs to the suburbs has left behind a population that has few options. Although undesirable underclass behaviors contribute to the unemployability of many ghetto residents, the fundamental problem is a shortage of jobs, which then feeds undesirable behaviors. The increasing isolation of these neighborhoods causes a divergence in values. Other institutions have declined with the neighborhoods and with burgeoning fiscal difficulties, which undermine the schools and the effectiveness of the police and the criminal justice system.

According to Wilson, inner-city ghetto neighborhoods lack basic opportunities and resources and have inadequate social controls. There is little low-skilled work available. There has been a decline in wages (adjusted for inflation). And there is no opportunity for economic advancement (entry-level jobs stay entry level). Although there has been economic growth, much of this has been growth of part-time jobs without benefits.

In the 1980s, crack cocaine invaded the cities and further worsened the ghetto neighborhoods. With crack came increases in drug trafficking and the widespread availability of weapons, especially handguns. Not only did the drug sellers have guns, but the residents then armed themselves as well. Young people have easy access to guns, and many have little self-control. There has been an explosion in homicide rates among minority youth, and homicide is the largest single cause of death among young African American males aged 15 to 19.[23]

In 2000, about 42 percent of those in poverty live in the central cities, compared to only one-third of the poor in 1959.[24] In 2000, the poverty rate in cities was 16 percent, double that of the suburban rate of 8 percent.[25] In some cities, poverty rates are much higher. For example, in 2004, Detroit was estimated to have a 34 percent poverty rate, El Paso 29 percent, and Miami 28.[26]

Increasing Numbers of Underclass   Aside from the general increase in poverty, in recent years there is greater concern over the growth of the underclass and underclass neighborhoods. We define the *underclass* as those living in concentrated poverty. The standard way to measure the underclass is to count all persons who live in a census tract where more than 40 percent of the population is in poverty. From 1970 through 1990, the number of poor people concentrated in ghetto neighborhoods was rising.[27] In 1990, about 10 percent of all city residents lived in underclass neighborhoods. This was twice the level cited for 1970. African Americans and Hispanics are much more likely to live in underclass neighborhoods. In 1990, almost one-fourth of all African Americans and one-sixth of the Hispanic population living in the central cities lived in underclass neighborhoods. It is important to recognize that not everybody who lives in an underclass neighborhood is living in poverty. However, all such residents are impacted by concentrated poverty.

Geographic Spread of Underclass Neighborhoods   Not only were more minorities concentrated in ghetto neighborhoods, but the neighborhoods were spreading spatially in the cities into the 1990s. Contiguous, nonghetto census tracts were identified as underclass in the 1980 and 1990 census. This can be illustrated by the case of Chicago. In 1990, Chicago had ten neighborhoods that were predominantly African American. Eight of these had poverty rates over 45 percent. However, in 1970, only two of these neighborhoods had poverty rates exceeding 40 percent (that is, underclass or ghetto poverty neighborhoods). Wilson points out that in 1990 in the largest 100 cities, one in seven census tracts was at least 40 percent poor. The underclass census tracts in cities had increased from 6 percent to 14 percent. This is double the number in 1970. Between 1970 and 1980, 579 census tracts became underclass, and another 624 changed between 1980 and 1990.[28]

Why did ghettos spread? It is not because of increased numbers of poor people needing more space but because of the exodus of the middle class, including minorities, from neighboring mixed neighborhoods. Underclass neighborhoods and adjacent neighborhoods have in many cases lost population as those who can leave do so. Predominantly African American neighborhoods in Chicago lost about half their population between 1970 and 1990. The impact of the geographic spread of underclass neighborhoods is severe, because in these neighborhoods, in a typical week, only about one in three persons over age 16 (adults) was employed. In neighborhoods that are not underclass, the average number of adults working in a typical week is more than 50 percent. The increasing scale of the ghetto contributes to fear of the city and to other urban ills, as large numbers of buildings become abandoned and deteriorate. Many are taken over as crack houses. In addition, the loss of the middle class eliminates role models and community leaders. This also erodes the economic base of the neighborhood, which can no longer sustain community businesses supplying services and goods (grocery stores, theaters, social life). As legitimate employment disappears, illegitimate economies take over, accelerating the deterioration of the neighborhood.[29]

Decline in Underclass, the 1990s Onward   Analysis of the 2000 census reveals that the underclass is declining in cities. A study by G. Thomas Kingsely and Kathryn L. S. Pettit of the Urban Institute found that

> Poverty became notably less concentrated in the 1990s. The share of the metropolitan poor who live in "extreme-poverty neighborhoods" (census tracts with poverty rates of 40 percent or more) had jumped from 13 to 17 percent in the 1980s but dropped all the way back to 12 percent in 2000.[30]

These findings were echoed in a study by Paul A. Jargowsky and Rebecca Yang (see Table 6.3). Jargowsky and Yang's measure of underclass is based on:

> the percentages of: (a) men not attached to the labor force, (b) teenagers who are high school drop outs, (c) families with children headed by women, and (d) households dependent on public assistance. [31]

TABLE 6.3   Underclass Census Tracts in 20 Largest Metropolitan Areas, 1990 and 2000

Name of MSA or PMSA	Year		Change	
	1990	2000	Number	Percent
New York, NY	125	60	−65	−52
Detroit, MI	99	38	−61	−62
Chicago, IL	87	57	−30	−34
Philadelphia, PA/NJ	51	28	−23	−45
Los Angeles, CA	40	9	−31	−78
Baltimore, MD	37	29	−8	−22
St. Louis, MO/IL	20	23	3	15
Houston, TX	16	7	−9	−56
Wash., DC/MD/VA/WV	12	7	−5	−42
Atlanta, GA	12	10	−2	−17
Dallas, TX	10	5	−5	−50
Minneapolis, MN/WI	10	3	−7	−70
Boston, MA/NH	9	4	−5	−56
Tampa, FL	9	6	−3	−33
Phoenix, AZ	8	13	5	63
Riverside, CA	5	7	2	40
San Diego, CA	2	0	−2	−100
Seattle, WA	1	2	1	100
Orange County, CA	0	0	0	0
Nassau, NY	0	0	0	0

Note: MSA = Metropolitan Statistical Area;
PMSA = Primary Metropolitan Statistical Area. Sorted in order of 2000 total population within MSA/PMSA boundaries.

Source: Paul A. Jargowsky and Rebecca Yang "The 'Underclass' Revisited: A Social Problem in Decline,"Brookings Institution Working Paper (May 2005), Table 7.
http://www.brookings.edu/dybdocroot/views/papers/200505jargowsky.pdf.

They found:

[T]he number of underclass neighborhoods declined by 32.5 percent from 1,148 census tracts in 1990 to 775 in 2000. This decline outpaced the 27 percent drop in high-poverty tracts. . . .

Far fewer persons lived in neighborhoods classified as underclass areas, declining from 3.4 million to 2.2 million.[32]

However, Jargowsky and Yang warn that it is too early to say the problem is solved.

Despite these dramatic changes in the underclass measure, it might be premature to conclude that the "social pathologies" that spurred the underclass debate of the 1980s—to use William Julius Wilson's memorable term—will soon join polio and smallpox on the list of eradicated diseases. The change in the underclass measure may be more dramatic than the underlying reality. In particular, the fact that the sharp decline is driven in part by the welfare dimension is a sword that cuts both ways. A positive view is that the strong economy and more paternalistic welfare laws helped many former residents of underclass neighborhoods into the labor market, with substantial benefits for them and their neighborhoods.

A negative view of the same facts would hold that the welfare poor have been forced into low-wage jobs, have just as little money , are less likely to have health care, and have less time to supervise their children. Proponents of the latter view would hold that the declines in the underclass noted in this paper are merely a statistical artifact of comparing welfare receipt from the legal context of 2000 to threshold levels based on a very different legal context.[33]

Still, on balance, the authors suggest that a strong economy, welfare reform, greater use of the Earned Income Tax Credit, and more dispersal of low-income housing in the city have in some combination substantially improved conditions in inner-city neighborhoods. However, the recession in 2001 could lead to slippage as we saw earlier that poverty rates, especially for minorities, have jumped in the last few years.

The Bipolar City—1970 to 1990s?

The 1970s and 1980s were decades of slow economic growth, declining central-city economies, and contracting opportunities that central cities offered their poorest residents. During the nineteenth- and twentieth-century period of urban European ethnic advancement, central cities grew faster than the rest of the economy, which was a major reason for European ethnic upward social mobility. Likewise, economic restructuring is a major reason for the very limited upward mobility of today's urban minorities.

Especially damaging to many older cities has been the decline of the industrial-production sector of the economy. Unskilled racial and Spanish-speaking minorities migrated by the millions into old industrial cities such as Buffalo, Cleveland, Detroit, Gary, and Pittsburgh, only to find that the industrial job market was starting to decline. Job growth was taking place disproportionately in the suburbs, but the minorities and immigrants were housed in the central cities, and the industrial cities could not expand their economic opportunities fast enough to absorb the influx of unskilled laborers who came looking for jobs in the urban factories. The new jobs in the city require high levels of education and skill.

We see, then, that the cities are facing a mismatch between (1) residents' skills and jobs available (jobs-skills mismatch) and between (2) residents' location and where new jobs are being created in the suburbs (jobs-spatial mismatch) (see Chapter 2). The Office of Technology Assessment reported on a ten-city study of jobs and education levels conducted by John Kasarda. He found that between 1970 and 1990 "the number of jobs held by people with less than a high school diploma declined by 602,000 while those jobs held by college graduates increased by 1,126,000."[34] The central cities tend to house large concentrations of disadvantaged people with low incomes and high poverty levels.

At the other pole of the bipolar city is a small elite of upper-income professionals who work in the sleek downtown office buildings and live in the gentrified high-income neighborhoods. Squeezed out between these two poles and fast disappearing, argue George Sternlieb and James W. Hughes, are the "middle groups who find both the lifestyles and economic opportunities of suburbia (and increasingly exurbia) affordable and much more fulfilling."[35]

In this pessimistic scenario, the central cities are losing middle-class people, losing jobs, and losing their dynamism as places of economic opportunity for their millions of low-income residents.[36] This scenario for cities was articulated succinctly by Norton Long, who said that the central city had become a "reservation for the poor, the deviant, the unwanted, and for those who make a business or career of managing them for the rest of society."[37] George Sternlieb compared the city to a sandbox for the poor, a place where society's problem people were given enough public programs to keep them busy while the real business of society got carried on in the suburbs.[38] The impoverished central city was increasingly surrounded by affluent and dynamic suburbs.

Disparities Between Central City and Suburbs

In 1960, for every dollar earned (per capita income) in the suburbs, central-city residents earned $1.05. In other words, central-city residents earned more than suburbanites. By 1990 this ratio had reversed, and for every dollar earned in the suburbs, only $.84 was earned by central-city residents.[39] Older central cities in the Northeast and Midwest were much more likely than newer ones in the South and West to be poorer than their suburbs. In the worst cases (Newark, Hartford, Cleveland, and Detroit), central-city income was $.56 or less for every dollar earned by suburbanites in 1990.

The Lewis Mumford Center released a report comparing cities and suburbs from 1990 to 2000 in the largest metropolitan areas on eight variables, including median household income, per capita income, poverty, college education, professional/white collar workforce, unemployment, homeownership, and vacant housing. According to the study, "on every indicator, the national average for cities compared to suburbs got worse during the 1990s."[40] In the highest-ranking city, Las Vegas, median household income in the city was $1.06 for every dollar earned in the suburbs (see Table 6.4). Las Vegas is a new boomtown—sprawling through the desert and encompassing the suburbs around it. To this extent, Las Vegas is a statistical artifact that masks the problems of traditional cities. An extreme example of these problems can be seen in the lowest ranking city Newark (50th), where only $.45 was earned in the city for every dollar earned in the suburbs (see Table 6.4).

An Urban Renaissance?

Although the economic prospects for central cities are portrayed rather grimly here, it would not be fair to leave the topic of central-city economies without noting that some observers have a much more optimistic viewpoint.[41] The urban optimists view commercial redevelopment as the cornerstone of their more hopeful view of the city. At the close of the twentieth century, corporations began to look more favorably upon expanding their facilities in central cities than they had at mid-century. Many cities have offered attractive incentives to encourage corporations to undertake central-city development. Some of this development deliberately took place in minority neighborhoods, where the corporate facilities could symbolize the company's concern for minority-employment problems. But the most visible sign of corporate investment in central cities has been in the construction of office buildings in the central business districts.

This approach was pioneered in the 1950s with the urban renewal programs in places such as Newark and New Haven. The pacesetters in the 1970s and 1980s were such architecturally stunning developments as Atlanta's Peachtree Center and Detroit's Renaissance Center. Miami, Buffalo, Washington, and Atlanta used federally available mass transit funds to start people movers and subway systems running through their downtowns. Chicago's Watertower Place (two marble-facade skyscrapers) literally transplanted the most luxurious retail shopping facilities from the downtown Loop to a new

TABLE 6.4 City-Suburban Disparities—Median Household Income

Rank 2000	Rank 1990	Metropolitan Area	2000 City	2000 Suburb	2000 Ratio	1990 City	1990 Suburb	1990 Ratio
1	2	Las Vegas, NV-AZ MSA	$44,069	$41,495	1.06	$40,077	$38,300	1.05
2	3	San Diego, CA MSA	$45,261	$48,389	0.94	$43,883	$46,923	0.94
3	7	Seattle-Bellevue-Everett, WA PMSA	$46,790	$54,911	0.85	$39,968	$50,758	0.79
4	4	Charlotte-Gastonia-Rock Hill, NC-SC MSA	$44,157	$47,164	0.94	$39,741	$40,836	0.97
5	8	Riverside-San Bernardino, CA PMSA	$37,711	$43,284	0.87	$39,273	$44,742	0.88
6	6	Greensboro—Winston-Salem—High Point, NC MSA	$37,867	$41,814	0.91	$35,486	$39,262	0.9
7	1	Phoenix-Mesa, AZ MSA	$42,683	$46,806	0.91	$39,546	$39,040	1.01
8	11	Fort Lauderdale, FL PMSA	$37,887	$41,667	0.91	$35,102	$40,195	0.87
9	9	Tampa-St. Petersburg-Clearwater, FL MSA	$34,950	$37,992	0.92	$30,684	$35,047	0.88
10	5	Raleigh-Durham-Chapel Hill, NC MSA	$43,540	$52,047	0.84	$39,542	$43,581	0.91
11	18	Portland-Vancouver, OR-WA PMSA	$39,799	$51,058	0.78	$34,104	$44,745	0.76
12	15	Orlando, FL MSA	$35,732	$42,141	0.85	$33,761	$39,935	0.85
13	10	Los Angeles-Long Beach, CA PMSA	$37,007	$47,361	0.78	$41,311	$49,146	0.84
14	13	Nashville, TN MSA	$38,519	$50,147	0.77	$35,917	$43,011	0.84
15	17	Norfolk-Virginia Beach-Newport News, VA-NC MSA	$39,493	$50,416	0.78	$38,536	$45,393	0.85
16	16	Fort Worth-Arlington, TX PMSA	$40,450	$51,250	0.79	$38,545	$46,158	0.84
17	32	San Francisco, CA PMSA	$55,221	$70,211	0.79	$43,367	$60,863	0.71
18	14	Austin-San Marcos, TX MSA	$41,510	$56,869	0.73	$33,232	$42,889	0.77
19	26	San Antonio, TX MSA	$36,148	$47,408	0.76	$31,831	$40,881	0.78
20	19	Salt Lake City-Ogden, UT MSA	$36,182	$51,988	0.7	$30,998	$43,367	0.71
21	12	Sacramento, CA PMSA	$37,049	$50,217	0.74	$37,490	$45,773	0.82
22	22	Denver, CO PMSA	$39,500	$54,985	0.72	$32,667	$47,324	0.69
23	24	Oakland, CA PMSA	$42,434	$63,037	0.67	$38,772	$58,447	0.66

(continued)

TABLE 6.4 City-Suburban Disparities—Median Household Income (continued)

Rank		Metropolitan Area	2000			1990		
2000	1990		City	Suburb	Ratio	City	Suburb	Ratio
24	29	New Orleans, LA MSA	$27,722	$39,556	0.7	$24,775	$36,244	0.68
25	21	Pittsburgh, PA MSA	$28,588	$38,558	0.74	$28,007	$35,969	0.78
26	20	Indianapolis, IN MSA	$38,922	$53,119	0.73	$37,199	$46,114	0.81
27	31	Washington, DC-MD-VA-WV PMSA	$45,498	$64,513	0.71	$44,153	$63,768	0.69
28	28	Kansas City, MO-KS MSA	$38,245	$51,259	0.75	$35,461	$45,695	0.78
29	27	San Jose, CA PMSA	$70,384	$83,314	0.84	$60,160	$69,031	0.87
30	30	Minneapolis-St. Paul, MN-WI MSA	$37,936	$57,661	0.66	$33,512	$52,545	0.64
31	25	Houston, TX PMSA	$36,557	$53,800	0.68	$35,114	$48,327	0.73
32	39	Miami, FL PMSA	$24,495	$39,044	0.63	$21,262	$40,206	0.53
33	33	Columbus, OH MSA	$37,331	$54,093	0.69	$33,868	$47,619	0.71
34	35	Orange County, CA PMSA	$50,252	$60,167	0.84	$52,153	$61,892	0.84
35	23	Dallas, TX PMSA	$38,325	$55,614	0.69	$36,396	$48,954	0.74
36	34	Providence-Fall River-Warwick, RI-MA MSA	$33,232	$49,106	0.68	$34,903	$47,794	0.73
37	36	Cincinnati, OH-KY-IN PMSA	$29,493	$49,027	0.6	$28,169	$43,622	0.65
38	37	Boston, MA-NH PMSA	$40,792	$59,129	0.69	$39,787	$57,149	0.7
39	38	Atlanta, GA MSA	$34,770	$53,268	0.65	$28,846	$48,465	0.6
40	45	Chicago, IL PMSA	$39,568	$58,912	0.67	$35,151	$56,339	0.62
41	40	St. Louis, MO-IL MSA	$29,599	$49,117	0.6	$27,646	$46,223	0.6
42	43	Milwaukee-Waukesha, WI PMSA	$33,738	$55,483	0.61	$32,627	$53,237	0.61
43	46	New York, NY PMSA	$38,069	$64,919	0.59	$38,835	$65,260	0.6
44	42	Buffalo-Niagara Falls, NY MSA	$24,932	$44,740	0.56	$24,666	$43,186	0.57
45	41	Philadelphia, PA-NJ PMSA	$29,947	$55,823	0.54	$31,509	$53,904	0.58
46	44	Baltimore, MD PMSA	$30,268	$56,190	0.54	$31,874	$55,059	0.58
47	48	Cleveland-Lorain-Elyria, OH PMSA	$27,427	$48,366	0.57	$25,332	$45,563	0.56
48	49	Detroit, MI PMSA	$30,397	$54,395	0.56	$26,579	$51,896	0.51
49	47	Hartford, CT MSA	$30,017	$54,884	0.55	$34,344	$57,177	0.6
50	50	Newark, NJ PMSA	$26,913	$60,414	0.45	$30,559	$60,210	0.51

Source: http://mumford.albany.edu/census/.

location a mile north, while the Loop has become mostly a jumble of massive office buildings. Boston rebuilt the historic Quincy Market into a chic downtown shopping area. And San Francisco's Fisherman's Wharf has been turned into a huge, sprawling collection of tourist-oriented businesses. Similar consumer-oriented projects were erected in Baltimore,[42] San Antonio, and Oakland.[43] St. Louis, a city that has received more than its share of bad press, was in the mid-1980s dubbed "Comeback City."[44]

In addition to corporate- and government-sponsored commercial redevelopment, many cities are also experiencing *gentrification*. This is the process whereby upper-middle-income and young people buy houses or apartment buildings in older neighborhoods of cities, rehabilitate the houses, convert apartment buildings into condominiums, and in general drive up property values. Gentrification has been widespread from Beacon Hill in Boston to Nob Hill in San Francisco. Although only a small number of people are involved, the process is significant because it brings more spending money into previously impoverished neighborhoods, improves the tax base of cities, and upgrades the physical appearance of the neighborhoods. It also leads to the founding of new restaurants, specialty shops, and other commercial activity that can profit from the higher incomes of these gentrifiers and make their neighborhoods more lively. The negative side of gentrification is that it displaces the previous, poorer residents of the gentrified neighborhoods and forces them to seek generally more expensive housing elsewhere in the city.[45] Although there is evidence that the central business districts have been revitalized in many cities, there is little evidence that the poor or minorities have directly benefited from this development.[46]

Paul S. Grogan and Tony Proscio's book, *Comeback Cities,* argues that urban scholars and pundits are too negative about city revitalization. The authors maintain that there has indeed been a turnaround in many cities but that it is not reflected in the traditional measures that researchers use to monitor the health of central cities or is hidden by the time lag in getting up-to-date census information on urban trends and conditions.

> The American inner city is rebounding—not just here and there, not just cosmetically, but fundamentally. It is the result of a fragile but palpable change in both the economics and the politics of poor urban neighborhoods. Though not yet visible everywhere, the shift is discernible in enough places to unsettle longstanding assumptions about the future of older urban communities.[47]

Grogan and Proscio are focusing not on the shiny new downtowns but on the inner-city poor neighborhoods. They point to four trends that underpin this new urban renaissance. First, community-based organizations have been working on rebuilding inner-city poor neighborhoods for decades, one block at a time. Second, businesses are rediscovering economic opportunities in these neighborhoods, investing in small retail shops, and starting new enterprises. Third, sharp declines in crime rates have made the cities safer for visitors as well as new residents. The fourth positive trend these authors point to is the demise of many of the large bureaucracies that used to regulate the lives of the poor in the inner city, including public housing and welfare. They hope that the school bureaucracies will be the next to collapse, thus allowing for more innovative and effective education that will foster upward mobility.[48]

Grogan and Proscio believe that urbanists overlook these trends because they are captive of the data they collect, which reveal (1) a middle-class exodus; (2) the end of work in the city for poor, unskilled, and low-educated workers, as well as the decline of businesses; (3) the physical expansion of ghettos in central cities; and (4) a "social implosion"—that is, the collapse of social order, the rejection of middle-class values, and the fiscal crisis of the city as it struggles to address spiraling problems without an adequate financial base. Thus researchers throw up their hands and suggest that the problems are impenetrable. The only solution is the return of the middle class and reduction of poverty, but no one can see how this can occur. The authors argue that just like downtowns, inner-city neighborhoods can recover. But first, they say, we must stop looking for the return of the middle class. Rather, they point to neighborhood revitalization without poverty reduction.[49]

They cite the South Bronx as an example of such renewed vitality. The neighborhood still suffers high poverty and has not seen large-scale development projects. Rather, the area has grown from within, via the hard work of groups in the area and with some modest assistance from outside. Crime is way down, housing has been rebuilt (but not large-scale public housing), and jobs have returned. The residents are still poor, but they live in a cleaner, safer, more healthful environment and have more economic opportunity and a better quality of life than they have had for decades. And all this was accomplished without a return of the middle class.[50]

Urban Economic Development Strategies

Earlier in the chapter, we described how economic restructuring and demographic changes had profound consequences for American cities. Central cities, especially in the Northeast and Midwest but also in the South and West, continue to grapple with the problems of central-city decline: a white middle-class exodus, loss of manufacturing jobs, concentrated poverty, urban decline, and related fiscal stress. In the industrial era, business was fixed in particular locales. But now, large multinational businesses are mobile. The corporation can relocate all or some of its operations from the central business district to the edge city in the suburbs, the Sunbelt, or even overseas. As Paul Kantor explains, this leads to economic dependence on private businesses' locating and expanding operations in the city,[51] which in turn gives business leverage over the city. City officials need these businesses to stay in the city in order to provide jobs for residents and revenue for city government. This is even more critical, now that the city can no longer rely on financial aid from the federal government to maintain city budgets or to pay for redeveloping abandoned areas of the city that are no longer needed for warehousing, manufacturing, or commercial activity. Leaders of the *dependent city* find it necessary to plan their city's role in the global economy more strategically so that they will have the resources to provide citizens with public services and a high quality of life.

There are two distinct aspects to *urban development policy:* redesigning the landscape of the city and conceiving an economic development strategy for the city or region. First are efforts to redesign the physical city by engaging in *urban redevelopment.* As population moved out of inner-city neighborhoods, many abandoned houses were left behind. As population declined and the population got poorer, businesses that served residents also fled to the suburbs or closed. This has left many neighborhoods and downtown streets with boarded-up homes or storefronts. Redeveloping this property is a major challenge for the cities. The urban "built environment" needs to be reshaped to meet the needs of a postindustrial economy and to find new uses for abandoned areas (railway yards, factories, warehouses, residential housing, and apartment units).

In Detroit, for example, as much as 30 percent of the city's land may be vacant. But many of these areas are *brownfield sites* polluted by toxic wastes, buildings with asbestos, or other contamination. Pittsburgh is estimated to have about 450 abandoned sites covering about two square miles of the city, many of which may be contaminated. Chicago has identified 2,000 brownfield sites that account for about 1,500 acres of land, and even Portland has found 40 sites totaling about 400 acres.

It is estimated that there are probably about 450,000 brownfield sites in the United States, many in the Northeast and Midwest. Cleaning these lands—clearing away factory buildings and warehouses—is expensive. Further, there are liability issues that make redevelopment problematic. For example, if a developer purchases land that later turns out to be contaminated, the developer, the investors, and the bank that provided financing may be responsible for cleaning up the pollution.[52]

Cities have made massive investments in convention centers, stadiums, aquariums, downtown shopping malls, performing arts centers, museums, and the like. These projects are usually justified by claims that they will stimulate employment, boost tourism, and increase revenues, as well as redevelop blighted and abandoned areas of the city.

Second, cities engage in economic development programs. These usually entail incentives to attract, retain, or expand business in a locality with the goal of increasing employment and revenues. Cities must decide on an organizational structure or process through which to implement economic development policies. Most cities created economic development departments and attempted to forge public-private partnerships with top local businesses. In some cases, cities relied on the private sector, such as the Chamber of Commerce, to identify and pursue a strategy for economic development of the community, be it a city, county, or metropolitan region. Cities created a range of economic development incentive programs and tools to recruit, expand, or retain businesses. Today, competition among cities for economic development is fierce, and many cities pay more than they get in order to land a new business or to keep a business in their community.[53]

The Business Climate Debate

Perhaps the most visible issue in development politics is the business climate. Mayors who pursue progressive policies are often accused of threatening a city's business climate. And political leaders in most states are vulnerable to the same charge if they press too hard on issues such as taxes or environmental protection that are resisted by the local business community. No political leader wants to be blamed if a major employer closes a large facility and cities a bad business climate.

What qualities it takes to create a positive business climate are not absolutely clear, and they may vary from one type of business to another. The Chicago-based industrial consulting firm Alexander Grant and Company publishes annual ratings of business climates for manufacturing firms. Those ratings focus on factors such as labor costs that are important to industrial manufacturing firms. Not surprisingly, states with strong unions and generous workers' compensation programs score poorly. By contrast, *Inc.* magazine rates state climates for small business. Labor cost is less important to small businesses than is state action to facilitate the investment of venture capital that can assist small firms as they get under way.[54]

What issues are most crucial in creating a favorable business climate? Taxes, labor costs, and the level of government expenditure on public services are the most politically controversial issues. Many business organizations in the high-tax and high-spending states of the Northeast and Midwest claim that the low-tax and low-spending states of the South and Southwest are more attractive to industry. According to this viewpoint, when firms decide to relocate or to expand, they often go to the South or West in order to avoid the "punitive" tax structures of the Northeast and Midwest.

Attempts to trace empirically and systematically the causes and effects of corporate relocations do not tend to support the tax structure theory. Although corporations continuously monitor their branch operations (deciding to open some new plants, expand some existing ones, and shut down others), they do not commonly relocate whole facilities from one state or region to another. One of the most widely respected studies of the impact of corporate in- and out-migrations on jobs was David L. Birch's study of over 2 million firms in the early and middle 1970s. He found that such migrations had a practically negligible impact on the number of jobs a state gains or loses.[55]

To the extent that firms do relocate facilities, to what extent do those relocations result from companies leaving a state to avoid high taxes? Roy Bahl surveyed numerous studies of the impact of taxes on decisions to relocate from one state to another and concluded, "The consensus of a great deal of such research would seem to be that taxes are not a major factor in interregional location,"[56] although taxes do affect relocation within a metropolis. State taxes are a relatively small percentage of a firm's income, and most firms can save relatively little on taxes by moving from one state to the next.

The limited impact of taxes on locational decisions was also revealed by Roger W. Schmenner's study of location decisions by 410 of the Fortune 500 companies. Schmenner found that "tax and financial incentives have little influence on almost all plant location decisions." At best they are "tiebreakers" when competing sites are otherwise equally desirable.[57]

More important than taxes is the cost of labor. States with low average wages, weak unions, so-called right-to-work laws that inhibit union strength, and low unemployment and workers' compensation benefits may have a significant advantage in attracting industry over states that are on the high side on all of those criteria. Offsetting this factor, however, is the fact that many firms also want a labor force that is relatively well educated and has a reputation for reliable, hard work. For this reason, a state that reduces taxes by cutting back on the public schools and higher education that produce quality workforces may in the long run undermine its business climate rather than improve it.

Finally, many criteria that may affect companies' location decisions are not directly under a state's control. Other things being equal, a moderate climate is more attractive than an extreme climate. Access to low-cost energy helped Texas attract industry during the energy-conscious 1970s. A region with a variety of first-class cultural, sports, and entertainment amenities is more attractive than a state without such amenities. And, perhaps most important, a region close to a firm's markets is more attractive than a region far from those markets.

To sum up, a state's business climate is composed of many variables that give each state its own peculiar combination of strengths and weaknesses. But seldom discussed is the question of how much difference the business climate actually makes in promoting a state's economy. If business climate were the single most important factor in economic development, states such as South Dakota and Mississippi would be among the highest in economic development, whereas states such as New York and California would be underdeveloped. In fact, the reverse is true. An overall comparison of the relationship between the Grant Thornton business climate rankings of 1985 and the number of jobs gained or lost in each state in the same year found no relationship between the two variables![58] Of the 24 states that gained the most jobs that year, 13 were in the 50 percent of states with the worst business climates.[59]

None of this information indicates that business climate is irrelevant to corporations when they make location decisions. Rather, it reflects the fact that corporations do not have unlimited discretion to move where they want. They are constrained by proximity to markets and suppliers, by availability of a competent workforce, and by other factors.

Incentives for Economic Development

In addition to facilitating a favorable business climate, states and communities also have a broad range of incentives to attract new industries and to retain established ones. Most states use public relations through advertising in business magazines. Most have established central agencies to coordinate business promotion efforts. And most states and communities provide a range of tactics to promote business. Some of the most prominent of these tactics are urban enterprise zones, a range of financial incentives, and venture-capital efforts.

Urban Enterprise Zones   Most states have set up *urban enterprise zones*. These are zones in blighted neighborhoods in which taxes are reduced and government regulations relaxed for any firm that will set up shop and employ local residents. Enterprise zones are set up in areas of the city that have a certain threshold of poverty (such as 25 percent). A firm that locates a facility in one of these zones and hires more than a certain number of employees receives tax breaks on property or income taxes.

Financial Incentives   Local governments are often very aggressive in promoting economic development, and over the years they have developed a variety of financial incentives to attract new business.[60] First among these incentives is probably the *tax abatement*—forgiving a firm's property taxes for a number of years if it expands in the particular city. Although the preponderance of the evidence suggests that they do not have much effect on the investment decisions of corporations,[61] tax abatements are widely used. Cities can also provide seed money to help firms locate within their boundaries. For example, suppose a firm wishes to expand in a city but is hampered by the lack of developable land. Using its powers of eminent domain, the city can force the owners of a desirable piece of land to sell and move out. Purchasing and clearing such land is extremely expensive, but cities have many sources of financial aid for this purpose. Cities are likely to use community development block grant (CDBG) funds from the federal government for this purpose. They can also raise money through their power to issue bonds. The two most popular types have been industrial development revenue bonds (IDRBs) and tax increment financing (TIF).

The IDRB allows the city to act as an intermediary to help a company raise development money at a cost lower than would be the case if the company had to go directly to the market and sell its own bonds. Because the interest earned by municipal bonds is exempt from federal income taxes (and usually from state income taxes in the state where the bond is issued), they carry lower interest rates than corporate bonds. In the past, a city might entice a corporation to expand by issuing IDRBs. The bonds were paid off by the revenues from the company's development project. This reduced the interest costs for most corporations without inflicting any cost on the city. The entire cost was paid by the federal government in the form of lower income tax revenues. Until 1987, IDRBs were the single most popular method of funding urban economic development. But in 1986, Congress put a cap on the amount of IDRBs that each state would be allowed.

Under *tax increment financing,* the city will declare a tax increment financing district in the neighborhood it wants to develop. The city will issue bonds to clear the land and entice a developer to come in and build some commercial structure on the site. Because the new structure will be more valuable than the older uses of the land, it will generate more property taxes. This increment, or increase, in property taxes generated will be used to pay off the tax increment financing bonds that were issued. Thus the new development will not bring new property taxes into the city's general revenues until after the TIF bonds are paid off. But the development itself may create new jobs for city residents and possibly improve the city's fiscal picture.

Venture Capital   A number of states today have *venture-capital* programs to invest start-up capital in new companies that have excellent prospects for growth. The Sky Computer Company of Lowell, Massachusetts, for example, badly needed capital in 1982 to market plug-in computer boards for scientific and engineering applications. The Massachusetts Technology Development Corporation (MTDC) then invested public funds in the company to help it get off the ground. Within three years the company's workforce expanded from 15 to 85, and its annual sales shot up to $10 million. By using its government-supplied venture capital for projects like this, the MTDC has been able to increase the number of jobs in the state. Between 1980 and 2000, the MTDC invested more than $45 million in venture capital in 100 companies, and claims to have created more than 10,500 jobs and $27.7 million in state income tax collections.[62] Although venture capital is extremely risky, the Massachusetts example shows that under the proper circumstances, it can produce benefits that far exceed its costs.

Assessing Urban Development Strategies

Cities are under so much economic and fiscal pressure that they have little choice but to do whatever seems likely to improve the local economy. Several questions should be asked, however, before a city enters into a public-private venture of the sort described here.

First, do the development projects result in a *net* increase in jobs? Development projects always generate new jobs. But they usually also destroy jobs that previously existed on the site. Before a city undertakes a public-private development project, it should ask whether the project will create more jobs than it destroys. It should alro ask whether the people who lose jobs will find new ones in the city.

Second, does the project bring a *net* fiscal benefit to the area? Wellston, Ohio, for example, suddenly got 980 new jobs when Geno's, Inc., decided to consolidate its $200-million-per-year pizza-making facilities in that city. To help Geno's locate in Wellston, the local county and the state of Ohio lent the firm over $5 million at a $1^7/_8$ percent interest rate. But soon after the new facility began operations, its waste products clogged the city sewerage system with a mass of cheese, meat, and other ingredients the consistency of toothpaste and the color of tomato soup. When the Environmental Protection Agency threatened to close down the plant as an environmental danger, Ohio had to give the firm $500,000 to find a way to clean up the wastes.[63] In the long run, Geno's may have been a net fiscal contributor to Wellston, the county, and the state. But in the short run, the inducements to locate there were very costly.

Third, does a public-private redevelopment project actually generate *new* economic activity, or does it just relocate activity that would have occurred anyway? Much of the redevelopment of the last several decades focused on central-city downtowns. In many cases, these investments would have been made even without the cities acting. However, they might have gone to the suburbs instead. Larger suburbs have learned that they too must compete for new development, so now they are also engaged in the game of offering a variety of tax or bond inducements to promote development. Many older regions probably had good reasons to redevelop their old, run-down central business districts. But from today's metropolitan-wide perspective, one has to ask whether it any longer makes sense to have cities competing with one another, offering tax incentives for development projects that in all likelihood would occur someplace in the same metropolitan area even if no government offered any inducement. As we will see in Chapter 8, American metropolises lack effective governmental institutions capable of planning and acting from such an area-wide perspective.

Fourth, what recourse will a city have if, after granting lucrative incentives to a firm, the firm eventually *moves out?* Yonkers, New York, in 1972 put up over $2 million of a $13 million public-financing package to help Otis Elevator build a modern factory and thus to keep its manufacturing facilities in that city. In the 1980s, Otis's parent company, United Technologies, began phasing out the factory and announced that it would have to be closed because it was technologically obsolete. The mayor charged that the firm had breached a contract and sued in court to get back the city's investment, but the city lost the suit.[64]

A related issue arose in Detroit, where in 1980 the city razed 1,100 homes in a neighborhood called Poletown. Having spent nearly $200 million to do this, Detroit offered the site to General Motors for $8 million and offered the company a $5.4 million annual property tax break to build an assembly plant on the site. General Motors built the plant, but at about that time the bottom fell out of the automobile market, and the employment levels at the plant did not match the promises that were made.[65] Given the vast number of public incentives bestowed on companies by cities in recent years, issues such as these are likely to recur. Unless a major court decision rules against such actions by companies, the cities will remain in a poor bargaining position. The tougher a city is when negotiating with a company, the less likely the company is to construct the facility the city wants so badly.

Fifth, what will be the *unanticipated consequences* of a redevelopment project? Although no one can predict the future, analysts ought to try to forecast what unintended side effects the project might have. Often community leaders are so eager to begin a project that will generate a lot of economic activity that they accept the developer's projections at face value, while downplaying the objections of critics. Nowhere was this clearer than in the case of Atlantic City, where casino gambling was adopted partly in the hope that it would revitalize the city. But George Sternlieb's account of the casinos' impact on Atlantic City shows that precious little revitalization occurred.[66] Atlantic City appears to have lost the gamble. The housing supply got tighter. The number of local services (such as supermarkets) declined and crime rose. The pervasive role of organized crime in the city also grew. The community development fund that was supposed to be set aside for renewal in the city never matched expectations. And few of the 40,000 jobs created by the casinos went to Atlantic City residents. Eighty percent of casino employees live in Atlantic City suburbs and surrounding communities. A 1985 survey found that 63 percent of the employees would not even think of moving into Atlantic City because of the crime, poor schools, and increased housing costs.[67]

Finally, whatever states and communities do, the prestigious business organization Committee for Economic Development (CED) urges them to do it within a broad economic strategy. The CED recommends that rather than skipping from construction project to construction project, states adopt a strategy to "define priority actions, to give cohesion to government actions, and to avoid actions which may be harmful to the economy."[68] The CED recommends that each state start with a diagnosis of its own economic conditions, its potentialities, and how it is affected by changing national economic conditions. The state must then develop a vision that focuses not on "the conventional emphasis on recruiting firms *to* the state, but [on] creating an environment that facilitates change and is conducive to development and entrepreneurship *within* the state."[69] Finally, states should take actions that are compatible with the diagnosis and the strategy.

Initially, many cities focused their efforts on attracting businesses, hoping to lure a corporate headquarters or industrial plant to their city. Cities offered relocating companies millions of dollars in tax abatements or other incentives. Some cities have attempted to build modern infrastructures and to offer a high quality of life that would appeal to corporate leaders. Cities also emphasized tourism to bring people back to the downtowns and revitalize the central business district. Many cities were unsophisticated in their economic development efforts, offering just about any business an incentive to come to the community. Realistically, only a few cities could hope to compete for corporate headquarters. Today, many cities have large and sophisticated economic development efforts with professional employees and more narrowly targeted economic development strategies.

Questions raised about the effectiveness of traditional economic development strategies and the beneficiaries of these programs have led some cities to pursue a more progressive strategy of economic development. David Imbroscio explains that more progressive policies might include municipal ownership of businesses, development of human capital, or community-based strategies. Cities have traditionally owned airports and convention centers; it is only a small step for them to own hotels, factories, or shopping centers. There are examples today of cities with an equity stake in, or ownership of, these kinds of endeavors. However, state constitutions often prohibit or limit cities engaging in these activities.[70]

Imbroscio explains that a community-based strategy involves creating "new community-owned and -controlled economic institutions, governed by democratic procedures, and usually based in neighborhoods suffering from prior disinvestment."[71] The best example would be a community development bank that targets loans for individuals and businesses in an underdeveloped (i.e., poor) neighborhood in the city. This would ensure that the poor benefit from development policies.

Human-capital development involves investing in upgrading the skills and knowledge of the workforce, not just in the physical infrastructure of the city. Knowledge-based businesses in the postindustrial economy require a high-quality labor force. Cities with poorly educated workers can hardly recruit these kinds of firms. If cities can improve the educational quality and skill level of the population through better public education and job training, they can improve their long-term prospects for economic development. This would also redirect benefits to the lower classes, who may not greatly benefit from existing development policies.

Change and Bias in the Urban Political Economy

The major change in the urban political economy in the last three decades has been solidification of the central-city mayor's role as a promoter of public-private partnerships seeking to increase economic activity in urban areas and to improve the city's fiscal base (see Chapter 7). Cities use a variety of strategies, from offering tax abatements to supplying seed money, to working out complicated lease-back arrangements. What biases, if any, permeate this urban political economy?

First, despite the infusion of new money into urban redevelopment projects, the economic benefits for the poor and minorities have been disappointing. As indicated earlier in this chapter, numerous central cities have experienced devastating losses in numbers of jobs over the past two decades. Even in the Sunbelt, where cities are still growing, population increases may have outpaced job increases, and most of the growth occurs on the expanding edge of the city, not in the low-income residential neighborhoods. Whatever the reason, the plight of those at the bottom of the urban hierarchy is today as bad as or worse than it was two or three decades ago.

Second, part of the reason for the lack of improvement in the cities' poverty statistics is the biases inherent in the urban redevelopment process itself. One of the most commonly used redevelopment tools, the industrial development revenue bond, for example, does not appear to have been used to stimulate economically depressed regions, despite the fact that the legislation establishing it usually names that as a prime objective. In Chapter 11 we will examine the Clinton administration's empowerment zone program, which was an effort to revitalize the poorest inner-city neighborhoods in the largest cities.

To examine how extensively IDRBs were aimed at depressed locations, Thomas A. Pascarella and Richard D. Raymond researched whether high-unemployment areas in Ohio used IDRBs more than low-unemployment areas, but they found no relationships.[72] IDRBs are used in at least 47 states, and they became so popular that by the mid-1980s they constituted 70 percent of all municipal bond issues, whereas in 1970 they constituted only 33 percent. The most common use of IDRBs has been for the installation of pollution-control equipment, for the construction of hospitals, and for the construction of publicly subsidized housing. They also are often used to finance fast-food franchises, discount store locations, and similar commercial facilities that have little developmental power. In short, the IDRB as often used does little to generate permanent, well-paying jobs in poverty-stricken neighborhoods. It was partly because of these disappointments that Congress in 1986 put limits on the number of IDRBs that a city could issue each year.

There are limits to what the city can raise money for, Paul E. Peterson has argued.[73] In Peterson's view, a city that tries to raise too much money for redistributive services for needy residents will drive its middle-income residents out to the less redistributive-oriented suburbs. Cities should focus on raising money for economic development, according to Peterson, and leave redistributive policies to the federal government.

Although many urbanists question Peterson's assertion, most cities accept the *city limits* thesis in their policy making. The most widely praised and successful redevelopment in the last several decades focused on economic activities in the mainstream of the nation's economy—primarily providing support and office space for service industries and retail commerce. Much has also gone into retaining or attracting manufacturing facilities. This has not reversed the decline of heavy industry in the Frostbelt, but it may have been helpful to industrialization efforts in the South and Southwest over the past decades. Urban redevelopment activities seem to be reinforcing the bipolar character of the city, which we discussed early in this chapter. Much public money has been spent supporting downtown projects and gentrification, but no one has yet found the formula that would provide enough economic opportunities to make a permanent dent in urban poverty. Small, owner-run retail establishments, which in the past assured the city of a substantial middle-class population, have been squeezed out.

A further bias in the urban political economy is related to the mechanisms for passing the costs of urban redevelopment on to the federal treasury. This may be a good or a bad development, depending on one's viewpoint, but the trend is clear. Much of the stimulus for urban redevelopment has come from the federal treasury in the form of direct appropriations from grants such as the community development block grant. Indirect subsidies such as the IDRB and lease-back and tax-increment financing have become even more important. These subsidies are not in the form of direct appropriations but in the form of tax reductions (*tax expenditures,* to use the federal budget jargon).

People have a difficult time evaluating much of the urban redevelopment and gentrification activities of the past decade. Remembering the seedy, run-down appearance of many big-city downtowns two decades ago, comparing them to the elaborate redevelopments in many of these same cities today, and noting the increased number of people, jobs, and activities, it is hard to say that the cities should not have initiated these projects. At the same time, however, many central-city residential neighborhoods have had trouble holding their own as their former middle-class occupants moved out to the suburbs, and today they are increasingly occupied with people subsisting on marginal incomes. Many cities are moving toward a bipolar status, as Sternleib and Hughes expressed it, and the urban redevelopment activities have not slowed that trend. They may even have hastened it.

SUMMARY

1. Economic restructuring and the rise of the global economy have had profound consequences for American cities. The postindustrial city is a dependent city—dependent on higher levels of government for financial aid and dependent on private business to create jobs, provide revenue, and physically redevelop the city.

2. Economically, the typical large American central city has become a bipolar city. At one pole is a large lower-income population, and at the other is a small elite of professionals working in sleek office buildings and often living in chic gentrified neighborhoods. Squeezed out are the middle-income families who did so much in the past to give city neighborhoods social stability. The bipolar city is much more prevalent in the Northeast and Midwest than in the South and Southwest.

3. Cities seek to cope with their fiscal and economic plight by promoting public-private redevelopment projects. These projects aim to increase the city's level of economic activity and to improve the tax base.

4. Three main biases were found in the contemporary urban political economy. First, the continuing high rate of poverty suggests that cities no longer provide the kind of economic opportunity for low-income minority residents that they did for earlier immigrants. Second, the urban redevelopment process, however necessary it may be for other reasons, offers slim hope of advancing the economic prospects for the urban minorities and the poor. Finally, much of the cost of urban redevelopment has been passed on to the federal treasury.

NOTES

1. H. V. Savitch, *Post-Industrial Cities* (Princeton, N.J.: Princeton University Press, 1987); John Kenneth Galbraith, *The New Industrial State* (Boston: Houghton Mifflin, 1967); and Daniel Bell, *The Coming of Post-Industrial Society: A Venture in Social Forecasting* (New York: Basic Books, 1973).

2. Lester C. Thurow, *The Zero-Sum Society: Distribution and the Possibilities for Change* (New York: Basic Books, 1980), pp. 7, 192.

3. U.S. Bureau of the Census, *Statistical Abstract of the United States: 2001,* Table 616, p. 400, Table 596, p. 384 (http://www.census.gov).

4. U.S. Bureau of the Census, *Statistical Abstract of the United States: 2006,* Table 601, p. 400 (http://www.census.gov).

5. U.S. Bureau of the Census, *Statistical Abstract of the United States: 2006,* Table 618, p. 414 (http://www.census.gov).

6. Richard Child Hill and Cynthia Negrey, "Deindustrialization in the Great Lakes," *Urban Affairs Quarterly* 22, no. 4 (June 1987): 580–597.

7. Paul Knox, "Globalization and Urban Economic Change," *Annals of the American Academy of Political and Social Science* 551 (May 1997), pp. 18–19. See also Paul Knox and Peter Taylor, eds., *World Cities in a World-System* (Cambridge, England: Cambridge University Press, 1995); Saskia Sassen, *The Global City: New York, London, Tokyo* (Princeton, N.J.: Princeton University Press, 1991).

8. Paul Knox, "Globalization and Urban Economic Change," p. 19.

9. Ibid., p. 21.

10. Ibid.

11. Saskia Sassen, *The Global City* (Princeton, N.J.: Princeton University Press, 1991).

12. James W. White, "Old Wine, Cracked Bottle? Tokyo, Paris, and the Global City Hypothesis," *Urban Affairs Review* 33 (March 1998): 451–478.

13. International Trade Administration, "Metro Area Exports" (http://www.ita.doc.gov/td/industry/otea/metro/Summary.html).

14. For more on the impact of globalization on American cities, see Peter Kresl and Gary Gappert, eds., *North America Cities and the Global Economy* (Thousand Oaks, Calif.: Sage, 1995). See also the special symposium published in *The Annals of the American Academy of Political and Social Science* 551 (May 1997).

15. Lester C. Thurow, "The Disappearance of the Middle Class," *New York Times,* February 5, 1984, p. F-3.

16. Arthur F. Jones, Jr., and Daniel H. Weinber, "The Changing Shape of the Nation's Income Distribution, 1947–1998," U.S. Bureau of the Census (June 2000).

17. Ibid., p. 10.

18. Joe Dalaker, "Poverty in the United States: 2000," U.S. Bureau of the Census (September 2001).

19. Source: U.S. Census Bureau, Figure 3, *Income, Poverty and Health Insurance Coverage in the United States: 2004,* p. 9 (http://www.census.gov/prod/2005pubs/p60-229.pdf).

20. Joe Dalaker, "Poverty in the United States: 2000," U.S. Bureau of the Census (September 2001).

21. *The Health and Human Services Poverty Guidelines,* 1997.

22. William Julius Wilson, *The Truly Disadvantaged: The Inner City, the Underclass, and Public Policy* (Chicago: University of Chicago Press, 1987).

23. Peter Dreier, "America's Urban Crisis: Symptoms, Causes, Solutions" in John Boger and Judith Wegner, eds., *Race, Poverty and American Cities* (Chapel Hill: University of North Carolina Press, 1996), p. 96.

24. William Julius Wilson, *When Work Disappears,* pp. 11–12. Joe Dalaker, "Poverty in the United States: 2000." U.S. Bureau of the Census (September 2001).

25. U.S. Department of Housing and Urban Development, *The State of the Cities* (June 2000).

26. U.S. Census Bureau, Places within United States, Percent of People Below Poverty Level, 2004 American Community Survey.

27. U.S. Department of Housing and Urban Development, "The State of the Cities" (June 1997), Exhibit 9.

28. William Julius Wilson, *When Work Disappears,* pp. 11–14; U.S. Department of Housing and Urban Development, "The State of the Cities" (June 1997), p. 34.

29. Ibid.

30. G. Thomas Kingsley and Kathryn L. S. Pettit, "Concentrated Poverty: A Change in Course," *Neighborhood Change in Urban America* No. 2, May 2003, p. 1 (Washington, D.C.: Urban Institute).

31. Paul A. Jargowsky and Rebecca Yang, "The 'Underclass' Revisited: A Social Problem in Decline," *Journal of Urban Affairs* 28 (2006): 57. This measure is taken from Erol R. Ricketts and Isabel V. Sawhill, "Defining and Measuring the Underclass," *Journal of Policy Analysis and Management* 7 (1988): 316–25.

32. "The Underclass Revisited," p. 61.

33. "The Underclass Revisited," pp. 64–65.

34. U.S Congress, Office of Technology Assessment, *The Technological Reshaping of Metropolitan America,* OTA-ETI-643 (Washington, D.C.: U.S. Government Printing Office, 1995), pp. 90–92.

35. George Sternlieb and James W. Hughes, "The Uncertain Future of the Central City," *Urban Affairs Quarterly* 18, no. 4 (June 1983): 456.

36. Ibid., pp. 455–572.

37. Norton Long, "The City as Reservation," *Public Interest* 25 (Fall 1971): 35. Long developed the same idea in his "City as Political Economy," *National Civic Review* 63, no. 4 (April 1974): 189–191.

38. George Sternlieb, "The City as Sandbox," *Public Interest* 25 (Fall 1971): 14–21.

39. Larry Ledebur and William Barnes, *Metropolitan Disparities and Economic Growth* (Washington, D.C.: National League of Cities, 1993).

40. John Logan, *The Suburban Advantage: New Census Data Show Unyielding City-Suburb Economic Gap, and Surprising Shifts in Some Places,* July 24. Albany, NY: Lewis Mumford Center for Comparative Urban and Regional Research. 2002: http://www.albany.edu/mumford/.

41. See especially Alexander Ganz and Thomas O'Brien, "The City: Sandbox, Reservation, or Dynamo?" *Public Policy* 21, no. 1 (Winter 1973): 107–124. For a journalistic account, see T. D. Allman, "The Urban Crisis Leaves Town," *Harper's* (December 1978): 41–56.

42. L. L. Berkowitz, "Economic Redevelopment Really Works: Baltimore, Maryland," *Urban Economic Development,* vol. 27, *Urban Affairs Annual Reviews,* eds. R. D. Bingham and J. P. Blair (Beverly Hills, Calif.: Sage, 1984).

43. Rochelle L. Stanfield, "Oakland's Comeback Aided by Economic Spillover from Thriving San Francisco," *National Journal* 15 (November 26, 1983): 2474–2476.

44. C. Prost, "Comeback City," *Planning* 51 (October 1985): 4–11.

45. Chester Hartman, Dennis Keating, and Richard L. Gates, with Steve Turner, *Displacement: How to Fight It* (Berkeley, Calif.: National Housing Project, 1982).

46. Marc V. Levine, "'A Third-World City in the First World': Social Exclusion, Racial Inequality, and Sustainable Development in Baltimore," in Mario Polése and Richard Stren, *The Social Sustainability of Cities 2000* (Toronto: University of Toronto Press, 2000), pp. 123–156.

47. Paul S. Grogan and Tony Proscio, *Comeback Cities* (Boulder, Colo.: Westview Press, 2000), p. 1.

48. Ibid., pp. 1–9.

49. Ibid., chap. 2.

50. Ibid., chap. 1.

51. Paul Kantor, *The Dependent City Revisited: The Political Economy of Urban Development and Social Policy* (Boulder, Colo.: Westview Press, 1995).

52. Office of Technology Assessment, pp. 228–229.

53. For overviews of economic development policy, see Edward Blakely, *Planning Local Economic Development: Theory and Practice* (Thousand Oaks, Calif.: Sage, 1994); David L. Imbroscio, "Economic Development" in Ronald K. Vogel, ed., *Handbook of Research on Urban Politics and Policy* (Westport, Conn.: Greenwood Press, 1997); Robert Bingham and Robert Mier, eds., *Dilemmas of Urban Economic Development: Issues in Theory and Practice* (Thousand Oaks, Calif.: Sage, 1997).

54. Dan Pilcher, "Assessing State Business Climates," *State Legislatures* 9, no. 8 (August/September 1983): 9–12; *St. Paul Pioneer Press and Dispatch,* October 23, 1983, p. D-1.

55. David L. Birch, *The Job Generation Process* (Cambridge, Mass.: M.I.T. Program on Neighborhoods and Regional Change, 1979), p. 21.

56. Roy Bahl, *The Impact of Local Tax Policy on Urban Economic Development* (Washington, D.C.: U.S. Department of Commerce, Economic Development Administration, Urban Consortium Information Bulletin, September 1980), p. 15.

57. Roger W. Schmenner, *Making Business Location Decisions* (Englewood Cliffs, N.J.: Prentice-Hall, 1982), pp. 50–51.

58. Data for jobs gained in 1985 from the Bureau of Labor Statistics. Data for business climates taken from Grant Thornton Company, *Survey of Manufacturing Climates, 1985* (Chicago: Grant Thornton Company, 1986).

59. Data reported in the *St. Paul Pioneer Press and Dispatch,* June 4, 1986, p. B-10.

60. Jane F. Roberts, "State Actions Affecting Local Governments: Upheaval for Fiscal Relations," *The Municipal Year Book: 1987* (Washington, D.C.: International City Management Association, 1987), pp. 56–57.

61. Stein, Sinclair, and Neiman review the relevant research on this question in their "Local Government and Fiscal Stress," p. 102; "MTCD's Role in Massachusetts Venture Capital," http://www.mtde.com/role.html.

62. Jane Carroll, "Economic Development Through Venture Capital," *State Legislatures* 11, no. 3 (March 1985): 24–25; "MTDC's Role in Massachusetts Venture Capital," http://www.mtdc.com/role.html.

63. *St. Paul Pioneer Press and Dispatch,* March 13, 1983, p. A-11.

64. *Minneapolis Tribune,* June 5, 1983, p. 6-D.

65. *New York Times,* March 15, 1981, p. 12; April 30, 1981, p. 23; *Minneapolis Tribune,* June 5, 1983, p. 6-D.

66. George Sternlieb and James Hughes, *Atlantic City Gamble* (Cambridge, Mass.: Harvard University Press, 1984).

67. *New York Times,* July 11, 1986, p. 11.

68. Committee on Economic Development, *Leadership for Dynamic State Economies* (New York: Committee on Economic Development, 1986), p. 6.

69. Ibid.

70. David Imbroscio, "Economic Development."

71. Ibid., pp. 265–266.

72. Thomas A. Pascarella and Richard D. Raymond, "Buying Bonds for Business: An Evaluation of the Industrial Revenue Bond Program," *Urban Affairs Quarterly* 18, no. 1 (September 1982): 73–89.

73. Peterson, *City Limits* (Chicago: University of Chicago Press, 1981).

CHAPTER 7

COMMUNITY POWER
AND LEADERSHIP

CHAPTER SYNOPSIS

The Classic Community Power Debates: *Elite Model; Pluralist Theory* • Revising Community Power—More Recent Scholarship: *Neo-Marxist and Growth Machines View of the Role of Business; A Unitary City Interest in Promoting Development?; Urban Regimes and Systemic Power; Converging Findings in Urban Political Economy* • Functional Feifdoms: *Fragmentation of the Local Public Sector; Strong Mayor as Antidote to Functional Feifdoms; Citizen Control (Decentralization) as Antidote to Unresponsive Local Bureaucracy; Bias and Consequences of Functional Feifdoms*

Who really runs American cities?

And for whose benefit?

These questions jump out when one reflects on the discussion of economic development in the previous chapter. Over the past three decades, many American cities have spent a great deal of public money (your tax money) and built up a huge amount of public debt (your debt) that will have to be paid off by future taxes (your taxes) in order to rebuild their downtowns and stimulate business investment. Whether or not these public actions achieve their goals, they will have an impact on your own quality of life in future years if you live within metropolitan America (as 80 percent of Americans do). For these reasons, it seems fair to ask, "Who really influences what governments do in American cities? And for whose benefit do they exert that influence?"

These questions are as troubling to urban scholars today as they have been for the last 50 years. Some people respond that cities are run by elite power structures. Others say that cities are run through the interactions of various interest groups and power centers. These two responses have been termed the *elitist model* and the *pluralist model* of community power, respectively. The elitist and pluralist models constitute the starting point for exploring the contest for dominance in American central cities. To understand this contest, we must examine these two models as well as some other important related changes taking place in urban politics—the emergence of what we will call functional fiefdoms, the challenge to strong mayoral leadership, and demands for community control and citizen participation in local governance.

Accordingly, this chapter will ask the following questions:

- Are the central cities dominated by a stratified power structure?
- What is meant by the emergence of functionally based governmental power, and why is the strong mayor proposed as an antidote for it?
- What is the nature of the charge that contemporary urban government is unresponsive to the citizenry, and why is community control proposed as an antidote for this alleged unresponsiveness?
- Does the organization of public power in the contemporary metropolis lead to consistent patterns of bias?

Are Central Cities Dominated by Stratified Power Structures?

Who runs American cities? Are they controlled by a unified, upper-status elite that usually operates behind the scenes and is capable of subordinating the formal governmental apparatus of the city to its own interests? In other words, is community power in city governance elitist? Or is control over the city divided among several competing groups and power centers? Is it pluralist? For 50 years elitists and the pluralists have debated basic methods of research, basic assumptions about the exercise of power, and basic conclusions about its dispersion.

The Elitist Model of Community Power

Although several sociological and anthropological community studies had commented on local politics,[1] the first community study that devoted itself exclusively to the exercise of power was Floyd Hunter's *Community Power Structure*.[2] His book is worth examining in some detail, because it establishes one major strand of basic research methodology and substantive conclusions that have influenced community studies since its publication in 1953. Hunter, a sociologist, set himself the task of answering the question "Who runs Regional City?" (for *Regional City,* read *Atlanta, Georgia*). To identify the leadership of Regional City, Hunter compiled lists of prominent civic leaders, government leaders, business leaders, and status leaders. He then selected a panel of six knowledgeable people to examine the lists and identify the most influential individuals and the most influential organizations on each list. From these selections, and after interviewing those identified, Hunter determined that 40 individuals were at the apex of the power structure in Regional City. Most of these 40 served on the boards of directors of the same corporations and belonged to the same social clubs. Beneath the top leadership was a cadre of what Hunter called "understructure personnel" who carried out the will and the instructions of the top power structure.

Not only did Hunter identify a top power structure in Regional City; he also contended that this power structure initiated most of the major developments that occurred in Regional City and that it successfully vetoed projects it disliked. Enterprising newspaper or journal writers lost their jobs when they disagreed with the power structure. Social-welfare professionals were carefully constrained not to raise issues such as public housing

---

Power in Regional City

As an example of how things were done in Regional City, Hunter describes how a top business leader named Charles Homer used a dinner meeting at an exclusive club to launch a project to establish an international trade council:

> When we meet at the Club at dinner with the other crowds, Mr. Homer makes a brief talk; again, he does not need to talk long. He ends his talk by saying he believes in his proposition enough that he is willing to put his own money into it for the first year. . . . The Growers Bank crowd, not to be outdone, offers a like amount plus a guarantee that they will go along with the project for three years. Others throw in. . . . I'd say within thirty or forty minutes, we have pledges of the money we need. In three hours the whole thing is settled, including the time for eating.
>
> We went into that meeting with a board of directors picked. The constitution was all written, and the man who was to head the council as executive was named . . . a third-stringer, a fellow who will take advice.
>
> The public doesn't know anything about the project until it reaches the stage I've been talking about. After the matter is financially sound, then we go to the newspapers and say there is a proposal for consideration. Of course, it is not news to a lot of people by then, but the Chamber committees and other civic organizations are brought in on the idea. They all think it's a good idea. They help to get the Council located and established. That's about all there is to it.

Source: From Floyd Hunter, *Community Power Structure* (Chapel Hill: University of North Carolina Press, 1953), pp. 173–174.

---

that might undermine the interests of the power structure. On certain key issues, such as limiting the supply of public housing, Hunter pictured the governor, the United States senators, the key state legislators, the party leaders, and other officials—with very few exceptions—as subordinated to the top power structure. Power, in Hunter's view, was cumulative. That is, power in one area of activity gave a person power in other areas as well (see the accompanying box).

Critiques of Hunter   In summary, Hunter described Atlanta as dominated by a very small and conservative business elite that acted to advance its own interests rather than the public benefit. Public officials were subordinated to this power structure, and power was cumulative. Because of this dominance of the city by a nongovernmental elite, Hunter's thesis is referred to as an elitist theory or *stratification theory* of community power.

When the book appeared, it provoked a furor in the academic community, particularly among political scientists, for, in a sense, Hunter's characterizing of governmental structures as totally subservient to economic structures made the traditional political scientists' concern over forms of city government seem irrelevant. If true power were to be found outside the governmental structure, what difference did it make whether the city government was organized under a strong mayor, a city manager, or a commission? Consequently, the appearance of Hunter's book precipitated a new rash of inquiry into the study of local government.[3]

Political scientists generally disagreed with Hunter's conclusion, but because no political scientist had conducted empirical studies that could refute Hunter's thesis, their strongest criticisms attacked his research methods and his assumptions about power.[4] By asking knowledgeable observers to identify the most influential leaders, said Hunter's critics, he had not really measured the exercise of power. He had merely measured the reputation for power.[5] Hence Hunter's approach to measuring community power was called the *reputational method*. To measure power validly, argued some of Hunter's critics, one would have to use a decision-making approach—that is, analyze the actual decisions through which power is exercised.

The Pluralist Model of Community Power

The first major empirical work that used a *decision-making* approach, rather than Hunter's reputational approach, to measure power was the study of New Haven by Robert Dahl in *Who Governs?*[6] Dahl deliberately set out to test the hypothesis that New Haven is governed by the kind of economic and social elite that Hunter had discovered in Atlanta. He isolated 34 important decisions in the three functional areas of urban renewal, education, and the selection of party nominees for mayor over a period of time that extended from 1941 to 1959. He established rigid criteria for defining the economic and social notables of New Haven. Contrary to Hunter's findings, Dahl discovered that in New Haven there was *no significant overlap* between the economic and social elites, that these elites had almost no influence on the decisions he studied, and that power in New Haven was *noncumulative* (that is, power in one functional area did not lead to power in other functional areas).

In the three issue areas that concerned him, Dahl conducted extensive interviews with 46 top decision makers. He found very few instances in which an individual person was involved in more than one major decision, let alone more than one issue area. The major exception to this was the mayor of New Haven, Richard C. Lee. Lee was a supreme political tactician, adept at bargaining with the leaders of all the major functional fiefdoms in New Haven plus some other leaders in federal and state agencies that had programs in New Haven. Through his bargaining skill, he was able to initiate and carry out the kinds of programs he envisioned for the growth and prosperity of the city. Dahl perceived Mayor Lee as occupying the critical position in what Dahl referred to as an "executive centered coalition" of a plurality of interest groups in New Haven. Because this view sees power as noncumulative and dispersed among several power centers, Dahl's theories about community power are called *pluralist* theories.

Early Refinements of the Two Models of Community Power

Following the publication of the initial studies by Hunter and Dahl, increasingly sophisticated research methods were used to examine every conceivable subtlety of these two models. Comparative studies of community power were conducted in more than one city,[7] and in some studies, reputational methods of analysis were combined with decision-making methods.[8] A survey of almost three dozen community power studies found that sociologists had an overwhelming tendency to use the reputational method, whereas political scientists were much more likely to use the decision-making method of analysis. Political scientists were also much less likely to come to stratificationist conclusions than were sociologists.[9]

Some of the early communities were studied again. Hunter revisited Atlanta a quarter-century later and found that little of basic importance had changed: "Fundamental power relationships have not altered."[10] New Haven was also revisited by the stratification theorist William G. Domhoff, who reanalyzed some of Dahl's data and came to the conclusion that fundamentally, New Haven really was run by an economic elite.[11]

In great measure the pluralists and the stratificationists were talking past one another, starting from different assumptions and leaving this "important area of study . . . in disarray," as Clarence N. Stone expressed it.[12] If Stone is correct that this large and growing body of research is in disarray, what conclusions can we draw about the contest for dominance in cities? Three conclusions in particular can be drawn with confidence. These concern the role of business, the importance of nondecisions, and the great variety of power relationships that exist.

The Role of Business   Subsequent research has tended to dispel the picture of top businesspeople operating as a cohesive clique and dominating city public affairs—the picture that Hunter presented of the businesspeople in Atlanta. However, it is conceivable that Hunter's observations of Atlanta were accurate for that time period and that businesspeople did indeed dominate the city's politics during the early 1950s.* Hunter's findings of business dominance are consistent with the overwhelming majority of early anthropological and sociological community studies, which asserted that they had found the same kind of business dominance over their cities that Hunter found in Atlanta. Particularly dominant were the owners of key businesses in one-industry towns. The classic example was the dominance of Muncie, Indiana, by the Ball family, referred to as Middletown and the X family, respectively, by Robert S. and Helen M. Lynd in their monumental works *Middletown* and *Middletown in Transition*.[13] In one famous passage, the Lynds quote a Middletown man's comments on the pervasive influence of the X family over all aspects of life in Middletown:

> If I'm out of work I go to the X plant; if I need money I go to the X bank, and if they don't like me I don't get it; my children go to the X college; when I get sick I go to the X hospital; I buy a building lot or house in an X subdivision; my wife goes downtown to buy clothes at the X department store; if my dog strays away he is put in the X pound; I buy X milk; I drink X beer, vote for X political parties, and get help from X charities; my boy goes to the X Y.M.C.A. and my girl to their Y.W.C.A.; I listen to the word of God in X-subsidized churches; if I'm a Mason I go to the X Masonic Temple; I read the news from the X morning newspaper; and, if I am rich enough, I travel via the X airport.[14]

Despite the protestations of the pluralists that stratificationists such as Hunter and the Lynds were exaggerating the business dominance of local politics,[15] many other cities in addition to Muncie and Atlanta seem to have had a particular business elite that dominated local affairs. United States Steel Corporation planned and built Gary,

---

*Edward C. Banfield argues that businesspeople may have dominated Atlanta in the early 1950s but that by the mid-1960s they were only one of two important blocs in the city. See his *Big City Politics* (New York: Random House, 1965), pp. 18–36. See also M. Kent Jennings, *Community Influentials: The Elites of Atlanta* (New York: Free Press, 1964).

Indiana, and exerted considerable influence over its government. The Mellon family had disproportionate influence in Pittsburgh. One-company mining towns often stayed under the control of their patrons for decades. And even today the Anaconda Corporation exerts extensive power over Butte, Montana.

Business interests were especially powerful in the rapidly growing cities of the Southwest. Houston probably exemplified this trend as much as any city:

> A land dealer and developer was mayor for 22 of the years between 1921 and 1957. In 1981, the mayor was a developer, one-third of the city council was in real estate or closely related fields, and the planning commission was composed mostly of developers, builders, and others tied to the real estate industry field.[16]

With this dominance over the city's political leadership positions, it is not surprising that the government of Houston during those years followed policies that were much more favorable to the city's real estate and land development interests than they were to the lower-strata residential neighborhoods or the minority communities. Accordingly, Houston had no zoning plan, scrimped on social services, was notorious for its inadequate bus system, and did its best to hold down property taxes in order to present a positive image for business.

Despite the examples of Houston, Middletown, and Atlanta, however, it is a mistake to think in terms of *a* unified business community. Any large metropolis is bound to have several business communities that compete with one another as much as they cooperate. For example, when Philadelphia first proposed an urban renewal program in the 1950s, the business community was split on the idea. The idea drew strong support from those parts of the business community that were locally oriented and stood to benefit from a rejuvenated downtown: law firms, local retailers, and banks. Businesses that were engaged in manufacturing for a nationwide market, however, as well as national retailers and the chamber of commerce, either had little interest in the plan or opposed it outright. An officer of one manufacturing corporation said, "It makes little difference to us what happens in the city. We do not have our homes here; we have no large plants located within the city limits; we have only an office building that we can close at any time that conditions within the city become too oppressive."[17]

This division of the business community in Philadelphia is common in most metropolises. In the years that have passed since the first community power studies were conducted, most sectors of the economy have come to be increasingly dominated by national corporations rather than local companies. This means that business leadership in a community is often bifurcated between a local elite of merchants and developers, who are very much interested in local affairs, and the managers of the national corporations, whose careers and interests impel them to pay more attention to the internal affairs of their corporation than to local politics.[18] Unless the corporation has a significant business reason to be interested in the local affairs of a community, the corporation executives often limit their involvement in local affairs to activities designed to do little more than maintain a positive corporate image. However, in cities where local affairs *do* affect the economic interests of national corporations, their managers are much more likely to become involved locally.[19]

Not only is the business sector divided between the owners of local businesses and the managers of national corporations; it is also divided into several functional categories. Few businesspeople exhibit much interest in civic affairs that lie beyond their functional sphere. Thus urban renewal agencies routinely seek out the advice and collaboration of real estate brokers and the financial community, whereas other kinds of businesspeople—such as retail merchants, automobile dealers, and shopping center owners—are often quite uninterested. Utilities seek to promote a city's population, income, and employment, whereas railroads often display little interest in city politics.[20] Because of this divergence of interests, the business community is not nearly so cohesive in its approach to local politics as Hunter's portrayal suggests. It is highly competitive. And the resources with which businesspeople can influence public affairs depend on the functional area involved, the issue, the interests of the businesspeople, and the homogeneity with which they can act.

The Importance of Nondecisions   If subsequent research on the role of businesspeople in city politics tended to dispel the stratificationist notion that they manipulate public affairs as one cohesive, well-organized bloc, it also found flaws in the decision-making approach to analyzing community power. Political scientists Peter Bachrach and Morton S. Baratz charged that its preoccupation with actual decisions ignores "the fact that power may be, and often is, exercised by confining the scope of decision-making to relatively 'safe' issues."

> Of course power is exercised when A participates in the making of decisions that affect B. But power is also exercised when A devotes his energies to creating or reinforcing social and political values and institutional practices that limit the scope of the political process to public consideration of only those issues which are comparatively innocuous to A. To the extent that A succeeds in doing this, B is prevented, for all practical purposes, from bringing to the fore any issues that might in their resolution be seriously detrimental to A's set of preferences.[21]

Such an exercise of power is referred to as coming to *nondecisions*. Nondecisions are much more difficult to identify and measure than actual decisions. The key area where nondecisions predominate is in preserving the dominant values, myths, and established political procedures of a community. Only certain kinds of questions are put on the agendas of the decision-making agencies. Other kinds of questions are never put on those agendas and hence never reach the point where decisions about them can be made.

Furthermore, some people have fewer resources for waging political battles than others. The people with fewer resources usually lose these battles, and they quite often are the poorest people in the city. Many issues stay in the realm of nondecisions because these people lack either the resources or the will to fight for them. In the words of Clarence Stone, "Because people have no taste for waging costly battles they are sure to lose, much goes uncontested."[22]

Although researchers have expressed doubts about the usefulness of the concept of nondecisions, pertinent examples have been cited in the literature on local politics.[23] In his study of New Haven, for example, Robert Dahl paid very little attention to the African American community because it did not figure in the major decisions he analyzed. Even the urban renewal decisions, which deeply touched the lives of large numbers of New Haven African Americans, were made without much input from the local black community. When a riot broke out in New Haven in 1967, some people began to ask why decisions had not been made on questions that African Americans themselves apparently considered important.[24] The answer seems to be that the African Americans did not constitute a strong enough interest group to have their demands placed on the decision-making agenda. The needs and demands of people who do not have the backing of strong interest groups and powerful civic leaders are likely to remain in the realm of nondecisions.

The Variety of Power Relationships   Finally, pluralists pointed out that power is structured differently in different communities and that the structures change over time. Atlanta of the 1990s is vastly different not only from the New Haven that Dahl studied but even from the Atlanta that Hunter studied in the early 1950s. For one thing, it has an African American majority today compared to only a black minority at the time of Hunter's analysis. Atlanta has had African American mayors for the past 30 years, an accomplishment that would have been impossible if the city's power structure had remained the same as the one described by Hunter. Not only do power structures change over time, but a city located in the middle of a large megalopolis will be subjected to outside political influences that will have less impact on a comparable city surrounded by a rural setting.[25]

Highly stratified power structures are most likely to be found where city leaders share a consensus on the role of government and where power is not shared extensively with the mass of the people. Highly stratified power structures are also most likely to be found in isolated communities dominated by a single industry, in small homogeneous communities, and in the South. Pluralist power structures are most likely to be found in metropolitan areas, in communities with a heterogeneous population, and in communities with a diversity of economic foundations and social cleavages.

Who Governs in the Age of Urban Restructuring?

By the end of the 1970s, the following three statements reasonably summarized the dispute over community power:

> The role of business is a great deal more complex than the elitists had portrayed it.
> But the existence of nondecisions gives business a larger role than pluralists generally admitted.
> And the structure of power relationships varies greatly from place to place and from time to time.

While these debates over community power were raging, the cities themselves were undergoing a dramatic restructuring that neither elitists nor pluralists could explain very well.[26] Especially prominent were the eruption of riots during the 1960s, the staggering economic decline of many cities, widespread fiscal stress in the late 1970s, a global economic restructuring that threatened the survival of the American city as a manufacturing center, and (more than anything) the impressive downtown and economic redevelopment schemes that blossomed across the land. In terms of their ethnic base, their economic base, and their physical appearance, American cities in the last third of the twentieth century experienced one of the greatest restructurings that had happened to any system of cities in history.

If the stratificationists were correct that a small group of business elites controlled the cities for their own benefit, why would these elites have collaborated with the economic disinvestment that has been so disastrous for so many cities? And why did so many of the economic redevelopment schemes appear to originate not in company boardrooms but in city halls? If the pluralists were correct in their optimistic view that a plurality of interest groups governed the city through competition and coalitions, then how do we explain the fact that the huge central-city underclass (as noted in Chapter 6) was almost always left out of the governing coalition? And how do we explain the fact that the economic redevelopment schemes have had so little payoff at the neighborhood level, where the rank-and-file members of the supposedly powerful interest groups lived?

These questions are very difficult to answer within the framework of early elitist or pluralist theories. But just as nature cannot tolerate a vacuum, the human mind cannot tolerate unexplainable facts. Thus it is not surprising that new theories emerged to answer the perplexing question of who governs in the current age of urban restructuring. As cities struggle to cope with the task of urban restructuring, who has the most influence? How is it exerted? And who benefits?

Dominance by Global Capital

One troubling set of answers came out of *neo-Marxist* schools of thought. In their view, as cities grapple with the challenge of urban restructuring, they respond to the dictates of the global capital markets. It is the market that governs. The city needs investment capital to prosper, and this fact puts city officials at the mercy of the global markets that control the investment of capital around the world. Cities must compete with one another to attract investment capital, and a fundamental problem facing many American cities (especially old manufacturing centers such as Detroit and Gary, Indiana) is that they simply are no longer competitive in the global marketplace. The evolution of capitalism has made the traditional American city obsolete. Richard Child Hill writes, "The city is forged upon the hearth of a given mode of production. . . . A particular city cannot be divorced from the encompassing political economy [within] which it is embedded and through which it manifests its particular function and form."[27]

From this viewpoint, the old industrial city of the Midwest was formed a century ago because labor-intensive industrial manufacturing required large numbers of workers to be assembled in concentrated areas. It was the job of city government to provide the infrastructure (streets, sewers, water supply, land preparation) that would enable this concentration of laborers to take place. It was also the job of the city to provide sufficient police protection and political services to keep the laborers from organizing collectively against the factory owners. For today's capital-intensive factory, however, large concentrations of workers are no longer needed. The Dodge plant at Poletown in Detroit employed many more workers at the height of its operations in the 1950s than have ever been, or are likely ever to be, employed by the Cadillac plant built on the same site in the 1980s.

Not only is today's factory capital-intensive rather than labor-intensive, but also capital is mobile: Corporations can move the production facilities out of troublesome locations into more receptive locations. Cities, by contrast, are stationary; you cannot move Detroit to the Sunbelt. Detroit, in fact, has been suffering for years from flight of capital out of the city as corporations have closed down plants in the city and built new ones in the suburbs, in the Sunbelt, or overseas. Between 1960 and 1976, Detroit lost 200,000 jobs, about 30 percent of all the jobs that had existed only 16 years earlier in 1960.[28]

In the late 1970s, when General Motors decided to invest $40 billion in building new automobile production plants, there were probably a hundred places around the globe, in addition to Detroit, where GM could profitably make the investments in new plants. The juxtaposition of the stationary city with highly mobile investment capital puts Detroit and every other city at a disadvantage in dealing with GM. Nowhere was this seen more clearly than in Detroit's bid to be selected as the site for GM's new Cadillac plant in 1980 and 1981. GM adopted an uncompromising take-it-or-leave-it attitude on the site specifications for the new plant. To produce the site, the city had to destroy a neighborhood (Poletown), suffer severe attacks on its public image as a result of that destruction, and spend over $200 million to turn the site over to GM. Realistically, this expenditure could not be justified in terms of anticipated increases in city revenues and the tax base.[29]

From a neo-Marxist perspective, the politics of urban redevelopment and the conflict between corporation and neighborhood is a contemporary replay of the class conflict in today's city. The corporation seeks to maximize profit and looks to the city government to prepare the infrastructure for the corporation's involvement. As in Poletown, this task often puts the city in the middle between the corporation and the city's own neighborhood residents. In this sense, the class struggle appears to be taking place today between capital and neighborhood as a substitute for the historical struggle between owner and worker.

These concepts of the neo-Marxists have come under severe criticism. Much of this theory is highly deductive in nature, with little foundation in systematic empirical research.[30] And some important case studies of redevelopment politics explicitly reject neo-Marxist explanations. An analysis of economic development politics in the New York region, for example, argues that huge development institutions such as the Port Authority of New York and New Jersey have policy agendas of their own that are quite independent of business leaders in the region.[31]

Growth Machine Theory

Despite these criticisms, the great contribution of the neo-Marxists to the community power debate was to take attention away from elites as behind-the-scenes conspirators in the city and to refocus attention on the larger politicoeconomic forces that influence city politics. For one school of thought, the most important of these forces is what sociologist Harvey Molotch called "a growth machine."[32] Molotch argues that local elites with substantial local land holdings, together with business interests that benefit from growth (e.g., bankers, developers, home builders, realtors, architects, engineers), dominate community policy making and that these leaders' common interest lies in promoting growth. Growth will make their land more valuable or increase profits of their businesses. To secure their investment, these local land-based elites dominate local government and seek to co-opt local political leaders by bringing them into the progrowth machine.

Growth machine theory differs from neo-Marxist theory in at least two key respects. First, the goal of the growth machine is *not to maximize profit* from selling goods and services in a national market, as is the goal of the corporation. Rather, the goal of the growth machine is to *maximize rental returns* through renting space to the businesses and people who will use the facilities built by the growth machine.[33] In this sense, from the viewpoint of the growth machine advocates in Detroit, the possibility that the city might never recover the $200 million it invested in the Poletown site was less bothersome than the prospect of nothing being built on the site. Whether or not the project is successful in the long run, the members of the growth machine also make immediate profits. Second, the growth machine is not composed of the national upper class or even of the leaders of the national corporations whose profits are not tied to any particular locale. Instead, the growth machine is a locally based elite focused on intensifying local development from which it profits. The members of the growth machine are local real estate owners, bankers, developers, construction unions, and central-city newspapers whose circulations and advertising revenues will expand with growth in the metropolis.

In dealing with the growth machine, city government plays two conflicting roles. First, it must support the growth machine's promotion of economic growth and redevelopment on the grounds that growth will bring in jobs for city residents and will make land in the region more valuable and increase city revenue. Second, because it represents people in local neighborhoods, city government often finds itself playing an intermediary role in the conflicts that arise when neighborhood residents oppose particular redevelopment projects. Molotch believes that the promise of jobs and increased revenues is an ideological prop of the growth machine but one that it fails to deliver. In most instances, Molotch believes the growth machine will profit from a particular project, such as a new stadium or downtown development. But in most instances, the jobs will be fewer, pay less, or cost more through incentives than they return to the community. Often the costs are paid by neighborhood residents who value *use* value over *exchange* value.

Occasionally, an *antigrowth coalition* may arise to challenge the dominant growth machine politics. Neighborhood residents in coalition with environmentalists may object to projects because they are too costly, because they will harm the environment, or because neighborhood residents will bear the burden while a privileged group will gain the benefits. For example, in an urban renewal project, a lower-income, minority group might be forced to move so that a company can build an office that creates jobs for white-collar managers. The antigrowth coalition, however, is often at a disadvantage in this battle over growth. Those who oppose growth or projects that claim to create many jobs for a community are often labeled kooks and accused of threatening the community's well-being. Ronald Vogel and Bert Swanson found that an antigrowth coalition in Gainesville, Florida, could not sustain itself even after gaining control of city government. The growth machine succeeded in shifting decisions to another arena—in this case the state—to prevent the antigrowth coalition from consolidating its gains.[34] Eventually, the growth machine was returned to power. By the time the antigrowth coalition learns of development plans, the decision is often so far along that it cannot be reversed. Vigorous study and questioning of business plans or incentive packages are often construed as harmful to the business climate.

Cities as a Unitary Interest

In contrast to the neo-Marxist and growth machine interpretations of urban decline and redevelopment is the concept of "unitary interest," which Paul E. Peterson spelled out in his highly influential 1981 book *City Limits*.[35] Like the neo-Marxists and the growth machine theorists, Peterson placed great emphasis on the role of investment capital in determining the fate of cities. Cities are in competition with one another to capture as much investment capital as they can. A city also has export industries (automobiles in Detroit, computer hardware and software in the Silicon Valley area, health services in Cleveland) that provide a lot of jobs and bring money into the city. The business leaders of the city, political leaders, and ordinary residents have a *unitary interest* in protecting those export industries and helping attract new investment capital that will help them expand in the future. Thus it is not a "growth machine" that impels the mayor to pursue downtown redevelopment. It is simply a mutual recognition of the best interests of all the city's residents.

Peterson's theory leads him to an extremely important normative conclusion, as we saw in Chapter 6. If city leaders have a unitary interest in promoting the city's export industries, then city government should limit its expenditures for redistributive social services and welfare services to a minimum; it should maximize expenditures that facilitate the unitary interest. Redistributive and welfare costs should be shifted to the national government.

This argument provides a powerful justification for the economic redevelopment activities of most cities, but like the other theories, it has been criticized.[36] It is not at all self-evident that a city in fact has an overarching unitary interest. The key interests of business leaders diverge sharply from those of political leaders. Although political leaders may care most about maximizing the city's export industries, the self-interest of most corporate leaders necessarily lies in maximizing the profits of their particular corporations, and in most instances this goal is divorced from the well-being of the cities in which the corporation resides. Finally, neighborhood residents might or might not benefit from downtown redevelopment. In fact, one could make a powerful argument that strengthening neighborhoods is a more important unitary interest of a city than is downtown redevelopment. If crime rates are low, the middle class is not moving out, city services are good, and schools are excellent, then a city will be a very attractive location for many kinds of businesses. This is precisely the situation in many suburban cities. But simply redeveloping the central-city downtown or putting in an automobile production plant will not necessarily pull in the middle class, improve the schools, reduce crime rates, or make the neighborhoods better places in which to live.

Different Regimes for Different Cities

One of the strongest critics of the idea of a unitary interest has been Clarence Stone, who argues that each city has a dominant coalition of interests that create an "urban regime."[37] He explains that *regimes* are "the informal arrangements by which public bodies [local governments] and private interests function together in order to be able to make and carry out governing decisions." Governing decisions include "manag[ing] conflict" in a community and making "adaptive responses to social change." The latter refers to whether a regime effectively adapts the community to changes in the economy and in society that are associated with economic restructuring. For example, how does the regime physically redevelop the city in the postindustrial economy and position the city to gain jobs and benefit from the rise of a global economy? A riot, the inability to restructure the local economy, or a fiscal crisis would be indicative of a failed regime.[38]

It is often the mayor who plays the key role in organizing a regime. This is because a mayor lacks the resources to govern on his or her own. The mayor finds that to redevelop the city physically or set economic development strategy, he or she must find partners. The mayor may be able to use the *power of eminent domain* (a city may take private property for public purposes if it compensates the owner) to clear an abandoned warehouse in the downtown. However, the mayor is usually dependent on private bankers, developers, and investors to build an office tower, downtown shopping mall, or other development on the site. Thus the mayor and the business community must enter into cooperative relationships to redevelop the city physically. Business cannot go it alone, either. The private actors may not be able to develop a site profitably if they have to pay a market price for the property, or they may not be able to assemble a large enough parcel on their own. In looking for partners, the mayor will look for groups already organized that have ready access to resources and can act immediately. In most communities, the best-organized group is usually the business community in a chamber of commerce or other business association. Neighborhood interests, minorities, and lower classes are usually unorganized, lack immediate access to resources, and have difficulty sustaining activity over several years.

The mayor is elected to office by the residents. But once in office, the mayor and other top political leaders can gain very few additional rewards from the city voters or their representative groups. Instead, it is the business elite and (to a lesser extent) other institutional elites who control access to most of the things that most reasonable mayors are likely to want: a thriving city economy, a successful administration, prestige, respect, and possibly postmayoral employment at a high salary. Ordinary voters can give a mayor none of these things. Thus a mayor's electoral coalition may be at odds with his or her governing coalition.

Because they control access to these goals that most reasonable mayors seek, business and institutional elites exercise *systemic power* over the city government.[39] Their exercise of power will seldom be overt, but the mayor will identify psychologically with the top institutional elite rather than with the masses. The mayor will anticipate the reactions of the elite to mayoral initiatives before the initiatives are taken. And it makes little difference whether the mayor is black, white, male, female, Democrat, or Republican. Mayors and high public officials generally "find themselves rewarded for cooperating with upper-strata interests and unrewarded or even penalized for cooperating with lower-strata interests."[40]

No better example of Stone's analysis could be offered than that of Mayor Dennis Kucinich, who was punished for aligning himself with Cleveland residents opposing the efforts of Cleveland banks to pressure the city into selling Muny Light to the Cleveland Electric and Illuminating Company in 1978 and 1979. As a result of Kucinich's opposition, the banks refused to roll over the city's debt, the city defaulted on loan payments, Kucinich was discredited, and he lost his reelection bid in 1979. His successor, George Voinovich, was much more cooperative with the business community, presided over considerable downtown redevelopment, enjoyed considerable respect as mayor, and held the office for more than a decade.[41]

What is at work in most cities, according to Stone's analysis, is a regime based on systemic power. There is no unitary interest binding the masses, the mayor, and the business elite. Rather, successful elected officials subtly and almost invisibly align themselves psychologically with the upper-strata interests of the area and keep themselves in power by convincing a majority of the average voters that all of this will benefit them in the long run.

What is important, in Stone's analysis, is to determine what sort of regime dominates in a given metropolis. The *entrepreneurial* or *corporate regime* is devoted primarily to downtown development policy, and in towns with corporate regimes, mayors will not have much success in reorienting the city's priorities toward serving its neighborhoods or its disadvantaged residents. Cities with a *progressive regime,* however, provide greater leeway for the mayor to expand services and shift priorities to neighborhoods. In Boston, for example, Mayor Raymond Flynn was able to follow several redistributive policies. He instituted a "linkage" program that required large developers to contribute to a trust fund ($70 million raised by 1987) that the city uses for housing and job-training purposes. Flynn also curbed the conversion of apartments into condominiums and required large residential development projects to earmark 10 percent of their space for low- and moderate-income renters.[42]

Community Power: A Summing Up

In the last analysis, there may simply be too many kinds of cities in the United States, and the urban restructuring that has been going on since the 1950s may be too complex, for any single theory to explain who governs the city. What is true of one city may not apply to a different one. Clarence Stone's analysis of the mayor's dependence on growth-oriented business elites for the success of his or her administration is probably accurate for Atlanta and for other cities with a corporate-dominated urban regime. Lawrence, Kansas, by contrast, has a strong tradition of citizen activism, and local residents for more than a decade successfully prevented the construction of a downtown shopping mall dearly desired by the city's local business leaders.[43] The growth machine there was clearly not dominant.

Not only does the nature of the urban regime differ from place to place, but different theories also lead us to focus on different aspects of the same event. This is why different observers can look at the same political event and draw completely incompatible conclusions. The case of Detroit's Poletown serves as a good example. From growth machine and neo-Marxist perspectives, Poletown is an unfortunate instance of Detroit's political leaders knuckling under to the demands of a multinational Fortune 500 corporation. From the viewpoint of unitary-interest theory, things worked out pretty well, because everybody in the city had an interest in having the city secure the jobs that would be required to build and operate the Cadillac plant in Poletown. But Bryan D. Jones and Lynn W. Bachelor look at the same facts and see something akin to old-fashioned pluralism.[44] First, they find no unitary interest between Detroit's or any city's business elite and the top political leaders. General Motors faced considerable competition from foreign automobile manufacturers, and GM's chief aim was to locate its new Cadillac production plant in a location that would contribute to the goal of competing successfully. This put GM's primary interest at odds with Mayor Coleman Young, whose primary interest was not

GM's profits but increasing the level of economic activity within the city of Detroit. In this sense, the mayor's job is akin to "making water run uphill; attracting capital where it would not normally flow . . . ; [getting] businessmen to do things that they would not do on their own."[45]

Although this situation clearly put GM in a privileged bargaining position, Mayor Young was by no means powerless. Indeed, the only reason why GM even considered the Poletown site in the first place was that Young had vocally badgered GM chairman Thomas Murphy about previous location decisions that had excluded Detroit.

In summary, Jones and Bachelor view the destruction of Poletown not as an example of either big capital trampling on the rights of a minority or a mayor systematically deferring to upper-strata interests rather than addressing lower-class needs. Instead, they view Poletown as an example of a democratically elected mayor, supported by the overwhelming majority of the city's residents, engaging in extremely effective political leadership to bring the city a very important economic resource that it would not otherwise have had.

Finally, neo-Marxist, growth machine, and unitary-interest theories share an excessively *deterministic* outlook. Unitary theory is deterministic in that it perceives a consensus among the residents, the business elite, and the political leaders that city government's primary concern is to protect the city's export industries. Neo-Marxism and growth machine theories perceive the same goal, attained by upper-strata interests co-opting the politicians, who in turn convince the lower-strata voters that these voters share in the interests of the upper strata. But in either view, "local policymaking on economic development issues becomes deterministic, barring occasional mistakes on the part of decision makers."[46] Mayors simply act out roles that are predetermined by the economic structure, much as a baseball player's role allows him to stand at the plate until he gets three strikes. Mark McGuire of the St. Louis Cardinals did the batter's job better than most (just as Coleman Young did the mayor's job better than most), but when McGuire (Young) is gone, the game still goes on as before. He is replaced by another batter (mayor) who enacts the same role without questioning the rules or even the point of the game.

Pluralists argue that this is too deterministic a view of city politics. In fact, considerable evidence shows that different political leaders may act in very different ways for many different purposes. For example, the fiscal policies that a city follows are greatly influenced by the quality of public-employee unions and their leadership.[47] And how cities adapt to fiscal retrenchment depends greatly on the ideological values of their mayors.[48] For all of these reasons, pluralists reject the all-encompassing nature of neo-Marxist, unitary-interest, and urban regime theories as an explanation for urban decline and redevelopment.

In summary, a rich variety of research has emerged in recent years seeking to explain the role of city government in the local political economy.[49] Neo-Marxists focus on contemporary twists to the historical class struggle. Growth machine theorists and urban regime theorists focus on a local, land-based elite and its relations with the local political system. Peterson's unitary-interest theory focuses on the proper role for city government to play in handling urban problems and on the very real limits confronting those governments. And pluralists generally tend to reaffirm city government's independence in these conflicts, asserting that it is not simply a passive actor playing out a predetermined role.

Still, there is some convergence among the theories: There is consensus among all researchers that both public and private leaders play a role in community decision making, that local decision-making structures may change over time, and that economic restructuring has circumscribed local autonomy but that local political leaders also have a great deal of latitude in how they respond to these pressures.[50] Whichever approach one uses to examine community power, the number of important decision makers one discovers is relatively small.* Also, the political influence of the important political participants derives from their positions of institutional leadership. The important participants are business leaders, labor leaders, party leaders, government leaders, and leaders of some other institutions that have a stake in the governmental process of their cities.

The Emergence of Functional Fiefdoms

Functionally Organized Power

One of the most striking aspects of the governmental process is the importance of functionally organized political power. The traditional general-purpose governmental structures (the city council and the mayor) have been bypassed to a considerable degree. Specially created governmental agencies have been given substantial authority to operate specific, key governmental functions. Each agency acquires governmental authority in its determined functional sector. It develops a professional bureaucracy that soon identifies its own set of vested interests. It is nominally run by a board of appointed officials who are often eager to demonstrate their independence from politics and to set new milestones in the functional area. In addition, outside of the governmental structure there are labor unions, church spokespersons, downtown business interests, racial organizations, highway lobbyists, construction contractors, teachers' organizations, professional organizations, and a host of other special-interest groups that establish ties with the agencies that operate the functions of most concern to them. Community-power researchers have not paid much attention to the rise of these functional fiefdoms and bureaucracies that may be more important to community decision making than are identified elites.

These ties between the professional bureaucracies and their related interest groups form what Paul Kantor called "islands of power"[51] or what Theodore J. Lowi called *functional feudalities*.[52] The feudal analogy is appropriate. Just as the elite noblemen in the Middle Ages enjoyed relative autonomy in the conduct of affairs within their fiefdoms, so for the past 50 years the elite bureaucratic officials have traditionally enjoyed considerable autonomy from effective outside interference by citizens and political parties (but not from members of Congress) in the conduct of their specialized operations. Just as the feudal nobility was not elected to its position of dominance but was maintained

---

*In his review of *Who Governs?* Floyd Hunter noted that despite Dahl's rejection of the elitist model, the actual number of participants in the large number of decision studies in New Haven never added up to more than 0.5 percent of the city's population. See his review of *Who Governs?* in *Administrative Science Quarterly* 6 (1961–1962): 517–518.

in it through a complex system of secular and ecclesiastical laws, the bureaucratic elite of the contemporary United States city is not elected to office but enjoys tenure through an equally complex system of laws and administrative rules. In Lowi's terms, the various functional feudalities constitute a "bureaucratic city-state."[53] The major inapplicability of the feudal analogy is that the fiefdoms of the Middle Ages were geographic in scope, whereas the fiefdoms of the contemporary bureaucracies are primarily functional in scope.

At the core of the functional fiefdoms are the administrative bureaucracies—what Lowi calls the *new political machines*. These new machines arose to perform service functions that the old political party machines were supposed to have performed. They also arose to perform new service functions (urban renewal, for example) that require more formalized administrative procedures than the old machines could provide.

A good example of a functional fiefdom in operation was the construction of urban freeways as part of the Interstate Highway System. This construction has largely occurred beyond the control of elected local officials. A federal highway trust fund was established in 1956 to earmark the revenue from federal gasoline taxes for the construction and maintenance of the Interstate Highway System. In addition, many states established their own highway trust funds. Both state and federal trust funds operated through state highway departments that, because of the automatic availability of the earmarked trust fund revenues, were able to become very independent of the policy preferences of mayors, governors, and state legislatures. Urban freeway planning was conducted by specialized technicians who showed very little regard for communities that might be broken up or displaced. Although freeways, bus service, and rapid-rail service are all interrelated components of urban transit systems, the highway planners were soon reinforced by highway construction lobbies. Together they were able to establish highway construction as the highest transit priority at the federal, state, and local levels. Given the rapid growth of automobile usage in the United States, this was not unreasonable. But the consequences for public transit were disastrous. In city after city, public transit ridership peaked in the late 1940s and declined throughout the 1950s and 1960s. It was not until the 1970s that the ridership on public transit began to increase[54] and cities began to fight successfully to gain some control over the location of their freeways.[55]

The Fiefdoms' Effects on City Government

Two major consequences have resulted from the proliferation of functional fiefdoms in American cities. First, this proliferation has inhibited, but not necessarily prevented, the exercise of unified political leadership in tackling urban problems. Second (as we will see later in this chapter), functional fiefdoms have compounded the problem of making urban government responsive to the citizenry.

Functional fiefdoms inhibit political leadership because political authority is so fragmented among competing agencies that establishing a clear-cut policy frequently becomes almost impossible. There often is no consensus among bureaucratic chiefs and public-employee unions on how programs should be run or even *whether* they should be run. This has been the case particularly in New York City, where, as political scientist David Rogers charges, "the centers of power . . . if indeed there are any, are in its municipal employees' unions and associations . . . [which] veto innovative social development programs almost as a reflex reaction."[56] In this kind of situation, it takes an extremely adept mayor to exercise unified leadership. The power of New York unions has declined considerably since that observation was made, but they still retain influence.

The result of functional fiefdoms in most cities is a juxtaposition of impressive power to act in urban redevelopment on the one hand with an inability to move dynamically on a myriad of social problems that afflict cities on the other. Detroit's functional fiefdom in redevelopment can work with GM to build a factory in Poletown and can work with Ford to build the impressive Renaissance Center. But the city government has been markedly unsuccessful in coping with high crime rates, high school dropout rates, deteriorating city services, and a fleeing white middle class.

This anomaly of powerful functional fiefdoms and weak ability to attack urban social problems exists in part because city governments have traditionally been weak. Although it is the most visible of urban governing institutions—and is the one institution that people hold responsible for solving urban ills—its authority to cope with those ills is sharply circumscribed not only by the existence of other powerful, competing institutions but also by law and by constitutions. A long-standing principle of municipal law holds that municipal governments can exercise only those powers specifically granted them by state legislatures or those powers indispensable for carrying out the responsibilities that the legislatures have assigned them. This principle is called *Dillon's rule,* after Judge John F. Dillon, who formulated it. Dillon stated, "Any fair, reasonable, substantial doubt concerning the existence of power is resolved by the courts against the [city government], and the power is denied."[57]

Consistent with Dillon's rule has been the historical tendency to minimize the number of functions a city government performs. Nearly all city governments are responsible for the traditional functions of police and fire protection, street maintenance, park maintenance, and the operation of water and sewer, zoning, building permits, and building inspection services. Only a small minority of cities, however, are responsible for other urban services such as welfare, courts, hospitals, or schools. The newer a city is, the fewer services it is likely to provide.[58] Furthermore, as new services (for example, airports, highway construction, and public welfare) have been created in the twentieth century, the tendency has been to insulate these services from mayors and city councils. The federal courts have tended to support federal programs that preempted local authority.[59]

For the past several decades, there has been a movement away from applying Dillon's rule and toward increasing the power of city governments. This so-called *home-rule movement* seeks to give each city a home-rule charter that authorizes the city to redraw its own charter and reorganize the structure of its government without the express permission of the state legislature. In a trend consistent with the home-rule movement, a number of states have begun giving their cities broader constitutional authority to act without getting prior permission from state legislatures.[60] Although these developments are not cure-alls for urban governing problems, they can be used to strengthen weak city governments.

The Strong Mayor as an Antidote to Functional Fiefdoms

Today, one of the major concerns of urban governance is overcoming the fragmentation of governmental authority into functional fiefdoms. The biggest step taken in that direction has been the drive to strengthen the big-city mayors.

Mayoral Strength and Weakness

In the view of strong-mayor advocates, the fragmentation of government authority is not so much a cause of mayoral weakness as it is an opportunity for skillful mayors to pyramid their power by bargaining with the various power centers, particularly with technical specialists in the bureaucracies and with downtown business leaders.[61]

If mayors are to become dynamic leaders, at least two things must happen. First, they must be given the legal and political resources to do their jobs. Jeffrey Pressman has identified seven factors that he calls the preconditions for strong mayoral leadership:

1. Sufficient financial resources with which a mayor can launch innovative social programs.
2. City jurisdiction in the vital program areas of education, housing, redevelopment, and job training.
3. Mayoral jurisdiction within the city government in those policy areas.
4. A salary sufficiently high that the mayor can work full-time at the office.
5. Sufficient staff support for the mayor for tasks such as policy planning, speech writing, intergovernmental relations, and political work.
6. Ready vehicles for publicity, such as friendly newspapers and television stations.
7. Politically oriented groups, including a political party the mayor can mobilize to help achieve particular goals.[62]

Unless mayors have these objective resources, claims Pressman, they are probably doomed either to frustration or to serving in a very minimal capacity.

In addition to these objective resources, an effective mayor must have a subjective vision of what needs to be done in the city—and of how it can be done. A mayor who has no vision of how the mayoralty can be used to improve the lives of the city's residents will not become a great mayor regardless of his or her objective resources. On the other hand, a very dynamic personality with a clear understanding of what can be accomplished may be able to have a lasting impact on the city, even if he or she lacks some of the resources identified by Pressman.

In trying to gain some understanding of the subjective vision of the mayor and mayoral leadership, John P. Kotter and Paul R. Lawrence studied mayors in 20 different cities during the 1960s and isolated several variables that contributed to mayoral success.[63] Of critical importance were setting a decision-making agenda, controlling their time, expanding their political alliances to attract new supporters, building a large staff to whom they could delegate tasks appropriately, and gaining political control over city government. If we juxtapose the objective preconditions with the subjective-vision dimension, we derive four types of leadership: the ceremonial mayor, the caretaker mayor, the program entrepreneur, and the crusader mayor. These are shown in Figure 7.1.

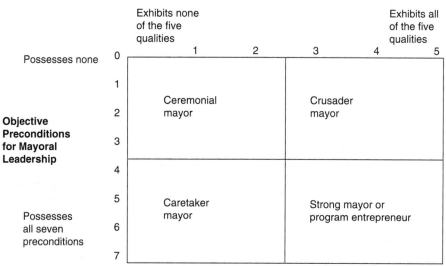

FIGURE 7.1   Styles of Mayoral Leadership

By juxtaposing the objective preconditions with the subjective vision for mayoral leadership, we can identify four major styles of mayoral leadership.

Source: This figure was composed by juxtaposing criteria developed in Jeffrey L. Pressman, "The Preconditions for Mayoral Leadership," *American Political Science Review* 66, no. 2 (June 1972): 511–574; John P. Kotter and Paul R. Lawrence, *Mayors in Action: Five Approaches to Urban Government* (New York: Wiley, 1974), chap. 7; and Douglas Yates, *The Ungovernable City* (Cambridge, Mass.: M.I.T. Press, 1977), p. 165.

The Ceremonial Mayor   Ceremonial mayors make little effort to set a decision-making agenda for dealing with city problems. They have no broad goals to be accomplished. Rather, they simply deal with problems individually. They have modest staffs and do not try to build new political alliances to cope with city problems. Rather, they rely on past friendships and personal appeals. In coping with mayoral tasks, ceremonial mayors try to tackle each task personally rather than delegating authority to others. As an example of a ceremonial mayor, Kotter and Lawrence point to Walton H. Bachrach of Cincinnati (1963–1967). They write of Bachrach,

> Walt was a very personable guy and just about everybody loved him. He'd walk down a crowded street and say hello to nearly everyone—by their first name.
>
> As mayor he spent nearly all of his time in ceremonial activities. He gave speeches at banquets, he welcomed conventions, he cut ribbons at all types of openings, he gave out keys to the city, and so on. He really looked the part and he played it with grace and dignity.[64]

The Caretaker Mayor   Like ceremonial mayors, caretaker mayors do not set an agenda of goals to be accomplished. They, too, simply deal with problems individually. They make more of an effort than ceremonial mayors to build political alliances and to surround themselves with loyal staffs, and they are more able to delegate authority to others, especially to the established bureaucracies.

The prototype of a caretaker mayor was Ralph Locher of Cleveland (1962–1967). Locher dealt with city problems via a nonsystematic approach. He let his own daily agenda be dictated by other people who placed demands on him and by regular office routines such as opening the mail and dictating letters. There is no evidence that Locher attempted to establish goals for any of Cleveland's broader social problems. He was simply a caretaker for the city. Locher himself said,

> You know, I suppose it could be said that Burke [a previous mayor] and I were custodial mayors. We tried to keep the city clean and swept and policed. Some say that wasn't enough. Let me just say this about that complaint. You can't nurture flowers and good thoughts and ideals when you're living in a rat-infested squalor and your city services aren't being done.[65]

The Program Entrepreneur   Program entrepreneurs are the most ambitious of all the mayoral types. Their agenda is much more detailed. They have broad goals and even a list of objectives or priority areas to be covered. Only a small portion of their daily work schedule is spent reacting to events. The rest is spent on activities tied into long-range and yearly objectives. Program entrepreneurs skillfully build political alliances and surround themselves with a substantial staff.

A prime example of a program entrepreneur is Richard C. Lee of New Haven, Connecticut (1954–1970). Lee built up a solid alliance comprising the major interest groups in the city—the city bureaucracy, federal renewal agencies, the city council, the business community, organized labor, the Democratic party, and Yale University.

Much of the basis for Lee's success was his strong political support in New Haven's Democratic party. With this strong political backing, he was assured of renomination and reelection, so he enjoyed a long tenure as mayor. The long-term mayor has advantages in dealing with the bureaucracy that the short-term mayor does not have.[66] It is easier for bureaucratic officials to oppose or ignore the wishes of short-term mayors, because they might not be around very long. One of Lee's first goals on becoming mayor was to establish control over the city departments and bureaucracies.[67] He was able to maintain control over New Haven's urban renewal projects, an achievement not duplicated by mayors in other cities such as Newark and New York.[68] At the heart of what Robert Dahl called an executive-centered coalition, Lee was able to line up business leaders, university leaders, union leaders, and other civic leaders behind his redevelopment goals.[69]

The Crusader-Mayor   In addition to the foregoing three mayoral styles, Douglas Yates has also identified a crusader-mayor.[70] The crusader style emerges when the mayor's office is occupied by an active, imaginative, ambitious personality who has a weak political power base. Yates points to New York City mayor John Lindsay as a crusader. Lacking the political strength to control the city bureaucracies and dominate the government, Lindsay adopted a crusading, symbolic style of leadership. During the riots of the 1960s, he went into the streets in the riot-torn sections and urged people to return to their homes. He traveled often to Washington to testify before congressional committees and to serve as a spokesperson for the nation's urban problems. He engaged in political battles with New York State governor Nelson Rockefeller. Despite the battles, the conflicts, and the publicity, however, it is hard to identify Lindsay with many significant accomplishments.

The Minority Mayor   Although she or he does not represent a distinct style of leadership, the minority mayor is a very visible and increasingly common phenomenon. Minority mayors have included African Americans such as the late Harold Washington (Chicago), Wilson Goode (Philadelphia), Thomas Bradley (Los Angeles), David Dinkins (New York), Coleman Young (Detroit), and Andrew Young (Atlanta); Hispanics such as Henry Cisneros (San Antonio) and Federico Peña (Denver); and women such as Kathy Whitmire (Houston) and Annette Strauss (Dallas).

Minority mayors may confront problems and opportunities that white mayors do not face. Writing particularly about black mayors, political scientist Peter K. Eisinger argues that they are faced with a problem of divided loyalties.[71] In their initial election campaigns, they usually win a small minority of the white vote,[72] which means that they rely on overwhelming support from black communities. But to initiate the economic development activities they seek, black mayors have to make alliances with upper-class and upper-middle-class whites who have the economic power to put economic development programs into action. The more minority mayors cater to their minority constituencies, the more problems they create with their economic development coalitions, and vice versa.

If minority mayors have special problems, they also have special opportunities to increase employment and business prospects for the minority populations. Eisinger's studies of black mayors show that they are indeed able to increase the number of blacks employed by city government at all levels.[73] A similar study among female mayors found that they are able to increase the number of women who hold city jobs.[74]

The Strengthening of Mayors

At the beginning of the 1980s, it did not seem likely that there would be enough resources for many mayors to serve successfully as program entrepreneurs, as Richard Lee did during the 1950s and 1960s. Federal community development funds did not grow as fast as inflation, and many local governments encountered strong voter resistance to big spending projects. Despite these fiscal problems, many mayors found imaginative ways to raise funds for economic development projects.

Considerable progress has also been made toward the seven objective preconditions for strong mayors that we have noted. Mayoral staffs have grown substantially over the past several decades,[75] as have mayors' bases of political support. A study of mayoral influence in 93 cities found that mayors with a strong political base of support tended to enjoy considerable success in getting their program proposals adopted.[76]

Finally, even where the mayor operates under difficult constraints, dynamic individuals have often exercised strong leadership by capitalizing on specific conditions in their cities. Two examples of this were Mayor Edward Koch of New York City and Mayor Pete Wilson of San Diego.

Edward Koch represents a peculiar type of mayor who comes to office at the precise moment when social upheaval provokes a major change in a city's governing coalition.[77] For Koch, that upheaval was New York City's fiscal crisis of the 1970s. Prior to the crisis, the mayor played a major role in balancing various functional fiefdoms that all demanded ever-larger pieces of the city budget. These fiefdoms included city council members, public-employee unions, city bureaucracies, neighborhood groups, and minority groups. So overwhelming was the total impact of these demands that one perceptive observer pronounced that city ungovernable.[78] The fiscal crisis, however, forced the demands of these groups to take a backseat to the concerns of fiscal solvency. Ed Koch was elected mayor in 1977, when the city's fiscal affairs were under the tight scrutiny of the Emergency Financial Control Board and the city was still several years away from balancing its budget and regaining access to the credit markets. Koch used the crisis to acquire greater control over the city's budget and over several quasi-independent city agencies, especially the city hospitals and the school system, and to create a political coalition that for the first time in nearly 20 years reduced the mayor's electoral dependence on the city's municipal unions and racial minority leaders.[79]

There was, however, a cost involved in Koch's use of the fiscal crisis to rejuvenate the mayor's office. The extensive budget cutbacks fell predominantly on the poor and on those who depended on the city's social services. At the same time that he cut back assistance to the poor, Koch utilized the whole gamut of tax incentives discussed in Chapter 6 to promote a building boom and extensive urban redevelopment. His business-oriented strategy precipitated shouting matches with the city's racial minorities, who accused him of racism and whom he counterattacked in equally acrimonious terms.[80] By 1989, Koch's combative style of leadership had run its course and he was defeated for reelection by the city's first African American mayor, David N. Dinkins.

Another dynamic mayor who exercised effective leadership in a weak situation was Pete Wilson of San Diego. In that city, a city-manager form of government had presided smoothly over a growth period of the city during the 1950s and 1960s. By 1970, San Diego had grown to nearly 700,000 people. Severe opposition arose to the ethos of unrestricted growth, and the city manager proved unable to negotiate effectively between the city's progrowth and no-growth political factions. This led to the emergence in the 1970s of Mayor Pete Wilson, who gradually strengthened the mayor's office, weakened the city manager, built a strong electoral coalition, and successfully balanced the city's competing progrowth and no-growth factions.[81]

In summary, there was a general awareness by the 1980s and 1990s that a need existed to strengthen central-city mayors if urban problems were to be addressed successfully. Some steps in this direction were taken in many cities during the 1970s— especially in curbing the functional fiefdom of urban renewal. Indeed, by the 1980s the mayor's office had become a much more prestigious place than it was in the past, often attracting dynamic candidates who were able to use the city as a stepping-stone to higher office. For example, San Diego's Pete Wilson and Indianapolis's Richard Lugar moved up to the United States Senate; Wilson went on to the governorship of California. President Clinton appointed two mayors to his cabinet, Henry Cisneros of San Antonio to HUD (1993–1997) and Federico Peña to Transportation (1993–1997) and later Energy (1997–1998). Today's mayor is likely to move on to higher office as a governor or United States representative, as a member of the cabinet, or as an ambassador. Another interesting phenomenon has been the number of women elected mayors of major cities in recent years.

Antidote to Nonresponsiveness: Decentralization

Charges of Nonresponsiveness

In addition to coping with the demands and interests of powerful functional fiefdoms, city governments must cope with the demands and needs of unorganized citizens, of smaller and less powerful groups, and of newly emerging power centers. When the urban political process is viewed from the perspective of these factors, it is often portrayed as something beyond the influence or even the understanding of ordinary citizens. Michael Parenti studied three unsuccessful attempts of the Newark Community Union Project (NCUP) to obtain major gains for the residents of a poor, African American neighborhood in Newark during the mid-1960s.[82] NCUP was organized by local black militants and white members of Students for a Democratic Society. Over a three-year period, NCUP attempted to get the city government to enforce the city's building codes and to install a traffic light at a particularly dangerous intersection. When these attempts failed, NCUP tried to elect new black candidates to the city council and the state legislature. But this attempt failed too. Throughout these efforts, the tactics employed by NCUP ranged from traditional voter registration and electioneering to protest activity and agitation that involved rent strikes, sit-ins, and blocking traffic at the intersection where the traffic light was desired. Although NCUP held together and persisted in its efforts for three years, none of its three major projects was successful.

Drawing on his observations of these unsuccessful experiences, Parenti describes the urban political process as seen from below. First, "there exists the world of the rulers and the world of the ruled." Second, one of the crucial elements of power is the capacity to set the agenda of the struggle, to determine that certain questions will not come up for consideration by government agencies. These are the so-called nondecisions. "Much of the behavior of Newark's officials can be seen as a kind of 'politics of prevention' . . . designed to limit the area of issue conflict." Third, Parenti rejects the pluralist concept of "latent power," which in this case would imply that the ghetto dwellers possess a latent or "potential power that would prevail should they choose to use it."[83] On the contrary, the resources of the poor are seen as infinitesimal in comparison to the resources of the interest groups. In contrast to Robert Dahl, who states that power is noncumulative, Parenti maintains that the *lack* of power is cumulative. Ghetto dwellers exist in a state of *cumulative inequalities* in which their unequal status in education, income, jobs, and discrimination all accumulate to reduce their potential collective political efficacy. Because of their cumulative inequalities, they are unable to translate their needs into effective demands. Politicians respond to *demands* more readily than they respond to citizens' needs, so the cumulative inequalities of the poor increase their difficulty in getting the government to meet their needs. Furthermore, politicians who do respond to ghetto dwellers' demands on certain kinds of issues such as the enforcement of building codes "might incur the wrath of high political leaders or powerful economic interests." For this reason, "party regulars have little inclination to entertain the kinds of issues" pushed by organizations such as NCUP, and "they also try to discredit and defeat those reformers who seek confrontations on such issues."[84]

Not all studies of attempts to mobilize the poor have been as pessimistic as Parenti's study, but a remarkable consensus exists on the extreme difficulties of organizing the poor to articulate their demands in ways that will oblige government agencies to respond positively. One of the most common political tactics of the poor has been protest activity. But a study of rent strikes and protest activity in New York found that protest as a tactic has severe limitations, particularly over the medium and long range.[85] Protest groups are inherently unstable and difficult to keep together. In order to get the attention of the mass media, protest leaders tend to overstate their strength and their accomplishments, only to lose credibility with reporters when they are unable to follow through on the statements and claims they make. In order for protests to be successful, the leaders have to capture the sympathy and often the financial support of third parties, particularly white liberals. This usually involves moderating their position or making compromises that lose them support from other members of the protesting groups. In the Harlem rent strikes of 1963 and 1964, government officials and slum landlords were able to use delaying tactics and wait for the indignation aroused by reportage of slum housing conditions to wane. When public interest declined, the rent strike coalition collapsed.[86]

Although the poor lack many of the resources of power, their powerlessness is not total and the power relations are not static. They do change. Changes have been most obvious in the arena of electoral politics. The number of African American elected officials increased dramatically from 1,469 in 1970 to 8,896 in 1999, and many of the cities with large African American populations now have African American mayors (see Table 5.2). Even where African Americans did not elect African American mayors, they have seen an increase in their collective political influence.[87]

What conclusions can we draw about this research into the powerlessness of the poor and the racial minorities? Three conclusions are warranted. First, African Americans, by engaging in community organization, direct political action, and electoral competition, have been able to get middle-class African American leaders drawn into the governing coalitions in most cities where African Americans constitute a substantial portion of the city population. Second, despite their being able to use this newfound power to make modest increases in African American public-sector employment, there is no systematic evidence that African American mayors have yet been able to make substantial improvements in the living conditions of the African American urban underclass.

Third, despite the African American success, there still is no systematic evidence that unorganized people, regardless of race, get any more positive reaction from city governments today than they did 40 years ago. Commentaries on certain white ethnic groups, poor white communities, and many big-city residents interviewed sporadically indicate that they also feel powerless to influence city politics.[88] This white powerlessness may not be limited to the poor; there may well be a sense of middle-class powerlessness as well. This sense of powerlessness within the city may be one reason for the white exodus to the suburbs. And for whites who cannot afford to move to the suburbs, there is often a frustrating sense of loss of control over their neighborhoods. In the Canarsie section of Brooklyn, these frustrations often exploded in acts of violence against blacks whom the whites saw as invading Canarsie.[89]

Decentralization as an Antidote to Nonresponsiveness

Given the widespread perception that city governments and their functional fiefdoms are not very responsive to unorganized city residents and their neighborhoods, it is not surprising that the past 40 years have seen a succession of decentralization proposals to give citizens more influence in the programs operated by the functional fiefdoms. To date, urban decentralization has evolved through three stages:

1. The Community Action and Model Cities programs of the 1960s
2. The community control movement of the late 1960s and early 1970s
3. A continuing emphasis on citizen participation and neighborhood revitalization in the 1980s and 1990s

Community Action and Model Cities Programs   The Community Action programs (CAPs) were created by the Economic Opportunity Act of 1964, and the Model Cities program was created two years later. Although important differences existed between these programs, they had three similar objectives: (1) to provide and improve public services for the poor, (2) to mobilize both public and private resources to cope with the problems of poverty, and (3) to engage the maximum feasible participation of the poor in carrying out the programs.

Participation of the poor was most advanced in the Community Action programs. Community action agencies (CAAs) were created to implement the Community Action programs. The CAAs were originally made independent of the city government, and neighborhood representatives dominated their boards of directors. But as time went on and as the federal funding agency (the Office of Economic Opportunity) was terminated, CAAs became highly dependent on local city halls for their survival. Although many cities have continued to fund their own CAAs, the CAAs now function more as an arm of city hall than as independent political organizations for the poor. Whatever merits they may have today in terms of delivering public services to the urban poor, they are clearly no longer a major force for decentralizing political influence to bring it to the neighborhood level.

Community Control   A second prescription in the 1960s and 1970s for making urban governments more responsive to the citizenry was that of sharing control over governmental services between centralized bureaucracies and community residents who receive the services. A wide variety of control-sharing schemes were advanced under a bewildering array of labels as diverse as community control, consumer representation, decentralization, little (neighborhood) city halls, neighborhood advisory councils, and neighborhood corporations. All are based on different assumptions about the nature of urban government, and all would have different results in dealing with the problem of bureaucratic unresponsiveness. In all community control plans, an important distinction must be made. Does the control-sharing plan simply decentralize the *delivery* of services? Or does it decentralize *political control* as well?[90]

There have been many instances of practical attempts to achieve decentralization of political control and/or delivery of services. Three of these have evoked the most interest among observers: (1) decentralization of education, (2) decentralization of city hall and public services, and (3) neighborhood advisory committees or councils.

Decentralization of Public Education   In central cities with large numbers of poor children or racial minorities, the public school systems have been resoundingly criticized as being unresponsive to children's needs.[91] Because of residential segregation, big-city schools have traditionally been racially segregated in fact, even though there may have been no laws demanding their segregation. Schools for the racial minorities were also commonly the oldest, shabbiest, and least adequately supplied with facilities. Teachers with enough seniority to have a choice tried to avoid teaching in the minority neighborhoods.

African American leaders attacked these problems for many years by seeking more school integration, but in few cities were they successful. Consequently, when the concept of decentralizing control over schools was advanced in the mid-1960s, it quickly won acceptance from those African Americans who despaired of ever getting truly integrated schools and at the same time deplored the inferior quality of the black schools. Local control of schools was also consistent with the then-growing philosophy of black separatism. Two of the most noteworthy experiments in decentralized control of schools occurred in New York City and Detroit.

In three of the most impoverished neighborhoods in New York City, the board of education established locally controlled demonstration districts to experiment with locally controlled schools. A local governing board was created in each district, and the members were chosen by popular election by residents of the district.

In the Ocean Hill–Brownsville district, an explosive controversy soon developed between the local governing board, the school bureaucracy, and the teachers' federation. When the governing board attempted to transfer some teachers out of the district and replace them with others, it ran into the solid opposition of the United Federation of Teachers. Because some of the teachers to be transferred out were Jewish, the local African Americans were accused of anti-Semitism, even though it should be noted that most of the retained teachers were also Jewish. A long, drawn-out struggle ensued in which the schools were closed by a teachers' strike and the police had to be brought in to preserve the peace. There was little popular support for the demonstration district's side of the strike outside the African American community, and even among blacks barely a majority supported it.* The strike proved so unpopular and divisive that the demonstration district experiment was brought to an end by the New York legislature in 1970. In its stead, 32 local school boards were created whose authority was sharply limited.[92]

In Detroit, the attempt to decentralize public schools also developed into an explosive controversy.[93] In 1969 the Michigan legislature passed a bill that created new local school boards that would be subordinate to the citywide board. The citywide board was dominated by liberals who were determined that decentralization would not be allowed to impede their plans for school integration. Consequently, they drafted a plan for local school boards in which about 9,000 pupils would be bused across local boundary lines in order to accomplish integration.

---

*Louis Harris conducted a survey of New Yorkers in April and May 1969. On a question of whether the teachers' federation was more right or the demonstration district governing board was more right, the ratios of the percentage favoring the teachers to the percentage favoring the governing board were 63 to 8 among Jews, 48 to 9 among Catholics, 35 to 20 among white Protestants, 21 to 12 among Puerto Ricans, and 14 to 50 among blacks (Louis Harris and Bert E. Swanson, *Black-Jewish Relations in New York City* [New York: Praeger, 1970], p. 132).

The public reaction was swift. Behind the leadership of a conservative board member who opposed integration, protests and demonstrations erupted. Under local pressure, the state legislature quickly revoked its 1969 law and passed a new law that outlawed such busing of students and mandated the decentralized school boards to be organized on the basis of neighborhood schools. That obviously meant that the schools would not be integrated. In addition, the new law gave each of the eight local school boards one representative on the previously at-large, citywide board of education. A recall petition was filed in June 1970, and in a special recall election, all the liberal members of the citywide board of education were removed from office and replaced with conservatives. The former conservative member who had led the anti-integration demonstrations was elected board president. Local neighborhood boards were given extensive sway to establish policies as they saw fit. In an African Ameirican district, a principal was removed. In another district, the local board was permitted to refuse to administer a statewide achievement test to students. And a district in a white region was allowed not to implement voluntary desegregation guidelines that had been established.

The decentralized schools in Detroit seemed to come much closer to the neighborhood government model of decentralization than did those in New York. Their net impact, however, was to impede integration in Detroit, inflame latent racial tensions, and cut back educational programs. They also failed to increase the representation of the poor or of the minorities in school policy making. As in New York, Detroit's local school board members came largely from middle-class professional, technical, and managerial positions.[94]

Perhaps in reaction to the experience of New York and Detroit, school decentralization efforts elsewhere have shied away from granting political control to subdistrict units. Instead, the tendency has been to expand the use of community advisory councils that give parents input into decision making on some curriculum matters and certain federal programs.

After the New York and Detroit experiments, most movement toward further decentralization stopped until the 1980s. During that decade, several prestigious national commissions sharply criticized the nation's public school system, the Reagan and Bush administrations pushed for voucher plans to help more children go to private schools, and some governors initiated highly publicized public school reform plans that included elements of decentralization. Chicago sought to rejuventate its poorly regarded system by creating local boards similar to those used in New York City and by decentralizing substantial authority to individual school principals and their staffs.

Little City Halls   A second approach to decentralization has been to establish little (neighborhood) city halls throughout the city. A little city hall is simply a mayoral branch office that seeks to expedite the provision of city services in neighborhoods and to improve ties with neighborhood residents. Little city halls were strongly recommended by the National Advisory Commission on Civil Disorders[95] as one means of lessening citizen alienation from the government. Forms of decentralized delivery of services were established in at least 75 cities, and least 25 of them were significant enough to be called little city halls.[96]

Neighborhood Advisory Councils   Similar to little city halls are the neighborhood advisory councils (NACs) established in St. Paul, Minnesota, in Washington, D.C., in

New York City, and in many other cities. The NAC plan typically divides a city into small geographic districts (17 in St. Paul, 36 in Washington, and 59 in New York City), provides funds for a neighborhood office and a full-time district manager, and allows for an elected or appointed representative board. Typically, councils are responsible for advising the central-city government on land use decisions, budgeting, and the delivery of services in the neighborhood. Where the NACs are elected, as in Washington, voting turnout rarely exceeds 20 percent of the registered voters,[97] and where they are appointed, as in New York City, there are inevitable complaints that the appointed board members do not reflect neighborhood views.[98]

Decentralization in the 1990s

By the late 1980s much of the thrust for community control had dissipated. The most advanced form of community control was that of Milton Kotler, who advocated dividing cities into neighborhood governments that would have legal authority to handle all neighborhood-level governmental issues.[99] But Kotler's model was not adopted anywhere.

More enduring were the moderate forms of control sharing. The New York City demonstration school districts, for example, disappeared very quickly when they attempted to exercise real power. The less powerful local school boards created after the Ocean Hill–Brownsville crisis, on the other hand, continue to function. One study of neighborhood programs in four midwestern states also found that neighborhood program participants expressed greater satisfaction with the program if it provided for only moderate levels of participation and if the program was moderate in scope rather than comprehensive.[100] Neighborhood advisory councils seemed to fit much better into the less militant mood of the 1990s.

Today there is some concern about how to revitalize neighborhoods without turning them into subcity governments. The American Institute of Architects called for a national growth policy based on preserving the quality of life in neighborhoods.[101] Mortgage-lending institutions came under attack for the practice of *redlining*—that is, making it difficult to get home mortgage loans in certain neighborhoods. Federal legislation attempted to curb redlining. Federal community development funds and public-housing funds under the 1974 Housing and Community Development Act made it easier to preserve buildings and to restore old neighborhoods of historic interest. This added impetus to the gentrification process of upper-middle-income people moving back into inner-city neighborhoods.

Decentralization—A Critique

Despite the eclipse of the community control movement in the 1980s, it would be a mistake to write it off entirely as a historical aberration of the 1960s. Some of its more moderate tenets (such as client representation and neighborhood advisory councils) are accepted practices in many cities today. Although these practices have not revolutionized the lifestyles of urban dwellers, they often have modified the plans of big-city institutions to make these plans more accommodating to local residents. Local groups in Boston and other cities halted the construction of freeways through their neighborhoods. And New York City's Office of Neighborhood Government seems to have had some success in making that city's bureaucracies more attentive to service-delivery problems at the district level.[102]

Control sharing has the potential to reduce citizen alienation from government. Giving citizens a voice in the management of their neighborhoods gives them an alternative to moving out to the suburbs when they become dissatisfied with the delivery of local public services.[103] Poorly organized or ineffectual control sharing, of course, can easily lead to bitter conflict that reduces confidence in government. But there is also evidence that meaningful and effective participation can increase satisfaction and trust in local government.[104]

There is also reason to believe that vibrant neighborhood politics makes the city more governable. Matthew A. Crenson studied neighborhood politics in Baltimore and concluded that it made several contributions to the effective government of that city. If neighborhood groups and a system of informal politics can be created, they can often deal with the hundreds of daily problems that arise in a big city (such as vandalism, people who fail to maintain their property, trash removal from private property, and even snow removal from alleys). This shields the central-city leaders from having their attention diverted in many different directions at once and enables them to focus their energies on the big problems of the city. By delegating "authority to a host of small-time operators . . . [the downtown leaders] will have more opportunities to behave like big-time operators themselves."[105]

Jeffrey Berry, Kent Portney, and Ken Thomson believe that we are in the midst of the rebirth of urban democracy in communities. In a book by that title, they examine neighborhood participation in Birmingham, Dayton, Portland, St. Paul, and San Antonio. Birmingham has 95 elected neighborhood councils to determine community development block grant expenditures and address community problems. In Dayton, there are 7 elected Priority Boards that provide a channel for dialogue between agencies of city government and neighborhoods. In Portland, 7 District Coalition Boards with their own staffs link 90 autonomous neighborhood associations, providing an institutionalized way for citizen participation to shape city policies. In St. Paul, 17 elected District Councils with staff and neighborhood offices make decisions on zoning, infrastructure investments, and city services within the neighborhoods. In San Antonio, a private group, Communities Organized for Public Service (COPS), has been able to gain a strong voice for Hispanics on issues of concern by using a confrontation strategy (protests and demonstrations).[106]

Berry, Portney, and Thomson are guardedly optimistic about the possibilities for participatory democracy in our cities. They identify three requirements for effective neighborhood participation. First, the citizens must be given real power to make decisions. Second, city officials must be given incentives and sanctions to encourage citizen participation. Third, these participation programs should be citywide. That is, if these neighborhood associations are to be seen as credible, they cannot be confined to low-income areas. This is a problem facing COPS in San Antonio. Berry, Portney, and Thomson find no evidence that neighborhood decision making limits the city government's ability to ensure that the broader community interests are not overtaken by narrower neighborhood interests.[107]

In conclusion, control sharing was one of the most creative concepts to come out of the turbulent decade of the 1960s. Although much more moderate and much less extensive, the concepts of citizen participation and neighborhood revitalization continue to have meaning as we enter the twenty-first century. The citizen participation movements have led to political mechanisms and expectations that will make it easier for citizens' groups in this new century to demand meaningful input into governmental decisions.

Bias in Contemporary Urban Government

Several themes about contemporary urban government have dominated the foregoing discussions:

- Although no consensus exists on whether elitist or pluralist theories of community power are more accurate, individual citizens are clearly much less influential than institutions.
- The institutional dominance of cities can be described in terms of the concept of functional fiefdoms. A functional fiefdom is an urban agency operating in some general arena of public affairs, consisting of its bureaucracy, its professional staff, its public-employee union, and its board or commission of directors; its counterpart agencies in the state and federal government; and the private businesses, labor organizations, and interest groups that serve as the agency's clientele.
- The functional fiefdoms pose enormous problems for the exercise of decisive political leadership in large cities.
- The existing structure and organization of power in urban areas, be it pluralist or stratified, is biased against people who are unorganized. This bias is felt most heavily by the poor and the racial minorities.
- Two entirely different remedies have been prescribed by social scientists and others as antidotes for the deficiencies of functional fiefdoms. For the weakness of inhibited political leadership, the antidote most often prescribed has been a strengthening of the big-city mayor. For the antipoor bias of the functional fiefdoms, the prescription has been some form of shared control with, or citizen control over, urban government.

The two antidotes appear to be contradictory, but a geographic decentralization of government can be consistent with strong mayoral leadership. Matthew Crenson's analysis of neighborhood politics in Baltimore suggests that the two antidotes are not necessarily contradictory. Effective politics at the neighborhood level helps to shield the mayor from dealing with petty squabbles and enables him or her to concentrate on the overriding citywide issues. Further, the mayor is likely to see the neighborhood groups as potential allies for his or her agenda. Following Clarence Stone's regime analysis, because organized neighborhood groups have institutional position and resources, the mayor may find them useful partners in the regime. In this case, urban regimes could become less dependent on organized business groups, leading to more progressive community policy making.[108]

The controversy over community control has exposed the biases of the status quo. The advocates of community control demand it not simply because they think that the bureaucracies are doing a bad job of helping the poor and the racial minorities. If that were the case, the problem could be remedied through the application of modern techniques of public administration and program analysis. Rather, in the writings of the advocates of community control, the functional fiefdoms are *inherently biased* against the interests of the disorganized, the poor, and the racial minorities. This is a direct result of the peculiar form of representative democracy that has developed in the United States. Legislatures and bureaucracies are most responsive to constituent and client groups and to citizens who participate in the political process. For a variety of reasons, the poor and the disorganized do not participate very well in these groups, in electoral activity, in campaigning activity, or in lobbying activity. The major institutional reason for their lack of participation is that there is no institutional mechanism that can mobilize them into action. The closest thing to such a mechanism has been the affiliation of organized labor, via the New Deal coalition, with the Democratic party. The labor unions can mobilize their members to vote and can pressure the government for legislation that will benefit their members. But no institution in American society has mobilized the poor and the disorganized in the same fashion.

In this view, then, the key failure of the bureaucratic state is that no institutional mechanism exists for representing the interests of the disorganized and the poor. And in this respect, community control is championed as the new institutional creation for accomplishing this representation directly in the administrative bureaucracy.

In fact, however, there is good reason to doubt that the poor would gain very much from community control. All the evidence we have reviewed to this point indicates that upper-status people participate in neighborhood politics more than lower-status people do. And Matthew Crenson argues that upper-status neighborhoods have more influence in city politics than lower-status neighborhoods have. "Decentralization achieved through community organizations would probably accentuate existing political inequalities between rich neighborhoods and poor neighborhoods."[109] The most effective thing that city governments can do for poor neighborhoods, asserts Crenson, is to encourage more middle-class people to move into those neighborhoods so that all of the city's neighborhoods will be more socially integrated. It is the middle-income people in generally poor neighborhoods who are most likely to engage in the informal politics that Crenson views as so favorable for city governability.

Bureaucratic decentralization has been accomplished without decentralizing control over policy. Steps have been taken to place token client representatives on the boards of public agencies without cutting into the autonomy of the bureaucracies involved. The proliferation of federal programs for compensatory education, health planning, community development, and so on has led to an equal proliferation of federally mandated and funded citizens' advisory councils. And despite the experiments with Model Cities and Community Action programs, no true neighborhood governments have been established. Instead, the emphasis has shifted from community control to neighborhood revitalization. Finally, whatever its revolutionary potential, the concept of neighborhood government via the Milton Kotler model clearly is not the wave of the future for American cities.

SUMMARY

1. Two competing theories of community power are the elitist, or stratificationist, theory and the pluralist theory. These theories can be traced to early research

conducted in Atlanta, Georgia, and New Haven, Connecticut. More recent community power research has modified the early elitist interpretations of the business community's role in community power, has attached greater importance to the concept of nondecisions, has shown that a variety of community power relationships exist, and has found that community power relationships can change over time. In the 1990s, the community power debate has been revived by neo-Marxist growth machine, unitary-interest, and urban regime theories and by a pluralistic counterattack.

2. A distinguishing feature of power in urban America has been functional fiefdoms. These are power relationships within specific functional sectors (urban renewal, for example) that involve bureaucratic officials at more than one level of government and private interests that work with those officials.

3. The emergence of functional fiefdoms has tended to inhibit unified political leadership in tackling urban problems and has compounded the problem of making urban government responsive to the citizenry.

4. Strong mayors have been proposed as antidotes to the fragmentation of power that occurs with functional fiefdoms.

5. Getting strong mayors requires giving mayors the objective legal and political resources they need to do their jobs and getting mayors who have a subjective vision of what must be done in the city and of how to do it.

6. To cope with the problems of making city government more responsive to citizens, experiments have been conducted with Community Action programs, Model Cities programs, and various schemes for community control and political decentralization.

7. Several biases were found in the contemporary patterns of urban government. Citizens are not so influential in urban politics as are institutions, particularly institutions tied into a functional fiefdom. This bias against citizens is especially pronounced against unorganized citizens. These biases have been exposed in the struggle over community control.

NOTES

1. See especially Robert S. Lynd and Helen M. Lynd, *Middletown in Transition* (New York: Harcourt, 1937); W. Lloyd Warner et al., *Democracy in Jonesville* (New York: Harper & Row, 1949); and August B. Hollingshead, *Elmtown's Youth* (New York: Wiley, 1949). A short summary and methodological critique of these early major works can be found in Nelson Polsby, *Community Power and Political Theory* (New Haven, Conn.: Yale University Press, 1963).

2. Floyd Hunter, *Community Power Structure* (Chapel Hill: University of North Carolina Press, 1953).

3. Lawrence J. R. Herson, "The Lost World of Municipal Government," *American Political Science Review* 51 (1957): 330–345.

4. T. J. Anton, "Power, Pluralism, and Local Politics," *Administrative Science Quarterly* 7 (March 1963): 425–454; Polsby, *Community Power and Political Theory;* Herbert Kaufmann and Victor Jones, "The Mystery of Power," *Public Administration Quarterly* 14 (Summer 1954): 2–5; Raymond E. Wolfinger, "Reputation and Reality in the Study of Community Power," *American Sociological Review* 25 (October 1960): 636–644; and Robert A. Dahl, "A Critique of the Ruling Elite Model," *American Political Science Review* 52 (June 1958): 463–469.

5. In particular, this is Polsby's critique. See *Community Power and Political Theory.*

6. Robert Dahl, *Who Governs? Democracy and Power in an American City* (New Haven, Conn.: Yale University Press, 1966).

7. See, for example, Delbert C. Miller, "Decision-Making Cliques in Community Power Structures: A Comparative Study of an American and an English City," *American Journal of Sociology* 64 (November 1958): 299–310; William H. Form and William V. D'Antonio, "Integration and Cleavage Among Community Influentials in Two Border Cities," *American Sociological Review* 24 (December 1959): 804–814; Robert Presthus, *Men at the Top: A Study in Community Power* (New York: Oxford University Press, 1964); and Robert E. Agger, Daniel Goldrich, and Bert Swanson, *The Rulers and the Ruled: Political Power and Impotence in American Communities* (New York: Wiley, 1964).

8. See, for example, Presthus, *Men at the Top;* Agger et al., *The Rulers and the Ruled;* and Linton C. Freeman et al., *Local Community Leadership* (Syracuse, N.Y.: University College, 1960).

9. John Walton, "Discipline, Method, and Community Power: A Note on the Sociology of Knowledge," *American Sociological Review* 31, no. 5 (October 1966): 684–689.

10. Floyd Hunter, *Community Power Succession: Atlanta's Policy-Makers Revisited* (Chapel Hill: University of North Carolina Press, 1980).

11. William G. Domhoff, *Who Really Rules? New Haven and Community Power Re-examined* (New Brunswick, N.J.: Transaction Books, 1978).

12. Clarence N. Stone, "Community Power Structure—A Further Look," *Urban Affairs Quarterly* 16, no. 4 (June 1981): 506.

13. Robert S. Lynd and Helen M. Lynd, *Middletown* (New York: Harcourt, 1929) and *Middletown in Transition.*

14. Lynd and Lynd, *Middletown in Transition,* p. 74.

15. Nelson Polsby in particular argues that the stratificationist conclusions of the elitists not only were inaccurate but also were inconsistent with much of the data that the authors recorded. See his *Community Power and Political Theory,* pp. 14–68.

16. Arnold Fleischmann and Joe R. Feagin, "The Politics of Growth-Oriented Urban Alliances: Comparing Old Industrial and New Sunbelt Cities," *Urban Affairs Quarterly* 23 (December 1987): 216.

17. Nancy Klemiewski, "Local Business Leaders and Urban Policy: A Case Study," *Insurgent Sociologist* 14, no. 1 (Winter 1987): 47.

18. Robert D. Schulze, "The Bifurcation of Power in a Satellite City," in *Community Political Systems,* ed. Morris Janowitz (New York: Free Press, 1961).

19. Ronald J. Pellegrin and Charles H. Coates, "Absentee-Owned Corporations and Community Power Structure," *American Journal of Sociology* 61 (March 1956): 413–419.

20. Edward C. Banfield and James Q. Wilson, *City Politics* (New York: Random House, 1965), pp. 261–276.

21. Peter Bachrach and Morton S. Baratz, "The Two Faces of Power," *American Political Science Review* 56, no. 4 (December 1962): 948.

22. Clarence N. Stone, "Social Stratification, Non-Decision-Making, and the Study of Community Power," *American Politics Quarterly* 10, no. 3 (July 1982): 293.

23. On the methods of researching nondecisions, see Matthew Crenson, *The Unpolitics of Air Pollution: A Study of Non-Decision-Making in the Cities* (Baltimore: Johns Hopkins University Press, 1971). Raymond Wolfinger finds the concept of nondecisions so fraught with methodological problems that it is virtually unresearchable. See his "Non-decisions and the Study of Local Politics," *American Political Science Review* 65, no. 4 (December 1971): 1063–1080. Frederick W. Frey takes a more optimistic view. See his "Comment: On Issues and Non-issues in the Study of Community Power," *American Political Science Review* 65, no. 4 (December 1971): 1081–1101. Other criticisms of nondecisions can be found in Geoffrey Debnam, "Nondecisions and Power: The Two Faces of Bachrach and Baratz," *American Political Science Review* 69, no. 3 (September 1975): 889–899; and Richard Merelman, "On the Neo-Elitist Critique of Community Power," *American Political Science Review* 62, no. 2 (June 1968): 451–460.

24. For example, see Bernard Asbell, "Dick Lee Discovers How Much Is Not Enough," *New York Times Magazine* 3 (September 1967): p. 6.

25. See Delbert C. Miller, *Leadership and Power in the BosWash Megalopolis* (New York: Wiley, 1975).

26. See Clarence N. Stone, "Paradigms, Power, and Urban Leadership," in *Leadership and Politics: New Perspectives in Political Science,* ed. Bryan D. Jones (Lawrence: University of Kansas Press, 1989), pp. 135–159. Stone views the pluralists as operating within a modernization paradigm, whereas the unitary-interest theorists, the structural Marxists, and growth theory adherents operate within an economistic paradigm.

27. See Richard Child Hill, "Crisis in the Motor City: The Politics of Economic Development in Detroit," in *Restructuring the City: The Political Economy of Urban Redevelopment,* ed. Susan Fainstein et al. (New York: Longman, 1983), pp. 98–102.

28. Richard Child Hill, "Fiscal Collapse and Political Struggle in Decaying Central Cities in the United States," in *Marxism and the Metropolis*, ed. William K. Tabb and Larry Sawyers (New York: Oxford University Press, 1978), pp. 213–240.

29. Several projections are analyzed in David Fasenfest, "Community Politics and Urban Redevelopment: Poletown, Detroit, and General Motors," *Urban Affairs Quarterly* 22, no. 1 (September 1986): 114.

30. See Michael Peter Smith, "Urban Structure, Social Theory, and Political Power," in *Cities in Transformation: Class, Capital, and the State,* vol. 26, *Urban Affairs Annual Review,* ed. Michael Peter Smith (Beverly Hills, Calif.: Sage, 1984), pp. 9–11.

31. Michael N. Danielson and Jamison Doig, *New York* (Berkeley: University of California Press, 1982).

32. Harvey Molotch, "The City as a Growth Machine: Toward a Political Economy of Place," *American Journal of Sociology* 82 (September 1976): 309–332. See also John Logan and Harvey Molotch, *Urban Fortunes: The Political Economy of Place* (Berkeley: University of California Press, 1987).

33. William G. Domhoff, "The Growth Machine and the Power Elite: A Challenge to Pluralists and Marxists Alike," in *Community Power: Directions for Future Research,* ed. Robert J. Waste (Beverly Hills, Calif.: Sage, 1986), p. 57.

34. Ronald K. Vogel and Bert E. Swanson, "The Growth Machine vs. the Antigrowth Coalition: The Battle for Our Communities," *Urban Affairs Quarterly* 25, no. 1 (September 1989): 63–85.

35. Paul E. Peterson, *City Limits* (Chicago: University of Chicago Press, 1981).

36. See especially Heywood T. Sanders and Clarence N. Stone, "Developmental Politics Reconsidered," *Urban Affairs Quarterly* 22, no. 4 (June 1987): 521–539.

37. Clarence N. Stone, "Summing Up: Urban Regimes, Development Policy, and Political Arrangements," in *The Politics of Urban Development,* ed. Clarence N. Stone and Heywood T. Sanders (Lawrence: University of Kansas Press, 1987).

38. Clarence Stone, *Regime Politics: Governing Atlanta, 1946–1988* (Lawerence: University of Kansas Press, 1989), p. 6.

39. Clarence N. Stone, "Systemic Power in Community Decision Making: A Restatement of Stratification Theory," *American Political Science Review* 74, no. 4 (December 1980): 978–990.

40. Ibid., p. 164.

41. Todd Swanstrom, *The Crisis of Growth Politics* (Philadelphia: Temple University Press, 1985).

42. Alan Digaetano, "Urban Political Regime Formation: A Study in Contrast," *Journal of Urban Affairs* 11, no. 3 (1989): 269.

43. Paul D. Schumacher, *Critical Pluralism, Democratic Performance, and Community Power* (Lawrence: University of Kansas Press, 1990). See also his "Cornfield Malls, Downtown Redevelopment and Democratic Performance," paper presented at a meeting of the Midwest Political Science Association, Chicago, April 1991.

44. Bryan D. Jones and Lynn W. Bachelor, with Carter Wilson, *The Sustaining Hand: Community Leadership and Corporate Power* (Lawrence: University of Kansas Press, 1986).

45. Ibid., pp. 206, 212.

46. Ibid., p. 8.

47. Pietro S. Nivola, "Apocalypse Now? Whither the Urban Fiscal Crisis?" *Polity* 14, no. 3 (Spring 1982): 375.

48. Terry Nichols Clark and Lorna Crowley Ferguson, *City Money: Political Processes, Fiscal Strain, and Retrenchment* (New York: Columbia University Press, 1983).

49. For recent efforts to appraise the community power field, see H. V. Savitch and John Clayton Thomas, eds., *Big City Politics in Transition* (Newbury Park, Calif.: Sage, 1991); Richard DeLeon, *Left Coast City: Progressive Politics in San Francisco, 1975–1991* (Lawrence: University of Kansas Press, 1992); Ronald K. Vogel, *Urban Political Economy: Broward County, Florida* (Gainesville: University Press of Florida, 1992); Peter Eisinger; "Theoretical Models in Urban Politics," Larry Lyon and Jason Miller, "Community," and Bert E. Swanson, "Power in Urban America" in *Handbook of Research on Urban Politics and Policy in the United States,* ed. Ronald K. Vogel (Westport, Conn.: Greenwood Press); David Judge, "Pluralism," Alan Harding, "Elite Theory and Growth Machines," and Gerry Stoker, "Regime Theory and Urban Politics" in *Theories of Urban Politics,* ed. David Judge, Gerry Stoker, and Harold Wolman (Thousand Oaks, Calif.: Sage, 1995).

50. See Ronald K. Vogel, *Urban Political Economy,* pp. 20–21.

51. Paul Kantor, *The Dependent City: The Changing Political Economy of Urban America* (Glenview, Ill.: Scott, Foresman, 1988), pp. 321–328.

52. Theodore J. Lowi, *At the Pleasure of the Mayor* (New York: Free Press, 1964). See especially chap. 7.

53. Theodore J. Lowi, "Machine Politics—Old and New," *Public Interest* 9 (Fall 1967): 86.

54. See the *Transit Fact Book: 1975–1976* (Washington, D.C.: American Public Transit Association, 1976), p. 32.

55. For an in-depth study of this in Boston and other cities, see Alan Lupo, Frank Colcord, and Edmund P. Fowler, *Rites of Way: The Politics of Transportation in Boston and the U.S. City* (Boston: Little, Brown, 1971).

56. David Rogers, *The Management of Big Cities* (Beverly Hills, Calif.: Sage, 1971), pp. 36–37.

57. John F. Dillon, *Commentaries on the Law of Municipal Corporations,* 5th ed. (Boston: Little, Brown, 1911), vol. I, sec. 237.

58. Roland J. Liebert, *Disintegration and Political Action: The Changing Functions of City Governments in America* (New York: Academic, 1976), p. 53. See also Thomas R. Dye and John A. Garcia, "Structure, Function, and Policy in American Cities," *Urban Affairs Quarterly* 14, no. 1 (September 1978): 103–126.

59. Supreme Court treatment of the impact of federal laws on state and local authority has spawned considerable research and writing. For some reactions, see Stephanie Beckes, "Boulder and NLC Revisited: An Introduction," *Intergovernmental Perspective* 9, no. 4 (Fall 1983): 5–6.

60. Doyle W. Buckwalter, "Dillon's Rule in the 1980s: Who's in Charge of Local Affairs?" *National Civic Review* 71, no. 8 (September 1982): 399–406.

61. See Alexander L. George, "Political Leadership and Social Change in American Cities," *Daedalus* 97, no. 4 (Fall 1968): 1194–1217; and Robert H. Salisbury, "Urban Politics: The New Convergence of Power," *Journal of Politics* 26, no. 4 (November 1964): 775–797.

62. Jeffrey L. Pressman, "The Preconditions for Mayoral Leadership," *American Political Science Review* 66, no. 2 (June 1972): 512–513, 522.

63. John P. Kotter and Paul R. Lawrence, *Mayors in Action: Five Approaches to Urban Governance* (New York: Wiley, 1974), chap. 7.

64. Ibid., p. 107.

65. Ibid., p. 111.

66. Norton Long, "The City as Reservation," *Public Interest* 25 (Fall 1971): 35.

67. Allan R. Talbot, *The Mayor's Game: Richard Lee of New Haven and the Politics of Change* (New York: Harper & Row, 1967), p. 29.

68. Jewell Bellush and Murray Hausknecht, "Entrepreneurs and Urban Renewal: The New Men of Power," *Journal of the American Institute of Planners* 32, no. 5 (September 1966): 289–297.

69. See Dahl, *Who Governs?* pp. 200–214; and Raymond E. Wolfinger, *The Politics of Progress* (Englewood Cliffs, N.J.: Prentice-Hall, 1974), pp. 157–202.

70. Douglas Yates, *The Ungovernable City* (Cambridge, Mass.: M.I.T. Press, 1977), p. 168.

71. Peter K. Eisinger, "Black Mayors and the Politics of Racial Advancement," in *Culture, Ethnicity, and Identity,* ed. William C. McReady (New York: Academic, 1983), p. 106.

72. In Ernest N. Morial's first election as mayor of New Orleans in 1977, he received only 19 percent of the white vote but 95 percent of the black vote. In Richard Arrington's first election as mayor of Birmingham in 1979, he won less than 15 percent of the white vote. Philadelphia's Wilson Goode won about 20 percent of the white vote in his 1983 victory. Chicago's Harold Washington won few white votes but an estimated 95 percent of the black vote in his 1983 election. In his 1987 reelection, Washington expanded his vote in white neighborhoods but still received a small minority of white votes.

73. Eisinger, "Black Mayors and the Politics of Racial Advancement," pp. 95–109.

74. Grace Hall Saltzstein, "Female Mayors and Women in Municipal Jobs," *American Journal of Political Science* 30, no. 1 (February 1986): 128–139.

75. Mayoral staffs in Boston and Philadelphia more than doubled during the 1960s, and by the mid-1970s, the New York mayor's office had a staff of over 1,000 people. See Arnold M. Howitt, "The Expanding Role of Mayoral Staff," *Policy Studies Journal* 3, no. 4 (June 1975): 363–369; and Peter Trapp, "Governors' and Mayors' Offices: The Role of the Staff," *National Civic Review* 63, no. 5 (May 1964): 242–249.

76. Wen H. Kuo, "Mayoral Influence on Urban Policy Making," *American Journal of Sociology* 79, no. 3 (November 1973): 637.

77. Robert F. Pecorella, "Fiscal Crises and Regime Change: A Contextual Approach," in *The Politics of Urban Development,* ed. Clarence N. Stone and Heywood T. Sanders (Lawrence: University of Kansas Press, 1987), pp. 52–72.

78. Douglas Yates, *The Ungovernable City.*

79. Martin Shefter, *Political Crisis/Fiscal Crisis: The Collapse and Revival of New York City* (New York: Basic Books, 1985), pp. 174–183.
80. Ibid., p. 180.
81. Glen Sparrow, "The Emerging Chief Executive: The San Diego Experience," *National Civic Review* 74, no. 11 (December 1985): 538–547.
82. Michael Parenti, "Power and Pluralism: A View from the Bottom," *Journal of Politics* 32, no. 3 (August 1970): 501–532.
83. Ibid., pp. 519, 521, 526, and 528.
84. Ibid., p. 529.
85. Michael Lipsky, *Protest in City Politics: Rent Strikes, Housing and the Power of the Poor* (Chicago: Rand McNally, 1970). See especially pp. 163–185.
86. Michael Lipsky, "Rent Strikes: Poor Man's Weapon," *Transaction* (February 1969): 10–15.
87. This was true in Florida. See James W. Button, *Blacks and Social Change: Impact of the Civil Rights Movement in Southern Communities* (Princeton, N.J.: Princeton University Press, 1989). It was also true in California. See Rufus P. Browning, Dale R. Marshall, and David H. Tabb, *Protest Is Not Enough* (Berkeley: University of California Press, 1984).
88. This is suggested by several commentaries on Chicago. Michael Novak charges that Poles and Italians are grossly underrepresented in executive positions in Chicago. He also charges that there are fewer Polish and Italian college students than there are black college students. See Michael Novak, "The New Ethnicity," *Center Magazine* 7, no. 4 (July–August 1974): 18–25. Studs Terkel's interview with Florence Scala, a leader of the unsuccessful movement to save the Hull House neighborhood from demolition, is a graphic example of the sense of powerlessness among whites. Studs Terkel, *Division Street: America* (New York: Avon, 1967), pp. 29–38. On Appalachian in-migrants into the city, see Todd Gitlin and Nanci Hollander, *Uptown: Poor Whites in Chicago* (New York: Harper & Row, 1970).
89. See Jonathan Rieder, *Canarsie: The Jews and Italians of Brooklyn against Liberalism* (Cambridge, Mass.: Harvard University Press, 1985).
90. See Eric Nordlinger, *Decentralizing the City: A Study of Boston's Little City Halls* (Cambridge, Mass.: M.I.T. Press, 1972), p. 9.
91. For some samples of this criticism, see Jonathan Kozol, *Death at an Early Age: The Destruction of the Hearts and Minds of Negro Children in the Boston Public Schools* (Boston: Houghton Mifflin, 1967); Bel Kaufman, *Up the Down Staircase* (Englewood Cliffs, N.J.: Prentice-Hall, 1964); Robert Coles, *Teachers and the Children of Poverty* (Washington, D.C.: Potomac Institute, 1970); and Herbert Kohl, *36 Children* (New York: New American Library, 1967).
92. Mario Fantini and Marilyn Gittell, *Decentralization: Achieving Reform* (New York: Praeger, 1973), pp. 48, 53–55.
93. Most of this account of decentralization in Detroit is taken from William R. Grant, "Community Control v. School Integration in Detroit," *Public Interest* 24 (Summer 1971): 62–79.
94. Fantini and Gittell, *Decentralization: Achieving Reform*, pp. 53–55.
95. National Advisory Commission on Civil Disorders, *Commission Report* (Washington, D.C.: U.S. Government Printing Office, 1968), pp. 32–33.
96. George J. Washnis, *Municipal Decentralization and Neighborhood Resources: Case Studies of Twelve Cities* (New York: Praeger, 1973). The 12 cities studied were Los Angeles, San Antonio, Kansas City (Missouri), Chicago, Norfolk, New York, Atlanta, Houston, Boston, Baltimore, Columbus, and San Francisco.
97. Jeffrey R. Henig, "The Political Consequences of Neighborhood Change," paper presented at the annual meeting of the American Political Science Association, Chicago, September 1–4, 1983.
98. Joseph Zimmerman, *Participatory Democracy: Populism Revived* (New York: Praeger, 1986), pp. 150–151.
99. Milton Kotler, *Neighborhood Government* (Indianapolis, Ind.: Bobbs-Merrill, 1969).
100. Richard L. Cole, "Citizen Participation in Municipal Politics," *American Journal of Political Science* 19, no. 4 (November 1975): 761–782.
101. John Hamer, "Neighborhood Control," *Editorial Research Reports* (October 31, 1975): 787–804.
102. John Mudd, "Beyond Community Control: A Neighborhood Strategy for City Government," *Publius* 6, no. 4 (Fall 1976): 113–136.
103. John M. Orball and Toru Uno, "A Theory of Neighborhood Problem Solving: Political Action vs. Residential Mobility," *American Political Science Review* 66, no. 2 (June 1972): 471–489.

104. Cole, "Citizen Participation in Municipal Politics," pp. 761–782.
105. Matthew A. Crenson, *Neighborhood Politics* (Cambridge, Mass.: Harvard University Press, 1983), p. 299.
106. Jeffrey Berry, Kent Portney, and Ken Thomson, *The Rebirth of Urban Democracy* (Washington, D.C.: The Brookings Institution, 1993), chap. 1.
107. Berry, Portney, and Thomson, *The Rebirth of Urban Democracy,* chap. 12.
108. See David Imbroscio, *Reconstructing City Politics: Alternative Economic Development and Urban Regimes* (Thousand Oaks, Calif.: Sage, 1997).
109. Crenson, *Neighborhood Politics,* p. 300.

PART FOUR

SUBURBIA AND THE
MULTICENTERED METROPOLIS

The most influential forces shaping the American metropolis in the last 50 years are associated with sprawl. In Chapter 1, we reported on a survey of scholars that highlighted the major influences that have shaped metropolitan development in the last half-century.[1] Among the forces propelling sprawl were the interstate highway system allowing people and businesses to flee the city along the highway corridors, federal mortgage guarantees and tax deductions making it more affordable to move to the suburbs, new large-scale suburban housing developments providing affordable housing for the middle classes on large lots, and the suburban mall providing a convenient alternative to the retail shopping in the city. Urban decline associated with loss of manufacturing jobs and race riots contributed to the urban exodus. In the next 50 years, much of the metropolitan challenge will revolve around problems related to sprawl. These include the need to develop "smart growth" policies to stop continued sprawl, to address the concentrated poverty and racial segregation related to sprawl, and to consider the appropriate political structure to govern metropolitan areas. It will be critical to ensure adequate infrastructure and public services to citizens, as well as democratic and representative governance arrangements that can address urban problems in the cities and suburbs.

Chapter 8 outlines the causes and consequences of sprawl. The transformation of the city into a metropolis led to new political structures to deal with the physical and social problems associated with suburban growth. Suburbs wanted to maintain political autonomy and independence, yet few suburbs were large enough or had enough resources to provide their own water, sewage disposal, roads, schools, and other physical systems needed for growth. Some metropolitan reformers have argued that the entire multicentered system of governance ought to be scrapped and replaced by a single metropolitan government. Other observers have argued that an effective system of governance could be achieved without creating a metropolitan government. Chapter 9 examines these arguments, the attempts to create metropolitan government, the patterns of bias associated with metropolitan reform, and the reasons for the successes and failures of metropolitan reform. In the absence of broad-scale success at creating metropolitan government, the last half-century has seen an emphasis on incremental change, metropolitan planning, and metropolitan policy-making agencies such as councils of government. These developments and their biases are discussed in Chapter 10 under the rubric of the new regionalism.

CHAPTER 8

URBAN SPRAWL

CHAPTER SYNOPSIS

The Suburbs and Sprawl: *Metropolitan Vision of Unlimited Low-Density Development (Sprawl); Problems with the Vision* • New Regionalist Agenda for the Metropolis: *Deemphasize "Structural" Fix of Government Restructuring; Smart Growth; New Urbanism* • In Defense of Sprawl: *Antisprawl Coalition Criticized as Elitist; Sprawl Ensures Affordable Housing; Lack of Empirical Evidence Underlying the Critique of Sprawl* • Distinctiveness of Suburban Politics: *Politics of Autonomy; Politics of Growth; Politics of Access* • Suburbia and the Challenge of Exclusion: *Taxes, Education, and Zoning; Housing and Exclusionary Zoning; Suburbs and Women; Consequences of Exclusion*

If there is any one distinguishing physical feature of the North American metropolis, it is the sprawl of the suburbs over the countryside. This sprawl is accentuated by the fact that control over zoning decisions—that is, specific uses for which land can be developed—is left in the hands of individual suburban municipalities (or county governments in the case of unincorporated areas). A study of zoning disputes in New York concluded that although individual zoning decisions "do not appear to have great significance by themselves, the total metropolitan development pattern is the result of a patchwork of local decisions, overlaid by transportation networks imposed by the state and federal governments."[2]

The multicentered metropolis hinders any efforts to control metropolitan growth, to channel the growth into areas designed for it, and to preserve other areas for permanent recreational green spaces or drainage, or even for vital groundwater recharge purposes. Despite the suburbs' lower population densities, they often have less park space or recreational space per capita than do the central cities. Typically, suburban growth has occurred before sewer and water lines were constructed, and this growth in many areas has thus posed a threat to the safety of the water supply. Furthermore, the outer suburbs are characterized by very low density, and the population concentrations are often separated by great distances. When low-density suburbs finally are forced to install public sewers and water supplies, the cost is much higher than it would have been if the growth had been planned in conjunction with the need for utilities. In the face of all this, suburban land use policies, particularly zoning laws, have been very unsuccessful in regulating where and under what conditions developers can build. Despite the ineffectiveness of suburban zoning controls, suburbanites tend to oppose vociferously any attempts to transfer zoning power to a higher level of government, such as the county.[3]

Ironically, the more that suburban sprawl continues, the more suburbanites are afflicted by the problems they sought to avoid by moving to the suburbs in the first place. Suburban gridlock is one of the most frustrating of these.

The Debate Over Sprawl

Sprawl conjures up images of traffic jams, single-family homes on large lots, ugly strip shopping centers along six-lane corridors, lack of sidewalks for pedestrians, and the like. There is no universally recognized definition of sprawl, although the term is generally used to mean low-density development on the edge of existing suburban development. Some studies of sprawl focus on the number of single-family detached dwelling units. The Environmental Protection Agency (EPA) in the past has defined sprawl as less than three houses per acre.*

This pattern of development leads to total dependence on the automobile for transportation. The amount of time Americans spend in traffic jams is growing. Analyzing 85 urban areas, *The 2005 Urban Mobility Report* finds that "the average annual delay for every person using motorized travel in the peak periods . . . climbed from 16 hours in 1982 to 47 hours in 2003."[4] Moreover, "the total congestion 'invoice' for the 85 areas in 2003 was approximately $63 billion" which was the value of "3.7 billion hours of delay and 2.3 billion gallons of excess fuel consumed."[5] To prevent increased congestion requires increasing roadway capacity and reducing bottlenecks. To increase capacity, they recommend building more streets and highways, more reliance on public transit, and better managing roadways through use of "high-occupancy vehicle lanes" and other operational improvements such as "freeway entrance ramp metering" (traffic signals), "motorists assistant patrols," "traffic signal coordination," and better "arterial street access management."[6] However, they warn that we must accept that large urban areas will have serious urban congestion problems. Even if all their recommendations were adopted, they say average delay per person would drop to only 44 hours per year.[7]

The Metropolitan Vision of "Unlimited Low-Density" Development

Anthony Downs argues that sprawl is promoted by the image of the suburban lifestyle as the ideal.[8] The American dream is a vision of the metropolis that inevitably leads to sprawl that is wasteful, inefficient, and unsustainable. Downs calls for a new metropolitan vision that focuses less on "unrestrained individualism" and puts community needs ahead of selfish private needs.[9] He identifies five specific elements of the metropolitan vision of sprawl that must be combated.

First, Americans want to own their own single-family home. Downs reports on a survey conducted in 1993 in which 86 percent of Americans said, "owning a home was

---

*U.S. Congress, Office of Technology Assessment, 1995. The Technological Reshaping of Metropolitan America (OTA-ETI-643). (Washington, D.C.: U.S. Government Printing Office).

better than renting," 83 percent said it "was a good investment," and 73 percent preferred a "single-family detached home with a yard."[10]

Second, Americans want their own car "on an uncongested road."[11] A community made up of single-family residences means that we are entirely dependent on the automobile for all transit needs.

Third, Americans want to work in low-rise office parks in landscaped settings with parking lots. These *edge cities* are found along interstate exits leading in and out of the central city.

Fourth, Americans want to live in "small communities with strong local governments" that "control land use, public schools, and other things that affect the quality of neighborhood life."[12]

Finally, Downs says that we want to live in "an environment free from the signs of poverty." Few will admit this or consciously acknowledge that it is a concern. Therefore, local governments prohibit the "construction of 'substandard' housing" and restrict the availability of subsidized housing for low-income residents. This means the primary source of housing for low-income residents is the "trickle-down" process whereby low-income residents take over housing that is no longer desired. This leads to the concentration of poverty in old, deteriorating neighborhoods in the older central city and inner suburbs. It also excludes low-income persons from suburbia.[13]

Problems of the Low-Density Vision

Downs identifies a number of problems stemming from this version of the American dream. The reality of suburban life is greatly at odds with its image. Rather than traveling the open roads portrayed in ads for suburbia, commuters confront and create serious traffic congestion, which leads to air pollution and expensive investment in new or expanded roads and highways. Suburbanites often blame this problem on the latest development project or the newest residents. However, it is their own behavior that is the problem. Restrictions on new growth may be imposed to combat the problems of suburban sprawl, but the fundamental source of the problem—the way the suburb is designed and built—is not challenged.

Downs identifies a number of problems stemming from sprawl. First, there is the "excessive travel" that results from the separation of housing from jobs. According to Downs, the low-density workplaces, commercial shopping, and single-family developments mean that jobs, homes, entertainment, and services are spread too far apart. Downs reports that in 1980 and 1990, about 30 percent of commuters traveled 30 minutes or longer to get to work. The time spent in the car and the distance traveled are increasing.[14] In 1990, only about 5 percent of commuters used mass transit. These numbers have gotten worse since Downs's study. This excessive travel leads to more air pollution and traffic congestion on the highway. It also means that individuals must sink a large share of their earnings into the purchase, maintenance, and insurance of automobiles. Transportation costs now make up a significant part of household expenditures (see Table 8.1). In addition, governments must fund new roads and maintain existing ones, which accounts for a large share of local expenditures and tax increases.

Second, there is a lack of affordable housing in the suburbs. Suburban development usually provides only "high-cost housing." This is often due to the regulations that are placed on new development. Unfortunately, lack of affordable housing leads to

TABLE 8.1   Household Spending on Transportation in 28 Metropolitan Areas

Rank	Metro Area	Transportation Expenditures	As Percent of Total
1	Houston–Galveston–Brazoria, TX	$8,840	22.1%
2	Atlanta, GA	$8,513	21.7
3	Dallas–Fort Worth, TX	$8,717	19.7
4	Miami–Fort Lauderdale, FL	$6,684	19.0
5	Detroit–Ann Arbor–Flint, MI	$6,710	18.8
6	Minneapolis–St. Paul, MN–WI	$8,683	18.4
7	Phoenix, AZ	$6,826	18.2
8	Philadelphia–Wilmington–Atlantic City, PA–NJ–DE–MD	$6,904	18.1
9	Kansas City, MO–KS	$6,489	18.1
10	Tampa–St. Petersburg–Clearwater, FL	$5,864	17.8
11	Anchorage, AK	$8,770	17.7
12	St. Louis, MO–IL	$6,489	17.6
13	Cleveland–Akron, OH	$6,384	17.5
14	Pittsburgh, PA	$6,331	17.5
15	Los Angeles–Riverside–Orange County, CA	$7,224	17.4
16	Denver–Boulder–Greeley, CO	$7,361	17.2
17	Seattle–Tacoma–Bremerton, WA	$7,387	17.1
18	Portland–Salem, OR–WA	$6,848	16.8
19	Cincinnati–Hamilton, OH–KY–IN	$6,145	16.7
20	Milwaukee–Racine, WI	$5,800	16.0
21	San Diego, CA	$6,319	15.8
22	Washington, DC–MD–VA	$7,207	15.4
23	Boston, MA–NH	$5,788	15.2
24	San Francisco–Oakland–San Jose, CA	$7,150	15.1
25	Chicago–Gary–Kenosha, IL–IN–WI	$5,436	14.9
26	Baltimore, MD	$5,236	14.7
27	New York–No. New Jersey–Long Island, NY–NJ–CT–PA	$5,956	14.5
28	Honolulu, HI	$6,136	14.4

Source: Reproduced from: Surface Transportation Policy Project/Center for Neighborhood Technology,
"Driven to Spend: The Impact of Sprawl on Household Transportation Expenses," 2000, p. 13
(http://www.transact.org/Reports/driven/default.htm).

concentration of poverty in the core. It also means that the low-wage earners who customarily fill service jobs (such as fast-food restaurant workers, store clerks, and lawn care workers) are in short supply. It is not just low-wage earners but moderate-income and professional workers as well who cannot live in the suburbs. For example, even firefighters, teachers, and mid-level managers earning $30,000 to $40,000 may have difficulty affording homes in the $250,000-or-more range. Downs points out that one-third of Americans are renters. Where are they to live in the suburbs? Low-density development does not include enough space for many Americans, because multifamily dwelling units are only a small part of most subdivisions. Even where they are built, they are often too expensive—and of course one must be able to afford a car.[15]

Housing regulations also raise the cost of housing beyond the means of many. These regulations both specify what materials can be used to build a house and establish minimum square feet and lot sizes. The rationale for regulation is to protect the public health and safety of the community. However, the regulations often have less to do with public safety than with ensuring a particular lifestyle favored by the middle class. This concern is usually framed in terms of protecting the property values of the community. However, as new urbanists (discussed later) point out, older neighborhoods in cities illustrate that single-family residences, small and medium-size apartment complexes, and small shops are not incompatible. The lack of affordable housing leads to the spatial mismatch between jobs (skills) and residences that we discussed in Chapter 6.

Third, Downs highlights the difficulty of "financing infrastructure fairly," including "new schools, roads, and sewage and water systems." There is a "lack of consensus" about how to finance the services and infrastructure needed to support suburban development. Impact fees on new development are often favored by long-term residents who say they should not have to pay for the added burden that new residents impose on the community. Thus general-obligation bonds are usually voted down. However, development fees raise the cost of housing, making the suburbs even more exclusive. More often than not, the battle over how to finance new infrastructure results in stalemate, and the needed infrastructure is not built.[16]

A fourth problem is the difficulty of placing *locally undesirable land uses* (LULUs) and the related *not in my back yard* (NIMBY) syndrome. There are many local governments in suburbia, and none wants to accept undesirable land uses such as airports, expressways, jails, garbage incinerators, landfills, homeless shelters, and so forth.[17]

Fifth is the "failure to compel people whose behavior generates significant social costs to pay for those costs directly."[18] For example, drivers who make many trips and create congestion on the roads do not pay for that privilege. One solution would be to impose pricing for road use— *peak hour road use pricing*. However, this is politically unlikely and could have the effect of penalizing the poor. Similarly, exclusionary zoning, which keeps out low-income residents, results in high social costs for those kept out and for society as a whole through more congested roads. However, Downs points out that the more affluent residents in their suburban cities avoid paying the cost of their exclusionary policies and pass it on to the rest of society.

A sixth problem is that too much open space is absorbed in pursuing the dominant vision for metropolitan America. Too many natural areas, wetlands, and farms are gobbled up. The low-density pattern of development and the roadways it necessitates consume much more space than more compact city development. This pattern also results in "bypassing parcels of vacant land" that otherwise would be used in the core cities.[19]

The net result of the dominant American vision is that we get sprawl and its related problems. Unfortunately, as a democracy, we have difficulty pursuing long-term strategies necessary to overcome sprawl, especially when so many derive short-term benefits from it. Downs believes that we must confront the vision itself if we are to change.

A New-Regionalist Agenda

Historically, government reorganization or central-city boundary adjustment was proposed to bring the suburbs back into the city. Then, the metropolitan city government or newly established metropolitan government would be able to plan the region's infrastructure, guide urban development, and ensure the efficient delivery of public services throughout the metropolis. For reasons discussed in Chapters 9 and 10, efforts to extend city boundaries or establish metropolitan governments have usually failed in the last century. Those concerned with addressing the continuing problems of sprawl, with achieving more coordinated metropolitan policy making, and with reducing disparities between central cities and suburbs are often called *new regionalists*. They are referred to as new regionalists because they eschew formal government restructuring. They are still "regionalists," but the "new" agenda is to develop effective regional policies or find ways to integrate existing fragmented governments in the metropolis. These entities could then pursue coordinated policies to attack further outward expansion and provide needed infrastructure such as landfills or incinerators, regional transportation, and the like. Thus policy solutions take precedence over efforts to reorganize government structure.[20] Chapters 9 and 10 address enhancing metropolitan governance. In this chapter, we focus on the new-regionalist policy agenda to counter sprawl and improve the design of suburbs.

Smart Growth

Many new regionalists have embraced "smart growth" as the solution. If governments planned better for growth and acted decisively to guide growth through infrastructure and tax policies, development that was more compact would occur, and natural areas and farmlands would be preserved. In 1997, the state of Maryland adopted smart growth legislation proposed by Governor Paris Glendening (see the accompanying box). A key component of the legislation was "priority funding areas." State aid for local governments would be directed toward targeted growth areas.

New Urbanism

Closely related to smart growth is *new urbanism*. New urbanists argue that Americans lack a "sense of place" and suffer "loss of community" living in the suburbs. As James Howard Kuntsler explains, the suburbs are poorly designed, cheaply built, and ugly.[21] Every city now looks the same. New urbanists argue that early builders respected history and built structures designed to last and fit in with their surroundings. Kunstler refers to this as "chronological connectivity [that] lends meaning and dignity to our little lives."[22] Kunstler argues that after 1945, we changed the way we built things. We talked about "design life" and spent little or no money on embellishing buildings. We built box schools with windows that did not open, relying on technology rather than "traditional solutions" to address issues such as weather and to provide lighting. The buildings turned their backs on the streets and neighborhoods and helped turn Americans off to their urban environment. Cities and towns lost their heart and soul as new suburbs blighted the landscape.

New urbanists seek to redesign suburbs to create a "sense of place" and "community." First, new urbanists say we need to eliminate or overhaul our zoning laws. Today's zoning regulations would outlaw most small-town "Main Streets." Nor would they allow the charming older neighborhoods that we cherish in cities to be built today. This is because zoning regulations now prohibit mixing single-family and multifamily dwelling units in the same area and require greater boundaries between commercial and residential areas. These kinds of neighborhoods were built because of "cultural

What Is Smart Growth?   *A Message from Governor Glendening*

Green pastures and lush forests, strong and friendly neighborhoods, prosperous businesses and family-supporting jobs, good schools and a healthy environment; these are the qualities we all want for Maryland, for now and generations to come. That is why in 1997 I proposed and the General Assembly passed the Smart Growth and Neighborhhod Conservation initiatives.

In a short time, we have made great progress. A series of financial incentives and neighborhood improvements already have encouraged companies and individuals alike to move back into our downtown areas. Job opportunities are springing from businesses that are using tax credits and brownfields cleanup assistance. Local governments and land trusts are teaming up to use our Rural Legacy and GreenPrint Programs to preserve thousands of acres of Maryland's farm lands and natural resource areas before they are lost forever to unplanned development.

Local governments have established their "Smart Growth Areas" to decide where, within their jurisdictions, they want State financial assistance with future growth. Establishment of these "Priority Funding Areas" will help State and local governments alike prioritize where they will allocate their funds.

Smart Growth Principles

- Mix land uses
- Take advantage of compact building design
- Create housing opportunities and choices
- Create walkable communities
- Foster distinctive, attractive communities with a strong sense of place
- Preserve open space, farmland, natural beauty, and critical environmental areas
- Strengthen and direct development toward existing communities
- Provide a variety of transportation choices
- Make development decisions predictable, fair, and cost-effective
- Encourage community and stakeholder collaboration in development decisions

Together, Smart Growth policies are setting a wise and prudent course for the future. They will save taxpayer dollars while reversing the debilitating economic, social and environmental costs caused by years of government supported sprawl development. For five decades, many of our cities have been in decline as our open space has been devoured by a growing migration from established neighborhoods. It is time to reverse these trends.

Smart growth will help restore our downtown economies, our sense of community and our environment. This is neither an easy nor a quick task. It will take a fundamental change in thinking. If our current growth patterns do not change, development will consume as much land in the next 25 years in central Maryland alone as it has during the entire 369-year history of our State. We must have a genuine sense of urgency. I am proud to say people from all walks of life are rising to meet this challenge. With your help, we will remain vigilant in our efforts to ensure that Maryland remains a great place to live, work and raise a family.

Parris N. Glendening, Governor

Source: Reproduced from http://www.smartgrowth.state.md.us/whatis.htm.

consensus" about the need for a corner grocery store, for Main Street buildings to be more than one story tall, and for sidewalks and trees on all roads.

New urbanists believe that zoning was a well-intentioned but harmful urban reform in the early twentieth century to protect neighborhoods from dirty and dangerous industrial development. They believe that zoning has been "taken to an absurd extreme" today.[23] Zoning no longer acknowledges the needs of "civic life." "Strict separation" of all activities was imposed, and the needs of the automobile were put ahead of all other concerns. Kunstler argues, "The model of the human habitat dictated by zoning is a formless, soulless, centerless, demoralizing mess. It bankrupts families and townships. It disables whole classes of decent, normal citizens. It ruins the air we breathe. It corrupts and deadens our spirit."[24]

Many (such as car dealers and builders) profit from this sprawl, but suburbanites begin to realize it is bad. Hence they oppose more growth that will result in more "traffic, bigger parking lots, and buildings ever bigger and uglier than the monstrosities" recently built. They become "NIMBYs" and stop new developments. This attitude results in leapfrogging, whereby sprawl moves even farther out. The new consensus is not to build anything. New urbanists say it is a consensus of fear.

New urbanists say there is a better alternative. People should try to make their own communities like Nantucket or St. Augustine—the kinds of towns they like to go to on vacations. This requires that we change the way the suburbs are built and redesign existing ones in accordance with new-urbanist principles. First, stop accommodating the automobile. Second, abandon zoning and build "compact, mixed use development" similar to the historic neighborhoods in inner cities. Third, increase density levels in urban neighborhoods, which will allow mass transit to work, create livelier communities, and ensure that sufficient population is available to support commercial establishments and services. Finally, recognize the importance of the street as an "outdoor room" in the neighborhood. New-urbanist ideas have been promoted by the Congress for the New Urbanism. The "Charter of the New Urbanism" presented in the accompanying box elaborates on the points made in Kunstler's article.

The Defense of Sprawl

Peter Gordon and Harry Richardson take aim at the critics of sprawl and the advocates of new urbanism. They argue that sprawl is another name for urbanization. "Cities around the world have grown outwards for almost all of recorded history as a result of cheaper travel, better communications, and greater affluence. Suburbia was not a post–World War II, or even a post-automobile, invention. But the strong demand for new housing in the late 1940s made the expansion appear new."[25] From their standpoint, the debate over sprawl is a clash of values over how the metropolis should develop. They argue that the empirical evidence does not support the claim of the "anti-sprawl coalition" that sprawl—that is, "low-density suburban living"—is bad or unsustainable. They reject the argument that insufficient farmland will be kept in production or that insufficient open space or natural areas will remain in the United States for future generations to enjoy.[26]

Charter of the New Urbanism

The Congress for the New Urbanism views disinvestment in central cities, the spread of placeless sprawl, increasing separation by race and income, environmental deterioration, loss of agricultural lands and wilderness, and the erosion of society's built heritage as one interrelated community-building challenge.

We stand for the restoration of existing urban centers and towns within coherent metropolitan regions, the reconfiguration of sprawling suburbs into communities of real neighborhoods and diverse districts, the conservation of natural environments, and the preservation of our built legacy.

We recognize that physical solutions by themselves will not solve social and economic problems, but neither can economic vitality, community stability, and environmental health be sustained without a coherent and supportive physical framework.

We advocate the restructuring of public policy and development practices to support the following principles: neighborhoods should be diverse in use and population; communities should be designed for the pedestrian and transit as well as the car; cities and towns should be shaped by physically defined and universally accessible public spaces and community institutions; urban places should be framed by architecture and landscape design that celebrate local history, climate, ecology, and building practice.

We represent a broad-based citizenry, composed of public and private sector leaders, community activists, and multidisciplinary professionals. We are committed to reestablishing the relationship between the art of building and the making of community, through citizen-based participatory planning and design.

We dedicate ourselves to reclaiming our homes, blocks, streets, parks, neighborhoods, districts, towns, cities, regions, and environment.

We assert the following principles to guide public policy, development practice, urban planning, and design:

The region: metropolis, city, and town

1. Metropolitan regions are finite places with geographic boundaries derived from topography, watersheds, coastlines, farmlands, regional parks, and river basins. The metropolis is made of multiple centers that are cities, towns, and villages, each with its own identifiable center and edges.

2. The metropolitan region is a fundamental economic unit of the contemporary world. Governmental cooperation, public policy, physical planning, and economic strategies must reflect this new reality.

3. The metropolis has a necessary and fragile relationship to its agrarian hinterland and natural landscapes. The relationship is environmental, economic, and cultural. Farmland and nature are as important to the metropolis as the garden is to the house.

4. Development patterns should not blur or eradicate the edges of the metropolis. Infill development within existing urban areas conserves environmental resources, economic investment, and social fabric, while reclaiming marginal and abandoned areas. Metropolitan regions should develop strategies to encourage such infill development over peripheral expansion.

(continued)

Charter of the New Urbanism *(continued)*

5. Where appropriate, new development contiguous to urban boundaries should be organized as neighborhoods and districts, and be integrated with the existing urban pattern. Noncontiguous development should be organized as towns and villages with their own urban edges, and planned for a jobs/housing balance, not as bedroom suburbs.

6. The development and redevelopment of towns and cities should respect historical patterns, precedents, and boundaries.

7. Cities and towns should bring into proximity a broad spectrum of public and private uses to support a regional economy that benefits people of all incomes. Affordable housing should be distributed throughout the region to match job opportunities and to avoid concentrations of poverty.

8. The physical organization of the region should be supported by a framework of transportation alternatives. Transit, pedestrian, and bicycle systems should maximize access and mobility throughout the region while reducing dependence upon the automobile.

9. Revenues and resources can be shared more cooperatively among the municipalities and centers within regions to avoid destructive competition for tax base and to promote rational coordination of transportation, recreation, public services, housing, and community institutions.

The neighborhood, the district, and the corridor

1. The neighborhood, the district, and the corridor are the essential elements of development and redevelopment in the metropolis. They form identifiable areas that encourage citizens to take responsibility for their maintenance and evolution.

2. Neighborhoods should be compact, pedestrian-friendly, and mixed-use. Districts generally emphasize a special single use, and should follow the principles of neighborhood design when possible. Corridors are regional connectors of neighborhoods and districts; they range from boulevards and rail lines to rivers and parkways.

3. Many activities of daily living should occur within walking distance, allowing independence to those who do not drive, especially the elderly and the young. Interconnected networks of streets should be designed to encourage walking, reduce the number and length of automobile trips, and conserve energy.

4. Within neighborhoods, a broad range of housing types and price levels can bring people of diverse ages, races, and incomes into daily interaction, strengthening the personal and civic bonds essential to an authentic community.

5. Transit corridors, when properly planned and coordinated, can help organize metropolitan structure and revitalize urban centers. In contrast, highway corridors should not displace investment from existing centers.

6. Appropriate building densities and land uses should be within walking distance of transit stops, permitting public transit to become a viable alternative to the automobile.

7. Concentrations of civic, institutional, and commercial activity should be embedded in neighborhoods and districts, not isolated in remote, single-use complexes. Schools should be sized and located to enable children to walk or bicycle to them.

8. The economic health and harmonious evolution of neighborhoods, districts, and corridors can be improved through graphic urban design codes that serve as predictable guides for change.

9. A range of parks, from tot-lots and village greens to ballfields and community gardens, should be distributed within neighborhoods. Conservation areas and open lands should be used to define and connect different neighborhoods and districts.

The block, the street, and the building

1. A primary task of all urban architecture and landscape design is the physical definition of streets and public spaces as places of shared use.

2. Individual architectural projects should be seamlessly linked to their surroundings. This issue transcends style.

3. The revitalization of urban places depends on safety and security. The design of streets and buildings should reinforce safe environments, but not at the expense of accessibility and openness.

4. In the contemporary metropolis, development must adequately accommodate automobiles. It should do so in ways that respect the pedestrian and the form of public space.

5. Streets and squares should be safe, comfortable, and interesting to the pedestrian. Properly configured, they encourage walking and enable neighbors to know each other and protect their communities.

6. Architecture and landscape design should grow from local climate, topography, history, and building practice.

7. Civic buildings and public gathering places require important sites to reinforce community identity and the culture of democracy. They deserve distinctive form, because their role is different from that of other buildings and places that constitute the fabric of the city.

8. All buildings should provide their inhabitants with a clear sense of location, weather and time. Natural methods of heating and cooling can be more resource-efficient than mechanical systems.

9. Preservation and renewal of historic buildings, districts, and landscapes affirm the continuity and evolution of urban society.

Source: Congress for New Urbanism: http://www.cnu.org.

Gordon and Richardson identify the key actors in the antisprawl coalition as environmentalists, for whom "only zero growth is acceptable" and "central city politicians" who "want to preserve their spheres of influence and make suburbanites feel guilty for eroding the viability of central cities." Downtown growth machine actors join the coalition in an effort to bolster their investments. "Redistributionists are also on board, sensing city-suburban disparities that can be mitigated by new 'regional' governments" (see Chapters 9 and 10).[27] The argument is consistent with Logan and Molotch's growth machine thesis (see Chapter 7). However, Gordon and Richardson add a new twist in suggesting that the antigrowth coalition of environmentalists and neighborhood groups has joined forces with the downtown growth machine against the suburban growth advocates under the banner of *new regionalism*.

Logan and Molotch might be encouraged by the new-regionalist agenda to undercut sprawl and value neighborhood use over continued wasteful development. However, Gordon and Richardson object that the antisprawl coalition is not in the public interest. They prefer to rely on the market for planning rather than on planners and politicians. In their view, the market is responding to the needs of consumers for more affordable housing and to a demand for better public services and healthier quality of life that can be enjoyed by families in the suburbs. They believe that the negative aspects of sprawl are overstated or nonexistent and, therefore, that restrictions on market processes are unwarranted.[28]

Several arguments are used to refute the "smart growth" policies advocated by the antisprawl coalition. First, sprawl ensures affordable housing. Where efforts to limit suburban growth occur, housing costs rise. Portland, Oregon, adopted an urban-growth boundary to limit outward urban expansion. A metropolitan government overlaying parts of three counties was established. It integrates land use, transportation, and infrastructure policies to ensure development that is more compact. This has reduced suburbanization and ensured that the central city is strong and vital. However, there is evidence that housing costs in Portland have risen greatly. According to Randy O'Toole of the Thoreau Institute,

> The urban-growth boundary and restrictions on new single-family housing have turned Portland from one the nation's most affordable markets for single-family housing in 1989 to one of the least affordable since 1996. Since 1990, the cost of an acre of land available for housing has risen from $20,000 to $200,000. According to the National Association of Homebuilders, in 1989 more than two-thirds of Portland households could afford to buy a median-priced home. Today it is around 30 percent.[29]

Critics of the antisprawl coalition lament that the new-regionalism agenda has been so successful in Portland. The result is an elitist vision of urban design that other communities would be well advised to reject.[30] For example, Gordon and Richardson cite a Fannie Mae survey that shows that "75–80 percent of households would prefer to live in a single-family home with a private yard."[31] This is exactly the type of housing that new regionalists hope to limit. Essentially, the opponents of the smart-growth policies argue that faulty premises underlie the critique of sprawl and the presumed lack of sustainability of existing and continued suburbanization (see the accompanying box). Gordon and Richardson argue that even the concern over lost farmland is misplaced because "urban development still absorbs less than 5 percent of the continental land mass."[32]

Distinctiveness of Suburban Politics

The pattern of metropolitan development that produced the suburbs also spawned a suburban politics distinct from that of central cities or nonmetropolitan areas.

Neglected Facts in the Sprawl Debate

1. The air is getting cleaner in spite of more people, more automobiles, and more vehicle miles driven. In the years 1979–1996, U.S. population grew by 29 percent, vehicles by 98 percent, and vehicle miles traveled (VMT) by 125 percent; yet, in the same interval . . . on-road vehicle emissions . . . declined.

2. Reductions in most air pollutants began well before the onset of federal environmental regulation.

3. Much more food is being grown on much less land. Cropland use in the United States peaked in 1930.

4. Suburb-to-suburb commuting and low-density settlement ease traffic congestion.

5. Inner-city poverty is not a consequence of low-density suburbs. Poverty is a human capital problem exacerbated by poor inner-city schools.

6. There are no clear infrastructure savings from high residential densities. The few available studies reveal a "U-shaped" cost function that bottoms at relatively low residential densities, below 1,250 people per square mile.

7. The social interactions of suburbanites are no different from central-city residents.

8. Providing expensive rail-transit systems does nothing for traffic congestion. After more than $360 billion of public subsidies, most of it to rail transit, over the last 35 years, per capita transit use in the United States is at a historic low. Yet new rail-transit systems are routinely proposed and built. This waste is explained by political pork-barrel. The overwhelming majority of Americans prefer personal transportation, a fact that planners and politicians continue to ignore.

9. The downtown revival stories may be much exaggerated. There have been many media reports about the revival of the central city in general and downtown in particular. Also, the 2000 census results have revealed remarkable resilience in several central cities. So, are the central cities coming back? . . . In the long run, the central cities require all the stars to come into constellation. The large majority of nontraditional households have to swear off children forever (no rational analysis can expect the vast majority of central-city schools to improve soon); central cities have to create their mini-Manhattans of good restaurants and recreational and cultural amenities; they have to address the other central-city social problems, apart from education; and significant job growth has to occur in downtowns. . . . There are serious doubts that this constellation can come into line.

Source: Excerpted from Peter Gordon and Harry W. Richardson, "The Sprawl Debate: Let Markets Plan," *Publius: The Journal of Federalism* 31 (Summer 2001): 143–144.

The Politics of Autonomy

First, suburbs are politically distinctive because of their quest for political autonomy—for a government that is small enough and close enough to home that the average citizen can have a personal impact on it. Robert Wood argues that suburbia is in essence an attempt to re-create Jeffersonian democracy on the fringes of the cities.[33] The outward growth of population and business *could have occurred* without the establishment of a ring of municipal governments surrounding the central city, and central cities *could have continued to grow* by annexing the newly settled areas. The fact that this did not occur reflects the strength of the political motivation to keep the new settlements separate from the old central cities.[34] This motivation was supported by scholars who argued that city governments function best if the cities are kept at a population range of 40,000 to 50,000,[35] a size that fits nicely into suburbia. Many people hoped that a proliferation of small, politically autonomous towns would enable their residents to have the best of two worlds: the intimacy of small-town government and the advantages of metropolitan facilities. Accordingly, one of the key themes that has pervaded many specific issues of suburban politics has been defending local autonomy from encroachment by big-city or metropolitan government.

This motivation behind suburbanization is similar in some respects to the motivation behind the demand for community control in central cities.[36] However, community control and the proliferation of suburban governments are very different in other respects. Even the most ardent advocates of neighborhood government within cities favor retention of an overall citywide government. The staunchest advocates of suburban government, however, have opposed an overall, metropolitan-wide government. Politically, then, suburbia is distinct in that there is no overall suburban or metropolitan government; there are many governments. Governmentally and politically, the metropolis has become multicentered.

The Politics of Growth

A second distinctive feature of suburban politics has been the politics of regulating metropolitan sprawl. Typically, someone would buy a farm within easy commuting distance of a city or a major employment center, subdivide the farm into suburban-size home lots, and contract with construction firms to put in a subdivision complete with houses and streets.[37] If the subdivision were far enough removed, the homes would get their water from wells and dispose of their waste through septic tanks. Eventually the high-density use of septic tanks would pollute the well water, and local governments would be called on to provide a community water supply as well as a sanitary sewer system. This growth would also necessitate other services. Storm sewers were often needed to prevent basements from flooding. In the North, snow had to be removed from the streets in winter. Police and fire protection had to be increased. Schools had to be built. Park space had to be bought and developed. Hospitals had to be provided.

The goals of autonomy and growth seemed to conflict. The goal of autonomy called for small-town suburban governments. However, providing the infrastructure for growth (highways, sewers, water supplies, hospitals, and schools) was too expensive for small-town governments to do on their own. If the system of autonomous small-town suburban governments was going to be maintained, some mechanisms had to be created to provide those expensive essential services. The creation of these mechanisms and the politics of managing growth was the second distinctive feature of suburban politics.

The Politics of Access

A third distinctive feature of suburbia is the politics of access. Especially in the larger and older metropolises, the suburbs do not house a proportionate share of racial minorities, low-income people, welfare recipients, or subsidized-housing tenants. On the contrary, these people are disproportionately housed in the central cities of the metropolises. Michael N. Danielson has argued that a series of legal mechanisms were used to keep low-income people out of the exclusive suburbs and penned up in the city or the poorer suburbs.[38] These exclusionary tactics have been employed largely in public education, in zoning, and in home construction and sales.

The Biases of Unrestricted Suburban Growth

The foregoing discussion makes it clear that some people receive benefits because of the decentralized political structure of the multicentered metropolis. Certain other people are disadvantaged.

The multicentered metropolis is biased to favor those who profit from uncontrolled sprawl, particularly land speculators, real estate developers, and large retailing enterprises. Local municipalities, which make zoning decisions in most metropolises, seldom turn down proposed real estate developments that will increase the local community's tax base, such as shopping centers and expensive single-family homes. Nor do they consider how the development fits into areawide growth patterns. In addition, once the overall permission for a shopping center is granted, specific decisions about the kinds of shops and their owners or managers may be left to the shopping center management, without input from the local municipality or from residents.

Although it is clear that the multicentered metropolis favors large-scale developers by granting them considerable autonomy in their operations, it is not so clear who is directly hurt by this process. Nor is it clear that the direct profits of development would be more widely shared if zoning decisions were made at the metropolitan rather than the municipal level.

A second bias may exist in the multicentered metropolis: a bias against the *public good*. To the extent that the "public good" consists of the objectives of minimizing pollution, protecting open space, equalizing the availability of public services, and equalizing access to housing, shopping, employment, and educational facilities, contemporary suburbia is probably biased against the public good. However, it is doubtful that universal agreement exists that embracing these objectives is in the public interest. Furthermore, many steps have been taken toward a number of these objectives in the past decade.

Third, the multicentered metropolis is biased against effective citizen input. With such a wide variety of government agencies operating within any given geographic region, concerned citizens may find it extremely difficult to express grievances effectively, because they do not know which agency has responsibility for their particular grievance. In theory, suburbanites are very close to their city council and their school board, and they are much more likely to know one of these officials personally than are central-city residents. But they also are likely to discover that some of the most important governmental activities that concern them—streetlight location, sewerage, transit service, welfare problems, and in some suburbs even water supply, fire protection, and police protection—are not handled by these local officials.

Suburbia and the Challenge of Exclusion

It is likely that the concentration of poor people and racial minorities in the central cities constitutes another bias of the multicentered metropolis. Three issues that dominate local suburban politics—taxes, schools, and zoning—affect exclusion and access. The issue of taxes inevitably arises, particularly when the suburb undergoes rapid development. Numerous expensive services must be provided, ranging from schools to police protection to sewers and water. Much of the revenue to provide these services comes from the local property tax. This tax accounts for 45 percent of all locally raised revenue.[39] In the central cities the property tax burden is spread across the entire city, but the property tax burden of suburbia varies from one suburb to another. Each suburban jurisdiction gets property tax revenue only from property within its boundaries. Consequently, suburbs are sensitive to the politics of attracting industry that pays more than its share of property taxes and of keeping out people (especially low-income families with school-age children) who will add more costs of providing services than they will add revenue to the property tax base. Furthermore, there is evidence that the greater the reliance on property taxes in a metropolitan area, the greater the disparities in income between suburbanites and central-city residents. The implication of this research is that suburbanites in these property-tax-reliant metropolises deliberately seek to keep low-income people out of their suburbs.[40]

Public education is a controversial issue for several reasons. As the central-city school systems were increasingly criticized for delinquency, segregation, racial unrest, and poor education over the past generation,[41] suburban schools came to be seen as places to escape these problems. Indeed, one reason why upper-middle-class professionals choose to live in suburbia is that they believe there will be decent schools where their children can be well educated and safe. Suburbanites, like central-city dwellers, feel that public education is much too important to become bound up with party politics. Yet several contradictory themes flourish in suburban school politics. On the one hand, a complex of factors impels the suburbs to provide expensive school facilities. Not only do parents want the best for their children, but also businesspeople and real estate brokers think that a reputation for good schools will attract upper-income residents with high-status professional occupations. On the other hand, good schools are expensive, and in most suburbs, bitter battles recur periodically over school expenditures. Tax-conscious citizens charge that their money is being wasted on superfluous frills. Much of this tax-conscious animosity is directed at teachers, especially if they are unionized and bargain militantly for better pay.

Finally, for the same reasons underlying the tax and school issues, zoning disputes always have the potential to disrupt the peace in the suburbs. Suburbs inevitably go through a phase of rapid growth. During this phase, subdividers and real estate developers construct and sell large numbers of houses. To service the new population, shopping centers and other facilities are built. This situation is always conducive to charges of conflict of interest, graft, sellouts to big developers, absence of planning, and dearth of public concern. The conditions under which developers are allowed to operate and the zoning restrictions that dictate what kinds of housing they can build inspire significant battles at this stage in the suburb's growth.

Exclusion and the Politics of Housing

Michael N. Danielson argues that racial and class segregation in the contemporary metropolis did not occur by accident. Rather, he sees them as resulting from a deliberate policy of exclusion.[42] The primary aim of the politics of exclusion is *class* homogeneity, not racial homogeneity. People in affluent neighborhoods do not want to cause property values to drop by allowing cheaper homes to be built nearby or by allowing nonaffluent neighbors to move in. Parents of children in affluent schools do not want their schools flooded with nonaffluent children. Nor do they want their children forcibly transported to less affluent schools. To achieve these exclusionary goals, suburbs can rely on several legal tools. The main ones, as discussed below, are exclusionary zoning, limited-growth zoning, strict subdivision requirements, strict building codes, nonimplementation of fair-housing legislation, and prohibitions against subsidized housing. And although the primary aim of these exclusionary devices may be class-based, they put a heavy burden on racial minorities because disproportionate numbers of the latter have low or moderate incomes.

The Strategies for Exclusion

Exclusionary Zoning   Zoning is the act of specifying what a piece of land may be used for. A zoning ordinance divides the city into different zones for different uses, reserving some zones for heavy industry, some for commerce, some for light industry, some for single-family homes, some for apartments, and so on. Nearly all suburbs of more than 5,000 people exercise zoning powers, and about half of the smaller ones also do so.[43]

There are two main ways in which zoning can be used to exclude low-income people. The first is to establish minimum lot sizes and building floor-space requirements. For example, during the 1960s, two-thirds of the developable residential land in Cleveland's suburban Cuyahoga County was zoned for half-acre or larger lots.[44] In addition to specifying large lots, zoning ordinances may also specify minimum lot width and a minimum number of square feet for any home built on the lot. By requiring that big houses be built on wide, large lots, zoning ordinances effectively inflate the cost of housing. This is because it costs more to buy a half-acre lot than a quarter-acre lot, more to build a house with 1,200 square feet of floor space than one with 900 square feet, and more to install sewers, curbs, and water lines in front of a 150-foot-wide lot than in front of a 60-foot-wide lot.

Large-lot zoning inflates the cost of new housing, so its net effect is to exclude people who cannot afford expensive houses. Because racial minorities have disproportionately low and moderate incomes, large-lot zoning imposes a special burden on them. The defenders of large-lot zoning argue, however, that it is needed to protect the value of other homes in the suburb. People who purchase $200,000 homes do not want someone building a $75,000 home next door to them.

A second exclusionary zoning tactic is to prohibit apartments with more than two bedrooms. The most exclusive suburbs prohibit apartments entirely. Relatively affluent suburbs permit apartments but prohibit three-bedroom apartments and require a high percentage of one-bedroom apartments in each complex. Michael Danielson reported that in 1976, "over 99 percent of all undeveloped land zoned for residential uses [in the New York metropolitan area] is restricted to single-family housing,"[45] thus excluding apartments.

Not only do these prohibitions discriminate against lower-income people unable to purchase a single-family home; they also discriminate against several categories of people who for one reason or another may not want to live in an entire house during certain periods of their lives—recently divorced people, young single adults, elderly people whose children have left home, and recently married couples. The rising numbers of people in these categories during the last several decades created an economic demand for multifamily buildings that has virtually forced the less exclusionary suburbs to permit apartment construction, townhouse construction, and condominium construction and conversion. Construction of multifamily units in suburbs during the 1960s and 1970s increased almost five times as fast as the construction of single-family homes.[46] Today, suburban multifamily complexes have become commonplace.

Limited-Growth Zoning   Limited-growth zoning consists of plans that limit the number of building permits issued each year. Although these are justified on aesthetic grounds (keeping the local community physically attractive) or on fiscal grounds (keeping down the costs of adding expensive public services), limits on growth are inherently biased against low- and moderate-income people.[47] By limiting the supply of houses while the demand for them is increasing, limited-growth zoning has the net impact of inflating the price of existing housing. This fact has led some observers to speculate that limited-growth zoning is a tool used by the well-to-do to keep out lower- and lower-middle-income people.[48]

However, a study of 97 northern California communities found that upper-income communities were no more likely to impose growth controls than were other communities,[49] and a study of voter reactions to a growth limitation initiative in Riverside, California, found that upper-status voters were no more likely than lower-status voters to support the growth control initiative.[50] The most noticeable difference between the advocates and the opponents of growth control was their attitude toward government's role in the economy generally. People with the liberal view that government should provide social services and protect the environment tended to support the growth control movement in Riverside, regardless of their socioeconomic status. On the other hand, people with a conservative view emphasizing individual property rights and a minimal government role tended to oppose growth control. If these California findings apply to the rest of the nation, they point to an interesting conclusion. Growth control has an exclusionary impact—even if the intent of its supporters is not necessarily to practice exclusion. Ironically, lower-income, nonhomeowning, environmentally concerned liberals may be supporting policies that work to their economic disadvantage.

Strict Subdivision Requirements   Along with zoning ordinances, municipalities also pass subdivision requirements that oblige developers to put in improvements such as streets, sewers, water lines, and other services whenever they build a new subdivision of homes. By assigning this responsibility to the developer, the city is spared the cost of paying for these improvements, and the purchasers of the homes are assured that they will not have to be added later at a much greater cost. In addition to necessary improvements such as streets, water lines, and sanitary sewers, subdivision ordinances may also require curbs, sidewalks, driveways, park space, storm sewers, and minimum setbacks of buildings from property lines. The more improvements that are required, the more expensive the subdivision becomes. Low-income and working-class suburbs often forgo many subdivision requirements.

Strict Building Codes A city's building code specifies the quality of construction and the types of materials that must be put into a new house. There is clearly a trade-off between holding down the cost of a new home and using expensive, high-quality construction materials and methods. People in wealthy suburbs often want very strict building codes to ensure that any new neighboring homes will not be cheap. People in low-income suburbs who envision that they might need to add an extension such as a room or a garage to their house are often content with lax building codes that will be cheaper to comply with. Strict building codes also tend to be favored by construction contractors and construction unions for the obvious reason that they generate larger sales and higher incomes.

When strict building codes and stringent subdivision requirements are combined with large-lot zoning or limited-growth zoning, the net impact on housing prices can be substantial. One researcher estimated that the impact of controls on land use and development in the San Francisco Bay area drove up the price of new housing units by 18 to 34 percent ($18,000 to $31,000).[51]

Discrimination in Housing The federal Fair Housing Act of 1968 prohibits discrimination in the sale or rental of housing. Most states and many municipalities passed comparable laws and have established human rights commissions to investigate complaints of discrimination. Although these actions have brought a great improvement in availability of housing to minorities, they have not, unfortunately, eliminated racial discrimination in housing. The Department of Housing and Urban Development (HUD) conducted surveys in the 1980s of housing market practices by sending out pairs of African American and white "auditors" to attempt to rent or buy housing units in 40 metropolitan areas and to keep track of any favorable or discriminatory treatment they received. These pairs of auditors were comparable in age, dress, and income. Systematically, favoritism was shown in about two-thirds of the audits, and the white testers were favored about twice as often as the African American testers.[52]

More recent research finds little has changed. George Galster and Erin Godfrey report on a study by HUD and the Urban Institute looking at 20 metropolitan areas.

> The results indicate that steering of all types is occurring when Black and White homebuyers are involved. In at least 12 to 15% of the cases, agents provided gratuitous commentary that gave more information to White homebuyers and encouraged them to choose homes in areas with more White and fewer poor households. Steering is less prevalent when Hispanic and White buyers are involved. We also found no evidence that steering declined over the last decade, despite toughening federal legislation in 1988.[53]

Not only do individual homeowners and landlords still discriminate, but so do mortgage-lending institutions. The Federal Reserve Board conducted a 1991 study of mortgage lending in seven of the largest metropolitan areas. Although two-thirds of African American mortgage applicants were approved, the study found that in the wealthiest income categories as well as in the lowest, African Americans and Hispanics were much more likely to be denied a mortgage than were whites or Asians in every one of the seven metropolitan areas. The areas with the worst records were Boston, Chicago, and Houston, whose rejection rate for African American applicants was about three times as high as it was for white applicants. The least discriminatory area was Los Angeles, where African Americans were rejected about half again as often as whites were.[54]

Finally, even in the absence of overt discrimination, real estate agents frequently engage in the practice of "steering" African American homebuyers away from predominantly white neighborhoods. A realtor can do this without breaking the law simply by not exerting as much sales effort to show a suburban house to racial minorities as he or she exerts in showing the same house to white buyers. Realtors do this in no small measure because they "qualify" prospective buyers as to the types of neighborhoods they can afford or are likely to be comfortable moving into. Although this undoubtedly saves the realtors from wasting time showing people homes they would not be likely to purchase, it also tends to perpetuate the segregation of neighborhoods along income lines.

Prohibiting Subsidized Housing   One effective way to keep out many low-income people is to refuse all attempts to build subsidized housing in the community (see the accompanying box). All that is needed to accomplish this is for the city council to fail to take the positive steps needed to add subsidized housing. Few suburbs have public-housing authorities that would be responsible for subsidized housing. In addition, private organizations seeking to use federal housing programs must get building permits before they can undertake their projects. Many suburbs do not look favorably on granting such permits if the subsidized housing units will be used for low- and moderate-income families. Yonkers, New York, for example, had such a consistent record of blocking the construction of public housing in white neighborhoods that a federal court imposed a fine on the city until it approved the building of 1,000 units of low- and moderate-income housing. The first day the fine was only $100, but the fine doubled each day, and within 15 days, exceeded $1 million per day. Facing the prospect of bankruptcy and the massive employee dismissals that would result from such fines, city officials finally relented and approved the project.[55]

Housing Without Exclusion

Exclusion—Some Caveats

The previous discussion points toward the conclusion that the suburbs do indeed engage in the politics of excluding racial minorities and low-income whites. Although the multicentered nature of the contemporary metropolis fosters exclusion, we should be very careful not to overgeneralize about what this means. In fact, we should specifically note some of the things that it does *not* mean.

Exclusion in Practice: The Case of Black Jack

How some of these exclusionary devices operate in practice can be seen in the case of a Missouri community with the fascinating name of Black Jack. In 1970 Black Jack was an unincorporated area of 2,900 people in St. Louis County. Although a number of apartment buildings existed in Black Jack, most residents lived in recently built single-family houses in the upper-middle price range. This prevailing upper-middle-income, single-family-home character of the community was threatened in 1969 when the Park View Heights Corporation (a church-sponsored nonprofit group) announced plans to construct 210 rental apartments under a federal program for moderate-income housing.[a]

When the plan was approved by HUD in 1970, the owners of single-family homes formed the Black Jack Improvement Association and swiftly organized a drive to incorporate as a municipality in order to transfer zoning control from the county to the local suburb. The county would be less inclined to use its zoning powers to keep subsidized housing out of Black Jack than would a locally elected city council. This blatantly discriminatory motivation for incorporation did not on the surface appear to be a sufficient reason for creating a new municipality in St. Louis County. Many local leaders felt that the county already suffered from an excess of suburban municipalities and governmental fragmentation. (There were 98 municipalities.) And even though leaders had been unsuccessful in their efforts to unify these fragmented governments, the county had since 1959 refused to grant any new incorporations. In accordance with this precedent, the St. Louis County planning department recommended against Black Jack's incorporation.

Despite this unfavorable setting for incorporation, political support came from neighboring suburbs that sympathized with the desire of Black Jack residents to preserve the upper-middle-class, single-family-home character of their community. The county approved the incorporation in August 1970, and within three months Black Jack residents drafted a charter, elected a city council, and passed a zoning ordinance disallowing any new multiple-family residential buildings.

As these political events unfolded, Black Jack residents followed a tactic that is very common in exclusionary zoning disputes. Residents never directly mentioned blocking racial integration as their reason for opposing the project. Rather, they argued on the economic grounds of preserving the value of their property. Nevertheless, as Michael Danielson points out, many of these economic arguments were euphemistic substitutes for direct arguments against racial integration.[b] Black Jack residents used *code words* that did not mention race but that evoked racial fears in the minds of neighboring suburban whites whose political support was needed for Black Jack's petition for incorporation. The most effective of these code words was *Pruitt-Igoe,* an infamous housing project in St. Louis that conjured up images of poor African American welfare recipients living in high-rise slum apartments amid crime, vandalism, and filth. To the sponsors of the project, opponents' peppering their argument with references to *Pruitt-Igoe* was simply another form of racial prejudice.[c]

Faced with what it believed to be blatant racial discrimination, the Park View Heights Corporation filed a suit against Black Jack. The incorporation of Black Jack and its new zoning ordinances were attacked as deliberate moves to prevent the housing project. Consequently the city was charged with violating the Civil Rights Act of 1964 and the Fair Housing Act of 1968.

(continued)

Exclusion in Practice: The Case of Black Jack *(continued)*

At this point, Black Jack became an issue in the national urban politics of the Nixon administration, whose stand on racial integration had not yet solidified. Civil rights groups, including the National Committee Against Discrimination in Housing, were pressuring the administration to take a strong stand on integrating both housing and schools. This was favored by HUD Secretary George Romney, who wanted the administration to weigh in against such blatant discrimination practices as those used in Black Jack. Attorney General John Mitchell, on the other hand, wanted the administration to remain aloof from such local matters. The Justice Department finally joined the suit against Black Jack but did so in a way that made it clear that it would support such suits only when there was blatant discrimination.

While this split was developing within the administration, the federal courts were striking down actions similar to those of Black Jack. Lackawanna, New York, for example, was not allowed to prohibit an African American subdivision in one of its white neighborhoods,[d] and Lawton, Oklahoma, was not allowed to zone out minorities or poor people.[e] The federal district court ruled against the Park View Heights Corporation, but in 1974 the federal circuit court reversed this ruling and struck down Black Jack's ordinances against the apartments.[f] This ruling was sustained by the United States Supreme Court.

As part of the court settlement, Black Jack was ordered to pay the Park View Heights Corporation $450,000 in damages. Black Jack residents apparently felt that this was a small price to pay to stop the project and buy out the corporation's option on the land. Although this ended the city's fight with the developers, another suit was filed by African American citizens of the St. Louis area. This suit was settled by a consent decree in 1982 whereby Black Jack agreed to adopt a fair-housing ordinance and complete construction on a 135-unit project very similar to the one it had opposed a decade earlier.[g]

Although the Black Jack cases ended happily for St. Louis minorities, they did not set a very useful legal precedent against exclusionary zoning generally. In Black Jack the racial discrimination had been so blatant that it was possible to prove to the court's satisfaction that the intent of city officials had been to discriminate on the grounds of race. But in cases where discrimination was less obvious, federal courts refused to strike down exclusionary zoning. In Arlington Heights, Illinois, for example, the United States Supreme Court refused to strike down an exclusionary zoning ordinance that barred an integrated, subsidized townhouse project, because no one could prove that the city officials had intended to discriminate racially.[h]

[a]Danielson, *The Politics of Exclusion* (New York: Columbia University Press, 1976), pp. 31–33, 84–85, 166–167, 184–186, and 231–233.

[b]Ibid., p. 90.

[c]*New York Times,* June 20, 1971.

[d]*Kennedy Park Homes v. City of Lackawanna,* 436 F.2d 108 (1971).

[e]*Dailey v. Lawton,* 425 F.2d 1037 (1970).

[f]*United States v. City of Black Jack, Missouri,* 508 F.2d 1179 (1974).

[g]*New York Times,* February 25, 1982, p. 12.

[h]*Arlington Heights v. Metropolitan Housing Development Corporation,* 429 U.S. 252 (1977).

First, the politics of exclusion does not mean that white suburbanites are racists or that they are unconcerned with the plight of the poor. Second, the politics of exclusion does not mean that all suburbs are exclusive. By definition, only a minority of suburbs can be exclusive. At most, 15 to 20 percent of the suburbs are "homogeneous high-income enclaves."[56] The vast majority of suburbs contain people who represent a wide range of incomes and occupations.

Third, the politics of exclusion does not always mean that affluent suburbia is a noose around the neck of the impoverished central cities. Although this may indeed be the case in some of the big, old metropolises of the Northeast and Midwest, it is not universally true. In the newer, smaller metropolises, the central cities may be more affluent than the suburbs. In addition, some of the sharpest fiscal disparities occur between rich and poor suburbs rather than between suburbia as a whole and the central cities.[57] Finally, even if all the exclusionary devices were removed and we lived in a world of perfect free choice, it seems likely that people would still cluster together in neighborhoods of homogeneous income, ethnic, and racial composition.

Having expressed these caveats, however, we are still left with a multicentered metropolis that is *not* a perfect model of free choice. It is characterized by some distinctive consequences and biases.

Development in a Nonexclusionary Setting

What would happen if suburbs dropped their exclusionary tools and simply let developers construct homes in response to people's demands? To investigate this, Michael Danielson and Jamison W. Doig compared development patterns in two New York metropolitan communities.[58] The northern suburbs of Westchester County began adopting large-lot zoning and other exclusionary land use tactics as early as 1912. The result has been to preserve most of the county's semirural atmosphere for a fairly affluent citizenry, the most successful of whom live in communities such as the very wealthy Scarsdale. To the extent that Westchester County has working-class or lower-middle-class people, they tend to concentrate in the old cities such as Yonkers. Most of Westchester County, however, stands as a model of how upper- and upper-middle-income elites can segregate themselves in communities that isolate them from urban problems.

In contrast to Westchester County's policy of exclusion, Danielson and Doig describe the development of Staten Island (the New York City borough of Richmond) during the 1960s. Until the 1960s, Staten Island remained about half undeveloped. Then the linking of Staten Island to Brooklyn, Queens, and Long Island (and through Brooklyn to Manhattan) by bridge in 1964 spurred a construction boom, and about 72,000 new residents were added by 1970. Land use in Staten Island was unfettered by any of the usual legal devices discussed earlier. New York City had no comprehensive land use plan for the island. Minimum lot sizes put no constraints on builders. In addition, no subdivision regulations were used.

Because of this situation, building contractors were not obliged to build big, expensive homes that would exclude moderate- and low-income people. They were free to respond to the demands of the market and build whatever types of houses would bring them the greatest profit. What they built were small, inexpensive homes packed together at the fairly high density of eight per acre. Although this practice was condemned by architectural critics for its lack of aesthetic concern, the houses were a big hit with working-class and lower-middle-class families that were excluded from Westchester and other suburbs but desperately wanted houses they could afford to buy.

Because there are so few studies of places like Staten Island that suburbanized without exclusionary controls, it is impossible to know for certain whether Staten Island is the model of what would happen if all exclusionary controls were removed. Rather, Staten Island and Westchester County exemplify the opposite extremes of a trade-off between having no controls on land use and having highly exclusionary controls. The less exclusionary a community makes its zoning laws, the better able builders are to respond to the demands of the market.

Inclusionary Zoning

As an antidote to the exclusionary impact of all the tactics we have reviewed, a number of states have begun forcing suburbs to adopt *inclusionary zoning* plans that will increase their low-income populations.[59] The leader of inclusionary zoning was New Jersey, whose supreme court obliged all municipalities to provide housing opportunities for low-income and moderate-income people. The court first imposed this burden on Mount Laurel, New Jersey, but in 1983,[60] after successful foot dragging on Mount Laurel's part, the court, in a decision popularly called Mount Laurel II, ordered all municipalities to discard zoning and subdivision restrictions not necessary to protect health and safety and to take affirmative steps to increase their units of low-income housing.[61] In response to these decisions, New Jersey's legislature created the Council on Affordable Housing to implement the state's inclusionary zoning policy and to resolve disputes.[62] Other states that have tried to promote inclusionary housing include Minnesota, Oregon, and Massachusetts.

Suburbs and Women

Do women in suburbs experience a lifestyle that is significantly better or worse than the lifestyles of central-city women? This is a very difficult question to answer, because there are so many different kinds of suburbs and such a great variety of women. Nevertheless, this question has drawn attention in feminist literature,[63] and at least four generalizations seem plausible.

First, the myth of homogeneous, white, upper-middle-income suburbia with its archetypal suburban family in which the husband brings home the paycheck and the wife devotes herself exclusively to the home is no longer accurate—if indeed it ever was. Some suburban women fit this image, but many suburban women work outside the home, are divorced parents, are widows, are single, or fall into any number of different life situations.

Second, some researchers argue that the suburbs were designed around this mythical image. With their low population density, their larger houses and yards, and their segregation of residential areas from commercial activities and busy streets, the suburbs encouraged only one female role: wife and mother.[64] Single parents, for example, are likely to find these same design features hindrances to their attempts to locate day care facilities, convenience stores within walking distance, and other needed services. Female-headed households, in fact, tend to settle in the central cities more frequently than in the suburbs.[65]

Third, for women without automobiles, and for women in one-automobile families, suburbia presents a major problem of access to stores, community facilities, and social services. Most suburbs are poorly served by public transportation. Even when bus service exists from the suburb to the central city, people are usually left to their own resources to travel around within the suburb itself. Without a car, a woman often must walk down a major highway with no sidewalks just to visit a supermarket, a drugstore, or a doctor's office.[66] This disadvantage is especially severe for older women and for women with young children. Not surprisingly, a number of researchers report a greater physical and social isolation among suburban women than among central-city women.[67]

Finally, there is some evidence that married suburban women are less satisfied with where they live than are central-city women, suburban men, or central-city men.[68] It is difficult to evaluate this evidence, however, because the people interviewed did not constitute representative samples of any large population groups, and the samples tended to be disproportionately upper-middle-income people. Nevertheless, the aspect of suburban living that was most appealing to the men was that they viewed it as a retreat—a place to get away from the tensions of their jobs. Women tended to like the informal socializing they found in suburbs, but they complained about isolation and a lack of stimulation in their suburban settings.

The Consequences and Biases of the Politics of Exclusion

Because of the housing boom that lasted from the end of World War II until the 1960s, the almost universal adaptation of the automobile as the basic means of mass transportation, the proliferating incorporation of suburban governments, and the decentralization not only of retail shopping but also of many kinds of employment opportunities, the central business district lost its dominance over the metropolis. More and more, the metropolitan areas became multicentered rather than centered on a single central business district. Los Angeles rather than New York became the model for the city of the future.

Politically, the multicentered metropolis is characterized by a series of geographic fiefdoms that feud with one another over commercial facilities and tax bases and that exercise almost unfettered control over zoning decisions. Individually, if a suburb is well located, it can maximize both high services and low taxes for its residents by behaving as a geographic fiefdom and yielding few concessions to its less fortunate neighbors. As Robert Wood points out, all suburbs have hoped to emulate this model.[69] From the vantage point of the metropolis as a whole, however, this geographic fiefdomization has several negative political consequences. Because these consequences are described in considerable detail in the following chapters, they will simply be outlined here.

Separation of Public Needs from Available Resources

Because local governments rely excessively on locally imposed property taxes for their local revenue, the division of the metropolis into hundreds of relatively small taxing units tends to separate the public needs from the available resources. The property tax revenue generated by an electric power plant or a factory or a shopping center goes only to the local governments that operate in that locality. This balkanization has especially caused problems in financing small suburban school districts and the school districts of central cities with a declining property tax base. If the school district area is very large—covering an entire central city or an entire county—it has schools located in affluent neighborhoods as well as in poor neighborhoods. It also has several large payers of property taxes within its boundaries. The residential areas of the *city,* including the poor neighborhoods, share in the property tax revenue generated by the factories, the central business district, and the commercial establishments. School districts are thus able to pool all of the available tax resources and redistribute them according to their priorities and their estimations of the public needs. If poor neighborhoods fail to get their fair share of these resources, the fault lies not in the lack of local resources but in the inequities of the established priorities.[70]

In most *suburbs,* however, the opposite situation prevails. There is no mechanism for sharing property tax resources. This fiscal imbalance has led to what the Advisory Commission on Intergovernmental Relations calls "the rise of lopsided communities."[71] The suburban school district with expensive homes, light industry, and elegant shopping centers will inevitably enjoy tremendous advantages over a neighboring school district that has lower-status homes, no industry, and no shopping centers.

These disparities in tax resources, it must be pointed out, do not derive from the nature of the multicentered metropolis itself as much as from the fact that the multicentered metropolis relies so heavily for its tax revenue on locally imposed property taxes. In order to alleviate these disparities, most states have taken steps to provide state aid to local school districts. The state aid normally derives from state sales taxes or income taxes and is normally distributed among the state's school districts according to complex formulas based on the numbers of pupils and the fiscal needs of the school districts. Moreover, as we noted earlier, several states have moved to reduce reliance on the property tax.

Despite attempts to reduce property tax inequities, most suburban municipalities and school districts in the United States still rely heavily on local property taxes for their revenue. As long as this remains the case, the multicentered metropolis will continue to separate public needs from available public resources. This separation will obviously continue to favor the residents of areas with the public resources (that is, suburbs with a substantial tax base) and to disadvantage the residents of both central cities and suburbs with a scanty tax base.

Biases

The poor and the racial minorities are most directly disfavored by suburban exclusion. Because the multicentered metropolis separates public needs from available resources, local governments in the metropolis are not able to apply all of their potential resources to programs that deal with the special problems of the poor and the racial minorities. Because local municipalities can use their zoning powers to exclude low-income residents, low-income families (both white and African American) are prevented from living near the places where the most dynamic growth is occurring both in jobs and in other economic opportunities—around the suburban shopping centers.

The suburbs are not promoting extensive integration either racially or socioeconomically.[72] This bias of the multicentered metropolis has had several results, particularly in public education. The poorest school districts are often peopled with lower-income residents and the most affluent school districts with upper-middle-income residents. In metropolises with large minority populations, central-city schools have higher percentages of minority pupils. Furthermore, the greater the proliferation of governments in a metropolis, the more likely that metropolis is to have large disparities in average income among its municipalities.[73]

Theoretically, this bias against the racial minorities and the poor does not necessarily have to result from the multicentered metropolis. It is conceivable that within the existing pattern of suburban development, property taxes could be equalized, minorities could be given access to the better school districts, transit systems could be built to give inner-city residents easy access to suburban job locations, low-income public housing could be made available in the suburbs, and exclusionary zoning could be minimized. However, the controversy that has erupted over attempts to put these measures into practice in places such as Black Jack and South Boston indicates that significantly reducing the bias will be extremely difficult. Considerable progress has been made over the past decade, and progress will probably continue to be made in years to come, especially with a number of states adopting fiscal equalization plans for school financing. On balance, however, the current state of governmental dispersion in the suburbs remains biased against the poor and the racial minorities. Some feminist thinkers also see suburbia as exhibiting distinct biases against women.

SUMMARY

1. Sprawl results from the American Dream of owning a single-family house in the suburbs. This leads to a pattern of metropolitan development that is low-density, is auto-dependent, and makes it costly to provide public services.

2. Current proposed solutions to sprawl include "smart growth" policies to limit further outward expansion and the "new urbanism" redesign of existing suburbs.

3. Not all agree that sprawl is bad. Defenders of sprawl critique the empirical evidence and elitist bias of the antisprawl coalition. In particular, they suggest that affordable housing is threatened by efforts to rein in sprawl.

4. The issues in suburban politics that often betray the politics of exclusion are taxes, schools, and zoning.

5. There are several legal tools that are brought to bear in the politics of exclusion. These range from large-lot zoning to prohibitions against subsidized housing. Normally these tactics are defended on economic or aesthetic grounds. Their practical effect is to exclude low- and moderate-income people. Because racial minorities have disproportionate numbers of low- and middle-income people, exclusionary politics place a heavy burden on the minorities.

6. Black Jack, Missouri, is an example of a community that incorporated and drafted an exclusionary zoning ordinance specifically aimed at keeping out a subsidized housing project that was expected to be heavily African American.

7. The settlement of Staten Island in the 1960s is an example of development in a nonexclusionary setting. Unhampered by the rigid requirements of exclusionary zoning, building contractors constructed thousands of homes that working-class and lower-middle-income people could afford.

8. Because school districts rely heavily on property taxes for their funding, they are particularly affected by the problem of fiscal disparities. Although the federal courts have not intervened in this issue, state courts in New Jersey, California, and elsewhere have actively sought to minimize fiscal disparities by reducing the heavy reliance of schools on the property tax.

9. The design of suburbia may have exclusionary effects on women. Specifically, the lack of public transit, the low-density housing, and social services less extensive than those in the central cities make it hard for many suburban women to gain access to commercial conveniences and to community facilities.

10. The existence of exclusionary politics does not mean that white suburbanites are racists, that all suburbs follow exclusionary policies, that the suburbs universally impose an economic burden on the central cities, or even that the metropolis would suddenly become integrated in terms of race and income if all the exclusionary devices were removed.

11. The existence of exclusionary politics in the multicentered metropolis does, however, have some definite consequences and biases. Its major economic consequence is that it separates public needs from available resources. Its major bias is against low- and moderate-income people and (consequently) against the racial minorities that have high percentages of low- and moderate-income people.

NOTES

1. Robert Fishman, "The American Metropolis at Century's End: Past and Future Influences," *Housing Facts and Findings* 1, no. 4 (Fannie Mae Foundation).
2. Raymond and May Associates, *Zoning Controversies in the Suburbs: Three Case Studies* (Washington, D.C.: U.S. Government Printing Office, 1963), p. 75 (Research Report no. 11, prepared for the consideration of the National Commission on Urban Problems).
3. Oliver P. Williams, Harold Herman, Charles S. Liebman, and Thomas R. Dye, *Suburban Differences and Metropolitan Politics: A Philadelphia Story* (Philadelphia: University of Pennsylvania Press, 1965), p. 294.
4. David Schrank and Tim Lomax, *The 2005 Urban Mobility Report* (Texas Transportation Institute, The Texas A&M University System, May 2005), p. 1 (http://tti.tamu.edu/documents/mobility_report_2005_wappx.pdf).
5. Ibid., p. 4.
6. Ibid., pp. 5–10.
7. Ibid., p. 11.
8. Anthony Downs, *New Visions for Metropolitan America* (Washington D.C.: The Brookings Institution, and Cambridge, Mass.: Lincoln Institute of Land Policy, 1994).
9. Ibid., p. 6.
10. Ibid., p. 6.
11. Ibid., p. 6.
12. Ibid., p. 6.
13. Ibid., p. 6.
14. Ibid., p. 8.
15. Ibid., p. 9.
16. Ibid., pp. 13–14.
17. Ibid., pp. 12–13.
18. Ibid., pp. 13–14.
19. Ibid., pp. 14–15.
20. H. V. Savitch and Ronald K. Vogel, "Paths to New Regionalism," *State and Local Government Review* 32, no. 3 (Fall 2000): 158–168.

21. James Howard Kunstler, "Home from Nowhere," *The Atlantic Monthly,* September 1996, p. 1 (http://www.theatlantic.com/issues/96 sep/kunstler/kunstler.htm).

22. Ibid., p. 3.

23. Ibid., p. 8.

24. Ibid., p. 9.

25. "Defending Suburban Sprawl," *Public Interest* 139 (Spring 2000), p. 65.

26. Ibid., p. 66.

27. Ibid.

28. Ibid. See also Peter Gordon and Harry W. Richardson, "The Sprawl Debate: Let Markets Plan," *Publius: The Journal of Federalism* 31 (Summer 2001): 131–149.

29. Randal O'Toole, "The Folly of Smart Growth," *Regulation* 24 (Fall 2001): 20–26. See also Richard A. Oppel, Jr., "Efforts to Restrict Sprawl Find New Resistance from Advocates for Affordable Housing," *New York Times,* December 26, 2000, p. A18.

30. Peter Gordon and Harry W. Richardson, "Critiquing Sprawl's Critics," *Policy Analysis No. 365,* Cato Institute, http://www.cato.org/pubs/pas/pa-365es.html.

31. "The Sprawl Debate," p. 140.

32. Ibid.

33. Robert C. Wood, *Suburbia: Its People and Their Politics* (Boston: Houghton Mifflin, 1958), p. 14.

34. Kenneth T. Jackson, "Metropolitan Government Versus Suburban Autonomy: Politics on the Crabgrass Frontier," in *Cities in American History,* ed. Kenneth T. Jackson and Stanley K. Schultz (New York: Knopf, 1972), pp. 442–462.

35. Daniel J. Elazar, "Suburbanization: Reviving the Town on the Metropolitan Frontier," *Publius* 5, no. 1 (Winter 1975): 33–80.

36. Joseph F. Zimmerman, *The Federated City: Community Control in Large Cities* (New York: St. Martin's Press, 1972), pp. 12–13. See also David C. Perry, "The Suburb as a Model for Neighborhood Control," in *Neighborhood Control in the 1970s,* ed. George Frederickson (New York: Chandler, 1973), pp. 85–99.

37. The classic account of developing a subdivision is Herbert J. Gans, *The Levittowners: Ways of Life and Politics in a New Suburban Community* (New York: Vintage, 1967).

38. Michael N. Danielson, *The Politics of Exclusion* (New York: Columbia University Press, 1976).

39. U.S. Bureau of the Census, *Statistical Abstract of the United States: 2000,* p. 302.

40. See John R. Logan and Mark Schneider, "Governmental Organization and City/Suburb Income Inequality, 1960–1970," *Urban Affairs Quarterly* 17, no. 3 (March 1982): 303–318; Scott A. Bollens, "A Political–Ecological Analysis of Income Inequality in the Metropolitan Areas," *Urban Affairs Quarterly,* no. 22 (December 1986): 221. The Logan and Schneider analysis was based on 1960 and 1970 census data; the Bollens analysis was based on 1980 census data.

41. For two examples of this criticism, see Jonathan Kozol, *Death at an Early Age: The Destruction of the Hearts and Minds of Negro Children in the Boston Public Schools* (Boston: Houghton Mifflin, 1967); or Bel Kaufman, *Up the Down Staircase* (Englewood Cliffs, N.J.: Prentice-Hall, 1964). For an analysis of the politics of suburban school systems, see David W. Minar, "Community Basis of Conflict in School System Politics," *American Sociological Review* 31 (December 1966): 822–835.

42. See Michael N. Danielson, *The Politics of Exclusion* (New York: Columbia University Press, 1976).

43. Ibid., p. 61.

44. Ibid.

45. Ibid., p. 53.

46. U.S. Bureau of the Census, *Census of Population and Housing 1970: General Demographic Trends for Metropolitan Areas, 1960 to 1970,* Final Report PHC(2)-1 (Washington, D.C.: U.S. Government Printing Office, 1971), p. 82.

47. Michelle J. White, "Self Interest in the Suburbs: The Trend Toward No-Growth Zoning," *Policy Analysis* 4, no. 2 (Spring 1978): 185–204.

48. John R. Logan, "Growth, Politics and the Stratification of Place," *American Journal of Sociology* 84, no. 2 (Summer 1978): 404–416.

49. William Protash and Mark Baldassare, "Growth Policies and Community Status: A Test and Modification of Logan's Theory," *Urban Affairs Quarterly* 18, no. 3 (March 1983): 397–412.

50. M. Gottdeiner and Max Neiman, "Characteristics of Support for Local Growth Control," *Urban Affairs Quarterly* 17, no. 1 (September 1981): 55–74.

51. David E. Dowall, *The Suburban Squeeze: Land Conversion and Regulation in the San Francisco Bay Area* (Berkeley: University of California Press, 1984), pp. 133–134.

52. See John F. Kain, "Housing Market Discrimination and Black Suburbanization in the 1980s," in *Divided Neighborhoods: Changing Patterns of Racial Segregation,* vol. 32, *Urban Affairs Annual Review,* ed. Gary A. Tobin (Beverly Hills, Calif.: Sage, 1987), pp. 82–83.

53. George Galster and Erin Godfrey, "Racial Steering by Real Estate Agents in the U.S. in 2000," *Journal of the American Planning Association* 71, no. 3 (Summer 2005): 251.

54. *Washington Post National Weekly,* October 28–November 3, 1991, p. 26.

55. *New York Times,* August 4, 1988, p. 13; August 10, 1988, p. 12; September 11, 1988, p. 1; and June 13, 1989, p. 22.

56. Mark Schneider and John Logan, "Fiscal Implications of Class Segregation," *Urban Affairs Quarterly* 16, no. 1 (September 1981): 29.

57. See Richard Child Hill, "Separate and Unequal: Governmental Inequality in the Metropolis," *American Political Science Review* 68, no. 4 (December 1974): 1560–1561; Myron Orfield, *American Metropolitics* (Washington, D.C.: The Brookings Institution, 2002).

58. Michael N. Danielson and Jameson W. Doig, *New York: The Politics of Urban Regional Development* (Berkeley: University of California Press, 1982), pp. 79–81, 105–108.

59. Barbara Taylor, "Inclusionary Zoning: A Working Option for Affordable Housing?" *Urban Land* 40, no. 3 (March 1981): 6–12.

60. For an analysis of the Mount Laurel case, see *New York Times,* June 21, 1983, p. 1; and June 22, 1983, p. 9.

61. *New York Times,* June 22, 1983, p. 9.

62. Harold A. McDougall, "From Litigation to Legislation in Exclusionary Zoning Law," *Harvard Civil Rights–Civil Liberties Law Review* 22 (1987): 623–663.

63. Genie N. L. Stowers, "Gender in the City," in *Handbook of Research on Urban Politics and Policy in the United States,* ed. Ronald K. Vogel (Westport, Conn.: Greenwood Press), pp. 109–125.

64. Janet K. Boles, "Making Cities Work for Women," *Urban Affairs Quarterly* 18, no. 4 (June 1983): 573–580.

65. Christine C. Cook and Nancy M. Rudd, "Factors Influencing the Residential Location of Female Householders," *Urban Affairs Quarterly* 20, no. 1 (September 1984): 78–97.

66. Rosalie G. Genovese, "A Women's Self-Help Network as a Response to Service Needs in the Suburbs," in *Women and the American City,* ed. Catharine R. Stimpson, Elsa Dixler, Martha J. Nelson, and Kathryn B. Yatrakis (Chicago: University of Chicago Press, 1981), p. 248.

67. See Sylvia Fava, "Women's Place in the New Suburbia," in *New Space for Women,* ed. Gerda R. Wekerle, Rebecca Peterson, and David Morley (Boulder, Colo.: Westview, 1980).

68. Boles, "Making Cities Work for Women," p. 574; and Susan Saegert, "Masculine Cities and Feminine Suburbs: Polarized Ideas, Contradictory Realities," in *Women and the American City,* pp. 100–104.

69. Wood, *Suburbia,* p. 9.

70. Wilbur R. Thompson, *A Preface to Urban Economics* (Baltimore: Johns Hopkins University Press, 1965), pp. 115–120.

71. Advisory Commission on Intergovernmental Relations, *Urban America and the Federal System* (Washington, D.C.: U.S. Government Printing Office, 1969), pp. 9–10.

72. A study of suburbs of Buffalo, New York, and Milwaukee, Wisconsin, found very little class integration. Richard F. Hamilton, *Class and Politics in the United States* (New York: Wiley, 1972), pp. 155–180.

73. Hill, "Separate and Unequal," p. 1560.

CHAPTER 9

METROPOLITAN GOVERNMENT

CHAPTER SYNOPSIS

The Scrap-the System-and-Start-Over Perspective: Chaotic Organization of Government in the Metropolis Is Antidemocratic; Fosters Lack of Accountability of Public Officials; Leads to Inefficient and Inequitable Distribution of Public Services; Solution Is Major Structural Reform • The Metropolitan-Governance-Without-a Metropolitan-Government Perspective: *Major Structural Reform Usually Fails; Many of the Problems Are Solvable by More Incremental Strategies; Empirical Studies Cast Doubt That Metropolitan Governments Provide More Efficient or Effective Services; Solution Is to Rely on Markets and Competition (Public-Choice Model) to Ensure Efficient and Effective Services* • Past Strategies to Attain Metropolitan Government: *Annexation, But Difficult in Most Places; City-County Consolidation, But Very Rare; Strengthen County Governments' Ability to Provide Urban Services; Two-Tier Metropolitan Government, But Abandoned in Toronto and Eroded in Miami* • Achievements of and Obstacles to Metropolitan Government: *Empirical Evidence on Performance of Metropolitan Government Is Mixed at Best; Social Lifestyle Issues Not Addressed; Impact on Minorities and the Problem of Dilution; Metropolitan Reform Politics (Most Efforts Fail)*

A major task of governments in metropolitan areas has been to cope with the consequences of the multicentered metropolis. At a *minimum*, pressures have increased rather than decreased on urban governments to provide services for growing populations in the suburbs. But the pressures on urban governments are rarely put in minimal terms. Urban governments are usually pressured by a variety of groups not only to provide at least minimal levels of service for all residents but also to equalize tax inequities, to find the resources to satisfy public needs, to control suburban sprawl, and to simplify the overlapping and complex structure of governments in metropolitan areas.

The Rationale for Metropolitan Reform

How urban governments should cope with the problems associated with the multicentered metropolis has been hotly debated. On one side of the issue are those who believe that the problems cannot be dealt with unless the whole system of government is scrapped and a new, general-purpose government established at the metropolitan level. On the other side are those who believe that adequate methods of governing the metropolis can be found without resorting to a metropolitan government as such. Scholarly study and broader concern by citizens and public officials of issues of metropolitan governance have grown greatly in the last few years after a decade or more of disinterest.[1]

263

The Scrap-the-System-and-Start-Over School of Thought

According to those who would scrap the whole contemporary system of metropolitan governments and start over, the flaws of the multicentered metropolis are so deeply rooted in its chaotic governmental structure that the structure itself must be rebuilt. The efficacy of the present governmental apparatus is brought into question. And the apparatus itself is seen as antidemocratic, as not accountable to the electorate, as inefficient, and as not conducive to meaningful citizen participation. This devastating indictment of the present system is presented by some distinguished scholars and prestigious organizations.

The argument that the present system is antidemocratic was made most forcefully, perhaps, by political scientist Robert Wood.[2] Participation in suburban political affairs is very limited. Election turnouts in suburban municipal elections are much lower than turnouts for corresponding elections in the central cities or even for elections to fill county offices. And the attempt of the suburbs to recapture the Jeffersonian ideal of small-town democracy very close to the people is misleading, because such small-town governments are seldom truly democratic. Even the famed town meetings of colonial New England tend to be dominated by a few local elites. For Wood, the "gargantuan" city provides a much better forum for the exercise of democratic values than does the proliferation of hundreds of small municipalities in suburbia.

The notion that small suburban governments are somehow closer to the people than large city governments is also challenged. Sociologist Scott Greer claimed that because the large city governments deal with more important issues than do small suburban governments, they dominate the media and capture people's attention. Suburban governments, in contrast, deal with such parochial issues that they "trivialize" local politics. Consequently, in the sense of getting people's attention and dealing with issues that are important to them, "the government of the greater urban polity is 'closer to the people'—they see its symbols with their morning coffee."[3]

Perhaps the most common complaint lodged against the multicentered metropolis is its seeming inability to equalize the costs and benefits of government.[4] In the 1960s and 1970s, the Advisory Commission on Intergovernmental Relations focused considerable attention on this issue, attributing many of the inequities to the fragmentation of governmental authority and recommending improvements in the structure of local government.[5] The commission especially recommended a reduction in the number of special districts and local governments and encouraged steps that would lead to metropolitan and regional-level governments.

Finally, and perhaps most forcefully, a general-purpose government at the metropolitan level is felt to be needed for reasons of efficiency, administrative competence, and matching the level of government with the level of problems.[6] Many metropolitan problems—such as water supply, sewage disposal, and air pollution—are areawide problems. To handle them on any other basis is to take indivisible problems and try to divide them up among many governments.[7] Metropolitan reformers complain that governance in these metropolitan areas is chaotic, is inefficient, and reveals "administrative impotence."[8] They propose to "consolidate the many political units under a single, overarching municipal government."[9]

Institutionally, the most prestigious advocate of metropolitan government in recent years has probably been the Committee for Economic Development (CED), an organization of civic-minded businesspeople. The CED was concerned about the two interrelated problems of efficiency at the metropolitan level and responsiveness to citizens at the local level. To meet these two needs, the CED recommended that governments in metropolitan areas be entirely reshaped into a two-tier, federative-type system. The upper-tier government would provide regional services and realize cost savings associated with economies of scale for expensive, capital-intensive services such as sewerage treatment. Lower-tier municipal governments would provide labor-intensive and more local services, such as policing and neighborhood parks. As an excellent example of how this should be done, the CED cited the reorganization of government in metropolitan Toronto in the 1950s.[10] Interestingly, as we shall see later in the next chapter, Toronto abandoned this experiment in favor of an amalgamation of the Toronto Metro and its municipalities.

Former Albuquerque Mayor David Rusk revived interest in creating metropolitan governments with the publication of his book *Cities Without Suburbs*.[11] Rusk's basic argument is that many cities are *inelastic*. They cannot grow or extend their borders, and consequently they face population loss, economic decline, and greater minority concentration, segregation, poverty, fiscal stress, and income disparities between the central city and suburbs. On the other hand, cities with high elasticity, such as Albuquerque, New Mexico, and San Antonio, Texas, do have the potential to expand their boundaries. In the past, Rusk has argued that the solution is to create metropolitan governments that tie the central cities to suburbs and allow the older city to capture the benefits of suburban growth. Many of the older cities of the Northeast and Midwest are inelastic. In part, this is a function of their being hemmed in by surrounding suburban cities and more restrictive state annexation laws. Rusk proposes that cities consolidate with their county governments in order to create metropolitan governments and reunite the central city with the suburbs.

The argument on behalf of city-county consolidation may be less relevant now than in the past. Metropolitan reformers hope to match boundaries of governments with service needs. However, metropolitan areas now extend well beyond the confines of a single county. Thus city-county consolidation no longer corresponds to a metropolitan government for the full metropolis.[12] As metropolises spread across state or international boundaries, the goal of metropolitan government appears even more remote. For example, San Diego's neighboring city, Tijuana, Mexico, lacks adequate sewage treatment facilities, which results in untreated sewage floating down the Tijuana River to San Diego beaches and agricultural land. Crop acreage has been reduced by one-third because of this pollution. But resolving the problem involves not only San Diego and Tijuana but also the governments of California, Mexico, and the United States.[13] It is difficult to imagine a scenario wherein a single over-arching metropolitan government would be proposed for San Diego and Tijuana to address the fragmented and inefficient urban services received by citizens in the larger metropolitan region that includes both cities. There are no examples of a metropolitan government straddling state boundaries, let alone international ones.

The Metropolitan-Governance-Without-a-Metropolitan-Government School of Thought

Despite these arguments for major surgery on the structure of governments in the metropolis, few major surgeries have been performed.[14] Seldom has anyone concluded that the Jeffersonian ideal of small-town democracy ought to be scrapped in suburbia and replaced with a general-purpose metropolitan government. Suburban residents are generally unconcerned about the proliferation of governments in the metropolis.[15] And rather than make sweeping changes in governmental structures, local officials usually prefer to make incremental changes when they become necessary in order to deal with specific problems that arise. These incremental changes tend to protect and preserve the status quo and to avoid any fundamental alterations in the governmental apparatus. The preference for an incremental approach seems to be shared by the voters, who usually turn down consolidation proposals unless a crisis is apparent. Further, as minorities have become more concentrated in central cities, they have questioned whether gaining access to revenues in the suburbs is worth the price of minority dilution.[16]

Criticisms of Metropolitan Government   It would be a mistake to think that metropolitan reform is opposed only by self-seeking, petty, small-time politicians. Some prominent scholars have raised several disturbing questions about the logic of making basic alterations in the government of the metropolis.

Political scientist Charles R. Adrian charges that reformers are unrealistic when they argue that metropolitan governments should be created so that needed services can be provided much more efficiently and economically.[17] The suburban "merchant or homeowner may value other things higher—in particular, access to decision-making centers and representatives of local government."[18] A study of suburbanites' attitudes in six different metropolitan areas also found that suburbanites were not greatly perturbed over the inadequacy of their public services. Even where they were concerned about the inadequacy of services, they seldom believed that a metropolitan government would improve the services.[19]

A study by William Lyons, David Lowery, and Ruth DeHoog challenges this view.[20] They compared attitudes among residents living in a consolidated city-county (Lexington, Kentucky) to attitudes in an unconsolidated metropolitan area (Louisville, Kentucky) and found higher levels of satisfaction with services in the consolidated metropolis. However, they did not examine residents' satisfaction with services in the central city of Louisville. It may be that residents living in unincorporated areas or in smaller, more limited suburban cities were less satisfied with the quality of public services than those in the central city.[21]

The reformers' belief that metropolitan government would save money through its professional administration and "economies of scale" is not very convincing to many opponents of metropolitan government. Public administration studies of selected public services tend to refute the notion that highly bureaucratized and centralized administration is more efficient than a proliferation of autonomous, smaller administrations that can compete with one another.[22] There may be a point of diminishing returns beyond which economies of scale do not save money. Some studies assert that costs per unit of services decrease up to about 50,000 people but not after that.[23] Some other studies put the point of diminishing returns much higher, in one case as high as 250,000 people.[24] Even at this level, however, the economies-of-scale argument fails to support creating a metropolis-wide government; the majority of the metropolitan population lives in metropolitan areas larger than 250,000 people.

Additionally, because the levels of public services in suburbia are likely to vary greatly, any attempts to equalize these services could only mean bringing the service levels of the poorer suburbs up to the levels of the richer suburbs. And this undoubtedly would mean more expenditures. Although nobody has conducted an extensive empirical analysis of this question, an appraisal of metropolitan government reforms in Toronto, Nashville, and Dade County, Florida, concluded that expenditures in fact had increased since the adoption of metropolitan government.[25] Even though expenditures increased, the services could still have been operating at greater efficiency than previously. But average voters are more likely to be concerned with the net impact of the services on their property tax bill than with internal administrative efficiencies or with the costs per capita of the services. And empirical evidence does indeed indicate that average suburbanites think that the creation of a metropolitan government would raise their taxes.[26]

Also, according to Adrian, the reformers' belief that professional administration is preferable to part-time amateur administration may be at odds with the preferences of the majority of suburbanites. To the homeowner, "amateur fire-fighters provide enough services to meet his demands."[27] Many of the volunteer services such as fire fighting perform an important symbolic function in suburbia. Countless suburbs in the United States view the volunteer fire department as a source of local civic pride, even if many now employ full-time professional staff.

Apart from the issue of whether the demand to create general-purpose metropolitan governments is based on realistic assumptions, a second question is whether one can even talk realistically of such an entity as a metropolitan community. Political scientist Norton E. Long has argued persuasively that such a thing as a metropolitan community exists only in the minds of planners and metropolitan reformers.[28] For most people, the sense of community in public policy rarely encompasses the entire metropolis.

Yet another question that has been raised is whether creation of a metropolitan government is necessary to correct the flaws of the multicentered metropolis. Opponents of metropolitan reform contend that many of these flaws can be corrected simply by continuing to tinker with the existing system. Many of the problems currently referred to as metropolitan problems involve only a portion of the metropolitan area. Thus it is questionable whether all the public water supply districts, for example, should be brought under one government. The same question may apply to such services as solid waste disposal, sewage treatment, public health, recreation, and police and fire protection.[29]

Finally, several important "value questions" are involved in restructuring metropolitan government, especially the argument that the costs and benefits of the government in any given metropolitan area ought to be equalized among areas. Should all services be equal throughout the metropolitan area? Or should all areas simply be required to provide minimal standards of services? Once the minimal standards are achieved, should wealthier areas be allowed to maintain levels of services that are above the minimum? Some critics say yes. But among the vital services involved are education, public health facilities, and libraries. Should some residents of the metropolis have inferior schools, hospitals, and libraries simply because they live in a portion of the metropolis that has no shopping center or commercial real estate, whereas other residents have superior schools, hospitals, and libraries simply because their area of the metropolis is benefited by such tax-generating establishments? On the other hand, given the spread of the metropolis outward, it may be that in some metropolitan areas, the central-city services and infrastructure are more extensive and of higher quality than those in the unincorporated areas or burgeoning suburbs and exurbs. In these cases, creating metropolitan government may entail reducing services for the central-city residents and redistributing them to the suburbanites.

The Public-Choice Model   The most influential argument against metropolitan government was presented by Vincent Ostrom, Charles M. Tiebout, and Robert Warren, who articulate what is called the *free-market* or *public-choice model* of metropolitan governance. Just as business firms compete with one another by producing or marketing goods, so do metropolitan municipalities compete with one another by producing or marketing public services. And this creates a "quasi-market choice for local residents in permitting them to select the particular community in the metropolitan area that most closely approximates the public service levels they desire." The net result is a "very rich and intricate 'framework' for negotiations, adjudicating, and deciding questions that affect their diverse public interests."[30]

The public-choice position was embraced by the Advisory Commission on Intergovernmental Relations in the late 1980s.[31] Fragmentation of the metropolis into hundreds of local governments was viewed as a virtue that facilitated market competition. This competition was said to promote low tax rates, overall high-quality basic services, and a good business climate. If a city government became too inefficient or provided poor services, citizens and businesses would "exit" the community. Thus one way to interpret the decline of large northeastern and midwestern cities was to postulate that they allowed services to deteriorate, interfered with the normal market functions by raising taxes too high, and allowed overregulation. Citizens and businesses exercised their option to relocate. Eventually, free-spending liberal mayors were replaced by more business-minded public officials who paid more attention to the economic base and improved services, luring back citizens and businesses and encouraging urban revitalization. Seen from this perspective, the market disciplined the cities and led to more efficient and effective delivery of public services. Intercity competition for economic development, if done rationally, is not harmful from this viewpoint.[32]

Three problems arise with using this free-market economy as the model for producing and distributing public services in the metropolis. First, the availability of certain public services becomes dependent on whether the citizen can afford to live in a given municipality. The school district with the highest per-pupil expenditures is likely to be found in the suburban areas with the most expensive homes. Citizens who cannot afford such homes have no free-market alternative to their "decision" not to take advantage of these superior expenditures on public education. Although some private goods may legitimately be distributed on the basis of higher-quality goods to different classes of recipients, public services are normally intended to be distributed indivisibly on an equal basis to all classes of recipients.[33] In the realm of public education, a persistent battle has been waged in state courts since 1971 over whether school financing can follow the free-market model.[34]

Second, the free-market model of metropolitan governance apparently assumes that the provision of public services needs no more governance than the provision of private goods and services. Even in the theoretical free-market model of the economy, however, some overall regulation of the economy is necessary, either by the government or by a supposedly invisible hand that guides the marketplace. If the provision of public municipal services in the metropolis performs according to free-market rules, then the regulation of public services of necessity becomes, as Matthew Holden has aptly phrased it, a problem in *diplomacy*.[35] To state that there is a limited analogy between metropolitan governance and either a free-market economy or international diplomacy is one thing; to posit it as a model for the way urban services ought to be provided in the metropolis is quite another. That transforms an empirical judgment into a normative judgment. Furthermore, it provides a theoretical justification for what is in most metropolises a very inequitable distribution of public services.

Finally, the free-market model of *metropolises* is valid only to the extent that the free-market model of the *economy* is valid. And if free-market economies ever existed in the world, they certainly do not exist today. To posit the free-market model as a norm to be adopted in the political sphere in urban America is to promote an economic model that does not exist even in the economic sphere.

Metropolitan Governance and Democracy   Finally, it is possible that the people want a multicentered metropolis. Simply by moving to suburbia, post–World War II Americans have chosen small-town governance. They have also rejected an overwhelming majority of metropolitan government referenda put before them. For services that the small suburban municipalities could not handle, voters preferred that these services be removed from the arena of partisan politics by establishing a big-business type of special-district organization to handle them on a supposedly nonpolitical basis. Establishing a metropolitan-level, general-purpose government would return politics to the administration of these services. In the words of Robert Wood, the choices of residents of the metropolis were limited to two: "Grassroots democracy or big business—no other vehicle is trustworthy in the United States."[36] Confronted with such an apparent array of citizen preferences for the multicentered metropolis, any arguments against it were often dismissed as elitist, antidemocratic, or politically naïve.

Strategies to Attain Metropolitan Government

Whatever the intellectual merits of the metropolitan-governance-without-a-metropolitan-government theory, metropolitan reformers have usually preferred a more radical approach that would scrap the whole system and start over. In practice, four types of metropolitan reorganization have occurred that meet some of the desires of the scrap-the-whole-system reformers:

- The first type has been central-city expansion through annexation or the use of extraterritorial powers.
- The second and third approaches, useful in metropolitan areas contained within one county, have been city-county consolidation and strengthening of the urban county.
- The fourth type of reorganization involves the creation of a two-tier form of government, the first tier responsible for areawide functions and the second tier responsible for local functions.

Annexation Strategies

Prior to World War I, metropolitan growth occurred largely through the expansion of the central-city boundaries via annexation of the outlying territories. As the city's boundaries expanded outward, most of the growing metropolitan population was kept within the new boundaries, and few municipalities were incorporated as autonomous suburbs on the fringes of the cities. The consolidation of incorporated municipalities occurred often during this period. Because of this frequent annexation to and consolidation with the central city, the growth of suburban fringe populations posed few problems until late in the nineteenth century. By 1900, however, successful annexation attempts became less popular and less frequent. Consequently, except for the South and Southwest, the growth of the central city through annexation peaked at about the time of World War I.

Central-city growth through annexation peaked in the early twentieth century largely because many state legislatures began requiring that annexations be approved by dual referenda of the voters both within the city doing the annexation and within the area to be annexed. In the Northeast and Midwest, suburbanites often voted against annexation in order to keep their distance from the large immigrant populations whom they blamed for the vice and corruption of central-city politics.[37] As a result, by the time the first phase of suburbanization ended during the Great Depression, the central cities of the Northeast and Midwest were mostly encircled by a ring of suburbs. Attempts by central cities to annex noncontiguous land beyond the ring of suburbs were generally frowned on by the courts.

Following World War II, many states relaxed their annexation restrictions, and a new phase of annexation took place. Much of this annexation has consisted primarily of suburbs and small cities annexing contiguous, unincorporated territory. More than 80 percent of annexations have been in the South and West.[38] State legislation plays a major role in the ability of cities to annex. For example, in 1963 Texas gave cities the power of *extraterritorial jurisdiction,* which is a city's legal right to control subdivision practices in unincorporated territories on its borders. Texas also allowed each city to annex up to 10 percent of its territory each year without referendum.[39] The most dramatic use of these powers was through "spoke" or "finger" annexation by cities such as San Antonio and Houston.[40] By annexing highway rights-of-way, the cities sent spokes or fingers out through the unincorporated suburbs and thus expanded their zones of extraterritorial jurisdiction. This kept those areas from incorporating as municipalities, and when their populations grew large enough to create a substantial tax base, they were annexed to the central city without referendum. These tactics enabled Houston and San Antonio to keep growing—and to capture the growing suburban tax base— while many northern and midwestern cities became increasingly surrounded by incorporated suburbs. San Antonio added 260 square miles in territory in the decades after World War II.[41] The growth of Houston through annexation was even more dramatic.

The practice of growth through annexation worked well for Texas cities until the 1970s, when, as we saw in Chapter 5, it came under attack from African Americans and Hispanics, who charged that annexation diluted their influence on the city government. By the 1980s, antiexpansion groups in both Houston and San Antonio had gained considerable influence, and the prospects for future growth through annexation appear to be limited.

City-County Consolidation

One metropolitan government approach that has been appealing to reformers is to consolidate the central city and county into one government. Such a plan necessarily works best in smaller metropolitan areas where the entire metropolis is contained in a single county. In the multicounty metropolitan areas, city-county consolidation would not create a metropolis-wide government, but it would go a long way toward reducing the fragmentation of government services.

In fact, consolidation of cities and counties was not uncommon in the nineteenth century—it occurred in New Orleans in 1805, in Philadelphia in 1854, in San Francisco in 1856, in New York in 1898, in Denver in 1904, and in Honolulu in 1907 (see Table 9.1). After the consolidation in Honolulu in 1907, however, there were no more consolidations until after World War II. According to the Advisory Commission on Intergovernmental Relations, only 17 of the 83 referenda on city-county consolidation passed between 1921 and 1979. In the 1980s, only 7 out of 27 consolidation efforts gained voter approval. In the 1990s, two additional consolidations occurred, one in 1990 in Athens–Clarke County (Georgia) and the other in 1997 in Kansas City–Wyandotte County (Kansas).

The most recent consolidation, Louisville–Jefferson County (Kentucky), took effect in January 2003. Counting Louisville, there have been only four successful consolidations in larger cities (250,000 or more people) since the early 1900s: Nashville–Davidson County (1962), Jacksonville–Duval County (1967), and Indianapolis–Marion County (1969). In Indianapolis, consolidated government was imposed by the state legislature without a voter referendum.[42]

Despite this pronounced lack of success, city-county consolidation was one of the most popular proposals for metropolitan reform in the last half-century. David Rusk's study *Cities Without Suburbs* led to a resurgence of interest and effort in city-county consolidation as a way to create metropolitan governments. And the recent approval of city-county consolidation in a referendum in Louisville, Kentucky, in November 2000 suggests that metropolitan reformers will continue to advocate merger. Because of this, the most important features of consolidation merit investigation. Three basic questions arise: Why was consolidation proposed in these larger metropolitan areas? How did consolidation change the structure of government and representation in elected bodies? How did it change the handling of public services?

TABLE 9.1   Consolidated Governments in Large Cities

1805	New Orleans–Orleans Parish
1854	Philadelphia–Philadelphia County
1856	San Francisco–San Francisco County
1898	New York–New York County
1904	Denver–Denver County
1907	Honolulu–Honolulu County
1962	Nashville–Davidson County
1967	Jacksonville–Duval County
1969	Indianapolis–Marion County
2003	Louisville–Jefferson County

Why Consolidation Was Proposed   Three background factors precipitated the consolidation movement. However, in the most recent consolidation approved in Louisville, none of these three background factors fit.

Breakdown of Public Service or Crisis   Most successful consolidations follow a breakdown in important public services or otherwise entail a crisis in the community. In Nashville, for example, the safety of the suburban water supply was threatened by the widespread use of septic tanks—one-fourth of which were faulty, according to one estimate—to dispose of waste. Serious problems also existed in providing adequate fire protection in the suburbs.[43] Because of inadequate fire departments, many suburbanites turned to private subscription for police and fire services. Several firms competed to provide fire protection in the suburbs, and the inconsistent quality of this fire protection made the cost of fire insurance higher in the suburbs than in the city. Things came to such a pass that in one instance, firefighters employed by a private fire company responded to the alarm of a burning house not to put out the fire—the burning house was not insured by their company—but to prevent the fire from spreading to a neighboring house, which *was* company-insured. They stood by and watched the one house burn to the ground.

In summary, Nashville's metropolitan area was characterized by sharp city-suburban political divisions, the existence of only a few areawide special districts, and deficiencies in the provision of public services in the suburbs. Taxable resources were distributed very unevenly throughout the metropolitan area. There was concern that county expenditures, which benefited primarily the urbanized area, were often duplicated by the city's expenditures.

Similar situations existed in the other areas where major consolidations occurred. Baton Rouge had been plagued by a proliferation of special districts and a sprawling of the population beyond the city's boundaries.[44] Jacksonville was threatened by a loss of accreditation of its school system and by a breakdown of its sewerage system, which was polluting the St. Johns River.[45]

The main exceptions to this principle were Indianapolis and Louisville, where no crisis existed. Through the creation of countywide service districts, Indianapolis had handled the problems of suburbanization with considerable success. The major complaint there seemed to be that the proliferation of these districts had gotten beyond the control of the elected county and city officials.[46]

In Louisville, a city-county compact was put in place in 1986, following two failed efforts at merger in 1982 and 1983 and a major annexation effort by the city in 1985 that was unsuccessful. The compact provided for joint agency services, tax sharing, and imposed a moratorium on new municipal incorporations or annexation. The compact also ended years of city-county competition for economic development and stilled suburbanites' fears of a city takeover.[47]

Louisville represents something of a Rustbelt success story, having successfully restructured its economy. At the time of the merger referendum (November 2000), Louisville's economy and fiscal health were strong. The crisis in Louisville was more of a perception of the city falling behind competitor cities such as Nashville and Indianapolis, which had merged. Also, the city continued to lose population through the 1990s, and leaders were concerned about consolidated Lexington–Fayette overtaking

Louisville in population to become Kentucky's largest city after the 2000 census. The city's business community viewed merger as a marketing issue to advance economic development. Finally, the newspaper and business community pointed to the continuing conflicts between the city and county. What was called for, they argued, was a single leader who could unify the community under one government. This matched the interests of a popular former mayor with ambitions of being the mayor of the new city of Greater Louisville, as well as those of Republicans, who were effectively blocked from winning office in the overwhelmingly Democratic city.[48]

Favorable Political Circumstances A second factor that facilitated city-county consolidation was the existence of special favorable political conditions. In Jacksonville–Duval County, the consolidation movement was accompanied by a long, drawn-out exposé of corruption in city government, which led to indictments of eight city government officials on counts ranging from grand larceny to bribery and perjury.[49]

In Nashville the passage of the consolidation charter in 1962 was linked not to public corruption but to voters' extreme dissatisfaction with the city officials. A very similar consolidation proposal had been resoundingly defeated by the voters just four years earlier. In the next four years, however, Nashville made an unpopular annexation of suburban land and forced suburbanites to purchase a green sticker for their automobiles if they wanted to drive them on city streets.[50] These actions led large numbers of suburbanites to support consolidation when it regained favor in 1962. By voting for consolidation, they were in effect casting a vote to throw out the unpopular rascals who inhabited city hall and who were responsible for the unpopular green-sticker tax.[51]

In Indianapolis, the special favorable political circumstance was a change in control of state and local government offices. When the Republicans regained control in 1968, local leaders got the legislature to pass a consolidation proposal called *Unigov*.[52] Implementation of Unigov was greatly facilitated by the fact that it needed no voter approval. The entire matter was handled in the state legislature.

In Louisville, there was no change in the political circumstance. Rather, Greater Louisville Inc. (the Chamber of Commerce) and the newspaper continued to beat the drum for city-county consolidation. The state legislative delegation responded by creating a task force (including the members of the state delegation, elected officials from Louisville and Jefferson County, and representatives of the small cities) to study the situation and recommend to the legislature whether to reform local government and put it to the voters in a referendum.

The mayor of Louisville and the judge-executive of Jefferson County were pressed to submit a reorganization plan in the fall of 2000. This plan, called *A Blueprint for City of Louisville and Jefferson County Government Reorganization*, was little more than a short PowerPoint presentation.[53] The task force seized the initiative and adopted it early in January 2001 with little or no discussion, and the legislature (at the behest of the local delegation) passed a bill for merger in the spring 2001 General Assembly meeting. It was then approved by the voters in a referendum in November 2001, to take effect in January 2003.

Absence of Many Small Cities The third factor that facilitated consolidation was that not very many incorporated areas existed in the suburbs. Nashville–Davidson

County had only 6 incorporated municipalities, and they were allowed to retain their separate existence. Baton Rouge had none. Jacksonville–Duval County had 4 small cities, which were allowed to retain their separate existence. Indianapolis–Marion County had 16 small suburbs that were consolidated together with the city of Indianapolis; 4 larger suburbs were allowed to retain their separate existence. Thus in none of these areas did consolidation pose a threat to any large suburban government.

There are 85 small cities in Jefferson County aside from the City of Louisville. The small cities and volunteer fire districts are specifically excluded from the merger. However, residents of the small cities do send representatives to serve on the consolidated council and also fully participate in elections for the mayor of the new city. Although Louisville deviates from the other cases in the large number of small cities, the blanket protection offered to small cities, along with the opportunity to have full representation on the new city's council, ensured that the merger would not threaten them.

Consolidation and Government Structure   The most visible governmental change in consolidated governments has been the creation of a new, countywide council to replace the previous city council and county board of commissioners. These new councils have usually been large (40 members in Nashville, 29 in Indianapolis, 19 in Jacksonville, and 26 in Louisville), and all except Louisville use a combination of at-large elections and single-member district elections. In all these cases, control over the new councils has gone, immediately or eventually, to the former suburbanites. In the case of Indianapolis, the Republicans got immediate dominance.

Consolidation also brought substantial reorganization in some places. The greatest reorganization came in Nashville, where many public services that had previously been performed separately by the city and the county were merged. Instead of two public health departments, for example, there was just one. However, consolidation does not always greatly reduce the degree of government fragmentation in the metropolis, even within the borders of the county government, nor does it necessarily lead to a better integrated administrative structure. In Jacksonville, for example, city-county consolidation led to the creation of several new independent authorities to provide services in Jacksonville–Duval. These public authorities now account for about 40 percent of all local spending in the county.[54]

The least complete integration of the governmental structure came in the Indianapolis–Marion County consolidation. According to Mark Rosentraub, although the 23 cities and towns were reduced to 5, there are still 9 townships, "11 school districts, more than 10 police departments, 8 fire departments, and 20 special service districts. The overlapping jurisdictions of these different service units yield more than 85 different taxing districts with the consolidated city."[55] The new government, Unigov, consisted of the same elected county officers who were there prior to the consolidation, and there was no change in several key services.[56] What Unigov did accomplish was to subordinate old county and city administrative agencies to the mayor. In the opinion of one observer, this has led to "a much stronger degree of coordination than previously existed."[57] But Unigov, often pointed to by the uninformed as an exceptional case of amalgamation (merger), is not a unified government. Indeed, "in some respects, the Unigov structure is even more complicated than that which it replaced."[58] In Louisville, city and county government were integrated. However, there remains a former Louisville fire department, which only serves residents of the former city. Also, the former city, unincorporated area, and small cities retain their former service levels. To facilitate passage, those who crafted the merger were deliberately vague about what services would be consolidated, leaving it to the new council to make these decisions.

Consolidation, Public Services, and Taxes   One of the most persistent features of the metropolitan political economy is the wide disparity between the quality of public services and the tax rates paid for these services. The five consolidated city-counties have dealt imaginatively with this problem by dividing the county into different service zones. Usually there is a *rural zone* that receives a minimum of public services and an *urban zone* that receives the maximum of public services. Because residents of the rural zone receive fewer services, they pay a lower property tax rate. The residents of the urban zone, who receive more services, pay a higher property tax rate. Provision is made for the urban zone's boundaries to expand as population grows in the rural areas.

In Nashville, for example, all county residents pay a tax to the general-services district.[59] This tax finances schools, public health facilities, police protection, courts, welfare, public housing, urban renewal, maintenance of streets and roads, libraries, enforcement of building codes, and traffic, transit, and refuse services. In addition, the more densely populated urban areas, which need more extensive provision of government services, constitute an urban-services district. Residents of these areas pay a higher tax rate, and for this they receive fire protection, intensified police protection, sewage disposal, water supply, street lighting, and street cleaning. The charter provides for a gradual expansion of the boundaries of the urban-services district as the population continues to grow in the suburbs.[60]

Similar types of service zones were established in Jacksonville, which also used two zones,[61] in Baton Rouge, which used three zones, and in Indianapolis, which used a complicated system of nine zones.[62] Depending on which zones a family lived in, it paid differing property tax rates to correspond to the service levels provided in those zones. Rosentraub has given Unigov a mixed review. On the one hand, he credits the new system with "the creation of a city large enough to attract and retain talented political leadership, the physical rebuilding of a downtown core area, and the stabilization of job levels in the downtown area." On the other hand, he finds that the costs of merger were disproportionately borne by those in the old city of Indianapolis, who had a higher tax burden.[63]

Again, Louisville's merger avoided addressing specific structural and service issues. Merger advocates promised that services would not be changed nor taxes raised as a consequence of the merger. Services would not be added for unincorporated residents unless new taxes were designated to pay for them. However, no urban-services districts were created in the merger bill passed by the voters to ensure continued provision of service in the old city.* Nor were any provisions included to create new service districts for areas that wanted enhanced urban services. This vagueness facilitated the merger's passage but left many gaps in the structure and operations of the newly merged government. The fear is that the existing city residents will see services diminish. It is thought

---

*The state legislature later amended the bill to include provision of an urban service district for the old city of Louisville to ensure that a higher property tax rate could continue in the former city's boundary.

that the new government may respond to the larger numbers of suburban residents outside the city, who lack urban services such as street sweeping and street lights and may be reluctant to see general funds go to city residents for services they themselves do not receive. There is no budget for the former city and there does seem to be an increase in capital expenditures for drainage projects and library branch expansion in the formerly underserved county areas funded from general funds or newly raised debt.

Strengthening the Urban County

In contrast to city consolidation, which is still a rare event, county governments themselves have grown increasingly important over the past few decades. Except for New England and a few other places such as New York City, counties have become the key governmental unit for providing social welfare services, health services, and many traditional urban services.

Traditional County Government   Despite being major service providers, most county governments have not been organized very effectively for the purpose of coping with urban ills. In particular, county government has lacked the capacity for decisive executive leadership. About 60 percent of all counties are governed by the traditional county governing body known as the board of commissioners or board of supervisors.[64] This board has responsibility for overseeing the operations of all the agencies and departments of the county. In practice, however, the boards of commissioners are usually ineffective in doing this. County agencies have tended to become autonomous, and very little coordination has existed between them. Big county agencies, such as welfare departments, public hospitals, public health bureaus, and highway departments, have tended to create large bureaucracies and have gained the autonomy that is characteristic of functional fiefdoms. The smaller agencies, such as tax assessors, license bureaus, registers of deeds, and bureaus of vital statistics, have in many instances become the patronage preserves of isolated political factions that strongly oppose centralized administrative control.

Especially where the head of such a department is elected (as is often the case with registers of deeds and sheriffs), the boards of commissioners have little leverage to oblige these fiefdoms to implement general public policies. Reformers see the fragmentation of the administrative structure and the lack of a unified executive in traditional county government structure as major impediments to county governments' taking on new service responsibilities in the era of the multicentered metropolis.[65]

Reforming County Government

In the last two decades, some communities pursued a strategy of reforming county government rather than undertaking more comprehensive restructuring, such as city-county consolidation or formal establishment of a two-tier metropolitan government. To the extent that a metropolitan area lies substantially within a county boundary, the strengthened urban county governments can serve as surrogates for metropolitan government.

The case of Broward County, Florida, illustrates this strategy.[66] Broward County in southeast Florida, home of the city of Fort Lauderdale, has grown rapidly and is now the fifteenth-largest county. Between 1950 and 1960, the population of Broward grew from 83,000 to 333,000; then it doubled to 620,100 by 1970 and to over 1 million by 1980. In 1990, there were 1.25 million residents, and in 2000, the county had more than 1.62 million people. By the early 1970s, Broward was one of the largest counties in the country. Yet, the county had a rather fragmented political and administrative structure. Within the county, there were 29 cities and the county government still operated with a rural mind-set and fragmented administrative structure. The county lacked a modern infrastructure—roads, parks, libraries, and schools—to serve the newly transplanted population.

In 1974 voters approved a home-rule charter that reformed county government. *Home-rule* is a greater grant of local authority by state government to make decisions about government organization and the powers and services of local government. This allows local governments more discretion and reduces their need to seek state legislative action to undertake new activities. One of the major changes in the Broward County's powers in the new home-rule charter was a provision for a countywide growth management plan linking development to the placement of services. Cities were required to make their land use plans consistent with the county growth management plan. This was an increase in the scope of services provided by county government; the county now had final authority over land use. Further, decision making in county government was unified under the county commission and appointed county administrator. The 65 departments that had reported to the county commission now were placed under the authority of the county administrator. In addition, the charter eliminated several constitutional officers, including a tax collector and county comptroller.

One of the first steps taken by the new reform county government was to propose, in 1978, a $238 million bond issue to upgrade the county's services. The county has assumed the role of regional service provider, focusing on services such as land use planning and development, regional parks, and a regional road network. The county also provides municipal services in the unincorporated area.

Most proposals for modernizing county government center on creating an *executive office* with the authority to subordinate disparate agencies to some form of centralized control. The elected county executive is analogous to the strong-mayor form of city government. As an elected official, the executive has a political base of support and is usually given considerable authority. County managers or administrators are analogous to city managers. They are directly accountable to the board of commissioners. Although they lack an electoral base of political support, they are given broad supervisory and budgetary control within the county government. This control varies quite a bit among county governments.

There is some evidence that larger, more urban counties have been more likely to reform their governments and create a stronger executive, whether elected or appointed. Among the largest counties—those with 423,000 to 8 million persons—54.2 percent have professional managers and 38.6 percent have elected executives.[67] There does appear to be a trend to shift from an appointed county manager to an elected-mayor (i.e., a strong-mayor) form of government in large urban counties. A continuing issue in Broward County has been whether to elect a county mayor while retaining the county manager form of government; at present, there is a chair of the commission. There has also been a study of formally adopting a strong-mayor form of government for the county. The largest county with an elected executive is Wayne County, Michigan (Detroit), which created the position in 1981 in response to a severe fiscal and political crisis. A county manager system had been used in Dade County, Florida, since 1957. However, voters approved a change to a strong-executive (mayor) form of government in 1996 (see p. 280).

Interestingly, the business elite has been a major force in promoting a stronger executive in many local communities. It seems that if county governments are to take on the role of regional governments, then a strengthened executive is needed to set the agenda and mobilize support behind it. The elected county mayor is in a better position than an appointed county manager or plural commissioners to forge a regime in the more politically and socially fragmented metropolitan communities of the early twenty-first century.

Two-Tier Government

The fourth form of metropolitan government is the two-tier approach, which was pioneered in Miami, Florida, and Toronto, Canada. Miami's two-tier government utilizes the existing county as the basis for metropolitan government, whereas Toronto's two-tier system established a true federative form. However, the two-tier model in Miami–Dade has come under serious pressure and operates quite differently than it did when first set up. And Toronto abandoned the two-tier approach in 1998 in favor of a consolidation.

Miami: A Two-Tier Urban County   In 1957 Dade County, Florida, established a two-tier form of metropolitan government that seemed to promise a solution to the problem of metropolitan governance. The movement to establish this government was promoted by an increasingly widespread belief among business and good-government leaders that intergovernmental antagonisms and excessive parochialism on the part of the county's 26 municipalities were seriously impairing the efficient provision of public services in the region. Traffic conditions in particular had become intolerable. There were no expressways or overpasses. Because each town could set its own speed limits and other traffic regulations, some towns became renowned locally for the fines they collected through speed traps.[68]

Civic leaders in Miami expressed open resentment at the parochialism practiced by some of the suburban communities, particularly Miami Beach. And the resentment was openly returned. When the mayor of Miami Beach denounced the plans for the new metropolitan government, a member of the Miami–Dade Chamber of Commerce retorted that Miami Beach was almost completely dependent on the city of Miami. "We Miamians furnish them with water, we burn their garbage, we house their servants, we furnish them with roads leading to Miami Beach . . . we even carry it to the ultimate extreme, we bury their dead."[69]

The city of Miami's government was plagued with charges of corruption. Police were accused of not enforcing the city's ordinances on gambling and vice. In contrast, the county government was relatively well regarded. Over the years, several public services had been transferred from municipal control to control by the county government. Given the good reputation of the county and the deteriorating reputation of the city government, when voters were presented with a new charter to broaden the county government's powers, there was enough support that the charter passed by a narrow margin of 44,404 to 42,620.

The new charter established a two-tier government. The county was given responsibility for what were deemed the areawide functions. These included mass transit, public health, planning, and some central police and fire services. Local functions (including police patrolling, public education, and control over local zoning and land use) were effectively left to local municipalities, special districts, or school districts. For some of these functions, the county was authorized to establish minimum service standards. If a local government failed to meet these standards, the county was empowered to take over the service.

This division of functions coincides very neatly with Oliver P. Williams's distinction between *systems maintenance* functions and *lifestyle* functions.[70] All the functions that were turned over to the county involved maintaining the physical operation of the metropolis—keeping the traffic flowing, the water unpolluted, and the public services in operation. The functions that had the most sensitive relationship to controlling people's access to the most highly prized social amenities of the region remained in the control of the local governments. This two-tier system of governance applied only in the municipalities. The unincorporated areas of the county retained a one-tier system in which the county government handled both local and areawide functions.

The new county charter also replaced the traditional commission style of government with a county-manager form of government. The county manager was given substantial executive responsibilities, and the county commissioners were removed from any direct control over the departments of government. The mayoral position was very weak, because the executive authority resided in the county manager. The city of Miami also was governed by a council-manager form of government.

The early years of the two-tier government were characterized by bitter conflicts between the county and the municipalities as the county sought to take over functions that had traditionally been performed by the municipalities.[71] The board itself was deeply divided over many of these issues, and as a consequence, it was not until 1965 that the Metro government entered a period of political stability. In the 1970s, the charter was amended to expand the county government's responsibilities, strengthen the manager, and provide for a charter review commission every five years.[72]

The performance of Miami–Dade (Metro) government has been mixed. In the almost 50 years since Metro was set up, the county has undergone dramatic changes that have undermined the two-tier model. First, the county population rose with the migration of people to the Sunbelt. Second, Miami and Dade County have absorbed massive immigration that has greatly increased diversity. In 1960 the city of Miami had an insignificant Hispanic population. By 2000 the city was more than 66 percent Hispanic. What had been the non-Latin white majority had fallen from 77 percent to just 11 percent of the population. Similar changes occurred in the county where the Hispanic population grew from about 5 percent to close to 57 percent of the population in 2000. Immigration was the major source of change; from 600,000 to 775,000 Cubans arrived between 1960 and 1990. Other immigrants introduced even more diversity. For example, about 80,000 or more Haitians arrived in the 1980s.

At the same time, the African American population grew modestly. In the city, African Americans went from about 22 percent of the population to 27 percent between 1960 and 1990 and dropped back to about 23 percent according to the 2000 census; in the county, the African American share of the population went from about 15 percent to

22 percent between 1960 and 1990 and in 2000 dropped back to 20 percent.[73] This increased diversity had led to serious racial and ethnic conflict, which was manifested in several riots in the 1980s. The reform-style metropolitan government with its county-manager system was more reactive than proactive in addressing these problems.[74]

The Metro government also was provided with an inadequate revenue base. Although Metro was given greatly expanded urban functions in 1957, it was not given the tax base it needed to perform these functions adequately. Because of a peculiarity of Florida law, Metro was denied such traditional urban fund-raising sources as excise taxes, franchise fees, a share of the state cigarette taxes, and the authority to impose taxes on utility bills.[75] Consequently, it was forced to rely almost exclusively on property taxes to finance the new services. This problem was eased considerably by broadening the county's revenue sources. By 1970–1971, the county's reliance on property taxes had diminished to the point where they provided only about a third of the total county revenue.[76] Even with this broadening of the fiscal base, however, considerable revenue problems remained.[77] The influx of immigrants has continued to challenge the county's finances.

The two-tier metropolitan model has been eroded. When it was created, about 35 percent of the population lived in the unincorporated areas; by 1990, more than half lived in the unincorporated area, a figure that is expected to grow to 60 percent by the year 2005. Already, then, more than half of the population has only one tier, the metropolitan (county) providing services. The proposers of the two-tier model never intended the Metro government to be a city government, but that is what it is for half the population. The charter review commission in 1984 found that more than half the commissioners' time was taken up with zoning matters in the unincorporated area. Yet Metro has been reluctant to use its powers to create additional cities.[78]

A number of structural changes have been made to Metro's government in order to try to remedy some of the problems and in response to a court challenge by minorities under the voting rights law. The original charter set up an 11-person commission elected from districts. This was later modified to 9 commissioners elected at large, including one as the mayor. In 1986, African Americans and Hispanics filed suit, claiming the election system was biased against minorities. There was only one case of a minority candidate having been elected to the commission without first having been appointed to fill a vacancy. The case was settled by the county in 1993 with the expansion of the commission to 13 members from single-member districts. In the first election after the changes, 4 African Americans and 6 Hispanic Americans won office. A chair and vice chair replaced the mayor while the county manager system was maintained. It is anticipated that Metro will now be more representative and responsive to minority concerns (with visible improvements in minority employment, for example).[79]

Miami–Dade voters approved a change in the charter to adopt a strong-mayor form of government effective in 1996. The 13 members of the commission continue to be elected in single-member districts. However, the mayor no longer serves on the commission and was granted veto power over legislation of the commission. Further, the county manager is now appointed and removed by the mayor, subject to approval of the county commission.[80] Underlying the shift in form of government was dissatisfaction with the lack of activism on the part of the Miami–Dade government and the county mayor during the Liberty City riots and other serious community crises in the 1980s.

The city of Miami survived a referendum to abolish the city in the fall of 1997. A petition drive led by more affluent and white residents in the Coconut Grove area had proposed the city's elimination, complaining of inefficient government and corruption. (Miami has been embroiled in financial scandals and corruption over the last several years.) This effort was defeated by about 5 to 1 in a light-turnout election. Hispanics turned out in greater numbers than African Americans to save the city. Obviously, had this measure succeeded, the two-tier model would have been transformed to more closely resemble a city-county consolidation. In the same election, Miami voters approved the adoption of a strong-mayor form of government to replace the council-manager form. Five commissioners are now elected from single-member districts, which ensures the election of an African American commissioner.[81]

It is hoped that these reforms in Miami and Dade County will help meet the community's needs in the next century and provide a greater institutional capacity for strong leadership by the new mayors of both governments. But the two-tier model has not been maintained. Genie Stowers suggested the need to reconceptualize how we think of Miami–Dade government:

> The region Metro Dade governs is still merely a county, not the full region. Although many consider Metro Dade County a regional government, it is more accurately described as neither a regional government nor . . . merely a metropolitan county government. Instead, it is a hybrid, perhaps called a "regional county" government. Its role goes beyond that of a traditional county government and even beyond a metropolitan county government in that it provides the entire county with some services and also supplies metropolitan services often provided by special districts. It is not quite a regional government because its powers stop at its limited borders. It provides some regional services but only within one county; therefore, it is a "regional county" structure.[82]

Toronto: A Federative Government Established and Abandoned   In contrast to Miami, Toronto created a *federative* government in which the city governments themselves were represented on the Metropolitan Council from the very beginning.[83]

Toronto was beset with the same problems of metropolitan growth that plagued United States metropolises. Governmental fragmentation made regional planning impossible. The metropolis was without adequate water and sewerage facilities, it had no modern, coordinated public transit system, and individual jurisdictions were unable to finance major projects.

In 1953, the Ontario Province Municipal Board, a quasi-judicial agency of the Province of Ontario, studied various plans for coping with these metropolitan problems and recommended a federal system that would guarantee the continued existence of the present municipalities in the Toronto area. On the basis of these recommendations, the Ontario Province legislature created the Metropolitan Council for the Toronto area. Originally, half of the members were municipal officials from the city of Toronto, and the other half were municipal officials from each of the 12 suburbs, making the system a federation.

Over time, however, the federative aspects of the arrangement weakened. In 1966, the 13 local municipalities were consolidated into 6 municipalities that were the constituent parts of the Metropolitan City of Toronto, and the size of the Metropolitan Council was expanded. In 1988 the model was significantly transformed by adopting direct election of all but six council members—the mayors of Toronto and the five suburban municipalities. A major concern had been that council members were representing parochial concerns in their home cities rather than a metropolitan public interest. The direct election of council members was expected to change that orientation, although a decision was made to have a chair of the council rather than an elected Metro mayor. The Metropolitan Council wards (districts) were periodically reapportioned to give greater representation to the suburban areas, which were growing faster than the city of Toronto.[84]

Toronto also sought to divide government services into those that were local and those that were regional. The Metropolitan Council was made responsible for providing the regionwide services—primarily property assessment, construction and maintenance of freeways and other transit, and development of regional parks. Schools were also considered an areawide function and were run by an areawide board of education chosen by the Metropolitan Council. Responsibility for local services, such as fire protection, police patrolling, and public health, was given to the six local municipalities. In fact, just as in metropolitan areas of the United States, there was a great deal of shared responsibility between the two levels. Metropolitan Toronto, for example, was responsible for trunk highways, whereas local municipalities were responsible for local streets.[85]

A general assessment of Metropolitan Toronto after almost two decades of operation indicated that two-level federation in the metropolitan area was a viable form of government. Nevertheless, there were some serious challenges facing Toronto that eventually led to its demise. First, the share of the region covered by the city of Toronto and Metropolitan Toronto had declined over the years as a consequence of suburbanization outside the boundaries of the metropolitan government. The boundaries of Metropolitan Toronto were not extended to capture this new growth. The regional government was no longer regional and the City of Toronto had decreased its share of population to just 27.8 percent of the Metro population.[86] The province of Ontario had created an Office of the Greater Toronto Area to promote and coordinate regional planning between the Toronto Metro and the four neighboring regional governments. This area of 2,600 square miles is only 21 percent urban and constitutes less than 1 percent of the province's land area, but it accounts for 40 percent of the province's population.[87] A natural solution would be to create a regional government for this territory. However, this would greatly threaten the province's authority.

A second problem was that the new elected Metropolitan Council was more willing to use powers that might antagonize the cities. Metro was taking greater initiative in shaping the metropolitan area's development, and this was upsetting the cities, including Toronto. Interlocal governmental relations were becoming more conflictual. The cities were concerned that Metro was interested in usurping municipal prerogatives.[88] These tensions were exacerbated by the province's reduction of financial aid to the local governments. The provincial government's solution was to amalgamate the cities and the Toronto Metro to create a mega-city. The regional boundaries have not been adjusted to extend the new city of Toronto to the growing suburbs covering the full Greater Toronto Area.

In creating the federated model, Toronto possessed one advantage that does not exist in any state in the United States. Both at the creation of Metro in Toronto and at the time of the divisive split over the transit system in 1963, a provincial government existed that was capable of taking decisive action. The closest approximation to this in the United States occurred in Indianapolis and the Twin Cities of Minneapolis and St. Paul, where the state legislature created the new metropolitan units without recourse to referenda. The ability of the province to act unilaterally ultimately led to the demise of the federated government in Toronto. In spite of the success of Toronto's federated form of government, this model was abandoned. The municipalities, including the City of Toronto, and the Metropolitan Toronto government were amalgamated (merged) into a single unified government in January 1 of 1998.*

Is Metropolitan Government an Improvement Over the Multicentered Metropolis?

To justify the time and energy spent trying to achieve metropolitan government, reformers at some point must ask whether these innovations are really an improvement over the multicentered metropolis in terms of better service delivery and better responsiveness to citizen demands. We can deal with this question by assessing the achievements of metropolitan government, its consequences and biases, and its impact on racial minorities.

Assessing the Achievements

Proponents of metropolitan reform can point to several improvements in public services following the enactment of reform. In Nashville and Jacksonville, the consolidated governments installed sewer lines and central water supply systems. In Indianapolis, Unigov brought significant improvements in sewer and transportation services and provided a broader tax base for financing sewer construction.[89] Miami's Metro also has significant accomplishments to its credit. Among them are a general land use plan for the area, a master plan for sewage treatment and water supply, and the construction of a rapid-rail transit system.[90]

Whether all of these achievements are due to metropolitan reform, however, is doubtful. There have not been any systematic comparisons of reformed metropolises with unreformed ones to sort out the differences. But one comparison of Jacksonville with nearby Tampa, Florida, concluded that city-county consolidation "produced no measurable impact on taxing and spending."[91] And a detailed study of the highly fragmented St. Louis, Missouri, metropolitan area did not find that the lack of metropolitan government deprived area residents of any important public services. When agreement existed that a service was needed, it was usually provided through voluntary interlocal agreements. As public-choice theorists (see p. 268) had predicted, St. Louis had achieved metropolitan *governance* in the absence of a metropolitan *government* through the tactic of intergovernmental cooperation.[92]

---

*A short-lived Greater Toronto Services Board was created to provide a way to link the core with the larger Greater Toronto Area. However, the board was disbanded after only two years.

The biggest failing of the St. Louis "governance without a government" arrangement was in coming to grips with the lifestyle and social access problems that put large numbers of the poor population and the racial minorities of St. Louis at a disadvantage.[93] But this has also been a failing of the areas that underwent metropolitan reform. On these critical social issues, metropolitan governments have probably fared no better than the multicentered metropolises.

The Consequences and Biases of Metropolitan Government

Annexation, city-county consolidation, strengthening the urban county, and two-tier government: What conclusions can be drawn about these devices for restructuring metropolitan government? Are they really effective mechanisms for coping with the consequences of the multicentered metropolis? Do they provide effective ways to respond to the needs of unorganized citizens as well as the demands of organized groups? And whatever the merits of these reorganizations, are they really indicative of change when so few consolidations have occurred, when so few metropolitan counties are using the most advanced form of county government, and when no U.S. metropolis has adopted a federative scheme of government? Have the reorganization movements really brought substantial change? Or have they been merely sound and fury, signifying nothing?

A response to these questions must first address the distinction between systems maintenance issues and the issues of social access. Metropolitan governments are uniformly much more successful in dealing with physical issues such as sewers, water supply, and parks and recreation than they are in dealing with social issues such as fiscal disparities, race relations, open housing, and the location of public, low-income housing in the suburbs. In terms of controlling metropolitan development and suburban sprawl, the metros do not seem to be much more effective than the governments in metropolitan areas where metros have not been created. The proliferation of suburban incorporations has been greatly slowed down, but only recently has suburban development been tied to any metropolitan development plans.

Metropolitan government also has some inherent biases. First, these governments have not eliminated the biases of the multicentered metropolis on social access issues of zoning, schools, and housing. Oliver Williams has drawn a distinction between these social access issues and systems maintenance functions, such as water supply and sewage disposal, that are essential for the sheer physical maintenance of the metropolis.[94] Although there has been little hesitation to give the metropolitan governments authority to perform the systems maintenance functions, there has been considerable reluctance to turning land use controls or residential zoning practices over to metropolitan-level agencies. This can be seen in the fact that in all four of these major metropolitan reformed governments, existing suburban municipalities were allowed to continue existing, their authority over zoning and land use decisions unimpaired. In fairness to these governments, however, it must be noted that the formation of metropolitan governments reduced the likelihood of future suburban incorporations and, in the unincorporated areas of the counties, did indeed create a metropolitan-level land use authority.

Second, metropolitan governments appear biased against citizen participation in their affairs. Voting turnouts for the election of metropolitan councils have usually been low. And not one of the metropolitan governments created to date has moved very effectively to involve citizens in its activities.

Third, because the leaders of many urban groups take metropolitan government seriously enough to oppose its formation, these leaders probably think that metropolitan government will be biased against their interests. The opposition by suburban municipal officials, special-district officials, and the administrative officers of city and county governments leads one to suspect that metropolitan government has the capacity to counter some of the existing biases toward the functional fiefdoms that now exist in the metropolis. Investigations of the impact of metropolitan government on African American communities indicate that the inevitable dilution of African American voting strength can be mitigated by certain structural arrangements to guarantee African Americans a voice in the resulting metropolitan government. Consequently, the evidence suggests that metropolitan government, if it is designed appropriately, does have the potential to make some noticeable alterations in the structure of bias toward the existing functional fiefdoms.

The Impact of Metropolitan Government on Racial Minorities

Creation of metropolitan governments threatens minorities—especially African Americans—with dilution of their voting power. In Jacksonville and Nashville, African Americans constituted a large and growing portion of the central-city populations prior to the consolidations and could reasonably have looked forward to wielding increasing influence over the city government, including possibly electing the mayor. Consolidation considerably reduced their percentage of the population. Similar situations have led African American leaders to oppose metropolitan reforms proposed in several metropolises. In Jacksonville, most African American leaders supported consolidation, but opposition came from two African American leaders who feared dilution of African American voting strength and from one African American who had been previously aligned with the old city government. African American voters approved the plan by a margin of 59 to 41 percent. In Nashville, the African American leadership was also divided, and here the African American electorate voted against the plan by a margin of about 56 to 44 percent.[95]

To preclude minority opposition to consolidation plans, proponents usually build in a district plan of representation and create a large council to ensure minority representation in the new merged government. This was true in Nashville, Indianapolis, and Jacksonville. In Nashville, African Americans had been guaranteed a district system of representation on the new council, and this was a marked improvement over the complete lack of representation they had suffered under the old at-large system of electing council members in Nashville.[96] In Indianapolis, Unigov's district system of electing council members not only ensured African Americans of representation on the new council but also gave the African American activists a stronger voice in both city and political-party affairs.[97] In Jacksonville, the district system of election also guaranteed some African American representation on the new council.[98]

However, it is also clear that African American political influence was greatly diluted. In Indianapolis, for example, African Americans were becoming a larger proportion of the city population. Then, after the creation of Unigov, African Americans were only 18 percent of the new consolidated city, but they were heavily concentrated in the core. This actually understates the loss of African American political influence. As William Blomquist explains,

> A strong case can be made . . . that the most important effect of Unigov on black political influence in Indianapolis was the shift in the balance of power between the two major parties. Even at the 1969 proportion of 27 percent, blacks were a substantial distance from majority status in the city population. However, black voters in Indianapolis overwhelmingly identified with the Democratic party; 90 percent of black votes regularly went Democratic. Black residents' 27 percent of the city's population was rapidly approaching half of the city's "normal Democratic vote" of 50 percent, and heavy Democratic votes in black wards occasionally proved decisive in city elections. . . .
>
> Given the black constituency's high level of voting cohesion, blacks in Indianapolis in 1969 were on the threshold of becoming the voting base and a dominant voice within the city's majority party. After Unigov, Indianapolis blacks not only were returned to minority status within the Democratic party, but the change in the Democratic party's fortunes meant that blacks became a minority within a minority party (Kirch, 1976; Schreiber, 1972). Blacks have associated disproportionately with a party that has proved unable to win a mayoral race or a council majority for the last 20 years.[99]

It is true that African Americans can get elected to the consolidated city-county council. But they are a small minority of Democrats with little direct influence in a Republican council. Blomquist finds that African Americans have not benefited from a broadening of the tax base. This is because Unigov does not provide services such as public assistance or public education. Further, "other services on which residents of the 'old city' depend—police and fire protection, and sanitation—were brought under the direction of the Republican mayor and council, while their tax bases remained fixed within the limits of their respective Special Service Districts."[100] Blomquist also suggests that the switch to Unigov had a detrimental effect on voting turnout. Turnout initially increased to 53 and 52 percent after Unigov was set up, but it then declined to between 29 and 39 percent in later years. Democratic voters seem to have reduced their participation since 1975.[101] Blomquist concludes, "Indianapolis residents appear to have learned that the real effect of the Unigov reorganization was to stack the odds so decidedly in favor of Republican candidates that Democrats have little or no chance of winning, and voters have adjusted their behavior in accordance with that expectation."[102] In November 1999, however, Democrats retook the mayor's office, ending 36 years of Republican rule. The council remains Republican, but by only a thin 15-to-14 margin.[103]

Bert Swanson finds that in Jacksonville, African Americans did not greatly benefit from the consolidation. Had the consolidation not taken place, African Americans would have enjoyed political dominance with their 57 percent share of the old city. The merger meant African Americans dropped to one-fourth of the new consolidated city. Although African Americans have won seats on the council in proportion to their share of the population, the consolidation has not reduced racial and economic disparities between the poor and minorities in the older city boundaries and the rest of the county, and there are still concerns that services are distributed unequally among neighborhoods.[104]

The picture is complicated, however. In some instances, the African American community may benefit even if African Americans have lost ground in some aspects of representation. In Indianapolis, Unigov has been much more successful than previous Democratic city administrations at getting federal grants for programs that operated primarily in African American neighborhoods.[105] This no doubt is due to the fact that the Republican-dominated Unigov was able to maintain good relations with the Republican administrations in Washington. In Jacksonville, observers report that both African American and white leaders view the postconsolidation system as "a vast improvement over preconsolidation days."[106] African American employment increased under the new consolidated government, and African American representatives have been appointed to every advisory board. Systematic efforts have been made to hire more African American police officers and firefighters. In contrast to an underrepresentation in the preconsolidation council, African American representation on the consolidated government council reflects the African American percentage of the area's population.

In Louisville, the promise to create six seats for African Americans on the new council was met. However, black representation still dropped from one-third of the former Board of Aldermen to less than one-fourth on the new council. More important, the city provided an institutional base for minority concerns to be heard. These voices may be drowned out by the suburban and white constituencies that will dominate the new city. A black council member was elected council president for one year from a black district outside the old city. However, even though the Democratic party has a majority on the council, 16 seats out of 26, twice the council has elected a Republican president from outside the old city.

The examples of metropolitan reorganization in these cities do not provide a definitive answer to the question of what minority populations can expect from metropolitan government. But they do indicate that the question is a good deal more complicated than simply asking whether metropolitan government will dilute the voting potential of African Americans.[107] However, the situation in Indianapolis also suggests that reformers underestimate the effects of minority dilution, especially given the strong correlation between race and party preference and its link to spatial organization of the metropolis. That is, African Americans are predominantly Democratic and concentrated in the central city. As we saw in Chapter 5, minorities need to be part of the dominant coalition on the council to attain policy preferences.

Some important trade-offs are involved. For Jacksonville African Americans, who already constituted 40 percent of the old city's population, consolidation meant delaying the day when they would constitute a majority and win the mayor's office. On the other hand, rejecting consolidation meant that Jacksonville would be relinquishing a claim on the rapidly growing tax base of suburban Duval County. This trade-off was expressed succinctly by a local African American leader who was subsequently elected to one of the consolidated government's at-large council seats: "I might have been the black mayor, but I would have been only a referee in bankruptcy."[108] An alternative perspective is offered by another set of observers: "At precisely that point in time when blacks threatened to wrest their share of political power from others, the rules of the game were changed."[109] Immediate influence in a viable government may be preferable to dominance over a nonviable one. But at some point, if the conditions of the poor and of African Americans in the original central city do not improve, or if segments of the community such as affluent suburbs can isolate themselves from the consolidation, what exactly has the trade-off accomplished?

Finally, metropolitan reorganizations could be structured in ways that would protect the interests of minorities.[110] For example, large councils elected from districts would ensure that African Americans had representation roughly proportionate to their numbers. On the other hand, holding elective office without wielding political influence is of questionable benefit. Perhaps African Americans and other minorities would be well advised to investigate carefully how a consolidation would affect their own group and community interest. This effect is likely to vary from community to community.

Why Is Metropolitan Government So Hard to Get?

If metropolitan governments are so great, then why are there so few of them? And why do three-fourths of all campaigns for metropolitan government go down to defeat? Five factors are important here: voter opposition in the suburbs and in most regions, levels of public dissatisfaction, lackluster campaigns for metropolitan reform, frequent opposition from minority leaders, and frequent opposition from local political elites.

Voter Opposition in the Suburbs and in Most Regions

Most metropolitan governments have been established in the South, partly because of the traditional reliance in the South on counties as the basic political and administrative units. Southern metropolises have typically been surrounded by fewer incorporated suburbs than have northern metropolises, so fewer local municipal officials have a vested interest that would be harmed by a metropolitan government. In both St. Louis and Cleveland, two of the largest areas to suffer defeat in attempting metropolitan reform, the officials of many suburbs could and did oppose the new charter.[111] In Miami, by contrast, the suburbanites are generally émigrés from other areas of the country rather than ex-residents of Miami. They therefore have fewer attachments to traditional political structures in Miami and fewer emotional ties to the Miami area.[112]

In the typical referendum on city-county consolidation, the suburban vote is usually against consolidation. Because passage normally requires separate majorities within the central city and suburbs (that is, concurrent majorities), suburban opposition is enough to kill the reform. This happened several times during the 1970s, including in Savannah, Georgia, in 1973; Albuquerque, New Mexico, in 1973; and Knoxville, Tennessee, in 1978.[113] In many cases suburban voters interpret metropolitan reform as an attempt by central-city officials to "grab" their tax base and deprive them of their autonomy. One study indicated that the single most important factor in the defeat of metropolitan reforms was the fear of increased taxes.[114]

Not Enough Public Discontent

In St. Louis, Cleveland, and some other cities where voter surveys were conducted,[115] voters were not markedly dissatisfied with the provision of government services. In Nashville, as we saw, voters *were* dissatisfied. And for several years prior to the charter reform, voters in Miami not only were concerned over tax inequities but also were upset about charges of corruption in police services in the city of Miami. It would seem, then, that substantial public discontent with public services creates a climate favorable to metropolitan reform if the proposed new governmental structure can offer some hope of reducing that discontent.

Lackluster Campaigns

A third major difference between the successful and the unsuccessful attempts at reform is closely associated with the level of discontent. The reform proposal has a much better chance for success if there is widespread public dissatisfaction with government officials, government agencies, government practices, or particular politicians. The new government can then be "sold" as a device for purging the government of its unpopular elements, and the campaign can be run as what Scott Greer terms a purification ritual.[116]

In Nashville, mayor Ben West was successfully blamed for the extremely unpopular green-sticker tax and the city's annexation moves. Thus a vote for the charter in 1962 could be sold as a vote against the mayor and his unpopular practices. In Miami, the charter proponents pointed out that the new charter government would be able to confront tax inequities and other aspects of government that elicited strong feeling in much of the county. In Cleveland and St. Louis, the charter proponents were unable to do either of these things, and they ran lackluster campaigns. Thus charter campaigns appear to have a better chance to succeed if their organizers can make a credible attack on some aspect or feature of the incumbents that is unpopular with a substantial part of the electorate. In the case of Louisville, the business community raised over $1 million and ran a modern professional media campaign and targeted mailings focusing on likely voters. Opponents were less well funded and ran more of a grassroots campaign.

Not Enough Minority Support

In the creation of metropolitan governments, the role played by the minority communities has often been very important. It was least important in the creation of the Miami–Dade County Metro and the Indianapolis Unigov. In Jacksonville, Nashville, St. Louis, and Cleveland, however, the role of the African Americans in particular was very important. In St. Louis, African Americans were important primarily by their absence. No effort was made to enlist their support for the district plan, and no support was forthcoming. In Cleveland, where the home-rule charter for the county was defeated by a very small margin, African American interests had been needlessly ignored. African American leaders campaigned against the charter, and African American wards voted resoundingly against it.

The most success in getting African American support came in Jacksonville and Nashville. In both places, African Americans were given important positions on the commissions that drafted the consolidation charters, and a large council elected from districts was created in order to maximize African American representation. The result of these concessions was that prominent African Americans supported the consolidation in both places. African American wards strongly supported consolidation in Jacksonville but rejected it narrowly in Nashville.

In particular, large councils in which the members are elected from districts rather than elected at large ensure some minority representation on the council. This assurance can be enhanced by promises to draw the council district lines so that the minority communities will have the maximum number of representatives warranted by their numbers. In addition, the charter can include guarantees for civil rights and equal opportunities in public employment. Such guarantees will be very important to those minority leaders who fear that the whole purpose of the metropolitan government is to deprive them of appointive positions and jobs in the city government. This strategy was followed in Louisville. African Americans were promised that at least 6 seats on the new council of 26 would be majority-minority. Election results suggest this threshold has been met. However, one-fourth of the seats on the new metro council is a significant decline from its prior one-third on the city council.

In short, when minority leaders were given reasons to support metropolitan reform, as in Jacksonville, they did so and were able to persuade a sizable proportion of minority voters to support reform as well. A number of things can be done to make reform more attractive to minorities. To begin with, metropolitan government promoters can include minority leaders in the planning, drafting, and promotion of the new charter. But appeals to local minorities must be grounded in reality. Minorities in a central city facing fiscal crisis may see the benefit of a consolidation that dilutes their numbers and potential dominance in the central city. Without such a crisis, the minority may not see the benefit of a unification that gives a white, suburban population political dominance, especially when the benefits of city-county consolidation or metropolitan government are uncertain. This was probably the case in Louisville, where the merger passed in spite of overwhelming opposition by black elected officials and the majority of the Board of Aldermen of the city of Louisville.

Opposition from Local Elites

Local political elites play a critical role in the passage or defeat of metropolitan reorganization proposals.[117] A reorganization plan would not seem to have much chance for passage unless there is a broad coalition of support from local government, business, civic, and media leaders. Division or opposition among these leaders is a signal to the voters that something is seriously wrong with the proposal.

Most of the factors that caused metropolitan reorganizations to be defeated in the 1950s and 1960s still prevail today. This was reflected in a commentary in the *National Civic Review* on the defeat of a proposed city-county consolidation in Salt Lake City, Utah, in November 1978:

> An analysis of the situation suggests the existence of some fundamental factors which laid the groundwork for the defeat: (1) unification lacked grassroots support, (2) abstract issues were rarely perceived, (3) justifications for unification were not inherently evident, and (4) political organizations required for success were missing.[118]

Although this explanation refers to Salt Lake City in 1978, one could easily apply it without changing a word to the earlier defeats of reorganization in Cleveland and St. Louis and more recently in places like Sacramento. In the past, metropolitan reformers failed to learn the lessons of history about how a campaign needs to be conducted and why the obstacles to reorganization are too overwhelming in most places.

However, the recent successful merger in Louisville suggests that at least in Louisville, they "got it." Here, the resources of the promerger forces were overwhelming and included raising more than $1 million to buy expensive television ads. There was a unified business leadership alongside top elected officials (e.g., state delegation leaders, the city mayor, and the judge-executive) and overwhelmingly promerger media coverage in news articles and the editorial pages. In addition, the merger was deliberately vague, avoided all controversial aspects, and protected small cities. Opponents were mercilessly attacked on the editorial pages. One was either for *unity* or against a better future for our children. The fact that the central city was economically and fiscally healthy meant that the suburbanites were not worried about bailing out a financially strapped city.

Of course, having sold merger, the media, and all these public and private leaders may have much to answer for. The new city appears to be on the verge of serious problems resulting from a plan poorly thought through or poorly developed, serious revenue shortages due to the merger, and high costs associated with equalizing salaries. Moreover, there is a real danger that promises to the residents of the former city of Louisville will not be kept, because there is no mechanism in place to ensure that services are not diminished. Although no new services are supposed to be extended to unincorporated areas or small cities without a new source of revenue to pay for them, the new council is dominated by suburban interests, and councilors may see little rationale for providing urban services in the city out of the general fund that their constituents do not get.[119]

Metropolitan Reform: Methodological Issues

Consideration of metropolitan government is complicated by several methodological difficulties.[120] First, many researchers and proponents of metropolitan government allow normative biases to influence their research and proposals. Proponents of metropolitan government continue to assert that consolidation or metropolitan government will result in more efficient and effective government in spite of the lack of evidence—and even contradictory evidence. They often propose metropolitan government as a panacea to all urban problems without analyzing whether this solution is the appropriate remedy to the specific problems facing a particular community. Public-choice researchers effectively point out the weaknesses in studies by advocates of metropolitan government. However, they fail to acknowledge that inequities exist in the financing and delivery of urban services and that few behave the way their assumptions require.

Second, real problems arise in defining the urban region. The way the region is defined has great consequences for the study of metropolitan governance. For example, if the metropolitan region is equated with the county, then metropolitan government exists virtually everywhere. On the other hand, if the metropolitan area is considered the unit for which a metropolitan government should exist, then metropolitan government is virtually nonexistent. Take the case of New York City, which consolidated with the five boroughs of New York in 1898. But the New York city-region is not treated as a consolidated city-county(ies) but as a fragmented region spanning three states. Defining the boundaries of a city-region for which a political jurisdiction should be created sounds easy. It is not.

Third, researchers, advocates, and opponents of metropolitan government often fail to define what is meant by *metropolitan government*. The governmental structures of Jacksonville, Indianapolis, Nashville, and Miami–Dade have little in common. Jacksonville is a consolidated city-county that is administratively unified but that comprises many independent public authorities and four independent suburban cities. Unigov is not a unified integrated metropolitan government. A supposed consolidation may not greatly reduce fragmentation. The label *metropolitan government* may conceal more differences than similarities among governments. The federated Toronto Metro differs greatly from the amalgamated new city of Toronto, although both are considered metropolitan governments and neither covered the full urban region in recent years.

Metropolitan Reform and Political Bias: Some Conclusions

The attempts to achieve metropolitan reform demonstrate certain political biases. The first of these is that attitudes of the general metropolitan population and of the leadership of many powerful interest groups seem biased toward the status quo rather than change; many more reform campaigns have been lost than have been won.

Second, the perceptible changes that have taken place suggest that the attitudinal biases are more inclined toward incremental and limited changes than toward drastic and far-reaching changes. Although (see Chapter 10) the reforms in the Twin Cities metropolitan area were far less extensive than complete consolidation of governments, they did nevertheless increase the capacity to deal with the metropolitan problems in their respective areas. And even though very few metropolitan counties have adopted the most advanced forms of urban county government (the county manager and the elected county executive), increasing numbers of metropolitan counties are adopting *some* reorganization proposals and assuming more responsibility for urban functions of government. Accomplishing limited reforms in metropolitan governance in an incremental fashion is apparently much easier than accomplishing sweeping reforms in one dramatic action.[121] This is the major lesson of the Twin Cities and Indianapolis—especially the Twin Cities, where creation of the Metropolitan Council was the culmination of years of incremental changes, and the council itself has been subject to incremental growth since its creation.

To the extent that the public mistrusts metropolitan government, the examples of Indianapolis and the Twin Cities also indicate that substantial changes can best be obtained by limiting the metropolitan reform proposals to those that can be accomplished by legislatures without requiring voter approval in referenda. Although this may seem to be an undemocratic attempt to circumvent the will of the electorate, some believe the legislature is actually a much more appropriate forum for crafting metropolitan changes. In a referendum, the electorate is given a simple yes-or-no choice over a charter that, more likely than not, has been drafted by a blue-ribbon committee of civic-minded reformers who lack electoral experience. Legislative committees, in contrast, are not limited to a take-it-or-leave-it option. They can debate every conceivable aspect of the proposal that any interest group or politician cares to raise.

Whether this method of dealing with metropolitan reform is less democratic than the referendum approach depends primarily on how democratic the legislative committees are in their procedures. If one accepts the Madisonian preference for representative government over direct democracy,[122] then seeking metropolitan reform through the legislative approach is not so much an attempt to skirt the will of the people as an attempt to provide a forum where the people's representatives can work effectively. But it is difficult to justify bypassing the local constituency in a system that places such a high value on localism. And state legislative decisions are more frequently the outcome of logrolling than of deliberative study and debate, and they are often heavily influenced by interest groups, elites, and campaign contributions.

Finally, proposals for reorganization of local government and resistance to them should be understood as barometers of power relations in a community. Increases or diminishment of the scope of government—including new services and regulatory power, changes to the boundaries of governments, and changes in the financing of government—often reflect a shift in the distribution of power in the community.[123] Urban service delivery systems and institutional structures have biases. Efforts to change the structure of government may change those biases in obvious or subtle ways. The pattern of bias changes with the government restructuring. A new elite often emerges or rises to ascendancy with the newly reformed government.

Very few metropolitan governments have been created. What has been the aftermath of the defeats of consolidation? If metropolitan government is rejected, what can be done? In fact, several options exist. And a considerable amount of incremental change has occurred. This will be examined in Chapter 10.

SUMMARY

1. The two main schools of thought about metropolitan reform are the scrap-the-system-and-start-over perspective and the metropolitan-governance-without-a-metropolitan-government perspective.

2. The strategies that have been implemented in an effort to attain metropolitan government have included central-city annexation, city-county consolidation, strengthening the urban county, and two-tier government.

3. Metropolitan governments have been more successful in addressing systems maintenance issues than in addressing the social access issues. Central-city African Americans have often opposed metropolitan reform on the grounds that it would dilute their voting strength.

4. Whatever the accomplishments of metropolitan governments, few attempts to institute them have succeeded. Campaigns for metropolitan reform have typically failed for several reasons: voter opposition in the suburbs, insufficient public discontent with the status quo, lackluster campaigns, and lack of support from minority leaders and other political elites.

5. The biases associated with metropolitan reform have included a bias in favor of the status quo in governmental organization and a bias of citizens toward incremental and limited change rather than drastic and far-reaching change. These biases have compounded the problems of getting metropolitan government.

NOTES

1. Three recent journal symposia on these issues are Frances Fisken and Donald F. Norris, eds., "Regionalism Reconsidered," *Journal of Urban Affairs* 23, no. 5 (2001); H. V. Savitch and Ronald K. Vogel, "New Regionalism and Its Policy Agenda," *State and Local Government Review* 32, no. 3 (2000); Richard W. Campbell and Dan Durning, "Is City County Consolidation Good Policy?" *Public Administration Quarterly* 24, no. 2 (2000).

2. Robert C. Wood, *Suburbia: Its People and Their Politics* (Boston: Houghton Mifflin, 1958), chap. 7 and pp. 232–241. On the concept of "Gargantua," see Robert C. Wood, "The New Metropolis: Green Belts, Grass Roots or Gargantua," *American Political Science Review* 52, no. 1 (March 1958): 108–122. See also his *1400 Governments: The Political Economy of the New York Metropolitan Region* (Cambridge, Mass.: Harvard University Press, 1961).

3. Scott Greer, *The Emerging City* (New York: Free Press, 1962), pp. 141, 149.

4. Wood, *Suburbia,* pp. 282–285.

5. Advisory Commission on Intergovernmental Relations, *Urban America and the Federal System* (Washington, D.C.: U.S. Government Printing Office, 1969), pp. 82–83.

6. Joseph F. Zimmerman, "Substate Regional Government: Designing a New Procedure," *National Civic Review* 61, no. 6 (June 1972): 286. Zimmerman writes, "Governmental irresponsibility exists in the typical substate region encompassing two or more counties. . . . A regional government is needed now in most metropolitan areas."

7. Luther Gulick, *The Metropolitan Problem and American Ideas* (New York: Knopf, 1962), p. 24.

8. Amos H. Hawley and Basil G. Zimmer, *The Metropolitan Community: Its People and Government* (Beverly Hills, Calif.: Sage, 1970), pp. 2–3.

9. Ibid., p. 3.

10. *Reshaping Government in Metropolitan Areas* (New York: Committee for Economic Development, 1970).

11. David Rusk, *Cities Without Suburbs,* 2nd ed. (Washington, D.C.: Woodrow Wilson Center Press, 1995).

12. Donald N. Rothblatt, "Summary and Conclusions," in *Metropolitan Governance Revisited,* ed. Donald N. Rothblatt and Andrew Sancton (Berkeley, Calif.: Institute of Governmental Studies, 1998), pp. 475–525; Robert L. Bish, "Local Government Amalgamations: Discredited Nineteenth-Century Ideals Alive in the Twenty-First" (Toronto, ON: C.D. Howe Institute, 2001), http://www.cdhowe.org; H. V. Savitch and Ronald K. Vogel, "Paths to New Regionalism," *State and Local Government Review* 32, no. 3 (Fall 2000): 158–168; Carolyn Cummins, Larry Ledebur, and William Barnes, "Divided Economies," paper presented at the annual meeting of the Urban Affairs Association, Detroit, April 2001.

13. Glen Sparrow and Dana Brown, "Black Water, Red Tape; Anatomy of a Border Problem," *National Civic Review* 75, no. 4 (July–August 1986): 214–218.

14. John C. Bollens et al., *Exploring the Metropolitan Community* (Berkeley: University of California Press, 1961), pp. 70–71. The surgical metaphor is Bollens's and Schmandt's.

15. Hawley and Zimmer, *The Metropolitan Community,* pp. 91–92.

16. John A. Powell, "Addressing Regional Dilemmas for Minority Communities," in *Reflections on Regionalism,* ed. Bruce Katz (Washington, D.C.: The Brookings Instituion, 2000); Myra Jones, "Remarks," in *Workshop in Metropolitan Governmental Strategies: Proceedings, 1990,* ed. C. James Owens (Fort Wayne; Ind.: School of Public and Environmental Affairs, Indiana University–Purdue University at Fort Wayne); Ronald K. Vogel, "Regionalism and Community: A View from the Central City," Paper presented at the Urban Affairs Association Annual Meeting, Toronto, April 1997.

17. Charles R. Adrian, "Metropology: Folklore and Field Research," *Public Administration Review* 21, no. 3 (Summer 1961): 148–157.

18. Ibid., p. 150.

19. Hawley and Zimmer, *The Metropolitan Community,* pp. 91–92.

20. *The Politics of Dissatisfaction: Citizens, Services, and Urban Institutions* (Armonk, N.Y.: M.E. Sharp, 1992).

21. Past surveys revealed that residents of Louisville have high levels of satisfaction with services. For example, a 1992 survey found that 64 percent were satisfied with the quality of the city's government, 81.9 percent were satisfied with police protection, and 78.4 percent were satisfied with neighborhood appearance. These data are from D. Mark Austin and Ronald K. Vogel, "Crime, Neighborhoods, and the Quality of Life," paper presented at the Urban Affairs Association, Indianapolis, April 1993.

22. Vincent Ostrom and Elinor Ostrom, "Public Choice: A Different Approach to the Study of Public Administration," *Public Administration Review* 31 (March 1971): 203–216; Edwin J. Benton and Darwin Gamble, "City/County Consolidation and Economies of Scale: Evidence from a Time-Series Analysis in Jacksonville, Florida," *Social Science Quarterly* 65 (March 1983): 190–198; Stephen Condrey, "Organizational and Personnel Impacts on Local Government Consolidation: Athens-Clarke County, Georgia," *Journal of Urban Affairs* 16, no. 4 (November 1994): 371–383.

23. Edward C. Banfield and Morton Grodzins, *Government and Housing in Metropolitan Areas* (New York: McGraw-Hill, 1958), p. 34.

24. Joseph F. Zimmerman, "Can Government Functions Be 'Rationally Assigned'?" *National Civic Review* 73, no. 3 (March 1983): 125–131.

25. Daniel R. Grant, "Metro's Three Faces," *National Civic Review* 55, no. 6 (June 1966): 317–324.

26. Hawley and Zimmer, *The Metropolitan Community,* pp. 95–96.

27. Adrian, "Metropology," p. 151.

28. Norton E. Long, "The Local Community as an Ecology of Games," *American Journal of Sociology* 64 (November 1958): 251–261. See also his *The Polity* (Chicago: Rand McNally, 1962), pp. 156–164.

29. Banfield and Grodzins, *Government and Housing,* p. 42.

30. Vincent Ostrom, Charles M. Tiebout, and Robert Warren, "Organizing Government in Metropolitan Areas: A Theoretical Inquiry," *American Political Science Review* 55, no. 4 (December 1961): 838, 842.

31. Advisory Commission on Intergovernmental Relations (ACIR), *The Organization of Local Public Economies* (Washington, D.C.: author, 1987); ACIR, *Metropolitan Organization: Comparison of the Allegheny and St. Louis Case Studies* (Washington, D.C.: author, 1993).

32. Fred Siegel, *The Future Once Happened Here: New York, D.C., L.A. and, the Fate of America's Big Cities* (New York: Free Press, 1997). Although Siegel does not directly adopt a public-choice perspective, his writing is consistent with this school of thought.

33. On the distinction between public and private goods, see Ostrom and Ostrom, "Public Choice: A Different Approach," pp. 206–207.

34. *Serrano v. Priest,* 5 Calif. 3d 584, 487 P.2d 1241 (1971).

35. Matthew Holden, Jr., "The Governance of the Metropolis as a Problem in Diplomacy," *Journal of Politics* 26 (August 1964): 627–647. See also Thomas R. Dye, "Metropolitan Integration by Bargaining Among Sub-Areas," *American Behavioral Scientist* 5 (May 1962): 11.

36. Wood, *Suburbia,* p. 84.

37. See Kenneth T. Jackson, "Metropolitan Government Versus Suburban Autonomy: Politics on the Crabgrass Frontier," in *Cities in American History,* ed. Kenneth T. Jackson and Stanley K. Schultz (New York: Knopf, 1972), pp. 442–446.

38. Henry G. Cisneros, "Regionalism: The New Geography of Opportunism," *Cityscape: A Journal of Policy Development and Research,* Special issue (December 1996): 39.

39. Stuart A. MacCorkle, *Municipal Annexation in Texas* (Austin: Institute of Public Affairs, University of Texas, 1965), pp. 28–36.

40. Arnold Fleischmann, "Sunbelt Boosterism: The Politics of Postwar Growth and Annexation in San Antonio," in *The Rise of the Sunbelt Cities,* vol. 14, *Urban Affairs Annual Reviews,* ed. David C. Perry and Alfred J. Watkins (Beverly Hills, Calif.: Sage, 1977), pp. 151–168; and "The Politics of Annexation: A Preliminary Assessment of Competing Paradigms," *Social Science Quarterly* 67, no. 1 (March 1987): 128–142.

41. Cisneros, "Regionalism," p. 36.

42. Vincent L. Marando, "City-County Consolidation: Reform, Regionalism, Referenda, and Requiem," *Western Political Quarterly* 32, no. 4 (December 1979): 409–422; Advisory Commission on Intergovernmental Relations, 1993.

43. Daniel R. Grant, "Urban and Suburban Nashville: A Case Study in Metropolitanism," *Journal of Politics* 17 (February 1965): 85. On the background to Nashville, see also Brett W. Hawkins, *Nashville Metro: The Politics of City-County Consolidation* (Nashville, Tenn.: Vanderbilt University Press, 1966); and David A. Booth, *Metropolitics: The Nashville Consolidation* (East Lansing: Institute for Community Development and Services, Michigan State University, 1963).

44. William C. Havard, Jr., and Floyd C. Corty, *Rural-Urban Consolidation: The Merger of Governments in the Baton Rouge Area* (Baton Rouge: Louisiana State University Press, 1964), pp. 146–147.

45. Melvin B. Mogulof, *Five Metropolitan Governments* (Washington, D.C.: Urban Institute, 1973), p. 22.

46. This point is made by R. Steven Hill and William P. Maxam in their article "Unigov: The First Year," *National Civic Review,* June 1971, 310–314, especially p. 310. See also York Wilbern, "Unigov: Local Government Reorganization in Indianapolis," in Advisory Commission on Intergovernmental Relations, *Report A-41: Substate Regionalism and the Federal System,* vol. II, *Regional Governance: Promise and Performance—Case Studies* (Washington, D.C.: U.S. Government Printing Office, 1973), pp. 49–51.

47. H. V. Savitch and Ronald K. Vogel, "Louisville: Compacts and Antagonistic Cooperation," in *Regional Politics: America in a Post-City Age,* ed. H. V. Savitch and Ronald K. Vogel (Thousand Oaks, CA: Sage), pp. 130–158.

48. H. V. Savitch and Ronald K. Vogel, "Metropolitan Consolidation versus Metropolitan Governance in Louisville," *State and Local Government Review* 32, no. 3 (Fall 2000): 198–212.

49. John M. De Grove, "The City of Jacksonville: Consolidation in Action," in Advisory Commission on Intergovernmental Relations, *Report A-41,* vol. II, pp. 19–20.

50. Daniel R. Grant, "Metropolitics and Professional Political Leadership: The Case of Nashville," *Annals of the American Academy of Political and Social Sciences* 353 (May 1964): 78.

51. Scott Greer, *Metropolitics: A Study of Political Culture* (New York: Wiley, 1963), pp. 7–18.

52. Howard W. Hallman, *Small and Large Together: Governing the Metropolis,* vol. 56, Sage Library of Social Research (Beverly Hills, Calif.: Sage, 1977), p. 85.

53. City of Louisville and Jefferson County.

54. Bert Swanson, "Jacksonville: Consolidation and Regional Governance" in *Regional Politics: America in a Post-City Age,* ed. H. V. Savitch and Ronald K. Vogel (Thousand Oaks, Calif.: Sage, 1996).

55. Mark S. Rosentraub, "City-County Consolidation and the Rebuilding of Image: The Fiscal Lessons from Indianapolis's UniGov Program" *State and Local Government Review* 32, no. 3 (Fall 2000): 182.

56. Joseph Zimmerman, "Metropolitan Reform in the U.S.: An Overview," *Public Administration Review* 30, no. 5 (September–October, 1970): 533.

57. Wilbern, "Unigov," p. 63.

58. William Blomquist and Roger B. Parks, "Unigov: Local Government in Indianapolis and Marion County, Indiana" in *The Government of World Cities: The Future of the Metro Model,* ed. L. J. Sharpe (New York: Wiley, 1995).

59. Grant, "Metropolitics and Professional Political Leadership," p. 79.

60. Ibid., p. 80.

61. Mogulof, *Five Metropolitan Governments,* p. 46; and De Grove, "The City of Jacksonville," p. 20.

62. Wilbern, "Unigov," pp. 61–62.

63. Rosentraub, p. 155.

64. National Association of Counties (NACO), "County Government: A Brief Overview" (Washington, D.C.: author, July 1996). The exact number of county governments that use the commission form of government is not clear; it may be from as many as 85 percent to as few as 40 percent. The particular source of data and definition used by researchers is a factor in different estimates. See Beverly Cigler, "County Governance in the 1990s," *State and Local Government Review* 27 (Winter 1995): 55–70; Jeffery Blake, Tanis Salant, and Alan Boroshok, *County Government Structure: A State by State Report* (Washington, D.C.: National Association of Counties, 1989); Victor DeSantis, "County Government: A Century of Change," in *Municipal Yearbook* (Washington, D.C.: International City Management Association, 1989), pp. 55–65.

65. On the weaknesses of traditional county government and proposals for reform, see Advisory Commission on Intergovernmental Relations, *Report M-61: For a More Perfect Union: County Reform* (Washington, D.C.: U.S. Government Printing Office, 1971); and Donald Menzel, ed., *The American County: Frontiers of Knowledge* (University: University of Alabama Press, 1996).

66. Ronald K. Vogel, *Urban Political Economy: Broward County, Florida* (Gainesville: University Press of Florida, 1992).

67. Susan MacManus, "Politics, Partisanship and Board Election: The Political Landscape Surrounding the Governing Boards of Large U.S. Counties in the 1990s," in *The American County: Frontier of Knowledge,* ed. Donald C. Menzal and John P. Thomas (University: University of Alabama Press, 1996).

68. Hallman, *Small and Large Together,* p. 96. See also League of Women Voters of the United States Education Fund, *Supercity/Hometown, U.S.A.: Prospects for Two-Tier Government* (New York: Praeger, 1974).

69. D. B. S. Paul, "Metropolitan Dade County Government: A Review of Accomplishments," from an address presented to the Local Government Law Section, American Bar Association, Miami Beach, Florida, August 8, 1965. The printed text can be found in Joseph F. Zimmerman, *Government of the Metropolis: Selected Readings* (New York: Holt, 1968), pp. 202–203.

70. Oliver P. Williams, *Metropolitan Political Analysis: A Social Access Approach* (New York: Free Press, 1971), pp. 86–93.

71. Grant, "Metro's Three Faces," p. 407.

72. "Dade County Reviews Charter," *National Civic Review* 71, no. 5 (May 1982): 265–266. The first charter review, in 1981, called for extending the two-tier system to the unincorporated areas of the county by creating limited-purpose municipalities there to handle zoning and purchase of services. This has not been done, however.

73. U.S. Bureau of the Census; Ronald K. Vogel and Genie N. L. Stowers, "Miami: Minority Empowerment and Regime Change," in *Big City Politics in Transition,* ed. H. V. Savitch and John Thomas (Beverly Hills, Calif.: Sage, 1991), pp. 116–118.

74. Ibid., pp. 119–120.

75. Irving G. McNayr, "A Report to the Chairman and the Members of the Board of County Commissioners," September 25, 1962. The printed text of this report can be found in Joseph F. Zimmerman, *Government of the Metropolis,* p. 199.

76. Aileen Lotz, "Metropolitan Dade County," in Advisory Commission on Intergovernmental Relations, *Report A-41,* vol. II, p. 10.

77. Mogulof, *Five Metropolitan Governments,* pp. 48–49.

78. Genie Stowers, "Miami: Experiences in Regional Government," in *Regional Politics: America in a Post-City Age,* ed. H. V. Savitch and Ronald K. Vogel (Thousand Oaks, Calif.: Sage Publications, September 1996), pp. 197–198.

79. Ibid., pp. 192, 196–197.

80. The Home Rule Amendment and Charter (as Amended Through March 12, 1996), Metropolitan Dade County, Florida.

81. Andres Viglucci, "Abolition Attempt Crushed, Miami to Be Run by Strong Mayor," *Miami Herald,* September 5, 1997, p. 1.

82. Stowers, "Miami: Experiences in Regional Government" in Savitch and Vogel, *Regional Politics: America in a Post-City Age,* p. 204.

83. This account relies heavily on *Reshaping Government in Metropolitan Areas,* pp. 7–83, and on Frank Smallwood, *Metro Toronto a Decade Later* (Toronto: Bureau of Municipal Research, 1963). For another analysis of the Toronto experiment, see Harold Kaplan, *Urban Political Systems: A Functional Analysis of Metro Toronto* (New York: Columbia University Press, 1967).

84. Lionel Feldman, "Metro Toronto: Old Battles—New Challenges," in *The Government of World Cities: The Future of the Metro Model,* ed. L. J. Sharpe (London: Wiley, 1995), p. 210; Frances Frisken, "Planning and Servicing the Greater Toronto Area: The Interplay of Provincial and Municipal Interests," *Urban Studies Working Paper* no. 12 (North York, Ontario: University of York, January 1990), pp. 19–20.

85. Frances Frisken, pp. 19–20.

86. Lionel Feldman, "Metro Toronto," p. 208.

87. Ibid., p. 214.

88. Ibid., pp. 217–219.

89. C. James Owen and York Wilbern, *Governing Metropolitan Indianapolis: The Politics of Unigov* (Berkeley: University of California Press, 1985), chap. 7.

90. Lotz, "Metropolitan Dade County," in Advisory Commission on Intergovernmental Relations, *Report A-41,* vol. II, p. 7. A less complimentary assessment is given in Mogulof, *Five Metropolitan Governments,* pp. 27–48, 59.

91. J. Edwin Benton and Darwin Gamble, "City/County Consolidation and Economies of Scale: Evidence from a Time Series in Jacksonville, Florida," *Social Science Quarterly* 65, no. 1 (March 1984): 190–198.

92. Roger B. Parks and Ronald J. Oakerson, "St. Louis: The ACIR Study," *Intergovernmental Perspectives* 15, no. 1 (Winter 1989): 10.

93. Donald Phares, "Bigger Is Better or Is It Smaller? Restructuring Local Government in the St. Louis Area," *Urban Affairs Quarterly* 25, no. 1 (September 1989): 5–17.

94. Williams, *Metropolitan Political Analysis,* pp. 86–93.

95. On Jacksonville, see Lee Sloan and Robert M. French, "Black Rule in the Urban South?" *Transaction* (November–December 1971): 29–34; and Advisory Commission on Intergovernmental Relations, *Report A-44,* vol. III, *The Challenge of Local Governmental Reorganization,* p. 102. On Nashville, see Hawkins, *Nashville Metro: The Politics of City-County Consolidation,* pp. 132–133.

96. Grant, "Metro's Three Faces," p. 403.

97. Wilbern, "Unigov," pp. 71–72.

98. Joan Carver, "Responsiveness and Consolidation: A Case Study," *Urban Affairs Quarterly* 9, no. 2 (December 1973): 246; and Vincent L. Marando and Carl Reggie Whitley, "City-County Consolidation: An Overview of Voter Response," *Urban Affairs Quarterly* 8, no. 2 (December 1972): 181–204, especially p. 190.

99. William Blomquist, "Metropolitan Organization and Local Politics: The Indianapolis–Marion County Experience," paper presented at the Midwest Political Science Association Annual Meeting, April 9–11, 1992, Chicago, pp. 25–26.

100. Ibid., p. 27.

101. Ibid., pp. 27–30.

102. Ibid., p. 32.

103. Ben White, "Democrats Turned Out Core Backers for Key Wins," *Washington Post,* November 6, 1999, p. A7; Indianapolis/Marion County City-Council Web page http://www.indygov.org/council/members.html.

104. Bert E. Swanson, "Jacksonville: Consolidation and Regional Governance," in Savitch and Vogel, *Regional Politics: America in a Post-City Age,* pp. 229–252.

105. Wilbern, "Unigov," p. 63.

106. De Grove, "The City of Jacksonville," p. 24.

107. This seems to have been the primary concern of much literature on the impact of metropolitan reorganization on the African American population. See Frances Fox Piven and Richard A. Cloward, "What Chance for Black Power?" *New Republic* 185, no. 13 (March 30, 1968): 23; and Lee Sloan and Robert French, "Race and Governmental Consolidation in Jacksonville," *Negro Educational Review* 2, no. 1 (April–July 1970): 72–78.

108. De Grove, "The City of Jacksonville," p. 24.

109. L. Sloan and R. M. French, cited in Bert E. Swanson, "Quandaries of Pragmatic Reform: A Reassessment of the Jacksonville Experience," *State and Local Government Review* 32, no. 3 (Fall 2000): 231.

110. Willis Hawley, *Blacks and Metropolitan Governance: The Stakes of Reform* (Berkeley: Institute of Governmental Studies, University of California, 1972).

111. On St. Louis's failure to achieve its metropolitan reform, see Robert H. Salisbury, "Interests, Parties, and Governmental Structures in St. Louis," *Western Political Quarterly* 13, no. 2 (June 1960): 500–501; Edward C. Banfield, *Big City Politics* (New York: Random House, 1965), pp. 121–124; Henry J. Schmandt, P. G. Steinbicker, and G. D. Wendel, *Metropolitan Reform in St. Louis* (New York: Holt, 1961); and Scott Greer, *Metropolitics: A Study of Political Culture* (New York: Wiley, 1963). On Cleveland's failure, see James A. Norton, *The Metro Experience* (Cleveland, Ohio: Press of Western Reserve University, 1963); Estal E. Sparlin, "Cleveland Seeks New Metro Solution," *National Civic Review* 69, no. 3 (March 1960): 143; and Richard A. Watson and John H. Romani, "Metropolitan Government for Metropolitan Cleveland: An Analysis of the Voting Record," *Midwest Journal of Political Science* 5, no. 4 (November 1961): 365–390.

112. Edward Sofen, *The Miami Metropolitan Experiment* (Bloomington: Indiana University Press, 1963), pp. 74–75.

113. *National Civic Review* 62, no. 8 (September 1973): 449; 63, no. 1 (January 1974): 32–33; and 68, no. 1 (January 1979): 43.

114. Sharon P. Krefetz and Alan B. Sharof, "City-County Merger Attempts: The Role of Political Factors," *National Civic Review* 66, no. 4 (April 1977): 178.

115. For sources on these surveys, see note 84. For surveys on experiences in addition to those of St. Louis and Cleveland, see Amos H. Hawley and Basil G. Zimmer, "Resistance to Unification in a Metropolitan Community," in *Community Political Systems,* ed. Morris Janowitz (Glencoe, Ill.: Free Press, 1961), pp. 164–167. A similar result emerged from a survey in Dayton, Ohio; see John C. Bollens et al., *Metropolitan Challenge* (Dayton, Ohio: Metropolitan Community Studies, 1959), p. 241.

116. Greer, *Metropolitics: A Study of Political Culture,* pp. 7–18.

117. Thomas A. Henderson and Walter A. Rosenbaum, "Prospects for Consolidation of Local Governments: The Role of Local Elites in Electoral Outcomes," *American Journal of Political Science* 17, no. 4 (November 1973): 695–720.

118. Doyle W. Buckwalter, "No on Merger for Salt Lake," *National Civic Review* 68, no. 3 (March 1979): 150–151.

119. H. V. Savitch and Ronald K. Vogel, "Metropolitan Consolidation versus Metropolitan Governance in Louisville," *State and Local Government Review* 32, no. 3 (Fall 2000): 198–212; H. V. Savitch and Ronald K. Vogel, "Suburbs Without a City: Power and City-County Consolidation," *Urban Affairs Review* 39, no. 6 (July 2004): 758–790.

120. Ronald K. Vogel, "Metropolitan Government," pp. 190–193; H. V. Savitch and Ronald K. Vogel, *Regional Politics: America in a Post-City Age,* chaps. 1 and 12.

121. See Thomas M. Scott, "Metropolitan Government Reorganization Proposals," *Western Political Quarterly* 21, no. 2 (June 1968): 489, 498–507.

122. *The Federalist Papers,* ed. Clinton Rossiter (New York: New American Library, 1961), No. 10, by James Madison, pp. 77–84.

123. Robert Agger, Daniel Goldrich, and Bert Swanson, *The Rulers and the Ruled* (New York: Wiley, 1964); Thomas Dye, "Community Power and Public Policy," in *Community Power,* ed. Robert Waste (Beverly Hills, Calif.: Sage, 1986).

CHAPTER 10

THE NEW REGIONALISM: TAKING "METROPOLITAN GOVERNANCE WITHOUT GOVERNMENT" SERIOUSLY

CHAPTER SYNOPSIS

The "New Regionalism" Agenda: *Structuring Governance Arrangements, Not Restructuring Government; Policies to Counter Sprawl and the Problems It Causes* • Regionalism and Lifestyles: *Easy Regionalism—Systems Maintenance Policies That Do Not Threaten Suburban Exclusiveness (e.g., Building a Regional Sewerage System); Hard Regionalism— Social-Access Policies That Threaten Upper-Middle-Class Suburban Lifestyles (e.g., Building Affordable Housing in the Suburbs)* • Weak Regionalism: *Origin of Metropolitan Planning; Councils of Government and Metropolitan Planning Organizations* • Stronger Regionalism: *Minneapolis–St. Paul Metropolitan Council; Portland Metro* • Assessing New Regionalism: *Effective Metropolitan Governance?; An Evolutionary Process; Bias—the Continuing Difficulty in Addressing Social-Access and Lifestyle Issues*

The great hopes for achieving metropolitan government were, as Chapter 9 demonstrated, pretty well dashed by the mid-1970s, but the problems of the multicentered metropolis have not disappeared. Nor have the demands to increase the capabilities of urban governments to deal with these problems. In fact, there is renewed interest in *regionalism*. In contrast to the mid-twentieth century, however, the thrust of these demands is seldom any longer to create metropolitan governments. Rather, the focus today is much more likely to be on *limited* reforms and limited attempts at cooperation. But this does not mean acceptance of the public-choice view that existing governing arrangements in the fragmented metropolis are satisfactory. Instead, the focus has shifted to promoting effective metropolitan governance while recognizing the unlikelihood of comprehensive restructuring.

The roots of this *new regionalism* are in the continuing population spread across the urban landscape (see Chapter 8). New suburban cities were created, and they tend to defend auto-dependent lifestyles, oppose public transit, and resist affordable housing. Sprawl into formerly rural and natural areas spawns environmental and infrastructure problems. Greater economic competition among cities brings pressure for strategic planning for the region. Higher-level governments can intervene, but state and federal governments lack the knowledge of local areas that they would need to make rational policies, and regional policies are not high on their agendas. Today, regional concerns are less about the efficiency of public services or the need for the city boundaries to match the metropolis. Instead, new regionalists seek to ameliorate the problems arising from sprawl and to stem continued outward expansion.

The new regionalist policy agenda includes (1) reducing fiscal disparities among local governments, (2) reducing racial and class (income) segregation, (3) reurbanizing the city, and (4) stemming the outward sprawl. New regionalist solutions include (1) tax sharing among local governments to reduce fiscal inequities, (2) affordable housing in the suburbs to reduce segregation and address the spatial mismatch between lower-income job seekers in the inner city and good-paying jobs in the suburbs, and (3) *smart-growth* policies whereby state and local governments stop investing resources to service growth that promotes sprawl and channel growth back to the central city.

New regionalists call for more resources and autonomy for local governments to address their problems. They seek to structure intergovernmental relations in such a way as to achieve new regionalist ends. They take a problem-oriented approach. If the major barriers to new regionalist policies are government structure, new regionalists will favor limited local government reorganization. However, new regionalists do not start with structure. Rather, they seek to enhance coordination among local governments and produce effective metropolitan governance. Thus they focus on *governance* rather than on *government* (see Table 10.1).

Historically, as we saw in Chapter 9, metropolitan reformers proposed metropolitan government as the solution to these problems. However, we also saw that even where metropolitan governments were established, they did not adopt regional policies on social access and lifestyle issues. New regionalism is based on the recognition that cities and suburbs are interdependent. Declining central cities undermine the metropolitan economy. On the other hand, there is a strong correlation between the economic health of the region as a whole and the health of the central city. The strongest metropolitan regions are anchored by strong central cities.[1] Thus, suburbs cannot go it alone.

TABLE 10.1   New Regionalism Definitions of Governance and Government

Government	Governance
Formal institutions, elections, and established decision-making processes	Harness existing institutions in new ways
Coercive power—command and control embedded in hierarchy	Sticks and carrots but focus on horizontal, not vertical, linkages
Stress centralizing features of regionalism	Stress decentralizing virtues of local cooperation

Source: H. V. Savitch and Ronald K. Vogel, "Paths to New Regionalism," *State and Local Government Review* 32, no. 3 (Fall 2000): 158–168.

New regionalists recognize that the metropolis has extended out well beyond the central city—or even the central county. Thus, even if major structural reform such as city-county consolidation were desirable, it is no longer a practical solution. It has proved almost impossible to create metropolitan governments within a single county. It is even less likely that the boundaries of governments can now be extended to capture the larger metropolitan region covering three or more counties and possibly crossing state or national boundaries. Thus, new regionalists aim to structure intergovernmental relations in such a way as to attain coordination and cooperation in providing urban services in the metropolitan region. New regionalists seek to devise new, flexible institutions for the metropolis. This might occur, for example, through interlocal government agreements to provide services or share taxes.[2]

This new regionalist view is gaining a number of adherents. A report by the National Committee on Improving the Future of U.S. Cities Through Improved Metropolitan Area Governance, 1996–1999 (see the accompanying box) eschewed traditional metropolitan reform in favor of a new regionalist approach. Though critical of the inequalities associated with the current pattern of metropolitan development (such as the income disparities between central city and suburbs), committee members were unimpressed by the record of achievement of metropolitan governments and skeptical that comprehensive structural reforms were possible in any event. Thus they focused on the kinds of reforms suggested above.[3]

As we consider the new regionalist agenda, four developments stand out:

- It has been easier to address the systems maintenance issues of metropolitan politics than the lifestyle issues.
- Under federal incentives, metropolitan planning has proliferated.
- New metropolitan institutions, the council of governments (COG), and metropolitan planning organizations (MPOs) have emerged.
- Through a process of incremental change, new models of metropolitan government have taken shape in Minnesota and Oregon.

New regionalist policies have been in place long enough for us to begin to assess whether a governance strategy may better address the problems that urban regions face and whether *metropolitan governance without government* is more than a public-choice model of voluntary cooperation.

A Matter of Lifestyles

One change that has come about is the increased willingness to turn control of certain kinds of governmental functions over to centralized metropolitan agencies. But not all governmental functions are being turned over. Oliver Williams has posited what is called the "lifestyle model" of metropolitan politics, a model that seems to fit contemporary trends in metropolitan governance. Williams states that where there is no outside intervention by the federal government, "policy areas which are perceived as neutral with respect to controlling social access may be centralized; policies which are perceived as controlling social access will remain decentralized."[4] The objectives of social access are the lifestyles of upper-middle-class suburban areas, particularly the lifestyles

The Committee on Improving the Future of U.S. Cities Through Improved Metropolitan Area Governance

The National Academy of Sciences set up a national commission to review evidence concerning the efficient and effective organization of metropolitan governance in the United States. The committee acknowledged inequalities arising from the present system of financing and providing urban services. However, the committee departed from traditional reform diagnoses and prescriptions as the excerpts below reveal.

- **Efficiency of Consolidated Government**

  The literature on the efficiency consequences of consolidated versus fragmented systems of local government (or large versus small units) is particularly extensive. . . . The preponderance of evidence indicates that small local governments (and thus metropolitan areas characterized by fragmentation) are more efficient for labor-intensive services, whereas larger units are more efficient for capital-intensive services (because of economies of scale) and for certain overhead functions. (p. 106)

- **Performance of Consolidated Government (Nashville, Jacksonville, and Indianapolis)**

  [C]onsolidation has not reduced costs . . . [and] it may have even increased local expenditures. (p. 106)

- **Effects of Consolidated Government on Reducing Disparities Between Central Cities and Suburbs and Whites and Blacks**

  [T]here are no systematic empirical studies. The evidence that does exist, however, suggests that these efforts have had no significant impact on redistributing income or on addressing the problems of the poor or racial minorities. (pp. 106–107)

- **Recommendation to Improve Metropolitan Governance**

  [W]hen a supra-local approach is desirable, existing overlaying units of governments can provide services, or special districts can be created to do so. When a regional approach or perspective is more appropriate, creation of such entities as the Portland Metropolitan Service District and the Minneapolis–St. Paul Metropolitan Council is desirable, if locally supported and politically feasible. If such entities are not likely to emerge (i.e., in most metropolitan areas), then we find most appropriate the use and expansion of existing metropolitan forums and agencies, such as councils of governments, metropolitan planning organizations, regional special-purpose authorities, and public-private alliances on the metropolitan level. It is possible that, over time, one or more of these will organically emerge into an institution that has the ability to make decisions for the entire region in several functional areas. (p. 129)

Source: Alan A. Altshuler, Harold Wolman, William Morrill, and Faith Mitchell, eds., *Governance and Opportunity in Metropolitan America* (Washington, D.C.: National Academy Press, 1999).

of the expensive suburban school districts and the exclusive residential areas. The devices that control access to these lifestyles thus become the issues over which suburbanites fight most vehemently to retain local control. And the public issues that most directly challenge the exclusivity of these lifestyles are busing of pupils for the purpose of achieving racial balance, low- and moderate-income public housing, zoning, and possibly the equalizing of fiscal disparities in the metropolis. Suburban officials show great reluctance to allow these issues to be controlled by a centralized metropolitan government.

In contrast to these lifestyle issues, many of the problems of the multicentered metropolis—such as sewerage, water supply, health facilities, and solid-waste disposal—represent what Williams labels the *systems maintenance* functions of government. Equal access to sewers does not threaten anybody's lifestyle in the suburbs, but it is essential to maintaining the health and safety of the majority of the population. As the seriousness of these systems maintenance problems began to be recognized, and as they began to be perceived as nonthreatening to the suburban lifestyle, municipal officials became less opposed to centralizing and coordinating their operations in agencies that were large enough to practice economies of scale. Even in metropolises such as Toronto, Miami, and the Twin Cities, where major metropolitan reorganizations have been achieved, the new governments have been much more effective in addressing physical-development issues than in addressing social issues, where questions of lifestyle are at stake.[5]

The major battles of metropolitan politics today are less over the forms of metropolitan governance than over the substance of issues that threaten suburban lifestyles. The tone may have been set in court battles over busing, the fiscal disparities inherent in relying on property taxes to finance public schools, and the extension of low- and moderate-income public housing into the suburbs.[6] These issues are just as volatile as we enter the twenty-first century as they have been in the past.

Metropolitan Planning

Because city planning is normally confined to the geographic areas within the city's municipal boundaries, it cannot cope with problems that transcend those boundaries, nor can it coordinate plans with those of neighboring communities. Most large metropolises today contain several suburban development nodes that are usually centered on huge shopping malls located at freeway interchanges. Sometimes called urban villages, periphery cities, or edge cities,[7] these nodes become powerful magnets that attract complexes of office buildings, other commercial development, and residential construction. And their impact on future development usually overpowers that of any suburban planning commission. Only a planning process that is metropolitan in scope could effectively control the impact of these periphery cities.

The first metropolitan plan was probably the regional plan for New York and its environs, sponsored by a private foundation in 1929. Key provisions of the plan were not implemented, however.[8] And left on their own, few other metropolises attempted to formulate their own metropolitan plans. Even as late as 1962 there were only 63 metropolitan planning commissions, and most of these concentrated on population studies and economic analyses rather than on trying to shape future metropolitan growth in a comprehensive fashion.

Federal Incentives   Whereas only 63 metropolitan planning commissions existed in 1962, by the end of the 1960s their number had tripled to almost 200, and today they exist in nearly all metropolitan areas. What sparked this proliferation of planning agencies was federal funding. The 1965 Housing and Urban Development Act authorized funds for research and planning by regional planning agencies, which could use the funds for a broad range of planning activities. The incentive of obtaining these funds spurred officials in many metropolises to create metropolitan planning agencies.

The creation of metropolitan planning agencies was also stimulated by a provision of the 1966 Demonstration Cities and Metropolitan Development Act (Model Cities Act) that required several kinds of federal grant applications to be reviewed by a metropolitan review agency before the federal government could award the grants. Furthermore, the review agencies were charged with ensuring that the grants would be used for purposes consistent with existing metropolitan development plans. Called the *A-95 review power* (after a budget agency document with that number), this provision was in effect until 1983, and it gave metropolitan planning bodies the first real potential power to enforce their development plans.[9]

Federal Impact on Metropolitan Planning   Despite the eventual demise of the A-95 process, the federal government had a significant impact on metropolitan planning. The availability of federal funds to underwrite planning, the emphasis on research, and the review power made it possible for metropolitan planning to be taken seriously for the first time in America. The metropolitan planning agencies now have the funds to hire professional staffs and to contract out particular jobs to consultants who specialize in given areas. The metropolitan planning agencies also now have a larger focus that enables them to tackle certain planning issues that the local municipalities are incapable of dealing with effectively. Some of these issues are land use, transportation, water supply, community facilities, air pollution, open-space preservation, and recreation.

The Impact and Politics of Metropolitan Planning

Despite the tremendous proliferation of metropolitan agencies since the 1960s, the impact of all this activity has been disappointing. David C. Ranney writes that these agencies "have not been able to bring about a metropolitan planning policy which is followed by the governments comprising the metropolitan areas."[10] Geographer John Friedmann asserts that "the manifest purpose of this style of planning [comprehensive development planning]—to shape the development of cities and nations in accord with a preconceived design, and to do so on the basis of functionally rational criteria—was not being accomplished. Where it was tried, and judged by its own claims, comprehensive planning turned out to be a colossal failure."[11]

One reason for the limited effectiveness of metropolitan planning can be traced to the estrangement between politicians and the professional planners. Although planners are really political actors, they have traditionally viewed themselves as self-styled guardians of the public good and as the promoters of long-range policies. But the planners inevitably confront politicians who are supposedly concerned with short-range private benefits for their constituents. This confrontation was described succinctly by Edward C. Banfield, who wrote, "No competent politician will sacrifice votes that may be needed in the next election for gains, however large, that may accrue to the public 10, 20, or 30 years hence."[12] Another reason for the limited effectiveness of metropolitan planning has been the absence of agreed-upon metropolitan goals that can be implemented through a metropolitan development plan. Planners may promote such goals, but they can implement them only if the goals are accepted by other political actors and if the planners themselves also control budgets, investment decisions, locational decisions, and zoning practices.

Some evidence indicates that the spate of metropolitan planning that has occurred since 1965 has apparently been little more than an exercise in drawing up plans merely to get federal money.[13] How useful such plans then become is questionable. One study by the Urban Land Institute found that of 102 cities surveyed that have a planning commission, only 10 made specific use of the plans produced by these commissions.[14]

Other inhibiting factors stem from the high value placed on local autonomy. Local officials fear that strong metropolitan plans will force on them development that they do not want and will deny them development that they may want. In particular, they are reluctant to allow control over zoning, public schools, and other lifestyle issues to be taken from local hands. Finally, the overwhelming majority of metropolitan planning agencies are not tied to a strong political base.[15]

Advocacy Planning

Historically, there was not much room in the planning process for citizen input. Certainly private real estate developers had little incentive to invite citizen participation in the planning of their projects. From the developer's viewpoint, citizen input is negative because citizens usually object to some feature of any project. And because most citizens do not even hear about projects until considerable money has been spent on them and they are presented to a planning commission or zoning board for approval, there is no mechanism for citizen input to be anything *but* negative.

Nor is this inhibition of citizen participation limited to private developers. Big-city planning staffs, highway planners, urban renewal planners, and metropolitan planning agencies tend to be just as unreceptive to citizen groups as are the private developers. Many federal programs require citizen participation in the planning process. But such participation is usually invited after the plan has been drafted, so "participation" means that the plan is presented at a meeting held for the purpose of enlightening the public. Quite often the result has been a widespread feeling of alienation and helplessness in the face of drastic neighborhood changes caused by construction of locally unwelcome freeways,[16] motels, commercial establishments, urban renewal projects,[17] university expansions, or any number of big projects. There is a basic tension between the traditional wish of the early-twentieth-century reformers to depoliticize politics and the Jeffersonian ideal of citizen participation.[18]

One proposal to remedy this citizen malaise has been *advocacy planning*. The major spokesperson for advocacy planning was city planner Paul Davidoff, who argued that the planning bureaucracies have aligned themselves with the prevailing local establishments and have neglected the legitimate needs of the poor and the racial minorities. To remedy this, Davidoff proposed that citizens' groups hire professional planners to prepare their own plans and propose them to the appropriate public agencies. In this way citizens can take the initiative and approach the city government with positive proposals. Because they are represented by a professional planner, they will not be overwhelmed by technical jargon.[19]

The Bias of Urban Planning

If the advocacy planners are correct in their charges, urban planning as such has an inherent conservative bias, especially in the areas of highway planning, urban renewal planning,[20] and comprehensive development planning, in which the planners have been responsive primarily to their respective bureaucracies and functional fiefdoms. Such planning is conservative because the plans reflect the biases of past decisions and seek to protect the agency and the program from future encroachment.[21] Herbert Gans argues that the dominant faction of the American Institute of Planners is conservative.[22] Finally, some observers argue that all planning, even advocacy planning, is inherently conservative because it seeks merely to reform existing institutional practices rather than to overthrow them.[23]

Most of the arguments for the conservatism of urban planning focus on city-level planning for highways or urban renewal. Metropolitan planning may be a more liberalizing force than these other kinds of planning, for it does represent a challenge to the status quo of municipal autonomy. And *if* the comprehensive metropolitan land use plans were implemented, they would have a sharp effect on the future of suburban sprawl. They would also, *if implemented,* broaden the social access to residences, schools, and jobs in the metropolis. The fact that they have not achieved these things testifies more to the strength of the status quo than to the conservatism of the metropolitan planners. In this sense the planners are exerting a liberalizing, not a conservative, influence on metropolitan politics. The plans would provoke a change in the power relations—a slow, incremental change to be sure, but change nevertheless.[24] Finally, surveys of planners suggest that planners are much more liberal than the general population and much more inclined to be Democrats than Republicans.[25]

Councils of Governments and Metropolitan Planning Organizations

For performing the metropolitan planning function and the former A-95 clearinghouse function of reviewing applications for federal grants, the most popular form of metropolitan agency has been the *council of governments* (COG). A council of governments is a voluntary association of local municipalities and counties that join forces for the purpose of coordinating their activities concerning regional problems. The *metropolitan planning organization* (MPO) has also become important in regional transportation planning. In many instances, the COG serves as the MPO, although this function may be carried out by a separate entity. The MPO is charged with developing short- and long-term transportation plans and with distributing federal and state transportation aid in accordance with these plans.

The Washington Metropolitan Council of Governments

A good example of a COG and the possibilities and limitations it offers is presented by the Metropolitan Washington Council of Governments.[26] This COG (the MWCOG) grew out of a cooperative effort in Washington, D.C., governance, which by the late 1950s was beginning to reach the limits of attacking areawide problems on a function-by-function basis.

There had been a long history of cooperation on functional activities in the Washington region. Eleven special authorities had been set up to regulate particular services in and around Washington. Considerable interstate and interjurisdictional agreement had been worked out on such matters as water supply, sewerage, roads, and recreational space. Nevertheless, most of these jurisdictional agreements had been adopted piecemeal for specific needs, and there was little coordination between them. Each organization was designed in functional terms, and within each functional sector there were often subregional jurisdictions. Maryland, Virginia, and the District of Columbia, for example, all had special agencies dealing with recreational open space. Most of these agencies were underfinanced, and no general body had planning or coordinating responsibility for the whole area.

In 1957 the Washington Metropolitan Regional Conference was organized, and five years later, in 1962, it changed its name to the Metropolitan Washington Council of Governments. Designed to stimulate cooperation among the federal government, the two states, and the various counties and municipalities involved, the MWCOG concentrated on noncontroversial issues such as demonstrating the need for mass transit, water supply, and pollution abatement.

The MWCOG developed an elaborate organization that has become typical of most COGs. Its ultimate governing body is the *conference,* which meets semiannually and has representation from each of the constituent unit governments. In between the semiannual meetings, policy is established by an executive board, and day-to-day operations are carried out by an executive secretary and staff. The MWCOG was originally financed by voluntary assessments from each of the constituent units of government, but since enactment of the 1965 Housing Act, these voluntary assessments have been supplemented with federal planning grants. It now has an annual budget of $10 million with 18 member governments and 120 employees.

During its early years, the MWCOG carried out a relatively successful program in the functions that have been referred to here as systems maintenance. Through its studies on transit, it recommended and saw created the National Capital Transportation Agency and subsequently the Washington Metropolitan Area Transit Commission, which has successfully undertaken the construction of Washington's subway. MWCOG also drew up the Year 2000 Regional Development Plan in an attempt to focus public attention on several land use problems created by extremely rapid population growth. On the lifestyle issues, MWCOG has been less successful, but it did create the United Planning Organization, which became the local community action agency once the federal antipoverty program was started in 1965.

A study of the MWCOG by Jeffrey Henig, David Brunori, and Mark Ebert confirms this view. The authors found that the major limitation the MWCOG faces is that it must avoid antagonizing member governments because they may withdraw from the coalition. As a consequence, the agency avoids controversial issues and focuses on programs that yield the constituent governments real benefits. Examples of such benefits include the MWCOG's ability to receive federal and state aid and distribute it to members and its role in providing contractual services. If the MWCOG did not exist, the area governments would lose out on hundreds of millions of dollars of assistance that is available only to regional agencies or that requires joint cooperative action by local governments in the metropolis. The MWCOG acts as the metropolitan planning organization (MPO) that makes it possible for local governments in the region to receive federal transportation aid (see the next section). The MWCOG also has a number of contractual relationships with member governments to model traffic patterns, analyze data, and research public policy issues of interest to members. There are many issues that require regional cooperation, and the MWCOG serves as a mechanism to pursue these. However, this works only on technical issues, such as developing plans to respond to emergency disasters or joint training of police and fire officers. In addition, the MWCOG offers a Cooperative Purchasing Program that saves members more than $1.8 million a year.

The authors explain that the main weakness of the MWCOG is inherent in the way the institution is structured. It is not a government in its own right. Because it is a voluntary association and because there is such great socioeconomic disparity between the central city (D.C.) and the suburban counties in Virginia and Maryland, it is difficult to reach consensus. In a few cases, local governments have withdrawn temporarily, and others have threatened to withdraw over the years. Examples of issues that have divided the COG and that, had they not been dropped, could have led to its demise include a gun control ordinance and a commuter tax proposed by D.C. The authors even find that economic development is divisive since it might benefit one member at the expense of another. The net effect is that the MWCOG is reactive and cannot act as a general-purpose regional government.[27]

The Growth of COGs

When the MWCOG was founded in 1957, there were only about half a dozen COGs in the country. By 1972 there were more than 300[28] and by 1980, 660.[29] This rapid increase was due primarily to the availability of federal government planning grants and to federal demands for a metropolitan review process. Many metropolitan planning agencies became councils of governments when the 1965 Housing and Urban Development Act made COGs eligible to receive grants for planning and research in a broad range of activities,[30] and by the 1970s, federal grants accounted for an estimated two-thirds of all COG expenditures.[31] A further federal stimulus, as we have noted, was the designation of COGs as the A-95 review agencies.

An Assessment of COGs

COGs offer some important advantages for intergovernmental cooperation. Not only are they relatively easy to create, they become a mechanism for studying metropolitan problems and formulating solutions to the problems. Most metropolitan areas had never had such a mechanism before the COG. The COG also may have more influence on local governments than some other agencies by virtue of the fact that it is composed of elected officials. Although its proposals may not be as far-reaching as those of institutions further removed from locally elected officials, the very fact that locally elected representatives on the COG have backed the proposals may increase their chances of acceptance.

Nevertheless, COGs are also extremely limited tools for metropolitan governance. Three limitations in particular stand out: the constituent-unit form of representation, the limitations on COGs' authority, and their lack of success in dealing with the social-access or lifestyle issues.

The fact that COG members are also officials of local governments means that COGs have a constituent-unit form of representation. This has caused disruptive bickering between the units of government in many COGs, but especially in San Francisco[32] and Cleveland.[33] In both places the problem was eventually solved by moving toward granting each city representation that was roughly proportional to its population. In Cleveland, this resolution was attained only after a bitter conflict in which the Department of Housing and Urban Development threatened to rescind the COG's status as the A-95 review agency.

If the representational problems of COGs can be solved by applying the one-person, one-vote principle to its constituents, the second major problem, that of sufficient authority, is not so easily solved. Constituent units are not usually willing to surrender power to a COG. In the Washington, D.C., COG, one of the constituent counties from the state of Maryland temporarily withdrew from the MWCOG in disagreement over the general direction of the organization. Cleveland temporarily withdrew from its COG. Because of this possibility of withdrawal, COGs cannot take decisive and effective action unless an overwhelming majority of members support any given proposal. And, of course, overwhelming majority support does not normally occur on the controversial lifestyle issues. Even in exercising the A-95 federal grant review power, COGs have been reluctant to exercise their authority to the fullest. A study of 11 COGs in Texas found that the review process was perfunctory. Only two COGs in Texas had ever made a negative review.[34] And political scientist Joseph F. Zimmerman asserts flatly that "no COG has solved a major problem."[35]

Finally, COGs have been ineffective in dealing with the social-access and lifestyle issues discussed at the beginning of this chapter. There are two reasons for this. First, the 1966 Model Cities Act, which created the review power, specifically limited it to "federal loans or grants to assist in carrying out open-space projects or for the planning or construction of hospitals, airports, libraries, water supply and distribution facilities, sewerage facilities and waste treatment works, highways, transportation facilities, and water development and land conservation projects within any metropolitan area."[36] This language clearly ignores the social-access issues of tax disparities, low-income public housing in the suburbs, and busing of pupils to achieve racial balance in the schools. The second reason for the weakness of COGs in dealing with lifestyle issues stems from the constituent-unit structure of COGs. This structure effectively grants a veto to the very suburban governments that do not want to lose control over the lifestyle issues. Consequently, the number of COG successes on social-access or lifestyle issues such as housing is very low. A study of 98 COGs, in fact, found that they rejected the idea that central-city problems should be one of their focal points.[37]

Because of all these weaknesses, it was widely assumed that COGs would suffer heavily when the Reagan administration abolished the A-95 review process and sharply reduced the federal planning grants that the COGs relied on so heavily. And indeed, 125 of the 660 COGs closed down under these pressures.[38] But the remainder adapted fairly well to the less favorable political environment of the 1980s. Although they relied on federal funds for 76 percent of their budgets on average in 1977, this fell to 48 percent by 1983. They made up most of that shortfall by getting more funds from state and local governments, grants from foundations, and service contracts from other agencies and institutions that were willing to pay for planning studies as well as technical and advisory services.[39] As a consequence, COGs have become much more resilient than was expected, and they seem to be filling a need for a centralized metropolitan agency to provide planning, studies, and technical services to other governments. But as we saw in the case of D.C., COGs are not full, general-purpose metropolitan governments.

Metropolitan Planning Organizations

Although the federal government weakened COGs by eliminating A-95 review and cutting federal planning grants, recent federal legislation has promoted regional transportation planning. The Clean Air Act Amendments of 1990 require urban areas to meet national air quality standards or face a number of sanctions.[40] The Intermodal Surface Transportation Efficiency Act (ISTEA) of 1991 and its successor Transportation Equity Act for the 21st Century (TEA-21) requires urban areas to have a designated metropolitan planning organization (MPO) that undertakes regional transportation plans. This MPO is to develop integrated transportation plans for the entire metropolitan area, taking into account the needs of different parts of the metropolis (e.g., central cities, suburbs) and the proper balance among different modes of transportation (e.g., mass transit, highways, bike paths). The goal of the legislation is to promote an "integrated transportation system" that not only integrates various modes of transportation but also links transportation planning to land use and infrastructure planning.[41] Federal transportation funds (surface transportation block grants under ISTEA) can be used only for projects that are included in the local MPO transportation plans.

The MPO function may be lodged in a COG. For example, the MWCOG performs this function in Washington, D.C., distributing about $250 million a year to member governments.[42] In other communities, the MPO function is housed in a separate agency or association. The actual body that carries out this function is determined by negotiation among local authorities and their respective states, subject to approval by the federal government. The ISTEA legislation requires the federal Department of Transportation periodically to certify that MPOs are adequately engaged in regional transportation planning. Regions that lack an MPO or fail to meet federal guidelines for regional transportation planning risk losing federal transportation aid.

There is evidence that federal promotion of regional transportation planning and air quality control has led to greater coordination of transportation planning and has fostered metropolitan governance even in the absence of metropolitan government. Alan Saltzstein's case study of the Los Angeles metropolis of 14 million people illustrates this. Los Angeles has a fragmented political structure spread over a five-county area with more than 200 cities, including the city of Los Angeles. ISTEA and the Clean

Air Act enhanced the status and powers of two regional actors—a council of government and a special district—to coordinate transportation planning and adopt policies to improve air quality within this fragmented metropolis.[43]

> The South Coast Air Quality Management District (AQMD) [a special district] develops and implements regional air quality plans, with the approval of state and federal agencies. Its authority includes plans for control of traffic congestion and land use; thus, it is directly involved in basic decisions of local government. The AQMD is governed by a board consisting of 12 representatives, 4 appointed by representatives of the five counties, 4 selected by the cities in the five counties, 1 additional selected by the cities in Los Angeles County, and 1 each appointed by the governor, the Assembly speaker, and the chair of the Senate Rules Committee.[44]

The Southern California Association of Governments (SCAG), a council of governments, is charged with "regional coordination" and serves as the region's MPO. Saltzstein describes the SCAG's function and structure as follows:

> The SCAG has a major role in developing the transportation and land use portions of the air plans developed by the AQMD. . . . In that capacity [as MPO], the SCAG has the power to recommend approval of individual projects proposed by cities if they are deemed in conformity with regional plans. The SCAG slowly has expanded its authority, changing from an advisory body to one with limited decision-making authority, particularly in transportation, air quality, and land use planning.
>   The SCAG is governed by a regional council of 70 elected officials. Sixty-three are selected by elected officials in districts, and seven are supervisors [county commissioners], one from each county and two from Los Angeles.[45]

The Clean Air Act and its amendments greatly enhanced the status of the AQMD, leading to an annual budget of $100 million with more than 1,000 employees in order to develop plans to reduce air pollution. The AQMD's powers are strong; it has "the power to issue permits and can fine industries that pollute." It also has "power over 'indirect' sources of pollution." In other words, the AQMD can restrict auto usage, which accounts for 60 percent of the air pollution in the Los Angeles metropolis, in order to reduce air pollution and conform to state and federal air pollution requirements.

> The plan is viewed by one expert as the most radical air quality plan in U.S. history (Rosenbaum, 1991, p. 170). It contains 24 compliance measures specifically aimed at local government control of indirect sources of pollution. Although the goal is pollution abatement, the effect is a regional plan that more rationally coordinates land use, transportation systems, and personal habits to reduce automobile usage and other sources of pollution.[46]

Compliance required local governments to take strong action to restrict land use development and regulate business and individual activity within their boundaries in order to reduce air pollution. For example, businesses might be required to alter employee work hours to reduce traffic congestion; individuals might be restricted in activities ranging from using a lawn mower to having a barbecue. If a locality did not comply, the AQMD could take over enforcement. According to Saltzstein, one-third of the cities had taken steps to comply with AQMD requirements by 1992. Local government objections to some of the measures they would have to enforce and more conservative appointments to the AQMD have shifted the emphasis from regulation to market incentives in the last few years.[47]

While AQMD was acting to regulate air pollution, under ISTEA, SCAG as the designated MPO was responsible for determining how about $1.36 billion for transportation would be spent. This led to greater effort to create a more balanced and efficient transportation system for the region including mass transit. AQMD as a regional actor was the stick to reduce auto usage; SCAG was the carrot.[48]

Thus regional institutions, bolstered by federal policies, did produce more effective regional transportation planning and reduced air pollution. However, this is a far cry from regional government. Single-function agencies cannot develop integrated policies or make "tradeoffs between fundamental values," such as clean air versus jobs. Saltzstein finds that the window for regional government and greater regional cooperation has closed. A regulatory approach carried out by an appointed staff in single-purpose agencies lacks sufficient political credibility and resources to overcome the centrifugal forces of this fragmented region.[49]

Evaluating MPOs

It is an open question whether ISTEA and TEA-21 will ultimately lead to stronger regional transportation planning. Major obstacles are that MPOs are not governments, may have boundaries that do not cover the full urban region, and may lack the technical and political competence to produce regional cooperation.[50] City and county governments are unlikely to place themselves under the authority of an MPO. If local self-interest conflicts with the regional MPO, the local response is likely to be an attempt to remove itself from the MPO. Still, initial studies, including the Los Angeles case, suggest that ISTEA has improved regional transportation planning and may have a role to play in fostering regionalism. One assessment reporting on an Advisory Commission on Intergovernmental Relations review of MPOs finds that

> ISTEA is having some success: decentralization is taking place; more stakeholders are getting involved; public involvement programs are becoming more common; and greater attention is being given to air quality, intermodal issues, long-range planning, and intergovernmental coordination."[51]

New regionalists are concerned not just that more cooperation occur but also that regional problems be addressed. A study of Louisville found that the MPO did enhance regional cooperation between Louisville and its suburbs, including Southern Indiana, in transportation planning. The MPO recommended that two new bridges be constructed to reduce traffic congestion and enhance economic development in the region. The cost will be approximately $1.8 billion. However, no consideration was given to the effects of building new bridges in accelerating sprawl into Southern Indiana. Moreover, there is concern that the project will lead to more decline in the urban core and will have disproportionate effects on poor and minorities in the city, including lack of access to new jobs and declining property values as people and businesses relocate to the newly opened lands in Southern Indiana. This will also reduce revenues in the central city and county. Here again, the case suggests that systems maintenance projects can gain regional support but social-access issues cannot. Interestingly, the newspaper accused those who raised the issue of race of being race baiters.[52]

Metropolitan Policy Making with Teeth

Although metropolitan planning, councils of government, and the metropolitan review process have not been very effective in coping with the problems of the multicentered metropolis, they could evolve into effective instruments for policy making at the metropolitan level. To go from a council of government with metropolitan planning and metropolitan review authority to a metropolitan agency with real teeth to make and enforce metropolitan policies would be only a series of small steps. During the 1970s, an evolutionary, incremental process took place in two areas that led in precisely that direction. In the Minneapolis–St. Paul, Minnesota, metropolitan area, one model of metropolitan policy making evolved, whereas a quite different model emerged in Portland, Oregon.*

Minneapolis–St. Paul: A Metropolitan Government Evolves

Powers of the Metropolitan Council   In essence the Twin Cities Metropolitan Council is a metropolitan planning and policy-making agency. The Metropolitan Council is made up of 17 members appointed by the governor to represent geographic districts roughly coterminous with two state senate districts. Council members are nonpartisan. The council was given four major powers.[53] First, as the metropolitan planning agency, it is responsible for preparing the metropolitan development guide. The development guide is a statement of policies on topics that range from the location of airports to solid waste disposal to the distribution of low-income housing throughout the suburbs to the channeling of future growth into predetermined locations in the region.

The council's second responsibility is reviewing the comprehensive development plans of the local governments in the region. Third, the council oversees and coordinates the metropolitan commissions and special districts. The council appoints the members of the three metropolitan commissions responsible for transit, waste control (sewers), and regional parks and open space. Although the council cannot appoint the members of the other two metropolitan commissions responsible for airports and sports facilities, it is empowered to review the budgets of these agencies and to veto capital expenditure projects. The Metropolitan Council has used this authority to bring the metropolitan districts in line with metropolitan policies for transit and airports.

The fourth power of the Metropolitan Council is to review applications from local governments and private organizations for many federal and state grant and loan guarantee programs. This power was used with some forcefulness in the Twin Cities to encourage local governments to cooperate with metropolitan policies. For example, in

---

*In some classification schemes, the Portland Metro and Minneapolis–St. Paul Metropolitan Council are treated as multicounty regional governments or as three-tier metropolitan governments (cities, counties, region). See National Academy of Public Administration, *Metropolitan Governance: A Handbook for Local Government Study Commissions* (U.S. Department of Housing and Urban Development, 1980); David Walker, "Snow White and the 17 Dwarfs: From Metro Cooperation to Governance," *National Civic Review* 76, no. 1 (January–February 1987): 14–17.

1973 the Metropolitan Council refused to review one suburb's application for park funds until that suburb came up with a plan for low- and moderate-income housing.[54]

Creation and Incremental Growth of the Metropolitan Council   The Metropolitan Council was established by legislative act in 1967. Prior to 1967, the Twin Cities region was plagued for many years by governmental fragmentation, tax inequities and disparities, and inconsistent provision of services throughout the region. The two central cities were ringed by more than 130 incorporated suburban municipalities. This made them very inelastic, to use David Rusk's terminology introduced in Chapter 9. Central-city annexation and city-county consolidation strategies were useless for coping with Minnesota's metropolitan problems. And the need to provide services in the suburbs led to a proliferation of municipalities, metropolitan agencies, special districts, and joint-powers agreements. The region had more than 300 governments with very little coordination between them, and the lack of coordination was beginning to produce a crisis in sewage disposal and water supply. A state health department investigation in 1959 discovered that 250,000 people in 39 suburbs were getting their drinking water from contaminated wells. More than 400,000 people used septic tanks rather than sewers.[55] When the Federal Housing Administration announced that it would no longer insure mortgages for homes that were not tied into central sewer and water systems, it became clear that some kind of metropolis-wide coordinating action was necessary.

Concerning the kind of action that was needed, at least 11 major groups put forward ideas to establish some form of metropolitan coordinating agency. Much interest was expressed in the Toronto federative experience, and several reformers traveled to Toronto to gain firsthand impressions of its operations, but federation was rejected as unsuitable and politically unfeasible. More conservative reformers were interested in establishing a council of governments for the Twin Cities.

Because of this evolution of consensus, metropolitan reform in the Twin Cities never went through a voting campaign. And the kinds of groups that surfaced in St. Louis, Cleveland, and other cities to defeat metropolitan reform schemes never argued against the creation of the Metropolitan Council. Suburban officials, although they may have viewed the new Metropolitan Council with suspicion, never organized themselves against its creation. In fact, their lobbying agency, the League of Minnesota Municipalities, put forward a proposal for the Metropolitan Council that was more far-reaching than the bill that eventually passed the legislature. County officials in the metropolitan area formed the Inter-County Council in 1966 to offer an alternative to the Metropolitan Council. And a chain of suburban newspapers vigorously opposed the idea of a metropolitan council with teeth and proposed that the legislature instead create a council of governments for the Twin Cities. But the very fact that these interests spoke of an alternative rather than merely opposing change indicates how much consensus existed about altering the status quo.

This lack of any significant opposition to the Metropolitan Council was explained by one observer as the result of a consensus of opinion that "something needed to be done, and [that] there was no push for a comprehensive home rule metropolitan government consolidation."[56] This lack of substantial opposition among the suburban officials might also have been a reflection of the particular nature of the political culture in Minnesota. This political culture has been described by Daniel J. Elazar as more moralistic than the political cultures of Cleveland or St. Louis. According to Elazar, a moralistic political culture is more receptive to expansive government for broad public purposes than are other types of political cultures found in the United States.[57]

Another very important factor was that the debate occurred in the forum of the legislature rather than in the forum of a voter referendum. When an issue comes to a referendum, the voter has only two choices: to vote for the issue or against it. For this reason, suburban newspapers, county officials, and municipal officials in the Twin Cities might have opposed such a referendum, just as similar officials had done elsewhere. But in the forum of the legislature, the normal process is one of negotiation, bargaining, and compromise rather than adamant opposition, especially when strong interest groups are pushing for action on an issue that clearly needs legislation.

A final important feature about metropolitan reform in the Twin Cities is the incremental nature of the way the reforms have occurred. As indicated earlier, the creation of the Metropolitan Council was the culminating event in a long history of developing a consensus that some areawide approach to metropolitan problems was needed. Nor did the metropolitan reform cease with the creation of the Metropolitan Council in 1967. In every legislative session since then, the council's powers have been expanded, refined, and clarified. If the only forum for debating the council's powers had been a referendum, it is highly unlikely that the council's powers would have continued evolving after its creation.

Reflection on the Twin Cities' approach to metropolitan governance reveals some advantages and some disadvantages. The major disadvantage is that a metropolitan reform enacted by a state legislature is not likely to be as far-reaching as one drafted by a charter commission and submitted to the electorate in a referendum. The interest groups that oppose metropolitan government are able to bargain with the legislators to dilute the scope of the reform. The Metropolitan Council created by the Minnesota legislature, for example, is not nearly as far-reaching a metropolitan government as are the governments that were created by referendum in Miami, Jacksonville, and Nashville.

A second disadvantage is that metropolitan government or governance imposed by state legislative action runs counter to the widely accepted value of local autonomy. There is no doubt that the state has the constitutional power to define and alter the system of local government. But the system of local government in the United States has always placed great value on local control and enhancing local democracy. State legislatures have embraced home rule, granting greater local discretion to city and county governments. State representatives have often found it politically unwise to tinker with local government powers; doing so often generates a backlash against them by city council members or county commissioners and upset residents who view state action as interference in local affairs. Changes imposed by the state legislature are legal, but the new governments may lack credibility and may have to work hard to overcome resistance engendered by the process, regardless of the wisdom and rationality of the governmental reform. Thus state-imposed changes are likely to be limited reforms to avoid overly antagonizing local sensitivities.

The major advantages are two. First, as we have noted, the legislative approach to metropolitan reform increased the likelihood of some kind of reform governance being established, because most city-county consolidation proposals and other metropolitan government proposals are defeated at the ballot box. A weak but legislatively created government may be better than no reform at all. Second, the legislative approach is more conducive to an incremental evolution of the powers of the metropolitan government once it is created. In contrast to the gradual refinement of powers of the Twin Cities Metropolitan Council, the Miami–Dade County Metro can change its charter only through a referendum. And Miami voters have not usually been receptive to changes; it was 1996 before they agreed to switch to an elected county executive, a move that will broadly strengthen the Metro.

Distinctive Features of the Twin Cities Model   The foregoing account makes apparent several distinctive features of the Twin Cities model of metropolitan government. First is the separation of policy making from administrative operations in the first three decades of the Metropolitan Council's existence. Until changes were made in 1994, the Metropolitan Council established policy for the region, but it did not operate anything. The bus system, for example, was run by the Transit Commission. The sewers were maintained by the Waste Control Commission and the airports by the Airports Commission. Exempt from operational and administrative responsibilities, the council was able to devote its attention to the overall policies that guide the operation of these various services.

A second distinctive feature of the Twin Cities model is that it avoided the most debilitating aspects of a council of governments. As noted earlier, many COGs were emasculated when member governments threatened either to withdraw or to not make their financial contributions. This would not be possible in the Twin Cities, because the local governments are not members of the Metropolitan Council in the first place. Most council districts overlap municipal boundaries, so council members do not represent specific municipalities. Also, the council has its own property tax authority, so it is not dependent on local governments for financial contributions.

Finally, the Twin Cities model is distinctive for the incremental, legislative approach that was taken to reform.[58] This provides for corrective feedback. Each time the state legislature increased the council's powers, those powers were tested in practice. In cases where the new authority was not working out well or created conflicts with other governmental units, the problem could be brought back to the next legislative session for fine-tuning. For example, in 1973 the Metropolitan Council and the Metropolitan Transit Commission were deadlocked over the question of who had the authority to plan for future transit development and whether that future development should rely on rapid-rail or expanded bus service. The legislature responded to this conflict with the Metropolitan Reorganization Act of 1974, which clarified the council's authority over the Transit Commission for policy-making purposes.

The Twin Cities: Successes and Failures   The Metropolitan Council had some noteworthy accomplishments in its first decade of existence. It solved the sewage crisis and developed a regional approach to solid-waste disposal. It succeeded in requiring wealthy suburbs to include low- and moderate-income housing in development plans. It blocked the Airport Commission from building a second international airport and the Metropolitan Transit Commission from building a rapid-rail system. One of its greatest successes was to pass in 1971 the Fiscal Disparities Act, which created a system of tax sharing among local governments in the metropolis, including the central cities. It developed a regional parks system, floating bonds to raise money and then turning the money over to the counties to buy, develop, and operate the parks. The council passed a Development Framework Plan that regulated development in the seven-county region and attempted to establish an urban growth boundary to contain suburban sprawl. The council gained the power to approve local comprehensive plans, which had to conform to the Development Framework Plan passed by the council. The council also had to review developments of "metropolitan significance" to ensure that major new developments were consistent with the Development Framework Plan. The municipalities themselves retained zoning powers and implemented the Metropolitan Council's policies.[59]

In spite of these impressive accomplishments, by 1990 there was serious doubt about the future of the Metropolitan Council. Despite the Metropolitan Council's vaunted powers to control development, the council was for all practical purposes bypassed in making some of the most important development decisions of the past decade, including decisions that led to a successful domed stadium, a failed racetrack, the largest shopping center in the United States on the site of the old stadiums, and a new downtown basketball arena. It also came under severe criticism for its shortcomings in transit planning and in overseeing the scandal-ridden Metropolitan Waste Control Commission. Because of this, the Metropolitan Council's extensive powers over the metropolitan districts began to look less impressive than they did in the 1970s, when the council had forced the Transit Commission to back down on plans for a rapid-rail system and the Airports Commission to back down on its plans for a second airport. As the Metropolitan Council celebrated its 20th birthday in 1987, it was looking more and more like a stodgy, mature bureaucratic agency than like the dynamic policy-making body it had been for its first decade of existence.[60]

Why did the Metropolitan Council's position erode in the last two decades? Three factors seem to be responsible. First, the nature of local decision making changed. The leadership structure, whether called a power structure or a regime (see Chapter 7), that supported the creation of the Metropolitan Council and helped ensure its success has faded. Turnover in the legislature, a decline of business elites associated with economic restructuring, and the increasing ideological basis of party politics have created a more pluralistic decision-making system less supportive of or committed to the council. A second factor is the lack of an independent institutional basis to provide strong metropolitan leadership. The council itself is highly dependent on the governor, who appoints the members. The council and the individual members who serve on it lack a political base to act independently in the metropolis. A third factor is the change in the type of issues confronting the council. At the time of its creation, the council was confronting infrastructure issues. More and more, the council has recently had to face social-access or lifestyle issues, which are more controversial and divisive. At the same time, counties have been modernized and strengthened and have increasingly challenged the Metropolitan Council for primacy over issues.

In 1994, the state legislature made three changes that significantly altered the Metropolitan Council. First, the bifurcated model of separating policy making from implementation was abandoned. For the first time, the Metropolitan Council was given the power not only to plan but also to implement its own policies. The transit operations and waste control were transferred directly to the Metropolitan Council; the agencies that had been carrying out these operations were eliminated. Second, the position of regional administrator was created to ensure professional administration—giving the Metropolitan Council the equivalent of a city manager for the seven-county region. Finally, the governor was given the power to dismiss Metropolitan Council members in addition to the power to appoint them.[61]

Two factors led to these changes. First, in 1993, a transit crisis had developed that revealed weaknesses in the system. The Metropolitan Council was over the Regional Transit Board (RTB), which planned transit, and the Metropolitan Transit Commission (MTC), which operated the bus system. Administrative and political differences led to conflict over the desirability of light rail, over a breakdown in delivering transit services to the disabled under a contract with a new provider of the service, and over the MTC board firing an administrator for the MTC whom the governor supported. Under the 1994 changes, both the RTB and the MTC were eliminated and their powers given to the Metropolitan Council.[62]

Second, a state legislator, Myron Orfield, had proposed a series of laws that were intended to address the growing disparities between the central cities and the suburbs. Among his proposals were that the Metropolitan Council be directly elected, that suburbs be required to provide for low- and moderate-income housing, that the council be empowered to restrict sewer and highway extension to suburbs that did not provide for such housing, and that a housing reinvestment fund be established and financed by the taxes raised on the increment of value of houses over $150,000; this fund would be used to underwrite affordable housing. These bills were vetoed by the Republican governor. A separate bill to create an elected Metropolitan Council failed by only a few votes in the House and Senate.[63] Although these bills did not pass, the debate and discussion that they provoked contributed to the passage of the other reforms. It appears that "a new metropolitan leadership regime might be emerging" that strengthens and nurtures the Metropolitan Council.[64] The newspapers, municipalities, and even some suburban Republican legislators supported the reforms, including some variation of Orfield's proposals. Representative Orfield has promoted building coalitions between central cities and suburbs as essential to the future of cities.[65]

The Metropolitan Council faces "three overriding challenges: the need to position the region to compete effectively in the changing global economy, the need to alleviate the growing central-city/suburban disparities that are seen to threaten the region's quality of life, and the need to gain better control over suburban sprawl."[66] Whether the Metropolitan Council can fill this role in the years to come remains to be seen. The fact that the council is so dependent on the governor is both a strength and a weakness. If the governor is interested in metropolitan issues, there is a ready vehicle for carrying out innovation. Likewise, the governor is a powerful ally for the Metropolitan Council. But if the governor is not interested in these issues, the council may languish. The more probable scenario is that the council will act as a state agency—in which case it is unlikely to meet the challenges it faces, because these require political risk taking.

Although the Twin Cities has created a truly distinctive model of metropolitan governance, it is important to remember that it still is not a true *metropolitan government* and consequently has important weaknesses in dealing with that area's metropolitan problems. The Minneapolis–St. Paul Metropolitan Council approach also illustrates that regional governance or government can be provided administratively by state government as opposed to an elected local government.

Portland: Uniting Metropolitan Planning with Service Delivery

In 1978, voters in the three-county Portland, Oregon, metropolitan area approved a metropolitan governing structure that has most of the powers of the Twin Cities Metropolitan Council and some others as well.[67] The Columbia Region Association of Governments (Portland's COG) and the Metropolitan Service District (a special district responsible for the zoo and for some other areawide functions, including solid waste) were combined into a single agency to be known as the Metropolitan Service District. The new Metropolitan Service District was given responsibility for areawide land planning, federal A-95 review, and direct provision of a limited number of services: sewage treatment, disposal of liquid and solid waste, public transit, the zoo, and drainage and flood control. The Metropolitan Service District also is empowered to assume authority at some future date over a number of other functions if that seems feasible. These functions were transit, sports facilities, criminal justice, open-space preservation, parks, water supply, and libraries. The Metropolitan Service District is governed by a seven-member board elected for four-year terms from single-member districts and an elected executive with veto power.

Like the Twin Cities model, the Portland model did not spring unexpectedly out of nowhere. The council of governments had existed for many years. In the early 1970s, a number of metropolitan services had been brought together under the Metropolitan Service District, making it one of the nation's few multifunctional metropolitan districts. In 1975, the National Academy of Public Administration began to study the possibility of forming a two-tier government in the region. Cooperating in the study was the 65-member Tri-County Local Government Commission, consisting of local officials and private citizens, who sent a two-tier proposal to the Oregon legislature in 1978. The legislature limited the new government's authority to the urbanized and urbanizing area of the three-county region and then submitted the proposal directly to voters in the three counties. They approved it by a margin of 55 to 45 percent. Ironically, the wording of the issue on the ballot ("Reorganize Metropolitan Service District, Abolish CRAG") led many voters to think that they were voting to abolish a metropolitan planning agency, not to create a more powerful one.[68]

As the new government began operating in 1979, it faced two major problems. First, it did not have a secure tax base, and Oregon at that moment was in the midst of a taxpayer revolt. To get a property tax levy, the Metropolitan Service District would need approval from the voters. Voters defeated such a proposal in 1980.[69] Metro has relied on fees generated from solid waste and zoo admission and on some other revenues. If voters approve, Metro can also levy a sales tax and income tax.[70] Its second problem concerned the thorny question of solid-waste disposal. The region did not have much suitable landfill space left for disposing of solid waste, and most communities did not want any more landfills in their own backyards. Metro, as the Metropolitan Service District is called in Portland, set the landfill problem as its highest priority and came up with a workable solution. It also attained control over the geographic sprawl of the urban population. Metro still faces a serious funding problem, however. Until that problem is resolved, it is unlikely to expand its operations.[71]

The Portland experiment has some notable distinguishing features. First, unlike the Twin Cities model, the Portland model had always given its metropolitan government operating as well as policy-making responsibilities. The new government is also elective, which gives it a source of legitimacy that the Twin Cities Metropolitan Council lacks. Second, the Portland model, like the Twin Cities model, has used an incremental approach to reform. As we have noted, considerable groundwork had been laid for the new government throughout the 1970s. Although the 1978 creation was much more than a simple incremental step, the full achievement of the Metropolitan Service District's potential seems destined to follow an incremental pattern.

Arthur Nelson suggests that the key to Metro's success is that it has limited its activities "to functions for which there is a consensus on a regional role."[72] Although generally positive in his assessment of Metro, he believes it should not be considered a full two-tier (or three-tier) metropolitan government. In reality, its only functions are "management of the zoo and regional landfills. . . . It does not provide regional water, sewer, police, airport services, parks (other than the zoo), public housing, cable television, or any related 'service.' It does not run the transit system, although it provides transportation planning services."[73] Nelson believes a more accurate description of Metro is as

> an "umbrella" under which a variety of policy-related functions are performed, but all services in the usual sense are provided by local or regional single-purpose governments. The elected board of Metro has no power to control the behavior of local governments; its primary authority . . . is coordinating planning. In this respect, its greatest single influence is in transportation planning because, as the region's staff to JPACT [Joint Policy Advisory Committee on Transportation, the designated MPO], it influences the allocation of federal transportation funds. . . .
>
> As an umbrella, Metro brings together local and regional interests under one roof, from coordinating a variety of issues ranging from fair share housing allocations to UGB [Urban Growth Boundary] adjustments to appropriating of transportation funds to simply creating consensus for new regional initiatives. In recent years, such initiatives have included comprehensive light rail planning, efforts to seek voter approval of general obligation bonds to acquire the development rights from farmland outside the UGB to preserve such land for farming in perpetuity, and selecting the site (with considerable political aplomb) for the region's $65 million Oregon Convention Center.[74]

Portland Metro's weaknesses may also be its strength. Lacking a strong financial base and having only limited services to provide, Metro could not rely on extensive authority or power to accomplish goals. It was not a threat to other local governments, so it could become an honest broker and mediate between the suburbs and the city of Portland. In time, Metro may become a fuller general-purpose regional government. As Paul Lewis points out, in 1992 voters approved a home-rule charter for Metro that, among other things, gives it authority over "matters of metropolitan concern."[75] The mere establishment of the Metropolitan Service District is an extraordinary achievement but one that other metropolitan areas may copy. Although it is not actually a general-purpose government such as that in Dade County, Florida, it could evolve into one, and it has the advantages of being truly regional in coverage (extending over a three-county area) and of being directly elected.

Assessing New Regionalism

After several years of dormancy, scholarly and community interest in metropolitan government and governance have been growing in the last decade. While advocates of metropolitan government and public-choice proponents have been engaged in academic discourse about the supposed benefits of each school of thought, metropolitan communities have struggled to develop cooperative arrangements to provide public services in the fragmented metropolis. The debate over which theory is correct, although it is of academic interest, largely misses the real issues facing the communities. The fate of central cities and that of suburbs are linked. Research by Larry Ledebur and William Barnes at the National League of Cities and by Hank Savitch and his associates points to the interdependence of cities and suburbs. Metropolitan economic performance is related to strong cities and suburbs.[76] And there is evidence that many metropolitan regions are attempting to develop mechanisms and regional institutions that provide greater coordination among area governments to plan growth and development, establish more efficient and effective regional services, place expensive infrastructure (e.g., bridges, sewerage systems, transit), and devise regional strategies for economic development.[77]

Even if metropolitan government is desirable—and that is an open question—it has proved nearly impossible to establish. Thus it is necessary to consider whether metropolitan governance can occur even in the absence of metropolitan government. But here, we do not mean as a function of market processes in the same way as public-choice advocates. We mean metropolitan governance that is carefully constructed and deliberately designed to bring about greater coordination and integration of public services in the metropolis. As I. M. Barlow explains,

> Metropolitan governance involves the governing of a metropolitan area without formal government at the metropolitan level. Instead, reliance is placed on special-purpose bodies, the joint efforts of local governments, and arrangements between levels of government. There is considerable fragmentation, both functional and territorial, and it is only by means of an array of institutional arrangements among the various agencies and governments that co-ordination and integration can be achieved. Metropolitan governance, therefore, is a system of governing in which intergovernmental relations—in the broadest sense—play a major role.[78]

David Walker has described a number of approaches to achieving greater coordination in urban service delivery. These range from informal cooperation to councils of government to special districts, annexation, the reformed urban county, and the actual establishment of metropolitan government.[79] What distinguishes metropolitan governance without government from the public-choice school is "that it moves the focus from cooperation . . . to a broader consideration of whether the metropolitan area or region can be said to be governed (i.e., to act in purposive, goal-directed ways)."[80] Barlow provides a standard to evaluate whether regional cooperation can be a substitute for metropolitan government.

> For an effective system, however, the relationships need to be such that they generate area-wide coordination and integration, and they need to be overseen by an "umbrella" body that has the capacity to view matters from a metropolitan perspective and to act in the metropolitan interest.[81]

It would seem that the Twin City Metropolitan Council and the Portland Metro meet these conditions to some degree. However, COGs are more questionable, because members may withdraw and tend to have a limited capacity to view matters from a metropolitan perspective.

Conclusions: Change and Bias in the Planning and Review Functions

The metropolitan planning and the metropolitan review process that have evolved since the mid-1960s represent a small but significant change in the politics of metropolitan governance. They illustrate well the incremental nature of urban political change. They represent change because they are a marked departure from the status quo. However, they represent *incremental* change; they are not as drastic or as far-reaching as the city-county consolidations, the urban-county governments, and the two-tier metropolitan governments discussed in Chapter 9. Because few such metropolitan governments were actually created, and because those that were created resulted from extraordinary conditions, no drastic, far-reaching changes have been wrought.

With drastic change unlikely and with the consequences of the multicentered metropolis still uncertain, the most successful innovations for governing the metropolis have been the combination of metropolitan planning and policy making. In some metropolises, such as Minneapolis–St. Paul, the federal review process has been augmented by state-granted review powers. In most metropolises, these functions have been given to the COGs. This change is incremental because it does not go very far, but it leaves open the possibility that the COG will evolve into a stronger institution, as happened in Portland.

The incremental nature of the review process can best be seen in the distinction between systems maintenance issues and lifestyle issues. The metropolitan review power has worked best on the systems maintenance issues and, in most metropolises, has not been applied well to lifestyle or social-access issues. This is incremental change because (so far) it touches only one small increment of the sum total of issues of metropolitan politics. As Oliver Williams suggested, the major cleavage in metropolitan politics today seems to be occurring over the question of equal access to upper-middle-class lifestyles as exemplified in the few exclusive suburbs. The cleavages are basically related to race and class. The issues that provoke these cleavages are zoning, the expansion of low- and moderate-income housing into certain suburbs, busing to achieve racial balance in the public schools, and the elimination of fiscal disparities in the metropolis.

Even when the A-95 review process was available, regional councils of government did not use their authority to remove the class and racial biases of the multicentered metropolis. Theoretically, they could do this effectively. Given the stipulation of the Intergovernmental Cooperation Act of 1968 that federal grants be consistent with the objectives of metropolitan planning, there is no theoretical reason why the A-95 review agencies could not have used their planning and review power to remove the biases of the multicentered metropolis. They could have written into their metropolitan plans provisions for low- and moderate-income housing in the suburbs, for example, or provisions for coordinated land use zoning, and then used their review power to deny unrelated federal grants to those municipalities that refused to follow the plan's provisions. The agencies could also lobby before the state legislatures to make significant modifications in tax disparities in the metropolis and to equalize the financing of public education.

Metropolitan planning agencies *could* do these things. But it is obvious that most metropolitan planning agencies, especially the COGs, did not do them and are not doing them. Because of the limitations on COGs that we noted earlier, COGs are unlikely to reverse the biases of the multicentered metropolis, although they have demonstrated that they can deal effectively with some of the systems maintenance problems. What authority they might have exercised seems to have been diminished even further by the elimination of the A-95 review power.

Finally, the most striking aspect of contemporary metropolitan politics has been the role of the federal government. The 1960s and 1970s saw the emergence of the federal government as a force behind change. Legislation in those years transformed the federal government from a stimulator of both the multicentered metropolis and the expansion of functional fiefdoms into a promoter of metropolitan planning and coordination. It is primarily from actions by the federal courts and by some agencies of the executive branch that substantial progress has been made in dealing with systems maintenance issues.

This trend toward increasing involvement of the federal government in metropolitan affairs came under intense criticism in the 1980s. The Reagan administration sharply reduced federal funding for metropolitan problems and sought to reduce the federal government's domestic role. These issues will be discussed in Chapter 11. The ISTEA and later the TEA-21, along with the Clean Air Act, have demonstrated again how federal laws and policies can foster regionalism and metropolitan governance. However, elimination of the Advisory Commission on Intergovernmental Relations has removed the major center for the study of intergovernmental relations and the ablest advocate of a greater federal role in promoting more effective regional governance. During the Clinton administration (1992–2000), HUD partially filled the gap in that under Secretary Cisneros and later Secretary Andrew Cuomo, HUD became a strong advocate for metropolitan partnerships between central cities and suburbs. Under the Bush administration, HUD has dropped this emphasis and played a more diminished role.

SUMMARY

1. Compared with traditional metropolitan reformers, new regionalists focus less on structure and more on regional problems. They call for adopting policies to counter sprawl and ameliorate its attendant problems, including traffic congestion, environmental degradation, and lack of affordable housing in the suburbs. They favor improved governance arrangements to ensure regional cooperation and coordination in metropolitan policy making but do not assume that market processes or voluntary cooperation will be sufficient to attain metropolitan governance.

2. Oliver Williams has posited a "lifestyle model" of metropolitan reform. According to this theory, the systems maintenance functions of government are sometimes turned over to metropolitan authorities, but in the absence of outside intervention, the lifestyle functions that control social access to upper-middle-class lifestyles are performed by local-level governments.

3. Metropolitan planning efforts date to the mid-1960s, when the federal government began to make planning grants available and also began to require a metropolitan plan in order for a region to be eligible for certain types of federal aid. To date, metropolitan planning has had limited effectiveness.

4. Because of the availability of federal funding and because of the federal (A-95) review required for federal grants, councils of government began to spread rapidly during the 1970s. Although COGs do perform planning and review functions, they have several inherent weaknesses, especially in dealing with lifestyle issues. Because local governments are represented in a COG, those local governments can paralyze the COG by threatening to withdraw or to withhold their voluntary financial assessments.

5. During the 1970s, two promising innovations for metropolitan policy making emerged in Minnesota and Oregon. The Minnesota model initially stressed the separation of policy-making authority from the actual administration of service delivery; this separation was eliminated in 1994. The Oregon model combined the planning and policy-making functions of COGs with the actual administration of service delivery.

6. The instruments of incremental change (metropolitan planning, COGs, and A-95 review) have a number of biases. They have not addressed the lifestyle issues of metropolitan politics nearly as well as the systems maintenance issues. They also may be biased in favor of the value systems of professional administrators rather than the value systems of traditional local-government politicians.

NOTES

1. H. V. Savitch and David Collins, "Ties That Bind: Central Cities, Suburbs, and the New Metropolitan Region," *Economic Development Quarterly* 7, no. 4 (November 1993): 341–359; William Barnes and Larry Ledebur, *The New Regional Economies* (Thousand Oaks, Calif.: Sage, 1998).
2. H. V. Savitch and Ronald K. Vogel, "Paths to the New Regionalism," *State and Local Government Review* 32, no. 3 (Fall 2000): 158–168.
3. Alan Altshuler, William Morrill, Harold Wolman, and Faith Mitchell, eds., *Governance and Opportunity in Metropolitan America* (Washington, D.C.: National Academy Press, 1999).
4. Oliver P. Williams, *Metropolitan Political Analysis* (New York: Free Press, 1971), p. 93.
5. This was noted in Chapter 9. For Miami, see Edward Sofen, *The Miami Metropolitan Experiment* (Bloomington: Indiana University Press, 1963). For Toronto, see Frank Smallwood, *Toronto: The Problems of Metropolitan Unity* (Toronto: Bureau of Municipal Research, 1963).
6. H. Paul Friesema, "Cities, Suburbs, and Short-Lived Models of Metropolitan Politics," in *The Urbanization of the Suburbs,* vol. 7, *Urban Affairs Annual Reviews,* ed. Louis H. Masotti and Jeffrey K. Hadden (Beverly Hills, Calif.: Sage, 1973), p. 242.
7. See Christopher B. Leinberger and Charles Lockwood, "How Business Is Reshaping America," *Atlantic* (October 1986): 43–57; Joel Garreau, *Edge City* (New York: Anchor Books).
8. For background on the New York Regional Plan of 1929 see Mel Scott, *American City Planning Since 1890* (Berkeley, University of California Press ,1969), pp. 260–265, 447–448.
9. For background on the evolution of the A-95 process, see Advisory Commission on Intergovernmental Relations, *Report A-42: Substate Regionalism and the Federal System,* vol. I, *Regional Decision Making: New Strategies for Substate Districts* (Washington, D.C.: U.S. Government Printing Office, 1973), pp. 140–166.
10. David C. Ranney, *Planning and Politics in the Metropolis* (Columbus, Ohio: Merrill, 1969), p. 104.
11. John Friedmann, "The Future of Comprehensive Urban Planning: A Critique," *Public Administration Review* 31, no. 3 (May–June 1971): 317.
12. Edward C. Banfield, "The Uses and Limitations of Metropolitan Planning in Massachusetts," in *Taming Megalopolis: How to Manage an Urbanized World,* vol. II, ed. H. Wentworth Eldredge (Garden City, N.Y.: Doubleday, 1967), pp. 712–714.
13. This charge was made of the Cleveland COG by Frances Frisken, "The Metropolis and the Central City: Can One Government Unite Them?" *Urban Affairs Quarterly* 8, no. 3 (June 1973): 395–422.

14. Rabinovitz, *City Politics and Planning,* p. 7.

15. Ranney, *Planning and Politics in the Metropolis,* pp. 104–107.

16. For an excellent discussion of citizen involvement in freeway controversies, see Alan Lupo, Frank Colcord, and Edmund P. Fowler, *Rites of Way: The Politics of Transportation in Boston and the U.S. City* (Boston: Little, Brown, 1971).

17. There are many excellent descriptions of the battles over urban renewal and urban renovation. One of the most readable, interesting descriptions of a resident's frustrations in fighting the destruction of the old Hull House neighborhood in Chicago unfolds in Studs Terkel's interview with Florence Scala in Studs Terkel, *Division Street: America* (New York: Avon, 1967), pp. 29–38. The battle over the expansion of the University of Chicago into the Hyde Park–Kenwood section is analyzed by Peter H. Rossi and Robert A. Dentler in *The Politics of Urban Renewal: The Chicago Findings* (New York: Free Press, 1961).

18. Thomas M. Scott, "Suburban Governmental Structures," in *The Urbanization of the Suburbs,* vol. 7, *Urban Affairs Annual Reviews,* ed. Louis H. Masotti and Jeffrey K. Hadden (Beverly Hills, Calif.: Sage, 1973), p. 236.

19. See Paul Davidoff, "Advocacy and Pluralism in Planning," *Journal of the American Institute of Planners* 31, no. 4 (November 1965): 331–338.

20. On highways, see Lupo, Colcord, and Fowler, *Rites of Way;* on urban renewal, see Jewell Bellush and Murray Hausknecht, eds., *Urban Renewal: People, Politics and Planning* (Garden City, N.Y.: Doubleday, 1969).

21. Thad L. Beyle and George T. Lathrop, eds., *Planning and Politics: Uneasy Partnership* (New York: Odyssey Press, 1970), p. 9.

22. Herbert Gans, *People and Plans: Essays on Urban Problems and Solutions* (New York: Basic Books, 1968), pp. 72–74.

23. See Alan S. Kravitz, "Mandarinism: Planning as Handmaiden to Conservative Politics," in *Planning and Politics: Uneasy Partnership,* ed. Beyle and Lathrop, pp. 240–267. See also Robert Goodman, *After the Planners* (New York: Simon & Schuster, 1971), pp. 171–175.

24. John W. Dyckman, "Social Planning in the American Democracy," in *Urban Planning in Transition,* ed. Ernest Erber (New York: Grossman, 1970), pp. 27–44, especially p. 28.

25. Michael L. Vasu, *Politics and Planning* (Chapel Hill: University of North Carolina Press, 1979), p. 175.

26. This account of the Washington Metropolitan Council of Governments is taken from Roscoe C. Martin, *Metropolis in Transition* (Washington, D.C.: U.S. Housing and Home Finance Agency, 1964), pp. 39–50.

27. Jeffrey Henig, David Brunori, and Mark Ebert, "Washington, D.C.: Cautious and Constrained Cooperation," in *Regional Politics: America in a Post-City Age,* ed. H. V. Savitch and Ronald K. Vogel (Thousand Oaks, Calif.: Sage, 1996), pp. 101–129.

28. Melvin B. Mogulof, *Governing Metropolitan Areas* (Washington, D.C.: Urban Institute, 1971), p. 1.

29. David B. Walker, "Snow White and the 17 Dwarfs: From Metro Cooperation to Governance," *National Civic Review* 76, no. 1 (January–February 1987): 14–27.

30. Royce Hanson, *Metropolitan Councils of Government,* report for the Advisory Commission on Intergovernmental Relations (Washington, D.C.: U.S. Government Printing Office, 1966), p. 27.

31. Alan Edward Bent, *Escape from Anarchy: A Strategy for Urban Survival* (Memphis, Tenn.: Memphis State University Press, 1972), p. 85.

32. Victor Jones, "Bay Area Regionalism: Institutions, Processes, and Programs," in Advisory Commission on Intergovernmental Relations, *Report A-41: Substate Regionalism and the Federal System, Regional Governance: Promise and Performance* (Washington, D.C.: U.S. Government Printing Office, 1973), pp. 75–110.

33. See Frisken, "The Metropolis and the Central City," pp. 395–422.

34. Philip W. Barnes, *Metropolitan Coalitions: A Study of Councils of Government in Texas* (Austin: Institute of Public Affairs, University of Texas, 1969), p. 67.

35. Joseph F. Zimmerman, "Can Governmental Functions Be 'Rationally Reassigned'?" *National Civic Review* 73, no. 3 (March 1983): 125–131.

36. Demonstration Cities and Metropolitan Development Act of 1966, sec. 204. Quoted in Barnes, *Metropolitan Coalitions,* p. 14. However, the Intergovernmental Cooperation Act of 1968 did grant review authority for social issues.

37. Frisken, "The Metropolis and the Central City," p. 399.

38. Walker, "Snow White and the 17 Dwarfs," pp. 14–27.

39. *Intergovernmental Perspectives* 10, no. 2 (Spring 1984): 4.

40. Edward Weiner, "Urban Transportation," in *Handbook of Research on Urban Politics and Policy in the United States,* ed. Ronald K. Vogel (Westport, Conn.: Greenwood Press).

41. Robert J. Dilger, "ISTEA: A New Direction for Transportation Policy," *Publius* 22 (Summer 1992): 67–78.

42. Henig, Brunori, and Ebert, "Washington D.C.: Cautious and Constrained Cooperation," in *Regional Politics,* ed. Savitch and Vogel, p. 111.

43. Alan Saltzstein, "Los Angeles: Politics Without Governance," in *Regional Politics,* ed. Savitch and Vogel, pp. 51–71.

44. Ibid., pp. 59–60.

45. Ibid., p. 60.

46. Ibid., p. 64.

47. Ibid., pp. 64–65.

48. Ibid., pp. 65–67.

49. Ibid., p. 70.

50. Bruce McDowell, "Reinventing Surface Transportation: New Intergovernmetal Challenges," *Intergovernmental Perspective* 18 (Winter 1992): 6–8, 18.

51. Robert Gage and Bruce McDowell, "ISTEA and the Role of MPOs in the New Transportation Environment: A Midterm Assessment," *Publius* 25 (Summer 1995): 133–154.

52. Ronald K. Vogel and Norman Nezelkewicz, "Metropolitan Planning Organizations and the New Regionalism: The Case of Louisville," *Publius: The Journal of Federalism* 32:1 (Winter 2002), pp. 107–129; H. V. Savitch, "Report 3: Ohio River Bridges Project: Sprawl and Urban Disinvestment" (Louisville; Ky.: Savitch and Vogel Consultants, 2002).

53. See John J. Harrigan and William C. Johnson, *Governing the Twin Cities Region: The Metropolitan Council in Comparative Perspective* (Minneapolis: University of Minnesota Press, 1978), pp. 39–64.

54. Ibid., p. 61.

55. Mogulof, *Governing Metropolitan Areas,* p. 82.

56. Stanley Baldinger, *Planning and Governing the Metropolis: The Twin Cities Experience* (New York: Praeger, 1971), pp. 120–124.

57. See Daniel J. Elazar, *American Federalism: A View from the States* (New York: Crowell, 1966), pp. 89–97. Elazar describes three political cultures in America. The individualistic culture has a utilitarian concept of government that prefers a minimal amount of governmental intervention in what are considered private, individual matters. The traditionalistic political culture is ambivalent toward governmental intervention in the private sphere and looks on officeholding as the perquisite of the social and economic elites. The moralistic political culture has no ambivalence about governmental intervention in the private sphere and believes that governments have a responsibility to act for the public good rather than the private.

58. See "Innovation by Increments: The Twin Cities as a Case Study in Metropolitan Reform," *Western Political Quarterly* 31, no. 2 (June 1978): 206–218.

59. John J. Harrigan, "Minneapolis–St. Paul: Structuring Metropolitan Government," in *Regional Politics,* ed. Savitch and Vogel, pp. 215–217.

60. See William C. Johnson and John J. Harrigan, "Political Stress and Metropolitan Governance: The Twin Cities Experience," *State and Local Government Review* 19, no. 3 (Fall 1987): 108–113.

61. Harrigan, "Minneapolis–St. Paul: Structuring Metropolitan Government," pp. 225–227.

62. Ibid., pp. 223–224.

63. Ibid., p. 225.

64. Ibid., p. 226.

65. Myron Orfield, *Metro Politics: A Regional Agenda for Community and Stability* (Washington, D.C.: The Brookings Institution and The Lincoln Land Institute, 1997).

66. Harrigan, "Minneapolis–St. Paul: Structuring Metropolitan Government," p. 206.

67. This account relies heavily on Anthony G. White, "Portland Merges Regional Agencies," *National Civic Review* 67, no. 7 (July 1978): 329; *New York Times,* March 22, 1979, p. A-16; and Carl Abbott, *Portland: Planning, Politics, and Growth in a Twentieth-Century City* (Lincoln: University of Nebraska Press, 1983), pp. 254–263; Arthur Nelson, "Portland: The Metropolitan Umbrella" in *Regional Politics,* ed. Savitch and Vogel, pp. 253–271.

68. Abbott, *Portland,* p. 262.

69. Ibid., p. 263
70. Nelson, "Portland," p. 254.
71. Interview with Portland Metropolitan Service District executive director Rick Gustafson at Portland, Ore., March 4, 1983.
72. Nelson, "Portland," p. 263.
73. Ibid., p. 266.
74. Ibid., pp. 267–268.
75. Paul G. Lewis, *Shaping Suburbia: How Political Institutions Organize Urban Development* (Pittsburgh: University of Pittsburgh Press, 1996), p. 191.
76. Larry Ledebur and William Barnes, "All in It Together: Cities, Suburbs and Local Economic Regions," (Washington, D.C.: National League of Cities, 1993); H. V Savitch, David Colins, and Dan Saunders, "Ties That Bind," pp. 341–357.
77. Neal Peirce, Curtis Johnson, and John Stuart Hall, *Citistates: How Urban America Can Prosper in a Competitive World* (Washington, D.C.: Seven Locks Press, 1993); Donald Rothblatt and Andrew Sancton, eds., *Metropolitan Governance: American/Canadian Intergovernmental Perspectives* (Berkeley: University of California Institute of Governmental Studies Press, 1993).
78. I. M. Barlow, *Metropolitan Government* (New York: Routledge, 1991), p. 294.
79. Walker, "Snow White and the 17 Dwarfs," pp. 14–27.
80. Ronald K. Vogel, "Metropolitan Government," in *Handbook of Research on Urban Politics and Policy in the United States,* ed. Ronald K. Vogel (Westport, Conn.: Greenwood Press, 1997), p. 189.
81. Barlow, *Metropolitan Government* p. 295.

PART FIVE

TOWARD AN URBAN POLICY

The federal government has had a marked effect on urban and metropolitan politics. However, that effect has changed dramatically from one presidential administration to the next. The overall impact of these changes has left the nation with a wide array of federal programs that impinge on the nation's cities but that are run independently of one another.

Because of this wide array of federal programs, it is often argued that a national urban policy is needed to tie the hundreds of separate urban programs into coherent operations that will focus on common objectives and rejuvenate urban America. In Chapter 11, we review the changing federal role in urban affairs. In Chapter 12, we speculate on the political changes that will probably shape metropolitan America in the twenty-first century.

CHAPTER 11

NATIONAL URBAN POLICY

CHAPTER SYNOPSIS

Evolution of the Federal Role in Urban Policy: *Grants-in-Aid System; Changes in the Federal Role*
• Impact of Presidents: *LBJ and the Expansion of the Federal Role; Nixon—the Effort to Reduce the Federal Role (New Federalism I); Carter—Failed Efforts to Shape a Coherent National Urban Policy; Reagan and the Conservative Approach: Contracting the Federal Role and "Abandoning" the Cities (New Federalism II); Clinton and the Neo-Liberal Approach: National Urban Policy on a Tight Budget; George W. Bush and Compassionate Conservatism: "Tough Love"* • Efforts to Shape a National Urban Policy: *Lack of a Coherent Agenda; Obstacles to Policy Making; Targeting People Versus Places; Content of National Urban Policy; Implementing Urban Policy* • Bias of Federal Involvement: *Lack of Responsiveness Toward Poor; Inability to Equalize Social Access to Middle-Class Lifestyle; Encourages Sprawl; Diminishes Accountability of Urban Governments; Idiosyncratic and Uncoordinated Intervention*

Dating from the 1930s, the intervention of the federal government in urban affairs is a relatively recent occurrence. Urban renewal and urban freeway systems resulted directly from federal activity. Urban welfare programs, criminal justice programs, and health care programs are heavily financed by the federal government. So extensive has the federal involvement become, and so far-reaching have been the changes in the nature of its involvement, that the changing federal role in urban affairs requires some detailed explanation.

Six broad changes can be seen in the evolution of the federal role:

- First was the invention of the grant-in-aid as a device for urban problem solving. This device saw its greatest expansion in the 1930s and the 1960s.
- Second were the grand designs of the Lyndon Johnson presidency: the waging of the War on Poverty and the creation of the Great Society that extended the New Deal legacy.
- Third were the Nixon administration proposals of revenue sharing and grant consolidation, as well as the attempts to reorient federal domestic programs away from the big-city Democratic officials favored under Johnson's Great Society and toward more Republican-oriented officials in suburbs, small towns, and state governments.
- Fourth was the attempt of the Carter administration to articulate a coherent national urban policy that could guide the hundreds of specific programs the federal government promotes in urban areas.

331

- Fifth were the efforts of the Reagan and Bush administrations to reduce the federal urban role through initiatives such as New Federalism, budget reductions, and regulatory cutbacks.
- Sixth were Clinton administration policies attempting to fuse traditional liberal targeted aid to poor neighborhoods in big cities with more conservative market-oriented strategies and welfare reform.

Although each presidency has contributed something new to the evolution of the federal urban role, these contributions did not always disappear as their sponsors left the White House. On the contrary, each change has been accompanied by the development of permanent constituencies that benefit from the new agencies and programs. These institutions, programs, and constituencies thus become a permanent feature of the urban political landscape. At the onset of George W. Bush's presidency, there was some indication that we might move in a seventh direction of "compassionate conservatism." However, the events of September 11, concerns over "homeland" security, and the Iraq War have trumped urban policy. Although Hurricane Katrina and the flooding of New Orleans momentarily returned America's attention to the unfinished urban agenda on race, poverty, and the plight of cities, this now seems to have faded from national attention.

Grants-in-Aid and the Federal Approach to Urban Problem Solving

Prior to the 1930s, there was very little involvement of the federal government in urban affairs or even in domestic affairs generally. The prevailing philosophy was *dual federalism,* the idea that the state and federal governments had separate realms of responsibilities.[1] Schools, public health, urban infrastructure, crime, and social welfare were primarily state responsibilities, and the federal government was not expected to take any initiatives in these policy areas.

This expectation ended with the Great Depression of the 1930s, however. With unemployment rates reaching 25 percent, banks failing left and right, and millions of middle-class families thrown into poverty, people clamored for federal action to cope with the economic catastrophe. Under the New Deal leadership of President Franklin D. Roosevelt, the federal government responded with a wide variety of initiatives ranging from greater regulation of the economy to the subsidizing of programs such as welfare that could be run by the states. For urban America, the most important federal initiative was the dramatic expansion of grants-in-aid as a mechanism to channel federal funds through the states into domestic programs.

Grants-in-Aid

A *grant-in-aid* is simply a federal payment to a state or local government to perform some specified activity. The state or local government usually must match a certain percentage of the federal funds and must adhere to program guidelines established by the federal government. Until 1930, there were only about ten such programs.

During the Great Depression of the 1930s, the number of grants-in-aid grew steadily.[2] They were used to finance highway construction, public works, public assistance, public housing, airport construction, hospital construction, vocational education, and many other projects. During the 1960s and 1970s, there was a greater emphasis than earlier on designing grant-in-aid programs to accomplish nationally defined objectives rather than to help state governments accomplish state objectives. Federal grants increased for social programs and environmental protection. Consequently, the number of grants-in-aid proliferated from 132 in 1960 to a high of 534 in 1981.

Grants-in-aid can be distinguished in terms of the narrowness or broadness of the purpose for which funds are granted. *Categorical grants* are specified for narrowly defined purposes, and they give recipient governments little discretion in spending the funds they receive. A *block grant* provides greater discretion in a functional area, such as education, and leaves it up to recipients to decide on exact allocations to specific programs. A third type of grant, *general revenue sharing* (GRS), was initiated in 1972 and gave local governments broad discretion to use their GRS funds in any way they wished, so long as it did not violate the law. Revenue sharing was aimed at providing fiscal aid, with few restrictions, to state and local governments. The state share was dropped in 1980. In 1987, the entire program was abolished as part of the Reagan budget cuts. Table 11.1 reports federal grants from 1980 to 2005. The amount of money transferred is more than $425 billion and helps support just about any activity a state or local government might undertake.

In addition to being classified according to the flexibility they give to local governments, grants-in-aid can also be distinguished in terms of how much discretion the federal granting agency has to deny grants to applicants that fail to meet the agency's specifications. If the federal agency has no discretion but must allot its funds to states or communities in accordance with a rigid formula established by Congress, then that grant is a *formula grant*. If the federal agency has lots of discretion to deny or award the grant, then that grant is called a *project grant*.

Evaluating Grants-in-Aid

The grant-in-aid system has been a controversial tool for involving the federal government in domestic problems, and federal grants have attracted as much criticism as praise. How well has the system of grants-in-aid worked in coping with America's urban and domestic problems? Not nearly as badly as its critics assert, but not as well as its advocates claim. We can evaluate grants-in-aid by comparing their positive effects with their negative ones.

The Positive Impact of Federal Programs   The federal grants-in-aid programs have had at least five positive features. First, these programs have stimulated the states and municipalities to address urban problems and spend considerable money on them. Second, the federal programs have provided some badly needed services. As Michael Reagan has pointed out, "To say that grants-in-aid funds account for over 20 percent of state-local revenues is to say that those governments would do one-fifth less for their citizens without federal aid."[3] Third, the multitude of federal programs have created a multitude of ways in which local governments could tie into federal funding, which is very

TABLE 11.1 Federal Aid to State and Local Governments—Selected Programs: 1980 to 2005

[In millions of dollars (91,385 represents $91,385,000,000). For year ending September 30. Includes trust funds.]

Program	1980	1990	1995	2000	2002	2003	2004	2005 est.
Grant-in-aid shared revenue[1]..............	91,385	135,325	224,991	284,659	351,550	387,386	406,330	425,793
Energy..	499	461	492	433	528	589	608	608
Natural resources and environment.......	5,368	3,745	4,148	4,595	5,085	5,593	6,009	6,121
Environmental Protection Agency[2].....	4,603	2,874	2,912	3,490	3,588	3,917	4,018	3,691
Agriculture......................................	569	1,285	780	724	750	800	995	981
Transportation....................................	13,022	19,174	25,787	32,222	40,998	41,029	41,471	43,870
Grants for airports[2].......................	590	1,220	1,826	1,624	2,860	2,681	2,958	3,041
Federal-aid highways[3]....................	9,208	14,171	19,475	24,711	29,833	29,960	29,791	31,457
Urban mass transportation[2]............	3,129	3,730	4,353	5,262	7,462	7,448	7,777	8,283
Community and regional development.......	6,486	4,965	7,230	8,685	10,501	15,082	12,604	14,941
Rural community advance program.......	325	139	333	479	740	800	797	792
Homeland security.............................	380	1,184	1,772	2,439	3,456	7,861	5,490	7,929
Community development fund.............	3,902	2,818	4,383	4,965	5,429	5,569	5,388	5,378
Education, training, employment, social services....................................	21,862	23,359	34,125	42,125	44,827	51,543	54,201	58,104
Education for the disadvantaged[4].......	3,370	4,437	6,785	8,511	9,211	11,204	12,417	14,524
School improvement programs[4].........	523	1,080	1,288	2,394	3,401	5,964	6,542	6,636
Vocational and adult education...........	854	1,287	1,449	1,448	1,742	1,908	1,909	1,963
Special education.............................	810	1,485	2,938	4,696	6,730	8,216	9,465	9,884
Social services-block grant................	2,763	2,749	2,797	1,827	1,780	1,740	1,762	1,764

(Continued)

TABLE 11.1 Federal Aid to State and Local Governments—Selected Programs: 1980 to 2005 (*Continued*)

Program	1980	1990	1995	2000	2002	2003	2004	2005 est.
Children and family services programs........	1,548	2,618	4,463	5,843	7,749	8,161	8,326	8,519
Training and employment services..............	6,191	3,042	3,620	2,967	4,206	4,291	3,883	3,372
Health............	15,758	43,890	93,587	124,843	158,677	173,814	189,883	203,253
Substance abuse, and mental health services[4]	679	1,241	2,444	1,931	2,193	2,171	2,241	2,297
Grants to states for medicald[4]..................	13,967	41,103	89,070	117,921	147,650	160,805	176,231	188,497
State children's health Insurance fund[4].......	(NA)	(NA)	(NA)	1,220	3,682	4,355	4,607	5,343
Income security............	18,495	35,189	55,122	63,200	81,508	86,476	85,983	89,317
Food stamp program[4]	412	2,130	2,740	3,508	3,949	4,162	4,204	4,410
Child nutrition program[4]	3,388	4,871	7,387	9,060	10,100	10,664	11,035	11,990
Temporary assistance for needy families[4].......	(NA)	(NA)	(NA)	15,464	18,749	19,352	17,725	18,099
Veterans benefits and services[4]	90	134	253	434	360	403	454	505
Administration of Justice............	529	574	1,222	5,120	5,826	4,498	5,084	3,641

NA Not available.

[1]Includes items not shown separately.

[2]Grants includes trust funds.

[3]Trust funds.

[4]Includes grants for payments to Individuals.

Source: U.S. Office of Management and Budget, *Historical Tables, Budget of the United States Government*, annual.

Reproduced from U.S. Census Bureau, Statistical Abstract of the United States: 2006, p. 275. http://www.census.gov/prod/2005pubs/06statab/stlocgov.pdf.

consistent with the fragmented nature of metropolitan governance. Michael Danielson has characterized this as a "system in which the many pathways to the national capital attract numerous metropolitan actors, each motivated by a different perspective of the urban landscape and none representing the metropolis as a whole."[4] It could be argued that the fragmented nature of the grants-in-aid program made federal aid more accessible than it would have been if it had all been centralized and coordinated.

Fourth, the federal urban programs have served as a stimulus to the local economy.[5] Urban renewal, highway construction, and housing programs have provided a great many jobs and have resulted in the investment of billions of dollars in local economies. Finally, and most important, grants-in-aid programs have enabled the federal government to deal with national problems. Problems of urban poverty, public welfare, urban transportation, and public housing are widely recognized as national problems, not local problems. Without the grants-in-aid programs, these problems would not be dealt with nationally. Each state or locality would have to cope with its portion of the problem on its own, isolated from other states and localities that are also trying to deal with their portions of the problem.

The Negative Impact of Federal Programs   Despite these positive contributions, the grants-in-aid approach to urban problem solving has been severely criticized. First, some federal programs have seriously aggravated the decline in central cities. The federally sponsored freeway systems and interstate highways led to the physical dispersion of shopping areas, which siphoned retail shoppers away from the central cities. Federal housing programs were supposed to eliminate slums, yet after a decade of New York's housing program, just as many people lived in slum housing as had lived there at the start. FHA/VA-insured home mortgages did provide a significant prop for the home mortgage system, but they also completely ignored community development. They stimulated growth in suburban areas that were already undergoing more growth than they could control. No attempt was made to set up a preferential condition for guaranteeing loans that would rank applicants according to community criteria rather than individual criteria. Such an approach would have forced local communities to establish criteria for land development and would have given local communities a strong incentive to support metropolitan planning.[6] Urban renewal programs were similarly implemented without any relation to metropolitan development planning.

Second, federal programs have led to extreme functional specialization. Third, and as a consequence of the first two negative impacts, federal programs have compounded the problems of accountability and control. Creating agencies that were semiautonomous and quasi-independent of mayors and elected local officials put the most important agencies for the physical development of a city beyond the reach of the local electorate.

Finally, the grants-in-aid have skewed state and local budgets into the areas determined by federal programs, and this has made it more difficult for state and local governments to address problems in areas not supported by grants-in-aid.[7] State and local officials complain about federal *mandates*. The independence of local governments has been restricted by federal or state governments mandating programs for local governments to implement without commensurate funding. These federal programs alone may add $50 to 100 billion to local spending without the money transferred to pay for them. Pietro Nivola of The Brookings Institution refers to this as the "shift and shaft" game played by national officials since they can claim they address problems without actually having to pay for them.[8]

Despite President Reagan's rhetoric about returning power to the states and communities, New Federalism did not bring about a decrease in federal mandates. During the 1980s, state or local governments were required by federal law among other things to remove asbestos hazards from local schools, raise the minimum drinking age from 18 to 21, implement stricter water pollution regulations, establish programs to protect workers against certain dangerous chemicals, and make reports on measures to protect more than 150 new endangered species.[9] A U.S. Conference of Mayors study estimated that 10 federal mandates cost cities $6.5 billion in 1993. President Clinton issued an executive order to reduce new unfunded mandates in 1993, and in 1995 the Unfunded Mandates Reform Act was passed. Although this law does not prohibit new mandates, it requires benefit/cost analysis for new regulations that impose an annual burden of $100 million or more on state and local governments. Agencies are also supposed to consult with state and local governments before the regulations are imposed.[10]

Not only does the federal government mandate programs, but so do the states. Most states, for example, require counties or cities to hire social workers to inspect and license day care providers, but the states do not supply the funds with which to hire these social workers or to pay for the other costs of implementing such an inspection and licensing program. When given a mandate such as this from the state, the local government must either raise local taxes or, if that is impossible, cut other programs in order to free up funds to run the mandated program. Because local governments may not cut programs mandated by the federal or state government, mandating has contributed to the declining autonomy of cities and other local governments.

The Evolution of Federal Urban Policy

Based largely, but not wholly, on the grants-in-aid approach to solving problems, the federal role in urban affairs has changed markedly from one presidential administration to the next. In the last half-century, the most significant changes took place during the Johnson years (mid-1960s) and the Reagan years (1980s).

Expansion of the Federal Role: Lyndon Johnson and the Great Society (1963–1968)

Of all the presidents, Lyndon Johnson had the most program-oriented approach to dealing with domestic problems. Challenging his fellow Americans to eradicate poverty and racial discrimination, Johnson called his presidency the Great Society and pushed through Congress a remarkable number of urban successes:

1. The creation of two cabinet-level departments to deal with urban problems. A number of transportation programs were brought together under the Department of Transportation (DOT). The Department of Housing and Urban Development (HUD) was created in 1965 to be the central agency for coordinating most federal urban programs.

2. The Elementary and Secondary Education Act of 1965. Not only did this act provide extensive funding for elementary and secondary education, but its Title I provision established the principle of compensatory education by earmarking funds for schools with large numbers of economically disadvantaged children.[11]

3. The Economic Opportunity Act of 1964. This act established the War on Poverty and the Office of Economic Opportunity (OEO). The OEO saw its purpose as creating experimental innovations that the established bureaucracies were too timid or too conservative to initiate. Its most controversial creation was the community action program (CAP), which sought to involve local citizens in the planning and implementation of programs designed to end their poverty.

4. The Fair Housing Act of 1968. This act outlawed discrimination in the sale or rental of housing.

5. Public Housing Legislation of 1968. This act called for six million publicly subsidized housing units by 1978. Unlike the 1949 housing act, the 1968 act was supported by appropriations.

6. Model Cities Act of 1966. This program sought to channel diverse federal programs into specific blighted neighborhoods and use these neighborhoods as models of what could be accomplished through careful planning and coordination of federal programs. This approach was highly imaginative, but it had some inherent defects that will be discussed later.

Through these massive programs, the Great Society significantly changed the relationship between the federal government and the urban centers. The Great Society broadened the federal urban involvement beyond the housing and urban renewal concerns that had dominated up to the 1960s.[12] The Great Society programs raised a whole series of issues, including participation of the poor in the planning and operation of programs, compensatory education, advocacy action in legal services and planning, equal opportunity in housing and employment, the role to be played by militant movements,[13] and a host of other social or human-related issues. This broadening of issues and programs forced the federal government to look seriously at coordinating all the programs it had unleashed. Under the Great Society, the grants-in-aid programs were designed for the first time to attain nationally defined objectives rather than state or locally defined objectives.[14]

As a result of Lyndon Johnson's Great Society programs, there was a dramatic expansion in the number of grants-in-aid from 132 in 1960 to nearly 400 when he left the White House in 1969. Grants-in-aid had contributed 12 percent of all state and local government revenue in 1960; by the end of Johnson's presidency, their contribution had grown to 23 percent.[15]

Despite this tremendous growth in federal programs during the 1960s and despite the magnitude of the expenditures involved, there was no consensus that these programs were improving the quality of life. And for the federal programs that operated in metropolitan areas, hardly a major program existed that was not under attack from one group or another. The federal grant programs themselves were accused of distorting the ability of states and localities to establish their own priorities.[16] The welfare programs were accused of breaking up families, destroying recipients' initiative, and condemning people to live their entire lives on permanent public welfare.[17] The urban renewal programs were accused of engaging in "Negro removal" and of destroying more housing than they replaced.[18] The Office of Economic Opportunity was accused by Nixon's urban advisor, Daniel Patrick Moynihan, of decimating the antipoverty program efforts through unthinking acceptance of the dogma of maximum feasible citizen participation.[19] The Model Cities programs were supposed to bring about a concerted interagency effort in target neighborhoods, but the funds were too few and were scattered over too many sites to have such an impact.[20] Even within the federal government, attempts to utilize federally owned land in key cities for the purpose of creating demonstration "new towns in town" were dismal failures.[21]

Not all of the federal programs were failures, of course, and many of the accusations were unfounded. There were also some startling success stories.[22] Legal-aid programs initiated procedures for using the courts to force changes in living conditions in urban slums. Community action programs trained a generation of African American youths in organizing techniques and pressure tactics. Head Start programs provided stimulating learning experiences for small children. Day care centers were established for parents who wished to work or needed to work.

But all these efforts did not eradicate poverty, rejuvenate the cities, or even provide a single city as a stunning success story that other cities could emulate. And when the moderately conservative Nixon came to the White House in 1969, he was influenced by his urban affairs adviser, Daniel Patrick Moynihan, who asserted, "Too many programs have produced too few results."[23]

Richard Nixon and the First New Federalism (1968–1974)

These criticisms of the Great Society fell on receptive ears when Richard M. Nixon moved into the White House in 1969. As a conservative, Nixon had no philosophical attachment to the many programs that proliferated during the Great Society years. Nor did he have any political motivation to support programs that primarily benefited big-city, lower-income, and racial minority constituencies. None of these constituencies had given Nixon a majority of their vote in 1968. Perhaps even more important was his philosophical commitment, as a conservative, to reverse the growth of federal power relative to that of the states. Nixon said in 1972,

> Do we want to turn more power over to bureaucrats in Washington in the hope that they will do what is best for all the people? Or do we want to return more power to the people and to the state and local governments so that people can decide what is best for themselves? It is time that good, decent people stopped letting themselves be bulldozed by anybody who presumes to be the self-righteous moral judge of our society. In the next four years, as in the past four, I will continue to direct the flow of power away from Washington and back to the people.[24]

Nixon sought to put this philosophy into practice through an ambitious attempt to curb the powers of the domestic-policy bureaucracies of the federal government and to strengthen the powers of state governments vis-à-vis the federal government. These efforts were expected to have a conservative impact, because the state governments were viewed as more conservative than the federal bureaucracies. Calling this effort the *New Federalism,* Nixon proposed to (1) establish a general revenue-sharing plan and (2) consolidate about a fifth of the categorical grant programs into six (later reduced to four) huge block grants.

General Revenue Sharing   Revenue sharing was enacted in 1972 to turn $5 billion in federal revenues over to state and local governments to use as they saw fit, with none of the strings that were attached to categorical grants or block grants. The state share was eliminated in 1980, and the entire program was abolished in 1987 as part of the Reagan administration's efforts to cut domestic spending. The revenue-sharing idea had first surfaced during the Kennedy administration but died for lack of political support. There were many arguments both for and against revenue sharing.* What appealed to Nixon was the hope that general revenue sharing would strengthen state and local governments and make it easier for them to perform needed urban services without having to rely on the initiative of federal grants-in-aid. For this reason, general revenue sharing fit neatly into Nixon's New Federalism plans to increase the authority of state governments while decreasing that of the federal government.

The Nixon Block Grants   A second key element of the New Federalism was the consolidation of several categorical grant programs into a few huge block grants. Nixon originally proposed in 1971 that Congress consolidate 129 categorical grant programs into 6 large block grants, which he called special revenue sharing. When Congress failed to do that, Nixon, in 1973, reduced the proposal from 6 special revenue-sharing packages to 4 (education, community development, law enforcement, and employment) that would consolidate only 70 categorical grants. So long as a state or locality spent its funds in the appropriate area, few restrictions were placed on how the funds were spent. From the conservative point of view, this had the advantage of allowing each state and locality to decide its own priorities for itself.

Before Congress could act on these proposals, Nixon in 1973 began unilaterally dismantling some of the programs that were subject to being phased out, and he impounded funds for some of the others. Because of these premature acts, Nixon ran into enormous congressional opposition. Instead of passing the special revenue-sharing programs, Congress passed two significant block grant consolidations in the fields of employment and community development.

The Community Development Block Grant   For urban redevelopment, the most important outcome of Nixon's New Federalism was the *community development block grant* (CDBG) program established by the 1974 Housing and Community Development Act.

---

*The arguments in favor of revenue sharing included the unreliability of some categorical grants, the tendency of categorical grants to become hard and narrow, and the hope that revenue sharing would make the states more viable fiscally. There were several major arguments against revenue sharing. The unit that spends the tax money should also raise the tax money. The availability of many categorical grant programs gives the local government many options from which it can choose. State governments are too inadequate, and in many cases too corrupt, to be trusted with the funds and discretion they would receive through revenue sharing. The notion that the states are laboratories for governmental innovation has been overworked. The states in actuality are no closer to the people than is the federal government. Particularly for racial minorities, the federal government has been more responsive than the state governments. Revenue sharing might mean less funds going to urban and metropolitan problems. Finally, in Michael Reagan's words, revenue sharing "moves us back to the level of separate state political cultures (and to the extent that the pass through is required, even to the level of separate local political cultures) as the context-setting environment in which public expenditure decisions will be made." Reagan, in *The New Federalism* (New York: Oxford University Press, 1972), summarizes the case for revenue sharing (pp. 92–101) and the case against revenue sharing (pp. 102–132); the quotation is from pp. 126–127.

This act consolidated seven urban categorical grants, including urban renewal and model cities, into a single block grant of $2.8 billion per year. The program has been renewed in succeeding years and continues to exist, although its funding was reduced in the Reagan–Bush administrations and more recently cut by one-fourth under Bush II.

Under the CDBG program, cities may use their block grant funds for a wide variety of purposes ranging from code enforcement to economic development projects. To get its funds, a community submits a community development plan that identifies its development needs and outlines a three-year program to meet those needs. Eighty percent of the CD funds were reserved for metropolitan areas. Under a complicated formula, each community of over 50,000 was automatically entitled to a specific sum. A "hold harmless" provision was inserted to protect big cities from receiving less than the annual average they had received under the consolidated programs over the preceding five years. Careful analysis of the first round of community development expenditures, however, showed that they redistributed federal money away from heavily Democratic big cities to more Republican-oriented suburbs and small cities. Of the 487 metropolitan communities entitled to receive CD funds, 204 got less money from CD funds than they had received under their old consolidated categorical grants. Of these 204 communities, 181 were central cities. Most of the communities that gained under the CD program were suburbs. Skokie, Illinois, for example, an affluent suburb of Chicago with virtually no racial minorities or people below the poverty line, had received nothing under the old categorical grants but received nearly half a million dollars during the first year of CD block grants.[25]

When the program was renewed in 1977, Congress rewrote the distribution formula to target a greater share of CDBG funds to distressed central cities. Over time, however, these attempts to target CDBGs failed, and as the 1980s wore on, distressed cities' share of CDBG funds declined.[26]

Although the community development program did create a cash loss to big cities, it had the positive feature of enabling them to recapture control over city redevelopment from the local public agencies (LPAs) that had dominated urban renewal. CD funds went directly to the city governments rather than to the LPAs and LHAs, as had occurred under the urban renewal and public housing programs. These agencies thus became more closely controlled by the mayors and city councils than they had been. They also were made more responsive to city residents. In order to get its CD funds, each city had to provide for citizen participation in planning CD expenditures. The quality of citizen participation has varied greatly, but there is little doubt that the CDBG program helped decentralize power in urban redevelopment away from Washington, away from the old urban renewal and public-housing functional fiefdoms, and toward locally elected executives and councils.[27]

The Carter Urban Policy: 1977–1980

More than any other president, Jimmy Carter sought to tie the melange of federal domestic programs together into a coherent urban policy that would target federal initiatives more effectively on the problems of big cities.[28] He appointed the cabinet-level Urban and Regional Policy Group, which spent a year studying federal urban programs. In March 1978, it gave him a list of 70 options on action to take on existing federal urban programs.

After making some modifications, Carter ended up approving a document that called for the "New Partnership" of the federal government, state governments, city governments, and private industry to cope with city problems. This New Partnership suggested the following remedies:

1. A national urban development bank that would channel investment funds into urban development projects.
2. Increased fiscal relief to help fiscally distressed cities.
3. An urban impact analysis that would force all federal agencies to delay domestic spending projects until it could be determined that they would not have an adverse impact on cities.
4. A renewed emphasis on economic revitalization of cities.[29]

If Lyndon Johnson's urban approach was characterized by providing social services directly to the poor, Carter's was characterized by stimulating corporations to invest in central cities, thus increasing job opportunities there and improving their economies. This economic revitalization would be achieved largely through tax credits, interest rate subsidies, and other incentives to get businesses to create jobs in cities and high-unemployment areas. Many of these incentives were to be administered by the National Development Bank, which would have the authority to provide more than $8 billion in loan guarantees to businesses and another $3.8 billion in interest rate subsidies.

In practice, Carter achieved very little of this modest program. Urban impact analysis was initiated by his presidential order, but observers cast doubt on whether it accomplished anything,[30] and it was rescinded by his successor, Ronald Reagan. The most significant, lasting achievement was the Urban Development Action Grant (UDAG) program, which permitted HUD to make project grants for economic development programs. Many cities used UDAG grants as seed money to clear blighted areas and entice corporations to locate factories, office buildings, and other developments on the sites. Through 1985, UDAG had disbursed $4 billion to nearly 2,700 projects in 2,200 cities.[31]

Reagan–Bush and the Return of New Federalism (1981–1992)

President Ronald Reagan's approach to urban policy was in essence embodied in the New Federalism he proposed. Reagan strongly believed that the best antidote to urban problems lay in a healthy national economy and that urban development projects were best left to market forces and the private sector rather than being directed by government programs such as UDAG, which had been so popular under the Carter administration. In this president's view, government development programs did not encourage the expansion of business; they merely shifted it from one location to another.[32] Rather than relocating jobs to depressed areas where huge numbers of unemployed people lived, Reagan preferred to let the people relocate to the places where jobs existed. Reagan's first budget director, David Stockman, was especially critical of urban development programs such as UDAG because "they encouraged companies to invest in high-cost and economically inefficient areas."[33] Although these ideas have considerable intuitive appeal, they rest on the dubious assumption that governments can do nothing to reverse the economic decline of faltering regions. But the experience of the Tennessee Valley Authority in the

1930s and 1940s as a major stimulant to economic growth in the Tennessee River region is evidence that governments can indeed stimulate declining regions if they have the will to do so.[34]

Urban Changes Under Reagan   The Reagan administration's views on urban policy were best synthesized, perhaps, by the 1982 *National Urban Policy Report*. This report argued for the need to "restore balance in our federal system of government"[35] by reducing federal authority over the states. It expressed doubt about the effectiveness of many previous urban programs, urged a reduction in federal urban funding, and called for increased reliance on the private sector to improve urban conditions.[36]

Consistent with his faith in the private-market economy as the solution to urban problems, Reagan's only urban program initiative focused on helping the private sector. This was his proposal for *urban enterprise zones*. As this plan was originally conceived, the Department of Housing and Urban Development would be allowed to designate up to 25 urban neighborhoods a year to qualify as enterprise zones. Any business firm that opened up in the qualifying zone would be eligible for special tax concessions from the local, state, and federal governments. Reagan also proposed reducing the minimum wage for the enterprise zones and relaxing federal regulations on environmental protection and on occupational safety and health.[37] With these concessions, businesses could be expected to move into the affected neighborhoods and create jobs for the residents.

Half of the states passed enterprise zone legislation. A national version of the plan was passed by Congress following the Los Angeles riot in 1992, only to be vetoed by President Bush because a provision of the bill raised taxes, something the president had promised not to do. Some critics noted that Puerto Rico had "a 35-year history as an 'enterprise zone.' Low wages and low taxation led to an economic boom in the 1950s and 1960s. But since 1970, disinvestment and stagnation had become the rule and in the 1990s in Puerto Rico, 30 percent of the population was unemployed."[38] As the centerpiece for national urban policy, enterprise zones have a fundamental conceptual flaw. If they do succeed in raising living standards within the enterprise zone, this will be accompanied by higher wages and eventually higher taxes. At that point, the corporations involved are likely to pack up their investments and move to some other low-wage, low-tax area.[39] In this respect, a national policy of enterprise zones would reinforce the disinvestment practices of corporations that seek to move to low-cost areas and, in the long run, would make it harder to raise living standards overall.

In addition to the urban enterprise zones, Reagan's urban approach also consisted of the various elements of his New Federalism. Like his Republican predecessor Richard Nixon, Reagan sought to reduce federal authority over state and local government. He said,

> My administration is committed heart and soul to returning authority, responsibility and flexibility to state and local governments. . . . The next years promise to be among the most exciting in the history of our intergovernmental system, as state and local governments assume responsibilities that have been preempted by the Federal Government over the past several decades.[40]

Central to the New Federalism were Reagan's budget cuts for domestic social programs and his efforts to *devolve* federal responsibilities to the states. Combined, these initiatives reduced the amount of federal money available for urban-related programs. By pushing 9 new block grants through Congress, the president shifted much responsibility and administrative control for 54 previously categorical grant programs from the federal government to the state capitals. At the same time that he cut the budgets of federal urban programs, Reagan also sought to reduce the federal strings attached to them. In the Community Development Block Grant program, for example, he reduced the number of pages of federal regulations on how CDBG funds could be spent from 52 to 2.[41] In the UDAG program, Reagan not only reduced the budget by a third but also gave communities greater discretionary power to use the funds for economic development rather than for a balance between that and neighborhood preservation projects, as the rules had previously required.

Finally, in addition to urban enterprise zones and New Federalism, the third part of Reagan's federal urban policy consisted of sharp budget cutbacks in direct urban programs (such as UDAG) and social welfare services (such as AFDC) that go disproportionately to central-city residents. The impact of these cuts on cities was severe. A survey of all cities with populations over 25,000 in four Midwestern states (Illinois, Indiana, Michigan, and Wisconsin) in 1982 found that the federal budget reductions under Reagan had a significant negative impact on these cities' ability to provide all the services they had previously offered. Nineteen percent of the cities reported elimination of city services because of the federal cutbacks. One-third of the cities reduced the level of city services. Twenty-three percent reported laying off employees. And 29 percent reported having to increase taxes in order to make up for the federal cutbacks.[42]

When Reagan left the White House in 1989, his approach to urban America was in essence continued by his successor, George Bush. Less ideological than Reagan, Bush was able to reach agreements with Congress on rewriting the Clean Air Act and the Civil Rights Act. He appointed a dynamic secretary of HUD, Jack Kemp, a strong advocate of privatizing public housing and enterprise zones. But for most of his years in office, Bush showed very little interest in urban affairs or even in domestic policy generally. His major domestic proposal was a cut in the capital gains tax, which he argued would stimulate economic growth and put more people to work. He also proposed turning more federal authority over to the states by consolidating 12 urban-related categorical grants into a new block grant.[43] Neither of these proposals passed Congress. As we noted earlier, Bush vetoed the enterprise program. As a result, most of the urban legacy of the Reagan–Bush years resulted from Reagan's efforts in the early 1980s rather than from Bush's efforts in the 1990s.

Reagan's Urban Legacy   What has Reagan's urban approach meant for American cities? What legacy has he left?

There is no doubt that Reagan had a greater impact on cities than any president since Lyndon Johnson. As a result of his New Federalism, the federal role in urban affairs has shrunk. This shrinkage has given cities and states greater independence to run domestic programs with less interference from Washington than they have had since the 1960s. And toward the end of his presidency, Reagan pointed to this as one of his major achievements. In a speech to the nation's governors, Reagan said that he hoped

> history will record that [I] not only talked about the need to get the federal government off the backs of the states but that [I] did, in fact, fight the use of federal grant-in-aid dollars . . . and sought to return power and responsibility to the states, where they belong.[44]

The cities have, however, paid a very high price for their renewed independence from Washington.[45] A survey of municipal finance officers in 1989 found that 86 percent of them received fewer federal dollars than they had at the beginning of the decade, in 1980. More than a third of them reported eliminating some city services or laying off city employees as a result of the cuts in federal aid. And generally they found themselves turning to regressive revenue sources such as user fees and sales taxes to make up for the losses in aid.[46] The net effect of Reagan's new federalism can be seen in Figure 11.1. Federal aid to the largest cities dropped from about 14 percent at the start of the Reagan years to less than 5 percent by the end of Bush's term in office. However, in fairness, it must be acknowledged that federal aid had already begun a downward slide in the Carter years. The figure also highlights the continuing important but often overlooked role of state governments in providing aid to municipalities.

Judged on its own terms, the Reagan urban legacy is a failure. The Reagan theory had been to solve urban problems primarily through national economic growth. The economy did indeed grow steadily for seven consecutive years (1983–1989) without a recession. And during those years, economic conditions within central cities did indeed improve. Inflation rates dropped markedly, poverty rates marginally, and unemployment rates significantly. But barely a dent was made in underlying urban problems such as poverty, social disorganization, crime, poor schools, and economic disinvestment. By the end of the Reagan administration, the basic underlying conditions affecting these problem areas in most cities were as bad as they had been at the start of his administration—if not worse.

In the eyes of Reagan's stronger critics, the judgment is even harsher. New construction of public housing was brought to a virtual standstill by his administration's unwillingness to compromise with Congress on housing policy. Federal cutbacks in social services and welfare programs placed a bigger burden on city and county governments to care for impoverished people. The huge income tax cuts of 1982–1984 went primarily to upper- and upper-middle-income people, with a mere pittance to urban lower-middle-income

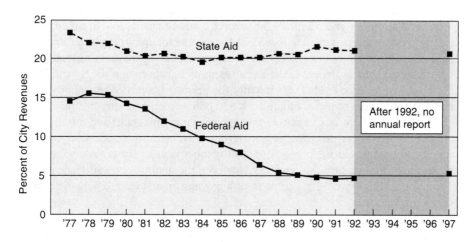

FIGURE 11.1   Trends in State and Federal Aid to Cities

Source: U.S. Bureau of the Census, *Government Finances: City Government Finances in (83–84 through 91–92), Finances of Municipal and Township Governments,* 1997. Courtesy of Michael Pagano, University of Illinois–Chicago.

people and the working poor. These tax and spending policies, as we saw earlier in Chapter 6, helped contribute to a long-term trend in which the national income is being redistributed away from the poor and toward the upper- and upper-middle-income groups. In the early years of Reagan's administration, city efforts to promote economic development were hampered by budget cuts in programs such as UDAG, CDBG, and the Economic Development Administration grant programs. Cities compensated for these cuts by increasing their reliance on tax incentives, especially IDRBs, to finance development projects and infrastructure rebuilding. But the Tax Reform Act of 1986 sharply limited the future use of IDRBs for development purposes.

In summary, Reagan's approach to urban policy was heavily marked by his own philosophical belief in laissez-faire: The best antidote to urban problems is economic growth. In fairness to Reagan's approach, it must be admitted that economic growth is indeed a precondition to solving urban problems. Without economic growth, there probably is no way to reduce urban poverty rates and unemployment rates. But the Reagan years show that economic growth by itself is not enough, for the eight years of Reagan's laissez-faire urban approach did nothing to tackle the underlying social problems that confront cities. Worse, the administration significantly reduced federal efforts to address those problems. As Demetrios Caraley reports, in an article entitled "Washington Abandons the Cities," between 1980 and 1990, urban grant programs to cities were cut by 46 percent, or $26 billion in constant 1990 dollars.[47] Revenue sharing and UDAGs, among other programs, were eliminated. Budget cuts of 57 percent decimated HUD, which was also embroiled in national scandals and corruption.[48]

Bill Clinton and a New Covenant with America's Communities

Contributing to George Bush's defeat was a serious economic recession. When Bill Clinton was elected to office in 1992, the mayors rejoiced. Although he came from a rural state (Arkansas) and presented himself as a new breed of Democrat who understood the limits of federal authority and resources, he favored a strong federal role in urban affairs. Once again mayors were invited to the White House. Clinton immediately demonstrated his concern for the plight of cities by appointing two popular mayors to cabinet positions: Frederico Peña of Denver to the Department of Transportation (DOT) and Henry Cisneros of San Antonio to HUD.*[49] Initially, the president appeared to embrace a U.S. Conference of Mayors proposal calling for a $30 billion economic stimulus plan to end the nation's recession through summer youth employment programs and infrastructure projects in the nation's cities. The bill was never passed because of concern over deficit reduction and the president's being distracted by other issues.† The economy recovered without the economic stimulus package. However, the nation's cities still faced severe problems, including skyrocketing crime rates, a growing urban underclass, homelessness, and inner-city decline.

---

*Secretary Cisneros stepped down at the end of Clinton's first term and was replaced by Andrew Cuomo, son of former Governor Mario Cuomo. Cisneros came under investigation for not disclosing, in his background check, personal payments he had made to a former mistress. This was undoubtedly a factor in his resignation.
†Immediately upon taking office, the president became embroiled in a debate over homosexuality in the armed forces that dominated the first few months of his presidency.

The Empowerment Zone Program—Cornerstone of Clinton's Urban Policy   President Clinton faced a dilemma. He favored a greater federal role in urban affairs but was hamstrung by the federal budget deficits and a political climate opposed to strong federal activism. His solution was the Empowerment Zone initiative passed by Congress in 1993.* On the one hand, this program embodied traditional liberal strategies to revitalize poor central-city neighborhoods through federal intervention to remake people and communities. On the other hand, the program embraced more conservative strategies to revitalize poor central-city neighborhoods through increasing economic opportunity by attaching *federal* enterprise zones (similar to Reagan and Bush proposals) and offering tax credits and incentives to increase private investment and business development. The program blends the liberal Great Society approach with the market-oriented approach of Reagan. The liberal strategy calls for directing capital into distressed communities by creating community development banks, improved services and infrastructure, social service assistance, and widespread grassroots participation to shape the redevelopment plans. The conservative strategy calls for reducing government regulation, promoting local entrepreneurialism, and emphasizing individual responsibility.[50]

Under the Empowerment Zone program, six cities were designated urban *empowerment zones* (EZs): Atlanta, Baltimore, Chicago, Detroit, New York, and Philadelphia/Camden. These six cities received grants of $100 million and were granted federal enterprise zones. Two cities (Los Angeles and Cleveland) were designated *supplemental empowerment zones* (SEZs) and received money from a different source, the Economic Development Initiative grant, for $125 million and $87 million. Another 64 cities were designated *enterprise communities* (ECs) and received $3 million. Some ECs (Oakland, Boston, Kansas City, and Houston) were also designated *enhanced enterprise communities* and were provided $22 million in addition to the $3 million provided to ECs. To obtain an EZ or EC grant, a city had to submit a strategic plan of how it would revitalize distressed neighborhoods. The strategic plan was to be a grassroots process not imposed by city government. To be eligible, the designated zone within a city with clear boundaries, and a majority of the population had to be below the poverty line. The zone could not include the central business district, nor could it exceed 20 square miles. The zones essentially targeted minority underclass neighborhoods. Each city had to develop a strategic planning process to allow local residents to determine the exact boundaries of the zone and the actual strategy for revitalizing the designated distressed community. The EZ/EC financing was provided through the Social Services Block Grant (SSBG) over a ten-year period.[51]

HUD promulgated a set of guidelines that outlined what had to be addressed in the plans. There were four main principles that were to underlie strategic plans:

- Creating economic opportunity for the EZ's residents
- Creating sustainable community development
- Building broad participation among community-based partners
- Describing a strategic vision for change in the community[52]

It was left up to communities to determine exactly what was proposed and what strategies were relied on. Communities could emphasize job training, job creation, crime control, creation of community development banks, business incubators, transportation

---

*This program was included in the Omnibus Budget Reconciliation Act of 1993 (OBRA 1993, P.L. 103-66).

systems to the suburbs, industrial parks, brownfield mitigation, or whatever other plans they could show would revitalize the affected neighborhoods. The exact process followed to determine plans and the content of the plans varied greatly among cities. HUD promised to allow communities great flexibility in how they used existing grant programs in pursuit of their strategic plans. Empowerment zones would become federal enterprise zones in addition to receiving their $100 million grants to implement their strategic plans. This would provide businesses relocating or expanding in the zones a $3,000 tax credit per employee, as well as additional tax benefits for capital investment and access to tax-exempt facility bond financing.[53] Designation as an EZ/EC also was supposed to result in greater priority in other federal grant programs. EZ and EC communities were encouraged to leverage funds through public-private partnerships.

The legislation establishing this program required continuous evaluation. Benchmarks and performance measures were required to monitor the progress of implementation. Cities had relatively short time spans to arrive at their strategic plans. The program guidelines were released in January 1994, and the strategic plans were to be submitted by June 1994. Some 290 communities applied for EZ/ECs.[54] Many more cities applied for EZs than could hope to receive them. It was almost a forgone conclusion which cities would get the EZs and there was much disappointment in cities that failed, receiving only $3 million after raising expectations in neighborhoods of $100 million. And even the $100 million is rather little federal assistance for completely turning around such distressed neighborhoods. Although the only significant new aid program, this amounts to as little as $200 per person per year over the 10-year period of the program. How much of this is new aid versus relabeled aid is also difficult to determine.

One concern raised by a General Accounting Office study was that the federal evaluation of this program was more oriented toward measuring program *outputs* to monitor implementation (e.g., number of loans provided by a community development bank, number of persons graduating from a job-training program) than toward measuring program *outcomes* (e.g., creating economic opportunity). In fact, according to the GAO,

> HUD officials agreed that the performance measures used in the EZ program were output-oriented and believed that these were appropriate in the short term. They believed that the desired outcomes of the EZ program are subject to actions that cannot be controlled by the entities involved in managing this program. In addition, the impact of the EZ program on desired outcomes cannot be isolated from the impact of other events. Consequently, HUD believed that defining outcomes for the EZ program was not feasible.[55]

Although HUD contracted for the evaluation studies of the EZ/EC program as required by Congress, its attitude as reported in the GAO study suggests that it was not particularly concerned with the results of the evaluation studies. This points to a fundamental difficulty in carrying out urban policy. If federal programs are so difficult to evaluate or if proponents are not committed to evaluation, how can we be sure when the programs are successful? On the other hand, if we insist on results within the first few years, it is unlikely that any program will be successful. And HUD's position realistically states the difficulties of identifying what factors account for community revitalization.

HUD did release, in 2002, an interim assessment report on five years of the empowerment zone/enterprise community program. According to HUD, "interim assessment findings were mixed." HUD pointed to "job growth" and an "improved business climate" across the EZ/EC sites. However, HUD acknowledged that "because there was a nation-wide economic upturn during the study period (1995–2000), it is difficult to attribute business growth and development exclusively to the EC/EZ initiative." Furthermore, only half of the businesses taking advantage of the tax incentives for locating in the six EZs saw the tax incentives as "important" or "somewhat important" in their location decisions.[56]

Aside from the EZ program, the Clinton administration pursued a number of *nonurban* policies that may have greater impact on urban revitalization and the plight of the poor in the cities than the formal urban policies that have been adopted. These include the failed national health care policy and the adopted crime bill and welfare reform bill.

Crime Bill of 1994   Fear of crime, especially violent crime in the cities, has been a major concern of citizens. As Susan Bennett points out,

> In 1994, 56 percent of respondents identified crime and violence as one of the country's two most serious problems. No other problem generated so much consensus. Although many factors contribute to this concern, a rising crime rate is certainly one (Flanagan and Maguire 1994: 152). From 1982 to 1992, the violent crime rate rose from 571.1 per 100,000 to 757.7 per 100,000. . . . Americans are more concerned, however, about changes in the kind of violence we are experiencing. Popular wisdom combines the crack explosion, youth gangs, assault weapons, and drive-by shootings in an image of urban violence. . . . At the same time, Americans doubt police capacity to protect them: 54 percent of respondents in a 1993 poll had either "not very much" confidence or no confidence in the police's ability to protect them from violent crime (Flanagan and Mcguire 1994: 165).[57]

The administration pushed two major crime bills. First, the Brady bill, passed by Congress in 1993, requires a waiting period of five days and a background check on those who would purchase a handgun. Second, the Violent Crime Control and Enforcement Act, often referred to as the crime bill, passed by Congress in 1994, imposes stricter punishments for violent crime, provides more prison funding, and (most important from the cities' standpoint) articulates a federal commitment to community-oriented policing, including a promise to put 100,000 new police on the streets of the nation's cities. The crime bill also banned 19 types of assault weapons.[58]

The professional model of policing found in most communities has been criticized as a reactive approach to policing that emphasizes responding to 911 calls. A new philosophy of policing (some would say a return to old-style policing), known as *community-oriented policing,* has been proposed to remedy this. It is based, at least in part, on the *broken windows* thesis advanced by James Q. Wilson.[59] Communities that permit *physical incivilities* or *social incivilities* are indicating a tolerance for crime and disorder. This leads to fear of crime and higher crime rates. Examples of physical incivilities include neighborhood physical decay and deterioration, such as broken windows and litter. Examples of social incivilities include disrespectful social interactions and inappropriate youth behavior (such as panhandling, drug use, or drinking on a street corner).[60] According to Susan Bennett,

> Three policies developed under the community policing umbrella: developing a partnership with communities and other agencies to handle problems; reestablishing the order maintenance role of police; and developing a proactive, problem solving approach to crime and quality-of-life problems. The expected benefits are extensive: improved job satisfaction among police officers, more effective use of police resources, improved police-community relations, empowerment of local communities, increased neighborhood viability, and reduction in fear of crime and [in] crime.[61]

Whether because of these policies or because of the improved economy, crime, especially violent crime, has peaked and is now plummeting in the nation's cities. Violent crime rates in the nation's largest cities jumped by 30 percent between 1985 and 1990. In San Diego, the increase was 72 percent. Violent crime rates dropped 40 percent in the nation's largest cities between 1990 and 2004. In a number of cities the drop exceeded 50 percent and in New York City it dropped 71 percent (see Figure 11.2). It is difficult to attribute these improvements directly to the crime policies of the Clinton

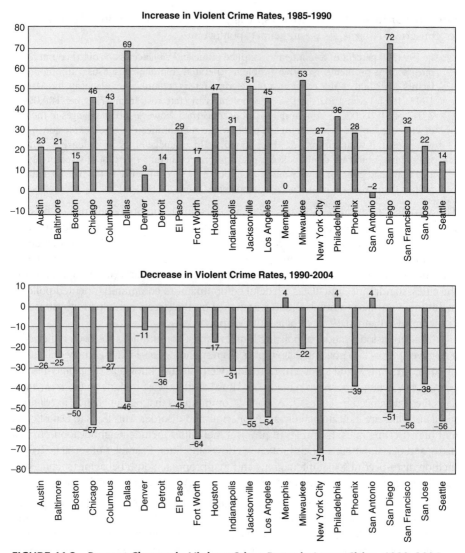

FIGURE 11.2   Percent Change in Violent Crime Rates in Large Cities, 1990–2004

Sources: FBI, Uniform Crime Reports, prepared by the National Archive of Criminal Justice Data Bureau of Justice Statistics–Data Online, http://www.ojp.usdoj.gov/bjs. Date of download: February 13, 2006.

administration, especially given that the declines began before the policies were instituted. On the other hand, community policing has proved popular and was adopted in many cities prior to the passage of the crime bills.[62] Other factors that may have played a role in the decline of violent crime in the big cities are increased incarceration rates, the aging of the baby boomers, the healthier economy, and the lessening of crack cocaine turf battles as drug markets stabilized in cities.

Welfare Reform   In 1996 the Republican Congress and Bill Clinton agreed on a new welfare program, Temporary Assistance to Needy Families (TANF), to replace Aid to Families with Dependent Children (AFDC).* As Sheila Zedlewski and Linda Giannarelli of the Urban Institute point out, this program differs in two significant ways from AFDC. First, under TANF, each state receives, for six years, a federal block grant equivalent to the amount it was receiving under AFDC prior to the change. AFDC was an entitlement program, which means that the federal and state governments had to fund whatever number of persons qualified for the program. Now the costs were fixed. If the number of poor seeking assistance were to increase, the states would have to shoulder the burden.

Second, the law is intended to "encourage work and discourage long-term welfare dependency."[63] States are free to design the welfare program as they see fit. They are constrained only by the amount of money available and by certain federal requirements, including a lifetime cap of five years on welfare and a requirement that welfare recipients work to receive benefits. As Zedlewski and Giannarelli point out, states that historically had higher AFDC funding will have more TANF funds and therefore more ability to finance innovative welfare programs. The federal government will continue to provide the $12 billion that it spent on AFDC in 1995, and for the first several years, states must maintain their $10 billion in expenditures.[64]

The ability of a state to meet the program requirements is closely related to the characteristics of its existing caseload and past AFDC generosity. The federal requirements were for 25 percent of the recipients to work in 1997 and 50 percent in 2002, excluding certain groups such as families with no adult. Twenty hours of work is required initially, to be increased to 30 hours. The more families on the welfare rolls that have no eligible adult, the easier it is for a state to meet federal work requirements, because these families are subtracted from the totals. States with higher numbers of these families without an eligible adult on welfare have fewer welfare recipients who must be moved into work to meet federal guidelines.[65] In addition, states that previously allowed welfare recipients to earn money may have an easier time, at least initially, in meeting work requirements; less than 10 percent of AFDC families had earnings in 1995. Later, however, these states will have problems with harder-to-place welfare recipients.[66]

In the short term, states did not face severe difficulties in meeting the requirements of the new law. Welfare rolls declined sharply in the first year of the program. For families, there was a 19 percent drop in welfare caseloads between August 1996 and September 1997. There was a 20 percent drop in the overall number of recipients in that time frame.[67] This provided states with a windfall, because they got to keep the funding level from prior years even though their caseloads were dropping. The caseloads have actually been dropping since January of 1993, which suggests that it was

---

*The Personal Responsibility and Work Opportunity Reconciliation Act of 1996.

not welfare reform but, rather, the improved economy that was the major factor in declining welfare rolls. The Department of Health and Human Services (HHS) points to a study by the Council of Economic Advisors on the factors underlying a drop in welfare rolls:

> According to the Council of Economic Advisors (CEA) analysis, over 40 percent of the reduction in the welfare rolls can be attributed to the strong economic growth during the Clinton Administration, nearly one-third can be attributed to waivers granted to states to test innovative strategies to move people from welfare to work, and the rest is attributed to other factors, which may include the Administration's expansion of the Earned Income Tax Credit, strengthened child support enforcement, and increased funding for child care.[68]

There is concern that remaining welfare recipients may be the most difficult to move into employment. In addition, transportation is a major hindrance to employing those on welfare, because the poor are concentrated in the cities and new job growth has been occurring in the suburbs. The Clinton administration proposed raising the minimum wage by at least $1 to $6.15 per hour, and there was discussion of the need for more child care aid and job training.[69] Underlying much of the concern about welfare reform is that moving people to work could cost more than the current welfare system. If states are reluctant to shoulder the additional burden, or are financially unable to do so, then what will happen to those forced off the welfare rolls? This population is heavily concentrated in central cities, so there is concern that the cities will have to absorb the added costs of caring for the poor who don't find work. When the economy was strong through the Clinton years, there was some optimism that welfare reform could work.

The economic slowdown in the first years of George W. Bush's presidency raised fears that welfare reform could have dire consequences for the cities in the future. TANF expired in 2002 and has been extended since then. According to the Department of Health and Human Services, caseloads continued to decline. In 2003, the number of individual recipients on TANF dropped 3 percent and the number of families declined by about 2 percent. However, there were some states with significant increases and decreases. For example, Arizona had a 13 percent increase in families on TANF and an 11 percent increase in individual recipients. Some states also had a large decrease. For example, Virginia saw a 70 percent drop in families and 62 percent decline in individual recipients.[70] Since TANF was adopted in 1996, the overall numbers of welfare recipients has declined by 60 percent for individuals and 54 percent for families.[71]

An Urban Institute report in 2005 reviews the nation's experience with welfare reform. The main findings with respect to welfare caseloads were that "more welfare recipients work while on welfare than in the past" going from about one-fifth in 1997 to one-third in 1999;[72] "employers are willing to hire welfare recipients,"[73] "many former welfare recipients work in low-wage jobs," paying "around $8.00 . . . above the $5.15 hourly federal minimum wage,"[74] and "about one-third of these workers have health insurance coverage through their jobs."[75]

The Urban Institute's ongoing research program in New Federalism focuses on case studies in 13 states. Drawing upon these cases, the report reviews the record of the states and finds they did focus on "work-first" with "job search and job-readiness activities" rather than "skills development and education."[76] The report found that states were flexible in administering the program so that recipients could still receive benefits while working. States also found that there were some recipients who were in need of greater attention such as those with "learning disabilities, mental or physical disabilities, substance abuse problems, and limited English language proficiency."[77] The report also found more nonprofit and workforce development organizations playing a greater role in welfare services.

Overall, the Urban Institute study says,

> information on how children fared in the years after welfare reform is consistent with a considerable body of evidence suggesting that children's outcomes were largely unchanged. Contrary to the fears of many, welfare reform, devolution, and an increase in parental work do not seem to have reduced children's well-being overall. More abused and neglected children have not entered the child welfare system, despite some predictions. At the same time, contrary to the hopes of others, aggregate improvements in parental earnings and reductions in child poverty have not—or not yet—consistently improved other outcomes for children.[78]

The years of the study do not reflect the recession years. So, it is still an open question whether the states will follow through on the commitment to fund welfare in hard times.

George W. Bush (2001–)

As a candidate, George W. Bush ran on a platform of *compassionate conservatism.* These ideas were shaped in part by Stephen Goldsmith, former mayor of Indianapolis. Goldsmith was noted for promoting privatization and infusing entrepreneurialism into city government. Under Goldsmith, city agencies had to bid for work against private businesses. Goldsmith also sought to involve community organizations and churches in revitalizing neighborhoods. These ideas meshed with those of candidate George W. Bush, and Goldsmith became a leading domestic advisor during the presidential campaign and following Bush's election.[79]

It is hard to pin down exactly what compassionate conservatism is. Its main thrust is to use the federal government to promote self-reliance. Myron Magnet, editor of *City Journal,* a policy journal published by the conservative think tank The Manhattan Institute, explains the philosophical base of compassionate conservatism as follows:

> Compassionate conservatism is above all an urban agenda. At its core is concern for the poor (who are concentrated in the cities) and an explicit belief that government has a responsibility for poor Americans. This is not a traditional Republican preoccupation. From Richard Nixon on down, the policy of Republican presidents toward the poor, especially the minority poor, has been, in Senator Moynihan's indelible phrase, benign neglect. Presidents Reagan and Bush similarly gave scant attention to poverty and urban issues. But in the 1990s, innovative big-city Republican mayors and urban-state governors have made solving these problems a top priority. Compassionate conservatism really is the effort to make these solutions central to national politics.
>
> If compassionate conservatism breaks out of the traditional Republican mold, it utterly rejects the liberal conventional wisdom about uplifting the poor that has reigned for over a generation. Compassionate conservatism, waving away the claim [that] liberal nostrums are the only possible expression of "compassion" for the poor, charges that liberal prescriptions, good intentions notwithstanding, have not only failed but have in fact

made the lot of the poor worse over the last 35 years. Why else, after decades of growing opportunity, are the worst-off more mired in dependency, illegitimacy, drug use, school failure, and crime than they were when the experiment began? How can this be, after decades of vigorous new job creation that has seamlessly integrated millions of low-skill immigrants into the mainstream economy, and after civil rights acts and a real cultural change have together opened the society to minorities as never before? A compassion whose main success is to make the self-styled compassionate feel good about their superior virtue is of limited value.[80]

Compassionate conservatives support workfare for welfare recipients. In addition, they would seek to "stop single women . . . from having babies in the first place by restigmatizing illegitimacy."[81] Under welfare reform passed in the Clinton era, 50 percent of welfare recipients are required to work. Bush proposed raising the number to 75 percent. Of course, liberals view this not as compassionate but merely as rhetoric that masks the harshness of conservative policies to make it more palatable to middle America.[82] Compassionate conservatism also embraces education reform. Deviating from traditional conservatism, which rejects a strong federal role that may eclipse state and local governments, the president called for the federal government to set standards for local education resulting in the adoption of *No Child Left Behind.*

In January 2001, President Bush created the White House Office of Faith-Based and Community Initiatives "to help the Federal Government coordinate a national effort to expand opportunities for faith-based and other community organizations and to strengthen their capacity to better meet social needs in America's communities."[83] However, the faith-based initiatives languished during the first year and were largely overtaken by the war against terrorism after September 11, 2001.

President Bush also succeeded in getting a major tax cut through Congress in June of 2001. This tax cut was intended to stimulate economic recovery and to reduce the burden on families. According to the Center on Budget and Policy Priorities (relying on Congressional Budget Office figures), the president's tax cuts, if made permanent, will reduce projected surpluses by almost $400 billion between 2003 and 2012. Moreover, the U.S. Treasury will lose $4 trillion from 2012 to 2022. The Center believes this money is needed to ensure the financial health of Social Security, Medicare, and Medicaid after the baby boomers retire. The Center believes this money may be "needed to ensure the solvency of the Trust Fund if deep Social Security benefit cuts are to be avoided." The Center also argues that the tax cuts favor those with higher incomes. The Center points to a Brookings study that found that the top 1 percent will receive 37 percent of the tax cuts.[84]

The most important long-term urban policy legacy of the George W. Bush administration will probably be related to the *War Against Terrorism.* A U.S. Conference of Mayors report projected that cities would spend $2.6 billion of their own resources to enhance local security between September 11 (2001) and December 2002.[85] Specific costs were associated with the following goals:

- Increase security and control access to city hall, police and fire facilities, schools, public utilities, water supply sources, and other public buildings and facilities through the addition of guards, gates, locks, access control systems, and surveillance equipment.
- Increase security at airports and port facilities.

- Increase security at public events.
- Improve communications within the city and with other jurisdictions.
- Enhance emergency operations centers and emergency management agencies, and create and/or activate special emergency response teams.
- Enhance hazmat response capabilities.
- Respond to reports of suspicious packages and mail.
- Train city staff in safe handling of mail.
- Provide better equipment to first responders.
- Expand training in responding to weapons of mass destruction and to nuclear, biological, and chemical threats.[86]

After the attacks on the World Trade Center and the Pentagon, President Bush created the Office of Homeland Security within the White House Executive Office. The president called for $3.5 billion to go to the nation's "'first responders'—our police, firefighters, and Emergency Medical Teams." Another $6 billion was requested to fight bioterrorism. Much of this money was intended for hospitals to bolster their ability to respond to attacks with biological agents such as anthrax or smallpox.[87] The assistance would come in the form of a block grant passed through the states. However, the mayors have called for the money to go directly to the cities. The mayors fear that the new war on terrorism has been waged at the expense of the prior war on crime, especially the Clinton crime bill, which supported putting more police officers on the street, promoted community policing strategies, and helped pay for technology to assist police departments in crime fighting. Bush sought to cut these funds by 80 percent, even while increasing funding for domestic security.[88]

Peter Eisinger found that costs to cities increased greatly immediately following the terrorism attacks. He reports:

> Because Congress did not appropriate any funds to help state or local governments defray the costs of these new responsibilities until March 2003, cities were reliant entirely on their own resources for nearly two years after September 11. None of this new activity came cheaply. Surveys conducted by the USCM estimate that cities had to spend $2.1 billion of their own funds in 2002 alone for first-responder overtime wages, new equipment, and additional personnel (U.S. Conference of Mayors 2002b). When the Department of Homeland Security raised the terror alert warning from yellow to orange as the war in Iraq began in March 2003, large and small cities all across the country increased their security spending by an estimated nationwide total of $70 million per week (U.S. Conference of Mayors 2003b). These expenditures came on top of existing homeland security outlays. One result of these added burdens is that 42% of the cities contacted in the summer 2002 NLC survey reported that they would be less able to meet their financial needs as a result of the additional security costs after September 11 (Baldassare and Hoene 2002).[89]

Whether the White House or the mayors prevail in the debate, domestic security concerns are clearly leading to an era of expanded funding for state and local government, with Washington playing an important role in both shaping priorities and providing money. However, the bulk of the work will have to be done by state and local governments. Moreover, the recession resulted in significant cuts in state aid to cities. A National League of Cities report finds that state aid dropped overall by 9 percent. However, some states cut aid more dramatically. Kansas reduced by 100 percent its aid to cities, California by 60 percent, and Texas by 47 percent.[90]

Kimberly Henrickson argues that the Bush administration has not been neglectful or hostile to cities as charged by critics. Rather, she argues Bush "has little to gain politically by putting forward an urban agenda." Instead, his policies emphasize "personal empowerment" rather than "urban renewal."[91] This would explain his recent $1 billion or 25 percent reduction in the Community Development Block Grant program, which the National League of Cities says "would be devastating to communities."[92] The U.S. Conference of Mayors call this "unwise and misguided."[93]

Can There Be a National Urban Policy?

Given the dramatic shifts in urban emphasis from one presidential administration to the next and the growing role of the states since 1980, it seems reasonable to ask what kind of urban policy role the federal government can in fact play. Are there any patterns to the successes and failures in the urban initiatives of Johnson, Nixon, Carter, Reagan, Bush, Clinton, and Bush (W.) that future presidents can learn from to improve their own prospects for success in the twenty-first century? Or would future presidents be better advised to concentrate on fields such as foreign policy, where their authority is less challenged, and stay out of the urban quagmire?

Some would rephrase the question from "*Can* there be a national urban policy?" to "*Should* there be a national urban policy?" The President's Commission for a National Agenda for the Eighties embarrassed Jimmy Carter when it said there was no need for a national comprehensive urban policy to help cities. Rather than assisting *places* that were experiencing deindustrialization, such as cities in the Northeast and Midwest, the commission recommended that federal aid help *individuals* move to growing areas with jobs. The Reagan administration later embraced this position, seeing the decline of some cities and the growth of others as market decisions. Rather than attempting to counter the market, the federal government took the view that it should respect market decisions.

Others favor nonurban policy over urban policy as a tactical decision rather than an ideological position:

> Some urbanists advocate a nonurban policy approach for pragmatic reasons (Kaplan 1995; Kaplan and James 1990). They argue that domestic programs targeted to people, rather than urban policies targeted to places have greater support among the public and ultimately benefit cities more than place-specific programs. Programs targeted at individuals (e.g., income support and job training) will reach inner-city residents without the programs being labeled urban policy. The argument is that the way to bring cities back into the mainstream is to promote policies that are aimed at individuals and universal.[94]

Simply put, there is not a large enough constituency to support urban programs, because most people now live in the suburbs. But many disagree with this position.

The Argument for a National Urban Policy

Although it might not be in the president's interest to get bogged down in the national infighting over urban policies, a national plan of action would certainly benefit cities and metropolitan areas. In sending more than $100 billion in grants-in-aid to communities of all sizes, the federal departments and agencies have become significant urban actors. Many observers feel that the federal government needs to articulate strongly a set of national urban policy goals and objectives to coordinate the formulation and implementation of all federal urban programs.[95] Programs deal with only specific aspects of the metropolis; without national goals, objectives, and priorities to tie the programs together, nothing provides overall guidance for all the federal urban programs. Consequently, the sheer magnitude of existing programs demands the articulation of national policy goals and objectives.

In addition to the need for guiding federal programs, there is a need for a national policy to address the dislocations created by imbalances in regional growth rates. During the early 1980s, for example, the industrial decline of the Midwest led to a significant migration of midwesterners to Texas, which was enjoying an oil boom. When the price of petroleum collapsed in the middle 1980s, Texas was suddenly faced with large numbers of displaced midwesterners who had lost their jobs in the Midwest and who now were losing their new jobs in Texas. The long-term migration of population to Texas and the rest of the Southwest over the past half-century also has other consequences that deserve to be addressed. Huge population buildups in desert and near-desert areas such as Phoenix, Las Vegas, and parts of southern California create ecological problems that they do not pose in other parts of the nation. As yet, the United States has no coherent urban policy that addresses these migration issues, the economic dislocations that precipitate them, and their consequences.

Finally and most important, a national urban policy is needed to come to grips with the widespread decay of central cities and the excessive concentration of poor people, especially poor racial minorities, in these cities.[96] These urban problems are national problems. The fundamental causes of urban problems are found in such unexciting statistics as the national ratio of births to deaths and national migration figures. Also, the number of people receiving welfare at any given time is very closely related to changes in the gross national product, and state and local governments acting individually can do very little to affect it. Nevertheless, they are left to cope with the problems that face most welfare recipients—the paucity of adequate housing, and the need for competent and often compensatory education, a variety of social services, and (in many instances) jobs. No given metropolis or state can hope to address the causal factors of these urban problems on its own. Only the national government can coordinate the efforts of states and municipalities so that they act in concert rather than in opposition to one another.

Why We Do Not Have an Urban Policy

Demonstrating the need for a national urban policy is much easier than creating one. Even formulating such a policy at the highest levels of government would not guarantee that it meant anything in practice, as the experience of the Carter administration clearly shows. The reason why it is so difficult to achieve a national urban policy is twofold, according to Peter Eisinger. First, political pluralism in the United States resulted in urban policy proposals under Nixon and Carter that were "great laundry lists of goals and programs that lacked internal coherence."[97] Each relevant interest group had its list of proposals, and many of these made it into the policy proposals of Nixon and Carter because of political pressures, regardless of whether the proposals interacted well together. Second, the commitment of the United States to the sanctity of the private sector has made it impossible to develop urban policy on the basis of principles of nationalized central planning, as is common in France, Great Britain, and much of western Europe.

Other obstacles to national urban policy include Americans' ambivalence toward urban areas, the declining influence of urban interests in Congress as a result of suburbanization, divergent and competing urban agendas (e.g., Sunbelt vs. Snowbelt), limited federal resources that preclude ambitious urban agendas, the incremental nature of the American political system, the complexity of urban problems (such as homelessness), and the weakness of HUD as a cabinet department with low prestige and weak capacity.[98] In fact, HUD was considered for possible elimination in 1994, and some believe that its demise would be more damaging for the "symbolic implications" than for the "functional implications."[99]

The Targeting Problem

No discussion of national urban policy can fail to note the problem of targeting federal aid to the regions and people that are supposed to benefit from the aid. No federal program illustrates the targeting problem better than the Model Cities program of 1966. For this reason it is worth discussing in some detail.

Model Cities as a Problem in Targeting   Shortly after assuming the presidency, Lyndon Johnson was advised by the Council of Economic Advisors chairman, Walter Heller, of a Kennedy administration proposal to completely rebuild blighted neighborhoods in a few cities on an experimental, demonstration basis.[100] All existing federal programs would be concentrated on those areas. They could be used as models of what concerted and coordinated federal action might accomplish by working in partnership with local government. Other cities would then institute similar programs to emulate the model. Johnson liked the idea but informed Heller that such a program would have to include more than just a few cities if it were ever to get through Congress. Johnson preferred something more grandiose. The presidential Metropolitan and Urban Affairs Task Force was formed and given responsibility for designing a Model Cities proposal. The task force criticized existing federal programs, including the Office of Economic Opportunity, for fragmenting logically related services. Included in the task force's final proposal was a suggestion that the federal government "adopt two or three large cities and in addition build a brand-new one in order to show what could be accomplished by well-conceived, large-scale, concerted effort."[101]

Although Johnson thought that this recommendation was too theoretical to send to Congress, he did approve the creation of a second task force in 1965 and charged it with making a practical proposal that could be implemented, and would show results, while he was still in office. The task force briefly considered the idea of concentrating all federal spending on just one demonstration city, but this approach was rejected because it would force Johnson's administration to choose between two of the most powerful Democratic supporters in the country: Mayor Richard Daley, who would propose Chicago, and labor leader Walter Reuther, who would propose Detroit. The task force also rejected a suggestion of five cities, because five cities would not attract enough members of Congress to vote for the bill. The task force report finally recommended that 66 demonstration cities be approved.

Cities would be invited to submit an application that would identify a neighborhood to be redeveloped by the demonstration cities treatment. The applicants would be judged on the quality of their plans for redeveloping the Model City area. Once the receiving cities were selected, two kinds of federal assistance would be available. First, the demonstration city neighborhoods would be eligible to receive all existing federal grants on a priority basis. Second, to make up any difference between what was available under existing programs and the costs of their demonstration cities experiment, they would receive supplemental grants on an 80:20 matching basis. That is, for every $80 of federal supplemental grants, the city government would have to provide $20. These supplemental grants would ensure cooperation of all the federal agencies. Because the locally approved demonstration cities program could get whatever supplemental grants it needed (at a cost of 20 percent), it would be in a good bargaining position to get other federal agencies to join in what promised to be a very glamorous program.

In 1966, 63 cities were chosen to participate in the first round of Model Cities grants. Although most grants went to big urban centers, a few were passed out to small towns in the home districts of key members of Congress. Smithfield, Tennessee, was an appropriate winning city; it was the hometown of the chairman of the House Appropriations Subcommittee that dealt with HUD's budget. Another appropriate winner was Pikesville, Kentucky, which was the hometown of another key subcommittee chairman. Montana, the home state of Senate Majority Leader Mike Mansfield, had two cities among the winners. And Maine, the home state of Senator Edmund Muskie, who had been the bill's floor leader, got three winners. To ensure that the program would not be blamed for political favoritism, Edward C. Banfield writes that "at least one large city represented in Congress by a Republican had to be on the list. Happily, one—Columbus, Ohio—was found."[102] The next year, another round of winners was chosen, more than doubling the total number of Model Cities to 150.

Early evaluations of the Model Cities programs suggested that they had enormous potential for accomplishing their goals for long-range planning, citizen participation, and coordination of federal programs.[103] However, Congress never appropriated the full amount of money authorized for Model Cities, and the amount of money actually spent never added up to the amount appropriated. Furthermore, the White House never lent its full prestige to the implementation of Model Cities. And the federal agencies in charge of the categorical grant programs were never as cooperative with the Model Cities planners as had been anticipated.[104]

In 1973 the Nixon administration impounded money that had been appropriated for Model Cities, thus bringing the program to a standstill, and the Housing and Community Development Act of 1974 consolidated Model Cities with six other urban grant programs into a large block grant for community development. This ended the Model Cities role as a coordinator of federal programs.

Other Targeting Problems   A critical defect of Model Cities was the inability of Congress to target federal funds where they could have a significant impact. That defect has also permeated several other federal domestic policy efforts. For example, a study of HUD and law enforcement grants to 20 medium-size cities found that instead of need, the most important factors in the selection of recipients were political and organizational. That is, the cities most adept at grantsmanship were likely to get the most grants.[105]

As Congress and the Nixon administration moved toward formula grants, revenue sharing, and block grants during the 1970s, federal urban aid was spread among so many different small communities that, as Paul R. Dommel criticized, "increasing amounts of this aid are coming under the influence of a new 'something for everyone' distribution politics."[106] The problem has persisted. An analysis of the Community Development Block Grant program discovered that despite congressional intent to target the money on communities suffering economic hardship, the number of communities eligible for the program grew from 590 in 1975 to 657 in 1980 and 814 in 1985. Between 1980 and 1985, the share of CDBG funds going to hardship communities declined, while the share going to well-off places increased. Detroit, one of the worst-off communities, saw its share of CDBG funds drop by 22.5 percent between 1980 and 1985, while well-off Hialeah, Florida, saw a 101 percent increase over the same period.[107] Federalism specialist David B. Walker commented wryly that Washington "couldn't target if it tried. It spreads the money around."[108]

The Content of a National Urban Policy

If a national urban policy were to be developed out of the current melange of urban programs, of what would it consist? Four particular issues are of the utmost importance.

Perhaps most important, a policy should be established on the distribution of future population growth and on interregional migrations. Although nobody really knows how many people can fit comfortably into the southern California megalopolis and into the other rapidly growing and water-short areas of the Southwest, southern California's shortfalls in water supply suggest that we may be approaching the limit under present technology. The federal government should discuss where the increased population should be housed and what kinds of realistic incentives can channel the interregional migrations into areas where they can best be accommodated.

Second, a national urban policy must confront the deterioration of the older central cities. Although hundreds of programs exist for these cities, many of them work at cross-purposes, and many still disrupt the governing capabilities of city governments. The federal government needs to decide what it wants for these urban centers, and the city governments need to define what they want for themselves. Unless broad policy goals and objectives can be formulated, and unless the means can be found to tie specific programs into these policy goals, federal involvement is likely to remain piecemeal and ad hoc.

Third, a national urban policy must demand that the federal government consistently confront the lifestyle issues of social access that we discussed in Chapter 10. Unless the gross inequities in the distribution of public goods and services in housing, jobs, and schools that characterize most metropolitan areas can be reduced, the nation probably cannot avoid the two-societies fate predicted by the Kerner Commission: "Our nation is moving toward two societies, one black, one white—separate and unequal."[109] Why should any parents who can afford the choice live in a neighborhood where their children must attend inferior schools and confront what they think is a relatively high probability of physical assault? And the answer, of course, is that very few people will live there if they can afford not to. For entirely rational reasons, they migrate into better neighborhoods where their children can have what they think are better and safer schools. And they strongly resist any efforts of local governments to make them share their advantages with the residents of less-advantaged neighborhoods. Continued federal pressure is thus an absolute must if the lifestyle issues are to be faced.

Fourth, a national urban policy must address the problems of suburban sprawl. Federally stimulated metropolitan planning has not done this. New-town proposals have not done it. Incalculably valuable natural resources of farmland, recreational space, open space, water supply, and natural beauty have been plowed under and paved over in the past 30 years. And over the next 20 years they will continue to be wasted unless federal incentives and priorities are established.

The four aspects of urban policy indicated here refer to *national* problems, not local problems. And the existence of national problems involving federal expenditures of more than $110 billion demands that national policies be articulated to guide the ways in which that money is spent.

The Process of a National Urban Policy

The implementing of national policies is just as important as their formulation, and it is apparent from earlier discussions that federal government programs have a mixed record of success in reaching their goals. Urban history in the 1960s and 1970s provides abundant examples of federal policies that failed to be implemented or were poorly implemented because the federal government did not have the means or the unity of purpose to carry them out. On the other hand, these same years also present abundant examples of federal initiatives that worked very well and accomplished their policy objectives. In order to assess whether the White House can fulfill its stated intentions of implementing a national urban policy, it would seem useful to try to distinguish between the kinds of policies that the federal government is currently capable of implementing and those that it is not. Some things it does well; other things it does poorly.

What the Feds Do Poorly   First there is the targeting problem. The federal government poorly implements policies that are adversely affected by traditional congressional logrolling. For example, the Model Cities program's prospects for success were seriously hampered from the beginning because its funds were spread among cities in so many congressional districts that no single Model City got enough funds to achieve its objectives. If the goal of Model Cities was in fact the creation of a demonstration project that all cities could emulate, then congressional logrolling hampered the attainment of that objective. Although the Clinton administration was more successful in concentrating resources on the six EZ cities, there is still concern that $100 million over ten years is not much of an investment even in those cities. Moreover, only $3.5 billion was set aside for direct EZ/EC expenditures for all the cities in the EZ/EC over a ten-year period. This is not a very large program in the overall national budget—or even in the budgets of recipient cities.

Second, coordination of federal policies has been a dismal failure. In the 1960s, the Office of Economic Opportunity was so far from being able to fulfill its legislative mandate to coordinate urban programs that it simply ignored the mandate and devoted itself to stimulating innovation and experimentation.[110] Model Cities was specifically created to coordinate federal programs at the neighborhood level, but its success at this was extremely limited.[111] The A-95 review process was devised to enable all federal grants to be coordinated at the metropolitan level, but the results were largely unencouraging, and A-95 was discontinued under the Reagan administration.[112] Federal regional councils were created as a coordinating device, but these too were largely ineffective,[113] and Reagan abolished them in 1983. The federal government has stimulated the creation of a plethora of metropolitan, substate, regional agencies whose goal is to plan and coordinate federal grant programs in water quality, criminal justice, health services, transportation, and land use. It is not clear how much effect all these coordinating agencies actually have on the delivery of services.

Third, the federal government has a spotty record of ensuring that federal funds are spent in compliance with federal guidelines. HUD in particular has not effectively overseen the use of credit provisions for new-town programs, the prohibition of discrimination in public housing, programs to stimulate home ownership among low-income families, or programs to stimulate urban rehabilitation.

What the Feds Do Well   In contrast to the foregoing activities, in which federal performance has been unsuccessful, there are many other federal activities in which the implementation process has worked very effectively. One example is transfer payments. *Transfer payments* are simply payments of cash from the federal treasury to individuals. They are called transfer payments because they in effect collect income taxes from some people and distribute (or transfer) those revenues to other people. The prime examples of transfer payments are Social Security and veterans' benefits. There may be disagreement about the adequacy of benefits or about whether Congress has attached too many obligations to the Social Security tax or about the general regressive nature of the Social Security tax, but once people qualify and register for Social Security benefits, the Social Security Administration accomplishes its objective of mailing checks to them with a minimum of disruption. Comparing the track records of the Social Security Administration and the Office of Economic Opportunity suggests that it is much easier to do an effective job of mailing checks to people badly in need of cash than it is to create programs that will help give those same people an effective voice in how their neighborhoods are run.

Second, the federal government operates some kinds of programs much better than others. Its most successful programs are characterized by (1) well-defined agency responsibilities, (2) tangible, measurable objectives, (3) adequate resources, and (4) the absence of strong opposition among interest groups or government agencies that could divert the program from its original intentions. The Apollo mission to land a man on the moon in the early, successful days of NASA clearly had these characteristics, but the antipoverty programs lacked them. In the Apollo program, NASA's responsibilities were clearly defined, the objective of placing a man on the moon was tangible and measurable, adequate resources were provided, and some of the most powerful interest groups in the country strongly supported the economic boost the program would give to the economy. In the federal antipoverty programs, a multitude of agencies had overlapping missions. The objectives were not tangible, and appropriations to meet them were inadequate. NASA was given much better control of the means to accomplish its program objectives than OEO or the related agencies were given to eliminate poverty.

Implications for Effective Policy

These statements comparing the things the federal government does well with those it does poorly are highly tentative. More systematic research is needed on the dynamics of implementing federal policies. If the foregoing analysis is valid, however, important implications follow for the success of national urban policies.

First, the coordination problem is horrendous. Nothing that has yet been tried has worked well. Under the Johnson administration, first the Office of Economic Opportunity and then the Department of Housing and Urban Development was named as the agency to coordinate all federal urban programs. The Nixon administration probably devoted more effort to coordinating and controlling urban policies than any other administration. Under Nixon, the Domestic Council was created to enable the White House to coordinate the formulation of domestic policies. The Domestic Council was to be chaired by the president, and membership consisted of the vice president and the heads of the major departments and agencies concerned with domestic affairs. To ensure that the policies formulated by the Domestic Council were actually carried out, the Office of Management and Budget was charged with evaluating the various domestic agencies in relation to the policies established by the Domestic Council. President Nixon, however, never exhibited the concern for urban problems that was needed to make this apparatus function effectively. His major policy considerations apparently centered on eliminating as many urban programs as possible and turning the funds for their operation over to the state governments. Under Carter, the federal emphasis switched from stimulating new services to facilitating private investment in the economic revitalization of cities.

A second barrier to successful urban policy is the traditional congressional logrolling process. How can programs such as Model Cities, Community Action, or mass transit have a measurable effect anywhere if the appropriations are never adequate and if the funds are parceled out to the districts of every rural or small-town congressional representative who happens to head a subcommittee?

The Bias of the Federal Involvement

Because the federal involvement in urban affairs is so massive and heterogeneous, it is difficult to categorize its overall biases. If some federal programs (such as public housing) seem biased toward the status quo, others (such as the Community Action programs) seem equally biased toward rapid social change. Furthermore, the multitude of federal programs makes it difficult to categorize an overall bias of the federal involvement in terms of individual group benefits. Each program generates its own constituency. And if the residents of low-income residential neighborhoods are often disproportionately injured by some federal programs (such as those supporting urban renewal and freeway construction), other federal involvements (such as transfer payments, Aid for Dependent Children, and day care centers) disproportionately benefit these low-income people.

In order to assess the overall bias of the federal involvement, a way is needed to calculate the *net bias* of federal programs, or their *net impact* on identifiable constituencies and on major urban and metropolitan problems. If the total of federal programs biased against some identifiable urban constituency (for example, poor

African Americans) were outweighed by the total of federal programs biased in favor of that constituency, then the net bias or net impact of federal programs would be biased in favor of that constituency. If the total of federal programs promoting social change were outweighed by the total of federal programs protecting the status quo, then the net bias or net impact of federal involvement would be biased against social change.

To translate the concept of net bias into operational terms is very difficult, however. The constituencies of urban programs are not easy to identify precisely, and the criteria for deciding whether a program works for social change or for the status quo are not clear. Consequently, the task of operationalizing the concept of net bias lies beyond the scope of this book. What follows, instead, is an effort to delineate five general patterns of federal involvement that strongly suggest a definite net bias. These patterns involve

The creation of interest groups for the urban poor and minorities

The attempts to equalize social access to middle-class lifestyles

The attempts to control suburban sprawl

The attempts to improve governmental accountability to the electorate

The attempts to subordinate urban programs to comprehensive national urban policies

Bias and the Creation of Interest Groups for the Urban Poor

Certain programs of Lyndon Johnson's Great Society were biased toward the creation of interest groups to represent the interests of the urban poor and of racial minorities. The Community Action programs and the Model Cities experiment greatly broadened the scope of community leadership in inner-city communities, particularly in the African American communities. This leadership has been far from unified, but it did not disappear with the demise of the War on Poverty. Consequently, as we move into the next century, the African American community is much better prepared than it was in previous decades to confront urban governments about their operation in African American neighborhoods. Particularly in relation to African American communities, the federal programs created in the 1960s have solidified a number of urban interest groups that cannot be ignored: the Urban League, the Urban Coalition, the Conference of Mayors, and most of the racial improvement groups such as the NAACP.

On the other hand, neither the national nor the state capitals is very responsive to the *unorganized* urban needy. Up to this point, the most disorganized urban communities have probably been Native Americans and the white, working poor. Neither group has benefited significantly from federal urban programs, which are biased toward more organized groups.

The revolutionary aspect of the New Deal in the 1930s was its institutionalization of organized labor as a mechanism for representing the interests of the working poor who were organized in unions. The major shortcoming of the Great Society during the 1960s was its inability to create a similar mechanism to represent the interests of those poor who were unorganized or were not part of the unionizable labor force.

Bias and Social Access to Middle-Class Lifestyles

A second net bias of the federal involvement has been against measures that would equalize social access to middle-class lifestyles. Federal housing programs illustrate this most clearly. Although some federal housing programs have indeed made it easier for moderate-income people to live in middle-class neighborhoods, and although public housing has provided living space for millions of low-income people, no housing program has had a very far-reaching impact on integrating communities along racial lines. Furthermore, as indicated by the data given in Table 11.2, the federal government provides more financial incentives to middle- and upper-middle-income homeowners than it does to lower-income people who benefit from public-housing rental programs.

The single biggest housing incentive is the deductibility of home mortgage interest on federal income tax returns. In 2004, this incentive saved homeowners $62 billion in federal income taxes. Funds for direct housing assistance in programs such as Section 8 and public housing, by contrast, amounted to only about one-third of that amount. In addition, Federal Housing Administration mortgage guarantees have been used overwhelmingly in the suburbs and have promoted little housing for the central-city poor or for racial minorities. Indeed, until the early 1960s, FHA loans were not given to African Americans. Traditional public housing has been confined largely to the poor neighborhoods of central cities and has increased racial segregation. Since 1974, however, public housing leased through Section 8 has contributed to spreading low-income housing throughout cities, so current federal housing policies may be less biased against social access than they were during the 1950s and 1960s.[114]

Bias and the Containment of Suburban Sprawl

Federal programs have a net bias against attempts to contain suburban sprawl. The major federal programs that aimed to contain it were the stimulation of metropolitan

---

TABLE 11.2 The Middle-Class Bias of Federal Housing Incentives in the Year 2004

Federal Incentives That Primarily Benefit Middle- and Upper-Middle-Income People	Billions of Dollars
Tax deductibility of home mortgage interest	$61.5
Tax deductibility of property tax payments	19.9
Capital gains exclusion on home sales	29.7
Total	**$111.1**

Federal Incentives That Primarily Benefit Low-Income People	Billions of Dollars
Direct expenditures for housing assistance	$36.6
Credit for low-income housing investment	3.7
Total	**$40.3**

Source: U.S. Bureau of the Census, *Statistical Abstract of the United States: 2006,* Tables 463, 469.
http://www.census.gov/prod/2005pubs/06statab/fedgov.pdf.

planning and councils of governments. However, these have been extremely weak control mechanisms. Furthermore, the federal funds invested in them are small compared to the federal funds invested in programs that *stimulate* suburban sprawl—especially guaranteed mortgages in the suburbs and the urban portion of the Interstate Highway System. The net effect of the federal involvement in urban affairs, then, has been to foster suburban sprawl.

Having noted the net bias against containing suburban sprawl and the net bias against equalizing access to middle-class lifestyles, however, we must also recognize that a number of federal initiatives over the past two decades do indeed seek to equalize access to middle-class lifestyles. The consistent commitments to affirmative action programs and to leased public housing should help equalize social access.

Bias and Governmental Accountability

Until at least the end of the 1960s, the net impact of government programs was clearly to diminish the accountability of urban governments to the electorate. Many grants-in-aid programs stimulated the proliferation of special districts. Many other programs stimulated the creation of semiautonomous housing and redevelopment authorities. Welfare programs have been administered under a Byzantine system of administrative rulings that practically eliminated the accountability of the programs to local elected officials.

The late 1960s and early 1970s, however, saw several coordinating devices aimed at making federal programs more accountable to identifiable officials. These devices include the A-95 review process, the stimulation of councils of governments (COGs), the federal regional councils, and the Community Development Block Grant program of the 1970s. This last item in particular has strengthened local elected officials' control over federally financed urban redevelopment. And the citizen participation provisions of the 1974 CD Block Grant program have also helped make the program more accountable to citizens' groups and neighborhood groups. In the 1980s, the Reagan administration downplayed coordination devices such as A-95 and COGs. But its New Federalism efforts supported the trend toward increasing the authority of state governors and legislators.

Bias and Policy Making

The net bias of the federal urban involvement works to protect urban programs and highly particularistic interests from subordination to systematic policies. This was shown repeatedly during the 1960s and 1970s. For example, the community development grant consolidation of 1974, as originally proposed by President Nixon, would have shifted influence away from those groups that are powerful at the national capital and toward those that are powerful at the state capitals. This would have been extremely detrimental to local big-city groups that had emerged around the Model Cities programs, the Community Action programs, and several others of the more than one hundred grants-in-aid programs that Nixon was going to consolidate into special revenue sharing. The results were predictable. These groups and their allies in Congress and the federal bureaucracies fought bitterly against the proposals. The net result was a substantial amount of consolidation—but consolidation crippled by a compromise that effectively diluted the concept of special revenue sharing and ensured the major urban bureaucracies in HUD, DOT, Health and Human Services (HHS), and Education, they would not suffer any setbacks. To give other examples, Carter's proposals for welfare reform, energy policy, and urban policy all were stymied by particular private interests unwilling to give in to Carter's perception of the public good. These examples suggest that very little incentive exists for any president to try to subordinate urban programs to national policy.

Conclusions

The federal involvement in urban affairs has evolved to the point where it makes a great deal of sense to coordinate urban programs under some form of executive-directed national urban policy. Ironically, the administration (Carter's) that worked the hardest to articulate such a policy enjoyed only modest success with it, whereas the administration (Reagan's) most vehemently opposed to articulating a national urban policy was one of the most successful in terms of reorienting the goals and purposes of federal involvement in urban affairs. The dynamics of the federal involvement thus suggest that several things will continue to happen as we move into the new millennium. First, attempts to make the melange of federal programs accountable to the White House and to local elected officials will probably continue. Second, these federal actions probably will not significantly improve the access of the poor to middle-class lifestyles or significantly alter suburban sprawl. Finally, the biases of the federal involvement that we have outlined will change very little.

SUMMARY

1. The main federal tool for coping with urban problems has been grants-in-aid. Two early grants-in-aid programs were public housing and urban renewal.
2. The most extensive outpouring of urban programs occurred during the administration of President Lyndon B. Johnson. In an initiative called the Great Society, his administration created two urban-related cabinet departments and sponsored the Elementary and Secondary Education Act, the Economic Opportunity Act, the Fair Housing Act, and the Model Cities Act.
3. During the presidential administration of Richard M. Nixon, national urban policy making focused on reversing some key programs of the Great Society and promoting a New Federalism based on general revenue sharing and grant consolidation.
4. President Jimmy Carter was the first president to articulate a specific urban policy. He did so in 1978, and his policies were characterized by the themes of economic revitalization, fiscal relief for distressed city governments, targeting of scarce federal resources to the most appropriate urban areas, and improvement of existing urban programs.
5. President Ronald Reagan sought only one new urban initiative: urban enterprise zones. However, his New Federalism, block grants, budget reduction, and regulatory changes had a marked impact on the federal urban role.

6. As a consequence of New Federalism, state governments have achieved a greater role in urban policy.

7. President Bill Clinton initiated the Empowerment Zone program to revitalize distressed inner-city neighborhoods while pursuing nonurban policies such as welfare reform and crime policy. In light of federal budget constraints, Clinton's urban initiatives are consistent with New Federalism and conservative market-oriented policies, while incorporating liberal agendas associated with Great Society programs.

8. President George W. Bush's "compassionate conservatism" seeks to use the federal government to promote traditional conservative values of self-reliance and the free-market system. The war against terrorism has somewhat overshadowed domestic concerns but implies a return to cooperative federalism in that state and local governments must carry out a large share of the domestic battle.

9. Several factors make it difficult to achieve a coherent and effective national urban policy. Some programs (such as the Apollo program) were implemented successfully by the federal government, but others (such as Model Cities) have been marked by much less success. It is important to distinguish between the things the federal government does well and the things it does poorly.

10. Because any given group both pays costs under some federal programs and benefits from other federal programs, the concept of net bias was introduced to sort out the patterns of bias. During the Great Society period, one bias of federal programs was to facilitate the creation of interest groups for the urban poor. On balance, however, federal housing, urban renewal, and transportation programs have not facilitated lower-class access to middle-class lifestyles. Federal policies have a net bias in favor of suburban sprawl, although a number of policies in recent years have been trying to contain that sprawl. Because of the proliferation of programs and special districts, federal policies have been biased against accountability of urban governments to the electorate. A number of developments since the 1960s, however, have attempted to promote greater accountability among urban governments.

NOTES

1. See Daniel J. Elazar, *The American Partnership* (Chicago: University of Chicago Press, 1962), p. 20.

2. Data on grants-in-aid are taken from *Significant Features of Fiscal Federalism 1982/83* (Washington, D.C.: Advisory Commission on Intergovernmental Relations, 1983), p. 66; and U.S. Bureau of the Census, *Statistical Abstract of the United States: 1991* (Washington, D.C.: U.S. Government Printing Office, 1991), p. 282.

3. Michael Reagan, *The New Federalism* (New York: Oxford University Press, 1972), p. 84.

4. Michael N. Danielson, *Federal-Metropolitan Politics and the Commuter Crisis* (New York: Columbia University Press, 1965), p. 189.

5. Roscoe C. Martin, *The Cities and the Federal System* (New York: Atherton, 1965), p. 146.

6. Robert C. Wood, *The Federal Government and the Cities* (Washington, D.C.: George Washington University Press, 1964), pp. 52–54.

7. Reagan, *The New Federalism*, pp. 87–88.

8. Pietro S. Nivola, 2003. "Fiscal Millstones on the Cities: Revisiting the Problem of Federal Mandates," Policy Brief #122. (Washington, D.C.: The Brookings Institution), p. 3.

9. *New York Times*, May 21, 1990, p. A-11.

10. U.S. Department of Housing and Urban Development, *Empowerment: A New Convenant with America's Communities—President Clinton's National Urban Policy Report* (Washington, D.C.: U.S. Government Printing Office, 1995) pp. 52–53.

11. Implementing the principle of compensatory education, however, proved very difficult. See Jerome T. Murphy, "The Education Bureaucracies Implement Novel Policy: The Politics of Title I of ESEA, 1965–1972," in *Policy and Politics in America*, ed. Allan P. Sindler (Boston: Little, Brown, 1973), pp. 160–198. See also Stephen K. Bailey and Edith K. Mosher, *ESEA: The Office of Education Administers a Law* (Syracuse, N.Y.: Syracuse University Press, 1968).

12. Suzanne Farkas, *Urban Lobbying* (New York: New York University Press, 1971), p. 60.

13. For a discussion of urban movements, see Norman I. Fainstein and Susan S. Fainstein, *Urban Political Movements: The Search for Power by Minority Groups in American Cities* (Englewood Cliffs, N.J.: Prentice-Hall, 1974).

14. James L. Sundquist, *Making Federalism Work: A Study of Program Coordination at the Community Level* (Washington, D.C.: The Brookings Institution, 1969), pp. 3–5.

15. U.S. Office of Management and Budget, *Special Analyses: Budget of the United States Government, Fiscal Year 1975* (Washington, D.C.: U.S. Government Printing Office, 1974), p. 210. FY 1973 grants-in-aid equaled 23.5 percent of state and local budgets. In FY 1961 they equaled 12.6 percent.

16. Criticisms of grants-in-aid as not enabling states to establish their own priorities can be found in many textbooks on state and local government. See Thomas R. Dye, *Politics in States and Communities* (Englewood Cliffs, N.J.: Prentice-Hall, 1969), pp. 471–472; and Duane Lockard, *The Politics of State and Local Government*, 2d ed. (New York: Macmillan, 1969), pp. 36–42.

17. For critiques of the welfare system, see Gilbert Y. Steiner, *The State of Welfare* (Washington, D.C.: The Brookings Institution, 1971); Frances Fox Piven and Richard A. Cloward, *Regulating the Poor: The Functions of Public Welfare* (New York: Pantheon, 1971); and Daniel P. Moynihan, *The Politics of a Guaranteed Income: The Nixon Administration and the Family Assistance Plan* (New York: Random House, 1973), especially chap. 2.

18. Jeanne Lowe, *Cities in a Race with Time: Progress and Poverty in America's Renewing Cities* (New York: Random House, 1968), pp. 232–233.

19. Daniel P. Moynihan, *Maximum Feasible Misunderstanding: Community Action in the War on Poverty* (New York: Free Press, 1969).

20. See Edward C. Banfield, "Making a New Federal Program: Model Cities, 1964–1968," in *Policy and Politics in America*, ed. Allan P. Sindler (Boston: Little, Brown, 1973) pp. 124–169.

21. Martha Derthick, *New Towns in Town: Why a Federal Program Failed* (Washington, D.C.: Urban Institute, 1972).

22. John E. Schwarz, *America's Hidden Success: A Reassessment of Public Policy from Kennedy to Reagan*, rev. ed. (New York: Norton, 1988). See also Sar A. Levitan and Rupert Taggart, "Great Society Did Succeed," *Political Science Quarterly* 91 (Winter 1976–1977): 601–618.

23. Daniel P. Moynihan, "Toward a National Urban Policy," *Public Interest* 17 (Fall 1969): 7.

24. Advisory Commission on Intergovernmental Relations, *The Failure of Federalism in the 1980s: M-126* (Washington, D.C.: Advisory Commission on Intergovernmental Relations, July 1981), p. 49.

25. Paul R. Dommel, "Distribution Politics and Urban Policy," *Policy Studies Journal* 3, no. 4 (June 1975): 370–374.

26. Paul R. Dommel and Michael J. Rich, "The Rich Get Richer, CDGB," *Urban Affairs Quarterly* 22, no. 4 (June 1987): 552–579.

27. See Raymond A. Rosenfeld, "Implementation of the Community Development Block Grant Program: Decentralization of Decision-Making and Centralization of Responsibility," paper presented to the Midwest Political Science Association, Chicago, April 21–23, 1977. See also Michael N. Danielson and Jaimison Doig, *New York*, "The Politics of Urban Regional Development," (Berkeley: University of California Press, 1982): chap. 9.

28. Marshall Kaplan, "National Urban Policy: Where Are We Now? Where Are We Going?" in *The Future of National Urban Policy*, ed. Marshall Kaplan and Franklin Jones, (Durham, N.C.: Duke University Press, 1990), p. 176.

29. See Myron A. Levine, "The President and National Urban Policy," paper presented at the 1979 Annual Meeting of the Northeastern Political Science Association, Newark, N.J., November 9, 1979.

30. Rochelle L. Stanfield, "Federal Policy Makers Now Must Ask: Will It Hurt Cities?" *National Journal* (July 21, 1979): 1203–1206.

31. Michael J. Rich, "Learning to Live with Less: Federal Aid for Housing and Community Development in the 1980s," *Urban Politics and Urban Policy Section Newsletter* 1, no. 1 (Summer 1986): 13.

32. Rochelle L. Stanfield, "Economic Development Aid—Shell Game or Key to Urban Rejuvenation?" *National Journal* (March 21, 1981): 497.

33. Ibid., pp. 494–495.

34. Norman J. Glickman, "Emerging Urban Policies in a Slow-Growth Economy: Conservative Initiatives and Progressive Responses in the United States," *International Journal of Urban and Regional Research* 5, no. 4 (December 1981): 492–527.

35. U.S. Department of Housing and Urban Development, *The President's National Urban Policy Report* (Washington, D.C.: U.S. Government Printing Office, 1982), p. 46.

36. Ibid., p. 66.

37. These proposals were enunciated by Reagan in various speeches. For the core of his message on enterprise zones, see *New York Times,* March 24, 1982: 14.

38. Richard Child Hill, "Market, State, and Community: National Urban Policy in the 1980s," *Urban Affairs Quarterly* 19, no. 1 (September 1983): 5–20.

39. Ibid., p. 12.

40. Ronald Reagan, *Federalism: The First Ten Months* (Washington, D.C.: The White House, 1981), p. 1.

41. Levine, "The President and National Urban Policy," p. 24.

42. David A. Caputo and Steven E. Johnson, "New Federalism and Midwestern Cities: 1981–1985," *Publius* 16, no. 1 (Winter 1986): 81–96.

43. Bruce D. McDowell, "Grant Reform Reconsidered," *Intergovernmental Perspective* 17, no. 3 (Summer 1991): 8–11.

44. President Ronald Reagan, speech to the National Governors' Association, August 8, 1988.

45. Richard L. Cole, Delbert A. Taebel, and Rodney V. Hissong, "America's Cities and the 1980s: The Legacy of the Reagan Years," *Journal of Urban Affairs* 12, no. 4 (1990): 345–360.

46. Ibid.

47. *Political Science Quarterly* 107 (1992): 1–30.

48. Ronald Berkman, *In the National Interest: The 1990 Urban Summit* (New York: Twentieth Century Fund Press, 1990); Robert Wood and Beverly Klimkowsky, "HUD in the Nineties: Doubt-Ability and Do-Ability," in *The Future of National Urban Policy,* ed. Marshal Kaplan and Franklin James (Durham, N.C.: Duke University Press, 1990).

49. Frank Shafroth, "Cisneros Plans Increased Role for Cities," *Nation's Cities Weekly* 16, no. 7 (February 15, 1993): 1–2.

50. Ronald K. Vogel, "National Urban Policy," in *Handbook of Research on Urban Politics and Policy in the United States,* ed. Ronald K. Vogel (Westport, Conn.: Greenwood Press, 1997), pp. 418–419.

51. General Accounting Office, "Community Development: Status of Urban Empowerment Zones" (Washington, D.C.: General Accounting Office, December 20, 1996).

52. Ibid.

53. U.S. Department of Housing and Urban Development, Office of Policy Development Research, *Empowerment: A New Covenant with America's Communities—President Clinton's National Urban Policy Report* (Washington, D.C.: U.S. Department of Housing and Urban Development, July 1995), pp. 43–45.

54. General Accounting Office, "Community Development: Status of Urban Empowerment Zones" (Washington, D.C.: General Accounting Office, December 20, 1996).

55. Statement of Stanley J. Czerwinski, associate director of the Housing and Community Development Issues, Resources, Community, and Economic Development Division, General Accounting Office, in testimony before the Subcommittee on Oversight, Committee on Ways and Means, House of Representatives, October 28, 1997, "Community Development: The Federal Empowerment Zone and Enterprise Community Program."

56. Office of Policy Development and Research, U.S. Department of Housing and Urban Development, "Five Years In: Assessing the EZ/EC Program," *Recent Research Results* (February 2002), http://www.huduser.org/periodicals/rrr/rrr_02B_2002/rrr02_02.html.

57. Susan Bennett, "Police, Crime, and Crime Prevention," in *Handbook of Research on Urban Politics and Policy in the United States,* ed. Ronald K. Vogel (Westport, Conn.: Greenwood Press, 1997), p. 339.

58. U.S. Department of Housing and Urban Development, *Empowerment: A New Covenant with America's Communities—President Clinton's Urban Policy Report,* pp. 42–43.

59. James Q. Wilson and George L. Kelling, "Broken Windows," *Atlantic Monthly* (March, 1982): 29–38.
60. Bennett, "Police, Crime, and Crime Prevention," p. 342.
61. Ibid., p. 349.
62. Robert Suro, "Drop in Murder Rate Accelerates in Cities," *Washington Post,* December 31, 1997, p. A1.
63. Sheila Zedlewski and Linda Giannarelli, *Diversity Among State Welfare Programs,* (Washington, D.C.: The Urban Institute, 1998), p. 1.
64. Ibid., p. 2.
65. Ibid., p. 2.
66. Ibid., pp. 3–6.
67. U.S. Department of Health and Human Services, The Administration for Children and Families, Office of Public Affairs, January 1998, "Total TANF families and recipients."
68. Department of Health and Human Services, Fact Sheet, August 12, 1997.
69. Peter Szekely, "Labor's Herman: Welfare Reforms Need More Time," Reuters, February 18, 1998.
70. U.S. Department of Health and Human Services, "Secretary Thompson Announces TANF Caseloads Declined in 2003," Press Release, August 23, 2004, http://www.hhs.gov/news/press/2004pres/20040823. html, downloaded February 17, 2006; U. S. Department of Health and Human Services, Administration for Children and Families, "Change in Numbers of TANF Families and Recipients from December 2002 to December 2003," http://www.acf.hhs.gov/TANF_data.htm, downloaded February 17, 2006.
71. U. S. Department of Health and Human Services, "Secretary Thompson Announces TANF Caseloads Declined in 2003," (Press Release) August 23, 2004, http://www.hhs.gov/news/press/2004pres/ 20040823.html, downloaded February 17, 2006.
72. Olivia A. Golden, *Assessing the New Federalism Eight Years Later* (Washington, D.C.: The Urban Institute, 2005), p. 8.
73. Ibid.
74. Ibid., p. 9.
75. Ibid.
76. Ibid., p. 10.
77. Ibid.
78. Ibid., p. 18.
79. Terry M. Neal, "Midwestern Mayor Shapes Bush's Message," *Washington Post,* June 5, 1999, p. A6, http://www.washingtonpost.com/wp-srv/politics/campaigns/wh2000/stories/goldsmith060599.htm.
80. Myron Magnet, "Solving President Bush's Urban Problem," *City Journal* 1, no. 1 (Winter 2001): 14–15, http://www.city-journal.org/html/issue_11_1.html.
81. Ibid., p. 18.
82. David Corn, "Bush Tells Welfare Mothers to Work More—How Pro-Family Is That?" *The Nation* (February 27, 2002), http://www.thenation.com/capitalgames/index.mhtml?bid=3&pid=20.
83. http://www.whitehouse.gov/news/releases/2001/01/20010129-2.html.
84. Joel Friedman, Robert Greenstein, and Richard Kogan, "The Administration's Proposal to Make the Tax Cut Permanent," Center on Budget and Policy Priorities (Washington, DC: Author), April 16, 2002 (revised).
85. U.S. Conference of Mayors, "The Cost of Heightened Security in America's Cities: A 192-City Survey," January 2002, http://www.usmayors.org/70thWinterMeeting/securitysurvey.pdf.
86. Ibid., p. 11.
87. "The President's Plan to Strengthen Our Homeland Security," The White House, News and Policies, http://www.whitehouse.gov/news/releases/2002/02/20020204-2.html.
88. U.S. Conference of Mayors, Press Release, April 10, 2002, "Mayors Ask Congress to Help Cities with Security Costs" http://www.usmayors.org/uscm/news/press_releases/documents/omalley_041002.pdf.
89. Peter Eisinger, The American City in the Age of Terror: A Preliminary Assessment of the Effects of September 11," *Urban Affairs Review 40* (September 2004): 118.
90. Michael A. Pagano and Christopher Hoene, "Fend-for yourself Federalism: The Impact of Federal and State Deficits on America's Cities," *Government Finance Review* (October 2003), 36–42.
91. Kimberly Hendrickson, "Bush and the Cities," *Policy Review* (August & September 2004): 77.
92. National League of Cities, "CDBG Cuts Would be Devastating to Communities," Press Release, February 11, 2006, http://www.nlc.org/Newsroom/Press_Room/8193.cfm, downloaded February 11, 2006.
93. The United States Conference of Mayors, "Statement of U.S. Conference of Mayors President Long Beach Mayor Beverly O'Neill on President Bush's Proposed FY-07 Budget" Press Release, February 7, 2006.

94. Ronald K. Vogel, "National Urban Policy," in *Handbook of Research on Urban Politics and Policy in the United States,* ed. Ronald K. Vogel, p. 420.

95. Daniel P. Moynihan, "Toward a National Urban Policy," *Public Interest* 17 (Fall 1969): 6; and Wood, *The Federal Government and the Cities,* pp. 52–54.

96. See Kaplan, "National Urban Policy: Where Are We Now? Where Are We Going?" p. 176; Robert Wood, "A Personal Commentary on the Perils of Multiple Authorship Even Among Friends," *Urban Affairs Review* 30, no. 5 (1995): 687–689; Paul Kantor, "A Case for a National Urban Policy: The Governmentalization of Economic Dependency," *Urban Affairs Quarterly* 26, no. 3 (1991): 394–415.

97. Peter K. Eisinger, "The Search for a National Urban Policy, 1968–1980," *Journal of Urban History* 12, no. 1 (November 1985): 3–24.

98. Vogel, "National Urban Policy," p. 422.

99. Robert Wood and Beverly Klimkowsky, "HUD in the Nineties: Doubt-Ability and Do-Ability," in *The Future of National Urban Policy,* ed. Kaplan and James (Durham, N.C.: Duke University Press, 1990), p. 275.

100. This account of the creation of the Model Cities program relies heavily on Banfield, "Making a New Federal Program," pp. 124–169.

101. Ibid., p. 129.

102. Ibid., p. 148.

103. Sundquist, *Making Federalism Work,* pp. 117–119.

104. Marshall Kaplan, *Urban Planning in the 1960's: A Design for Irrelevancy* (New York: Praeger, 1973), pp. 110–111.

105. Alan Saltzstein, "Federal Categorical Aid to Cities: Who Needs It Versus Who Wants It," *Western Political Quarterly* 30, no. 3 (September 1977): 377–383.

106. Paul R. Dommel, "Distribution Politics and Urban Policy," *Policy Studies Journal* 3, no. 4 (June 1975): 370–374.

107. Paul R. Dommel and Michael J. Rich, "The Rich Get Richer: The Attenuation of Targeting Effects of the Community Development Block Grant Program," *Urban Affairs Quarterly* 22, no. 4 (June 1987): 552–579.

108. Interview between David B. Walker and the author (Harrigan), Washington, D.C., December 29, 1983.

109. National Advisory Commission on Civil Disorders, *Report* (Washington, D.C.: U.S. Government Printing Office, 1968), p. 1.

110. Sundquist, *Making Federalism Work,* pp. 74, 78, 81.

111. Kaplan, *Urban Planning in the 1960's,* pp. 109, 118; and Banfield, "Making a New Federal Program," pp. 124–169.

112. See Chapter 10. See also Melvin B. Mogulof, *Governing Metropolitan Areas* (Washington, D.C.: Urban Institute, 1971).

113. Mogulof, *Federal Regional Councils* (Washington, D.C.: Urban Institute, 1970).

114. A calculation by the Office of Technology Assessment came to a similar conclusion about the nature of bias in subsidies for low- versus middle- and upper-income housing benefits, although it arrived at a higher expenditure level for both. It finds that, as Table 11.2 shows, about two-thirds more is spent on middle- and upper-income housing benefits. "[T]he cost of homeownership is subsidized through the federal tax code—by deductions of mortgage loan interest, capital gains tax deferment, and property tax payments. The amount of the subsidy is not insignificant. It is projected for 1995 that the federal outlay for homeownership deductions will be $83.2 billion. By contrast, subsidies for renters (usually low-income renters) in the form of public housing and rental assistance will total $24.9 billion. . . . Not only do homeowners receive more benefits than renters, but high-income owners receive more than low- and moderate-income owners. In 1993, households with annual incomes of more than $100,000 received 38.9 percent of homeowner subsidies, even though they represent only 5 percent of the population." U.S. Congress, Office of Technology Assessment, *The Technological Reshaping of Metropolitan America,* OTA-ETI-643 (Washington, D.C.: U.S. Government Printing Office, September 1995), p. 200.

CHAPTER 12

POLITICAL CHANGE IN THE METROPOLIS OF THE FUTURE

CHAPTER SYNOPSIS

State of America's Cities • Unlikelihood of National Urban Policy •
Technological and Demographic Effects on the Metropolis of the Future: *Scenario 1:
Return to the City; Scenario 2: Return to the Countryside; Scenario 3: Continued Sprawl* •
Conclusion: *Twentieth-Century Metropolitan Growth Based on Cheap Energy and Growing
Economy; Increased Access of Racial Minorities to Middle-Class Lifestyles in Last Half
of Twentieth Century Based on Growing Economy; Suburbanization and Minority
Gains Predicated on Economic Growth, But Is It Sustainable in the Future?*

If present-day urban trends in the United States continue for another decade, what are the probable consequences? In order to answer that question, this chapter will make conservative projections about the developmental and political consequences of certain existing trends:

- First, we offer a summary of the present state of cities in America, highlighting signs of the improvements in our nation's cities and metropolitan areas, as well as concerns that persist as we enter the twenty-first century.
- Second, we give reasons why we are unlikely to witness the adoption of drastic national urban policies.
- Third, we project recent demographic and technological trends into the near future to show what changes can be expected by the year 2020. That is, how will the metropolis of 2020 differ from today's metropolis?
- Fourth, we speculate about the political consequences of these changes. How will we be governed in the year 2020? And what major changes in political processes will have occurred?

The State of America's Cities

The U.S. Department of Housing and Urban Development (HUD) released a series of *State of the Cities* reports in the 1990s evaluating current conditions facing U.S. cities.[1] In the 1970s and 1980s, American cities faced severe challenges, including population loss, job loss, increased poverty, and spiraling crime rates. These trends were more pronounced in the Northeast and Midwest, but cities in the Sunbelt were not immune. Table 12.1 presents a snapshot of these troubling conditions and trends facing American cities at the end of the twentieth century.

In the last decade of the century, the situation of American cities improved. For example, the 1997 HUD report revealed that unemployment rates had declined to 6.5 percent in the largest 50 cities, compared to 4.2 percent in the suburbs. Although the disparity between central cities and suburbs continued, this was a much-improved situation compared to the 9.2 percent unemployment these cities suffered in 1993.[2] In addition, a new optimism has returned to many cities. These reports highlighted declining rates of violent crime (see Chapter 11) and improved job growth and economic opportunity in the cities.

However, HUD reports also focused on the growing disparities between the central cities and the suburbs. Job growth is higher in the suburbs, the poor and minorities are more concentrated and isolated in the central cities, and the middle class continues to migrate to the suburbs. The image of the city in the American mind has become

TABLE 12.1   Selected Statistics for Large U.S. Cities

	1960	1970	1980	1990	2000
Percent of U.S.population	26.1%	22.5%	20.9%	20.1%	20.2[b]
Percent minority population	18.9	24.1	37.1	40.1	48.7[c]
Unemployment rate	5.5	4.7	7.3	8.1	5.4[d]
Percent employed in manufacturing	25.3	22.1	17.4	14	10.7[e]
Median family income as percent of U.S. median family income	106.7	100.4	92.6	87.5	87.9[f]
Family poverty rate	17.2	11	13.6	15.1	16.1[g]
Percent population in census tracts with more than 40% poverty	8	5.1	8.1	10.8	10.3[h]
Female-headed families with own children as percent of all families	7.9[a]	10.4	13.8	14.5	—

[a]Estimated.

[b]Largest 100 cities, U.S. census data assembled by authors.

[c]All central cities, from HUD, SOCDS data system.

[d]Largest 50 cities, Bureau of Labor Statistics, 2001.

[e]Largest 100 cities, Brookings Institution Living Cities Interactive Databooks.

[f]All central cities in 1999, U.S. Bureau of the Census, American FactFinder, GCT-P14. Income and Poverty in 1999: 2000 Data Set.

[g]All central cities, U.S. Bureau of the Census.

[h]Largest 50 cities, Alan Berube and Bruce Katz, "Katrina's Window: Confronting Concentrated Poverty Across America," (October 2005), Appendix A (p. 10).

Source: U.S. census data for 1960, 1970, 1980, 1990, as compiled by John D. Kasarda, *Urban Underclass Database Machine Readable Files,* Social Science Research Council, New York, 1992 and 1993 (except as noted). Calculations by U.S. Department of Housing and Urban Development.

Note: The table is reproduced from U.S. Congress, Office of Technology Assessment, *The Technological Reshaping of Metropolitan America,* OTA-ETI-643 (Washington, D.C.: U.S. Government Printing Office, September 1995), p. 88. Data are based on the 100 largest MSA central cities in 1980 with the exceptions of Anchorage; Fort Lauderdale; Jackson, Mississippi; Jersey City; Newark; and Amarillo, for which tract-level data were not available in 1960. Therefore, the data are based on 94 central cities. The last column is updated by the authors from HUD State of Cities Database, the U.S. census, and the Bureau of Labor Statistics.

associated with decline, poverty, and crime. As Professor David Ames and his colleagues put it, "The central city was where urban problems were isolated and contained."[3] In contrast, the image of suburbs is that of growth, a good quality of life, and affluence. "It is this disparity between central cities and suburbs that has come to define the urban crisis today."[4] Indeed, images of New Orleans in the aftermath of the flood reminded Americans of the depth of problems in inner cities.

HUD also warned of two looming threats to cities in the future: welfare reform and immigration approaching record levels. HUD pointed to the need to create new jobs in the nation's cities to provide work for those no longer on the welfare rolls. Given that most new jobs are created in the suburbs and that welfare recipients are concentrated in the cities, there is concern over whether the cities can meet this challenge, especially with the economic boom years of the 1990s now past. Unanticipated in any of HUD's reports is the threat posed to cities by terrorism, both international and domestic. This threat will probably overshadow every other aspect of domestic and urban policy in the next few years.

The poor response to Hurricane Katrina also reminds us that cities still are vulnerable to natural disasters. However, one reason the hurricane was so devastating was the degree of concentrated poverty in New Orleans. It was the poorest residents who were left behind to weather the storm. About 38 percent of the poor in New Orleans live in underclass neighborhoods (neighborhoods with 40 percent or more living in poverty). Among African Americans, 43 percent live in these concentrated poverty neighborhoods.[5] In this sense, Table 12.1 can be misleading. Urban problems in the aggregate appear to be declining but that may distort the overall urban conditions of particular cities.

The Unlikelihood of a National Urban Policy

Barring some unforeseen nuclear or ecological catastrophe, the migration and urban development patterns traced in Chapter 2 seem likely to continue well into the twenty-first century. Coherent and enduring urban growth policies are no more likely to be achieved in the next decade than they were in previous decades. The reasons are deeply rooted in the structure of the American political system and in the nature of the American political culture.

The structure of the American political system has several features that impede the articulation and implementation of long-range policy goals for the kind of urban society we want to become. Foremost among these features are *federalism* and the *separation of powers*. Although the national government is still the dominant policy maker in the American federal partnership, national policies are carried out 50 different ways in 50 different states, and the New Federalism developments of the 1980s and welfare reform in the 1990s enhanced state independence even further. The separation of powers makes different branches of the government responsive to so many different constituencies that achieving a consensus on controversial matters among all the branches and agencies of government becomes nearly impossible.

Furthermore, Congress and the executive agencies in particular are organized around the performance of specific service and regulatory functions that have their own interest-group clienteles. This organization of government and private structures around specific service and regulatory functions gives the government a preference for making specific decisions that are related to specific projects. Even within given sectors of public life (veterans' benefits, for example), it is very difficult, once a service is established, to get either Congress or the appropriate executive agencies to make policy evaluations of the program in relation to its objectives and its performance.

In some functional sectors of public life, a long-range policy goal can be articulated and all efforts and programs subordinated to the achievement of that goal. The Apollo program and the specific decision to place an astronaut on the moon are prime examples of this.[6] In the operation of urban programs, however, there is no consensus on long-range policy goals to which separate programs can be subordinated. As a result, several hundred federal programs have proliferated in the metropolises in an uncoordinated, unplanned way. In more than one instance, the objectives of one program have been undone by the objectives of other programs. The New Federalism proposals of the Nixon and Reagan administrations were offered to give state and local governments more policy control over their usage of federal aid. However, studies found a tendency to recategorize the block grants,[7] and poor coordination seems just as much of a problem today as it was in the past.

Finally, the tradition of logrolling in Congress has been detrimental to urban programs such as Model Cities, in which program success depended on large appropriations being made for a few carefully selected sites. In order to ensure the votes needed for passage, the number of Model Cities had to be increased so much that few cities received adequate resources to carry out a successful program. Although these geographic considerations have not necessarily proved detrimental to programs that are not organized on a geographic basis (such as the Apollo program), they do work to the disadvantage of programs designed to benefit certain locations. The population shift to the Sunbelt and the suburbs has further reduced the urban constituencies in Congress. This is because reapportionment has resulted in there being fewer representatives from cities, and presidential elections are decided in the suburbs rather than the cities. This means urban areas are disadvantaged in policy making.

These structural impediments to the creation of a long-range national urban policy are reinforced by certain prominent values of the American political culture. By *American political culture* we mean the sum total of beliefs, attitudes, opinions, and expectations about the way the American political system does function and should function.[8] Foremost among the aspects of the American political culture that impede the establishment of a national urban policy is a deep-rooted distrust of centralized control over domestic problems. Much of this stems from the colonial heritage and the Jeffersonian ideal of small-town democracy. It also stems from reaction against the corruption of the urban political machines. As a result, governmental authority in urban areas has been deliberately fragmented. One semiautonomous agency is given operating responsibility for one functional service sector, another semiautonomous agency is given operating responsibility for another functional service sector, and so on. The ideal of small-town democracy is resurrected in urban America by the proliferation of relatively small municipalities in the suburbs. General-purpose governments at the metropolitan level are so few and so difficult to establish that they cannot be considered a practical way of ending the fragmentation of government authority in most metropolises.

Considerable centralization of authority has been achieved on a function-by-function basis in the area of key services needed to maintain the physical existence of the metropolis. However, on issues concerning access to middle-class lifestyles, such as zoning, school integration, and the construction of low-income public housing in the suburbs, there has been a strong reluctance to centralize control at the metropolitan level. Federal programs have supported the functional organization of authority and the creation of suburbia itself.

This inability to formulate a national urban policy and to form a national consensus about national objectives for our urban areas is perhaps the most apparent conclusion to be drawn about the governance of metropolitan America. Closely related to this lack of consensus is the lack of political power to confront directly some of the most obvious urban and metropolitan problems, particularly the lifestyle problems. We do not lack imaginative proposals; if anything, we are embarrassed by a wealth of imaginative proposals that we have not been able to implement effectively. What has been sorely lacking is the organization of political power to make the programs work over the long run.

Of course, the events of September 11, 2001, have the potential to alter urban development patterns. On the one hand, they may accelerate the decentralized pattern of urban development if corporations seek to reduce risk by decentralizing operations and avoiding tall buildings. Insurance costs, building code changes, and enhancing city first-responding capabilities could raise business costs and reduce the desirability of locating in central business districts. If terrorist incidents became commonplace or even if levels of anxiety were heightened enough, recent successes in central-city revitalization could be undermined. Although we have seen great increases in oil prices, there is no indication as of yet that Americans are changing their residential and business location decisions.

Technological and Demographic Effects on the Metropolis of the Future

A key question about the future of the metropolis concerns its technological viability beyond the next generation. The viability of the contemporary metropolis is contingent on the availability of highly developed technologies for transit, transport, supply, employment, and the provision of public services. The vulnerability of the contemporary metropolis is demonstrated at least once a year when some major central city undergoes a strike by transit workers, garbage collectors, teachers, police officers, or other public employees. The famous northeastern blackout of 1965 demonstrated how easily a whole network of metropolises can be paralyzed simply by an electrical failure. More recently, utility privatization experiments in California led to insufficient electrical power supply and soaring prices. Periodic lines at the gasoline pumps during the 1970s, combined with escalating costs of gasoline, fuel oil, and other petroleum-based products, demonstrated just how dependent the whole system of metropolises is on reliable supplies of gasoline, fuel oil, and natural gas. In trying to speculate on the viability of the contemporary metropolis as we move further into the twenty-first century, we must make certain assumptions about the state of the economy and the availability of energy sources.

First, it seems likely that there will be sufficient petroleum, natural gas, and electrical energy to maintain the physical existence and continued expansion of the contemporary metropolises for the next few decades. (A war in the Middle East could alter this.) Second, although continued expansion of the metropolis is physically possible, it is becoming increasingly expensive. The sources of petroleum, natural gas, and electrical energy will eventually become much more costly to exploit than they were in the past. Ecological concerns will continue to require investments to reduce air pollution, to restore polluted waterways, and to reclaim land that will be strip-mined for coal.

All of these factors will reduce the amount of money available for discretionary spending and for improving individual standards of living. This, in turn, will limit the number of people who can afford to buy houses in and commute by auto from a new tier of suburbs created by developers who will want to leapfrog beyond the existing suburbs. Thus leapfrog development will probably slow down in the twenty-first century. Recent years have already seen a slowdown in the movement to small cities just beyond the metropolis. This may be a signal that leapfrog development itself is beginning to reach a limit. Ultimately, leapfrog development will stop—but probably not within the next decade. However, federal, state, and local subsidies to peripheral development in the form of tax deductions and infrastructure placement (such as highways) mean that the residents and businesses of these suburbs on the fringe do not bear the full cost of services and infrastructure. If these subsidies are not reduced, sprawl is likely to continue.

Third, the expansion of the job market will probably continue in the pattern of the past quarter-century. That is, the private job market will expand most rapidly in the suburbs, while the public-service job market will expand most rapidly in the central cities.

Predicting what effects these assumed conditions will have on metropolitan development is, of course, impossible. But one or some combination of three scenarios seems most likely.

One possibility that has been predicted in the media is an implosion in which the suburban populations begin migrating back into the central cities. In fact, recent years have seen a significant "gentrification" process, as upper-middle-income professionals have bought up old homes in run-down city neighborhoods and have begun restoring them. For a variety of reasons, however, only a small percentage of the suburban population is likely to do this. Despite the increased costs of leapfrog development because of the economic and energy factors we have noted, leapfrogging is still likely to be cheaper for big developers than buying previously developed central-city land, destroying the buildings there, and clearing the sites for new construction. Furthermore, millions of workers now have jobs in the suburbs, and moving back into the central city will not necessarily put them closer to their places of employment. For all of these reasons, the preconditions that would sustain a massive in-migration into the central cities do not exist.

A second possible scenario, which has also been suggested by the media, is a genuine migration back to the country, where families can live much more independently of natural-resource shortages than they can in the large metropolises. *The Last Whole Earth Catalog*[9] implies that such a movement is possible. And the Sunday supplements of the big-city newspapers periodically feature articles about young families who give up the comforts of the metropolitan rat race for idyllic, primitive homesteads in the wilderness. These publications suggest that it might be possible to create another golden age of thriving, small family farms. Small may be beautiful,[10] but it does not seem likely to be the destiny of the present generation of Americans. A massive movement back to the farm is no longer possible. In the nineteenth-century age of small and thriving family farms, most of the arable land was originally not owned by private individuals. It was given by the federal government under the terms of the Homestead Act. Today the most arable portions of rural land are privately owned, and they are increasingly owned by corporations that want either to cultivate them or to exploit their mineral wealth. Furthermore, as agricultural exporting becomes increasingly important to the national economy, arable farmland will become much too valuable an asset to be used merely for subsistence farming. For all these reasons, not much land will be available for the increasing millions of metropolitan people who might wish to abandon the metropolis.

The back-to-the-country movement is likely to be limited in the future, as it is now, to three groups of people. One very small group consists of dropouts from the metropolitan rat race who actually try to "live off the land." The second, not much larger, group consists of a new generation of nonfarmers and part-time farmers. These are professionals—doctors, lawyers, writers, artists, teachers, and others—who can afford the time and the cost of absenting themselves from the metropolis for days or weeks at a time. They often live in expensively refurbished farmhouses in places (such as northern New England and the Blue Ridge Mountains) from which they can drive back to the metropolis on a few hours' notice. The third group consists of those people who move to growing small towns that have once again become economically viable thanks to the decentralizing impact of new communications technology.

The third possible scenario, and the one most likely for most of the population over the next decade, consists of continued metropolitan sprawl. Since 1970 there has been a net out-migration of metropolitan residents to small towns and new-tier suburbs just beyond the current metropolitan boundaries. As metropolitan sprawl has continued, the number of metropolitan areas has increased.

The sprawl of the next decade is likely to proceed much more slowly than the sprawl of the past, because more rigorous land use controls have been imposed and because no-growth and slow-growth movements took hold in many areas in the 1980s. But the metropolis of 2020 is not likely to be very much different from the metropolis of 1995—except that it will be larger and more spread out.

Beyond the year 2020, some basic alterations will have to be made in the patterns of metropolitan growth. Economically exploitable energy resources, on which the current technology of metropolitan growth depends, are not inexhaustible. Major changes in the technology of transit and of home heating may have to be made. Whenever such changes have occurred in the past, they have always had a stupendous impact on the patterns of urbanization. The railroads made the coal and canal towns of early-nineteenth-century Pennsylvania obsolete. The automobile, the interstate highway, and the airplane made most of the late-nineteenth-century railroad towns obsolete. And when newly emerging technology is applied to transit and to home heating, it is likely to have a major impact on many contemporary suburbs and certain metropolises. Even now, if it were economically feasible, considerable electrical energy could be generated from solar cells and the burning of processed solid waste. The application of solar heating and of "energy-conscious" building construction methods could reduce dependence on natural gas for home heating. Natural gas itself could be supplemented by methane gas generated from human and animal waste. Personalized rapid transit could reach all but the neighborhoods of the lowest densities. High-speed, short-distance train travel between cities could diminish contemporary reliance on energy-intensive air travel. Telecommuting could drastically alter business and residential location decisions and the spatial organization of the metropolis.

As some of these methods are applied, the face and structure of the metropolis are certain to begin changing in ways that are not apparent now. By the year 2020, these physical changes will just be emerging and may not be very perceptible. Beyond that date it is not possible to project very well.

Ultimately, demographic changes may have the greatest effect in reducing sprawl. A report entitled *Emerging Trends in Real Estate—1999* by Pricewaterhouse-Coopers and the Urban Land Institute finds that

> Not-so-subtle demographic changes are encouraging people to seek city lifestyles over suburban. . . . As baby-boomers become empty nesters, their children move into the expanding ranks of Generation Xers. . . . Both groups are gravitating to cities. Graying boomers can be closer to work and take advantage of urban amenities. . . . The 20-somethings, meanwhile, have graduated from hanging out at the mall. City nightlife and social interaction offer more possibilities, interest, and excitement.[11]

More recent reports including 2006 find these trends continuing leading to greater emphasis on urban in-fill.

Conclusions

In the past 50 years, two basic changes have occurred in the interplay between metropolitan politics and economic growth. First, post–World War II metropolitan growth was contingent on the availability of cheap energy and on the ability of the economy to sustain both the mass production of single-family homes in a suburban leapfrog development pattern and a mass-consumption economy of continuously improving standards of living for most urban and suburban residents. The oil crises of 1973–1974 and 1978–1979 cast doubt on the assumption that enough resources will be available under current technology to satisfy metropolitan needs for energy over the long run. Although economic growth has continued unabated through most of the last decade, it is unclear whether this has translated into an improved standard of living for individuals, because many jobs are now part-time and because workers lack job security and benefits and have seen little real growth in wages.

A second basic change in coming urban conditions is related to the role of the racial minorities. In post–World War II metropolitan growth, the vast majority of racial minorities were systematically excluded from access to middle-class lifestyles. The urban upheavals of the 1960s reflected the demand of the leaders of these minorities that this systematic exclusion be ended. It is doubtful that this exclusion can be ended by the traditional method of relying on continued growth in the size of the economic pie. It cannot be ended without some redistribution of income to the lower half of the income earners and without major alterations in the distribution of political power in the metropolis. Hence urban political issues in the future will be much more intricately involved with national political issues and with economic issues than they ever have been before.

What the political complexion of the metropolis will look like *beyond* the year 2020 is highly conjectural, but certain trends seem likely to persist. One of the constants will be the long-range dwindling of supplies of certain natural resources that have been essential for the development of the modern industrial economy. If these long-range shortages mean, as many people are predicting, that we will move from an economy of abundance to an economy of scarcity, then the lifestyle issues of urban politics will undoubtedly assume increasing importance. If the benefits of the metropolis have proved impossible to equalize during the greatest growth boom that the country has ever seen, how can they be equalized when the supply of those benefits grows relatively smaller rather than larger each year?

If the long-range shortages of natural resources do in fact lead to a long-range leveling off of the national economy while the metropolitan population continues to increase, then demands will probably increase for both greater federal intervention and the centralization of political authority in general-purpose, metropolitan governments that can exert some control over the functional fiefdoms. Although it is difficult to imagine urban issues becoming any more explosive in the future than they were during the middle and late 1960s, the seeds for explosive politics are certainly present in the trends we have discussed. Leaders of the new urban minorities will understandably fear the freezing of their racial and ethnic groups into a permanent urban underclass. White lower-middle- and working-class people will fear an end to their social mobility. Upper-middle-class and professional people will fear the loss of their affluent lifestyles. The leaders of functional fiefdoms will rigidly oppose control-sharing schemes that will diminish their own influence over urban governments, and they will support citizen representation schemes that give the appearance of shared control so long as the substance of their control is unaffected.

Of course, none of this is inevitable. The entire scenario is predicated on the assumption that natural-resource shortages will cause a permanent contraction in the growth of the American economy before the lifestyle issues of urban politics can be settled. Perhaps, instead, technological and economic adjustments to the scarcity of natural resources will be made before supplies dwindle to the crisis stage. Maybe American business will become more competitive in the world arena, and the decline of America's industrial sector will reverse itself. Maybe the lifestyle issues will be settled. Maybe population growth will cease. Maybe the traditional American practice of muddling through with piecemeal, ad hoc remedies for specific problems will continue to suffice in the future as it has in the past. Maybe a national urban policy will be formulated to deal with these matters. Maybe the present generation of economic and political leaders will act with more foresight and selflessness over the next decade than they have in the past.

But then again, maybe they won't. And maybe it's up to you.

NOTES

1. U.S. Department of Housing and Urban Development, http://www.huduser.org/publications/polleg/tsoc.html.
2. U.S. Department of Housing and Urban Development, *The State of the Cities* (Washington, D.C.: HUD, June 1997), p. 17.
3. David Ames, Nevin Borwn, Mary Helen Callahan, Scott Cummings, Sue Smock, and Jerome Ziegler, "Rethinking of American Urban Policy," *Journal of Urban Affairs* 14 (1992): 199.

4. Ronald K. Vogel, "National Urban Policy," in *Handbook of Research on Urban Politics and Policy in the United States,* ed. Ronald K. Vogel (Wesport, Conn.: Greenwood Press, 1997), p. 411.

5. Alan Berube and Bruce Katz, "Katrina's Window: Confronting Concentrated Poverty Across America," The Brookings Institution (October 2005), Table 1, p. 3.

6. This distinction between the efficacy of the Apollo program and the inefficacy of urban programs is elaborated by Anthony J. Catanese, *Planners and Local Politics: Impossible Dreams,* vol. 7, Sage Library of Social Research (Beverly Hills, Calif.: Sage, 1974), pp. 55–60.

7. Advisory Commission on Intergovernmental Relations, *Report A-62, Summary and Concluding Observations: The Intergovernmental Grant System: An Assessment and Proposed Policies* (Washington, D.C.: U.S. Government Printing Office, June 1978), p. 6.

8. A more detailed discussion of the concept of political culture can be found in Gabriel A. Almond and Sidney Verba, *The Civic Culture: Political Attitudes and Democracy in Five Nations* (Boston: Little, Brown, 1965), chap. 1, "An Approach to Political Culture." A short compendium of survey research findings of American opinions on a variety of issues over the past generation was compiled by Rita James Simon, *Public Opinion in America: 1936–1970* (Chicago: Rand McNally, 1974). The acquisition of political attitudes and the transmission of the political culture to new generations are referred to as *political socialization.* For a discussion of these processes, see Kenneth P. Langton, *Political Socialization* (New York: Oxford University Press, 1969).

9. Portola Institute, *The Last Whole Earth Catalog* (New York: Random House, 1971). See the catalog's statement of purpose, p. 1.

10. Ernst F. Schumacher, *Small Is Beautiful: A Study of Economics as If People Mattered* (New York: Harper & Row, 1973).

11. Pricewaterhouse Coopers and Lend Lease Real Estate, Inc., excerpted in Sprawl Guide, http://www.plannersweb.com/sprawl/solutions_demog.html.

INDEX